LUKE 1–9

WISDOM COMMENTARY

Volume 43A

Luke 1–9

Barbara E. Reid, OP, and
Shelly Matthews

Amy-Jill Levine
Volume Editor

Barbara E. Reid, OP
General Editor

A Michael Glazier Book

LITURGICAL PRESS
Collegeville, Minnesota

www.litpress.org

A Michael Glazier Book published by Liturgical Press

1   2   3   4   5   6   7   8   9

Library of Congress Cataloging-in-Publication Data

Names: Reid, Barbara E., author. | Matthews, Shelly, author.
Title: Luke / Barbara E. Reid, OP, and Shelly Matthews ; Amy-Jill Levine, volume editor ; Barbara E. Reid, OP, general editor.
Description: Collegeville, Minnesota : Liturgical Press, 2021. | Series: Wisdom commentary; volume 43A-B | "A Michael Glazier Book." | Includes bibliographical references and index. | Contents: Volume 1. Luke 1-9 — Volume 1. Luke 10-24. | Summary: "This commentary on Luke provides a feminist interpretation of Scripture in serious, scholarly engagement with the whole text, not only those texts that explicitly mention women. It addresses not only issues of gender but also those of power, authority, ethnicity, racism, and classism"— Provided by publisher.
Identifiers: LCCN 2020030815 (print) | LCCN 2020030816 (ebook) | ISBN 9780814681671 (hardcover) | ISBN 9780814688151 (hardcover) | ISBN 9780814681923 (epub) | ISBN 9780814681923 (mobi) | ISBN 9780814681923 (pdf) | ISBN 9780814688403 (epub) | ISBN 9780814688403 (mobi) | ISBN 9780814688403 (pdf)
Subjects: LCSH: Bible. Luke—Commentaries. | Bible. Luke—Feminist criticism.
Classification: LCC BS2595.53 .R45 2021 (print) | LCC BS2595.53 (ebook) | DDC 226.4/077—dc23
LC record available at https://lccn.loc.gov/2020030815
LC ebook record available at https://lccn.loc.gov/2020030816

Contents

List of Abbreviations   vii

List of Contributors   xi

Foreword: *"Come Eat of My Bread . . . and Walk in the Ways
of Wisdom"*   xvii
Elisabeth Schüssler Fiorenza

Editor's Introduction to Wisdom Commentary:
"She Is a Breath of the Power of God" (Wis 7:25)   xxi
Barbara E. Reid, OP

Authors' Introduction: A Feminist Commentary on
an Ambiguous Gospel   xli

Luke 1:1-80   An Orderly Account for Lovers of God   1

Luke 2:1-52   Divine Love Becomes Incarnate   63

Luke 3:1-38   Beloved Son of God and All God's Children   97

Luke 4:1-44   Prophetic Mission Declared; Divided Responses   117

Luke 5:1-39   Male Disciples Called; Female Disciples
in the Shadows   165

Luke 6:1-49   Multitudes of Women and Men
Are Healed and Hear   195

Luke 7:1-50   Wisdom's Children Justified   221

Luke 8:1-56   Galilean Women Followers and Financiers   247

Luke 9:1-62   The Cross That Should Not Be Taken Up   277

Works Cited   297

Abbreviations

AB	Anchor Bible series
ABD	*Anchor Bible Dictionary*. Edited by David Noel Freedman. 6 vols. New York: Doubleday, 1992.
ABRL	Anchor Bible Reference Library
AnBib	Analecta Biblica
ANTC	Abingdon New Testament Commentaries
AYBD	Anchor Yale Bible Dictionary
BAR	*Biblical Archaeology Review*
BBC	British Broadcasting Company
BCE	Before the Common Era
BDAG	Walter Bauer, Frederick William Danker, William Arndt, F. Wilbur Gingrich, *A Greek-English Lexicon of the New Testament and Other Early Christian Literature*, 3rd ed. (Chicago: University of Chicago Press, 2001).
BDB	Brown, Francis, S. R. Driver, and Charles A. Briggs, *A Hebrew and English Lexicon of the Old Testament*
BETL	Bibliotheca Ephemerium Theologicarum Lovniensium
Bib	*Biblica*
BibInt	*Biblical Interpretation*
BibInt	Biblical Interpretation series

BibRev	*Bible Review*
BibSem	The Biblical Seminar
BJRL	*Bulletin of the John Rylands University Library of Manchester*
BJS	Brown Judaic Studies
BR	*Biblical Research*
BTS	Biblical Tools and Studies
BZNW	Beihefte zur Zeitschrift für die neutestamentliche Wissenschaft
CahRB	Cahiers de la Revue biblique
CBA	Catholic Biblical Association of America
CBQ	*Catholic Biblical Quarterly*
CBQMS	Catholic Biblical Quarterly Monograph Series
CE	Common Era
CIL	*Corpus Inscriptionum Latinarum*
CurTM	*Currents in Theology and Mission*
ECL	Early Christianity and Its Literature
EJL	Early Judaism and Its Literature
EPRO	Études préliminaires aux religions orientales dans l'empire romain
FCB	Feminist Companion to the Bible
FCNTECW	Feminist Companion to the New Testament and Early Christian Writings
FSR	Feminist Studies in Religion
FT	*Folia Theologica*
GBS	Guides to Biblical Scholarship
GNS	Good News series
HNT	Handbuch zum neuen testament
HSM	Harvard Semitic Monographs
HTR	*Harvard Theological Review*
HTS	Harvard Theological Studies

IFT	Introductions in Feminist Theology
Int	*Interpretation*
JBL	*Journal of Biblical Literature*
JDS	Judean Desert Studies
JECS	*Journal of Early Christian Studies*
JES	*Journal of Ecumenical Studies*
JFSR	*Journal of Feminist Studies in Relgion*
JJS	*Journal of Jewish Studies*
JPS	Jewish Publication Society
JR	*Journal of Religion*
JRE	*Journal of Religious Ethics*
JSNT	*Journal for the Study of the New Testament*
JSNTSup	Journal for the Study of the New Testament Supplement Series
JSOT	*Journal for the Study of the Old Testament*
JSOTSup	Journal for the Study of the Old Testament Supplement Series
JTS	*Journal of Theological Studies*
LHBOTS	The Library of Hebrew Bible/Old Testament Studies
LNTS	Library of New Testament Studies
NCBC	New Cambridge Bible Commentary
NICNT	New International Commentary on the New Testament
NovT	*Novum Testamentum*
NT	New Testament
NTS	*New Testament Studies*
OBT	Overtures to Biblical Theology
OECS	Oxford Early Christian Studies
OT	Old Testament
PBS	Public Broadcasting System
PRSt	*Perspectives in Religious Studies*
PTMS	Pittsburgh Theological Monograph Series

RelSRev	*Religious Studies Review*
SBL	Society of Biblical Literature
SBLDS	Society of Biblical Literature Dissertation Series
SBLMS	Society of Biblical Literature Monograph Series
SBLStBL	Society of Biblical Literature Studies in Biblical Literature
SBLSymS	Society of Biblical Literature Symposium Series
SemeiaSt	Semeia Studies
SNTSMS	Studiorum Novi Testamenti Societas Monograph Series
SP	Sacra Pagina
SSEJC	Studies in Scripture in Early Judaism and Christianity
SymS	Symposium Series
TDNT	*Theological Dictionary of the New Testament.* Edited by Gerhard Kittel and Gerhard Friedrich. Translated by Geoffrey W. Bromiley. 10 vols. Grand Rapids: Eerdmans, 1964-1976.
ThTo	*Theology Today*
TS	*Theological Studies*
TSAJ	Texte und Studien zum antiken Judentum
VT	*Vetus Testamentum*
WCS	Wisdom Commentary series
WUNT	Wissenschaftliche Untersuchungen zum Neuen Testament

Contributors

Helen F. Bergin is a New Zealand Dominican sister. Her religious congregation was begun in 1871 by the arrival into Dunedin, New Zealand, of eleven Dominican sisters from Ireland. Helen was born in Wellington, NZ, as the eldest in a family of eight children. She completed doctoral studies in theology at The Catholic University of America, Washington, DC. Helen has taught theology at the national seminary in Dunedin, at the University of Auckland, and in many parishes. Feminist Theology, Trinity, and Introduction to Theology have been among regular courses that she has enjoyed teaching.

Stephen Bevans is a priest in the missionary congregation of the Society of the Divine Word (SVD) and is Louis J. Luzbetak, SVD, Professor of Mission and Culture, Emeritus, at Catholic Theological Union, Chicago. He is the author and editor of some twenty books, among which are *Models of Contextual Theology* (Orbis Books, 2002), *An Introduction to Theology in Global Perspective* (Orbis Books, 2009), and *Essays in Contextual Theology* (Brill, 2018). He is a member of the World Council of Church's Commission on World Mission and Evangelism.

Stephanie Buckhanon Crowder is vice president of academic affairs/academic dean at Chicago Theological Seminary. She is the first woman and first African American to hold this position in the institution's history. As associate professor of New Testament, Stephanie is a noted Bible scholar, versatile speaker, and prolific author. Dr. Crowder earned a bachelor of science degree summa cum laude in speech pathology/

audiology from Howard University; a master of divinity degree from United Theological Seminary; and master of arts and doctoral degrees in religion from Vanderbilt University. Dr. Crowder has contributed to *The Covenant Bible Study and Video Series* and *True to Our Native Land: An African American New Testament Commentary*, and most recently *Parenting as Spiritual Practice and Source for Theology*. Her second book is *When Momma Speaks: The Bible and Motherhood from a Womanist Perspective* (Westminster John Knox, 2016).

Acacia Chan holds a master of arts in religion from Yale Divinity School. She is currently pursuing a PhD in religious studies with a concentration in religions of the ancient Mediterranean at the University of Texas at Austin. Her current research interests include ancient literary remixes within apocryphal literature, Asian American feminism, and ancient humor. She is also a junior editor for *Glossolalia*, Yale's graduate journal of religion.

Mila Díaz Solano, O.P., is a native of Peru. She ministered in a rural parish of the Central Andes and in the diocesan program of formation in social doctrine of the church in Peru. She worked in the Theological Department of the Instituto Bartolomé de las Casas (IBC) Peru in 2017. Mila has taught Scripture at the Seminary Juan XXIII in Lima, Peru, and at Mundelein Seminary in Illinois. She is currently serving as a councilor for the Dominican sisters of Springfield, Illinois, and is completing a doctorate in biblical studies at the École biblique et archéologique française de Jérusalem.

Febbie C. Dickerson is ordained clergy and associate professor of New Testament at American Baptist College in Nashville, Tennessee. She holds a PhD in religion from Vanderbilt University. Her publications include *Luke, Widows, Judges, and Stereotypes* (Lexington/Fortress, 2019); "Yehud, Persia, and Liberating Christological Exegesis in Light of the Book of Malachi," *Testamentum Imperium* (Online International Journal, 2018); and "Acts 9:36-43: The Many Faces of Tabitha, A Womanist Reading," in *I Found God in Me: A Womanist Biblical Hermeneutics Reader*, ed. Mitzi J. Smith (Cascade Books, 2015). Her current research is in the area of labor, debt, and wages in the New Testament.

Elizabeth Dowling is an independent biblical scholar living in Ballarat, Australia. After completing her doctoral studies in theology at the Melbourne College of Divinity (2005), she lectured in biblical studies at

Australian Catholic University for more than ten years. She specializes in the study of the New Testament, in particular the Gospel of Luke, reading from an ecofeminist perspective. Elizabeth is the author of a monograph, *Taking Away the Pound: Women, Theology and the Parable of the Pounds in the Gospel of Luke*, LNTS 324 (T&T Clark International, 2007), as well as numerous journal articles and book chapters. She is a member of the Institute of Sisters of Mercy of Australia and Papua New Guinea.

Anne Elvey is a researcher, poet, and editor living in Melbourne, Australia, on what is Boonwurrung Country. She is author of *The Matter of the Text: Material Engagements between Luke and the Five Senses* (Sheffield Phoenix, 2011) and *An Ecological Feminist Reading of the Gospel of Luke: A Gestational Paradigm* (Edwin Mellen, 2005), and coeditor of *Ecological Aspects of War: Engagements with Biblical Texts* (Bloomsbury T&T Clark, 2017). Her most recent poetry collection is *On Arrivals of Breath* (Montrose, VIC: Poetica Christi, 2019). Anne is an honorary research associate with Trinity College Theological School, University of Divinity.

Ma. Marilou S. Ibita is an associate professor in the Theology and Religious Education Department at the De la Salle University, Manila, Philippines, and a visiting professor at the University of Leuven, Belgium. One of her research interests is to explore how biblical scholarship can help achieve the United Nations Sustainability Development Goals, particularly Goal No. 2: Zero Hunger. She recently published "The Agricultural Parables in Mark 4: An Ecological-Economic Reading" in *Reading the Gospel of Mark in the Twenty-First Century: Method and Meaning*, ed. Geert van Oyen, BETL 301 (Leuven: Peeters, 2019).

Marcie Lenk received her PhD from Harvard University in 2010 with a dissertation titled "*The Apostolic Constitutions*: Judaism and Anti-Judaism in the Construction of Christianity." She lives in Jerusalem, where she has served as the academic director of Bat Kol Christian Institute for Jewish Studies. She teaches patristics at the *Studium Theologicum Salesianum* at Ratisbonne Monastery, and Jewish and Christian texts at Ecce Homo Convent and the Tantur Ecumenical Institute. She served for six years as director of Christian leadership programs at the Shalom Hartman Institute. Dr. Lenk organizes educational programs for Jews and Christians (and people of other faiths) to understand and appreciate the basic texts, ideas, history, and faith of the Other.

Rabbi Dalia Marx is the Rabbi Aaron D. Panken Professor of Liturgy and Midrash at HUC-JIR's Taube Family Campus in Jerusalem and teaches in various academic institutions in Israel and Europe. A tenth generation in Jerusalem, Marx earned her doctorate at the Hebrew University and her rabbinic ordination at HUC-JIR in Jerusalem and Cincinnati in 2002. She is involved in various research projects and is active in promoting liberal Judaism in Israel. Marx is the author of *When I Sleep and When I Wake: On Prayers between Dusk and Dawn* (Yediot Sfarim, 2010, in Hebrew), *A Feminist Commentary of the Babylonian Talmud* (Mohr Siebeck, 2013, in English), and *About Time: Journeys in the Jewish-Israeli Calendar* (Yediot Sfarim, 2018, in Hebrew), and she is the coeditor of several books. Marx lives in Jerusalem with her husband Rabbi Roly Zylbersztein, PhD, and their three children.

Alice Matthews is a 2018 graduate of Smith College, currently enrolled in the dual master's degree program in arts administration and policy and modern and contemporary art history at the School of the Art Institute of Chicago. She has special interest in prioritizing accessibility and inclusion within museums and art institutions.

Carmen M. Nanko-Fernández is professor of Hispanic theology and ministry at the Catholic Theological Union in Chicago (USA). A Latin@ Catholic theologian, her publications include the book *Theologizing en Espanglish* (Orbis Books, 2010), numerous book chapters, journal articles, and digital media on Latin@ theologies, im/migration, and sport and theology. Her theological and pastoral commentaries appear in *The Bible Today* (May 2014); *Lectionary Homiletics* (2008–2015); *Feasting on the Word: Preaching the Revised Common Lectionary Year A* (Westminster John Knox, 2010); *Feasting on the Gospels* series (Westminster John Knox, 2014–2015) for which she also served on the editorial board. Nanko-Fernández developed and is an author and editor for the multivolume *Disruptive Cartographers* series, mapping theology *latinamente*, forthcoming with Orbis Books (English) and Editorial Verbo Divino (Español).

Michael Patella is a Benedictine monk and holds a license in Sacred Scripture from the Pontifical Biblical Institute in Rome and a doctorate in Sacred Scripture from the École biblique et archéologique française in Jerusalem. Fr. Michael is a professor of New Testament at Saint John's University in Collegeville, Minnesota, where he also serves as the seminary rector and director of the School of Theology's Holy Land Studies program. He chaired the Committee on Illumination and Text for *The Saint John's Bible*, for which he wrote *Word and Image: The Hermeneutics of* The Saint John's Bible. In addition, he has published in the area of Luke–Acts, Paul, Mark, and angels and demons.

Katherine A. Shaner is associate professor of New Testament at Wake Forest University School of Divinity and author of *Enslaved Leadership in Early Christianity* (Oxford University Press, 2018). In classrooms, in faith communities, in the public square, she challenges leaders to listen for voices of people who are left out of biblical texts and histories of justice. She works with archaeological materials from modern-day Turkey, Greece, and Israel to understand embodied contexts of ancient religious communities. She teaches courses across the New Testament and early Christian history that explore the theological, social, and political implications of biblical interpretation.

Antonio D. Sison, CPPS, associate professor of systematic theology at Catholic Theological Union, earned his PhD at the Catholic University of Nijmegen, Netherlands, and is committed to contextual, intercultural, and aesthetic approaches to doing theology. His authored books include *World Cinema, Theology, and the Human* (Routledge, 2012) and *Screening Schillebeeckx: Theology and Third Cinema in Dialogue* (Palgrave Macmillan, 2006); among his published chapters are contributions to *The Bible in Motion: A Handbook of the Bible and Its Reception in Film* (De Gruyter, 2016) and *The Routledge Companion to Religion and Film* (2009). He was the featured keynote lecturer at the 2018 Association for Southeast Asian Cinemas Conference (ASEACC) in Yogyakarta, Indonesia.

Mitzi J. Smith is the J. Davison Philips Professor of New Testament at Columbia Theological Seminary in Decatur, Georgia. Smith has authored / coauthored and edited / coedited seven books and many essays and articles. Her latest books are *Minoritized Women Reading Race and Ethnicity: Intersectional Approaches to Constructed Identity and Early Christian Texts* (Lexington, 2020), *Toward Decentering the New Testament: A Reintroduction* (Cascade, 2018), and *Womanist Sass and Talk Back: Social (In)Justice, Intersectionality and Biblical Interpretation* (Cascade, 2018).

C. Vanessa White, DMin, is associate professor of spirituality and ministry at Catholic Theological Union in Chicago. She is co-director and a member of the summer faculty of Xavier University of Louisiana's

Institute for Black Catholic Studies in New Orleans, LA. Her articles have appeared in *New Theology Review, U.S. Catholic, America,* and CNN.org as well as a chapter, "Black Catholic Response to *Amoris Laetitia,*" in *Amoris Laetitia: A New Momentum for Moral Formation and Pastoral Practice,* ed. Grant Gallicho and James F. Keenan (Paulist Press, 2018), 12–21. She is a contributor to *Give Us This Day,* a daily prayer booklet published by Liturgical Press. Her research is focused on the intersections of spirituality and praxis and is attentive to issues of discernment, health, women's spirituality, diversity/intercultural dialogue, leadership development, spiritual and ministry formation, spiritual practices, lay ministry, and adult faith formation.

Brittany E. Wilson is associate professor of New Testament at Duke University Divinity School. She is the author of *Unmanly Men: Refigurations of Masculinity in Luke–Acts* (New York: Oxford University Press, 2015) and *The Embodied God: Seeing the Divine in Luke–Acts and the Early Church* (Oxford University Press, forthcoming). Her work focuses on issues related to embodiment, gender, and the senses within the New Testament and the ancient world more broadly.

Foreword

"Come Eat of My Bread . . . and Walk in the Ways of Wisdom"

Elisabeth Schüssler Fiorenza
Harvard University Divinity School

Jewish feminist writer Asphodel Long has likened the Bible to a magnificent garden of brilliant plants, some flowering, some fruiting, some in seed, some in bud, shaded by trees of age old, luxurious growth. Yet in the very soil which gives it life the poison has been inserted. . . . This poison is that of misogyny, the hatred of women, half the human race.[1]

To see Scripture as such a beautiful garden containing poisonous ivy requires that one identify and name this poison and place on all biblical texts the label "Caution! Could be dangerous to your health and survival!" As critical feminist interpretation for well-being this Wisdom Commentary seeks to elaborate the beauty and fecundity of this

1. Asphodel Long, *In a Chariot Drawn by Lions: The Search for the Female in the Deity* (London: Women's Press, 1992), 195.

Scripture-garden and at the same time points to the harm it can do when one submits to its world of vision. Thus, feminist biblical interpretation engages two seemingly contradictory insights: The Bible is written in kyriocentric (i.e., lord/master/father/husband-elite male) language, originated in the patri-kyriarchal cultures of antiquity, and has functioned to inculcate misogynist mind-sets and oppressive values. At the same time it also asserts that the Bible as Sacred Scripture has functioned to inspire and authorize wo/men[2] in our struggles against dehumanizing oppression. The hermeneutical lens of wisdom/Wisdom empowers the commentary writers to do so.

In biblical as well as in contemporary religious discourse the word *wisdom* has a double meaning: It can either refer to the quality of life and of people and/or it can refer to a figuration of the Divine. Wisdom in both senses of the word is not a prerogative of the biblical traditions but is found in the imagination and writings of all known religions. Wisdom is transcultural, international, and interreligious. Wisdom is practical knowledge gained through experience and daily living as well as through the study of creation and human nature. Both word meanings, that of capability (wisdom) and that of female personification (Wisdom), are crucial for this Wisdom Commentary series that seeks to enable biblical readers to become critical subjects of interpretation.

Wisdom is a state of the human mind and spirit characterized by deep understanding and profound insight. It is elaborated as a quality possessed by the sages but also treasured as folk wisdom and wit. Wisdom is the power of discernment, deeper understanding, and creativity; it is the ability to move and to dance, to make the connections, to savor life, and to learn from experience. Wisdom is intelligence shaped by experience and sharpened by critical analysis. It is the ability to make sound choices and incisive decisions. Its root meaning comes to the fore in its Latin form *sapientia*, which is derived from the verb *sapere*, to taste and to savor something. Hence, this series of commentaries invites readers to taste, to evaluate, and to imagine. In the figure of *Chokmah-Sophia-Sapientia-Wisdom*, ancient Jewish Scriptures seek to hold together belief in the "one" G*d[3] of Israel with both masculine and feminine language and metaphors of the Divine.

---

2. I use wo/man, s/he, fe/male and not the grammatical standard "man" as inclusive terms and make this visible by adding /.

3. I use the * asterisk in order to alert readers to a problem to explore and think about.

In distinction to traditional Scripture reading, which is often individualistic and privatized, the practice and space of Wisdom commentary is public. Wisdom's spiraling presence (*Shekhinah*) is global, embracing all creation. Her voice is a public, radical democratic voice rather than a "feminine," privatized one. To become one of Her justice-seeking friends, one needs to imagine the work of this feminist commentary series as the spiraling circle dance of wisdom/Wisdom,[4] as a Spirit/spiritual intellectual movement in the open space of wisdom/Wisdom who calls readers to critically analyze, debate, and reimagine biblical texts and their commentaries as wisdom/Wisdom texts inspired by visions of justice and well-being for everyone and everything. Wisdom-Sophia-imagination engenders a different understanding of Jesus and the movement around him. It understands him as the child and prophet of Divine Wisdom and as Wisdom herself instead of imagining him as ruling King and Lord who has only subalterns but not friends. To approach the N*T[5] and the whole Bible as Wisdom's invitation of cosmic dimensions means to acknowledge its multivalence and its openness to change. As bread—not stone.

In short, this commentary series is inspired by the feminist vision of the open cosmic house of Divine Wisdom-Sophia as it is found in biblical Wisdom literatures, which include the N*T:

> Wisdom has built Her house
> She has set up Her seven pillars . . .
> She has mixed Her wine,
> She also has set Her table.
> She has sent out Her wo/men ministers
> to call from the highest places in the town . . .
> "Come eat of my bread
> and drink of the wine I have mixed.
> Leave immaturity, and live,
> And walk in the way of Wisdom." (Prov 9:1-3, 5-6)

---

4. I have elaborated such a Wisdom dance in terms of biblical hermeneutics in my book *Wisdom Ways: Introducing Feminist Biblical Interpretation* (Maryknoll, NY: Orbis Books, 2001). Its seven steps are a hermeneutics of experience, of domination, of suspicion, of evaluation, of remembering or historical reconstruction, of imagination, and of transformation. However, such Wisdom strategies of meaning making are not restricted to the Bible. Rather, I have used them in workshops in Brazil and Ecuador to explore the workings of power, Condomblé, Christology, imagining a the*logical wo/men's center, or engaging the national icon of Mary.

5. See the discussion about nomenclature of the two testaments in the Editor's introduction, pages xxxvii–xxxviii.

Editor's Introduction to Wisdom Commentary

"She Is a Breath of the Power of God" (Wis 7:25)

Barbara E. Reid, OP
General Editor

Wisdom Commentary is the first series to offer detailed feminist interpretation of every book of the Bible. The fruit of collaborative work by an ecumenical and interreligious team of scholars, the volumes provide serious, scholarly engagement with the whole biblical text, not only those texts that explicitly mention women. The series is intended for clergy, teachers, ministers, and all serious students of the Bible. Designed to be both accessible and informed by the various approaches of biblical scholarship, it pays particular attention to the world in front of the text, that is, how the text is heard and appropriated. At the same time, this series aims to be faithful to the ancient text and its earliest audiences; thus the volumes also explicate the worlds behind the text and within it. While issues of gender are primary in this project, the volumes also address the intersecting issues of power, authority, ethnicity, race, class, and religious belief and practice. The fifty-eight volumes include the books regarded as canonical by Jews (i.e., the Tanakh); Protestants (the "Hebrew Bible" and the New Testament); and Roman Catholic, Anglican, and Eastern

Orthodox Communions (i.e., Tobit, Judith, 1 and 2 Maccabees, Wisdom of Solomon, Sirach/Ecclesiasticus, Baruch, including the Letter of Jeremiah, the additions to Esther, and Susanna and Bel and the Dragon in Daniel).

A Symphony of Diverse Voices

Included in the Wisdom Commentary series are voices from scholars of many different religious traditions, of diverse ages, differing sexual identities, and varying cultural, racial, ethnic, and social contexts. Some have been pioneers in feminist biblical interpretation; others are newer contributors from a younger generation. A further distinctive feature of this series is that each volume incorporates voices other than that of the lead author(s). These voices appear alongside the commentary of the lead author(s), in the grayscale inserts. At times, a contributor may offer an alternative interpretation or a critique of the position taken by the lead author(s). At other times, they may offer a complementary interpretation from a different cultural context or subject position. Occasionally, portions of previously published material bring in other views. The diverse voices are not intended to be contestants in a debate or a cacophony of discordant notes. The multiple voices reflect that there is no single definitive feminist interpretation of a text. In addition, they show the importance of subject position in the process of interpretation. In this regard, the Wisdom Commentary series takes inspiration from the Talmud and from *The Torah: A Women's Commentary* (ed. Tamara Cohn Eskenazi and Andrea L. Weiss; New York: URJ Press and Women of Reform Judaism, The Federation of Temple Sisterhoods, 2008), in which many voices, even conflicting ones, are included and not harmonized.

Contributors include biblical scholars, theologians, and readers of Scripture from outside the scholarly and religious guilds. At times, their comments pertain to a particular text. In some instances they address a theme or topic that arises from the text.

Another feature that highlights the collaborative nature of feminist biblical interpretation is that a number of the volumes have two lead authors who have worked in tandem from the inception of the project and whose voices interweave throughout the commentary.

Woman Wisdom

The title, Wisdom Commentary, reflects both the importance to feminists of the figure of Woman Wisdom in the Scriptures and the distinct wisdom that feminist women and men bring to the interpretive process. In the Scriptures, Woman Wisdom appears as "a breath of the power of God, and a pure emanation of the glory of the Almighty" (Wis 7:25), who was present and active in fashioning all that exists (Prov 8:22-31; Wis 8:6). She is a spirit who pervades and penetrates all things (Wis 7:22-23), and she provides guidance and nourishment at her all-inclusive table (Prov 9:1-5). In both postexilic biblical and nonbiblical Jewish sources, Woman Wisdom is often equated with Torah, e.g., Sirach 24:23-34; Baruch 3:9–4:4; 38:2; 46:4-5; 2 Baruch 48:33, 36; 4 Ezra 5:9-10; 13:55; 14:40; 1 Enoch 42.

The New Testament frequently portrays Jesus as Wisdom incarnate. He invites his followers, "take my yoke upon you and learn from me" (Matt 11:29), just as Ben Sira advises, "put your neck under her [Wisdom's] yoke and let your souls receive instruction" (Sir 51:26). Just as Wisdom experiences rejection (Prov 1:23-25; Sir 15:7-8; Wis 10:3; Bar 3:12), so too does Jesus (Mark 8:31; John 1:10-11). Only some accept his invitation to his all-inclusive banquet (Matt 22:1-14; Luke 14:15-24; compare Prov 1:20-21; 9:3-5). Yet, "wisdom is vindicated by her deeds" (Matt 11:19, speaking of Jesus and John the Baptist; in the Lukan parallel at 7:35 they are called "wisdom's children"). There are numerous parallels between what is said of Wisdom and of the *Logos* in the Prologue of the Fourth Gospel (John 1:1-18). These are only a few of many examples. This female embodiment of divine presence and power is an apt image to guide the work of this series.

Feminism

There are many different understandings of the term "feminism." The various meanings, aims, and methods have developed exponentially in recent decades. Feminism is a perspective and a movement that springs from a recognition of inequities toward women, and it advocates for changes in whatever structures prevent full flourishing of human beings and all creation. Three waves of feminism in the United States are commonly recognized. The first, arising in the mid-nineteenth century and lasting into the early twentieth, was sparked by women's efforts to be involved in the public sphere and to win the right to vote. In the 1960s and 1970s, the second wave focused on civil rights and equality for women. With the third wave, from the 1980s forward, came global feminism and the emphasis on the contextual nature of interpretation. Now a fourth wave may be emerging, with a stronger emphasis on the intersectionality of women's concerns with those of other marginalized groups and the increased use of the internet as a platform for discussion and activism.[1] As feminism has matured, it has recognized that inequities based on gender are interwoven with power imbalances based on race, class, ethnicity, religion, sexual identity, physical ability, and a host of other social markers.

Feminist Women and Men

Men as well as nonbinary people who choose to identify with and partner with feminist women in the work of deconstructing systems of domination and building structures of equality are rightly regarded as feminists. Some men readily identify with experiences of women who are discriminated against on the basis of sex/gender, having themselves had comparable experiences; others who may not have faced direct discrimination or stereotyping recognize that inequity and problematic characterization still occur, and they seek correction. This series is pleased to include feminist men both as lead authors and as contributing voices.

Feminist Biblical Interpretation

Women interpreting the Bible from the lenses of their own experience is nothing new. Throughout the ages women have recounted the biblical stories, teaching them to their children and others, all the while interpreting them afresh for their time and circumstances.[2] Following is a very brief sketch of select foremothers who laid the groundwork for contemporary feminist biblical interpretation.

One of the earliest known Christian women who challenged patriarchal interpretations of Scripture was a consecrated virgin named Helie, who lived in the second century CE. When she refused to marry, her

---

1. See Martha Rampton, "Four Waves of Feminism" (October 25, 2015), at http://www.pacificu.edu/about-us/news-events/four-waves-feminism; and Ealasaid Munro, "Feminism: A Fourth Wave?," https://www.psa.ac.uk/insight-plus/feminism-fourth-wave.

2. For fuller treatments of this history, see chap. 7, "One Thousand Years of Feminist Bible Criticism," in Gerda Lerner, *Creation of Feminist Consciousness: From the Middle Ages to Eighteen-Seventy* (New York: Oxford University Press, 1993), 138–66; Susanne Scholz, "From the 'Woman's Bible' to the 'Women's Bible,' The History of Feminist Approaches to the Hebrew Bible," in *Introducing the Women's Hebrew Bible*, IFT 13 (New York: T&T Clark, 2007), 12–32; Marion Ann Taylor and Agnes Choi, eds., *Handbook of Women Biblical Interpreters: A Historical and Biographical Guide* (Grand Rapids: Baker Academic, 2012).

parents brought her before a judge, who quoted to her Paul's admonition, "It is better to marry than to be aflame with passion" (1 Cor 7:9). In response, Helie first acknowledges that this is what Scripture says, but then she retorts, "but not for everyone, that is, not for holy virgins."[3] She is one of the first to question the notion that a text has one meaning that is applicable in all situations.

A Jewish woman who also lived in the second century CE, Beruriah, is said to have had "profound knowledge of biblical exegesis and outstanding intelligence."[4] One story preserved in the Talmud (b. Ber. 10a) tells of how she challenged her husband, Rabbi Meir, when he prayed for the destruction of a sinner. Proffering an alternate interpretation, she argued that Psalm 104:35 advocated praying for the destruction of sin, not the sinner.

In medieval times the first written commentaries on Scripture from a critical feminist point of view emerge. While others may have been produced and passed on orally, they are for the most part lost to us now. Among the earliest preserved feminist writings are those of Hildegard of Bingen (1098–1179), German writer, mystic, and abbess of a Benedictine monastery. She reinterpreted the Genesis narratives in a way that presented women and men as complementary and interdependent. She frequently wrote about the Divine as feminine.[5] Along with other women mystics of the time, such as Julian of Norwich (1342–ca. 1416), she spoke authoritatively from her personal experiences of God's revelation in prayer.

In this era, women were also among the scribes who copied biblical manuscripts. Notable among them is Paula Dei Mansi of Verona, from a distinguished family of Jewish scribes. In 1288, she translated from Hebrew into Italian a collection of Bible commentaries written by her father and added her own explanations.[6]

Another pioneer, Christine de Pizan (1365–ca. 1430), was a French court writer and prolific poet. She used allegory and common sense

3. Madrid, Escorial MS, a II 9, f. 90 v., as cited in Lerner, *Feminist Consciousness*, 140.

4. See Judith R. Baskin, "Women and Post-Biblical Commentary," in *The Torah: A Women's Commentary*, ed. Tamara Cohn Eskenazi and Andrea L. Weiss (New York: URJ Press and Women of Reform Judaism, The Federation of Temple Sisterhoods, 2008), xlix–lv, at lii. See Excursus on Mary Magdalene and Beruryah at Luke 24:1-12.

5. Hildegard of Bingen, *De Operatione Dei*, 1.4.100; PL 197:885bc, as cited in Lerner, *Feminist Consciousness*, 142–43. See also Barbara Newman, *Sister of Wisdom: St. Hildegard's Theology of the Feminine* (Berkeley: University of California Press, 1987). See further comments on Hildegard at pp. 160–61.

6. Emily Taitz, Sondra Henry, Cheryl Tallan, eds., *JPS Guide to Jewish Women 600 B.C.E.–1900 C.E.* (Philadelphia: JPS, 2003), 110–11.

to subvert misogynist readings of Scripture and celebrated the accomplishments of female biblical figures to argue for women's active roles in building society.[7]

By the seventeenth century, there were women who asserted that the biblical text needs to be understood and interpreted in its historical context. For example, Rachel Speght (1597–ca. 1630), a Calvinist English poet, elaborates on the historical situation in first-century Corinth that prompted Paul to say, "It is well for a man not to touch a woman" (1 Cor 7:1). Her aim was to show that the biblical texts should not be applied in a literal fashion to all times and circumstances. Similarly, Margaret Fell (1614–1702), one of the founders of the Religious Society of Friends (Quakers) in Britain, addressed the Pauline prohibitions against women speaking in church by insisting that they do not have universal validity. Rather, they need to be understood in their historical context, as addressed to a local church in particular time-bound circumstances.[8]

Along with analyzing the historical context of the biblical writings, women in the eighteenth and nineteenth centuries began to attend to misogynistic interpretations based on faulty translations. One of the first to do so was British feminist Mary Astell (1666–1731).[9] In the United States, the Grimké sisters, Sarah (1792–1873) and Angelina (1805–1879), Quaker women from a slaveholding family in South Carolina, learned biblical Greek and Hebrew so that they could interpret the Bible for themselves. They were prompted to do so after men sought to silence them from speaking out against slavery and for women's rights by claiming that the Bible (e.g., 1 Cor 14:34) prevented women from speaking in public.[10] Another prominent abolitionist, Isabella Baumfree, was a former slave who adopted the name Sojourner Truth (ca. 1797–1883) and quoted the Bible liberally in her speeches[11] and in so doing challenged cultural assumptions and biblical interpretations that undergird gender inequities.

---

7. See further Taylor and Choi, *Handbook of Women Biblical Interpreters*, 127–32.

8. Her major work, *Women's Speaking Justified, Proved and Allowed by the Scriptures*, published in London in 1667, gave a systematic feminist reading of all biblical texts pertaining to women.

9. Mary Astell, *Some Reflections upon Marriage* (New York: Source Book Press, 1970, reprint of the 1730 edition; earliest edition of this work is 1700), 103–4.

10. See further Sarah Grimké, *Letters on the Equality of the Sexes and the Condition of Woman* (Boston: Isaac Knapp, 1838).

11. See, for example, her most famous speech, "Ain't I a Woman?," (quoted on pp. 25–26 below) delivered in 1851 at the Ohio Women's Rights Convention in Akron, OH; http://www.fordham.edu/halsall/mod/sojtruth-woman.asp.

Another monumental work that emerged in nineteenth-century England was that of Jewish theologian Grace Aguilar (1816–1847), *The Women of Israel*,[12] published in 1845. Aguilar's approach was to make connections between the biblical women and contemporary Jewish women's concerns. She aimed to counter the widespread notion that women were degraded in Jewish law and that only in Christianity were women's dignity and value upheld. Her intent was to help Jewish women find strength and encouragement by seeing the evidence of God's compassionate love in the history of every woman in the Bible. While not a full commentary on the Bible, Aguilar's work stands out for its comprehensive treatment of every female biblical character, including even the most obscure references.[13]

The first person to produce a full-blown feminist commentary on the Bible was Elizabeth Cady Stanton (1815–1902). A leading proponent in the United States for women's right to vote, she found that whenever women tried to make inroads into politics, education, or the work world, the Bible was quoted against them. Along with a team of like-minded women, she produced her own commentary on every text of the Bible that concerned women. Her pioneering two-volume project, *The Woman's Bible*, published in 1895 and 1898, urges women to recognize that texts that degrade women come from the men who wrote the texts, not from God, and to use their common sense to rethink what has been presented to them as sacred.

Nearly a century later, *The Women's Bible Commentary*, edited by Carol A. Newsom and Sharon H. Ringe (Louisville: Westminster John Knox, 1992), appeared. This one-volume commentary features North American feminist scholarship on each book of the Protestant canon. Like Cady Stanton's commentary, it does not contain comments on every section of the biblical text but only on those passages deemed relevant to women. It was revised and expanded in 1998 to include the Apocrypha/Deuterocanonical books, and the contributors to this new volume reflect the global face of contemporary feminist scholarship. The revisions made in the third edition, which appeared in 2012, represent the profound advances in feminist biblical scholarship and include newer voices. In both the second and third editions, *The* has been dropped from the title.

12. The full title is *The Women of Israel or Characters and Sketches from the Holy Scriptures and Jewish History Illustrative of the Past History, Present Duty, and Future Destiny of the Hebrew Females, as Based on the Word of God.*

13. See further Eskenazi and Weiss, *The Torah: A Women's Commentary*, xxxviii; Taylor and Choi, *Handbook of Women Biblical Interpreters*, 31–37.

Also appearing at the centennial of Cady Stanton's *The Woman's Bible* were two volumes edited by Elisabeth Schüssler Fiorenza with the assistance of Shelly Matthews. The first, *Searching the Scriptures: A Feminist Introduction* (New York: Crossroad, 1993), charts a comprehensive approach to feminist interpretation from ecumenical, interreligious, and multicultural perspectives. The second volume, published in 1994, provides critical feminist commentary on each book of the New Testament as well as on three books of Jewish Pseudepigrapha and eleven other early Christian writings.

In Europe, similar endeavors have been undertaken, such as the one-volume *Kompendium Feministische Bibelauslegung*, edited by Luise Schottroff and Marie-Theres Wacker (Gütersloh: Gütersloher Verlagshaus, 2007), featuring German feminist biblical interpretation of each book of the Bible, along with apocryphal books, and several extrabiblical writings. This work, now in its third edition, has recently been translated into English.[14] A multivolume project, *The Bible and Women: An Encyclopaedia of Exegesis and Cultural History*, edited by Irmtraud Fischer, Adriana Valerio, Mercedes Navarro Puerto, Christiana de Groot, and Mary Ann Beavis, is currently in production. This project presents a history of the reception of the Bible as embedded in Western cultural history and focuses particularly on gender-relevant biblical themes, biblical female characters, and women recipients of the Bible. The volumes are published in English, Spanish, Italian, and German.[15]

Another groundbreaking work is the collection The Feminist Companion to the Bible Series, edited by Athalya Brenner (Sheffield: Sheffield Academic, 1993–2015), which comprises twenty volumes of commen-

---

14. *Feminist Biblical Interpretation: A Compendium of Critical Commentary on the Books of the Bible and Related Literature*, trans. Lisa E. Dahill, Everett R. Kalin, Nancy Lukens, Linda M. Maloney, Barbara Rumscheidt, Martin Rumscheidt, and Tina Steiner (Grand Rapids: Eerdmans, 2012). Another notable collection is the three volumes edited by Susanne Scholz, *Feminist Interpretation of the Hebrew Bible in Retrospect*, Recent Research in Biblical Studies 7, 8, 9 (Sheffield: Sheffield Phoenix, 2013, 2014, 2016).

15. The first volume, on the Torah, appeared in Spanish in 2009, in German and Italian in 2010, and in English in 2011 (Atlanta: Society of Biblical Literature). Five more volumes are now available: *Feminist Biblical Studies in the Twentieth Century*, ed. Elisabeth Schüssler Fiorenza (2014); *The Writings and Later Wisdom Books*, ed. Christl M. Maier and Nuria Calduch-Benages (2014); *Gospels: Narrative and History*, ed. Mercedes Navarro Puerto and Marinella Perroni; Amy-Jill Levine (English ed.) The Bible and Women: An Encyclopedia of Exegesis and Cultural History, New Testament 2.1 (Atlanta: SBL Press, 2015); *The High Middle Ages*, ed. Kari Elisabeth Børresen and Adriana Valerio (2015); and *Early Jewish Writings*, ed. Eileen Schuller and Marie-Theres Wacker (2017). For further information, see http://www.bibleandwomen.org.

taries on the Old Testament. The parallel series, Feminist Companion to the New Testament and Early Christian Writings, edited by Amy-Jill Levine with Marianne Blickenstaff and Maria Mayo Robbins (Sheffield: Sheffield Academic, 2001–2009), contains thirteen volumes with one more planned. These two series are not full commentaries on the biblical books but comprise collected essays on discrete biblical texts.

Works by individual feminist biblical scholars in all parts of the world abound, and they are now too numerous to list in this introduction. Feminist biblical interpretation has reached a level of maturity that now makes possible a commentary series on every book of the Bible. In recent decades, women have had greater access to formal theological education, have been able to learn critical analytical tools, have put their own interpretations into writing, and have developed new methods of biblical interpretation. Until recent decades the work of feminist biblical interpreters was largely unknown, both to other women and to their brothers in the synagogue, church, and academy. Feminists now have taken their place in the professional world of biblical scholars, where they build on the work of their foremothers and connect with one another across the globe in ways not previously possible. In a few short decades, feminist biblical criticism has become an integral part of the academy.

Methodologies

Feminist biblical scholars use a variety of methods and often employ a number of them together.[16] In the Wisdom Commentary series, the authors will explain their understanding of feminism and the feminist reading strategies used in their commentary. Each volume treats the biblical text in blocks of material, not an analysis verse by verse. The entire text is considered, not only those passages that feature female characters or that speak specifically about women. When women are not apparent in the narrative, feminist lenses are used to analyze the dynamics in the text between male characters, the models of power, binary ways of thinking, and the dynamics of imperialism. Attention is given to how the whole text functions and how it was and is heard, both in its original context and today. Issues of particular concern to women—e.g., poverty, food, health, the environment, water—come to the fore.

16. See the seventeen essays in Caroline Vander Stichele and Todd Penner, eds., *Her Master's Tools? Feminist and Postcolonial Engagements of Historical-Critical Discourse* (Atlanta: Society of Biblical Literature, 2005), which show the complementarity of various approaches.

One of the approaches used by early feminists and still popular today is to lift up the overlooked and forgotten stories of women in the Bible. Studies of women in each of the Testaments have been done, and there are also studies on women in particular biblical books.[17] Feminists recognize that the examples of biblical characters can be both empowering and problematic. The point of the feminist enterprise is not to serve as an apologetic for women; it is rather, in part, to recover women's history and literary roles in all their complexity and to learn from that recovery.

Retrieving the submerged history of biblical women is a crucial step for constructing the story of the past so as to lead to liberative possibilities for the present and future. There are, however, some pitfalls to this approach. Sometimes depictions of biblical women have been naïve and romantic. Some commentators exalt the virtues of both biblical and contemporary women and paint women as superior to men. Such reverse discrimination inhibits movement toward equality for all. In addition, some feminists challenge the idea that one can "pluck positive images out of an admittedly androcentric text, separating literary characterizations from the androcentric interests they were created to serve."[18] Still other feminists find these images to have enormous value.

One other danger with seeking the submerged history of women is the tendency for Christian feminists to paint Jesus and even Paul as liberators of women in a way that demonizes Judaism.[19] Wisdom Commentary

17. See, e.g., Alice Bach, ed., *Women in the Hebrew Bible: A Reader* (New York: Routledge, 1999); Tikva Frymer-Kensky, *Reading the Women of the Bible* (New York: Schocken Books, 2002); Carol Meyers, Toni Craven, and Ross Shepard Kraemer, eds., *Women in Scripture* (Grand Rapids: Eerdmans, 2001); Irene Nowell, *Women in the Old Testament* (Collegeville, MN: Liturgical Press, 1997); Katharine Doob Sakenfeld, *Just Wives? Stories of Power and Survival in the Old Testament and Today* (Louisville: Westminster John Knox, 2003); Mary Ann Getty-Sullivan, *Women in the New Testament* (Collegeville, MN: Liturgical Press, 2001); Bonnie Thurston, *Women in the New Testament: Questions and Commentary*, Companions to the New Testament (New York: Crossroad, 1998).

18. J. Cheryl Exum, "Second Thoughts about Secondary Characters: Women in Exodus 1.8–2.10," in *A Feminist Companion to Exodus to Deuteronomy*, FCB 6, ed. Athalya Brenner (Sheffield: Sheffield Academic, 1994), 75–97, at 76.

19. See Judith Plaskow, "Anti-Judaism in Feminist Christian Interpretation," in *Searching the Scriptures, vol. 1: A Feminist Introduction*, ed. Elisabeth Schüssler Fiorenza with Shelly Matthews (New York: Crossroad, 1993), 1:117–29; Amy-Jill Levine, "The New Testament and Anti-Judaism," in *The Misunderstood Jew: The Church and the Scandal of the Jewish Jesus* (San Francisco: HarperSanFrancisco, 2006), 87–117.

aims to enhance understanding of Jesus as well as Paul as Jews of their day and to forge solidarity among Jewish and Christian feminists.[20]

Feminist scholars who use historical-critical methods analyze the world behind the text; they seek to understand the historical context from which the text emerged and the circumstances of the communities to whom it was addressed. In bringing feminist lenses to this approach, the aim is not to impose modern expectations on ancient cultures but to unmask the ways that ideologically problematic mind-sets that produced the ancient texts are still promulgated through the text. Feminist biblical scholars aim not only to deconstruct but also to reclaim and reconstruct biblical history as women's history, in which women were central and active agents in creating religious heritage.[21] A further step is to construct meaning for contemporary women and men in a liberative movement toward transformation of social, political, economic, and religious structures.[22] In recent years, some feminists have embraced new historicism, which accents the creative role of the interpreter in any construction of history and exposes the power struggles to which the text witnesses.[23]

Literary critics analyze the world of the text: its form, language patterns, and rhetorical function.[24] They do not attempt to separate layers

20. For an overview of the work of Jewish feminists see Mara H. Benjamin, "Tracing the Contours of a Half Century of Jewish Feminist Theology," *JFSR* 36 (2020): 11–31.

21. See, for example, Phyllis A. Bird, *Missing Persons and Mistaken Identities: Women and Gender in Ancient Israel* (Minneapolis: Fortress, 1997); Elisabeth Schüssler Fiorenza, *In Memory of Her: A Feminist Theological Reconstruction of Christian Origins* (New York: Crossroad, 1983); Ross Shepard Kraemer and Mary Rose D'Angelo, eds., *Women and Christian Origins* (New York: Oxford University Press, 1999).

22. See, e.g., Sandra M. Schneiders, *The Revelatory Text: Interpreting the New Testament as Sacred Scripture*, rev. ed. (Collegeville, MN: Liturgical Press, 1999), whose aim is to engage in biblical interpretation not only for intellectual enlightenment but, even more important, for personal and communal transformation. Elisabeth Schüssler Fiorenza (*Wisdom Ways: Introducing Feminist Biblical Interpretation* [Maryknoll, NY: Orbis Books, 2001]) envisions the work of feminist biblical interpretation as a dance of Wisdom that consists of seven steps that interweave in spiral movements toward liberation, the final one being transformative action for change.

23. See Gina Hens-Piazza, *The New Historicism*, GBS, Old Testament Series (Minneapolis: Fortress, 2002).

24. Phyllis Trible was among the first to employ this method with texts from Genesis and Ruth in her groundbreaking book *God and the Rhetoric of Sexuality*, OBT (Philadelphia: Fortress, 1978). Another pioneer in feminist literary criticism is Mieke Bal (*Lethal Love: Feminist Literary Readings of Biblical Love Stories* [Bloomington: Indiana University Press, 1987]). For surveys of recent developments in literary methods,

of tradition and redaction but focus on the text holistically, as it is in its present form. They examine how meaning is created in the interaction between the text and its reader in multiple contexts. Within the arena of literary approaches are reader-oriented approaches, narrative, rhetorical, structuralist, post-structuralist, deconstructive, ideological, autobiographical, and performance criticism.[25] Narrative critics study the interrelation among author, text, and audience through investigation of settings, both spatial and temporal; characters; plot; and narrative techniques (e.g., irony, parody, intertextual allusions). Reader-response critics attend to the impact that the text has on the reader or hearer. They recognize that when a text is detrimental toward women there is the choice either to affirm the text or to read against the grain toward a liberative end. Rhetorical criticism analyzes the style of argumentation and attends to how the author is attempting to shape the thinking or actions of the hearer. Structuralist critics analyze the complex patterns of binary oppositions in the text to derive its meaning.[26] Post-structuralist approaches challenge the notion that there are fixed meanings to any biblical text or that there is one universal truth. They engage in close readings of the text and often engage in intertextual analysis.[27] Within this approach is deconstructionist criticism, which views the text as a site of conflict, with competing narratives. The interpreter aims to expose the fault lines and overturn and reconfigure binaries by elevating the underling of a pair and foregrounding it.[28] Feminists also use other post-

---

see Terry Eagleton, *Literary Theory: An Introduction*, 3rd ed. (Minneapolis: University of Minnesota Press, 2008); Janice Capel Anderson and Stephen D. Moore, eds., *Mark and Method: New Approaches in Biblical Studies*, 2nd ed. (Minneapolis: Fortress, 2008); Michal Beth Dinkler, *Literary Theory and the New Testament*, AYBRL (New Haven: Yale University Press, 2019).

25. See, e.g., J. Cheryl Exum and David J. A. Clines, eds., *The New Literary Criticism and the Hebrew Bible* (Valley Forge, PA: Trinity Press International, 1993); Edgar V. McKnight and Elizabeth Struthers Malbon, eds., *The New Literary Criticism and the New Testament* (Valley Forge, PA: Trinity Press International, 1994).

26. See, e.g., David Jobling, *The Sense of Biblical Narrative: Three Structural Analyses in the Old Testament*, JSOTSup 7 (Sheffield: University of Sheffield Press, 1978).

27. See, e.g., Stephen D. Moore, *Poststructuralism and the New Testament: Derrida and Foucault at the Foot of the Cross* (Minneapolis: Fortress, 1994); *The Bible in Theory: Critical and Postcritical Essays* (Atlanta: Society of Biblical Literature, 2010); Yvonne Sherwood, *A Biblical Text and Its Afterlives: The Survival of Jonah in Western Culture* (Cambridge: Cambridge University Press, 2000).

28. David Penchansky, "Deconstruction," in *The Oxford Encyclopedia of Biblical Interpretation*, ed. Steven McKenzie (New York: Oxford University Press, 2013), 196–205.

modern approaches, such as ideological and autobiographical criticism. The former analyzes the system of ideas that underlies the power and values concealed in the text as well as that of the interpreter.[29] The latter involves deliberate self-disclosure while reading the text as a critical exegete.[30] Performance criticism attends to how the text was passed on orally, usually in communal settings, and to the verbal and nonverbal interactions between the performer and the audience.[31]

From the beginning, feminists have understood that interpreting the Bible is an act of power. In recent decades, feminist biblical scholars have developed hermeneutical theories of the ethics and politics of biblical interpretation to challenge the claims to value neutrality of most academic biblical scholarship. Feminist biblical scholars have also turned their attention to how some biblical writings were shaped by the power of empire and how this still shapes readers' self-understandings today. They have developed hermeneutical approaches that reveal, critique, and evaluate the interactions depicted in the text against the context of empire, and they consider implications for contemporary contexts.[32] Feminists also analyze the dynamics of colonization and the mentalities of colonized peoples in the exercise of biblical interpretation. As Kwok Pui-lan explains, "A postcolonial feminist interpretation of the Bible needs to investigate the deployment of gender in the narration of identity, the negotiation of power differentials between the colonizers and

---

See, for example, Danna Nolan Fewell and David M. Gunn, *Gender, Power, and Promise: The Subject of the Bible's First Story* (Nashville: Abingdon, 1993); David Rutledge, *Reading Marginally: Feminism, Deconstruction and the Bible*, BibInt 21 (Leiden: Brill, 1996).

29. See David Jobling and Tina Pippin, eds., *Semeia 59: Ideological Criticism of Biblical Texts* (Atlanta: Scholars Press, 1992); Terry Eagleton, *Ideology: An Introduction* (London: Verso, 2007).

30. See, e.g., Ingrid Rosa Kitzberger, ed., *Autobiographical Biblical Interpretation: Between Text and Self* (Leiden: Deo, 2002); P. J. W. Schutte, "When *They, We,* and the Passive Become I—Introducing Autobiographical Biblical Criticism," *HTS Teologiese Studies / Theological Studies* 61 (2005): 401–16.

31. See, e.g., Holly E. Hearon and Philip Ruge-Jones, eds., *The Bible in Ancient and Modern Media: Story and Performance* (Eugene, OR: Cascade, 2009).

32. E.g., Gale Yee, ed., *Judges and Method: New Approaches in Biblical Studies* (Minneapolis: Fortress, 1995); Warren Carter, *The Gospel of Matthew in Its Roman Imperial Context* (London: T&T Clark, 2005); *The Roman Empire and the New Testament: An Essential Guide* (Nashville: Abingdon, 2006); Elisabeth Schüssler Fiorenza, *The Power of the Word: Scripture and the Rhetoric of Empire* (Minneapolis: Fortress, 2007); Judith E. McKinlay, *Reframing Her: Biblical Women in Postcolonial Focus* (Sheffield: Sheffield Phoenix, 2004).

the colonized, and the reinforcement of patriarchal control over spheres where these elites could exercise control."[33] Methods and models from sociology and cultural anthropology are used by feminists to investigate women's everyday lives, their experiences of marriage, childrearing, labor, money, illness, etc.[34]

As feminists have examined the construction of gender from varying cultural perspectives, they have become ever more cognizant that the way gender roles are defined within differing cultures varies radically. As Mary Ann Tolbert observes, "Attempts to isolate some universal role that cross-culturally defines 'woman' have run into contradictory evidence at every turn."[35] Some women have coined new terms to highlight the particularities of their socio-cultural context. Many African American feminists, for example, call themselves *womanists* to draw attention to the double oppression of racism and sexism they experience.[36] Similarly, many US Hispanic feminists speak of themselves as *mujeristas* (*mujer* is Spanish for "woman").[37] Others prefer to be called "Latina feminists."[38] As a gender-neutral or nonbinary alternative, many today use Latinx. *Mujeristas*, Latina and Latinx feminists emphasize that the context for their

33. Kwok Pui-lan, *Postcolonial Imagination and Feminist Theology* (Louisville: Westminster John Knox, 2005), 9. See also, Musa W. Dube, ed., *Postcolonial Feminist Interpretation of the Bible* (St. Louis: Chalice, 2000); Cristl M. Maier and Carolyn J. Sharp, *Prophecy and Power: Jeremiah in Feminist and Postcolonial Perspective* (London: Bloomsbury, 2013); L. Juliana Claassens and Carolyn J. Sharp, eds., *Feminist Frameworks and the Bible: Power, Ambiguity, and Intersectionality*, LHBOTS 630 (London: Bloomsbury T&T Clark, 2017).

34. See, for example, Carol Meyers, *Discovering Eve: Ancient Israelite Women in Context* (New York: Oxford University Press, 1991); Luise Schottroff, *Lydia's Impatient Sisters: A Feminist Social History of Early Christianity*, trans. Barbara and Martin Rumscheidt (Louisville: Westminster John Knox, 1995); Susan Niditch, *"My Brother Esau Is a Hairy Man": Hair and Identity in Ancient Israel* (Oxford: Oxford University Press, 2008).

35. Mary Ann Tolbert, "Social, Sociological, and Anthropological Methods," in *Searching the Scriptures*, 1:255–71, at 265.

36. Alice Walker coined the term (*In Search of Our Mothers' Gardens: Womanist Prose* [New York: Harcourt Brace Jovanovich, 1967, 1983]). See also Katie G. Cannon, "The Emergence of Black Feminist Consciousness," in *Feminist Interpretation of the Bible*, ed. Letty M. Russell (Philadelphia: Westminster, 1985), 30–40; Renita Weems, *Just a Sister Away: A Womanist Vision of Women's Relationships in the Bible* (San Diego: Lura Media, 1988); Nyasha Junior, *An Introduction to Womanist Biblical Interpretation* (Louisville: Westminster John Knox, 2015).

37. Ada María Isasi-Díaz (*Mujerista Theology: A Theology for the Twenty-First Century* [Maryknoll, NY: Orbis Books, 1996]) is credited with coining the term.

38. E.g., María Pilar Aquino, Daisy L. Machado, and Jeanette Rodríguez, eds., *A Reader in Latina Feminist Theology* (Austin: University of Texas Press, 2002).

theologizing is *mestizaje* and *mulatez* (racial and cultural mixture), done *en conjunto* (in community), with *lo cotidiano* (everyday lived experience) of Latina women as starting points for theological reflection and the encounter with the divine. Intercultural analysis has become an indispensable tool for working toward justice for women at the global level.[39]

Some feminists are among those who have developed lesbian, gay, bisexual, and transgender (LGBT) interpretation. This approach focuses on issues of sexual identity and uses various reading strategies. Some point out the ways in which categories that emerged in recent centuries are applied anachronistically to biblical texts to make modern-day judgments. Others show how the Bible is silent on contemporary issues about sexual identity. Still others examine same-sex relationships in the Bible by figures such as Ruth and Naomi or David and Jonathan. In recent years, queer theory has emerged; it emphasizes the blurriness of boundaries not just of sexual identity but also of gender roles. Queer critics often focus on texts in which figures transgress what is traditionally considered proper gender behavior.[40]

Feminists have also been engaged in studying the reception history of the text[41] and have engaged in studies in the emerging fields of disability theory (see p. 42, n. 4 in authors' introduction for examples) and of children in the Bible (for examples, see notes in the commentary at 9:43b-48 and 18:15-17).

39. See, e.g., María Pilar Aquino and María José Rosado-Nunes, eds., *Feminist Intercultural Theology: Latina Explorations for a Just World*, Studies in Latino/a Catholicism (Maryknoll, NY: Orbis Books, 2007). See also Michelle A. Gonzalez, "Latina Feminist Theology: Past, Present, and Future," *JFSR* 25 (2009): 150–55. See also Elisabeth Schüssler Fiorenza, ed., *Feminist Biblical Studies in the Twentieth Century: Scholarship and Movement*, The Bible and Women 9.1 (Atlanta: Society of Biblical Literature, 2014), who charts feminist studies around the globe as well as emerging feminist methodologies.

40. See, e.g., Bernadette J. Brooten, *Love Between Women: Early Christian Responses to Female Homoeroticism* (Chicago: University of Chicago Press, 1996); Mary Rose D'Angelo, "Women Partners in the New Testament," *JFSR* 6 (1990): 65–86; Deirdre J. Good, "Reading Strategies for Biblical Passages on Same-Sex Relations," *Theology and Sexuality* 7 (1997): 70–82; Deryn Guest, *When Deborah Met Jael: Lesbian Feminist Hermeneutics* (London: SCM, 2011); Teresa Hornsby and Ken Stone, eds., *Bible Trouble: Queer Readings at the Boundaries of Biblical Scholarship* (Atlanta: Society of Biblical Literature, 2011); Joseph A. Marchal, "Queer Studies and Critical Masculinity Studies in Feminist Biblical Studies," in *Feminist Biblical Studies in the Twentieth Century: Scholarship and Movement*, ed. Elisabeth Schüssler Fiorenza, The Bible and Women 9.1 (Atlanta: Society of Biblical Literature, 2014), 261–80.

41. See Sharon H. Ringe, "A History of Interpretation," in *Women's Bible Commentary*, 5; Marion Ann Taylor and Agnes Choi, eds., *Handbook of Women Biblical Interpreters: A Historical and Biographical Guide* (Grand Rapids: Baker Academic, 2012); Yvonne Sherwood, "Introduction," in *The Bible and Feminism: Remapping the Field* (New York: Oxford University Press, 2017).

Feminists also recognize that the struggle for women's equality and dignity is intimately connected with the struggle for respect for Earth and for the whole of the cosmos. Ecofeminists interpret Scripture in ways that highlight the link between human domination of nature and male subjugation of women. They show how anthropocentric ways of interpreting the Bible have overlooked or dismissed Earth and Earth community. They invite readers to identify not only with human characters in the biblical narrative but also with other Earth creatures and domains of nature, especially those that are the object of injustice. Some use creative imagination to retrieve the interests of Earth implicit in the narrative and enable Earth to speak.[42]

Biblical Authority

By the late nineteenth century, some feminists, such as Elizabeth Cady Stanton, began to question openly whether the Bible could continue to be regarded as authoritative for women. They viewed the Bible itself as the source of women's oppression, and some rejected its sacred origin and saving claims. Some decided that the Bible and the religious traditions that enshrine it are too thoroughly saturated with androcentrism and patriarchy to be redeemable.[43]

In the Wisdom Commentary series, questions such as these may be raised, but the aim of this series is not to lead readers to reject the authority of the biblical text. Rather, the aim is to promote better understanding of the contexts from which the text arose and of the rhetorical effects it has on people in contemporary contexts. Such understanding can lead to a deepening of faith, with the Bible serving as an aid to bring flourishing of life.

Language for God

Because of the ways in which the term "God" has been used to symbolize the divine in predominantly male, patriarchal, and monarchical modes, feminists have designed new ways of speaking of the divine. Some have called attention to the inadequacy of the term *God* by trying

---

42. E.g., Norman C. Habel and Peter Trudinger, *Exploring Ecological Hermeneutics*, SymS 46 (Atlanta: Society of Biblical Literature, 2008); Mary Judith Ress, *Ecofeminism in Latin America*, Women from the Margins (Maryknoll, NY: Orbis Books, 2006).

43. E.g., Mary Daly, *Beyond God the Father: A Philosophy of Women's Liberation* (Boston: Beacon, 1973).

to visually destabilize our ways of thinking and speaking of the divine. Rosemary Radford Ruether proposed God/ess, as an unpronounceable term pointing to the unnameable understanding of the divine that transcends patriarchal limitations.[44] Some have followed traditional Jewish practice, writing G-d. Elisabeth Schüssler Fiorenza has adopted G*d.[45] Others draw on the biblical tradition to mine female and non-gender-specific metaphors and symbols.[46] In Wisdom Commentary, there is not one standard way of expressing the divine; each author will use her or his preferred ways. The one exception is that when the tetragrammaton, YHWH, the name revealed to Moses in Exodus 3:14, is used, it will be without vowels, respecting the Jewish custom of avoiding pronouncing the divine name out of reverence.

Nomenclature for the Two Testaments

In recent decades, some biblical scholars have begun to call the two Testaments of the Bible by names other than the traditional nomenclature: Old and New Testament. Some regard "Old" as derogatory, implying that it is no longer relevant or that it has been superseded. Consequently, terms like Hebrew Bible, First Testament, and Jewish Scriptures and, correspondingly, Christian Scriptures or Second Testament have come into use. There are a number of difficulties with these designations. The term "Hebrew Bible" does not take into account that parts of the Old Testament are written not in Hebrew but in Aramaic.[47] Moreover, for Roman Catholics and Eastern Orthodox believers, the Old Testament includes books written in Greek—the Deuterocanonical books, considered Apocrypha by Protestants.[48] The term "Jewish Scriptures" is inadequate because these

---

44. Rosemary Radford Ruether, *Sexism and God-Talk: Toward a Feminist Theology* (Boston: Beacon, 1993).

45. Elisabeth Schüssler Fiorenza, *Jesus: Miriam's Child, Sophia's Prophet; Critical Issues in Feminist Christology* (New York: Continuum, 1994), 191 n. 3.

46. E.g., Sallie McFague, *Models of God: Theology for an Ecological, Nuclear Age* (Philadelphia: Fortress, 1987); Catherine Mowry LaCugna, *God for Us: The Trinity and Christian Life* (San Francisco: Harper Collins, 1991); Elizabeth A. Johnson, *She Who Is: The Mystery of God in Feminist Theological Discourse* (New York: Crossroad, 1992). See further Elizabeth A. Johnson, "God," in *Dictionary of Feminist Theologies*, ed. Letty M. Russell and J. Shannon Clarkson (Louisville: Westminster John Knox, 1996), 128–30.

47. Gen 31:47; Jer 10:11; Ezra 4:7–6:18; 7:12-26; Dan 2:4–7:28.

48. Representing the *via media* between Catholic and reformed, Anglicans generally consider the Apocrypha to be profitable, if not canonical, and utilize select Wisdom texts liturgically.

books are also sacred to Christians. Conversely, "Christian Scriptures" is not an accurate designation for the New Testament, since the Old Testament is also part of the Christian Scriptures. Using "First and Second Testament" also has difficulties, in that it can imply a hierarchy and a value judgment.[49] Jews generally use the term Tanakh, an acronym for Torah (Pentateuch), Nevi'im (Prophets), and Ketuvim (Writings).

In Wisdom Commentary, if authors choose to use a designation other than Tanakh, Old Testament, and New Testament, they will explain how they mean the term.

Translation

Modern feminist scholars recognize the complexities connected with biblical translation, as they have delved into questions about philosophy of language, how meanings are produced, and how they are culturally situated. Today it is evident that simply translating into gender-neutral formulations cannot address all the challenges presented by androcentric texts. Efforts at feminist translation must also deal with issues around authority and canonicity.[50]

Because of these complexities, the editors of the Wisdom Commentary series have chosen to use an existing translation, the New Revised Standard Version (NRSV), which is provided for easy reference at the top of each page of commentary. The NRSV was produced by a team of ecumenical and interreligious scholars, is a fairly literal translation, and uses inclusive language for human beings. Brief discussions about problematic translations appear in the inserts labeled "Translation Matters." When more detailed discussions are available, these will be indicated in footnotes. In the commentary, wherever Hebrew or Greek words are used, English translation is provided. In cases where a wordplay is involved, transliteration is provided to enable understanding.

Art and Poetry

Artistic expression in poetry, music, sculpture, painting, and various other modes is very important to feminist interpretation. Where possible, art and poetry are included in the print volumes of the series. In

---

49. See Levine, *The Misunderstood Jew*, 193–99.

50. Elizabeth Castelli, "*Les Belles Infidèles*/Fidelity or Feminism? The Meanings of Feminist Biblical Translation," in *Searching the Scriptures*, 1:189–204, here 190.

a number of instances, these are original works created for this project. Regrettably, copyright and production costs prohibit the inclusion of color photographs and other artistic work.

Glossary

Because there are a number of excellent readily available resources that provide definitions and concise explanations of terms used in feminist theological and biblical studies, this series will not include a glossary. We refer you to works such as *Dictionary of Feminist Theologies*, edited by Letty M. Russell and J. Shannon Clarkson (Louisville: Westminster John Knox, 1996), and volume 1 of *Searching the Scriptures*, edited by Elisabeth Schüssler Fiorenza with the assistance of Shelly Matthews (New York: Crossroad, 1993). Individual authors in the Wisdom Commentary series will define the way they are using terms that may be unfamiliar.

A Concluding Word

In just a few short decades, feminist biblical studies has grown exponentially, both in the methods that have been developed and in the number of scholars who have embraced it. We realize that this series is limited and will soon need to be revised and updated. It is our hope that Wisdom Commentary, by making the best of current feminist biblical scholarship available in an accessible format to ministers, preachers, teachers, scholars, and students, will aid all readers in their advancement toward God's vision of dignity, equality, and justice for all.

Acknowledgments

There are a great many people who have made this series possible: first, Peter Dwyer, director of Liturgical Press, and Hans Christoffersen, publisher of the academic market at Liturgical Press, who have believed in this project and have shepherded it since it was conceived in 2008. Editorial consultants Athalya Brenner-Idan and Elisabeth Schüssler

Fiorenza have not only been an inspiration with their pioneering work but have encouraged us all along the way with their personal involvement. Volume editors Mary Ann Beavis, Carol J. Dempsey, Gina Hens-Piazza, Amy-Jill Levine, Linda M. Maloney, Song-Mi Suzie Park, Ahida Pilarski, Sarah Tanzer, and Lauress Wilkins Lawrence have lent their extraordinary wisdom to the shaping of the series, have used their extensive networks of relationships to secure authors and contributors, and have worked tirelessly to guide their work to completion. Four others who have contributed greatly to the shaping of the project are Linda M. Day, Mignon Jacobs, Seung Ai Yang, and Barbara E. Bowe of blessed memory (d. 2010). Editorial and research assistant Susan M. Hickman provided invaluable support with administrative details and arrangements. I am grateful to Brian Eisenschenk and Christine Henderson who assisted Susan Hickman with the Wiki. I am especially thankful to Lauren L. Murphy and Justin Howell for their work in copyediting; and to the staff at Liturgical Press, especially Colleen Stiller, production manager; Stephanie Lancour, production editor; Julie Surma, desktop publisher; Angie Steffens, production assistant; and Tara Durheim, associate publisher.

Authors' Introduction

A Feminist Commentary on an Ambiguous Gospel

To Write a Feminist Commentary

To explain our approach to writing a feminist commentary, we begin with a negative: To write *as a feminist* should not be equated with writing *as a woman*. Such an equation works from two mistaken assumptions: first, that "woman" is a unitary category, that all women are essentially the same and share a universal common perspective; second, that all women share a perspective that is "naturally" feminist. Easy equations between women and feminists are problematic insofar as they overlook the fact that not all women challenge patriarchal/kyriarchal[1] systems of oppression. Some openly embrace and support them.[2]

---

1. Throughout this commentary, *kyriarchy*—rule of the masters or lords—will often be used in place of *patriarchy*—rule of the fathers. Kyriarchy is a neologism first introduced by Elisabeth Schüssler Fiorenza as a better term than patriarchy for theorizing domination and oppression, in that it facilitates the understanding that power relations are pyramidal and interlocking, rather than simply binary. Those with most power in society are at the top of the pyramid—as masters or lords, and not all men are equally empowered. See, for example, Elisabeth Schüssler Fiorenza, *Wisdom Ways: Introducing Feminist Biblical Interpretation* (Maryknoll, NY: Orbis Books, 2001), 102–34.
2. In the US context, Phyllis Schlafly (1924–2016) has epitomized the antifeminist woman. Schlafly, a constitutional lawyer and political activist, was known for

Though we both identify as women, it is not our gender identity that makes this a feminist commentary but rather our politics.[3] This is a feminist project, first, because we recognize that in kyriarchal cultures, both ancient and modern, women and other nondominant persons are commonly subject to oppressions by those who rule over them by means that include silencing, denigration, impoverishment, enslavement, sexual abuse, and other forms of physical violence such as maiming and killing. Further, we recognize that these oppressions are not just the product of individuals engaging in random acts of bad behavior but that they owe to the kyriarchal nature of social institutions—political, religious, economic, legal—such that we might speak of this oppression as systemic or, more colloquially, as "baked into the system." Finally, it is feminist because in our commentary, insofar as our partial vision allows,[4] we identify and

---

staunchly conservative social and political views, including opposition to the Equal Rights Amendment to the US Constitution. In the realm of dystopian fiction, consider the antiwoman, "pro-Gilead" Aunt Lydia in Margaret Atwood's *The Handmaid's Tale* (New York: Alfred A. Knopf, 2006). Aunt Lydia is responsible for the "reeducation" of handmaids into docile receptacles for the sperm of the male heads of household. She spews misogynistic arguments throughout the novel. Thus, she demonstrates how women can be complicit in the most egregious forms of patriarchal rule.

3. Here we take our inspiration from the Black feminist theorist bell hooks, who stresses the importance of politics over identity in the work of liberation and thus argues that the phrase "I advocate feminism" serves better than "I am a feminist" to communicate feminist perspectives and struggles. See bell hooks, *Feminist Theory: From Margin to Center* (Boston: South End Press, 1984), 28–30. See also Elisabeth Schüssler Fiorenza's distinction between the "logic of identity" and the logic of democracy/praxis in *But She Said: Feminist Practices of Biblical Interpretation* (Boston: Beacon, 1992), 102–32.

4. Of course, our own social locations and limited perspectives constrain our identification of what is liberating and what is oppressive in the biblical text. Readers should recognize these evaluations as partial and limited and always subject to further debate. For one instance of how criteria for what constitutes liberation can change as new evaluative paradigms come into view, consider feminist interpretation of the story of the Canaanite woman in Matthew 15:21-28. While this pericope was often celebrated as a triumph of the missionary impulses of the Jesus movement in feminist work from the 1980s and 1990s, Musa W. Dube subsequently provided a strong critique of the colonizing impulse in that celebration, from her postcolonial perspective. See Musa W. Dube, *Postcolonial Feminist Interpretation of the Bible* (Atlanta: Chalice, 2000). For a more recent example of a new evaluative paradigm coming into view, consider the impact of disability studies on biblical interpretation. While it once may have been standard to celebrate biblical stories of healing from physical impairment as stories of "liberation," disability scholars now question how conditions such as blindness or deafness are stigmatized vis-à-vis the "normate" body. See, for instance, Candida R. Moss and Jeremy Schipper, eds., *Disability Studies and Biblical Literature* (New York: Palgrave MacMillan, 2011); Sarah J. Melcher, Mikeal C. Parsons, and Amos Yong, eds., *The Bible*

critique instances of such oppression while embracing aspects of the text that can serve as resources in our struggles for liberation.

As a feminist commentary this volume takes special interest in narratives of women in Luke, but our analysis is not restricted to the question of women alone. We also incorporate gender analysis, a mode of study that pays attention to how notions of masculinity or femininity are understood and valued in a given text.[5] In the ancient world gender was typically conceived on a sliding scale, with dominant forms of masculinity, such as those attained by elite statesmen and valiant warriors, on the highest end of the scale. Clustered on the lower, feminine end of the scale were not just women but also "unmanly men," including male slaves and nonelite men. Though masculinity was valued over femininity, it was not something that automatically accrued to anyone born with male genitalia. Rather, it had to be achieved through acts of dominance, such as superior speaking skill or physical mastery of a weaker opponent. In ancient sources, gradations of masculinity and femininity were commonly organized around questions of insertion and reception, "where those with more power ideally and phallically penetrated those with less."[6]

We utilize gender analysis when we take up Luke's narratives of Satan and the demonic, where we take note of this gospel's special emphasis on the virility of Jesus and his male disciples in their heroic combat with

---

and Disability: A Commentary, Studies in Religion, Theology, and Disability (Waco, TX: Baylor University Press, 2017); Anna Rebecca Solevåg, *Negotiating the Disabled Body: Representations of Disability in Early Christian Texts*, ECL 23 (Atlanta: SBL Press, 2018).

5. For gender analysis of Luke, see Mary Rose D'Angelo, "The ANHP Question in Luke-Acts: Imperial Masculinity and the Deployment of Women in the Early Second Century," in *A Feminist Companion to Luke*, ed. Amy-Jill Levine with Marianne Blickenstaff, FCNTECW 3 (Sheffield: Sheffield Academic, 2002), 44–69; Shelly Matthews, "The Weeping Jesus and the Daughters of Jerusalem: Gender and Conquest in Lukan Lament," in *Doing Gender—Doing Religion: Fallstudien zur Intersektionalität im frühen Judentum, Christentum und Islam*, ed. Ute E. Eisen, Christine Gerber, and Angela Standhartinger, WUNT 302 (Tübingen: Mohr, 2013), 385–403; Brittany E. Wilson, *Unmanly Men: Refigurations of Masculinity in Luke–Acts* (New York: Oxford University Press, 2015); Caryn A. Reeder, *Gendering War and Peace in the Gospel of Luke* (Cambridge: Cambridge University Press, 2019); Brittany E. Wilson, "Masculinity in Luke–Acts: The Lukan Jesus and Muscular Christianity," in *Luke–Acts*, ed. James P. Grimshaw, Texts@Contexts (London: T&T Clark, 2019), 23–33; Christopher B. Zeichmann, "Gender Minorities in and under Roman Power: Race and Respectability Politics in Luke–Acts," in Grimshaw, *Luke–Acts*, 61–73.

6. For this quotation, see Jason Edwards, *Eve Kosofsky Sedgwick*, Routledge Critical Thinkers (New York: Routledge, 2009), 21. For an important analysis of ancient Roman gender ideology, with attention to issues of penetration, see Bernadette J. Brooten, *Love Between Women: Early Christian Responses to Female Homoeroticism* (Chicago: University of Chicago Press, 1996).

Satan (see commentary on Luke 9:37-43; 10:1-20; 11:14-26; 22:31-32). We will also ask whether the depiction of all of Jesus's women followers as having been penetrated by demons (Luke 8:1-3) is a means of underscoring their femininity/weakness.[7] We raise the question of the gender of Jesus himself as we consider the import of his weeping at the sight of Jerusalem (19:41) and also as we consider the crucifixion narrative of Luke 23. With respect to the former passage, we will argue that this depiction of Jesus weeping does not feminize him, as it conforms to a literary topos of acceptable "manly" tears (see commentary on Luke 19). With respect to the crucifixion, we note that there was no surer way to feminize an ancient person than to penetrate them, and crucifixion was a quintessential from of Roman penetration and humiliation.

Furthermore, as several strands of feminist theory have taught us, including Black feminist theory, intersectional feminist theory, and transnational feminist theory, we regard gender as only one facet of identity and recognize that oppression cannot be analyzed along the axis of gender alone.[8] This is because systemic oppressions are produced by the intersection of multiple identity factors, including gender, sexuality, (dis)ability, class, race, nationality, religion, and citizenship. The influence of these identity markers on questions of domination and oppression cannot be treated in isolation, as if they were akin to pearls on a necklace or slices of a pie. Rather, because these identity nodes intersect, the resulting force of oppression for those bearing nondominant status markers is multiplied.

As an illustration of how this intersectionality bears on our analysis of Luke, consider the following: While Joanna the wife of Herod's steward Chuza (8:3), the widow who offers her copper coins to the treasury in the temple (21:2-4), the slave-girl who challenges Peter during Jesus's trial (22:56-57), and the daughters of Jerusalem admonished by Jesus on his way to be crucified (23:28-31) are all women, their respective identities are also inflected by factors such as wealth, marital status, slavery, and Lukan prejudice against Jerusalemites. All of these factors, and not merely their gender, weigh into questions of where these women stand with respect

---

7. For a gender analysis of these Lukan passages on Satan and the demonic, see also Shelly Matthews, "'I Have Prayed for You . . . Strengthen Your Brothers' (Luke 22:32): Jesus's Proleptic Prayer for Peter and Other Gendered Tropes in Luke's War on Satan," in *Petitioners, Penitents, and Poets: On Prayer and Praying in Second Temple Judaism*, ed. Timothy J. Sandoval and Ariel Feldman, BZAW 524 (Berlin: de Gruyter, 2020), 231–46.

8. See, for instance, hooks, *Feminist Theory*; Kimberlé Crenshaw, *On Intersectionality: Essential Writings* (New York: New Press, 2000); Uma Narayan, *Dislocating Cultures: Identities, Traditions and Third World Feminism* (New York: Routledge Press, 1997).

to kyriarchal structures. Because each of these wo/men[9] bears multiple identity markers and stands in a different relationship to oppression, each passage raises a different set of questions for analysis and evaluation.

Because we are aware of the multiaxial nature of oppression, we will also highlight passages in the Third Gospel that bear on other questions of power and domination, such as status, (dis)ability, and prejudice owing to racial, ethnic, and religious difference, even when women, or gender issues, are not in view. Because the Third Gospel contains numerous passages that can be read to support anti-Judaism, and because anti-Judaism has long plagued Christian biblical commentary, including feminist Christian biblical commentary, we attempt to be especially attuned to this problem in our analysis.

Coauthors

Like many of the volumes in Wisdom Commentary series, this one has two principal coauthors. While sharing much in common, we also have our differences. Shelly Matthews is an ordained United Methodist minister and has been teaching at the Brite Divinity School since 2011. Born to a farm family of European ancestry in a sparsely populated region of North Dakota, she is a first-generation college graduate. The tiny Methodist church she attended in the Dakotas became an escape hatch to a considerably wider world owing to the UMC's connectional process that binds small local churches to a global Methodist community and to its generous funding for theology students. She gravitated to the wing of the church committed to justice issues, as articulated in the UMC's

---

9. In order to signal our awareness that not all women are the same, and that in patriarchal/kyriarchal cultures nonelite men are often negated as women, we will sometimes employ the term wo/men rather than women when analyzing particular texts. This interrupted or broken spelling of the term reminds us that women are not unitary but fragmented according to the multiple factors of their identity. It also enables recognition that marginalized men, "unmen," and nonbinary persons can also be included under the sign.

Here we acknowledge our indebtedness to Elisabeth Schüssler Fiorenza, who proposed this way of writing wo/men "in order to lift into critical consciousness the linguistic violence of so-called generic male-centered language. . . . To use 'wo/men' as an inclusive generic term invites male readers both to think twice and to experience what it means not to be addressed specifically." She also uses the term "to avoid an essentialist depiction of 'woman' and to stress the instability of the term. Wo/man is defined not only by gender but also by race, class, and colonial structures of domination. Thus, 'wo/men' can also be equivalent of 'subordinated people'" (*Ephesians*, WCS 50 [Collegeville, MN: Liturgical Press, 2017], xlv); see also Schüssler Fiorenza, *Wisdom Ways*, 107–9.

statement of social principles.[10] While earning her master of divinity degree at Boston University School of Theology, she took several courses with Holocaust survivor and Nobel laureate Elie Wiesel. Concerns with the legacy of Christian anti-Judaism in the post-Holocaust era have continued to fuel her study of biblical texts. Study with Elisabeth Schüssler Fiorenza at the Harvard Divinity School has also been a foundational influence for her. Though she loves engaging with Christian Scripture constructively, with an eye both to teaching and to proclamation, she aims still to be an unflinching critic of kyriarchy interwoven into the Scriptures and into the history of their interpretation.

Barbara Reid is a Roman Catholic Dominican sister of Grand Rapids, Michigan. She is from the US Midwest, born in Detroit, and has been teaching at Catholic Theological Union, a Roman Catholic graduate school of Theology and Ministry in Chicago, since 1988. Being White, from a lower middle-class background, with advanced education, and with the security provided by the religious congregation to which she belongs, she regards herself as privileged. She also considers herself most fortunate to have had many experiences of living with and interacting with people in cultures and places very different from her own, having lectured in over a dozen other countries and teaching students at CTU who come from all over the world. Fluent in Spanish (her undergraduate major), she especially appreciates the many opportunities she has had to interact with people in Latin America. Some of those experiences will be brought into the commentary. Keenly aware of the restrictions in her religious tradition that prevent women from being ordained and from taking on many leadership positions in the church, she nonetheless has found encouragement and freedom to develop her feminist lenses and advocate for change as she works within the Roman Catholic Church.

This commentary has been greatly enriched by our collaboration. As the introduction by the general editor, Barbara, notes, there is no one way of doing feminist biblical interpretation and no singular interpretation of a given text by feminists. We often saw different things in the same text. Most of the time we agreed with one another even as we appreciated the richer insights gained in conversation. In a few instances where we hold strongly different positions and/or where one of us has offered distinctive views on the question in previous publications, we indicate these distinctions. While in most of the commentary we have woven our comments together,

10. For the current statement of the Social Principles of the United Methodist Church, see http://ee.umc.org/what-we-believe/social-principles-social-creed.

one of us having done the initial drafting and the other having added her comments, discerning readers will be able to detect which of us took the lead in drafting which sections, as our writing styles are different. Rather than attempting uniformity of style, we let our diverse voices interweave.

Although we are both White women, we rely on the work of womanists and Latina, Asian, South Asian, African, and Middle Eastern feminists. This will be evident both in the works we cite and in the contributing voices in the excurses. While we recognize that differences in social location lead to different ways of being feminist, for expedience we use "feminist" throughout the commentary in a way that intends to include diverse perspectives.[11]

We turn now to introductory questions concerning the author, composition, date, place, genre, structure, and major theological themes of the Third Gospel.

The Author of the Gospel

The ascription ΕΥΑΓΓΕΛΙΟΝ ΚΑΤΑ ΛΟΥΚΑΝ, "Gospel according to Luke," appears at the end of 𝔓[75], a papyrus considered the Gospel's oldest existing manuscript. There is no additional external evidence for the evangelist's identity. Writing at the end of the second century, Irenaeus identifies the third evangelist with "Luke, the beloved physician" (Col 4:14), Paul's coworker (Phlm 24; 2 Tim 4:11).[12] Some current scholars still hold that position,[13] while others, ourselves included, do not think the author of our gospel, whom we will call "Luke," was personally acquainted with Paul.[14]

---

11. See also comments about distinctive approaches by womanists, Latina feminists, etc. under the subtitle "Methodologies" in the general editor's introduction.

12. Irenaeus, *Haer.* 3.1.1 and 3.14.2–3.

13. E.g., Ben Witherington III, *The Acts of the Apostles: A Socio-Rhetorical Commentary* (Grand Rapids: Eerdmans, 1998), 56–57.

14. There are substantial divergences between the portrait of Paul in Acts (if the author of Luke and Acts is the same) and that which emerges in Paul's own letters. As for the gospel's supposed traces of vocabulary and medical knowledge (W. K. Hobart, *The Medical Language of St. Luke* [London: Longmans Green, 1882]), these can be found in the works of other ancient Greek authors, as shown by H. J. Cadbury, *The Style and Literary Method of Luke*, HTS 6/1 (Cambridge, MA: Harvard University Press, 1920). Some scholars interpret the "we" passages in Acts (16:10-17; 20:5-15; 21:1-18; 27:1–28:16) as evidence that Luke was present with Paul on those sea voyages; others, ourselves included, consider them a literary device (e.g., Susan M. Praeder, "Acts 17:1–28:16: Sea Voyages in Ancient Literature and the Theology of Luke–Acts," *CBQ* 46 [1984]: 683–706).

What we can surmise about the evangelist comes from the gospel itself and the Acts of the Apostles.[15] The polished Greek and use of Greco-Roman literary forms indicate that the author had advanced education and was likely a native speaker of Greek. The author's extensive knowledge of the Septuagint (LXX), the Greek translation of the Hebrew Scriptures, is evident in the numerous allusions and direct citations. In order, first, to have received this education and, second, to have had the leisure to write, the author would have had to be a person of independent means or, more likely, a retainer of a well-to-do person. In the preface (1:1-4), Luke adopts the position of a subordinate to Theophilus, which may well reflect the evangelist's actual social status.[16]

Cracks have appeared in the long-held consensus that Luke was a Gentile, writing for Gentiles.[17] For instance, pointing to Paul's exchange with Agrippa in Acts 26:24-29 as an appeal to those who shared this king's worldview, Loveday Alexander has suggested that Luke was likely writing for Diaspora Jews.[18] Arguing that "Luke was equipped with a cultural basic knowledge that was profiled in an unmistakably Jewish manner," Michael Wolter has proposed that Luke was raised in a Jewish family and was thoroughly integrated into a Jewish milieu.[19] Though our commentary does not hinge on pinning down the ethnic identity of the

---

15. We consider the author of Luke to be the same as that of Acts. The author of Acts presents this work as the second volume by the same author as the gospel: "In the first book, Theophilus, I wrote . . ." (Acts 1:1). Theophilus is also the addressee in Luke 1:3. Scholars who question the authorial unity of the two volumes include Mikeal C. Parsons and Richard I. Pervo, *Rethinking the Unity of Luke and Acts* (Minneapolis: Fortress, 1993); Patricia Walters, *The Assumed Authorial Unity of Luke and Acts: A Reassessment of the Evidence*, SNTSMS 145 (Cambridge: Cambridge University Press, 2009).

16. Amy-Jill Levine and Ben Witherington III, *The Gospel of Luke*, NCBC (Cambridge: Cambridge University Press, 2018), 7–8.

17. Werner Georg Kümmel, in his 1973 introduction to the New Testament, had proclaimed that Luke's Gentile identity was an indisputable fact. See *Einleitung in das Neue Testament*, 17th ed. (Heidelberg: Quelle und Meyer, 1973), 118. Recent commentators who assume that Luke is Gentile include François Bovon, *Luke 1: A Commentary on the Gospel of Luke 1:1–9:50*, trans. Christine M. Thomas, Hermeneia (Minneapolis: Fortress, 2002), 8; Richard Pervo, *Acts*, Hermeneia (Minneapolis: Fortress, 2009), 5–12.

18. Loveday Alexander, "The Acts of the Apostles as an Apologetic Text," in *Apologetics in the Roman Empire: Pagans, Jews, and Christians*, ed. Mark Edwards, Martin Goodman, Simon Price, and Christopher Rowland (Oxford: Oxford University Press, 1999), 15–44, esp. 43.

19. Michael Wolter, *The Gospel According to Luke: Volume 1 (Luke 1–9:50)*, trans. Wayne Coppins and Christoph Heilig (Waco, TX: Baylor University Press, 2016), 11. See also Rick Strelan, *Luke the Priest: The Authority of the Author of the Third Gospel* (Aldershot: Ashgate, 2008), who argues that the author was a Jewish priest, writing for pious Jews.

author or first audience, our own concerns with Luke's harsh polemic against nonbelieving Jews (see below) lead us to conclude that, even if the author is Jewish, this identity does not lead in the end to a sympathetic rendering of traditional Jewish practice and teaching. Likewise, even if the first audience were Jewish, they were also Jews whom Luke freely subjected to this anti-Jewish polemic. Thus, we come again to the recognition that one's identity does not necessarily guarantee a predictable set of political-religious practices and beliefs. This is as true for the question of ethnic identity as it is for the question of gender, to which we now turn.

Because of the number of episodes in the Third Gospel that feature women, some scholars have proposed that the third evangelist was a woman.[20] Since there is evidence in Greek and Latin literature that some women had the education, skills, and opportunity to write, such a proposal is not entirely out of the question (see excursus on women's authorship).[21] But still, if the author of Luke is actually female, she takes

---

20. E.g., E. Jane Via, "Women in the Gospel of Luke," in *Women in the World's Religions: Past and Present*, ed. Ursula King (New York: Paragon House, 1987), 49–50 nn. 37–40. Similar assertions have been made about the book of Ruth, the story of Joseph and Aseneth, certain chapters of the *Testament of Job*, and portions of *The Acts of Paul and Thecla*. See Mary R. Lefkowitz, "Did Ancient Women Write Novels?," in *"Women Like This": New Perspectives on Jewish Women in the Greco-Roman World*, ed. Amy-Jill Levine, EJL 1 (Atlanta: Scholars Press, 1991), 199–219. Elisabeth Schüssler Fiorenza suggests that the author of the Gospel of John might have been a woman (*In Memory of Her: A Feminist Theological Reconstruction of Christian Origins* [New York: Crossroad, 1984], 333).

21. William V. Harris (*Ancient Literacy* [Cambridge, MA: Harvard University Press, 1989]) observes that we shall never know how many people in the Roman world were literate, and he assumes that the majority were illiterate. In societies in which illiteracy is widespread, a higher proportion of women than men are illiterate (23). Obstacles to literacy include the price and availability of writing materials, lack of network of schools, and lack of eyeglasses. Ross Shepard Kraemer ("Monastic Jewish Women in Greco-Roman Egypt: Philo Judaeus on the Therapeutrides," *Signs* 14 [1989]: 342–70) shows that "While it is unlikely that very many women, Jewish or otherwise, would have been so highly educated, the evidence from papyri, inscriptions, and literature suggests that at least some women in Alexandria and in other communities with substantial Jewish populations in this period were well educated" (350). Alan R. Millard (*Reading and Writing in the Time of Jesus* [Washington Square: New York University Press, 2000]) shows that writing was ubiquitous in Herodian Palestine, and used widely in the affairs of daily life, religious and secular (228). He estimates a high literacy rate among Jewish males who were expected to be able to read from the Scriptures in synagogue services (157) (as Jesus is portrayed in Luke 4:18). Although he does not take up the topic of women's literacy, he speculates that Joanna, wife of a high official of Herod Antipas (Luke 8:1-3) would have been used to writing (223). Millard also notes the importance of the archive of papyrus documents

on a male persona, as the verb παρηκολουθηκότι, "investigating" (1:3), referring to the writer's activity, is a masculine participle. Further, if the author is a woman, she is a woman who very much favors kyriarchy and works to uphold it, as will be evident throughout this commentary.

> ### Women's Authorship in Antiquity
>
> While women authored poetry, epigrams, letters meant for public circulation, and philosophical treatises in antiquity,[22] only fragments of their work still exist, along with references in works by male authors to female writing.[23] We wonder whether we have works by women where the author is anonymous or in other cases pseudonymous, that is, a female author who writes under a male penname. Such measures could ensure greater acceptance and readership of her work.[24]

discovered in 1960 in the Judean desert that belonged to Babatha (115). The Babatha archive contains deeds of gift, purchase and sale, marriage, and the like, written between 93 and 132 CE. These not only attest to Babatha's literacy but also give insight into the activities in which she was involved, such as ownership and management of property and involvement with monetary transactions. See further Naphtali Lewis, Yigael Yadin, and Jonas C. Greenfield, *The Documents from the Bar Kokhba Period in the Cave of Letter. I. Greek Papyri*, JDS (Jerusalem: Israel Exploration Society, 1989). See also Catherine Hezser, *Jewish Literacy in Roman Palestine*, TSAJ 81 (Tübingen: Mohr Siebeck, 2001); Chris Keith, *Literacy: New Testament*, Oxford Bibliographies Online (New York: Oxford University Press, 2015). On Jesus's literacy, see Chris Keith, *Jesus' Literacy: Scribal Culture and the Teacher from Galilee*, Library of Historical Jesus Studies 8, LNTS 413 (New York: T&T Clark, 2011).

For an analysis of contemporary disparities in literacy between males and females, see https://looker.com/blog/data-of-women-education-and-literacy-around-the-world.

22. Lefkowitz ("Did Ancient Women Write Novels?," 214) notes that no prose known to be written by a woman survives from the first centuries CE.

23. For examples from both Jewish and Christian sources, see Ross Shepard Kraemer, "Women's Authorship of Jewish and Christian Literature in the Greco-Roman Period," in Levine, *"Women Like This,"* 221–42; Ross Shepard Kraemer, *Unreliable Witnesses: Religion, Gender, and History in the Greco-Roman Mediterranean* (Oxford: Oxford University Press, 2011); Lefkowitz, "Did Ancient Women Write Novels?," 199–219; Jane McIntosh Snyder, *The Woman and the Lyre: Women Writers in Classical Greece and Rome* (Carbondale: Southern Illinois University Press, 1989).

24. Contemporary examples include French novelist Amantine Lucile Aurore Dupin (1804–1876), who used the name George Sand; English novelist, poet, and journalist Mary Ann Evans (1819–1880), who adopted the name George Eliot; British writer Violet Paget (1856–1935) who went by Vernon Lee; and Danish author Baroness Karen Christenze von Blixen-Finecke (1885–1962), who took the pen name Isak Dinesen.

Determining whether an ancient writing could have been authored by a woman is a complex task. Mary Lefkowitz has analyzed epigrams, prose treatises, and poetry written by women from the classical Greek, Hellenistic, and Roman periods and notes certain traits that recur in them. Unlike the poems of men who write about women, women's poems about women tend to describe "women's thoughts about aspects of their lives not connected with marriage or sexuality."[25] They emphasize women's love for other women, especially childhood companions and daughters. They say little or nothing about men. Male authors, by contrast, tend to call attention to themselves "or to those aspects of women's lives that are specifically concerned with men, like marriage."[26] Similarly, Jane McIntosh Snyder finds in her study of four women poets of Hellenistic Greece—Anyte, Nossis, Moero, and Erinna—that "women writers of postclassical Greece treated not only some of the standard themes characteristic of contemporary male writers— epitaphs for a fallen solder, praise of the dead, dedications to gods and goddesses, references to poets of the past, descriptions of pastoral scenes, and so on— but also themes which can be identified particularly with the female experience in the ancient world," such as descriptions of children's play, weaving, emotional attachment and commitment between women, Baukis (the poor woman to whom Zeus and Hermes appeared in Greek mythology), and the special relationship between women and the goddess Aphrodite. These subjects are "almost wholly absent from the works of their male contemporaries."[27]

But the assumption that only women can write sympathetically about women or portray women who take initiative in a positive light is itself problematic. Ross Kraemer observes, "Much feminist research has demonstrated the degree to which many if not most women inculcate the dominant, misogynist values and perspective of

---

25. Lefkowitz, "Did Ancient Women Write Novels?," 213. Stevan Davies proposes that women authored several early Christian apocryphal acts, based on the fact that women, not men, play central roles and are not denigrated (*The Revolt of the Widows: The Social World of the Apocryphal Acts* [Carbondale: Southern Illinois University Press, 1980]). Dennis R. MacDonald (*The Legend and the Apostle: The Battle for Paul in Story and Canon* [Philadelphia: Westminster, 1983]) argues that, in their current form, these works are more likely to have been collected and edited by men.

26. Lefkowitz, "Did Ancient Women Write Novels?," 214.

27. Snyder, *The Woman and the Lyre*, 98.

their own cultures into their self-understanding."[28] When it comes to the Gospel of Luke, the kinds of features Mary Lefkowitz and Jane Snyder have identified in works by female authors are lacking. Whether that tells us anything about the author is not possible to say with certitude.

As we continue to call the author of the gospel "Luke" throughout this commentary, we ask our readers to remember the uncertainties surrounding this author's identity.

Nossis and Erinna: Women Poets of Hellenistic Greece

We know only a scant amount of the works of Greek women poets from Hellenistic times (323 BCE–30 BCE). One was Nossis of Locri (a Greek colony founded in southern Italy in the seventh century BCE). Twelve epigrams[29] of Nossis survive. Written around 300 BCE, "they reflect a distinctly female world centered around the worship of Hera and Aphrodite."[30] In the following epigram, Nossis celebrates the delights of Eros (the Greek god of sexual desire):[31]

Nothing is sweeter than Eros.
All other delights
hold second place—I spit out
from my mouth even
honey.
Nossis declares this: whoever
Cypris[32] has not loved
Does not know what sort of
blossoms her roses are.

In the next epigram, Nossis sees herself as following the tradition of the famous ca. seventh-century female poet Sappho:

Stranger, if you sail toward
Mytilene[33] of the beautiful
dances

---

28. Kraemer, "Women's Authorship," 233.

29. "The epigram was a short poem in elegiac couplets, that is, pairs of lines of which the first was a hexameter line and the second a shorter line derived from the hexameter. Originally the epigram had served the limited purpose of epitaph, . . . but in the Hellenistic period, epigrams had come to be used to treat any number of subjects—laments, dedications, love affairs, family pets, and so on" (Snyder, *The Woman and the Lyre*, 66).

30. Ibid., 77.

31. These poems are from ibid., 77–78, 87.

32. Another name for Aphrodite, the goddess associated with love, beauty, pleasure, passion, and procreation.

33. Mytilene, founded in the eleventh century BCE, is the capital city and port of the island of Lesbos.

to be inspired by the flower of
Sappho's charms,
Say that the land of Locri gave
birth to one dear to the Muses,
and when you have learned
that my name is Nossis,
go your way.

We know more about another poet, Erinna, from the praise she receives from male authors than from her own writing, as all that has survived are three epigrams and the partial remains of a longer poem. Biographical information about her is sketchy. From the male authors who write about her, such as Asclepiades (who was born around 320 BCE), we surmise that Erinna wrote around 300 BCE. Her reputation endured at least into the first century CE,

as this epigram by Antipater of Sidon (writing 20 BCE–20 CE) shows:

Erinna is a writer of few verses,
nor is she wordy in
her songs,
but she received this brief epic
from the Muse.
So she does not fail to be
remembered, nor is she
confined
under the shadowy wing of
black night.
But we, O stranger, we
wither away in heaps—the
numberless
myriads of later singers.
Better the small murmuring of
the swan than the
cawing of jackdaws sounding
all through the spring
clouds.

Sources

The author acknowledges not being an eyewitness (1:2). That Luke used the Gospel of Mark as one source is virtually certain, since much of what Luke recounts occurs in the same language and sequence as Mark. Luke also seems to have used a source containing sayings of Jesus to which Matthew also had access. To date, no ancient copy of this source has been found, though it appears to have been a written source, as there are some 278 verses that occur in the First and Third Gospels in the same order and with similar wording. Because the existence of an independent sayings source used by both Matthew and Luke was first hypothesized in German biblical scholarship, it is commonly referred to as "Q," from the German word for source, *Quelle*. While a number of biblical scholars are coming to doubt the existence of Q and, instead, suggest that Luke had access not only to Mark's Gospel but also to Matthew's,[34] we regard the

---

34. See, for instance, Mark Goodacre, *The Case against Q: Studies in Markan Priority and the Synoptic Problem* (Harrisburg, PA: Trinity Press International, 2002).

arguments in support of Q more convincing than alternative constructions of the relationships among the first three gospels.[35]

There is also material unique to Luke, which likely came from a separate source and was not simply the product of the evangelist's own creativity. For example, there was likely a source from which Luke obtained
information about the Herodian family whose members appear more
frequently in Luke (and Acts) than in the other gospels.[36] Finally, the
evangelist may have had access to traditions that were preserved and
shaped in circles of women disciples, highlighting their interactions with
Jesus and their contributions to the early communities of believers.[37]

The Synoptic Problem

As noted above, Luke likely draws on Mark as a source for his gospel,
along with a collection of sayings, Q, that is used also in the Gospel of Matthew. The proposal that two sources, Mark and Q, were used by the authors of both Matthew and Luke is commonly known as the "two-source
hypothesis." The two-source hypothesis has long been regarded by many
scholars as the best solution to "the Synoptic problem," the question of
how to account for the relationships between Matthew, Mark, and Luke,
given their various commonalities and differences. Both authors of this
commentary assume the two-source hypothesis in their study of Luke.

Is there any feminist stake in engaging the Synoptic problem? Inas-
much as feminists value multiple voices over claims to a monolithic tra-

---

35. For John Kloppenborg's earliest challenge to Goodacre's proposal, see "On
Dispensing with Q? Goodacre on the Relation of Luke to Matthew," *NTS* 49 (2003):
210–36. The debate has continued. For recent assessment of that debate, with important bibliography, see Mogens Müller and Heike Omerzu, eds., *Gospel Interpretation
and the Q-Hypothesis*, LNTS 573 (London: Bloomsbury T&T Clark, 2018).

36. The gospel narrative begins by dating the story to the time of King Herod of
Judea (1:5). This reference is to Herod "the Great," who ruled between 37 and 4 BCE.
Herod (Antipas), his son, tetrarch of the Galilee, appears in Luke 3:1, 19; 8:3; 9:7, 9;
13:31; 23:7-12, 15; Acts 4:27. References to Herod Agrippa (the grandson of Herod
the Great and Mariamne and son of Aristobolus), who was king of Judea from 41 to
44 CE, appear in Acts 12:1-12, 20-23. Acts 13:1 introduces his son, Herod Agrippa II,
who, like Herod Antipas is also called "Herod the tetrarch." Later, Luke calls him
"King Agrippa" (Acts 25:13, 24, 26; 26:2, 19, 27). Acts 23:35 mentions this Herod's
praetorium as the place where Paul is held in custody.

37. For the argument that canonical passion narratives originate in stories created
in women's gatherings both to mourn and to find meaning in the death of Jesus, see
Marianne Sawicki, *Seeing the Lord: Resurrection and Early Christian Practices* (Minneapolis: Fortress, 1994); Kathleen E. Corley, *Maranatha: Women's Funerary Rituals and
Christian Origins* (Minneapolis: Fortress, 2010).

dition, the answer may be yes. As John Kloppenborg notes, the proposal that eliminates Q and argues that Mark was used by Matthew, and then Luke used both of these gospels, assumes "a high degree of continuity between the historical Jesus and the practices and dogmatic views of the early Jesus movement and a high degree of uniformity among various streams of primitive Christianity thereafter."[38] Feminists tend to get better leverage within frameworks that assume our texts and traditions are multilayered rather than uniform. Such a framework allows us more easily to tease out minority voices, alternate views, and struggles against forces that both silence wo/men and inscribe kyriarchal perspectives as if they were monolithic—as if they were the only ones that matter.[39]

Date

Scholarly consensus dates the Gospel of Luke to the middle of the 80s CE. This chronology depends in part on the hypothesis that Luke used Mark as a source and that Mark dates to near 70 CE, either in the immediate run-up to or the immediate aftermath of the war between Rome and Judaea.[40] This dating also depends on the fact that Luke is aware of, and finds inadequate, other accounts of the story of Jesus, including that of Mark (Luke 1:1-14).

While our commentary does not require a more precise dating, Shelly has noted that assigning the completion of Luke to a fixed first-century date does not account for the multiple indications that the gospel text remained fluid for several centuries. The late second-century teacher Marcion, whose popularity was so great that Christian heresiologists devoted entire tomes to railing against him, possessed a form of Luke's Gospel that did not contain chapters 1 and 2.[41] Furthermore, the manuscript tradition

---

38. John S. Kloppenborg, "Conceptual Stakes in the Synoptic Problem," in Müller and Omerzu, *Gospel Interpretation and the Q-Hypothesis*, 13–42, here 42.

39. For a recent feminist analysis of Q, see Sara Parks, *Gender in the Rhetoric of Jesus: Women in Q* (Lanham, MD: Fortress Academic, 2019).

40. See, e.g., Joseph A. Fitzmyer, *The Gospel According to Luke I–IX*, AB 28 (Garden City, NY: Doubleday, 1981), 53–57.

41. The traditional explanation for Marcion's abbreviated gospel, offered by Tertullian in the late second/early third century, is that Marcion excised the first two chapters of canonical Luke because he rejected the material's allusion to the Septuagint, Jewish ritual practices, and positive views of bodily concerns like pregnancy, parturition, and circumcision. Increasingly this view has been challenged by those who note Marcion's redactional tendencies bend in the direction of conservation rather than mutilation. One alternative explanation for the absence of Luke 1 and 2

attests several variants, clustered especially in the final three chapters of Luke, which suggests that the ending to the gospel was a source of contention for at least three centuries.[42] Finally, Shelly's agreement with a recent cluster of arguments for dating of the book of Acts to the second century, and possibly as late as 130 CE, leads her to ask whether the Third Gospel also reflects concerns of a developing second-century form of early Christianity.[43]

As with the issue of sources, we ask here whether anything about dating the gospel matters in a feminist reading. The answer is similar: thinking about the gospel as fluid, as an open book that was subject to reworking, and thus whose final form was contested, moves us from a framework that assumes a high degree of continuity and uniformity within developing Christian tradition to a framework allowing for multiplicity and contest—for struggle among competing viewpoints concerning what constitutes "gospel." To acknowledge this contest is to acknowledge multiple voices—including minority voices eventually suppressed by developing orthodoxy—and feminists tend to be concerned to bring as many voices into the conversation as possible. As this commentary shows in its discussion of the gospel's earliest and latest chapters, recognizing variant versions raises questions of immediate

---

in Marcion's gospel is that the first two chapters are a later, perhaps anti-Marcionite addition to the gospel. For discussion and entry into this debate, see Shelly Matthews, "Does Dating Luke–Acts into the Second Century Affect the Q Hypothesis?," in Müller and Omerzu, *Gospel Interpretation and the Q-Hypothesis*, 245–65, esp. 253–60; Andrew Gregory, *The Reception of Luke and Acts in the Period before Irenaeus*, WUNT 2.169 (Tübingen: Mohr Siebeck, 2003), 173–209; Jason D. BeDuhn, *The First New Testament: Marcion's Scriptural Canon* (Salem, OR: Polebridge, 2013), 78–92; Joseph B. Tyson, *Marcion and Luke–Acts: A Defining Struggle* (Columbia: University of South Carolina Press, 2006).

42. For the argument that the Third Gospel was an "open book," subject to considerable expansion and reworking in the first three centuries of the Common Era, see D. C. Parker, *The Living Text of the Gospels* (Cambridge: Cambridge University Press, 1997), 148–74. Some of the most well-known textual variants where verses are lacking in these later chapters of Luke include Luke 22:20, Jesus's taking a second cup after the Last Supper; Luke 22:43-44, Jesus's sweat is like drops of blood and he is supported by an intervening angel; Luke 23:34a, Jesus's prayer for forgiveness of his crucifiers.

43. For discussion, see Matthews, "Dating Luke–Acts into the Second Century?" For instances where Luke appears to reflect second-century concerns, consider his inclusion of Roman soldiers as potential baptizees of John the Baptist (3:14); the totalizing nature of assertions that Jesus fulfills Scripture in its entirety (24:27); the distinctive emphasis on Jesus's resurrection *in the flesh* (24:39).

interest to feminists—particularly as these variants concern the value of flesh, the body, birth, the nature of resurrection, and the question of who is authorized to speak as legitimate witness to the resurrection. (See commentary on chapters 1–2 and 24.)

Place

The oldest tradition about the locale in which Luke was writing dates to the second century. An extratextual Prologue to the gospel asserts that Luke was a native of Antioch in Syria.[44] Scholars have suggested other locations, including Ephesus,[45] Caesarea, the Decapolis, Pisidian Antioch, Philippi, and Cyrene (identifying the evangelist with Lucius of Cyrene of Acts 13:1).[46] We do not think that determining the precise setting is essential to our interpretation. What we conclude is that the audience for the gospel appears to be Greek-speaking, urban, predominantly Gentile Christian, with a significant number of prosperous members, including rich women patrons.[47]

Genre

Both the gospel and Acts exhibit features of popular Greco-Roman literary types: biographies, monographs, histories, antiquities, apologies, and historical novels.[48] In addition, they are suffused with biblical language, imagery, settings, and character types.

---

44. This tradition is reiterated by Eusebius (*Hist. eccl.* 3.4.6) and Jerome (*De vir. ill.* 7).

45. See remarks by Linda M. Maloney in her forthcoming commentary on *Acts of the Apostles* in the Wisdom Commentary series.

46. Justin R. Howell, *The Pharisees and Figured Speech in Luke–Acts*, WUNT 2.456 (Tübingen: Mohr Siebeck, 2017), devotes a chapter to evaluating proposals for Judea, Ephesus, and Antioch in Syria for the provenance of Luke–Acts. He summarizes: "All we can conclude is that the author lived and wrote somewhere within the Mediterranean basin, possibly Antioch" (71).

47. Shelly Matthews, *First Converts: Rich Pagan Women and the Rhetoric of Mission in Early Judaism and Christianity* (Stanford, CA: Stanford University Press, 2001).

48. Richard I. Pervo (*The Gospel of Luke*, The Scholars Bible [Salem, OR: Polebridge, 2014], 1) sees the gospel as a biography, like other ancient lives of prophets, philosophers, leaders, and holy persons. Dennis R. MacDonald thinks that the evangelist was aware of the *Aeneid* and shaped the narrative structure and development of the gospel to rival it (*Luke and Vergil: Imitations of Classical Greek Literature*, The New Testament and Greek Literature, vol. 2 [Lanham, MD: Rowman & Littlefield, 2015]). See also Marianne Palmer Bonz, *The Past as Legacy: Luke–Acts and Ancient Epic* (Minneapolis: Fortress, 2000).

In Lukan studies the identification of genre has often been pegged to the question of the gospel's "historical reliability," with more conserving scholars assigning this work to the genre of ancient history as an indication of its accuracy.[49] While both of us will engage with the gospel for purposes of historical reconstruction, neither of us sees a direct line between Luke's narrative and "what really happened." We recognize that ancient narrators, including Luke, are much more concerned with matters of usefulness,[50] with inculcating particular values in readers, and with communicating "good news" rather than with questions of accuracy that one might expect from modern historians or journalists. For example, the episode with Martha and Mary (10:38-42) is more of a vehicle for Luke to inculcate his preferred behavior for women than it is a precise record of something that happened in the life of Jesus.

Structure

Like the other Synoptic Gospels, Luke's narrative has two major parts: Jesus's ministry in the Galilee (4:14–9:50) and his journey to, ministry in, and execution in Jerusalem (9:51–23:56). It is likely that Luke has taken the literary-theological schema from Mark. It is also more probable that Jesus traveled often to Jerusalem, as John 2:13; 7:10; 12:12 and even Luke 2:41-51 indicate. Luke presents Jesus's public ministry as preceded by preparatory episodes (3:1–4:13), infancy narratives (1:5–2:52) and a formal Prologue (1:1-4). The work concludes with the finding of the empty tomb by the women disciples and the appearances and ascension of the risen Christ (24:1-53).[51] Particularly important for feminists is to note Luke's framing of the gospel narrative with powerful prophetic women in chapters 1 and 2 (unique to this gospel) and the faithful presence and proclamation of women disciples in the final two chapters. In addition, Luke alone introduces women disciples during the Galilean ministry, and their presence is implied in the journey to Jerusalem. In this latter

---

49. See, e.g., Todd Penner, *In Praise of Christian Origins: Stephen and the Hellenists in Lukan Apologetic Historiography* (New York: T&T Clark, 2004), 104–222.

50. On the influence of the *chreai* or "useful example," an ancient Greek rhetorical form, on gospel composition, see David B. Gowler, "The Chreia," in *The Historical Jesus in Context*, ed. Amy-Jill Levine, Dale C. Allison Jr., and John Dominic Crossan, Princeton Readings in Religion (Princeton: Princeton University Press, 2006), 132–48.

51. This outline follows essentially that of Sharon H. Ringe, *Luke*, Westminster Bible Companion (Louisville: Westminster John Knox, 1995), v–xi.

section, there are also uniquely Lukan episodes and parables that feature women. How to evaluate the rhetorical impact of the appearance of women at key junctures in the gospel is a question we take up at the end of this introduction.

Theological Themes

The distinct theological emphases in the Third Gospel include stress on the fulfillment of Scripture, salvation, prayer, the dangers of wealth, association with tax collectors and sinners, the power of the Spirit, table companionship, and journeying. Luke uses these themes to invite the reader into an understanding of and commitment to Jesus. Each theme is explained more fully in the commentary the first time it appears.[52]

Yet two other important Lukan perspectives require more extensive elaboration, in part because of the harm certain interpretations have created: Luke's attitude toward Jews who do not follow Jesus and the evangelist's portrayal of women.

The Lukan Attitude toward Jews

The question of whether or not the Gospel of Luke (and Acts) may be considered anti-Jewish remains debated among scholars. For those who would defend Luke against the charges of anti-Judaism, the following arguments have been marshalled: (a) Luke cannot be considered anti-Jewish because he values many Jewish institutions, including the temple and the priesthood (see especially Luke 1–2; 24:52–53), and the Jewish Scriptures; (b) Luke directs his polemic not at "the Jews" writ large but rather at smaller groups, such as the Jewish leaders or residents of Jerusalem, who alone are responsible for Jesus's crucifixion; (c) Luke is writing "within Judaism," and therefore his polemic against Jews needs to be understood as intramural, akin to the polemic that could be hurled by an angry prophet like Jeremiah against his own people.[53]

---

52. For further treatment of fulfillment of Scripture see comments at 4:21; salvation at 1:47; prayer at 11:2; the dangers of wealth at 16:1; association with those on the margins at 4:16; the power of the Spirit at 3:22; table companionship at 14:1; journeying at 9:51; and women disciples at 5:30.

53. For a summary of various positions in scholarship at the end of the twentieth century, see Mark Allan Powell, *What Are They Saying about Luke?* (New York: Paulist Press, 1989), 51–59; Joseph B. Tyson, ed., *Luke–Acts and the Jewish People: Eight Critical*

We find each of these positions problematic. First, Luke's privileging of Jewish institutions such as the temple and Jewish texts is better understood as appropriation rather than appreciation. Typically for Luke, as for later Christian apologists, the value of the Jewish tradition, up to the time of Jesus, is that it either aligns with or points to Jesus, as the fulfillment of Jewish prophecy, Jewish worship, Jewish Scripture. We note instances of this phenomenon as we proceed in our commentary, but to cite a few examples here: Luke 24:27 proclaims that all of the Jewish Scriptures are fulfilled by Jesus, who is the promised messiah ("Then beginning with Moses and all the prophets, he interpreted to them the things about himself in all the scriptures"; similarly 24:44). (Non-messianic) Jews outside of the Jesus-following group—both then and now—would deny this Christocentric reading of their Scriptures. Likewise, the temple is highlighted as locus of revelation and of worship both at the beginning of Luke (1:8-20; 2:21-40, 46-49) and at its end (24:52-53). In these cases the worship is linked with Christocentric concerns.

With respect to the argument that Luke is depicting only some Jews, not all Jews, as harboring murderous intentions toward Jesus and his followers: Luke depicts the Jewish leaders as initiating Jesus's crucifixion while "the people" are divided (see the various responses of "the people" in Luke 22–23). But Luke's demonization of those leaders as Satan's henchmen is quite stark (22:3-6, 53). Furthermore, especially when we also consider the book of Acts, the repeated accusations that "the Jews" killed Jesus and then continued to persecute Jesus's followers suggests that Luke aims to paint many, if not all, nonbelieving Jews as murderous enemies. The depiction of Jews as aggressively hostile toward Jesus and his followers sometimes focuses on the leaders in Jerusalem, but the hostility is not contained there. Rather, as the gospel moves from Jerusalem to Rome, this hostility flows from Jerusalem outward.

Finally, with respect to the argument that Luke's polemic is intramural/intra-Jewish, we note that the standard for right conduct and/or repentance in Luke is closely tied to acceptance of Jesus as the mes-

---

Perspectives (Minneapolis: Augsburg, 1988). See also Robert C. Tannehill, "Israel in Luke–Acts: A Tragic Story," *JBL* 104 (1985): 69–85; David Tiede, " 'Fighting against God': Luke's Interpretation of Jewish Rejection of the Messiah Jesus," in *Anti-Semitism and Early Christianity: Issues of Polemic and Faith*, ed. Craig Evans and Donald Hagner (Minneapolis: Fortress, 1993), 102–12; Michael Wolter, *Das Lukasevangelium*, HNT 5 (Tübingen: Mohr Siebeck, 2008); Mark Kinzer, *Jerusalem Crucified, Jerusalem Risen* (Eugene, OR: Cascade, 2018).

siah.[54] Such a Jesus-centered view of Judaism seems to us at best a form of proto-supersessionism, and it lays the groundwork for the full-blown Christian supersessionism[55] that will come, as the boundaries between Jews and Christians become more firmly fixed.[56]

We write in dangerous times, where recognition of anti-Judaism in Christian Scriptures and subsequent Christian theology has been used for harmful ends. In the US context, we witness the increasing visibility of anti-Jewish hate crimes, including murder. We are aware that some of those who have committed these crimes have used the New Testament to justify their actions, thus joining a centuries-long chain of Christian Jew-hatred.[57] Therefore, identification of passages within Luke as anti-Jewish must go hand in hand with criticism of that anti-Jewishness. This aspect

54. This factor distinguishes Luke from Jeremiah, for whom "repentance" means *returning* to proper Torah observance. Luke is asking not for return but for a turn to something new, namely, a confession of Jesus as Christ. See Amy-Jill Levine, "Anti-Judaism and the Gospel of Matthew," in *Anti-Judaism and the Gospels*, ed. William R. Farmer (Harrisburg, PA: Trinity Press International, 1999), 9–36; compare also Amy-Jill Levine's comments in Levine and Witherington, *Gospel of Luke*, 118–24.

55. Supersessionism asserts that the covenant made with Moses and the Jewish people is superseded or replaced by the new covenant made with followers of Jesus. A significant repudiation of such an approach was made by Roman Catholics at Vatican II when *Nostra Aetate*, the Declaration on the Relation of the Church to Non-Christian Religions, was issued (1965). It declared, "God holds the Jews most dear for the sake of their Fathers; He does not repent of the gifts He makes or of the calls He issues" (10), and it urged mutual understanding, respect, and dialogue. Subsequently, there have been sustained efforts at dialogue and building relations between Jews and Christians. For the full text, see http://www.vatican.va/archive/hist_councils/ii _vatican_council/documents/vat-ii_decl_19651028_nostra-aetate_en.html.

56. For elaboration of these arguments, see Shelly Matthews, *Perfect Martyr: The Stoning of Stephen and the Construction of Christian Identity* (New York: Oxford University Press, 2010); *The Acts of the Apostles: Taming the Tongues of Fire*, Phoenix New Testament Guides (Sheffield: Sheffield Phoenix, 2013); reissued as *The Acts of the Apostles: An Introduction and Study Guide; Taming the Tongues of Fire*, T&T Clark Study Guides to the New Testament (London: Bloomsbury T&T Clark, 2017); "The Weeping Jesus and the Daughters of Jerusalem," 385–403.

57. For example, the shooter who murdered Jews at the Poway Synagogue in California in April 2019 included within his screed against Jews charges that their deaths are deserved because of "their persecution of Christians of old (including the prophets of ancient Israel—Jeremiah, Isaiah, etc.), members of the early church (Stephen—whose death at the hands of the Jews was both heart-wrenching and rage-inducing)," and referred to "their role in the murder of the Son of Man—that is the Christ." https://www.memri.org/reports/anti-jewish-manifesto-john-t-earnest-san -diego-synagogue-shooter.

of Christian Scripture, like androcentricism, ableism, or heterosexism should be assessed as antithetical to human flourishing.[58]

Luke: Friend of Women or Most Dangerous Book in the Bible?

Feminists are not of one mind about the Gospel of Luke. Some find this gospel to be their best ally; others think it is the most dangerous of all. Still others see it as somewhere in between.

It is because more women appear in the Gospel of Luke than in the other canonical gospels that interpreters in the second wave of feminism, in the 1970s and 1980s, gravitated toward this gospel, seeing Luke as the friend of women.[59] Only in Luke do we find the stories of Elizabeth (1:5-7, 24-25, 39-45, 57-66), Mary (1:26-56; 2:1-52; Acts 1:14), Anna (2:36-38), the widow of Nain (7:11-17), the woman who had been a sinner who showed great love (7:36-50), the woman bent double (13:10-17), the women of Jerusalem lamenting Jesus on the way of the cross (23:26-32), and the parables of the woman who searches for a lost coin (15:8-10) and of the widow demanding justice before an unjust judge (18:1-8). While Mary Magdalene appears in the passion and empty tomb narratives in all four gospels, only Luke introduces her as part of Jesus's Galilean ministry as well, and only Luke recounts the financial support she and Joanna, Susanna, and the other Galilean women provided to Jesus (8:1-3). Martha and Mary play an important role in John 11:1–12:12, but Luke has a unique vignette in which they appear (10:38-42), wherein Jesus announces that the (silent) Mary who listens to his teaching has "chosen the better part" over Martha's "service." Luke also includes the stories found in Mark and Matthew about Simon's mother-in-law (Luke 4:38-39 // Mark 1:29-34 // Matt 8:14-17), Jairus's daughter and the woman with a hemorrhage (Luke 8:40-56 // Mark 5:21-43 // Matt 9:18-26), a widow who gives her "whole life" (Luke 21:1-4 // Mark 12:41-44), and the parable of the woman who hides yeast in dough (Luke 13:20-21 // Matt 13:33).

---

58. For recent work on Christian anti-Judaism by Jewish feminist scholars focused on the Gospel of John, see Adele Reinhartz, *Cast out of the Covenant: Jews and Anti-Judaism in the Gospel of John* (Lanham, MD: Lexington Books/Fortress Academic, 2018); Amy-Jill Levine, "Christian Privilege, Christian Fragility, and the Gospel of John," in *The Gospel of John and Jewish-Christian Relations*, ed. Adele Reinhartz (Lanham, MD: Lexington Press, 2018), 87–111.

59. See above, p. xxiii–xxiv in the general editor's introduction, for an explanation of four contemporary waves of feminism.

In his second volume, Luke gives us the traditions about the women disciples in the upper room (Acts 1:14), Sapphira (5:1-11), Tabitha/Dorcas (9:36-43), Lydia (16:13-15, 40), the slave girl of Philippi (16:16-24), Damaris (17:34), Priscilla (18:2, 18, 26), and Philip's four daughters who were prophets (21:8-11).

The abundance of stories featuring women led Alfred Plummer to remark, "The Third Gospel is in an especial sense the Gospel for women. . . . All through this Gospel they are allowed a prominent place, and many types of womanhood are placed before us."[60] In addition, some scholars, noting Luke's construction of parallel pairs[61] of stories of men and women, have concluded that Luke regards women and men as equals. Robert O'Toole, for example, asserts, "Men and women receive the same salvific benefits. God, Christ, and the disciples act in their lives in similar fashion. Women and men have similar experiences and fulfill similar functions. They believe and proclaim the gospel message."[62]

From the late 1980s forward, however, feminist interpreters began to see that Luke's portrait of women is ambiguous[63] at best and dangerous at worst.[64] Elisabeth Schüssler Fiorenza was one of the first to show that although Luke knew of women prophets, leaders, and missionaries, he

---

60. Alfred Plummer, *The Gospel According to S. Luke*, 5th ed., ICC (Edinburgh: T&T Clark, 1981; first ed. 1901), xlii–xliii. See Robert J. Karris, "Women and Discipleship in Luke," *CBQ* 56 (1994): 2 n. 4 for a list of scholars who hold that Luke has a favorable view of women. See also the introduction by Amy-Jill Levine in the volume she edited with Marianne Blickenstaff, *A Feminist Companion to Luke*, FCNTECW 3 (Sheffield: Sheffield Academic, 2002), 1–22.

61. See Veronica Koperski, "Is 'Luke' a Feminist or Not? Female-Male Parallels in Luke–Acts," in *Luke and His Readers: Festschrift A. Denaux*, ed. Reimund Bieringer, Gilbert van Belle, and Joseph Verheyden, BETL 182 (Leuven: Leuven University Press, 2005), 25–48, who outlines the work of eight scholars and shows how their lists of pairs vary and that they reach different conclusions about how the pairs function. For some, the pairs present women as having equal status with men; others find a double message in that although women are full members of the Christian community, they have separate spheres of action from men. For some authors, the pairs depict a subordination of the women's group to the men's.

62. Robert F. O'Toole, *The Unity of Luke's Theology: An Analysis of Luke–Acts*, GNS 9 (Wilmington, DE: Glazier, 1984), 120. For a fuller treatment and for our evaluation of the function of these pairs, see the excursus "Gender Pairs" at 2:21-40.

63. E.g., Mary Rose D'Angelo, "Women in Luke–Acts: A Redactional View," *JBL* 109 (1990): 441–61; Turid Karlsen Seim, *The Double Message: Patterns of Gender in Luke–Acts* (Nashville: Abingdon, 1994).

64. Jane D. Schaberg, "Luke," in *The Women's Bible Commentary*, ed. Carol A. Newsom and Sharon H. Ringe (Louisville: Westminster John Knox, 1992), 275–92.

typically refrains from granting them speech or placing them in active roles.[65] Similarly, Mary Rose D'Angelo examined depictions of women in Luke and concluded that his purpose is to restrict and control them: beyond the infancy narratives, where "women prophets belong to the exotic biblical past,"[66] no woman speaks except to be corrected by Jesus[67] or disbelieved (24:11). Women are beneficiaries of Jesus's ministry and engage in charitable works[68] but are seen to have "chosen the better part" when they remain silent and receptive (10:42). Jane Schaberg demonstrates that in Luke "women are included in Jesus' entourage (8:1-3) and table community, but not as the equals of men."[69] Luke "shows only the men empowered to speak and act and bear responsibility within the movement."[70] In the third edition of *Women's Bible Commentary,* Jane Schaberg and Sharon Ringe show that the actual numbers belie the impression of the prominence of women: in Luke the named men outnumber the named women by more than 13 to 1;[71] in Acts the individual men named outnumber the women by 4 to 1; male groups outnumber the female groups by almost 14 to 1.

In her analysis of the way Luke portrays women's discipleship in the gospel and Acts, Barbara[72] has shown that while there are women who receive the word, believe, are baptized, follow Jesus, and host house churches, there are no narratives showing individual women disciples as called, commissioned, enduring persecution, or ministering by the power of the Spirit. Women in the gospel and Acts do not imitate Jesus's mission of preaching, teaching, healing, exorcising, forgiving, or praying. Only male disciples are depicted in these roles. Women in the Third Gospel

---

65. Schüssler Fiorenza, *In Memory of Her,* 50.

66. D'Angelo, "Women in Luke–Acts," 460.

67. Ibid., 452. See Luke 10:41-42; 11:27-28; 23:28.

68. D'Angelo, "Women in Luke–Acts," 455, notes that Tabitha and the widows with her are shown administering charity in Acts 9:36, 39, 40.

69. Schaberg, "Luke," 291. Based on the use of διακονία for eucharistic table service and for proclamation of the word (e.g., Rom 11:13; 15:31; 1 Cor 12:5; 2 Cor 4:1; 5:18; Acts 6:1, 4), Schaberg thinks there may be a tradition behind Luke 8:2-3 and Mark 15:41 that women were significant figures in the table community and the intellectual activity that marked the original movement (287).

70. Ibid., 281.

71. We note, however, that naming does not always signify importance; e.g., the unnamed centurion at the crucifixion (23:47).

72. Barbara E. Reid, *Choosing the Better Part? Women in the Gospel of Luke* (Collegeville, MN: Liturgical Press, 1996), 21–54.

are healed by Jesus, are objects of his compassion, and listen to the word, but nothing is related about how their discipleship is enacted, except for Mary Magdalene and her companions, whose financial ministry (8:1-3) is portrayed as an ancillary service to the mission of Jesus and his twelve chosen male apostles in gratitude for their healing.

In the Acts of the Apostles, although women, including Mary the mother of Jesus (1:14), are present at Pentecost, those said to be filled with the Spirit, directed by the Spirit, or mediating the power of the Spirit include only males: Peter (4:8; 10:19, 44; 11:12, 15; 15:8), David (4:25), Stephen (6:3, 5, 10; 7:55), Philip (6:3; 8:29, 39), Prochorus, Nicanor, Timon, Parmenas, Nicolaus (6:3-5), Barnabas (11:24; 13:1-2, 4), Symeon, Lucius, and Manaen (13:1-2), Paul (9:17; 13:4, 9; 16:6, 7; 19:21), Judas (15:32), Silas (15:32; 16:6, 7), Timothy (16:6, 7), Agabus (11:28; 21:11), the apostles and presbyters (15:28), twelve men in Ephesus (19:6-7), and the Ephesian elders (20:22, 23, 28). In Acts 9:36, Luke describes Tabitha, the only person in the New Testament expressly identified as a disciple (μαθήτρια), as having been "devoted to good works and acts of charity." Her ministry is one that is silent and behind the scenes, making tunics and clothing (9:39). Luke indicates his awareness that Philip's four daughters are gifted with prophecy, a tradition for which the church historian Eusebius provides more details and suggests that their charism was once widely celebrated (*Eccl. Hist.* 3.31). Yet, in Luke's narrative, they do not speak (Acts 21:9).

Since Luke claims to have investigated "everything accurately from the very first, to write an orderly account" (1:3), it is likely that he knew of women's presence, struggles, and agency in the early apostolic ministries, including instances of their leadership. Paul's letters make abundant references to such women.[73] Luke, no doubt knowing of such women, restricts them to silent, passive, supporting roles. For him, women and men have different ways of being disciples.

Recognizing that there is truth to both positions—that Luke includes women who are prophets, faithful followers, hearers and proclaimers of the word, and ministering out of their financial resources, while at the same time restricting their roles and subordinating them to men—a

---

73. E.g., Phoebe, deacon and leader of the church at Cechreae (Rom 16:1-2); Junia, notable among the apostles (Rom 16:7); Mary, Tryphaena, Tryphosa, and Persis, coworkers of Paul (Rom 16:6, 12); Prisca, a coworker who "risked her neck" for Paul and was host of a house church at Corinth and then Ephesus (Rom 16:3-4); Euodia and Syntyche, coworkers of Paul who struggled at his side in promoting the gospel (Phil 4:2-4); and Nympha, head of a house church in Colossae (Col 4:15).

number of feminist scholars have focused on the ambiguity, the "double message," as Turid Karlsen Seim labeled it.[74] We agree that a dual approach to the gospel is needed. We must both enter into it to appreciate it and "stand apart from it in order to assess its truth and helpfulness."[75] The gospel contains both challenge and promise.[76] Luke's rhetorical aim might be to silence women's voices and occlude their agency in the *basileia*[77] movement. But the evangelist's control of the narrative is not total. We can find traces of women's agency, struggle, and voice within the gaps and fissures in the text; in comparing Luke's portrayal of women to their depictions in other sources, such as the letters of Paul, the other canonical gospels, and extracanonical sources such as the Gospel of Mary; and by reading Luke's rhetoric against the grain. Indeed, as we

74. Seim, *The Double Message*; Turid Karlsen Seim, "The Gospel of Luke," in *Searching the Scriptures: A Feminist Commentary*, ed. Elisabeth Schüssler Fiorenza with Ann Brock and Shelly Matthews (New York: Crossroad, 1994), 728–62; "Feminist Criticism," in *Methods for Luke*, ed. Joel B. Green, Methods in Biblical Interpretation (Cambridge: Cambridge University Press, 2010), 42–73; Marinella Perroni, "Disciples, Not Apostles: Luke's Double Message," in *Gospels: Narrative and History*, ed. Mercedes Navarro Puerto, Marinella Perroni; English translation ed. Amy-Jill Levine, The Bible and Women: An Encyclopedia of Exegesis and Cultural History, New Testament 2.1 (Atlanta: SBL Press, 2015), 173–213. F. Scott Spencer, *Salty Wives, Spirited Mothers, and Savvy Widows: Capable Women of Purpose and Persistence in Luke's Gospel* (Grand Rapids: Eerdmans, 2012), analyzes the female characters in Luke's Gospel, aiming "to tilt feminist scholarship toward a slightly more positive—though still critical—evaluation of the *creative agency and capable activity* of women in Luke's Gospel" (x, emphasis original). By striking a "more celebratory than lamentable chord," he hopes to encourage "more direct liberating readings of Luke today" (x) by steering "a middle course between the extreme poles of skepticism, on the left, and fideism, on the right" (20).

75. Jane D. Schaberg and Sharon H. Ringe, "Gospel of Luke," in *Women's Bible Commentary*, ed. Carol A. Newsom, Sharon H. Ringe, and Jacqueline E. Lapsley, 3rd ed. (Louisville: Westminster John Knox, 2012), 493. See also Claudia Janssen and Regene Lamb, "Gospel of Luke: The Humbled Will Be Lifted Up," in *Feminist Biblical Interpretation. A Compendium of Critical Commentary on the Books of the Bible and Related Literature*, ed. Luise Schottroff and Marie-Theres Wacker, trans. Lisa E. Dahill, Everett R. Kalin, Nancy Lukens, Linda M. Maloney, Barbara Rumscheidt, Martin Rumscheidt, and Tina Steiner (Grand Rapids: Eerdmans, 2012), 647–48, who caution that "hasty generalizations are to be avoided" and propose that Luke "should be understood as a document testifying to a dynamic process of working out differences over questions of equal rights; it shows evidence of conflicts that had to be worked through in everyday life."

76. Schaberg and Ringe, "Gospel of Luke," 493.

77. See commentary at 4:1-13 on the meaning of *basileia*, typically translated as "kingdom."

shall see, Luke's multiple strategies for suppressing women's leadership should be recognized as evidence for it. Using feminist critical methods, we can expose and challenge Luke's patriarchal biases, and so we can re-contextualize and reinterpret the text.[78] Rather than let Luke provide final answers, we must allow the text to stimulate valuable questions about women's place and legacy in the early Jesus movement and point to issues that demand rethinking today, including the restriction of women from certain ministries and forms of leadership in the church.[79]

78. That the methods, presuppositions, and conclusions of scholars analyzing gender in Luke vary considerably is quite evident in the fourteen essays edited by Amy-Jill Levine with Marianne Blickenstaff in *A Feminist Companion to Luke*.

79. Schaberg and Ringe, "Gospel of Luke," 493.

Luke 1:1-80

An Orderly Account for Lovers of God

To Most Excellent Theophilus (1:1-4)

The Third Gospel is the only canonical gospel that begins with a formal preface addressing a named reader, explaining the purpose of the account (διήγησις), and including an authorial "I."[1] This account of events "that have been fulfilled among us" is less a list of historical details than a narrative connecting past and present events of God's saving action toward humankind and pointing to its future unfolding.[2] Others have told the story of Jesus, but we must tell it again, in our own words, and say what it means to us and to our communities in each new time and place. No one tells the whole story; we all have our biases and emphases. As we interpret Luke's story in this commentary,

---

1. See Loveday Alexander, "Luke's Preface in the Context of Greek Preface Writing," *NovT* 28 (1986): 48–74, and her fuller study, *The Preface to Luke's Gospel: Literary Convention and Social Context in Luke 1.1-4 and Acts 1.1*, SNTSMS 78 (Cambridge: Cambridge University Press, 1993). Alexander, examining Greek prose prefaces from the fourth century BCE to the second century CE, shows that Luke's preface is more akin to explanatory prefaces found in ancient scientific texts than in ancient historiographies.

2. See comments at 4:16-30 on the theme of fulfillment of Scripture in Luke.

1

Luke 1:1-4

1:1Since many have undertaken to set down an orderly account of the events that have been fulfilled among us, 2just as they were handed on to us by those who from the beginning were eyewitnesses and servants of the word, 3I too decided, after investigating everything carefully from the very first, to write an orderly account for you, most excellent Theophilus, 4so that you may know the truth concerning the things about which you have been instructed.

we come with a feminist[3] critical lens, as we try to point to ways in which the narrative can either inhibit or contribute to the full flourishing of all people and all creation.

Luke dedicates the gospel to Theophilus, whose name means "lover of God" or "beloved by God." Whereas Theophilus could have been an actual patron[4] who commissioned the work,[5] his name suggests also a broader audience of any who love God. The adjective κράτιστε, "most excellent," indicates an ideal reader of high status,[6] so we wonder if Luke had in mind an audience likewise of high status.[7] Yet among the gospel's

---

3. See the general editor's introduction for definitions of feminism and the authors' introduction for what we mean by a feminist approach to biblical interpretation.

4. Loveday Alexander ("What if Luke Had Never Met Theophilus?," *BibInt* 8 [2000]: 161–70) notes that dedicating texts was a literary convention and does not necessarily imply a relationship between the author and dedicatee. Nonetheless, she finds possible that Theophilus was the catalyst for the production of Luke and Acts and suggests that Theophilus could have been the head of a house-church who provided a place where Luke's Gospel could be performed, not unlike a Greco-Roman *symposium*. While we find the scenario of a "historical Theophilus" plausible, we part with Alexander in her proposal that Luke is writing primarily for a Jewish Diaspora community. We think that Luke was writing for a predominantly Gentile audience (see the authors' introduction). Dennis R. MacDonald (*Luke and Vergil: Imitations of Classical Greek Literature*, The New Testament and Greek Literature, vol. 2 [Lanham, MD: Rowman & Littlefield, 2015], 5) argues that the name Theophilus is fictitious. Dedicatory prefaces are frequent in ancient writings, and MacDonald thinks Luke is imitating Vergil's dedication of the *Aeneid* to Augustus, the *divi filius*, "son of the divinized" Caesar. See further Dennis R. MacDonald, *Two Shipwrecked Gospels: The Logoi of Jesus and Papias's Exposition of Logia about the Lord*, ECL 8 (Atlanta: SBL, 2012), 52–56.

5. On women patrons, see comments at 8:1-3.

6. The same word is used to address the Roman governor, Felix, at Acts 23:26.

7. Greg Carey observes that though the gospel is "designed to challenge insiders and welcome outsiders, Luke does so from the perspective of the prosperous, the male, the religious insider, and the righteous person" (*Luke: An Introduction and Study*

audience would also have been people who were poor, those who serve at the table as well as those who seek the place of honor at the table (14:7-24). For the "most excellent" hearers, whether elite women or men of note, poor people may be merely objects spoken about who illustrate Jesus's teachings. These teachings will have a different impact on hearers who are of lower social status, as we will point out in our commentary.

The word ἀσφάλεια (v. 4) connotes assurance that the story told will be acceptable, rather than disturbing, to the reader's core values. The NRSV translation "truth" misses this nuance. As Brigitte Kahl points out, "ἀσφάλεια/*securitas* was a core concept in Roman state ideology."[8] Luke writes so that Theophilus "might be reassured" concerning things about which he has been instructed.

As feminists, we are suspicious of the reassurance Luke offers. Luke's interest in presenting an "orderly account" for the purpose of "reassuring" the "most excellent" Theophilus signals that Luke will be polishing up or idealizing the events, the main characters, and the traditions passed on in his sources to make them more suitable to an audience of Theophilus's status. We see several instances of such idealization when we compare Luke to Mark, which is widely recognized as one of Luke's sources. For example, Luke has enhanced the portrait of John the Baptist. According to Mark, the Baptist appears out of nowhere, wears a scratchy coat of camel hair, and eats locusts and honey. That is, he appears as an eccentric figure. Luke both eliminates comments on John's dress and diet (3:2-3) and provides John an extremely respectable lineage—a father from the priestly order of Abijah, and a mother whose descent is traced back to Aaron. Furthermore, Luke enhances Jesus's standing by eliminating Mark's reference to Jesus as a carpenter (Mark 6:3) and presenting Jesus as literate (4:16-30).[9] Similarly, we suspect that Luke has transformed accounts from Mark and possibly other sources about women by putting restrictions on women's roles and omitting stories, such as that of the Syro-Phoenician woman (Mark 7:24-30) // Canaanite woman (Matt 15:21-28), that Luke found inappropriate.

Guide; All Flesh Shall See God's Salvation, T&T Clark's Study Guides to the New Testament [London: Bloomsbury T&T Clark, 2017], 88).

8. Brigitte Kahl, "Reading Luke against Luke: Non-Uniformity of Text, Hermeneutics of Conspiracy and the 'Scriptural Principle' in Luke 1," in *A Feminist Companion to Luke*, ed. Amy-Jill Levine with Marianne Blickenstaff, FCNTECW 3 (Sheffield: Sheffield Academic, 2002), 70–88, esp. 75 n. 11.

9. See Chris Keith, *Jesus' Literacy: Scribal Culture and the Teacher from Galilee*, Library of Historical Jesus Studies 8, LNTS 413 (New York: T&T Clark, 2011).

Luke acknowledges reliance on eyewitnesses and "servants of the word" (1:2).[10] He depicts women among the eyewitnesses: Mary Magdalene, Joanna, Susanna, Mary the mother of James, and other Galilean women (Luke 8:1-3; 23:49, 55-56; 24:1-11).[11] As "servants of the word," Mary Magdalene, Joanna, Mary the mother of James, and the other women announced (ἀπήγγειλαν) to the eleven and all the rest what they had experienced and heard from the angel at the empty tomb (24:9), and they repeatedly told (ἔλεγον)[12] this to the apostles (24:10).[13] Moreover, women have always been catechists by their instructing others in the faith.[14] Whether Luke consulted women eyewitnesses or whether those who catechized Theophilus (1:4) included women is an open question.

Righteous and Childless Elizabeth (1:5-7)

Elizabeth and Zechariah are the lead characters in the first vignettes. Only in recent years have commentators, particularly feminists, given attention to Elizabeth rather than to the intriguing story of Zechariah's

---

10. See the authors' introduction, pp. liii–liv, for a fuller treatment of the evangelist's sources.

11. All the gospels depict Galilean women as witnesses of the crucifixion and as the ones who discover the empty tomb. Only Luke shows them accompanying Jesus during the Galilean ministry (see our comments on 8:1-3). On the differences in the number and names of the women, see comments at chaps. 23 and 24.

12. The imperfect tense of ἔλεγον indicates repeated telling, not a one-time announcement.

13. Carolyn Osiek, "The Women at the Tomb: What Are They Doing There?," *Ex Auditu* 9 (1993): 97–107, reprinted in *A Feminist Companion to Matthew*, ed. Amy-Jill Levine with Marianne Blickenstaff, FCNTECW 1 (Sheffield: Sheffield Academic, 2001), 203–20, argues that the memory of the women's role at the empty tomb "was so persistent that it . . . must indicate that something actually happened that Sunday morning at the tomb" (220). See further comments at 24:1-12.

14. Acts of the Apostles and the Epistles include several references to women teachers: Priscilla and Aquila took aside Apollos, an eloquent preacher who was well-versed in the Scriptures, and "explained [ἐξέθεντο] the way of God to him more accurately" (Acts 18:26). First Timothy 2:12 restricts women teachers: "I permit no woman to teach or have authority over a man." On the principle that prescriptions against a behavior suggest that this behavior is taking place, we cite this passage also as evidence of women teachers. Second Timothy speaks of the faith of Timothy's grandmother, Lois, and mother, Eunice, that now lives in him (1:5), implying it was they who taught him. See also 2 Timothy 3:15, which infers that the knowledge Timothy has of the sacred writings came from his mother and grandmother. The author of the letter to Titus instructs women to "teach what is good" (καλοδιδασκάλους, 2:3).

⁵In the days of King Herod of Judea, there was a priest named Zechariah, who belonged to the priestly order of Abijah. His wife was a descendant of Aaron, and her name was Elizabeth. ⁶Both of them were righteous before God, living blamelessly according to all the commandments and regulations of the Lord. ⁷But they had no children, because Elizabeth was barren, and both were getting on in years.

muteness and his later proclamation.[15] At the outset, what Luke says of Zechariah is matched by what he says of Elizabeth. Both are named, from priestly lineage, righteous before God, getting on in years, and childless.

Elizabeth is named, while the majority of women in the Bible go unnamed or are identified only as the mother, daughter, or wife of an important male. Unnamed women in the gospel include the widow of Zarephath (4:26, also unnamed in 1 Kgs 17:7-16), Simon's mother-in-law (4:38-39), the widowed mother in Nain (7:11-17), a woman who anoints Jesus's feet (7:36-50), many of the "other" Galilean women who followed and ministered (8:3; 23:55-56; 24:10), a woman with a hemorrhage and the daughter and wife of Jairus (8:40-56), a woman bent for eighteen years (13:10-17), Lot's wife (17:32, also unnamed in Gen 19:26), a widow who gives her all (21:1-4), the women of Jerusalem who lament Jesus on the way of the cross (23:26-32), and possibly the companion of Cleopas (24:13). With the exception of Simon's mother-in-law, Jairus's daughter and wife, the woman healed of hemorrhages, and the widow in the temple, all are characters who appear only in Luke's Gospel.[16] One feminist critique of the anonymity of women characters is that it makes them invisible.[17] Likewise, identifying women in terms of their relationship to a man makes

15. E.g., Raymond E. Brown, "The Annunciation to Zechariah, the Birth of the Baptist, and the Benedictus (Luke 1:5-25, 57-30)," *Worship* 62 (1988): 482–96. Surveys by Brown, "Gospel Infancy Narrative Research from 1976 to 1986: Part I (Matthew)," *CBQ* 48 (1986): 468–83; "Gospel Infancy Narrative Research from 1976 to 1986: Part II (Luke)," *CBQ* 48 (1986): 660–80, show no studies on Elizabeth. An example of a feminist retrieval of Elizabeth's story is found in the reflection by Diana Scholl (Elisabeth Schüssler Fiorenza, *But She Said: Feminist Practices in Biblical Interpretation* [Boston: Beacon, 1992], 193–94), who places Elizabeth center stage and focuses on Elizabeth's personal power and strength rather than her failure to reproduce.

16. No person is named in gospel healing stories.

17. Elaine M. Wainwright, *Shall We Look for Another? A Feminist Rereading of the Matthean Jesus*, The Bible and Liberation (Maryknoll, NY: Orbis Books, 1998), 149 n. 2.

him the central one and masks the importance of the woman. Adele Reinhartz, however, has shown that the anonymity of biblical characters is more complex.[18] Namelessness can be a means of effacing identity, of turning a person into a function. Alternatively, it may emphasize the dissonance between a character and their stereotypical role, as when Potiphar's wife or the cannibalistic mothers of 2 Kings 6 act in ways that are contrary to what is expected of wives and mothers. Anonymity can also enhance pathos, as in the stories of the Levite's concubine (Judg 19) or Jephthah's daughter (Judg 11) illustrate. In addition, not all name-less characters are insignificant, as exemplified by the centurion in Luke 23:47. For us, naming Elizabeth, along with giving her speech while her husband goes mute, has the effect of bringing her to the foreground as a character who reliably communicates God's word. Her name, אֱלִישֶׁבַע, which means "My God is the one by whom to swear," or "my God is satiety, fortune," points to her being a woman who depends on God and who will be filled to satisfaction by God.

Luke emphasizes that both Elizabeth and Zechariah were "righteous [δίκαιοι] before God, living blamelessly according to all the command-ments and regulations of the Lord." For Jews, the Torah, the first five books of the Bible, reveals how to respond in concrete action to God's love. The commandments and regulations outlined in the Torah are a gift and a privilege, not a burden or impossible to keep, as 1:6 affirms.[19] The Bible rarely describes women as "righteous."[20] The only woman of whom the term is used in the Old Testament[21] is Tamar when her father-in-law Judah, whom she has tricked into impregnating her, declares

---

18. Adele Reinhartz, *"Why Ask My Name?" Anonymity and Identity in Biblical Narrative* (New York: Oxford University Press, 1998).

19. Note also Paul's assertion that "as to righteousness under the law" he was "blameless" (Phil 3:6). Contrast the speech of Peter in Acts 15:10 suggesting that the yoke (of the law) was something "neither our ancestors nor we have been able to bear." This is a characterization of the law that Jews in Luke's day would not have recognized.

20. In the LXX, δίκαιος, which translates Hebrew צַדִּיק, is used of God (Pss 7:12; 114:5; Isa 45:21; Jer 12:1; Dan 9:14; 2 Chr 12:6), Noah (Gen 6:9), Job (Job 1:1), Daniel (4 Macc 16:21), Ishbaal, the son of Saul (2 Sam 4:11), and the Servant of God (Isa 53:11). In the New Testament, God is called δίκαιος (John 17:25; Rom 3:26; 2 Tim 4:8; 1 John 1:9); as is Jesus (Matt 27:19; 27:24 [some *mss*, e.g., א, K, L, W]; Luke 23:47; Acts 3:14; 7:52; 22:14; 1 Pet 3:18; 1 John 2:1, 29; 3:7), Joseph (Matt 1:19), John the Baptist (Mark 6:20), Zechariah (Luke 1:5), Simeon (Luke 2:25), Joseph of Arimathea (Luke 23:50), Cornelius (Acts 10:22), Abel (Heb 11:4; 1 John 3:12), and Lot (2 Pet 2:7).

21. See pp. xxxvii–xxxviii in the general editor's introduction for an explanation of the term "Old Testament."

her to be "more in the right than I" (Gen 38:26). In the New Testament, Elizabeth is the only woman to whom the term is applied. The Bible's androcentric focus on righteous men is interrupted by Elizabeth and Tamar, who are also are exemplary in the godly virtue of righteousness, that is, they strive for right relation with God and other people. Today, in light of ecofeminist thinking, we would broaden that striving to include right relation with all creation.

The word δίκαιοι, "righteous," also arcs forward to Jesus's crucifixion, where the centurion, seeing Jesus die, declares him δίκαιος (23:47). This connection is obscured in the NRSV translation as "innocent" (see comments at 23:47). Luke's story begins and ends with righteous ones who suffer.

The pairing[22] of statements about Elizabeth and Zechariah ends with Luke's assertion that Elizabeth's infertility, not Zechariah's, is the cause of their childlessness (1:7: ἡ Ἐλισάβετ στεῖρα). Elizabeth is one of a long line of biblical women facing infertility: Sarah (Gen 16:1), Rebecca (Gen 25:21), Rachel (Gen 30:1), the mother of Samson (Judg 13:2), Hannah (1 Sam 1–2), and the woman of Shunem (2 Kgs 4:8-37).[23] In these biblical instances, it is always the woman who is said to be infertile, and it is she who bears the shame of childlessness, not her husband.[24] While 1 Enoch 98:14 (165 BCE) makes a connection between infertility and sinfulness on the part of a woman, there is no hint of such in the biblical stories, especially in the case of Elizabeth, as Luke has stated that she observed all the commandments (1:6). One important commandment in Scripture is God's directive in Genesis 1:28, "Be fruitful and multiply, and fill the earth." Luke implies that Elizabeth and Zechariah have tried to fulfill this command, but as in all the stories of biblical women who are infertile, it is God who controls fertility and infertility. Calling attention to Elizabeth's and Zechariah's age highlights the likelihood that they will remain childless without divine help. It also underscores their faithfulness to God for many long years despite their childlessness.

---

22. See 2:36-38 for comments on Luke's gender pairs.

23. In addition, there is a story in 4 Ezra 9:43-45 of a woman who was infertile for thirty years before giving birth and the story of Anna in the apocryphal *Protoevangelium of James* (c. 145 CE), who was infertile and whose prayer for a child is finally heard by God and she conceives Mary, the mother of Jesus.

24. See Tal Ilan, *Jewish Women in Greco-Roman Palestine* (Peabody, MA: Hendrickson, 1996), 111–12, for instances in rabbinic literature that recognize the possibility that not the woman but her husband may be to blame for infertility.

Elizabeth Will Bear a Son (1:8-23)

Attention shifts to Zechariah performing his priestly service in the temple. Elizabeth is also of priestly lineage, a daughter of Aaron,[25] but Exodus 40:13-15 restricts priestly functions to Aaron's sons. For Christians whose denomination restricts priesthood to males, it is important to know the lengthy tradition of female priests in both Judaism and Christianity when considering changes in contemporary practice. Feminists who have identified and interpreted evidence of women priests include Bernadette Brooten, Ross Shepard Kraemer, Ute Eisen, Mary Ann Rossi, and Carolyn Osiek.[26]

The angel of the Lord (1:10) who appears to Zechariah, identifies himself as Gabriel (1:19) and is the first of many divine messengers in the Gospel. Gabriel appears also to Mary at 1:26-38; a comforting angel appears during Jesus's prayer on the Mount of Olives in 22:43;[27] and two men in dazzling clothes speak with the women at the empty tomb in 24:4. Their function is to interpret events from the divine perspective.

---

25. ἐκ τῶν θυγατέρων, translated in the NRSV as "a descendent," is literally "one of the daughters." Also, Elizabeth's name underscores her Aaronic lineage, since the only Elizabeth in the Old Testament was Aaron's wife (Exod 6:23).

26. For inscriptional evidence on women as priests, see Bernadette J. Brooten, *Women Leaders in the Ancient Synagogue: Inscriptional Evidence and Background Issues*, BJS 36 (Chico, CA: Scholars Press, 1982), 73–99. Brooten analyzes three ancient Jewish inscriptions in which a woman bears the title *hiereia/hierissa* that range in age from the first century BCE through possibly the fourth century CE. On women priests in the Isis cult, see Sharon Kelly Heyob, *The Cult of Isis among Women in the Graeco-Roman World*, Études préliminaires aux religions orientales dans l'Empire romain 51 (Leiden: Brill, 1975), esp. 81–110. See Ross Shepard Kraemer, *Her Share of the Blessings: Women's Religions among Pagans, Jews, and Christians in the Greco-Roman World* (New York: Oxford University Press, 1992) on women's religious offices in Greco-Roman pagan settings, including priesthood (80–92), and on Jewish women's religious lives and offices in the Greco-Roman diaspora (106–27). See also sixteen inscriptions naming priestesses from Greece and Rome dating from the first through the fourth century CE in Mary R. Lefkowitz and Maureen B. Fant, *Women's Life in Greece and Rome: A Sourcebook in Translation*, 2nd ed. (Baltimore: Johns Hopkins University Press, 1992), 300–306. For epigraphic and literary evidence for women presbyters/priests in early Christianity, see Ute E. Eisen, *Women Officeholders in Early Christianity: Epigraphical and Literary Studies*, trans. Linda M. Maloney (Collegeville, MN: Liturgical Press, 2000), 116–42; Mary Ann Rossi, "Priesthood, Precedent, and Prejudice: On Recovering the Women Priests of Early Christianity," *JFSR* 7 (1991): 73–94; Kevin Madigan and Carolyn Osiek, eds., *Ordained Women in the Early Church: A Documentary History* (Baltimore: Johns Hopkins University Press, 2005).

27. Verses 43-44 are lacking in some manuscripts; the NRSV includes them, but in double brackets to signal their questionable authenticity. See comments at 22:43-44 about the authenticity of these verses.

[8]Once when he was serving as priest before God and his section was on duty, [9]he was chosen by lot, according to the custom of the priesthood, to enter the sanctuary of the Lord and offer incense. [10]Now at the time of the incense offering, the whole assembly of the people was praying outside. [11]Then there appeared to him an angel of the Lord, standing at the right side of the altar of incense. [12]When Zechariah saw him, he was terrified; and fear overwhelmed him. [13]But the angel said to him, "Do not be afraid, Zechariah, for your prayer has been heard. Your wife Elizabeth will bear you a son, and you will name him John. [14]You will have joy and gladness, and many will rejoice at his birth, [15]for he will be great in the sight of the Lord. He must never drink wine or strong drink; even before his birth he will be filled with the Holy Spirit. [16]He will turn many of the people of Israel to the Lord their God. [17]With the spirit and power of Elijah he will go before him, to turn the hearts of parents to their children, and the disobedient to the wisdom of the righteous, to make ready a people prepared for the Lord." [18]Zechariah said to the angel, "How will I know that this is so? For I am an old man, and my wife is getting on in years." [19]The angel replied, "I am Gabriel. I stand in the presence of God, and I have been sent to speak to you

Zechariah questions Gabriel, but the consequences for doing so are quite different than for Mary (1:34-38). Zechariah is left mute for not believing, while Mary receives a fuller explanation. Some scholars resolve this disparity by interpreting Mary's question as a request for further information, not an expression of disbelief: she asks *how* it will come about, not for proof that what Gabriel says is true. This explanation seems to us an overread. Another explanation is that Zechariah's culpability is in asking for a sign.[28] Elsewhere in the gospel, sign seekers test Jesus (11:16) and Jesus calls them an evil generation (11:29-30). This explanation also falls short: asking for a sign is not always a bad thing; indeed, in Isaiah 7:11, God tells King Ahaz to ask for a sign. Frequently, God offers signs (e.g., to Moses, Exod 3:12; to Samuel, 1 Sam 10:2; to Ahaz, Isa 7:11) and does not rebuke persons who request them (e.g., Gideon, Judg 6:36-40; Hezekiah, 2 Kgs 20:8). We interpret Zechariah's inability to speak as a narrative device that opens the way for Elizabeth's and Mary's voices to be heard. There is a twist, in that Zechariah, a priest, a mediator between God and the people, would be expected to explain

28. Frederick W. Danker, *Jesus and the New Age: A Commentary on St. Luke's Gospel,* rev. and exp. ed. (Philadelphia: Fortress, 1988), 32.

and to bring you this good news. [20]But now, because you did not believe my words, which will be fulfilled in their time, you will become mute, unable to speak, until the day these things occur."

[21]Meanwhile the people were waiting for Zechariah, and wondered at his delay in the sanctuary. [22]When he did come out, he could not speak to them, and they realized that he had seen a vision in the sanctuary. He kept motioning to them and remained unable to speak. [23]When his time of service was ended, he went to his home.

the new divine act; instead it is Elizabeth who articulates what God is doing at the conception of John (1:24-25).[29]

A contemporary example of how silencing men's voices allows women to be heard is in the practice adopted by the women's Bible study groups in the Diocese of San Cristóbal de las Casas, México. In a context where women customarily keep silence and defer to men when they are in mixed gatherings, the leaders of the women's groups have insisted that only the women speak. If men are allowed to attend, it is with their agreement to keep silent. In this way, the women have been able to learn how to express freely their own understanding of the Scriptures and how God is working in their lives (for an example of their reflections, see excursus at 1:38: "What God Has Determined for Us").

A Literal "Lukan Silence": Zechariah's Loss of Voice in Luke 1:5-25

Feminist interpreters often highlight the relative silence of women in Luke's narrative. Luke assigns far more "speaking roles" to his male characters, and when he does include female characters, he often does so to silence them, a tendency that Elisabeth Schüssler Fiorenza famously coined "the Lukan silence." Yet while Luke arguably promotes silence for women in a variety of implicit ways, he begins his two-volume work by narrating the explicit silencing of a man. In the opening scene of his birth narrative (Luke 1:5-25), Luke silences a man in a very

29. Sharon H. Ringe, *Luke*, Westminster Bible Companion (Louisville: Westminster John Knox, 1995), 30. Ringe sees this as part of a Lukan pattern of reversals, e.g., the powerful brought down from their thrones and the humiliated lifted up (1:52), the hungry filled with good things and the rich sent away empty (1:53); the rich man suffering in Hades and the poor Lazarus held at Abraham's bosom (16:19-31).

concrete way, for here the priest Zechariah, the father of John the Baptist, literally loses his ability to speak.

Zechariah's silence contributes to the sharp reversal he undergoes in this scene, for Zechariah begins as a faithful, praiseworthy man (1:5-7) but ends as a man who is punished and identified as lacking faith (1:19-23). Zechariah's reversal turns around the question he poses to the angel Gabriel after receiving the news of his impending fatherhood: "How will I know that this is so? For I am an old man, and my wife is getting on in years" (1:18). In response to this question, Gabriel rebukes Zechariah and tells him that he will not be able to speak until the birth announcement is fulfilled because he did not believe Gabriel's words (1:20). Gabriel's rebuke is surprising because Zechariah's response has precedent: it not only repeats information provided earlier by the narrator (1:7) but also mirrors the question the patriarch Abraham asked God in Genesis 15:8. Unlike Zechariah, Abraham receives no rebuke. Unlike Zechariah, Mary also receives no rebuke when she poses her own question to Gabriel regarding the feasibility of her impending motherhood just a few verses later (1:34). Gabriel simply answers her question instead of reprimanding her (1:35-37), and Mary herself concludes the scene by having the last word (1:38).

Zechariah's silence becomes all the more surprising when viewed through the lens of ancient understandings of masculinity. In the Greco-Roman world, men expressed their "manliness" through controlling their own speech and the speech of others. Men could be silent were the silence self-imposed, but being silenced by an outside source undermined a man's manhood. Such an infliction signaled a loss of self-control— one of the cardinal virtues of "manly men"—and also situated men among women, whose "proper" purview was silence, especially in public spaces. Given that Luke's narrative was written in a culture where "true" men had to assert their voices to maintain their manliness, it is suggestive, therefore, that Luke lingers on Zechariah's loss of voice. Indeed, Zechariah remains mute throughout the duration of Elizabeth's pregnancy, a fact that Luke notes at various junctures (e.g., 1:24, 40, 56). More, Zechariah's silence opens up space for both Elizabeth and Mary to speak. Elizabeth's direct discourse concludes Luke's opening scene when she rightly identifies God as the source of her reversal of circumstances (1:25), and Elizabeth's and Mary's speeches continue to dominate the next few scenes as well, culminating in Mary's famous *Magnificat* (1:26-56).

Zechariah's silence is temporary, for he eventually regains his voice when he sings a song of praise after his son is born (1:67-79). While a feminist reader may interpret Zechariah's restoration as a return to patriarchal norms, Elizabeth's speech enables Zechariah's restoration. Directly prior to his song, Elizabeth exercises her own voice in a public space when she rejects the paternal name "Zechariah" that her relatives and neighbors try to impose on her child (1:59-62). Only when Zechariah agrees with his wife's words (to the surprise of the crowd!) is his mouth opened and he is able to join his voice with the faithful witness of Elizabeth and Mary (1:63-64, 67-79).

Zechariah's reversals involving speech, silence, and gender norms coincide with the theme of reversal found in Luke–Acts as a whole, a theme that Mary programmatically expresses in her *Magnificat* (1:52-53). Yet Zechariah's reversals also anticipate Luke's expectations concerning how men are to act as members of "the Way." As the father of one who "prepares the way," Zechariah prepares readers for how men in Luke's narrative do not always conform to ancient conceptions of what makes a "manly man."

Brittany E. Wilson

God's Favor to Elizabeth (1:24-25)

The focus now shifts to Elizabeth, who makes two important theological assertions. The first is that her pregnancy is God's doing (1:25).[30] Second, she acclaims that God delights not in people's suffering but rather in taking away their humiliation (ὄνειδός, "disgrace," 1:25).[31] This declaration anticipates the central message of the *Magnificat*,[32] where

30. Joel S. Baden ("The Nature of Barrenness in the Hebrew Bible," in *Disability Studies and Biblical Literature*, ed. Candida R. Moss and Jeremy Schipper [New York: Palgrave Macmillan, 2011], 13–27) shows that in the OT fertility and infertility are both due to God's action. He finds that except for Genesis 20:17-18, barrenness is less the result of human sin than a lack of divine blessing. See further Candida R. Moss and Joel S. Baden, *Reconceiving Infertility: Biblical Perspectives on Procreation and Childlessness* (Princeton: Princeton University Press, 2015).

31. The question of how to understand God's goodness and power in relation to the suffering of the innocent/righteous is a critical one, which will be taken up in more detail in chap. 22. One important assertion in 1:25 is that God does not send or will suffering.

32. Claudia Janssen and Regene Lamb, "Gospel of Luke: The Humbled Will Be Lifted Up," in *Feminist Biblical Interpretation: A Compendium of Critical Commentary on the Books of the Bible and Related Literature*, ed. Luise Schottroff and Marie-Theres Wacker, trans. Lisa E. Dahill, Everett R. Kalin, Nancy Lukens, Linda M. Maloney,

Luke 1:24-25

24After those days his wife Elizabeth conceived, and for five months she remained in seclusion. She said, 25"This is what the Lord has done for me when he looked favorably on me and took away the disgrace I have endured among my people."

Mary similarly sings of how God "has looked with favor" on her humiliation (1:48) and lifts up all the humiliated (1:52). While Luke does not specify the source of Elizabeth's disgrace, the narrative sequence implies that, despite her uprightness in keeping all the commandments (1:6), she endured unmerited contempt because of her childlessness, like Sarah did from Hagar (Gen 16:4-5) and Hannah from Peninnah (1 Sam 1:6).[33] Such treatment of women who long for children makes their pain doubly difficult to bear.

One way in which Elizabeth's story is different from Old Testament stories of women who are infertile is that she is not shown as taking any direct action to remedy the situation. Rachel Havrelock has shown that there is a pattern in the stories of Sarah, Rebekah, Rachel, Leah, Hannah, the mother of Samson, and the Great Woman of Shunem that parallels that of the male heroes in the patriarchal narratives and that the covenantal promises of innumerable descendants are not fulfilled until these women take action to forge their own relationship to the God of the covenant.[34] The pattern of male journeys involves departure, tests, and visual or auditory encounters with God as they seek to conquer, claim, and sanctify land. The steps of the journey for women who are infertile are: (1) barrenness, (2) statement of protest, (3) direct action,

---

Barbara Rumscheidt, Martin Rumscheidt, and Tina Steiner (Grand Rapids: Eerdmans, 2012), 650.

33. See Moss and Baden, *Reconceiving Infertility*, 27–42, on the pressure to procreate in agricultural societies, such as ancient Israel, to have more hands to work, to give a safety net to the parents, and to continue the family lineage. They also explore the shame experienced by infertile women such as Sarah, Rachel, and Hannah, made even more intense by living in the same home with their fertile rivals (which is not to say that Sarah's experience of shame excuses her treatment of Hagar her slave, who is under grave duress in the household).

34. Rachel Havrelock, "The Myth of Birthing the Hero: Heroic Barrenness in the Hebrew Bible," *BibInt* 16 (2008): 154–78; on the pattern of biblical male journeys, see Ronald S. Hendel, *The Epic of the Patriarch: The Jacob Cycle and the Narrative Traditions of Canaan and Israel*, HSM 42 (Atlanta: Scholars Press, 1987).

(4) encounter with God, (5) conception, (6) birth, (7) naming. The women do not accept the status quo and voice their protests to their husband and/or to God (Sarah in Gen 16:2; Rachel in Gen 30:1; Leah in Gen 30:15-16; and Hannah in 1 Sam 1:10). Actions follow, such as giving a surrogate to their husband (Sarah and Hagar in Gen 16:3; Rachel and Bilhah in Gen 30:3; Leah and Zilpah in Gen 30:9), by which the women who are infertile claim the body of another as an extension of their own.[35] Subsequently, there is an encounter with and response from God, often framed as God remembering, listening, and opening the womb (Gen 30:17, 22; 1 Sam 1:19). The final elements in the pattern are the birth and naming of the child. "The giving of a name affords the mothers the opportunity to tell their story of movement from the barrenness to fertility and to perpetuate their experience through the child's ascribed identity."[36] Although the mother is "quickly whisked off stage"[37] after the birth of the son, memory of her persists "through the record of her deeds and continues to exert influence through the name she bestows on her child."[38]

Havrelock makes a case for the agency of the women in the stories she analyzes: "The movement from barrenness to fertility depends on articulation, assertion and action as well as a heroic daring."[39] Reading Luke's story of Elizabeth against the stories Havrelock studies, we see Luke's tendency to diminish women characters. In the case of Elizabeth, there is no such articulation or action; in 1:24-25, she is a passive recipient of God's favor, thus conforming to Luke's ideal for women.

We see very little in the story of Elizabeth and Zechariah's childlessness, and the eventual gift to them of their son John, that might speak to contemporary struggles with infertility. Those today who wish for children but who cannot conceive might take some solace that Luke recognizes the pain such unfulfilled desire can cause. They might appreciate the sensitive character portrait of Elizabeth as one who has experienced her inability to conceive as "a disgrace" she has endured (v. 25) if they have experienced their own pain in these terms. But we cannot imagine

---

35. Havrelock, "The Myth of Birthing the Hero," 166. The landmark work on the plight of Hagar, the first surrogate in Genesis, is Delores S. Williams, *Sisters in the Wilderness: The Challenge of Womanist God-Talk*, ann. ed. (Maryknoll, NY: Orbis Books, 2013).

36. Havrelock, "The Myth of Birthing the Hero," 176.

37. Esther Fuchs, "The Literary Characterization of Mothers and Sexual Politics in the Hebrew Bible," in *Women in the Hebrew Bible: A Reader*, ed. Alice Bach (New York: Routledge, 1999), 127–40; here 137.

38. Havrelock, "The Myth of Birthing the Hero," 178.

39. Ibid.

that these small narrative details assuage in any significant way the deep pain childlessness can cause for those wanting children. Further, we reject the biblical view that God intentionally "closes wombs," along with any proposal that infertility is a punishment from God. We do not believe in a God who intentionally causes such suffering.

Mary's Prophetic Call and Response (1:26-38)

Many Christians see in this scene a Mary who is a docile, sweet, compliant servant, totally submissive to God's will, and therefore a model for women to emulate. Barbara stands among many feminist scholars who have argued, instead, that Mary is a strong woman who has a direct encounter with God, who does not hesitate to question, and who does not need the mediation of a man to accomplish God's purposes. These feminists propose that Luke depicts Mary as a prophet,[40] aligning her with the powerful women prophets in the Old Testament. This passage has the same elements as call stories of Old Testament prophets.[41]

---

40. Barbara E. Reid, "Prophetic Voices of Mary, Elizabeth, and Anna in Luke 1–2," in *New Perspectives on the Nativity*, ed. Jeremy Corley (London: T&T Clark, 2009), 37–46; Barbara E. Reid, "Women Prophets of God's Alternative Reign," in *Luke–Acts and Empire: Essays in Honor of Robert L. Brawley*, ed. David Rhoads, David Esterline, and Jae Won Lee, PTMS (Eugene, OR: Pickwick Papers, 2010), 44–59. See also Ivone Gebara and Maria Clara L. Bingemer, *María, Mujer Profética: Ensayo teológico a partir de la mujer y de América Latina* (Madrid: Ediciones Paulinas, 1988); N. Clayton Croy and Alice E. Connor, "Mantic Mary? The Virgin Mother as Prophet in Luke 1.26-56 and in the Early Church," *JSNT* 34 (2011): 254–76, outline references to Mary as prophet in the early church fathers, 268–69. See also Beverly Roberts Gaventa, *Mary: Glimpses of the Mother of Jesus*, Studies on Personalities of the New Testament (Columbia: University of South Carolina Press, 1995); Alice L. Laffey, "Images of Mary in the Christian Scriptures," in *All Generations Shall Call Me Blessed*, ed. Francis A. Eigo (Villanova, PA: Villanova University Press, 1994), 39–71; Richard I. Pervo, *The Gospel of Luke*, The Scholars Bible (Salem, OR: Polebridge, 2014), 22: "The story seems more like the report of a prophetic calling than a simple announcement." Mary is not only important for Christians but also revered in Muslim tradition. Muslim feminist Hosn Aboud, "'*Idhan Maryam Nabiyya*' ('Hence Maryam Is a Prophetess'): Muslim Classical Exegetes and Women's Receptiveness to God's Verbal Inspiration," in *Mariam, the Magdalene, and the Mother*, ed. Deirdre Good (Bloomington: Indiana University Press, 2005), 183–96, outlines how medieval Andalusian exegetes argued for the prophethood of Maryam, mother of Jesus, and then compares her to Muhammad.

41. For a comparison of the calls of Moses (Exod 3:1-12), Gideon (Judg 6:11-24), Isaiah (Isa 6:1-13), Jeremiah (Jer 1:4-10), and Ezekiel (Ezek 1:1–3:11) to Luke 1:26-38, see the table by Croy and Connor, "Mantic Mary?," 259. Bea Wyler, "Mary's Call,"

[26]In the sixth month the angel Gabriel was sent by God to a town in Galilee called Nazareth, [27]to a virgin engaged to a man whose name was Joseph, of the house of David. The virgin's name was Mary. [28]And he came to her and said, "Greetings, favored one! The Lord is with you." [29]But she was much perplexed by his words and pondered what sort of greeting this might be. [30]The angel said to her, "Do not be afraid, Mary, for you have found favor with God. [31]And now, you will conceive in your womb and bear a son, and you will name him Jesus. [32]He will be great, and will be called the Son of the Most High, and the Lord God will give to him the throne of his ancestor David. [33]He will reign over the

Comparing the call of Moses (Exod 3:1-12) and that of Mary, we note first that the encounter with God's messenger takes place in the midst of ordinary everyday life. Moses was simply tending his father-in-law's sheep when God's angel appeared to him in a flame of fire out of a bush (Exod 3:1-2). Mary appears to be an ordinary Galilean woman about to be married when Gabriel appears to her.[42]

The angel's salutation, Χαῖρε, is not only the common greeting "hail" but also means "rejoice." In the context of a prophetic call, it recollects prophecies of Zephaniah (3:14), Joel (2:21), and Zechariah (9:9). Gabriel calls Mary κεχαριτωμένη, "favored one" (1:28, 30); not only males like Noah, Moses, Gideon, and Samuel are favored by God.[43] Gabriel then articulates the prophetic mission (1:31-33). Authentic prophets initially resist their commissions and offer sound objections to it.[44] Prophets know that they risk rejection and suffering (e.g., Num 11:1-15; Jer 18:18; 20:1-6; see Jesus's remark that Jerusalem kills the prophets and stones those who are sent to it in Luke 13:34). In the following chapter, Simeon prophesies the pain Mary will endure (2:35).

---

in *A Feminist Companion to the Hebrew Bible in the New Testament*, ed. Athalya Brenner, FCB 10 (Sheffield: Sheffield Academic, 1996), 136–48, sees a similar call to Sarah (Gen 18:9-14) and Manoah's wife (Judg 13:2-20).

42. In two other instances in the OT an angelic messenger appears to a woman: Hagar (Gen 16:7-16) and Samson's mother (Judg 13:1-25).

43. Noah (Gen 6:8), Moses (Exod 33:12-17), Gideon (Judg 6:17), and Samuel (1 Sam 2:26). The term also foreshadows the "favor [χάρις] of God" that is upon Mary's son (2:40, 52) and the favorable or gracious words (λόγοις τῆς χάριτος) he utters (4:22).

44. See Exod 3:11; 4:10; Jer 1:6; Amos 7:14.

house of Jacob forever, and of his kingdom there will be no end." [34]Mary said to the angel, "How can this be, since I am a virgin?" [35]The angel said to her, "The Holy Spirit will come upon you, and the power of the Most High will overshadow you; therefore the child to be born will be holy; he will be called Son of God. [36]And now, your relative Elizabeth in her old age has also conceived a son; and this is the sixth month for her who was said to be barren. [37]For nothing will be impossible with God." [38]Then Mary said, "Here am I, the servant of the Lord; let it be with me according to your word." Then the angel departed from her.

God's messenger then issues a promise of divine assistance: "nothing will be impossible with God." [45] The messenger next gives the prophet a tangible sign: for Moses, it is his brother Aaron, who will act as his spokesman (Exod 4:15); for Mary, it is the pregnancy of her relative, Elizabeth (1:36). The prophet then assents and fulfills the mission with which she or he has been entrusted (Exod 4:15-18; Luke 1:38).

Although Luke does not explicitly call her a prophet, in contrast to Anna (2:36-38),[46] Mary functions as one when she utters a prophecy in the next scene. She stands on the shoulders of other women prophets who went before: her namesake, Miriam (Exod 15:20), Deborah (Judg 4:4), Huldah (2 Kgs 22:14; 2 Chr 34:22), the unnamed mother of Isaiah's child

45. Compare promises of divine assistance: Exod 4:15; Jer 1:8; Isa 6:5-8. "Nothing will be impossible with God" echoes God's words to Abraham (Gen 18:14) and to the prophet Zechariah (8:6) concerning the restoration of Jerusalem, as well as Job's declaration (42:2) at the end of his ordeals.

46. The only other references to female prophets in the NT are to the four virgin daughters of Philip (Acts 21:9), the women prophets of Corinth (1 Cor 11:5), and a "false" woman prophet in Rev 2:18-28. Women such as Mary Magdalene (John 20:11-18) and the Samaritan woman (John 4:4-42) act as prophets by proclaiming the word and bringing people to faith in Jesus and are called such in early church tradition but are not so named in the gospels. In addition, the woman who anoints Jesus (Mark 14:3-9) does a prophetic action akin to Samuel's anointing of Saul and David as king (1 Sam 10:1; 16:13). In Luke's version of the anointing woman (7:36-50), it is Jesus, not the woman, who is the prophet. In the early third century, Hippolytus of Rome wrote in his commentary on the Song of Songs (25:6-7) that the women who meet the risen Christ "were made apostles to the apostles, having been sent by Christ." Origen (ca. 185–253/54) referred to the Samaritan woman as an apostle and evangelist: "Christ sends the woman as an apostle to the inhabitants of the city because his words have inflamed this woman" (*Comm. S. Jean* 4.26–27).

(Isa 8:3), No'adiah (Neh 6:14), and unnamed daughters who prophesy (Joel 3:1-2; Ezek 13:17; 1 Chr 25:3-5).[47]

N. Clayton Croy and Alice E. Connor hypothesize that the reason that Luke does not call Mary a prophet is that he avoids associating Mary with practices in Greco-Roman antiquity that relate virginity and prophecy.[48] In Delphi, for example, the Pythia who delivered Apollo's oracle was a virgin, thought to be in a state more pure, more receptive to penetration by the god or oracular spirit.[49] Descriptions in ancient sources (e.g., Virgil, *Aen.* 6.77–80) of the act of possession by the prophetic spirit often have sexual overtones, another thing that Luke wants to avoid associating with Mary. We find this hypothesis credible. In addition, we think that Luke's agenda is to diminish the voices of women prophets so that those of men come to the fore, assuring Theophilus-type readers (1:3-4) that there is nothing disorderly about the Jesus movement.[50] The only women who are called prophets in Luke and Acts are Anna (2:36-38) and Philip's

---

47. The Talmud (b. Meg. 14a-b) also recognizes Sarah, Hannah, Abigail, and Esther as prophets. See further Wilda C. Gafney, *Daughters of Miriam: Women Prophets in Ancient Israel* (Minneapolis: Fortress, 2008).

48. Croy and Connor, "Mantic Mary?," 270. Greco-Roman sources that speak of women virgin prophets at the oracle of Delphi include Lucan, *Astr.* 21; Diodorus Siculus 16.26; Plutarch, *Def. orac.* 437C-D; Strabo, *Geogr.* 9.3.5. Some sources, e.g., Lycophron, *Alexandra* 1279; Pausanias, *Descr.* 10.12.6, refer to the Sybil as a virgin prophet. Most often she is depicted as an aged woman, "a functional virgin" (e.g., Hermas, *Vis.* 8 [2.4]; Ovid, *Metam.* 14.101–53). See Mary F. Foskett, *A Virgin Conceived: Mary and Classical Representations of Virginity* (Bloomington: Indiana University Press, 2002), 36–40; Antoinette Clark Wire, *The Corinthian Women Prophets: A Reconstruction through Paul's Rhetoric* (Minneapolis: Fortress, 1990); Jill E. Marshall, *Women Praying and Prophesying in Corinth: Gender and Inspired Speech in First Corinthians*, WUNT 2.448 (Tübingen: Mohr Siebeck, 2017).

49. Foskett, *A Virgin Conceived*, 68–70; Mary F. Foskett, "Virginity as Purity in the Protoevangelium of James," in *A Feminist Companion to Mariology*, ed. Amy-Jill Levine with Maria Mayo Robbins, FCNTECW 10 (Edinburgh: T&T Clark, 2005), 67–76; Croy and Connor, "Mantic Mary?," 265. Virginity can also signify single-minded devotion, as in Paul's exhortation to virgins to remain unmarried and so be solely "anxious about the affairs of the Lord," in contrast to married women who are "anxious about the affairs of the world, how to please her husband" (1 Cor 7:34). Other examples where virginity is associated with prophecy include the Sibyl and vestal virgins of Rome.

50. See the authors' introduction on Luke's overall treatment of women; on Luke's desire to tame and limit prophecy, see Mary Rose D'Angelo, "(Re)Presentations of Women in the Gospel of Matthew and Luke–Acts," in *Women and Christian Origins*, ed. Ross Shepard Kraemer and Mary Rose D'Angelo (New York: Oxford University Press, 1999), 188–89.

four daughters (Acts 21:9), none of whom is given speech. In the gospel, once Jesus begins his public ministry, he takes over the role of prophet.[51]

Inserted into Their Reality and Inspired by God: Female Prophets of the Old Testament

The significant role that prophetic women play in Luke's accounts must be viewed as a continuation of the public influence of women prophets in ancient Israel. The texts of the Old Testament mention only five women holding a prophetic title. Nevertheless, there are biblical references to anonymous women who exercised prophetic roles (e.g., in Ezek 13:17-23). Also, other women are described as performing actions that can be associated with prophecy: those at the entrance of the tent of meeting (Exod 38:8 and 1 Sam 2:22), the medium of Endor (1 Sam 28:3-25), and the daughters of Heman (in 1 Chr 25:1-7). Women prophets appear deeply inserted into the reality of their people and/or nation. Sent by God and committed especially to the most vulnerable, they prophesied through oracles, songs, and symbolic actions. They also advised or warned leaders and kings.

The reference to Maryam appears during the process of the configuration of Israel as a people (in Exod 2; 15:20-21; Num 12; 20:1; 26:59; 1 Chr 5:29/6:3; and Mic 6:4). Maryam is portrayed as a sister, daughter, and collaborator with God's project of life within a human regime of death (Exod 2). She also remained in the memory of the people as a significant leader of the journey through the desert, together with Moses and Aaron (Num 12; 20:1; 26:59; 1 Chr 5:29/6:3; Mic 6:4). Evidence of the love of the people for Maryam is highlighted in the story about their refusal to move until she was freed from leprosy (Num 12:15). Fulfilling her prophetic role, Maryam sings or "interprets theologically" (ותען) that the event at the Reed Sea was a salvific action provided by the hand of God (Exod 15:20-21).

Deborah's prophetic contribution is found in the book of Judges 4–5. The Deuteronomist presents her as a נביאה, "woman prophet," in Judges 4:4. She is also recognized as a judge and called לפידות, "Lapidot-woman," which can mean a woman "from the city of Lapidot," a woman "married

---

51. The emphasis on Jesus as prophet is strongest in the Third Gospel. See Luke 4:18-19 (echoing Isa 61:1-2) and the parallels with Elijah and Elisha: Luke 4:25-26; 7:2-10 // 2 Kgs 5:1-14; Luke 7:11-17 // 1 Kgs 17:17-24; 2 Kgs 4:18-37; Luke 9:10-17 // 2 Kgs 4:42-44; Exod 16:4-36; Luke 9:51; 24:51 // 2 Kgs 2:11; Luke 13:33-35; 22:64; 24:19.

to Lapidot" (a man), or a "torch-fire woman."[52] Deborah was involved in the political and social life of her community. She was the initiator, the brains, and the inspiration for her people.[53] She pronounced an oracle of military victory (4:6-7) and the fate of Sisera (4:9), and she called Barak to persevere (4:14). In the song attributed to her (in Judg 5), Deborah is designated as "mother of Israel." A similar title, "father of Israel," was given to Elijah (2 Kgs 2:12) and Eliakim (Isa 22:21), indicating their authority and role as protectors of the community.[54] Deborah's song proclaimed the victory of the most vulnerable among the nations. Her song links her to Maryam's prophetic action.

During the golden age of prophecy and contemporaneously with the prophet Isaiah, we find the reference to an anonymous female prophet in Isaiah 8:3. The accounts in Isaiah 7–8 show that Judah was being pressured by Syria and Samaria to join them against Assyria. Isaiah, following the command of God, approached the unnamed woman prophet. The verb קרב, "come near, approach,"

emphasizes the movement of a husband toward his wife. It seems, however, that she was granted the title, not for being Isaiah's wife, but rather for her action. Isaiah and she bore a child. The name of the child, "Maher-Shalal-Hash-Baz" (meaning "Swift is booty, speedy is prey"), constitutes their symbolic action. It warned Ahaz that if he joined the Syro-Ephraimite coalition, Judah would be destroyed.

References to Huldah, her prophetic title, and contribution are found in 2 Kings 22:14-20 // 2 Chronicles 34:22-28. Huldah was sought to interpret a scroll discovered in the temple. She was chosen probably because she lived among those who experienced and processed theologically the disaster of the Northern Kingdom in the Mishneh (second quarter of Jerusalem). Also, she seems to be well known because her husband's name, occupation, and lineage were registered (in 2 Kgs 22:14 // 2 Chr 34:22). Huldah was a prophet of the Word. Her oracles contain the introductory formula "Thus says YHWH" and the concluding formula "Word of YHWH." Her first oracle, which

---

52. Mieke Bal, *Death and Dissymmetry: The Politics of Coherence in the Book of Judges* (Chicago: University of Chicago Press, 1988), 209.

53. Athalya Brenner, *The Israelite Woman: Social Role and Literary Type in Biblical Narrative* (London: Bloomsbury, 2014), 63.

54. Tikva Frymer-Kensky, "Deborah 2," in *Women in Scripture: A Dictionary of Named and Unnamed Women in the Hebrew Bible; The Apocryphal/Deuterocanonical Books, and the New Testament*, ed. Carol Meyers, Toni Craven, and Ross Shepard Kraemer (Grand Rapids: Eerdmans, 2000), 67.

was probably reworked after the exile (2 Kgs 23:15-17), addressed the people and presumed the inevitability of a catastrophe. Her second oracle (in 2 Kgs 23:18-20a) confirmed Josiah's piety and humility before YHWH and communicated a promise that he would be buried "in peace" (with his ancestors). Huldah's intervention was taken seriously by Josiah, who initiated and continued eagerly a religious reform (2 Kgs 23 // 2 Chr 34:29-33).

Noadiah's name, prophetic title, and level of influence in Jerusalem during the Persian period is found in a short prayer attributed to Nehemiah in Nehemiah 6:14. She is mentioned together with an anonymous group of prophets who were frightening Nehemiah. It seems that her prophetic function was exercised in deep solidarity with the poor and the marginalized of her time: the population that was affected by the nationalist and separationist perspective of the returnees from exile. We have no record of her words but apparently Nehemiah could not co-opt her or the rest of the prophets to support his nationalist cause.[55]

The prophetic action of these five women and of many other women made clearer the signs of God's presence in the history of Israel and prepared the people to receive the fulfilment of salvation.

Mila Díaz Solano

While artistic renditions frequently depict Mary praying when Gabriel appears to her, and despite the frequency with which Luke inserts this theme,[56] Luke says nothing here about her piety. Unlike Zechariah, who is in the temple when Gabriel appears to him (1:8), Mary is at home, going about her ordinary business. Such will also be the pattern when her son encounters fishermen who are washing their nets when he calls them to be his disciples (5:2).

Mary's name, Μαριάμ, is the Greek equivalent of the Hebrew מרים, Miriam, the name of Moses's sister, who was a prophet (Exod 15:20; Num 12:2; Mic 6:4).[57] It was also one of the most common names for Jewish women

55. Cf. Robert P. Carroll, "Coopting the Prophets: Nehemiah and Noadiah," in *Priests, Prophets, and Scribes: Essays on the Formation of Heritage of Second Temple Judaism in Honour of Joseph Blenkinsopp*, ed. Eugene Ulrich, JSOTSup 149 (Sheffield: JSOT, 1992), 96.

56. See excursus at 11:2 on the pervasiveness of prayer in Luke.

57. See further Deirdre Good, "What Does It Mean to Call Mary Mariam?," in Levine and Robbins, *A Feminist Companion to Mariology*, 99–106.

in the Second Temple period in Galilee and Judea[58] and may also evoke the memory of Mariamme, the Hasmonean princess married to Herod and executed by him in 29 BCE. The murder of Mariamme, her brother Aristobulus, and Mariamme's two sons by Herod in 7 BCE ended the Hasmonean dynasty. Inscriptions and documents from Galilee and Judea show a marked rise in Hasmonean names in the first century CE.[59] Parents were naming their babies John, Simon, Judas, Salome, or Mariamme as an expression of their nationalistic hopes for independence. Mary's parents, by giving her a name that had previously been uncommon in Galilee and Judea, express their Hasmonean sympathies.[60] Mary is well disposed to hear and accept a prophetic call and to articulate not only what God has done for her people in the past but their future hopes for liberation (1:46-55).

Luke provides no information about Mary other than her name, the name of her town, and that she is a virgin engaged to a man named Joseph. He says nothing of her genealogy, other than the fact that Elizabeth is a relative. This lack of detail contrasts with the lineages Luke provides for Elizabeth and Zechariah (1:5), Joseph (1:27),[61] and the prophet Anna (2:36). Joel Green suggests that this surprising lack may be to stress Mary's insignificant social status.[62]

Determining the socioeconomic status of Galileans of the late Second Temple period is a difficult endeavor. Douglas E. Oakman, who argues from sociological models drawn from peasant studies, asserts that "the historical context of Jesus . . . reflects a social and economic situation in which exploitative urbanism, powerful redistributive central institutions like the Roman state and Jewish temple, concentration of land holdings in the hands of a few, rising debt, and disrupted horizontal relations in society were becoming the norm."[63] Other scholars, who base their con-

58. Tal Ilan, "Notes on the Distribution of Jewish Women's Names in Palestine in the Second Temple and Mishnaic Periods," *JJS* 40 (1989): 186–200.

59. Margaret H. Williams, "Palestinian Jewish Personal Names in Acts," in *The Book of Acts in Its Palestinian Setting*, ed. Richard Bauckham (Grand Rapids: Eerdmans, 1995), 79–113.

60. Marianne Sawicki, *Crossing Galilee: Architectures of Contact in the Occupied Land of Jesus* (Harrisburg, PA: Trinity Press International, 2000), 137–40.

61. Although the Greek is ambiguous, most understand "of the house of David" to modify Joseph, not Mary, in accord with Luke 2:4; 3:23, 31.

62. Joel B. Green, "The Social Status of Mary in Luke 1,5–2,52: A Plea for Methodological Integration," *Bib* 73 (1992): 457–72.

63. Douglas E. Oakman, *Jesus and the Economic Questions of His Day*, Studies in the Bible and Early Christianity 8 (Lewiston, NY/Queenston, Ont.: Mellen, 1986), 211. See also Douglas E. Oakman, "Execrating? Or Execrable Peasants!," in *The Galilean*

clusions on archaeological evidence, claim that both cities and villages in the Galilee during the Hellenistic and early Roman periods enjoyed a fair degree of economic prosperity.[64] Because of the fragmentary nature of the archaeological data and the limitations of sociological models, it is not possible to reach a sure conclusion about what would have been the socioeconomic status of the majority of Galileans in the late Second Temple period.[65] What we can say is that Luke portrays Mary after her marriage to Joseph, not as a poor peasant, but as one who had sufficient income to be able to travel to Jerusalem every year for the feast of Passover (Luke 2:41). Luke lacks references to Joseph and Jesus being woodworkers (τέκτων, NRSV: "carpenter," applied to Joseph in Matt 13:55 and to Jesus in Mark 6:3), but a likely scenario is that Mary, Joseph, Jesus, and the rest of the family would have been engaged in part-time farming in addition to Joseph and Jesus plying their trade among the villagers of Nazareth and possibly the nearby Sepphoris, being built by Herod Antipas as his capital.[66] They may have been poor, but theirs "was not the grinding, degrading poverty of the day laborer or the rural slave."[67]

Virginal Conception

Luke calls attention to Mary's sexual status by repeating παρθένος, "virgin," in verse 27 along with her assertion ἄνδρα οὐ γινώσκω, "I do

---

Economy in the Time of Jesus, ed. David A. Fiensy and Ralph K. Hawkins, ECL 11 (Atlanta: SBL, 2013), 139–64; the recent Marxist analysis of Roland Boer and Christina Petterson, *Time of Troubles: A New Economic Framework for Early Christianity* (Minneapolis: Fortress, 2017); and John Dominic Crossan, *The Historical Jesus: The Life of a Mediterranean Jewish Peasant* (San Francisco: HarperSanFrancisco, 1991), 43–71.

64. E.g., these essays in Fiensy and Hawkins, *The Galilean Economy in the Time of Jesus*: Mordechai Aviam, "People, Land, Economy, and Belief in First-Century Galilee and Its Origins: A Comprehensive Archaeological Synthesis," 5–48; C. Thomas McCollough, "City and Village in Lower Galilee: The Import of the Archeological Excavations at Sepphoris and Khirbet Qana (Cana) for Framing the Economic Context of Jesus," 49–74; Sharon Lea Mattila, "Revisiting Jesus' Capernaum: A Village of Only Subsistence-Level Fishers and Farmers?," 75–138. John P. Meier, *A Marginal Jew: Rethinking the Historical Jesus*, vol. 1: *The Roots of the Problem and the Person*, ABRL (New York: Doubleday, 1991), 282, notes that "the reign of Herod Antipas (4 B.C.–A.D. 39) in Galilee was relatively prosperous and peaceful, free of the severe social strife that preceded and followed it."

65. David A. Fiensy, "Assessing the Economy of Galilee in the Late Second Temple Period: Five Considerations," in Fiensy and Hawkins, *The Galilean Economy in the Time of Jesus*, 165–86, outlines both the positive contributions and the limitations of archaeology and sociological models and asserts that both are needed.

66. Meier, *A Marginal Jew*, 1:279–80.

67. Meier, *A Marginal Jew*, 1:282.

not know / have relations with man" (1:34). What is not entirely clear, however, is whether Luke intends to describe a virginal conception. The future-tense verbs in verses 31-33 allow for the possibility that Gabriel is announcing the conception of Jesus that would occur in the natural way after Mary and Joseph marry.[68] In setting forth Jesus's genealogy, Luke writes, "He was the son (as was thought) of Joseph" (3:23). The phrase "as was thought" does not appear in parentheses in the early Greek manuscripts; the punctuation is the choice of the NRSV translation team. It can be understood either as an assertion that Joseph was indeed Jesus's biological father or that the notion was mistaken.

Andrew T. Lincoln proposes the coexistence of two perspectives in Luke: one that asserts the virginal conception of Jesus (1:34-37) and another that presents Joseph as Jesus's father, through whom he has Davidic ancestry (1:27, 32; 2:4, 7, 11; 2:27, 33, 41-51; 3:23-38; 4:22). He demonstrates that it was a convention for ancient biographers to juxtapose "two different sorts of tradition, one natural and one miraculous, about their subjects' origins." Thus, "Luke holds with the earliest Christian formulations that Jesus was of the seed of David and Joseph's son, but he also holds that in the light of his resurrection Joseph's son was vindicated as God's Son."[69] Jane Schaberg argues that Luke writes, indirectly, of an illegitimate conception of Jesus—thus Mary was seduced, or more probably raped, by a man other than Joseph, to whom she was betrothed.[70] Both hypotheses are plausible, but the evidence does not allow a sure conclusion. Moreover, Luke's intent is not to convey the historical circumstances of Jesus's birth but to make a theological and christological assertion.[71] As Elizabeth Johnson explains,

---

68. Joseph A. Fitzmyer ("The Virginal Conception of Jesus in the New Testament," *TS* 34 [1973]: 567–70) espoused this interpretation but later changed his position. See also *Mary in the New Testament: A Collaborative Assessment by Protestant and Roman Catholic Scholars*, ed. Raymond E. Brown et al. (Philadelphia: Fortress; New York: Paulist Press, 1978), 120.

69. Andrew T. Lincoln, *Born of a Virgin? Reconceiving Jesus in the Bible, Tradition, and Theology* (Grand Rapids: Eerdmans, 2013), 20, 23.

70. Jane D. Schaberg, *The Illegitimacy of Jesus: A Feminist Theological Interpretation of the Infancy Narratives* (San Francisco: Harper & Row, 1987). See also Michael Pope, "Gabriel's Entrance and Biblical Violence in Luke's Annunciation Narrative," *JBL* 137 (2018): 701–10, on biblical rape and biblical impregnation *topoi* in Luke 1. In a subsequent study, "Luke's Seminal Annunciation: An Embryological Reading of Mary's Conception," *JBL* 138 (2019): 791–807, Pope contends that "Luke imports the notion of semen into the infancy narratives by employing language and imagery from both biblical and Greco-Roman literature but prohibits a literal reading of Jesus's conception in Mary's womb" (795).

71. Raymond E. Brown, *The Birth of the Messiah: A Commentary on the Infancy Narratives in Matthew and Luke* (Garden City, NY: Doubleday, 1977), 517.

"The virginal conception of Jesus . . . signifies theologically that Jesus' origin lies in the initiating decree of the loving God, so that his existence is not explainable in terms of the inner forces of this world alone."[72]

Feminist interpreters differ in how they see Mary's virginity. Some associate Mary's virginity with "a misogyny that reifies male power over women, subordinates female sexuality and creativity to a virginal ideal, and perpetuates the notion of femininity as passive receptivity."[73] Other feminists find it offensive that exalting Mary's virginal conception denigrates women who bear children in the normal way. Still others find in Mary's virginity a positive expression of female autonomy and power.[74] The famous speech of Sojourner Truth (see insert) captures this sense. We find value in both strategies: resistance against misogyny and reclamation of female power are transformative when used in tandem.

Ain't I a Woman?[75]

Well, children, where there is so much racket there must be something out of kilter. I think that 'twixt the negroes of the South and the women at the North, all talking about rights, the white men will be in a fix pretty soon. But what's all this here talking about?

That man over there says that women need to be helped into carriages, and lifted over ditches, and to have the best place everywhere. Nobody ever helps me into carriages, or over mud-puddles, or gives me any best place! And ain't I a woman? Look at me! Look at my arm! I have ploughed and planted,

---

72. Elizabeth A. Johnson, "The Symbolic Character of Theological Statements about Mary," *JES* 22 (1985): 312–35; here 315 n. 6.

73. Foskett, *Virgin Conceived*, 2. See also Nancy J. Duff, "Mary, Servant of the Lord," in *Blessed One: Protestant Perspectives on Mary*, ed. Beverly Roberts Gaventa and Cynthia L. Rigby (Louisville: Westminster John Knox, 2002), 62.

74. Foskett, *Virgin Conceived*, 63–68.

75. https://sourcebooks.fordham.edu/mod/sojtruth-woman.asp. Sojourner Truth, born Isabella (Belle) Baumfree (c. 1797–November 26, 1883), was an African American abolitionist and women's rights activist. She was born into slavery in Ulster County, New York, but escaped with her infant daughter to freedom in 1826. She went to court to recover her son in 1828 and became the first Black woman to win such a case against a White man. She gave herself the name Sojourner Truth in 1843 after she became convinced that God had called her to leave the city and go into the countryside "testifying the hope that was in her." "Ain't I A Woman" is her best-known speech and was delivered extemporaneously at the Ohio Women's Rights Convention in Akron, Ohio, in 1851. In 2014, she was included in Smithsonian magazine's list of the "100 Most Significant Americans of All Time."

and gathered into barns, and no man could head me! And ain't I a woman? I could work as much and eat as much as a man—when I could get it—and bear the lash as well! And ain't I a woman? I have borne thirteen children, and seen most all sold off to slavery, and when I cried out with my mother's grief, none but Jesus heard me! And ain't I a woman?

Then they talk about this thing in the head; what's this they call it? [member of audience whispers, "intellect"] That's it, honey. What's that got to do with women's rights or negroes' rights? If my cup won't hold but a pint, and yours holds a quart, wouldn't you be mean not to let me have my little half measure full?

Then that little man in black there, he says women can't have as much rights as men, 'cause Christ wasn't a woman! Where did your Christ come from? Where did your Christ come from? From God and a woman! Man had nothing to do with Him.

If the first woman God ever made was strong enough to turn the world upside down all alone, these women together ought to be able to turn it back, and get it right side up again! And now they is asking to do it, the men better let them.

Obliged to you for hearing me, and now old Sojourner ain't got nothing more to say.

Sojourner Truth

Active Agency and Free Choice (1:38)

Many feminists see Mary as exercising what womanist Diana Hayes calls "outrageous authority"[76] as she dialogues with God's messenger and freely chooses to assent to the mission entrusted to her. Gabriel speaks directly to her, without the mediation of her father or intended husband, much as an angel spoke directly to Hagar (Gen 16:7-12) and to Samson's mother (Judg 13:3-5). It is a conversation in which both participate. Self-possessed, Mary questions the angel.[77] Although the future-tense verbs in Gabriel's explanation to her (1:31-33, 35) might suggest that everything is divinely determined, the case is rather that as with the prophets in the Old Testament, none of what the angel announces can be accomplished

76. Diana L. Hayes, *And Still We Rise: An Introduction to Black Liberation Theology* (New York: Paulist Press, 1996), 173.

77. F. Scott Spencer (*Salty Wives, Spirited Mothers, and Savvy Widows: Capable Women of Purpose and Persistence in Luke's Gospel* [Grand Rapids: Eerdmans, 2012], 71) observes that Mary "displays remarkable moxie and agency in challenging Gabriel and the appropriation of her womb." See above at 1:18 for various interpretations of Zechariah's question.

without Mary's consent. Just as Jesus invites disciples but cannot compel anyone to follow him (see Luke 18:18-25), so God's power needs Mary's receptivity in order to accomplish the divine will. Gabriel is not delivering a decree from a dictatorial patriarch but an invitation from One who is able to work through those who have a disposition of hospitality toward God.[78] Mary's choice invites reflection on women's rights to choose in every arena that concerns their own lives and those of their family and community.

Reproductive Justice: More Than a Woman's Right to Choose

One of the most fraught questions in feminist theology is reproductive choice. Some feminists are ardent defenders of a pro-life stance that opts for the preservation of the life of the fetus in all circumstances.[79] Others, such as Beverly Wildung Harrison, argue that a woman's well-being is a decisive, morally relevant concern that must be considered. She advances that abortion is a positive moral good in many cases.[80] More recently, theologians such as Cristina L. Traina show that the moral issues surrounding unwanted pregnancy are much more complex than a simple choice between the right of the mother over her body and the right of the fetus to be born.[81] Likewise, Tina Beattie demonstrates that absolutist positions do not adequately deal with questions of relationality, consciousness,

78. Kalbryn A. McLean, "Calvin and the Personal Politics of Providence," in *Feminist and Womanist Essays in Reformed Dogmatics*, ed. Amy Plantinga Pauw and Serene Jones (Louisville: Westminster John Knox, 2006), 122–24.

79. E.g., Feminists for Life: https://www.feministsforlife.org/.

80. Beverly Wildung Harrison, *Our Right to Choose: Toward a New Ethic of Abortion* (Boston: Beacon, 1983).

81. Cristina L. Traina, "Between a Rock and a Hard Place," *JRE* 46 (2018): 658–81; Patricia Beattie Jung, "Abortion: An Exercise in Moral Imagination," *Reproductive Health Matters* 1 (1993): 84–86, lists five competing responsibilities to consider by both potential mothers and fathers: (1) an obligation to sustain their own physical, mental, and emotional health, both for their own sake as intrinsically valuable persons and for the sake of others; (2) obligations to other family members, especially to other dependents; (3) communal and vocation-related responsibilities and obligations; (4) a responsibility to support their child's life; (5) an obligation to serve their child's best interest. To be born is not self-evidently in the best interest of every fetus. In addition to abortion, there is also the question of the use of contraception. See, e.g., Emily Reimer Barry, "On Women's Health and Women's Power: A Feminist Appraisal of *Humane Vitae*," *TS* 79 (2018): 818–40.

and community that must be in the foreground. She argues for "a gradual shift in emphasis from the primacy of a woman's right to choose in the first trimester to the right to life of the foetus in the third trimester."[82] She concludes with a reflection on Mary's awakening of maternal consciousness at the annunciation and sees in her a symbol of eschatological hope as "the new Eve."[83] Margaret D. Kamitsuka reflects on how Mary's choice in the annunciation offers a different way for women to imitate Mary than the way pro-life Christians

---

82. Tina Beattie, "Catholicism, Choice, and Consciousness: A Feminist Theological Perspective on Abortion," *International Journal of Public Theology* 4 (2010): 51–75, here 51. Tina Beattie also makes this important observation: "The fact that the modern church has adopted an absolutist position on abortion and contraception, while continuing to respect individual conscience on matters of war and the death penalty (albeit with a strong sense of abhorrence), suggests that this may have more to do with the changing status of women in modern society than with a genuine concern for the unborn child. (One might, for example, point to the vast numbers of children—born and unborn—killed in Iraq but, while the church has not declared that war just, neither has it threatened excommunication to those who take part in it.)

"The recent entry of large numbers of women into the previously masculine domains of theology and politics threatens to destabilize ancient and unchallenged assumptions about the meaning of life and the body, sex and death, law and freedom, because all too often when men have reflected upon these questions, they have written their reflections upon the mute and passive bodies of the female sex. It is not surprising that we are currently experiencing a backlash in which ecclesial misogyny is masked by a *faux* concern for embryonic life, while vast numbers of fully formed and conscious human beings continue to be sacrificed on the altars of economic, military, political and religious expediency" (75).

In critiquing the church's absolutist position on abortion, Beattie also recalls the work of Carol Gilligan (*In a Different Voice: Psychological Theory and Women's Development* [Cambridge, MA: Harvard University Press, 1982]) that demonstrated how men tend to approach moral decision-making by appealing to absolute principles rooted in beliefs about individual autonomy and freedom, whereas women are more likely to reflect in terms of relationality and care.

For comments on the church's intimidation of those who criticize the current teaching, see Kate M. Ott, "From Politics to Theology: Responding to Roman Catholic Ecclesial Control of Reproductive Ethics," *JFSR* 30 (2014): 138–47.

83. See also her prior work with sustained reflection on Mary-Eve symbolism: Tina Beattie, *God's Mother, Eve's Advocate: A Marian Narrative of Women's Salvation* (London: Continuum, 2002). Space does not allow us to discuss adequately Mary-Eve symbolism. We have concerns that this kind of comparison often rests on dualistic contrasts and stereotypes that are antithetical to feminist liberationist approaches.

use her to bolster an antiabortion stance.[84] She sees Mary's *fiat* not as an instantaneous acceptance of motherhood but as the culmination of a process that included perplexity (1:29), questioning (Gabriel), seeking advice (from Elizabeth), and continuing to ponder (2:19).

We agree with those scholars who recognize the complexities in moral decision-making and who see in Mary one whose experience is closer to contemporary women's realities. In addition, we note that when it comes to pregnancy and child rearing, the range of options for a woman with economic means and education living in a country with laws that ensure her equal treatment is vastly different from the choices open to women who are poor, illiterate, and lack legal protection.[85] Moreover, in patriarchal cultures, male imposition of their will on females is the norm, a force difficult to overcome for even the strongest of women.

In her comparison of the character of Mary in Luke with the contemporary experiences of surrogate mothers in India, Sharon Jacob demonstrates well the multiple constraints on women's choices. She sees these similarities between Mary and surrogate mothers: "Both conceive without the physical presence of a male; their conception takes place only after their *consent*; they are impregnated by a third party who hails from a superior realm; and finally, their *willingness* to participate in an anomalous birth is driven by their desire to better

84. Margaret D. Kamitsuka, "Unwanted Pregnancy, Abortion, and Maternal Authority: A Prochoice Theological Argument," *JFSR* 34 (2018): 41–57. There are numerous Catholic and evangelical Christian pro-life websites that use Mary to bolster their position, e.g., Jennifer LeClaire, "What if Mary had Chosen Abortion?," *Charism News*, December 18, 2015: https://www.charismanews.com/opinion/watchman-on -the-wall/53920-what-if-mary-had-chosen-abortion; Rev. Mark H. Creech, "What if Mary Had Known about Abortion?," *Christian Post*, December 17, 2012: https://www .christianpost.com/news/what-if-mary-had-known-about-abortion.html.

85. Recognition that the health and thriving of parents and children, especially in communities of color, have to do with factors beyond the narrower questions of choice and abortion, and includes issues such as poverty and the mass incarceration of reproductive-aged people, Black activist Loretta Ross has spearheaded a movement under the framework of reproductive justice, rather than simply "choice." The movement for reproductive justice affirms three principles: the right to have a child, the right *not* to have a child, and the right to parent children in environments where they are safe and able to flourish. See Loretta Ross and Rickie Solinger, *Reproductive Justice: An Introduction* (Oakland: University of California Press, 2017). For an engagement with Ross's work in religious studies, see Rebecca Todd Peters, *Trust Women: A Progressive Christian Argument for Reproductive Justice* (Boston: Beacon, 2018).

the situation of their people or their families."[86] For Indian surrogate mothers, economic emancipation is contingent on their acceptance of enslavement to another. Likewise, Mary is neither fully free nor fully enslaved (see excursus on "Slave of the Lord"). Mary is not a monolithic character; she remains ambivalent, not fully fashioned as either subject or object.[87]

Empowered and Being Overpowered (1:35)

In Gabriel's assurance that "the Holy Spirit will come upon you,[88] and the power of the Most High will overshadow you" (v. 35), some readers have heard resonances of how they have been overpowered and raped. While recognizing the force of those readings, we offer here a more optimistic reading as well. The verbs ἐπελεύσεται, "come upon," and ἐπισκιάσει, "overshadow," have no sexual connotation; rather, they evoke God's protective and empowering presence. The Holy Spirit's power is not a harmful one;[89] it creates, sustains, and re-creates new life.[90] The Spirit that hovered over the chaotic waters at creation (Gen 1:2) and that brings rebirth to God's people (Ezek 36:26; John 3:3-5) comes upon Mary with that same generative force without usurping her own partnership in the creative process.[91] Likewise, the overshadowing of the Most High need not suggest overpowering. The Septuagint uses the verb ἐπισκιάζειν, "overshadow," in relation to the cloud of God's presence that settled on the wilderness tabernacle (Exod 40:35, LXX); the term signals divine protection and guidance for Israel. Just as the glory of the

86. Sharon Jacob, *Reading Mary Alongside Indian Surrogate Mothers: Violent Love, Oppressive Liberation, and Infancy Narratives*, The Bible and Cultural Studies (New York: Palgrave Macmillan, 2015), xii (italics in the original).

87. Ibid., 93, 113. See also Moss and Baden, *Reconceiving Infertility*, 160–61, who see Mary, the self-described slave, as "cast in the role of Hagar. She is the slave girl, the vessel, the mechanism by which God's son would be born. . . . Luke does not want us to see Mary as the bride of God. She is the favored vessel chosen to carry his Son; she plays the role of the surrogate."

88. The Spirit that comes upon Mary is the same prophetic Spirit that came upon Saul (1 Sam 10:10), rested on Elijah (see Luke 1:17) and Elisha (1 Kings 2:9-10, 15-16), filled Micah (Mic 3:8), and fills her son (3:22; 4:18) and his followers, both female and male (Acts 2:17-18).

89. Although in Luke 11:22 ἐπέρχομαι connotes a violent assault on a strong man by one stronger, the context of 1:35 precludes such a nuance.

90. See excurses at 3:22 on feminist understandings of the Spirit.

91. Spencer, *Salty Wives*, 71.

Lord filled the tent of meeting, so the divine presence is with Mary. The term also foreshadows Jesus's empowerment and divine guidance for his mission when the "Holy Spirit descended upon him" at his baptism (3:22), and the cloud symbolizing God's presence overshadowed Jesus and the disciples at the transfiguration (Luke 9:34). The Israelites, Mary, Jesus, and his disciples all remained free to follow or not the directives of the overshadowing divine presence.

The Slave of the Lord (1:38, 48)

Mary's response, "Here am I," is the ideal response of those whom God chooses as prophets and leaders in the Old Testament,[92] and her self-designation as δούλη κυρίου, literally, "slave of the Lord" (1:38, 48), proleptically fulfills the Pentecost promise in Acts 2:18, where Peter declares, "Even upon my slaves, both men and women [τοὺς δούλους μου καὶ τας δούλας μου], in those days I will pour out my Spirit; and they shall prophesy" (quoting Joel 3:1). Furthermore, her words "let it be with me according to your word" foreshadow those of her son on the Mount of Olives, "not my will but yours be done" (Luke 22:42), showing her to be a model of one who hears God and obeys. But we find Mary's self-designation δούλη κυρίου, "slave of the Lord," highly problematic.

As helpful as it may be to see Mary as linked to the lineage of faithful servants of God, a major problem with the expression "slave of God" remains. We concur with the assessment of Elizabeth A. Johnson: "The master-slave relationship, now totally abhorrent in human society," is "no longer suitable as a metaphor for relationship to God, certainly not in feminist theological understanding. . . . Slavery is an unjust, sinful situation. It makes people into objects owned by others, denigrating their dignity as human persons. In the case of slave women, their masters have the right not only to their labor, but to their bodies, making them into tools of production and reproduction at the master's wish. In such circumstances the Spirit groans with the cries of the oppressed, prompting persons not to obey but to resist, using all their wiles."[93]

---

92. E.g., Abraham (Gen 22:1); Samuel (1 Sam 3:4, 5, 6, 8).
93. Elizabeth A. Johnson, *Truly Our Sister: A Theology of Mary in the Communion of Saints* (New York: Continuum, 2003), 255. See also Clarice J. Martin, "Womanist Interpretation of the New Testament: The Quest for Holistic and Inclusive Translation and Interpretation," in *I Found God in Me: A Womanist Biblical Hermeneutics Reader*, ed. Mitzi J. Smith (Eugene, OR: Cascade, 2015); Jennifer Glancy, *Slavery in Early Christianity* (New York: Oxford University Press, 2002); Sandra R. Joshel and Sheila Murnaghan, *Women and Slaves in Greco-Roman Culture: Differential Equations* (London: Routledge, 1998).

TRANSLATION MATTERS

Mary's self-designation, δούλη κυρίου, literally means "slave of the Lord." Most translations render it as "servant" (NJB, NEB, TEV, NIV, REB, CEB), some as "handmaid" (RSV, JB, NAB), others as "maidservant" (NKJV). These translations mask the reality of the literal translation. The question of how to translate δούλος (male slave) and δούλη (female slave) when they appear in the Bible is complex and is of special concern to womanist biblical scholars, owing to the history of African American enslavement. For ancient Greek literature outside of the Bible, δούλος/δούλη is generally translated as "slave." On the other hand, with the rise of interest in liberation theology, reader-response theory, and the question of how contemporary readers *hear* ancient texts, concern has been expressed about the deep pain associated with the word "slavery" for African American readers of the Bible. As womanist scholar Clarice Martin frames this question, does hearing the term "slave" in a reading of Scripture "recall an image that is painfully reminiscent of that legacy [of slavery]? Is the use of the term *infradignitatem* (beneath one's dignity)? Would it not be better . . . to translate *doulos* regularly as the more euphemistic 'servant'?"[94] Martin answers these questions with a resounding "no!" in no small part because the euphemistic translation "servanthood" minimizes the cruelty of slavery. But the debate is still a live one for translation committees working to render the Bible into English, who are sensitive both to the text in its ancient context and to the resonance of the text in contemporary worshiping communities.[95]

In his World Day of Peace message on January 1, 2015, titled "No Longer Slaves But Brothers and Sisters,"[96] Pope Francis named the present-day forms of slavery, such as persons detained against their will in inhuman

---

94. Martin, "Womanist Interpretations of the New Testament," 19–41, here 23. See also Jacquelyn Grant, "The Sin of Servanthood and the Deliverance of Discipleship," in *A Troubling in My Soul: Womanist Perspectives on Evil and Suffering*, ed. Emilie M. Townes, The Bishop Henry McNeal Turner Studies in North American Black Religion 8 (Maryknoll, NY: Orbis Books, 1993), 199–218.

95. Of course we recognize that slavery is both an ongoing problem and an international issue, rather than merely a phenomenon of the antebellum period of the United States. Further, we recognize the intersections of slavery and sexual abuse. One important organization that aims to provide "the knowledge and framework needed to recognize and acknowledge past collaboration in slavery; to engage in restorative justice for slavery; and to create sexual ethics untainted by slave-holding values" is the Feminist Sexual Ethics Project, https://www.brandeis.edu/projects/fse/about/index.html.

96. For the full text: http://www.vatican.va/content/francesco/en/messages/peace /documents/papa-francesco_20141208_messaggio-xlviii-giornata-mondiale-pace -2015.html.

working conditions, those forced into prostitution, and young girls and women victims of terrorist groups used as sex slaves. He named as a deeper cause of slavery the corruption of the human heart that allows one person to reject the humanity of another and treat that one as an object. Other root causes of slavery include poverty, armed conflicts, criminal activity, and corruption on the part of people willing to do anything for financial gain. Pope Francis recognized the immensity of the task of combatting these, as he urged all people of goodwill—individuals, institutions, intergovernmental organizations, and businesses—to enter into a shared commitment to end slavery in all its forms.

Although Pope Francis spoke eloquently of the necessity of all people to see others as siblings who share the same nature, dignity, and origin, and thus counter any impulses to subjugate another, he did not address the way that the metaphor of master and slave to describe our relationship with God may also contribute to a mentality that allows real slavery to continue. In our view, reading Mary's self-identification as slave could have a positive effect if it means that she, as a person who is not a slave, chooses to identify with, accompany, and advocate for those who actually are slaves,[97] thus able to effect change for them, a task to which many contemporary women religious have devoted themselves.[98] But we doubt that is the rhetorical effect Luke intended for Mary's self-declaration; nor do we think that most contemporary readers see Mary that way. The master-slave metaphor on Mary's lips rather reinforces a spirituality of subservience and servitude, which in turn creates a tension between her acquiescence to servility while at the same time accepting a prophetic mission in which she proclaims liberation from powers that dominate (1:46-55).

Most pernicious is when women choose servility out of a misdirected sense of self-sacrificial love or notions that God intended for women to

---

97. Slavery was all too real in first-century Roman Judea and Galilee. Mary's home in Nazareth (1:26) was just a few short miles from Sepphoris, whose inhabitants were enslaved by the Romans after they revolted at the death of Herod in 4 BCE (Jos., *J.W.* 2.68; *Ant.* 17.289). Enslavement could also be the fate of those unable to meet Rome's excessive taxation.

98. One of many examples is the launching in 2007 of the International Network of Religious Against Trafficking in Persons by more than thirty leaders of women's religious congregations from twenty-six countries. See Dennis Sadowski, "Women Religious Vow Solidarity in Fight Against Human Trafficking," *America*, October 31, 2018, https://www.americamagazine.org/politics-society/2018/10/31/women-religious-vow-solidarity-fight-against-human-trafficking.

be subservient to the powerful males in their lives (see sidebar: "What God Has Determined for Us"). Kathleen Gallagher Elkins advances that self-sacrifice can at times be a strategic choice from a position of power. Relating Mary to the madres de la Plaza de Mayo, who risk physical and verbal violence as they demand justice concerning their husbands, fathers, and sons who disappeared during Argentina's "dirty war" (1975–1984), Gallagher Elkins sees in both Mary and the madres maternal self-sacrifice that is strategic. The situation is not of their choosing, but they exercise their agency in response to it.[99]

What God Has Determined for Us

Women in the Diocese of San Cristóbal de las Casas, México, have journeyed toward greater freedom and joy through their participation in women's Bible study groups under the direction of the Diocesan Council for Women (CODIMUJ). Learning to question traditional biblical interpretations that reinforced their subservience to men, they have discovered their own agency and new understandings of God.

"The worst thing was that we women regarded the situation in which we served everyone else and never did anything for ourselves as natural and that God made it this way. We believed that this is just the way things are; there is nothing that can be done about it. We felt trapped; we never thought of ourselves as having value in ourselves, or of being capable and free to make choices and decisions about our own lives. Sorrowful, solitary, silent, and enclosed: this was our reality inside our homes in our daily lives—lives that we did not choose and that we thought we had no way to change. In our prayer we would cry to God asking why he had determined this life for us. Our faith did not help us change anything; we believed that God had decided that it should be so. All the suffering we endured we accepted as our way of carrying the cross."

Voices of women of CODIMUJ[100]

---

99. Kathleen Gallagher Elkins, *Mary, Mother of Martyrs: How Motherhood Became Self-Sacrifice in Early Christianity* (Indianapolis: FSR Books, 2018), 21.

100. CODIMUJ is the acronym for Coordinación Diocesana de Mujeres in the Diocese of San Cristóbal de las Casas in the state of Chiapas, México. Instigated by Bishop Samuel Ruiz, work with women in the diocese by women religious began in the mid-1960s, and eventually a grassroots network of women's Bible study groups developed. These reflections are recorded in *Con Mirada, Mente y Corazón de Mujer* (México, D.F.: CODIMUJ, 1999), 17–22.

Mariological and Christological Significance

While many interpreters of 1:26-38 focus on its Christological significance, it is equally important to attend to the character of Mary, the main
character of the gospel's first two chapters. Although she appears only
once more in the gospel (8:19-20) and once again in the opening of Acts
(1:14), Mary plays a critical role for Luke's story of Jesus.

Elizabeth and Mary: The Companionship of Women (1:39-45)

Hasty Departure (1:39)

Mary's hasty departure for Judea is often interpreted as an indication
of her eagerness to share her joy and to help her aged, pregnant relative.[101] The expression μετά σπουδῆς ("with haste"), however, in classical
Greek denotes "an inner condition of the soul, a dynamic process of
the mind" rather than a physical sense of rapid movement.[102] Blaise
Hospodar proposes that the translation "in a serious mood of mind"
captures better the sense of μετά σπουδῆς.[103] Another nuance is suggested
by the Greek translations of the Old Testament, where it "often has overtones of terror, alarm, flight, and anxiety."[104] For example, in Exodus
12:11 (LXX), the Israelites who are about to flee Egypt are instructed to
eat the Passover lamb μετά σπουδῆς ("hurriedly"); Psalm 78:33 speaks
about what befalls unrepentant sinners: "their days vanish like a breath
and their years in terror [μετά σπουδῆς; LXX]."[105] Jane Schaberg finds that
μετά σπουδῆς may be a clue "that points toward a situation of violence
and/or fear in connection with Mary's pregnancy, or at least to the idea
that she is depicted as reacting with anxiety or inner disturbance to the
pregnancy."[106] It is easy to imagine the anxiety Mary would have had in
the small town of Nazareth once her pregnancy became known. With
others talking about her and looking askance, it is no wonder she goes
to Judea to spend time with her relatives there. Alternatively, we can also

101. This interpretation is found as early as St. Ambrose's fourth century *Commentary on Luke* (Lib. 2, 19.22–23, 26–27; CCL 14:39–42).
102. Blaise Hospodar, "META SPOUDES in Lk 1.39," CBQ 18 (1956): 14–18, here 17.
103. Ibid., 18.
104. Schaberg, *Illegitimacy*, 89. The only other instance in which the expression
occurs in the NT is Mark 6:25, where Herodias's daughter returns to the king
μετά σπουδῆς, "immediately," to ask for the head of John the Baptist.
105. See Schaberg, *Illegitimacy*, 89 for further examples.
106. Ibid., 90.

³⁹In those days Mary set out and went with haste to a Judean town in the hill country, ⁴⁰where she entered the house of Zechariah and greeted Elizabeth. ⁴¹When Elizabeth heard Mary's greeting, the child leaped in her womb. And Elizabeth was filled with the Holy Spirit ⁴²and exclaimed with a loud cry, "Blessed are you among women, and blessed is the fruit of your womb. ⁴³And why has this happened to me, that the mother of my Lord comes to me? ⁴⁴For as soon as I heard the sound of your greeting, the child in my womb leaped for joy. ⁴⁵And blessed is she who believed that there would be a fulfillment of what was spoken to her by the Lord."

imagine that people reacted with compassion and care to Mary's unexpected pregnancy (see reflection by Stephanie Buckhanon Crowder at 1:38-45 on "Another View of Community Mothering") and that her haste to go to Judea is out of concern for her aging pregnant relative Elizabeth.

Traveling Alone (1:39)

Luke makes no mention of anyone accompanying Mary on this journey of slightly more than one hundred miles. For a woman to make such a journey alone would have been highly improper and dangerous. The image of the frightened, solitary, pregnant woman traveling on her own evokes that of many women who have had to flee for their lives from abusive situations. Not all women have a relative across the border or a sense of divine protection. Some commentators squelch such a frightening image in Mary's case by presuming that Joseph accompanied her. A popular fourteenth-century writer, Ludolph of Saxony, says that a train of virgins and angels accompanied Mary to protect her.[107]

Wise Mentor (1:40-45)

When Mary arrives, she enters the "house of Zechariah," but it is Elizabeth she greets. Still mute, Zechariah plays no role in this scene. Elizabeth does all the speaking. While we know a number of readers who envision Mary as the stronger one, who travels to help her elderly relative, we see in the scene Elizabeth as the wise mentor to the younger woman. Both

107. *Vita Domini nostri Jesu Christi ex quatuor evangeliis.*

women are in an unenviable position. Both endure suffering due to the peculiar timing of their pregnancies. Elizabeth has had a long history of being faithful to God and is just the one to help Mary respond with trust to what God is doing in this messy situation.

A Prophetic Cry (1:42-45)

When Elizabeth hears Mary's greeting, she is filled with the Holy Spirit and prophesies. Although Luke does not call her a prophet, he aligns her with others who are filled with the Holy Spirit and so designated: John (1:15, 76), Zechariah (1:67), Simeon (2:25), and Jesus (4:1, 18-19). Elizabeth makes her proclamation "with a loud cry" (κραυγῇ μεγάλῃ). While "a loud cry" seems out of place in the narrative setting inside a house, it signals a prophetic announcement, pointing forward to the "loud shout" (φωνῇ μεγάλῃ) of the multitude of Jesus's disciples as he enters Jerusalem (19:37).

Elizabeth pronounces a threefold blessing. First, she declares to Mary, "Blessed are you among women" (1:42). This declaration echoes that of Deborah, who sings, "Most blessed of women be Jael" for slaying Sisera (Judg 5:24). Likewise, Uzziah sings Judith's praises for beheading Holofernes, "O daughter, you are blessed by the Most High God above all other women on earth" (Jdt 13:18). Brittany Wilson notes that while the blessedness of Jael and Judith came from violently murdering an enemy, "Mary ushers in a new age, in which women are called most blessed for their acts of peace rather than for their acts of violence." Moreover, "Mary's peaceful servanthood foreshadows the life and death of her son, Jesus the κύριος, who overcomes violence through peace."[108] We challenge this reading. There is more violent content in Luke 1–2 than Wilson acknowledges and thus less disjuncture between Mary and these women from the Old Testament (see the excursus below on Luke 1–2 as anti-Marcionite).[109]

Elizabeth then proclaims the blessedness of the fruit of Mary's womb (1:42) and a third time declares Mary blessed, this time for her belief in the fulfillment of God's word to her (1:45). Mary's blessedness is not only in bearing Jesus but in hearing and acting on the word of God, a prominent Lukan theme. Mary exemplifies not only the importance of motherhood but also the crucial qualities needed for discipleship and

---

108. Brittany E. Wilson, "Pugnacious Precursors and the Bearer of Peace: Jael, Judith, and Mary in Luke 1:42," *CBQ* 68 (2006): 436–56; here 437–38.

109. See Matthews, *Perfect Martyr*, 43–53.

for prophesying. This point will surface again when a woman in a crowd raises her voice and says to Jesus, "Blessed is the womb that bore you and the breasts that nursed you!" (11:27). Jesus's response, "Blessed rather are those who hear the word of God and obey it" (11:28), turns attention to the prime importance of hearing and acting on God's word.[110]

Elizabeth declares Mary and her child as blessed and a source of divine blessing for all. Mary accepts this affirmation acclaiming, "from now on all generations will call me blessed" (1:48). Not all pregnant women feel themselves "blessed," particularly if the pregnancy was unplanned, unwanted, or the result of rape. Elizabeth's words of benediction can be an invitation to women in any difficult situation to experience blessing and be able to bless others.

Roman Catholics very often call Mary "Blessed Mother" while Protestants have been hesitant to call her "blessed" and in some cases have avoided any reflection on or appropriation of Mary at all. This stems from a wariness about elevating Mary to a position beyond that of the rest of Christians or making her equal to Christ or God.[111] Recently, Protestant theologians and biblical scholars are thinking in new ways about Mary, "blessing her and being blessed by her," finding that "to call Mary blessed is to recognize the blessedness of ordinary people who are called to participate in that which is extraordinary."[112]

Companioning Prophets

Both Elizabeth and Mary are depicted as prophets, but unlike many of the Bible's male prophets, they are not portrayed as solitary figures who alone mediate between God and the people (like Moses in Exod 34:28; or Elijah in 1 Kgs 19:10). Rather, as Mary and Elizabeth discern God's word and act on it, they are companions like Ruth and Naomi (Ruth 1–4) and Moses's mother and sister and Pharaoh's daughter (Exod 2:1-10). Although there is a kind of one-upmanship in the step-parallelism

110. See further comments at 11:27-28.

111. Gaventa and Rigby, "Introduction," in *Blessed One: Protestant Perspectives on Mary*, 5. At Vatican II, Roman Catholics reasserted the belief that Mary is first among the disciples, placing reflections about her in the Dogmatic Constitution on the Church, *Lumen Gentium* (so named for its opening line: "Christ is the Light of Nations," issued in 1964) 52–69, rather than issue a separate document on Mary as had first been proposed. Elizabeth A. Johnson, a Roman Catholic theologian, also underscores this understanding of Mary in *Truly Our Sister*.

112. Gaventa and Rigby, *Blessed One*, 5.

between the stories of the births of their two sons,[113] there is no competition between Elizabeth and Mary, as there is in other narratives of births of biblical heroes, such as that between Sarah and Hagar (Gen 16, 21), Leah and Rachel (Gen 29–31), and Peninnah and Hannah (1 Sam 1).[114] The companionship of Elizabeth and Mary is mirrored by that of the Galilean women who cooperate in financing Jesus's ministry (8:3), work together to prepare the spices and ointments for his burial (23:56), go with one another to the tomb, and together announce to the Eleven and all the rest the message entrusted to them by the heavenly messengers (24:1-11).[115] Elizabeth and Mary, who support one another on their journey with God, can serve as a model for women, especially those in churches that do not ordain women, who seek spiritual companionship from other women rather than male clergy.

Another View of Community Mothering

We live for the we.[116] As this is the title of a book on the power of Black motherhood, I borrow the line to place womanist maternal thought in conversation with Mary's visit to Elizabeth. A pregnant, uncertain Mary spends months learning maternal ways from one who is further along in years and in her own pregnancy. As they are both with child, Mary and Elizabeth no longer exist for themselves. Their lives are motherly mingled with the occupants of their womb. The in utero beings growing in these mothers will change the landscape of their communities, towns, and macrocosm. Mary and Elizabeth "live for the we" of their unborn children, their locales, and each other.

Whereas the gospel writer does not depict Elizabeth as displaying any reservation about her maternal path, Mary's motherly misgivings are profound. Thus, immediately after resolving to "let it be," she seeks a fellow mother-to-be,

---

113. John Dominic Crossan, *Jesus: A Revolutionary Biography* (San Francisco: HarperSanFrancisco, 1994), 5–10.

114. Athalya Brenner, "Female Social Behavior: Two Descriptive Patterns within the 'Birth of the Hero' Paradigm," *VT* 36 (1986): 257–73.

115. Not all female partnerships are for doing good. Mark (6:14-29) and Matthew (14:1-12) narrate Herodias and her daughter's machinations that bring about the death of John the Baptist, an episode that Luke does not recount.

116. Dani McClain, *We Live for the We: The Political Power of Black Motherhood* (New York: Bold Type Books, 2019).

Elizabeth. For three months Mary learns from and, yes, grows with her kinswoman. Mary does not have to traverse the mother road alone. Employing the language of communal mother, I aver that Elizabeth helps to mother Mary as both women come to terms with their own maternal status.

My womanist maternal interpretation brings to the forefront voices of African American mothers within this racial, ethnic, spiritual, and sociological context, whether the mothers are biological or women who for one reason or another take responsibility for another's child.[117] This umbrella also includes community mothers, those deemed as the matriarchal figure in a neighborhood or larger geopolitical network.

Community mothers may or may not have given birth. Their "seed" is the many women, men, and children who do not have voice to tell of their own economic plight or the skills to navigate social hardship and class conundrum. The progeny of the community mothers includes anyone who needs an advocate to remonstrate against racial discrimination and class prejudice. Marching to the beat of Mary Church Terrell, Nannie Helen Burroughs, Mary MacLeod Bethune, and mothers of the movement,[118] these activist matriarchs yield a clarion call for a new day and a new order. Cheryl Townsend Gilkes notes, "Community mothers are the guardians of community political traditions. Their ability to function as power brokers stemmed from their leadership within the historical African American women's movement and organizations."[119]

Mary and Elizabeth are Jewish. Womanist maternal thought underscores motherhood through an African American

117. Stephanie Buckhanon Crowder, *When Momma Speaks: The Bible and Motherhood from a Womanist Perspective* (Louisville: Westminster John Knox, 2016), 13.

118. Sabrina Fulton, mother of Trayvon Martin; Cleopatra Cowley, mother of Hadiya Pendleton; and newly elected Georgia Congresswoman, Lucia McBath, to name a few, now occupy this maternal seat. Trayvon Martin was killed by a neighborhood watch participant later found not guilty of his murder: https://www.nytimes.com/2012/04/02/us/trayvon-martin-shooting-prompts-a-review-of-ideals.html. A stray bullet from a gang member silenced Hadiya Pendleton on a playground near her home: https://www.chicagotribune.com/news/local/breaking/ct-met-hadiya-pendleton-mother-father-20180827-story.html. A driver shot into the truck where Jordan Davis was sitting with friends, killing him: https://atlantablackstar.com/2018/07/27/the-murder-of-her-son-jordan-davis-prompted-her-activism-now-shes-won-the-congressional-primary-in-georgia/.

119. Cheryl Townsend Gilkes, *If It Wasn't for the Women: Black Women's Experience and Womanist Culture in Church and Community* (Maryknoll, NY: Orbis Books, 2001), 65.

lens. Nevertheless, there is a maternal appropriation that embraces racial identities and cultural contexts. Mary is a young woman with little status. Elizabeth is her literary foil and social antithesis. She is a wife of "old age" married to a priest. It is this status that allows for Elizabeth's consideration as a community mother and guardian of tradition. In essence, Luke wants to show the distinct social locations of Mary and Elizabeth.

The gospel writer clearly describes Elizabeth's reversal of fortune. Her pre-pregnancy shame is now pregnancy favor. Coupled with social footing, she has mother(less) experience to share. She knows the brisk nature of public embarrassment. Her task now is to buttress others from such chagrin. Mary becomes the recipient of Elizabeth's communal mother covering.

The very act of giving birth during the first century was dangerous. Mortality in childbirth was high and affected both rich and poor women, especially mothers in their early teens.[120] A woman in the Greco-Roman world dare not go the maternal road alone. Elizabeth sojourns with Mary.

As she is about to give birth to a son, Mary first dons a daughter's posture. Under the maternal wings of Elizabeth, Mary allows a community mother to do her work. A married mother-to-be provides social nurturing, protection, and advocacy for a pregnant, unwed teenager. Theirs is an intergenerational, "we-molded," womanist maternal model. Elizabeth engages in a form of parental sojourning with a young Mary as she learns how to be Mom to the Most High.

Stephanie Buckhanon Crowder

Mary's Prophetic Proclamation (1:46-56)

The focus returns to Mary as she first exults in what God has done for her personally (vv. 47-49) and then acclaims God's saving acts for all Israel (vv. 50-55). This victory hymn rounds out the depiction of Mary as prophet. Along with the other canticles in Luke 1–2, the *Magnificat* was a hymn that circulated in the Christian communities before Luke inserted it into the gospel. Mary's song echoes that of the prophet Miriam, her namesake, who led the Israelites in singing and dancing[121] after their

120. Joel B. Green, "Setting the Context: Roman Hellenism," in *The World of the New Testament: Cultural, Social and Historical Contexts*, ed. Joel B. Green and Lee Martin McDonald (Grand Rapids: Baker, 2013), 182.

121. As Gafney (*Daughters of Miriam*, 6) shows, prophets not only declare oracles but also engage in "intercessory prayer, dancing, drumming, singing, giving and

Luke 1:46-56

⁴⁶And Mary said,
"My soul magnifies the Lord,
    ⁴⁷and my spirit rejoices in God my
        Savior,
⁴⁸for he has looked with favor on the
    lowliness of his servant.
    Surely, from now on all generations
        will call me blessed;
⁴⁹for the Mighty One has done great
        things for me,
    and holy is his name.
⁵⁰His mercy is for those who fear him
    from generation to generation.
⁵¹He has shown strength with his arm;
    he has scattered the proud in the
        thoughts of their hearts.

⁵²He has brought down the powerful
    from their thrones,
    and lifted up the lowly;
⁵³he has filled the hungry with good
        things,
    and sent the rich away empty.
⁵⁴He has helped his servant
        Israel,
    in remembrance of his mercy,
⁵⁵according to the promise he made
        to our ancestors,
    to Abraham and to his
        descendants forever."
⁵⁶And Mary remained with her
        about three months and then
        returned to her home.

escape from the Egyptians (Exod 15:1-21).[122] There are also echoes of the victory hymns of Judith (Jdt 16:1-17) and Deborah (Judg 5) and of Hannah's song (1 Sam 2:1-10). These songs all celebrate God's intervention, sometimes in desperate situations, with divine saving power. They are among the oldest traditions preserved in the Bible, and thus one might argue that women were the first biblical theologians.[123]

---

interpreting laws, delivering oracles on behalf of YHWH (sometimes in ecstasy, sometimes demonstratively), resolving disputes, working wonders, mustering troops and fighting battles, archiving their oracles in writing, and experiencing visions."

122. It is likely that the whole Exodus hymn was originally attributed to Miriam, and not simply v. 21, which mirrors v. 1. First Samuel 18:7 shows that women were the leaders of the victory songs and dances. George J. Brooke, "A Long-Lost Song of Miriam," *BAR* 20 (1994): 62–65, proposes that a separate Song of Miriam, partially suppressed in the book of Exodus has survived in part in a Qumran text, 4Q365. See also Rita J. Burns, *Has the Lord Indeed Spoken Only Through Moses? A Study of the Biblical Portrait of Miriam*, SBLDS 84 (Atlanta: Scholars Press, 1987); Phyllis Trible, "Bringing Miriam Out of the Shadows," *BibRev* 5 (1989): 14–25; J. Gerald Janzen, "Song of Moses, Song of Miriam: Who Is Seconding Whom?," *CBQ* 54 (1992): 211–20. For a detailed analysis of parallels between the songs of Mary and Miriam, see Barbara E. Reid, *Taking Up the Cross: New Testament Interpretations through Latina and Feminist Eyes* (Minneapolis: Fortress, 2007), 103.

123. Carol Meyers, "Miriam, Music, and Miracles," in *Mariam, the Magdalen, and the Mother*, ed. Deirdre Good (Bloomington: Indiana University Press, 2005), 27–48, here 41.

These hymns, the *Magnificat* included, are not sweet lullabies.[124] They proclaim divinely wrought vanquishing of the ruling powers, victory for God's own people in the past, and a vision for God's power and protection in bringing forth a different future. Frequent recitation of Mary's song and the prevalence of images of Mary as a docile, compliant maiden have dulled for us the power of her words. "They have lost their power to stun and offend."[125] Not so for Christian base communities and liberation theologians in Latin America, for whom the *Magnificat* has served as a rallying cry for political and social change from the 1980s forward.[126] This image of Mary with a raised clenched fist trampling a skull and a snake captures this sense.[127]

124. See Reid, "Women Prophets of God's Alternative Reign," 44–59.

125. Lisa Wilson Davison, *Preaching the Women of the Bible* (St. Louis: Chalice, 2006), 91.

126. See, for example, Gustavo Gutiérrez's chapter on the Magnificat, "Holy Is God's Name," in *The God of Life*, trans. Matthew J. O'Connell (Maryknoll, NY: Orbis Books, 1991), 164–86, originally published as *El Dios de la vida* (Lima, Perú: Instituto Bartolomé de las Casas), 1989.

127. This image by Ben Wildflower accompanied an article in the *Washington Post* on December 20, 2018, by D. L. Mayfield, "Mary's 'Magnificat' in the Bible Is Revolutionary: Some Evangelicals Silence Her," https://www.washingtonpost.com/religion/2018/12/20/marys-magnificat-bible-is-revolutionary-so-evangelicals-silence-it/.

The Significance of Imperial Language in the Magnificat: Two Readings

The titles Mary attributes to God—κύριος, "Lord" (v. 46); σωτήρ, "savior" (v. 47); and ὁ δύνατος, "the Mighty One" (v. 49)—evoke claims made on behalf of the Roman emperors. For example, the *Discourses* of Epictetus[128] name the emperor ὁ πάντων κύριος καῖσαρ, "Caesar, lord of all" (*Disc.* 4.1.12). A well-known image from the Sebasteion in Aphrodisias shows the deified emperor receiving in one hand a cornucopia of fruits from the earth and in the other a steering oar, signifying his status as all powerful over both land and sea.[129] An inscription from Aeraephiae in Boeotia gives Nero the title ὁ τοῦ παντὸς κόσμου κύριος, "lord of the whole world."[130]

128. The *Discourses* of Stoic philosopher Epictetus are a series of informal lectures written down by his pupil Arrian around 108 CE.
129. See R. R. R. Smith, *Aphrodisias VI: The Marble Reliefs from the Julio-Claudian Sebasteion at Aphrodisias* (Darmstadt: von Zabern, 2013).
130. C. Kavin Rowe, "Luke–Acts and the Imperial Cult: A Way through the Conundrum?," *JSNT* 27 (2005): 279–300, esp. 292–93; Steve Walton, "The State They Were In: Luke's View of the Roman Empire," in *Rome in the Bible and the Early Church*, ed. Peter Oakes (Grand Rapids: Baker Academic, 2002), 1–41; John Dominic Crossan, *God and Empire: Jesus against Rome, Then and Now* (San Francisco: HarperSanFrancisco, 2007), 15–25.

Beginning with Julius Caesar, Roman rulers were commonly hailed with the term σωτήρ, "savior."[131] Julius Caesar, for example, was described as "the god made manifest . . . and common savior of human life." Augustus was called "a savior who put an end to war" and "savior of the entire world." Claudius was said to be "savior of the world" and "god who is savior and benefactor."[132]

The significance of Luke's employment of terms honoring God and Jesus that were also used to honor Roman emperors is much debated.[133] We take up this debate in greater detail at 2:14, "Good News of Peace to All." Here we note that both of us have worked on this question in the past and have taken different approaches. Barbara has read the *Magnificat* as a clear instance where Luke is countering Roman imperial values by offering Jesus's service in humility as a contrast to imperial power and arrogance. Shelly has agreed that there is contrast between imperial power and the power of Luke's God, but she sees Luke reinscribing imperial power rather than overturning it. We offer both readings here, recognizing that both might be compelling ways that lead to feminist critique of dominating power. Readers, of course, can activate different meanings in a text. As we have noted above, liberation theologians and base Christian communities in Latin America have recognized the subversive potential that Barbara's reading of the *Magnificat* allows. Shelly's reading, which sees reinscription of imperial power in the *Magnificat*, may explain why many Christians can celebrate the *Magnificat* as a vindication of "our side" while condemning the Other.

Mary Prophesying God's Alternative Reign

Barbara reads Luke's use of these titles as having political implications: Luke evokes the titles of Lord, Savior, and Mighty One used of Roman

---

131. Lance Byron Richey, *Roman Imperial Ideology and the Gospel of John*, CBQMS 43 (Washington, DC: CBA, 2007), 85. Only Luke among the Synoptic evangelists uses σωτήρ (Luke 1:47; 2:11; Acts 5:31; 13:23) and σωτηρία (Luke 1:69, 71, 77; 19:9; Acts 4:12; 7:25; 13:26, 47; 16:17; 27:34; 28:28). In the Fourth Gospel they occur only at John 4:22, 42. For more on σωτήρ and σωτηρία, see comments at 2:11.

132. Walton, "The State They Were In," 27 n. 86.

133. For a 2015 review of myriad scholarly positions, see Michael Kochenash, "Review Essay: Taking the Bad with the God; Reconciling Images of Rome in Luke–Acts," *RelSRev* 41 (2015): 43–51.

emperors in order to counter them explicitly.[134] Luke would certainly have been aware that these titles were used in imperial circles; he acknowledges as much in Acts 25:26, where Festus refers to the emperor as ὁ κύριος.[135] Conversely, the opening line of the *Magnificat* proclaims that it is God who is ὁ κύριος. Luke then uses κύριος some two hundred more times in the gospel and Acts in reference to God and Jesus.[136] Luke also contrasts the manner in which Gentiles exercise their lordship with Jesus's way: "The kings of the Gentiles lord it over [κυριεύουσιν] them; and those in authority over them are called benefactors. But not so with you; rather the greatest among you must become like the youngest, and the leader like one who serves" (22:25-26).[137]

The acclamation of God as "the Mighty One," ὁ δυνατός (v. 49),[138] highlights the contrast between Roman power and the divine might (δύναμις) of Israel's God. God's power is that which protects the vulnerable, as Gabriel assures Mary (1:35). It resided in Elijah and John the Baptist in enabling them "to turn the hearts of parents to their children, and the disobedient to the wisdom of the righteous, to make ready a people prepared for the Lord" (1:17; quoting Mal 3:1). It is what impels Jesus throughout his mission (4:14) to do good, to heal (5:17; 6:19; 8:46; Acts 10:38), and to cast out unclean spirits (4:36). Jesus's "deeds of power" (δυνάμεις) bring repentance (Luke 10:13) and cause his disciples to acclaim him the "king who comes in the name of the Lord" (19:37) and "a prophet mighty [δυνατός] in deed and word before God and all the people" (24:19).[139]

---

134. Reid, "Women Prophets of God's Alternative Reign," 44–59. Compare also Amanda C. Miller, *Rumors of Resistance: Status Reversals and Hidden Transcripts in the Gospel of Luke* (Minneapolis: Fortress, 2014).

135. Rowe, "Luke–Acts and the Imperial Cult," 293–94.

136. Ibid., 294. See further comments on Jesus as Lord at 2:11.

137. While the *Magnificat*'s insistence on God being Lord, not Caesar, and Jesus's lordship is later shown to be servant leadership, it is problematic from a feminist point of view to call God or Jesus "Lord." See excursus at 6:46.

138. This title is also used of YHWH in Zeph 3:17; Ps 89:9 (LXX).

139. These examples are of Luke's use of ὁ δυνατός and δύναμις, all of which relate to male exercise of power. There are also instances in the gospel when women exercise power, for example, when the woman suffering from hemorrhages touches the fringe of Jesus's clothes, causing him to ask who touched him, for he "noticed that power had gone out" from him (8:46). On feminist understandings of power, see excursus at 4:1-13.

God of the Magnificat: A Warrior God Seeking Revenge Against Enemies

Luke's use of Roman imperial titles is a breathtaking assertion of contrast and reversal: it is not Caesar but Jesus who is Lord and Savior. In Shelly's reading, the contrast and reversal is not necessarily an assertion that Luke's God is nonviolent or always on the side of the most vulnerable. Even in the *Magnificat*, "showing strength with his arm" and "bringing down the powerful from their thrones" are reflections of a God who inflicts violence. These are images of a warrior God seeking revenge against enemies.

While emphasis on Jesus and/or God as the true κύριος is often read as an explicit contrast with the power and values of the Roman Empire, these titles can be employed to affirm kyriarchal[140] structures. For example, Peter's affirmation that Jesus is Lord of all in Acts 10:36 is part of the justification that only the twelve apostles are authentic witnesses to the resurrection, and thus only they are the authorized spokesmen for the church (Acts 10:34-43).[141] As Shelly will also argue concerning the saying on leadership and reversal (Luke 22:25-26), even this saying about greatest and least does not have a fully egalitarian thrust in the context of the Lukan Last Supper, where it is followed immediately by a more hierarchical affirmation of the Twelve as those who will "sit on the thrones judging the twelve tribes of Israel" (22:30).

In short, while affirming that the *Magnificat* can be read, and has been read, as a celebration of God's siding with the oppressed and against the oppressive ruling powers, we must caution that sometimes Luke's appropriation of Roman imperial titles for Israel's God, and for Jesus as savior, seems more like mimicry, or imitation of Roman views of power, rather than an overturning of such views. From both perspectives, feminists challenge Roman views of power.

Lifting Up the Humiliated (1:52)

What is Mary's "humiliation" (ταπείνωσις) that God has "looked upon" (ἐπέβλεψεν, 1:48) remains unclear. Part of the difficulty resides with the translation of ταπείνωσις. Most English translations render it "lowliness" or "humility." Many interpreters see a reference to Mary's spiritual humility;

---

140. See above n. 1 in the author's introduction on kyriarchy.
141. See Shelly Matthews, "Fleshly Resurrection, Authority Claims, and the Scriptural Practices of Lukan Christianity," *JBL* 136 (2017): 163–83, here at 175.

for example, it expresses "her unworthiness to be the mother of the Davidic Messiah and the Son of God."[142] Others, such as Elizabeth A. Johnson, suggest it refers to her social position: "Young, female, a member of a people subjected to economic exploitation by powerful ruling groups, afflicted by outbreaks of violence, she belongs to the semantic domain of the poor in Luke's gospel, a group given a negative valuation by worldly powers."[143] Luise Schottroff understands Mary's ταπείνωσις as part of her people's degradation, most especially that suffered by women. "The *degradation of* women and the *degradation of the people* belong together."[144] For Schottroff, the *Magnificat* is "a prophetic announcement of the people's liberation. . . . The two pregnant women beat the drum of God's world revolution." Schottroff uses the metaphor of "beating the drum" in order to emphasize the contradiction between the way Mary's humility has been "drummed into our heads" and the actual prophetic and revolutionary nature of the *Magnificat*. "The woman Mary represents in her fate and prophecy God's option for the poor,[145] an option that is decided in

---

142. E.g., Joseph A. Fitzmyer, *The Gospel According to Luke I–IX*, AB 28 (Garden City, NY: Doubleday, 1981), 367.

143. Johnson, *Truly Our Sister*, 265. See also Green, "The Social Status of Mary," 457–72. See comments at 1:26 on the social status of Galileans at the time of Mary and Jesus.

144. Luise Schottroff, *Lydia's Impatient Sisters: A Feminist Social History of Early Christianity*, trans. Barbara and Martin Rumscheidt (Louisville: Westminster John Knox, 1995), 193; italics are Schottroff's. The book was originally published in German: *Lydias ungeduldige Schwestern: Feministische Sozialgeschichte des frühen Christentums* (Gütersloher: Kaiser/Gütersloher, 1994). Schottroff, a pioneer in feminist liberationist Bible interpretation, died in 2015 at the age of eighty. She was professor of New Testament in Mainz, Kassel, Berkeley, and New York. Her socio-historical work in early Christianity and in reclaiming the Jewish context of Christian Scriptures was groundbreaking. She, along with her husband Willy Schottroff and her close friend Dorothee Soelle, was formative in shaping post-Holocaust Christian theology in Germany, both on the academic and congregational level.

145. Latin American liberation theologians, such as Gustavo Gutiérrez (*A Theology of Liberation: History, Politics, and Salvation* [Maryknoll, NY: Orbis Books, 1973]), coined the phrase "preferential option for the poor" to express the necessary choice for all Christians to work in solidarity and justice first and foremost for and with those who are poor and disadvantaged and to try to look at the world from their perspective. The Latin American bishops' conferences at Medellín (1968) and Puebla (1979) strongly endorsed this perspective. In response to those who misinterpret "preferential option for the poor" to mean that there is competition for God's love between rich and poor, Gutiérrez explains that, "in fact, the concept displays the *universality* of God's love for all—a love that, in a world structured to the benefit of the powerful, extends *even* to the least among us. . . . Like a mother who tends most tenderly to the weakest

the option for women."[146] Schottroff insists that, in the future, ταπείνωσις has to be translated differently, as "humiliation" or "degradation" or "oppression," and that as "maiden slave" Mary must be understood as God's messenger and prophet.[147] She notes that when Paul refers to himself as God's slave (e.g., Rom 1:1), "No Christian ear hears 'humility'; one rather hears 'officebearer.' "[148] So should Mary also be understood in Luke 1:26-56 as one who serves God by exercising a prophetic mission.

TRANSLATION MATTERS

The noun ταπείνωσις (1:48) primarily means "humiliation, experience of a reversal in fortunes, abasement," and metaphorically "lowliness, humility, humble station" (BDAG, 990; Liddell-Scott, 1757). The verb ταπεινόω means "to humble, abase" and also "to violate" a woman (Liddell-Scott, 1757). Most modern English translations of Luke 1:48 choose the metaphorical sense: "lowliness" (NRSV, NABRE), "low estate" (RSV), "lowly state" (NKJV), "humble state" (NET, NASB, NIV). Only NJB renders it "humiliation," which we consider the correct nuance, based on its usage in the LXX for the sexual humiliation of a woman (see citations in the commentary below on "Lifting Up the Humiliated"). In the one other occurrence of ταπείνωσις in Luke's writings, NRSV translates it as "humiliation": the Ethiopian eunuch is reading the passage from Isaiah 53:8, which speaks of the God's servant: "In his humiliation justice was denied him" (Acts 8:33).[149]

---

and threatened of her children, so it is with God's care for the poor" (Michael Griffin and Jennie Weiss Block, eds., *In the Company of the Poor: Conversations with Dr. Paul Farmer and Fr. Gustavo Gutiérrez* [Maryknoll, NY: Orbis Books, 2013], 28–29; italics in the original).

146. Schottroff, *Lydia's Impatient Sisters*, 199.

147. Ibid., 200.

148. Ibid.

149. The NRSV also translates ταπείνωσις as "humiliation" in Phil 3:21. In the only other occurrence of the noun in the New Testament, the NRSV translates "being brought low" (Jas 1:10). In all other instances of the verb (Matt 18:4; 23:12; Luke 3:5; 14:11; 18:14; 2 Cor 11:7; 12:21; Phil 2:8; 4:12; Jas 4:10; 1 Pet 5:6), the NRSV translates "made low" or "humble," e.g., "all who exalt themselves will be humbled [ταπεινωθήσεται], and those who humble themselves [ὁ ταπεινῶν ἑαυτὸν] will be exalted" (Luke 14:11; similarly Luke 18:14). See the forthcoming study by Andrew Davis, "The End of Humiliation in LXX Isa 40:2," in *Forget Not God's Benefits (Ps 103:2): A Festschrift in Honor of Leslie J. Hoppe, OFM*, CBQ Imprints (Washington, DC: Catholic Biblical Association of America), where he shows that the meaning "to belittle, humiliate, or oppress" accounts for most uses of ταπείνωσις in the LXX, where it occurs most often as a translation of Hebrew עֳנִי ("suffering, affliction").

There are a number of instances in the LXX where ταπεινόω refers to the sexual humiliation of a woman: the rape of Dinah (Gen 34:2), the abuse of the Levite's concubine (Judg 19:24; 20:5), Amnon's rape of Tamar (2 Kgs 13:12, 14, 22, 32), and the Babylonians' raping of the wives in Zion and the virgins in the cities of Judah (Lam 5:11).[150] Noting these references together with Deuteronomy 22:23-27, concerning the punishment for a man who has violated (ἐταπείνωσεν, v. 24) a virgin, Jane Schaberg argues that Luke 1:48 alludes to Mary having been sexually violated.[151] The *Magnificat* declares that God looks upon her humiliation and reverses it.

In our estimation, it is not possible to extrapolate Mary's historical circumstances from the wording of the *Magnificat*. As we noted above, the hymn was in circulation in the early Christian communities, with its adaptations and echoes of Hannah's prayer (1 Sam 1:11) and Miriam's victory song after the Exodus (Exod 15:1-21).[152] Ταπείνωσις likely came into the *Magnificat* from Hannah's prayer, "O LORD of hosts, if only you will look on the misery [LXX: ταπείνωσις; Heb.: עָנִי] of your servant" (1 Sam 1:11). For the early Christians who sang the *Magnificat*, Mary gave voice to and identified with whatever forms of humiliation they endured, whether social, political, or sexual, and affirmed with her that God would look with mercy on them and lift them from it.

Jane Schaberg, the Illegitimacy of Jesus, Feminist Courage, Patriarchal Backlash

In 1987 the Catholic feminist biblical scholar Jane Schaberg published a book arguing that Jesus was conceived illegitimately during the time Mary was betrothed to Joseph, likely the result of rape. Schaberg's argument, based on her engagement with historical-critical exegetical methods, proposed that traces of this historical circumstance were preserved in the gospels of both Matthew and Luke. Her work, also a deeply theological undertaking, proposed that the gospel authors wished to

---

150. Schaberg, *Illegitimacy*, 100, points out these references. See also Deut 21:14; 22:24; Isa 51:21, 23; Ezek 22:10-11.

151. Schaberg, *Illegitimacy*, 100.

152. See further Fitzmyer, *The Gospel According to Luke I–IX*, 358–59, who argues that the canticles of Mary, Zechariah, and Simeon are from an earlier Jewish Christian tradition that Luke has taken over. The *Magnificat* is "a mosaic of OT expressions drawn from the LXX," dependent especially on the Song of Hannah (1 Sam 2:1-10), and much of the hymn does not suit Mary specifically (359).

demonstrate how God could vindicate the oppressed by having the messiah born from a rape victim. Schaberg's feminist theological concerns are obvious from her dedication of the book to "the millions of women who have borne illegitimate children, and to those often 'fatherless' children." Acknowledging that her critics questioned the title, *The Illegitimacy of Jesus*, as "unnecessarily inflammatory," she pushed back with the argument that "the title . . . tells what the book is about in a way that no other title could. The gospels themselves are sensational and scandalous. Familiarity with them and certain bland interpretations obscure that aspect."[153]

Backlash ensued. Scholars nationally and locally shunned her; popular reviews of the book led to a stream of hate mail; her car was set on fire. Trauma from that hate impacted Schaberg throughout her life, even though she developed several coping mechanisms to withstand it. Her courage through those hateful times continues to inspire those who are targets of hate mail, or worse, for taking controversial stands on issues of gender, sexuality, and the church.[154]

Feminist biblical scholarship has become considerably more mainstream than it was in 1987, as, for instance, this publication of the Wisdom Commentary series with a respected Catholic press demonstrates.[155] Schaberg's book has been reprinted several times, including in an expanded twentieth-anniversary edition, containing insightful retrospectives. But the potential for violent reaction to feminist work remains. As Schaberg reflects on the interlocking sexist structures of society, church, and academy:

> I know that jokes at parties, ridicule of women faculty and candidates, harassment that went unchallenged, and lack of concern for employment equity were always clear signals that none of us is safe. The nature of backlash deserves close examination: it is not irrational outbursts, individual acts of cowardice and lack of leadership, pompous posturing, opportunities for cruelty. Rather . . . these are

---

153. Schaberg, *Illegitimacy*, x.

154. Jane Schaberg died of cancer in 2012. Her final collection of essays was published posthumously. See Jane Dewar Schaberg, *The Death and Resurrection of the Author and Other Feminist Essays on the Bible*, ed. Holly E. Hearon, The Bible in the Modern World 51 (Sheffield: Sheffield Phoenix, 2012).

155. It has been particularly gratifying that eight of the first twenty volumes published in Wisdom Commentary series have won awards from the Catholic Press Association and the Association of Catholic Publishers, helping to diffuse some of the backlash against feminism.

all political acts, carefully calculated to intimidate; hortatory acts, intended to announce boundaries and serve as a warning.[156]

The experience of Jane Schaberg is not unique. When the Wisdom Commentary was conceived in 2008, the atmosphere toward feminists in the Catholic Church was becoming increasingly hostile. In December 2008, the Vatican initiated an apostolic visitation "in order to look into the quality of the life" of women religious in the United States. This came on the heels of a doctrinal investigation of the Leadership Conference of Women Religious (LCWR)[157] announced in April 2008. Among its top three concerns were the "prevalence of certain radical feminist themes incompatible with the Catholic faith." In 2011, Elizabeth A. Johnson, distinguished professor of theology at Fordham University, one of the foremost Catholic feminist systematic theologians, came under public scrutiny when the US Conference of Catholic Bishops' Committee on Doctrine declared that many of the conclusions in her book *Quest for the Living God: Mapping the Frontiers in the Theology of God* (New York: Continuum, 2007) were "incompatible with Catholic teaching." Johnson wrote a response in which she said that "in several key instances [the bishops] radically misinterpret what I think, and what I in fact wrote."[158] Another renowned Catholic feminist theologian, Margaret Farley, professor emerita of Christian ethics at Yale Divinity School, also came under fire from the Congregation for the Doctrine of the Faith[159] when they declared in June 2012 that her book, *Just Love: A Framework for Christian Sexual Ethics* (New York: Continuum, 2006), was "not consistent with authentic Catholic theology" and should not be used by Roman Catholics.

We cannot predict whether our own commentary will stir up anger in any way comparable to what Schaberg faced. On the one hand, from the perspective of those who work on some of the cutting edges of the field of

---

156. Jane Schaberg, *The Illegitimacy of Jesus: A Feminist Theological Interpretation of the Infancy Narratives*, exp. 20th ann. ed. (Sheffield: Sheffield Phoenix, 2006), 8–9.

157. The LCWR is an association of the leaders of congregations of Catholic women religious in the United States. As of 2020, the conference has about 1,350 members, who represent nearly 80 percent of the approximately 44,000 women religious in the United States.

158. James Martin, "Elizabeth Johnson's Response," *America*, March 31, 2011, https://www.americamagazine.org/content/all-things/Elizabeth-johnsons-response.

159. The Sacred Congregation for the Doctrine of the Faith is the office in the Vatican that is responsible for safeguarding the doctrine on faith and morals.

biblical scholarship, such as intersectional minoritized feminist approaches,[160] approaches employing ethno-spatial reasoning,[161] or queer biblical criticism,[162] our own commentary might well be perceived as conventional. On the other hand, we live at a time in which rightwing Christians wield enormous political power worldwide and unite in agreement that women should not be permitted to interpret Scripture.[163] We not only interpret but include critique of the kyriarchal logic of the Gospel of Luke as we evaluate the text. Though we do not do so for the purpose of invoking hostile reactions, we would not be surprised to receive them.

There are three other instances in which the combination of divine "looking upon," ἐπιβλέπω, with ταπείνωσις, "humiliation," occur in the LXX. In 1 Samuel 1:11, Hannah prays for God to look upon (ἐπιβλέπω) the misery (ταπείνωσις) of God's servant (δούλη) and grant her a male child.[164] Likewise, in 1 Samuel 9:16, when Samuel is shown whom to anoint to be ruler over Israel to save them from the Philistines, God says, "I have seen [ἐπέβλεψα] the suffering [ταπείνωσιν] of my people." When the Israelites are threatened with destruction from the Assyrian commander

160. Mitzi J. Smith and Jin Young Choi, *Minoritized Women Reading Race and Ethnicity: Intersectional Approaches to Constructed Identity and Early Christian Texts* (Lanham, MD: Lexington Books, 2020).

161. Jennifer T. Kaaland, *Reading Hebrews and 1 Peter with the African American Great Migration: Diaspora, Place, Identity* (London: Bloomsbury T&T Clark, 2019).

162. Jimmy Hoke, *Under God? Romans in Feminist and Queer Assemblages*, ECL (Atlanta: SBL Press, forthcoming).

163. In 2018, the second year of the US Republican presidential administration of Donald Trump, the BBC journalist Owen Amos reported that his cabinet regularly engages in Bible study and that, in this first cabinet-level Bible study in the United States in more than one hundred years, no woman is allowed to lead. As Amos reports, the conservative Christian organizer of the study, Ralph Drollinger, justifies this exclusion by explaining, "There is a prohibition of female leadership in marriage and female leadership in the church. And those are clear in scripture." Owen Amos, "Inside the White House Bible Study Group," BBC News, April 8, 2018, http://www.bbc.com/news/world-us-canada-43534724.

164. In two other instances ταπείνωσις refers to affliction suffered by childless women, which God alleviates by giving them a son. In Genesis 16:11, God heeds the affliction (ταπείνωσις) of Hagar, and she conceives Ishmael. In Genesis 29:32 God sees the affliction (ταπείνωσις) of Leah, and she bears Reuben. These references shed less light on Luke 1:48, since Mary's affliction is caused not by infertility but by her conception of a son before having relations with her husband-to-be, Joseph.

Holofernes, they implore God to "have pity on our people in their humiliation [ταπείνωσιν], and look kindly [ἐπίβλεψον] today on the faces of
those who are consecrated to you" (Jdt 6:19). Just as in these instances,
God looks mercifully on Mary (v. 48) and all those who are humiliated
(ταπεινούς, v. 52) and raises them up. This claim also has political overtones
in that it paints God in contrast to the agents of imperial Rome who maintained the submission of their subjects through means of humiliation.[165]

Mary, following the lead of Elizabeth, who exulted in God's removal
of her humiliation by saying, "This is what the Lord has done for me
when he looked favorably [ἐπεῖδεν] on me and took away the disgrace
[ὄνειδος][166] I have endured among my people" (1:25), confidently prophesies God will do the same for her and for all humiliated people. The
Magnificat voices the dream that no more will anyone, especially women,
be humiliated by sexual violation, economic exploitation, or any other
form of violent degradation.

Mercy and Meals

One way in which God lifts up the humiliated is by filling "the hungry
with good things" while sending "the rich away empty" (v. 53).[167] In
first-century Judea and Galilee, people struggled to have enough food,
even as Roman imperial propaganda boasted that its citizens enjoyed
abundance. As Warren Carter describes,

> Food was about power. Its production (based in land), distribution,
> and consumption reflected elite control. Accordingly, the wealthy and
> powerful enjoyed an abundant and diverse food supply. Quality and
> plentiful food was a marker of status and wealth . . . that divided elites
> from nonelites. It established the former as privileged and powerful
> and the latter as inferior and of low entitlement. The latter struggled
> to acquire enough food as well as food of adequate nutritional value.
> For most, this was a constant struggle. And it was cyclic whereby most

165. See Richard A. Horsley, *Jesus and Empire: The Kingdom of God and the New World
Disorder* (Minneapolis: Augsburg Fortress, 2003), 30–31, who lists crucifixion, levying
tribute, and erecting Roman standards among the means of humiliation employed
by the Romans.

166. This same combination of ὁράω, "to see," and ὀδύνη, "misery," is found in
Exodus 3:7-8, where God says, "I have observed [εἶδον] the misery of my people who
are in Egypt. . . . Indeed, I know their sufferings [ὀδύνην], and have come down to
deliver them."

167. See the excursus "Luke and Riches" at 16:1.

dropped below subsistence levels at times throughout each year. Food, then, displayed the injustice of the empire on a daily basis.[168]

That God's mercy is manifest in feeding hungry people is a theme that recurs throughout the gospel. Jesus declares blessed those that hunger now and assures them that they will be satisfied (6:21). He feeds a hungry crowd of five thousand at 9:10-17, a foreshadowing of the Last Supper (22:14-22), where he offers himself in the form of bread and wine. In the Third Gospel, Jesus is frequently found in meal settings, providing not only physical sustenance but also, as did Woman Wisdom (Prov 8–9), teaching that nourishes the spirit.[169]

Feeding the hungry can still be a dangerous, subversive activity, as is seen in the example of the women who ran community soup kitchens and supplied milk for children during the reign of terror of the *Sendero Luminoso* ("Shining Path") in Perú in the 1980s and 1990s. The women's vocal denunciations of the violence of *Sendero* and their strong support among the people made them a threat to the terrorist organization. Juana López, coordinator of the *Vaso de Leche* ("Glass of Milk") program for children, was murdered in 1991; twenty-nine more leaders were killed in 1992. One of the most notorious examples was that of María Elena Moyano: on February 15, 1992, she was gunned down in front of her children and other women, and her corpse was then blown up with dynamite. María Elena's friend tells how the rallying cry voiced in the *Magnificat* may be acted upon today: "Presently in Perú we, as women, have taken on a political role of more importance than ever before in the history of the country. We are leaders, citizens, women's rights activists, organizers, and mobilizers of the grassroots efforts to survive, to overcome the crisis, and to protect the life and livelihoods, as well as the democratic spaces and values that have cost us so much effort to construct."[170] These mothers in Perú, identifying with Mary in the

---

168. Warren Carter, *The Roman Empire and the New Testament: An Essential Guide* (Nashville: Abingdon, 2006), 109–10. Carter's assessment is akin to the position of Oakman, that Galileans were struggling peasants. See the discussion on Mary's social status at 1:26 for other possible interpretations.

169. In some episodes Jesus is host (9:10-17; 22:14-20), while at others he is a guest (5:30; 7:36; 10:38; 14:1; 19:7).

170. *The Autobiography of María Elena Moyano: The Life and Death of a Peruvian Activist*, a translation of *María Elena Moyano: en busca de una esperanza*, ed. Diana Miloslavich Tupac, trans. Patricia S. Taylor Edmisten (Gainesville: University Press of Florida, 2000), https:// ufdcimages.uflib.ufl.edu/AA/00/01/16/41/00001/AutobiographyMoyano.pdf.

Magnificat, link physical nourishment with a political vision and action for well-being for all. They understand well what Dom Helder Cámara (1909–1999), archbishop of Recife, Brazil, observed: "When I give food to the poor, they call me a saint. When I ask why they are poor, they call me communist."[171]

The divine "mercy" (ἔλεος) of which Mary sings (vv. 50, 54) is more than a compassionate feeling; it is expressed in concrete saving actions by God and by those who are devoted to God, from Abraham and Sarah to all their descendants (v. 55).[172] From a feminist perspective, the hope is that saving actions result not simply in a reversal of fortunes, so that those who were previously enthroned and powerful are now debased or outside the realm of salvation, as in the parable of the rich man and Lazarus (16:19-31). Rather, a feminist aim would be a simultaneous movement of relinquishment of power, privilege, and status on the part of those who are rich and powerful and empowerment on the part of those who are humiliated and hungry, which can result in a leveling of goods and power.[173] The Acts of the Apostles says the first Christian communities attempted this: "All who believed were together and had all things in common; they would sell their possessions and goods and distribute the proceeds to all, as any had need" (Acts 2:44-45; similarly 4:32-37). Christian communities of women and men religious today still try to live in this manner. In Israel, kibbutzim (plural of "kibbutz," קיבוץ, "gathering, clustering"), collective communities that began in 1909, also have a similar aim. These efforts keep alive the hope of equitable distribution, still an unrealized hope in most places.

In the remainder of the gospel, divine mercy is manifest to Elizabeth in the birth of her son (1:58) and is a refrain in Zechariah's canticle (1:72, 78). Jesus enacts mercy by healing people afflicted with leprosy (17:13) and blindness (18:38, 39). He teaches his disciples to be merciful by loving enemies, doing good, and giving to those who beg without expecting recompense (6:27-36). He exhorts his followers to emulate a hated Samaritan who "did mercy" (ὁ ποιήσας τὸ ἔλεος) to a wounded Jewish

171. Zildo Rocha, *Helder, O Dom: uma vida que marcou os rumos da Igreja no Brasil* (Petrópolis: Editora Vozes, 2000), 53.

172. For Israel, "saving" generally means from present oppression, e.g., "God will save Zion and rebuild the cities of Jerusalem" (Ps 69:35). See further comments on savior and salvation in chap. 2.

173. Elisabeth Schüssler Fiorenza, "'Waiting at Table': A Critical Feminist Theological Reflection on Diakonia," in *Diakonia: Church for the Others*, ed. N. Greinacher and N. Mette, Concilium 198 (Edinburgh: T&T Clark, 1988), 84–94.

traveler (10:37) and tells a parable about a tax collector who went home justified after praying for mercy (18:13).

The question arises: if God is all merciful and if we are likewise to be merciful, what about justice? How can God (and we) be both merciful and just? Doesn't it revictimize a person who has been hurt if a perpetrator is let off with mercy? What is the point of trying to live faithful to God's commands (as Elizabeth and Zechariah, 1:6) if the Holy One mercifully saves all—even the most egregious of sinners? Pope Francis offers this insight: "Justice and mercy . . . are not two contradictory realities, but two dimensions of a single reality that unfolds progressively until it culminates in the fullness of love."[174] This approach can be called feminist in that it breaks down dualistic ways of thinking: justice and mercy are not opposites but two dimensions of a single reality. Pope Francis explains further: mercy is God's way of reaching out to the sinner, offering that one a new chance.[175] St. Thomas Aquinas has a similar approach: God acts mercifully, not by going against divine justice, but by doing something more than justice; "Thus a man who pays another two hundred pieces of money, though owing him only one hundred, does nothing against justice, but acts liberally or mercifully. . . . Hence it is clear that mercy does not destroy justice, but in a sense is the fulness thereof."[176] While neither Pope Francis nor St. Thomas Aquinas can be accused of being feminists, their insights on the relationship between justice and mercy resonate with feminist thinking.

Diana Hayes Speaks of Mary

Black Catholic womanist theologian Diana Hayes writes, "It is perhaps, in their reinterpretation of the role and presence of Mary, the mother of God, that Black Catholic Women can make the most significant contribution. Too often seen as a docile, submissive woman, Black Catholic womanists, instead, see a young woman sure of her God and of her role in God's salvific plan. She is a woman who, in her song (Luke 1:46-55), proclaims her allegiance with God and with her brothers and sisters with whom she lived, as a

174. Pope Francis, *Misericordiae Vultus* 20, accessible online at: http://www.vatican.va/content/francesco/en/apost_letters/documents/papa-francesco_bolla_20150411_misericordiae-vultus.html.

175. Pope Francis, *Misericordiae Vultus* 21.

176. Thomas Aquinas, *S.T.* 21 art. 3 available at: http://www.newadvent.org/summa/1021.htm.

Jew under Roman oppression, a poor and marginalized existence similar to the existence of Blacks in the church for so long. They relate to her by sharing in her experiences as women who are also oppressed but who continue to bear the burden of faith and to pass on that faith to generations to come. . . . Mary accepted a singular call from God to stand out as 'blessed among all women.' As a young, pregnant, unwed woman who had many difficult questions to answer within her community, she still had the courage to say a powerful and prophetic 'yes' to God that shattered all of time. She is a role model, not for passivity, but for strong, righteous, 'womanish' women who spend their lives giving birth to the future."[177]

A Homebound Prophet and the Order of Time (1:56)

At the conclusion of the *Magnificat*, Luke says that Mary returned home after about three months (1:56). In light of the reference to Elizabeth being in her sixth month at the time of the annunciation to Mary (1:36), Luke means us to understand that Mary stayed with Elizabeth until the birth of her child. Luke completes the scene that focuses on Mary by having her exit (1:56) before resuming Elizabeth's story in 1:57.[178]

The time marker at the end of the *Magnificat* also signals an important shift. Brigitte Kahl shows that there are different measurings of time that crisscross in the first chapters of Luke. There is political/historical time, "the days of King Herod of Judea" (1:5); biological/individual time, "getting on in years" (1:7, 18); religious/cultic time, "when he [Zechariah] was serving as priest" (1:8, 23), "the time of the incense offering" (1:10), and "his delay in the sanctuary" (1:21); and finally the onset of messianic time (1:13-17), a radically changed time that begins with the silencing of Zechariah. Kahl sees a strong connection between time order and gender relations in Luke 1: "Historical political time, measured in terms of the rulers in power, and Temple time, structuring the cultic obligations and also the lifetime of an exclusively male priesthood, were patriarchal understandings of time. The same is essentially true of biological and biographical time, which is oriented by paternity and male progeny. But now, the beginning of the time of God's promise is posited most

177. Diana L. Hayes, "And When We Speak: To Be Black, Catholic, and Womanist," in *Taking Down Our Harps: Black Catholics in the United States*, ed. Diana L. Hayes and Cyprian Davis (Maryknoll, NY: Orbis Books, 1998), 113–14.
178. Fitzmyer, *The Gospel According to Luke I–IX*, 362.

dramatically in a time roster that is gynocentric."[179] With the time-break that begins at 1:24 and extends to 1:57 "comes a fundamental reversal of the entire structure of patriarchal domination on the level of narrative interaction. For the entire nine months, *pater familias* Zechariah is not seen or heard. During this interval, the hitherto prevailing patriarchal order of space and time in his household is transformed from top to bottom by two women and two unborn sons. The patriarchal house of Zechariah . . . becomes a mother's and children's house in which sisterliness and brotherliness reign in place of 'paternal power' (*patria potestas*). The initiative to act and speak lies exclusively with the women."[180]

Beginning with 1:59, however, the order of time is once again constituted by the male,[181] as Zechariah regains his voice and takes over the naming and interpreting. Mary does not speak again in the gospel, except to voice her anguished query to her twelve-year-old son after finding him in the temple (2:48). The initial portrayal of Mary as a prophet called by and interacting directly with God's messenger, asking questions and answering for herself, traveling alone to Judea, being blessed by Elizabeth, and proclaiming a powerful prophecy of God's favor to her and to all her people gives way to that of a silent ponderer (2:19, 51). Like most other women in Luke and Acts, Mary speaks only within the confines of a home (1:40). Public proclamation is reserved to men. It is Jesus who brings into the open the prophetic themes of the *Magnificat* (4:18-19). Nonetheless, Luke has placed powerful women's voices in the beginning of the narrative, and 1:24-57 is a "main connecting thread for the subsequent reading of the entire Lukan corpus. It is a 'key,' so to speak, that determines, like a clef in music, how patriarchal texts can and must be transposed in a manner that does justice to women and the poor."[182] As readers who resist Luke's silencing of women, we "read Luke against Luke," keeping in memory the voices of Elizabeth and Mary.

While most Christians celebrate Mary's obedient yes to God's call, it is equally important to pass on the dangerous memory of her insistent no to all that debases God's own, whether in public or private ways. However important public proclamation and actions, we cannot underestimate the power of prophetic women who equip their family members from inside their homes with stories and songs that envision an alternative rule by divine mercy.

---

179. Kahl, "Reading Luke against Luke," 70–88, here 79.
180. Ibid., 79–80.
181. Ibid., 87.
182. Ibid., 88.

Finding One's Voice (1:57-80)

At 1:57 the focus shifts again to Elizabeth. Although the birth of John is accomplished by both Zechariah and Elizabeth, she is at the center: "she bore a son" and "her neighbors and relatives . . . rejoiced with her" (1:57-58). Zechariah does not come into view until they propose his name for the child, to which Elizabeth voices strong objection. Contrary to the impression given by Luke 1:59, it was not up to the neighbors and family to decide on a name. As with Jesus, God is the one who gives John his name, as Gabriel instructed Zechariah (1:13).[183] When and how Elizabeth learned of this name is not narrated; most likely Luke intends for us to imagine that Zechariah wrote it down for her, as he does for the neighbors and relatives (1:63), giving us an image of Elizabeth as a literate woman.[184] When the neighbors and relatives are about to name the child after his father, Elizabeth strongly intervenes, "By no means! [οὐχί ἀλλά] He is to be called John" (1:60). Οὐχί ἀλλά is a strong formulation and implies more than a polite difference of opinion.[185] It is an emphatic corrective. Although Elizabeth faithfully follows the divine directive to name her child John, her friends and relatives turn to Zechariah. We can read Zechariah's response as affirming Elizabeth's authority and even submitting himself to her,[186] but what becomes evident as the narrative progresses is that here begins the reassertion of the patriarchal voice. From this point forward, women's voices go mute.

---

183. In the Old Testament, sometimes the mother names her child: Eve names Cain (Gen 4:1) and Seth (Gen 4:25); Lot's daughters name their sons Moab and Ben-ammi (Gen 19:37-38); Leah names Reuben, Simeon, Levi, and Judah (Gen 29:32-35); Rachel names Dan and Naphtali, born to her slave Bilhah (Gen 30:6, 8), and her own son Ben-oni, whom Jacob renames Benjamin (Gen 35:18); Bat-Shua names Onan and Shelah (Gen 38:4-5); Samson's mother names him (Judg 13:24); Hannah names Samuel (1 Sam 1:20). Sometimes the father does the naming: Seth names Enosh (Gen 4:26); Adam named Seth (Gen 5:3); Lamech names Noah (Gen 5:28-29); Abram names Ishmael (Gen 16:15), although an angel appears to Hagar and tells her to name him thus (16:11), and Isaac (Gen 17:19); Moses names Gershom (Exod 2:22); Gideon names Abimelech (Judg 8:31).

184. See comments on women's literacy in the authors' introduction, pp. l–lii.

185. Mark Coleridge, *The Birth of the Lukan Narrative: Narrative as Christology in Luke 1–2*, JSNTSup 88 (Sheffield: JSOT, 1993), 106 n. 2. See also Karl Allen Kuhn, "Deaf or Defiant? The Literary, Cultural, and Affective-Rhetorical Keys to the Naming of John (Luke 1:57-80)," *CBQ* 75 (2013): 486–503, esp. 489. See Luke 12:51; 13:3, 5; 16:30, where the same formulation οὐχί ἀλλά occurs, with an emphatic sense: "by no means" (BDAG, 742).

186. Kahl, "Reading Luke against Luke," 83.

57Now the time came for Elizabeth to give birth, and she bore a son. 58Her neighbors and relatives heard that the Lord had shown his great mercy to her, and they rejoiced with her.

59On the eighth day they came to circumcise the child, and they were going to name him Zechariah after his father. 60But his mother said, "No; he is to be called John." 61They said to her, "None of your relatives has this name." 62Then they began motioning to his father to find out what name he wanted to give him. 63He asked for a writing tablet and wrote, "His name is John." And all of them were amazed. 64Immediately his mouth was opened and his tongue freed, and he began to speak, praising God. 65Fear came over all their neighbors, and all these things were talked about throughout the entire hill country of Judea. 66All who heard them pondered them and said, "What then will this child become?" For, indeed, the hand of the Lord was with him.

67Then his father Zechariah was filled with the Holy Spirit and spoke this prophecy:
68"Blessed be the Lord God of Israel,
    for he has looked favorably on
        his people and redeemed
        them.
69He has raised up a mighty savior
    for us
    in the house of his servant David,
70as he spoke through the mouth of
    his holy prophets from of old,

After a break from patriarchal time where women's voices prevailed (1:24-57), Zechariah's prophecy reasserts patriarchal time. His canticle echoes that of Mary and Elizabeth in structure, vocabulary, and themes. For readers like Theophilus, Zechariah's proclamation gives assurance (1:3), along with the lengthy male speeches in Acts, that male voices prevail over the subversive women's speeches.

In the flow of Luke's first chapter, female prophets take center stage. They readily believe, and they first articulate God's saving action toward them individually and toward their people, while the male priest stands mute in the shadows. When Zechariah does speak, much of what he says echoes what they have already proclaimed. In many contexts, ancient and modern, it is more usual for women to find themselves in Zechariah's role, unnoticed and silent while male voices prevail. It is not often that a man needs help to find his voice.[187] Luke has crafted the chapter so that the women's prophetic utterances are validated by the priest and family patriarch before they can be accepted by the people. Many competent,

187. See further Reid, *Taking Up the Cross*, 118–19.

Luke 1:57-80 (cont.)

⁷¹that we would be saved from our enemies and from the hand of all who hate us. ⁷²Thus he has shown the mercy promised to our ancestors, and has remembered his holy covenant, ⁷³the oath that he swore to our ancestor Abraham, to grant us ⁷⁴that we, being rescued from the hands of our enemies, might serve him without fear, ⁷⁵in holiness and righteousness before him all our days. ⁷⁶And you, child, will be called the prophet of the Most High; for you will go before the Lord to prepare his ways, ⁷⁷to give knowledge of salvation to his people by the forgiveness of their sins. ⁷⁸By the tender mercy of our God, the dawn from on high will break upon us, ⁷⁹to give light to those who sit in darkness and in the shadow of death, to guide our feet into the way of peace." ⁸⁰The child grew and became strong in spirit, and he was in the wilderness until the day he appeared publicly to Israel.

faith-filled, articulate, prophetic women still face this dynamic today. We are hard pressed to find examples where male utterances are not accepted until validated by a woman.

As the chapter closes, two women prophets set the stage for the remainder of the gospel. Not only repositories for John and Jesus, they actively interpret the divine perspective of what is happening through them.[188]

188. Turid Karlsen Seim, *The Double Message: Patterns of Gender in Luke–Acts* (Nashville: Abingdon, 1994), 176.

Luke 2:1-52

Divine Love Becomes Incarnate

She Gave Birth to Her Firstborn Son (2:1-7)

Luke situates Jesus's birth in historical time and place as he did with the annunciation of the birth of John the Baptist (1:5).[1] The problem is that the historical details do not add up. There was no empire-wide census conducted during the reign of Caesar Augustus (27 BCE–14 CE). Quirinius did conduct a census, but not until he became governor of Judea in 6 CE, which does not fit Jesus's birth occurring during the reign of Herod, who died in 4 BCE. Luke's purpose is more theological and literary than historical.[2] By linking Jesus's birth with a decree of the Roman emperor carried out by the local governor, Luke

---

1. At regular intervals, Luke names Roman rulers and Jewish leaders who collaborated with them (Luke 1:5; 3:1-2, 19; 8:3; 9:7, 9; 13:1, 31; 20:20, 22-26; 23:1-5, 7-12, 13-25, 52). On the historical value of Lukan writings, see Joseph A. Fitzmyer, *The Gospel According to Luke I–IX*, AB 28 (Garden City, NY: Doubleday, 1981), 14–18, who shows that Luke's historical concern serves a theological end: to show the events he narrates as fulfillment of God's plan.

2. For more details on ways to resolve the historical discrepancies, see Raymond E. Brown, *The Birth of the Messiah: A Commentary on the Infancy Narratives in the Gospels of Matthew and Luke* (Garden City, NY: Doubleday, 1977), 547–55; Fitzmyer, *The Gospel According to Luke I–IX*, 393–94, 399–405; Amy-Jill Levine and Ben Witherington III, *The Gospel of Luke*, NCBC (Cambridge: Cambridge University Press, 2018), 55.

²·¹In those days a decree went out from Emperor Augustus that all the world should be registered. ²This was the first registration and was taken while Quirinius was governor of Syria. ³All went to their own towns to be registered. ⁴Joseph also went from the town of Nazareth in Galilee to Judea, to the city of David called Bethlehem, because he was descended from the house and family of David. ⁵He went to be registered with Mary, to whom he was engaged and who was expecting a child. ⁶While they were there, the time came for her to deliver her child. ⁷And she gave birth to her firstborn son and wrapped him in bands of cloth, and laid him in a manger, because there was no place for them in the inn.

reminds readers that Jesus is born in a land where imperial might holds sway. Were Jesus to "reign over the house of Jacob forever," and were his kingdom to have no end, as Gabriel announced (1:33), a power struggle would be inevitable. Luke does not make the conflict as immediately dramatic as does Matthew, who narrates Herod's command to slaughter all the babies in the region of Bethlehem (Matt 2:1-18), but the clash of kingdoms is set nonetheless.

Within the Roman Empire, taking a census[3] was not a benign act; the count was done so that Rome could exact taxes and military service (Jews were exempt from the latter). Josephus describes the agitation that occurred when Rome deposed Herod the Great's son, Archelaus, from serving as tetrarch of Judea, annexed Judea to Syria, and established direct Roman rule. Josephus records that the Jewish population was alarmed when Quirinius declared that they had to register their property, but the high priest entreated them to comply, and so most did. Others followed Judas the Galilean in revolt.[4]

While the historical details do not add up, the story is a convenient way for Luke to explain how Mary and Joseph, who reside in Nazareth (1:32), bring their son into the world in Bethlehem, the "city of David,"

---

3. For the census in the Old Testament, see Exod 30:11-16; Num 1–2, 26, 31; Josh 8:10; 1 Sam 11:8; 13:15; 15:4; 2 Sam 18:1; 24:1-10; 1 Chr 21. In Exod 30 and 2 Sam 24, danger and punishment are associated with census taking, whether it is for usurping a divine prerogative (see Ps 147:4) or some other cause. See Shira Golani, "Is There a Consensus That a Census Causes a Plague?" https://thetorah.com/is-there-a-consensus-that-a-census-causes-a-plague/.

4. Josephus, *Ant.* 18.1. (See also Acts 5:37.) See Brown, *Birth of the Messiah*, 547–55.

a birthplace fit for a king. Within this story world, details pertaining to family relations and reasons for travel are minimal.

Being Counted

In the ideal form of democracy, to be counted is to have voice, and feminists advocate for this kind of counting. We wish for women to be counted not only by recognizing our physical presence but also by hearing our voices and taking seriously the skills and talents we have to contribute in every arena. A famous biblical example of women not being counted is found at the end of the episode where Jesus feeds a multitude. Mark says, "Those who had eaten the loaves numbered five thousand men" (6:44; similarly, Luke 9:14). Matthew adds: "And those who ate were about five thousand men, besides women and children" (14:21). To count women in, one feminist strategy is always to ask, "Where were the women?" If women aren't mentioned in the text, we don't presume they were absent.

Not all forms of counting take place for democratic representation or human flourishing. In imperial Rome, the purpose of census-taking was taxation, and there is evidence that Roman tax levies in the provinces may have pushed vulnerable populations to, and sometimes beyond, the brink of desperation.[5] In our own time, "being counted" can also provoke fear. As we are writing this chapter, the United States is approaching a new decennial census to be taken in 2020, and fears are rampant in communities of immigrants. Because the census may include a question about citizenship, people who are not US citizens are terrified that the US Census Bureau may cooperate with the Immigration and Customs Enforcement agency (ICE), and they could face deportation.[6] Many people refuse to open the door or to speak with the Census Bureau agents. In the 2010 census, an estimated 1.5 million people went uncounted.[7]

---

5. Douglas E. Oakman, *Jesus and the Economic Questions of His Day*, Studies in the Bible and Early Christianity 8 (Lewiston, NY/Queenston, Ont.: Mellen, 1986); Roland Boer and Christina Petterson, *Time of Troubles: A New Economic Framework for Early Christianity* (Minneapolis: Fortress, 2017).

6. See, e.g., Kevin G. Andrade's article in the *Providence Journal* on July 5, 2018: http://www.providencejournal.com/news/20180705/fear-of-census-common-for-immigrants-in-ri.

7. See CBS News, "2010 Census Missed 1.5 Million Minorities," May 22, 2012, https://www.cbsnews.com/news/2010-census-missed-15-million-minorities/.

Those undercounted include not only immigrants but also people who are homeless. The US Department of Housing and Urban Development (HUD) estimated their number to be roughly 554,000 in January 2018.[8] The fastest growing segment of homeless people are women and families, 84 percent of which are families headed by women.

In Luke's narrative, there is no hint of fear or resistance to the census. Luke wants to provide assurance (1:4) that Jesus-followers and those who are part of his story are not a threat to the empire. Joseph and Mary comply despite the danger posed by the imminent birth.

Joseph's actions and decisions are the focus of 2:4-5. Luke does not say whether Joseph consulted Mary in making the decision that she would accompany him. Since women were not subject to military conscription and if Mary did not own property, she would not have needed to go along. A compassionate reading of Joseph's motive would be that as he weighed the risks of travel when Mary was so close to delivery, he decided in favor of them being together.

Verses 6-7 highlight Mary's role. She gives birth to her firstborn son,[9] wraps him in bands of cloth, and lays him in a manger. Wrapping the infant in bands of cloth (2:7) creates an inclusion with the end of the gospel, where Jesus's dead body is taken down from the cross and wrapped in a linen cloth (23:53).

Their lodging is not at an inn,[10] πανδοχεῖον, such as the one in the parable of the Samaritan and the injured traveler (10:34). Rather, Mary and Joseph stay in a κατάλυμα, the same word used for the guest room where Jesus celebrates Passover with his disciples (22:11).[11] Whether the Bethlehem guest space is rented or in the home of a friend or relative, Luke does not say. On a practical level, the place where animals were fed afforded Mary and Joseph more seclusion, but on a theological level, placing the newborn in a feeding trough in Bethlehem (meaning "house of bread") symbolizes that he will be food for a hungry world. There are

---

8. http://thedataface.com/2018/01/public-health/american-homelessness.

9. Note that it is *her* firstborn, not *their* firstborn. And in Luke's account, there is no hint of Joseph's distress over Mary's pregnancy, as in Matt 1:18-24.

10. Many colorful tales have grown around the innkeeper. In some he is heartless and cruel; in others he and his wife are tender and kind to the expectant couple. None has a basis in the biblical text.

11. See Luke 19:7 where the cognate verb καταλῦσαι is rendered "to be the guest of."

many dining scenes in the gospel that will build on this theme,[12] where acceptance or rejection of Jesus is in the foreground.

Jesus: The Only Child of a Perpetual Virgin or a Boy with Siblings?

The term προτότοκος, "firstborn," in 2:7 points ahead to 2:23, where the principle that the firstborn male shall be consecrated to the Lord is said to be "written in the law of the Lord."[13] Jesus is firstborn, but not necessarily the *only* child of his mother Mary. Other New Testament texts presume that Jesus has siblings, including Galatians 1:19, which names James as the brother of Jesus, and Mark 6:3, which names four brothers of Jesus and indicates that he has sisters as well.[14] The mention of siblings suggests Mary gave birth to children in addition to Jesus, as would have been typical for a married woman in her time, if she were lucky enough to escape early death in childbirth. Because these references to Jesus's siblings are offered up in early sources incidentally, without apology and without awareness of the doctrine of the perpetual virginity of Mary that will develop in Christian orthodoxy, we accept these references as historical.

As Christian orthodoxy consolidates, however, it becomes increasingly important to assert that Mary was a perpetual virgin and that Jesus, her "firstborn," was an only child. Church fathers explain away biblical references to brothers and sisters as pointing instead either to Jesus's "cousins"[15] or to children Joseph

---

12. E.g., 5:29-32; 7:36-50; 9:10-17; 14:1-24; 19:1-10; 22:14-20.

13. Luke 2:23 is a paraphrase of Exod 13:2.

14. Other mentions of Jesus's siblings in the New Testament include Mark 3:31-32; Matt 12:46-50; 13:55; Luke 8:19-21; John 2:12; 7:3-10; Acts 1:14. On Jesus's siblings in Luke, see comments at Luke 8:19-20. James the brother of Jesus is mentioned also in Josephus (*Ant.* 20.199–203), and he holds a prominent place in extracanonical Christian tradition as well (see Eusebius, *Hist. eccl.* 2.23.4–18; and the Pseudo-Clementine *Recognitions*, 1.27–71). The extracanonical Gospel of Thomas, somewhat puzzlingly, names Thomas as Jesus's twin brother. For one attempt to account for the historical place of Jesus's family members, see Richard Bauckham, *Jude and the Relatives of Jesus in the Early Church* (London: T&T Clark, 2004). For consideration of James the brother within Christian traditions of martyrdom, see Shelly Matthews, *Perfect Martyr: The Stoning of Stephen and the Construction of Christian Identity* (New York: Oxford University Press, 2010), 79–97.

15. This view is found in Jerome's tract *Against Helvidius*, which dates to ca. 383 CE and became the predominant position of Christianity in the West, while the view that the brothers and sisters were children of Joseph by a previous marriage was the dominant position in the East. See John P. Meier, *A Marginal Jew: Rethinking the Historical Jesus*, vol. 1: *The Roots of the Problem and the Person*, ABRL (New York: Doubleday, 1991), 318–32.

had with a previous wife (this is the view presented already in the Protoevangelium of James, dated to the mid-second century CE). The doctrine of the perpetual virginity of Mary (before, during, and after the birth of Jesus) was a subject of discussion until the late fourth century, when a consensus emerged. The Fifth Ecumenical Council held at Constantinople in 553 speaks of Mary as *aeiparthenos*, "ever virgin." As we have noted in our commentary on chapter 1, from a feminist point of view, the doctrine that Mary gave birth in an exceptional manner, unreproducible by any other human mother, is deeply problematic (see comments under the heading "Virginal Conception," at 1:26-38). The teaching both denies to Mary the human bodily experience of sexuality and idealizes a form of motherhood that is impossible for any other human mother to obtain.[16]

Deep Incarnation

The phrase "deep incarnation," coined by Danish theologian Niels Gregersen,[17] "is starting to be used in theology to indicate the radical divine reach in Christ through human flesh all the way down into the living web of organic life with its growth and decay, amid the wider processes of evolving nature that beget and sustain life. As he writes, 'In Christ, God enters into the biological tissue of creation in order to share the fate of biological existence. . . . In the incarnate One, God shares the life conditions of foxes and sparrows, grass and trees, soil and moisture.' The saving God became a human being, who was part of the wider human community, which shares the membrane of life with other creatures, all made from cosmic material, and vulnerable to death and disintegration. . . . As a densely specific expression of the love of God already poured out in creation, the

16. For further feminist reflection on Mary, see Elizabeth A. Johnson, *Truly Our Sister: A Theology of Mary in the Communion of Saints* (New York: Continuum, 2003); Diego Irarrázaval, Susan Ross, and Marie-Theres Wacker, eds., *The Many Faces of Mary*, Concilium 2008, no. 4 (London: SCM, 2008); Kathleen Gallagher Elkins, *Mary, Mother of Martyrs: How Motherhood Became Self-Sacrifice in Early Christianity* (Indianapolis: FSR Books, 2018), 1–33; and our comments in chap. 1 on Virginal Conception.

17. Niels Henrik Gregersen, ed. *Incarnation: On the Scope and Depth of Christology* (Minneapolis: Fortress, 2015).

incarnation brings God near in a different way to the whole of earthly reality and its corporal and material dimensions—all of earth's ecosystems, plants and animals, and the cosmos in which planet Earth dynamically exists. For Christian faith, the one ineffable God who creates the heavens and the earth is free enough to participate personally in the created world this way, and loving enough to want to do so."[18]

Good News for All the People (2:8-20)

The first ones to hear the good news of the birth of the child are ordinary people,[19] not magi who come from afar as in Matthew 2:1-12. The shepherds are out in the open field, watching over their flock. While in androcentric imagination, the shepherds receiving the message are assumed to be men, women could also be shepherds in the biblical period (see Gen 29:6, 9 where Rachel is keeping her father's sheep).[20]

The shepherds can suggest divine care and protection (Ps 23; Ezek 34:11-16) and leaders of Israel (Ezek 34:1-15; Jer 3:15; 23:1-4). Some leaders, such as Moses (Exod 3:1) and David (1 Sam 16:11), were actual shepherds before being called to pastor people. Jesus will invoke this image when he calls his disciples "little flock" (12:32), and he implicitly likens himself to a shepherd who goes to great lengths to search out the one lost sheep of the flock (15:1-7).[21]

18. Elizabeth A. Johnson, *Creation and the Cross: The Mercy of God for a Planet in Peril* (Maryknoll, NY: Orbis Books, 2018), 184–87.

19. Interpretations that make the shepherds sinners or unclean have no basis in the text.

20. The task of tending flocks of sheep is often assigned to women, even today. For example, there continue to be women shepherds in Israel to this day, e.g., among the Bedouin in the Negev: https://www.alamy.com/stock-photo-israel-negev-desert-mitzpe-ramon-female-bedouin-shepherd-and-her-herd-140899717.html. For a 2014 United Nations report on the perseverance of female shepherds in Somaliland, see https://blogs.un.org/blog/2014/01/07/the-women-shepherds-of-somaliland/. For a 2019 newspaper feature on women shepherds in New Zealand, see https://www.nzherald.co.nz/the-country/news/article.cfm?c_id=16&objectid=12282266.

21. The parallel in Matthew 18:10-14 is addressed to the disciples and instructs them on the kind of leadership they are to exercise. John 10:1-21 offers a discourse on Jesus as the Good Shepherd.

Luke 2:8-20

⁸In that region there were shepherds living in the fields, keeping watch over their flock by night. ⁹Then an angel of the Lord stood before them, and the glory of the Lord shone around them, and they were terrified. ¹⁰But the angel said to them, "Do not be afraid; for see—I am bringing you good news of great joy for all the people: ¹¹to you is born this day in the city of David a Savior, who is the Messiah, the Lord. ¹²This will be a sign for you: you will find a child wrapped in bands of cloth and lying in a manger." ¹³And suddenly there was with the angel a multitude of the heavenly host, praising God and saying,

¹⁴"Glory to God in the highest heaven,

and on earth peace among those whom he favors!"

¹⁵When the angels had left them and gone into heaven, the shepherds said to one another, "Let us go now to Bethlehem and see this thing that has taken place, which the Lord has made known to us." ¹⁶So they went with haste and found Mary and Joseph, and the child lying in the manger. ¹⁷When they saw this, they made known what had been told them about this child; ¹⁸and all who heard it were amazed at what the shepherds told them. ¹⁹But Mary treasured all these words and pondered them in her heart. ²⁰The shepherds returned, glorifying and praising God for all they had heard and seen, as it had been told them.

Las Pastorelas[22]

Las pastorelas, the shepherds' plays, emerged from theater practices used in catechesis by Spanish missionaries to evangelize the first peoples of the Americas. These performances, rooted in Luke 2:8-20, enact the story of the shepherds' encounter with the good news from the angels and their decision to head to Bethlehem. Integrating medieval nativity plays with Indigenous traditions of ritual drama, these performances, over time, moved from the churches to the streets as more profane aspects were scripted into the plays. Today variations can be found during the Christmas season presented at venues in Mexico and the United States, especially in the Southwest. Increasingly performed in theaters or cultural centers, some are still sponsored by churches, and others are even staged by locals in their backyards and barrios.

22. Some material in this contribution first appeared in Carmen Nanko-Fernández, "Theological Reflections: Luke 2:1-14, (15-20)," *Lectionary Homiletics* (December 2011): 27–28.

The pastorelas imaginatively narrate the tale of the shepherds' journey to Bethlehem as one fraught with interference by the devil who seeks to distract them from their destination. The misadventures of the shepherds occur via temptations courtesy of the devil, who in some versions is accompanied by minions. Laced with humor, thanks in part to the antics of the devil and the earthiness of the shepherds, pastorelas counteract overly romanticized portrayals of the nativity by dealing with the reality of sin. The shepherds, male and female, are accessible and relatable to their audiences who can see themselves in their silliness, vulnerabilities, and struggles. The plays often reflect the lived experiences of contemporary communities suffering with the social evils and political and personal demons that trouble their own time and place—everything from racism to immigration to corruption to abuse. Pastorelas are characterized by improvisation, bawdy language, ludic and comic behavior—a blend of social satire and morality play wrapped up in a nativity story. Latino theologian Alejandro García-Rivera contends that it is precisely the "biting humor," the comic dimension, that "underlines

what is basically a commentary on evil."[23]

These performances situate the incarnation in a complex world where the power of evil must be contended with individually and collectively. In this sense pastorelas embrace the more challenging dimensions of the good news by depicting the struggles entailed in responding to that good news in daily life. While the shepherds eventually make their way, with the help of the angels, to behold the child of God and bring their simple gifts, the journey is not an easy one.

Pastorelas fill in the blanks, enflesh the shepherds, and embellish the nativity with local details that in effect make us all shepherds heeding the angels' tidings. They remind us of the fullness of the humanity of those early witnesses to divine revelation, of the humanity the incarnated word chooses to share, of the challenges and temptations that can compromise our haste to respond to the invitation. Pope Francis adds another dimension to what it means to be shepherds. Through various media he specifically teaches ministers, bishops, theologians, and evangelizing communities that they are all called to be shepherds, so embedded with their sheep that they bear their

23. Alejandro García-Rivera, "The Whole and the Love of Difference: Latino Meta-physics as Cosmology," in *From the Heart of Our People: Latino/a Explorations in Catholic Systematic Theology*, ed. Orlando O. Espín and Miguel H. Díaz (Maryknoll, NY: Orbis Books, 1999), 69.

scent.[24] What often gets lost in the appropriation of this dictum is the radical vulnerability that such a call requires. To smell as the sheep do makes the shepherd not only familiar to the flock but indistinguishable to those who prey on sheep. In other words, to be a shepherd is to accompany in a way that puts one at risk to share in the threats, struggles, anxieties, and dangers that our communities endure as well as the joys and hopes.

Carmen Nanko-Fernández

Good News of Peace to All (2:10)

One of the most significant shifts in New Testament studies at the end of the twentieth century involved widespread recognition that biblical authors employ terminology for Jesus that was also used across the Roman Empire to affirm the beneficence of Roman emperors.[25] The angel's message to the shepherds concerning the birth of Jesus is a prime example of Luke's employment of such terms. In verse 11, in addition to the distinctly Jewish term Messiah (or Christ), the angel proclaims Jesus as "Savior" and "Lord," two titles often used to acclaim Roman emperors (see comments at 1:46-56 on the titles "Lord" and "Savior" for emperors).

The proclamation of "good news," εὐαγγέλιον (v. 10), as the result of a prodigious birth (v. 11), leading to peace on earth (v. 14), reads almost as if Luke has borrowed directly from the Priene calendar inscription. This inscription, set up to commemorate the decision by an assembly of Greek cities in Asia Minor to honor Caesar Augustus and dated to 9 BCE, celebrates the birth of Caesar Augustus as owing to divine providence and as ushering in a new era of "good news," εὐαγγέλιον. Augustus is hailed

---

24. Pope Francis in "Homily, Chrism Mass" (March 28, 2013); *Evangelii Gaudium* (November 24, 2013) 24; "Letter to Faculty of Theology of the Pontifical Catholic University of Argentina" (March 3, 2015); "Address to the Central American Bishops," Panama (January 24, 2019).

25. For an early forerunner to this conversation, see Adolf Deissmann, *Light from the Ancient East: The New Testament Illustrated by Recently Discovered Texts of the Graeco-Roman World*, trans. Lionel R. M. Strachan (London: Hodder & Stoughton, 1910). See, for example, Helmut Koester, *Introduction to the New Testament*, vol. 1: *History, Culture and Religion of the Hellenistic Age*, 2nd ed. (New York: DeGruyter, 1995); John Dominic Crossan, *The Historical Jesus: The Life of a Mediterranean Jewish Peasant* (San Francisco: HarperSanFrancisco, 1991); Richard A. Horsley, *Jesus and the Spiral of Violence: Popular Jewish Resistance in Roman Palestine* (San Francisco: Harper & Row, 1987).

as having "made war to cease" and as one who will "put everything [in peaceful] order."[26] A similar inscription from Halicarnassus (2 CE–14 CE) celebrates Augustus as "savior of the whole human race," because "Land and sea have peace, the cities flourish under a good legal system, in harmony and with an abundance of food, there is an abundance of all good things, people are filled with happy hopes for the future and with delight at the present."[27]

Another detail of this pericope that echoes Roman imperial thinking is the "heavenly army" that joins with the angel to proclaim the "peace" that is to come on earth. While the phrase πλῆθος στρατιᾶς οὐρανίου (v. 13) is commonly translated into English as "a multitude of the heavenly host," στρατιᾶς is the Greek word for army. Thus, as the Roman peace is accomplished through conquest and subjugation, so the peace of the Lord Jesus born in Bethlehem somehow involves a multitude of soldiers as well.[28]

While consensus holds that Luke employs language that is recognizable from Roman imperial propaganda the debated question is, to what end? Though some read Luke as making an explicit and subversive contrast between the "good news" of Jesus and the "good news" of Rome here and throughout his gospel,[29] we typically align with those who emphasize that Luke's overarching rhetorical aim is to reassure his readers, rather than to incite them to engage in politically subversive action.[30] Thus, we do not believe that Luke means to challenge directly the earthly reign of Caesar by this announcement of a new Lord and Savior who will establish peace on earth with the help of his heavenly army—at least not anytime soon.[31] Here, as in several instances we point

---

26. Frederick W. Danker, *Benefactor: Epigraphic Study of a Graeco-Roman and New Testament Semantic Field* (St. Louis: Clayton, 1982), 217.

27. *The Collection of Ancient Greek Inscriptions in the British Museum* IV, ed. Gustav Hirschfeld (London, 1893), no. 894, cited in Klaus Wengst, *Pax Romana: And the Peace of Jesus Christ* (Philadelphia: Fortress, 1987), 9.

28. For an argument concerning the inseparability of peace from war in the logic of the Pax Romana, and its implications for Luke's Gospel, see Caryn A. Reeder, *Gendering War and Peace in the Gospel of Luke* (Cambridge: Cambridge University Press, 2019).

29. Richard S. Cassidy, *Society and Politics in the Acts of the Apostles* (Maryknoll, NY: Orbis Books, 1987); Richard A. Horsley, *The Liberation of Christmas: The Infancy Narratives in Social Context* (New York: Crossroad, 1989).

30. See our comments on the preface, Luke 1:1-4.

31. Luke defers the question of political messianism at Luke 24:21a: "But we had hoped that he was the one to redeem Israel"; and Acts 1:6b, "Lord, is this the time when you will restore the kingdom to Israel?" which the resurrected Jesus deflects in 1:7.

to in our commentary, Luke seems to employ language of "kingship," "peace," "redemption," and "salvation" as applying to a spiritual realm that is distinct from the realm of the Roman Empire. And, as the example of a heavenly army singing about peace illustrates, sometimes Luke's proclamations concerning redemption and salvation reinscribe Roman imperial categories rather than overturn them.

Caveats are necessary: First, Luke is not uniformly focused on spiritual matters to the exclusion of material needs. For example, the counsel of John the Baptist to soldiers and tax collectors in 3:10-14 contains specific exhortation for ethical practice that would provide material benefit to those without coats and food and to those cheated by tax collectors and extorted by soldiers. Likewise, the Sermon on the Plain (Luke 6:20-49) contains ethical exhortations that would alleviate suffering of the downtrodden if put into practice. The "salvation" that Jesus announces to Zacchaeus (19:1-10) manifests itself in charitable gifts to the poor. Passages such as these demonstrate that even if Luke is not aiming to subvert empire, this gospel shows concern for the suffering caused by imperial practices of economic extraction.[32]

Second, while Luke aims for a narrative that does not threaten the political status quo, his readers might take his narrative in different directions. The angelic announcement of "Peace on earth" might be directed by Luke to peace in the distant future or to an "inner" peace that does not disturb the ruling powers. Still, as with the *Magnificat* (see also our comments on 1:46-55), the themes of peace, goodwill, and good news in the announcement to the shepherds can captivate (and have captivated) readers to hope and to work for the manifestation of these ideals in this world, in spite of Luke's repeated deferrals.[33]

With respect to the story of Pentecost in Luke's second volume (Acts 2), Shelly has argued: "Luke attempts to tell a story of the orderly descent of the Spirit, but such a phenomenon is not particularly conducive to order. Because Luke is 'playing with fire' here, we can identify places where the

---

32. See comments at 1:26 on the competing views on the economic status of Galileans. While the data so far do not allow us to say with certainty what was the historical situation in the Galilee at the time of Jesus, we can say that Luke shows knowledge of the oppressiveness of Roman taxation throughout the empire.

33. See, e.g., Gustavo Gutiérrez, *The God of Life*, trans. Matthew J. O'Connell (Maryknoll, NY: Orbis Books, 1991), 126, who insists that peacemaking, which goes hand in hand with the establishment of authentic justice, is an essential task of Christians in this life. He quotes the Latin American bishops' document from Medellín (*Peace*, 14): "Peace is not found, it is built" (127).

flames have escaped the boundaries he has erected in his attempt to contain it."[34] We see a similar process in Luke's attempt to bring order to his story of Jesus in the Third Gospel, where the author frequently resorts to powerful promises of good news, salvation, and peace, drawing from the Jesus tradition, the Old Testament, and also Roman imperial discourse of beneficence. On the one hand, Luke repeatedly suggests that these images are not part of a program of political subversion enacted by Jesus or the followers of the "the Way."[35] On the other hand, the promises are powerful enough that some readers might understand them as having broader implications than Luke himself allows—including salvation and liberation in material and political terms.[36]

Savior for Whom and from What? (2:11)

When Christians today think of Jesus as savior, most associate salvation with rescue from sin.[37] The title savior[38] carried other nuances for the gospel's first hearers. Acclamations of God as savior, such as that of

---

34. Shelly Matthews, *The Acts of the Apostles: An Introduction and Study Guide; Taming the Tongues of Fire*, T&T Clark Study Guides to the New Testament (London: Bloomsbury T&T Clark, 2017), 82.

35. Compare the declarations of Jesus's innocence in the passion in Luke 23:4, 14, 22, 40, 47 and the refutation of charges of subversion in Acts 18:14-15; 19:37; 23:9; 26:31-32.

36. Debates about the relationship of Luke(–Acts) to empire are without end. See Michael Kochenash, "Review Essay: Taking the Bad with the God; Reconciling Images of Rome in Luke–Acts," *RelSRev* 41 (2015): 43–51. For Luke's imitation of imperial themes in Acts, see Drew W. Billings, *Acts of the Apostles and the Rhetoric of Roman Imperialism* (Cambridge: Cambridge University Press, 2018). Reeder (*Gendering War and Peace*, 14) reads Luke's Gospel as offering an "implicit alternative to Rome" that sometimes becomes "explicit."

37. In Matt 1:21, the angel tells Joseph that Mary "will bear a son, and you are to name him Jesus, for he will save his people from their sins." In Luke 1:77, Zechariah sings of John the Baptist's giving "knowledge of salvation to his people by the forgiveness of their sins." In a speech in Acts 5:31, Peter says of Jesus: "God exalted him at his right hand as Leader and Savior that he might give repentance to Israel and forgiveness of sins." Ben Witherington III (*The Acts of the Apostles: A Socio-Rhetorical Commentary* [Grand Rapids: Eerdmans, 1998]) notes that what most ancients looked for was "salvation from disease, disaster, or death in this life, and the 'redemption' many pagans cried out for was redemption from the social bondage of slavery, not the personal bondage of sin" (821).

38. Only Luke among the Synoptic evangelists uses σωτήρ (Luke 1:47; 2:11; Acts 5:31; 13:23) and σωτηρία (Luke 1:69, 71, 77; 19:9; Acts 4:12; 7:25; 13:26, 47; 16:17; 27:34; 28:28). In the Fourth Gospel they occur only at John 4:22, 42. See comments on "savior" at 1:47.

Mary in 1:47, are found throughout the Old Testament as authors praise God for rescue from slavery and exile, from the hands of their enemies, and for providing life's necessities (e.g., Deut 32:15; Isa 12:2; Ps 62:2, 6).[39] Another use of the term in the Old Testament is when God raises up a "savior" (מושיע) such as the judges Othniel (Judg 3:9, 15), Ehud (Judg 3:15), and Shamgar (Judg 3:31).[40] Although the word "savior" or "deliverer" is not used of Jael, Deborah, and Judith, their actions in rescuing Israel from its enemies certainly depict them as such.

Greek and Egyptian gods, such as Poseidon, Leda, Zeus, Athena, Apollo, Aesclepius, Hercules, Isis, and Serapis, were also called saviors, not only for delivering people in times of distress, but also for their ongoing protection and preservation of the city and its citizens. "Savers of life" could also be human beings, such as doctors, philosophers, and statesmen. Under the Ptolomies and Seleucids (third and second centuries BCE), Hellenistic rulers were revered as "saviors,"[41] and in Roman imperial times, there is an increase in the use of this title for the emperor (see comments at 1:47).

Why people in the first-century Greco-Roman world came to acclaim Jesus as savior remains a difficult question. While the term might properly be ascribed to an emperor who wields enormous power, the humble origins of Jesus and his ignominious death seem a far cry from that kind of power. And for Greek and Roman polytheists, what might Jesus offer that the other savior gods did not? For women in particular, what might attract them to a male savior, when goddesses such as Isis, one of the most popular deities since the eighth century BCE,[42] embodied female power over life and death and protected women in all their various passages through life? One answer to these questions is that the shift in the empire from Isis devotion to veneration of Jesus as Savior was only gradual and that multiple loyalties to various savior gods including Isis, along with accompanying syncretistic religious practices, persisted for centuries.[43] Some might even say that veneration of Isis as savior leaves

---

39. The Hebrew root is ישע, rendered σωτήρ in the LXX.

40. See also Neh 9:27.

41. For primary references on each of these uses of σωτήρ, see Werner Foerster, σωτήρ in *TDNT* 7 (1971), 1004–5.

42. Having originated in Egypt, the cult of Isis became widespread in the Roman Empire by the early first century CE.

43. See Josephine Massyngbaerde Ford, *Redeemer—Friend and Mother: Salvation in Antiquity and in the Gospel of John* (Minneapolis: Fortress, 1997), 45; Gail Paterson Corrington, *Her Image of Salvation: Female Saviors and Formative Christianity*, Gender and the Biblical Tradition (Louisville: Westminster John Knox, 1992), especially chap. 2

its mark in iconography of the Madonna and Child, which imitates the depictions of Isis with her son Horus.

Isis and Horus[44]

Mary with baby Jesus[45]

on Isis. See also Sharon Kelly Heyob, *The Cult of Isis among Women in the Graeco-Roman World*, EPRO 51 (Leiden: Brill, 1975), and C. J. Bleeker, "Isis as Saviour Goddess," in *The Saviour God: Comparative Studies in the Concept of Salvation*, ed. S. G. F. Brandon (Manchester: Manchester University Press, 1963), 1–16. For an excellent treatment of the choices faced by women in Thessalonica, see chap. 3, "Forget Demeter and Isis— Even if Most Women Rely on Them," in Florence Morgan Gillman's commentary on *1 Thessalonians*, WCS 52 (Collegeville, MN: Liturgical Press, 2016), 57–68.

44. https://commons.wikimedia.org/wiki/File:Isis_and_Horus_MET_45.4.4_002.jpg.
45. https://commons.wikimedia.org/wiki/File:Maestro_del_codice_di_san_giorgio, _madonna_col_bambino_su_un_trono,_1320-30_ca..JPG.

Anointed One (2:11)

Christos (χριστός, "Christ"), rendered in 2:11 as "Messiah" in the NRSV, means "anointed one" and is the Greek translation of the Hebrew משׁיח (*māšîaḥ*). In the Old Testament, משׁיח was used of anointed agents of God for service to and protection of Israel, such as kings (Saul, 1 Sam 10:1; David, 1 Sam 16:13) and priests (Aaron and his sons, Exod 29:21).[46] Though the word *christos* is not employed, many recognize in the anointing of Jesus on the head by an anonymous woman (Mark 14:3 // Matt 26:7) a gesture similar to Samuel's anointing of Saul and David (1 Sam 10:1; 16:13). Through this gesture, which both echoes these actions by prophets on behalf of kings and prepares Jesus for his burial (Mark 14:8), the nameless woman communicates symbolically one of Mark's most important but paradoxical messages: Jesus is both a king and one who will be crucified. Other stories of women and anointing (though with ἀλείφω rather than *christos* terms) place them in more traditional and/or subservient roles. In Mark's Gospel, Mary Magdalene, Mary the mother of James, and Salome go to the tomb of Jesus so that they might anoint him (16:1).[47] In Luke and John, a woman anoints Jesus's feet (Luke 7:36-50; John 12:1-8). While there are these few instances of women performing anointing, none is the recipient of an anointing.[48]

Can a Male Savior Save Women?

"Can a male savior save women?" This is Rosemary Radford Ruether's provocative question in her influential book *Sexism and God-Talk*.[49] It is a question that ultimately challenges the significance of Jesus's maleness for the Christian understanding of the doctrine of the incarnation and for Christian soteriology. If Jesus's maleness is indeed significant, then Gregory Nazianzen's famous dictum against Apollinarius would exclude women from being fully and truly saved: "What has not been assumed has not been healed."[50]

---

46. See Fitzmyer, *The Gospel According to Luke I–IX*, 197–200, for a fuller treatment on the meaning of "Christ" in Luke and the development of the title into a second name for Jesus.

47. This Markan detail conflicts with the story he has already told of the body already prepared for burial by the woman who anoints Jesus in 14:3-9.

48. See excursus and illustrations at 23:26 on representations of crucified women as *Christa*.

49. Rosemary Radford Ruether, *Sexism and God-Talk: Toward a Feminist Theology* (Boston: Beacon, 1983), 116–38.

50. Gregory Nazianzen, Letter 101, "To Cledonius the Priest against Apollinarius," in ed. Philip Schaff and Henry Wace, *A Select Library of Nicene and Post-Nicene Fathers,*

Closer study reveals that Jesus's maleness is not the crucial factor in God's taking on human flesh and revealing the divine in Jesus's life, ministry, death, and resurrection. Early texts, creeds, and baptismal formulas profess that in Jesus God has become "a human being" (*anthrōpos, homo*) or has become "flesh" (*sarx, caro*). Never do these texts speak of incarnation as God becoming a male human being (*anēr, vir*). The Prologue of John's Gospel, for example, proclaims that "The Word became *flesh* [*sarx*]" (John 1:14). The Nicene and the Apostles' Creeds affirm that Jesus became "incarnate" as a "human being." Thus, it is the humanness of Jesus that is revelatory and salvific, not his male sex or gender.[51]

Recent theology that takes seriously cosmic and biological evolution—a development that has been endorsed by many feminist theologians—has uncovered another aspect of the witness of the Christian tradition in reference to the incarnation. In becoming a human being of *flesh*, Jesus reveals God as connected with the *whole* of creation. In Jesus, in other words, God saves *creation*, not just people. Jesus is like us in all things except sin (see Heb 4:15), but "the atoms comprising his body were once part of other creatures . . . kin to the flowers, fish, frogs, finches, foxes, the whole community of life that descended from common ancestors in the ancient seas."[52] And those atoms, like everything else in the universe, are made of stardust.[53] God saves us in Jesus through the power of the Holy Spirit by God's solidarity with all that is.

Finally, God's saving action cannot be "encapsulated 'once-for-all' in the historical Jesus."[54] Jesus of Nazareth, raised from the dead, is now the Christ and so is beyond sex and gender. Jesus the Christ continues to save through the women and men of the church, who are his body in the world and who share and prolong his mission (see, e.g., 1 Cor 12:12-31; Gal 2:19-21; 3:27). As Ruether writes: "Christic personhood continues in our sisters and

---

vol. 7 (Grand Rapids: Eerdmans, 1955), 440, col. 2. Apollinaris of Laodicea taught that Jesus had a fully human body but a divine mind and so was not fully like human beings—Christ had not assumed full humanity. Apollinaris was condemned by the First Council of Constantinople in 381. Gregory's dictum evoked Athanasius of Alexandria's insistence that if Jesus was not fully God, then human beings have not been fully redeemed. See Walter Kasper, *The God of Jesus Christ* (New York: Crossroad, 1984), 183.

51. See e.g. Heinrich Denzinger's *Enchiridion symbolorum: definitionum et declarationum de rebus fidei et morum*, 34th ed. (Barcinone: Herder, 1965), 40–44, 125, 150.

52. Johnson, *Creation and the Cross*, 185–86.

53. See Denis Edwards, *Breath of Life: A Theology of the Creator Spirit* (Maryknoll, NY: Orbis Books, 2004), 13–15.

54. Ruether, *Sexism and God-Talk*, 138.

brothers. . . . We can encounter Christ *in the form of our sister.* Christ, the liberated humanity, is not confined to a static perfection of one person two thousand years ago. Rather, redemptive humanity goes ahead of us, calling us to yet incompleted dimensions of human liberation."[55]

Stephen B. Bevans, SVD

Earth and Highest Heaven (2:14)

The image of the universe reflected in Luke 2:14 locates God's abode in the heights of heaven (see Job 16:19; Ps 148:1; Sir 26:16; 43:9), above the heavens where the angels dwell; below is a flat earth, where humans and creatures dwell, and below that is the underworld, the abode of the dead. In this cosmology, God and angels descend to Earth to communicate with human beings and then go back up (Luke 2:15). Today we know that the universe is incomprehensively large and vastly different from the biblical view. "Extrapolating from a series of observations made by the Hubble telescope . . . scientists figure there are at least 100 billion galaxies, each

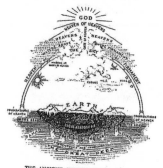

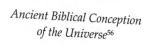

Ancient Biblical Conception of the Universe[56]

Photo of the cosmos from the Hubble telescope[57]

55. Ibid., 138. Recent critiques of the binary male-female necessarily expand Ruether's construction.

56. https://commons.wikimedia.org/wiki/File:The_ancient_Hebrew_conception _of_the_Universe.JPG.

57. https://en.wikipedia.org/wiki/NGC_6503#/media/File:NGC_6503_(2015-06-10).jpg.

comprised of billions of stars, and no one knows how many moons and planets, all of this visible and audible matter being only a fraction of the matter and energy in the universe. Earth is a medium-sized planet orbiting a medium-sized star toward the edge of one spiral galaxy."[58] With this conception of the cosmos, it is no longer possible to consider heaven as up in the sky.

In the angels' message, Earth and highest heaven stand in parallelism, not in opposition; the divine radiance and peace extend to every sphere.

Making Known and Pondering Within (2:17, 19)

After the angels depart, the shepherds decide to go to Bethlehem to see for themselves what has taken place. Seeing, a prominent theme in the gospel, is both physical sight (4:18; 7:21; 18:35) and a metaphor for understanding that leads to belief in Jesus (e.g., 7:20-23). After seeing Mary, Joseph, and the child, the shepherds make known what had been told them about the child (v. 17) and glorify and praise God for all they had heard and seen (v. 20). Luke does not say to whom they made known what they had seen and heard, only that it evoked amazement from all (v. 18), a frequent reaction to Jesus's words and deeds in Luke.

While the shepherds spread the word outward, Mary holds all these happenings within and ponders their meaning (2:19). The word συνετήρει, rendered "treasured" in the NRSV, means more than simply storing something away. It has the nuance "to preserve against harm or ruin, to protect, defend" and "to keep in mind, be concerned about."[59] Mary's action is not in the least passive.[60] Like the shepherds who keep watch

---

58. Elizabeth A. Johnson, *Ask the Beasts: Darwin and the God of Love* (London: Bloomsbury, 2014), 113.

59. BDAG, 975. Beverly Roberts Gaventa notes that it has the nuance of worrying. This is the word that appears in the LXX of Gen 37:11 when Jacob worries about Joseph's troublesome dreams and in Dan 7:28 when Daniel frets over the meaning of an apocalyptic vision ("'All Generations Will Call Me Blessed': Mary in Biblical and Ecumenical Perspective," in *A Feminist Companion to Mariology*, ed. Amy-Jill Levine with Maria Mayo Robbins [Cleveland: Pilgrim Press, 2005], 127).

60. Anne F. Elvey, *An Ecological Feminist Reading of the Gospel of Luke: A Gestational Paradigm* (Lewiston, NY: Edwin Mellen, 2005), 137. This is contrary to the way Jane Schaberg and Sharon Ringe see Mary in Luke 2 rendered as "model listener (2:19), a dependent contemplative heroine (2:33-35, 51), who never initiates any action. . . . what Luke considers a woman's perfect response to the word of God: obedient trust and self-sacrifice" (Jane D. Schaberg and Sharon H. Ringe, "Gospel of Luke," in *Women's Bible Commentary*, ed. Carol A. Newsom, Sharon H. Ringe, and Jacqueline E. Lapsley, 3rd ed. [Louisville: Westminster John Knox, 2012], 504).

(φυλάσσοντες, 2:8),[61] Mary guards all that has occurred,[62] putting things together, connecting, and interpreting.[63] Like a feminist theologian, she continually interprets what God is doing in her life and that of her family and her people.[64]

Bonnie J. Miller-McLemore offers valuable observations about Mary's pondering in 2:19 and 2:51 as involving three aspects of mothering: attention, anguish, and amazement. Pondering first involves focusing one's attention, "which requires a kind of patient, anticipatory 'waiting upon truth,' a holding openness."[65] Mary attends both to what God is doing in the messiness of her life and to what her child experiences, with an attitude of holding and keeping rather than acquiring or possessing her child's life. A second aspect of maternal pondering involves anguish. "Mothering involves loss. It demands a constant giving up and letting go."[66] In the case of Mary, this anguish is all the more profound due to the mission of her son. Between the two references to Mary's pondering (2:19, 51), Luke places Simeon's oracle about Mary's anguish (2:34-35). Traditional interpretations of Mary as "the perfect example of self-sacrificial

---

61. Elvey (*An Ecological Feminist Reading of the Gospel of Luke*, 126) notes that the combination φυλάσσω φυλακάς, which occurs only here in the New Testament, is also found in the LXX of Num 1:53; 3:7; 8:26; 18:4-5 in the context of Levitical responsibility for the tent of meeting, where the expression "refers to both the guarding of the tent and the performance of liturgical duties as an act of keeping. The Lukan use of φυλάσσω . . . φυλακὰς to describe the activity of the shepherds allows a reading which re-inscribes as sacred space, or tent of meeting, the countryside near Bethlehem, where the shepherds will soon encounter a divine messenger (2:9)."

62. The phrase τὰ ῥήματα ταῦτα, "these words," includes more than what was said; ῥῆμα also signifies an event that can be spoken about, as in 2:15 (BDAG, 905).

63. The verb συμβάλλουσα, "pondered," is a compound verb from συν, "with," and βάλλω, "to throw, put," so that it means putting things together, connecting, and interpreting. In the NT, it occurs only in Luke and Acts, where it also means "to discuss or debate" and "to meet" (Luke 14:31; Acts 4:15; 17:18; 18:27; 20:14). See Elvey, *An Ecological Feminist Reading of the Gospel of Luke*, 133; F. Scott Spencer, *Salty Wives, Spirited Mothers, and Savvy Widows: Capable Women of Purpose and Persistence in Luke's Gospel* (Grand Rapids: Eerdmans, 2012), 83–88.

64. The verbs συνετήρει ("treasured," 2:19) and διελογίζετο ("pondered," 1:29) are in the imperfect tense, meaning that these are habitual, ongoing actions. At 2:51, Luke repeats that Mary "treasured all these things [διετήρει πάντα τὰ ῥήματα ταῦτα] in her heart."

65. Bonnie J. Miller-McLemore, " 'Pondering All These Things': Mary and Motherhood," in *Blessed One: Protestant Perspectives on Mary*, ed. Beverly Roberts Gaventa and Cynthia L. Rigby (Louisville: Westminster John Knox, 2002), 97–114, here 107.

66. Ibid., 108.

love conceal her real distress."[67] Finally, maternal pondering also contains a certain amount of awe—sheer amazement at the miracle of birth and the way one's child develops. The amazement of all those who heard about her son from the shepherds (2:18) and of those who hear him in the temple (2:47) feeds into Mary's own amazed ponderings (2:19, 51).

Mary's keeping of these words/things anticipates the Galilean women at the empty tomb, who are told by the angelic figures to remember what Jesus had told them and they "remembered his words [ἐμνήσθησαν τῶν ῥημάτων αὐτοῦ]" (24:8). The whole of the Lukan narrative is framed by women who keep the word, pondering, remembering, connecting, interpreting, and announcing it.

Male and Female Prophets in the Temple (Luke 2:21-40)

Mary and Joseph, like Elizabeth and Zechariah (1:6), are observant Jews who circumcise their son on the eighth day after his birth (Lev 12:3); they also follow Gabriel's instruction (1:31) to name him Jesus. Ἰησοῦς is a Greek form of the Hebrew name יהושע, Joshua, "YHWH is salvation."[68] Mary and Joseph travel to Jerusalem to present Jesus in the temple to the Lord. The reference to *their* purification is puzzling, since according to Leviticus 12:2-6, only the mother incurs ritual impurity in giving birth. Ritual purification is not a matter of cleansing from sin. Amy-Jill Levine explains:

> Impurity, which is not to be confused with sin, was a daily factor in Jewish life: one is impure because of menstruation or ejaculation, childbirth, or burial of a corpse. Purity marks matters of life and death. To regain the status of purity, which was needed to enter the Jerusalem Temple, people practiced certain rituals, such as bathing; in some cases, such as being cured from leprosy, sacrifice was also mandated. Attending to purity concerns allows practitioners to sanctify the body as well as to mark all times of either the beginning of life or its cessation.[69]

In Christian tradition, particularly Roman Catholic, Anglican, and Orthodox, a ceremony for the churching of women after childbirth developed that echoes this Jewish purification ritual. The woman would

---

67. Ibid., 109.
68. BDB, 3091. See Fitzmyer, *The Gospel According to Luke I–IX*, 347, for the evolution of the meaning of the name.
69. Levine and Witherington, *The Gospel of Luke*, 64.

Luke 2:21-40

²¹After eight days had passed, it was time to circumcise the child; and he was called Jesus, the name given by the angel before he was conceived in the womb.

²²When the time came for their purification according to the law of Moses, they brought him up to Jerusalem to present him to the Lord ²³(as it is written in the law of the Lord, "Every first-born male shall be designated as holy to the Lord"), ²⁴and they offered a sacrifice according to what is stated in the law of the Lord, "a pair of turtledoves or two young pigeons."

²⁵Now there was a man in Jerusalem whose name was Simeon; this man was righteous and devout, looking forward to the consolation of Israel, and the Holy Spirit rested on him. ²⁶It had been revealed to him by the Holy Spirit that he would not see death before he had seen the Lord's Messiah. ²⁷Guided by the Spirit, Simeon came into the temple; and when the parents brought in the child Jesus, to do for him what was customary under the law, ²⁸Simeon took him in his arms and praised God, saying,

²⁹"Master, now you are dismissing
   your servant in peace,
   according to your word;
³⁰for my eyes have seen your
   salvation,

kneel in the vestibule of the church with a lighted candle, be sprinkled with holy water, and be led by the priest by the edge of his stole into the church. She would then kneel before the altar and receive a blessing. The focus of the prayer is thanksgiving to God for delivering the mother from the perils of childbirth and ongoing divine protection of both the mother and child.[70] Few Christians observe this ritual today. One of Barbara's students remembers participating in it after the birth of her first child. She found it very disturbing, feeling that it implied there was something "dirty" about childbirth, from which she needed to be cleansed. The gesture of leading her into church holding the edge of the priest's stole was insulting to her, as if she were a tethered animal. Finally, since she and her husband shared in every moment of the birthing process, it was unsettling that the prayers were directed only to her.

Contemporary Christian feminists have created rituals for welcoming and blessing that emphasize joy at the creation of new life, hopes for the

70. See http://www.newadvent.org/cathen/03761a.htm for a description of the traditional Catholic ritual; http://anglicanhistory.org/liturgy/old_catholic_ritual /churching.html for the Anglican ritual; see https://orthodoxdeaconess.org/wp -content/uploads/2016/03/Churching-Part-I.pdf on the Orthodox ritual. Other Christian denominations did not have such a practice.

[31]which you have prepared
in the presence of all
peoples,
[32]a light for revelation to the
Gentiles
and for glory to your people
Israel."
[33]And the child's father and mother were amazed at what was being said about him. [34]Then Simeon blessed them and said to his mother Mary, "This child is destined for the falling and the rising of many in Israel, and to be a sign that will be opposed [35]so that the inner thoughts of many will be revealed—and a sword will pierce your own soul too."
[36]There was also a prophet, Anna the daughter of Phanuel, of the tribe of Asher. She was of a great age, having lived with her husband seven years after her marriage, [37]then as a widow to the age of eighty-four. She never left the temple but worshiped there with fasting and prayer night and day. [38]At that moment she came, and began to praise God and to speak about the child to all who were looking for the redemption of Jerusalem.

[39]When they had finished everything required by the law of the Lord, they returned to Galilee, to their own town of Nazareth. [40]The child grew and became strong, filled with wisdom; and the favor of God was upon him.

child's future, remembrance of the ancestors, and blessing of both parents. For some Christian feminists, these rituals are more meaningful than traditional rites of baptism, which stress the sin that needs to be removed from the infant and which ignore the role of the mother in the child's birth.[71]

Jewish feminists have likewise created new rituals, including *brit banot* ("covenant of the daughters") or *simḥat bat* ("celebration of a daughter") to parallel the circumcising of male infants. What began experimentally in Reform communities in the early 1970s is now widely practiced. While there are many variations, typically there is an introductory greeting and blessing and then a washing ritual. Then follows the naming of the daughter and prayers of benediction. The ritual ordinarily concludes with a celebratory meal.[72]

In addition to the purification ritual, Mary and Joseph bring Jesus to Jerusalem to present him to the Lord. This gesture imitates Hannah's

71. See, e.g., Diann L. Neu, *Women's Rites: Feminist Liturgies for Life's Journey* (Cleveland: Pilgrim Press, 2003), 89–98. See further comments at 3:21.
72. See Ramon Einat, "Ritual: A Feminist Approach," *Jewish Women: A Comprehensive Historical Encyclopedia*, March 1, 2009, Jewish Women's Archive, https://jwa.org/encyclopedia/article/ritual-feminist-approach; "Brit Banot" in Jewish Lifecycle, http://jewishwebsight.com/lifecycle/brit.html.

bringing Samuel to the temple after promising him to God (1 Sam 1:22-24). Before Hannah conceived Samuel, she had vowed to God while praying in the temple that, were she given a son, she would dedicate him as a Nazirite until the day of his death (1 Sam 1:11). After weaning the child, she fulfills this promise by entrusting Samuel to Eli, the priest, and saying, "as long as he lives, he is given to the LORD" (1 Sam 1:28). The allusion to Hannah and Samuel suggests that Mary also gives Jesus over to God's work, something he will claim as an adolescent in the next scene (2:49). Unlike Hannah who makes the vow and gives over her son to Eli, Mary will struggle to understand why Jesus remains in the temple (Luke 2:50).

Gender Pairs (2:25-38)

In the temple, Mary and Joseph encounter two prophets, Simeon and Anna. Luke has many pairs of similar characters, one female and one male, including the following:[73]

Zechariah	Mary	Luke 1:11-20/26-38, 46-55/67-79
Simeon	Anna	Luke 2:25-35/36-38
Naaman	Widow in Zarephath	Luke 4:27/25-26
Jairus's daughter	Widow's son	Luke 8:40-56/7:11-17
Jairus	Woman with the issue of blood	Luke 8:40-41, 49-56/43-38
Men of Nineveh	Queen of the South	Luke 11:32/31
Man healed on sabbath	Woman healed on sabbath	Luke 14:1-6/ 13:10-17
Abraham's son	Abraham's daughter	Luke 19:9/13:16
Man sowed seed	Woman hid yeast	Luke 13:18-19/20-21
Sheep owner with sheep	Woman with coins	Luke 15:3-7/8-10
Men sleeping	Women milling	Luke 17:34/35
Peter at tomb	Women at tomb	Luke 24:12/1-11
Aeneas	Tabitha	Acts 9:32-35/36-42

73. This list is based on that of Turid Karlsen Seim, *The Double Message: Patterns of Gender in Luke–Acts* (Nashville: Abingdon, 1994), 15.

Some scholars see these pairs as pointing to "both the inclusiveness of the Christian Gospel and the spiritual equality of men and women in the Christian community."[74] We, however, see that these pairs distinguish women from men in a way that distances and segregates them and, in some instances, affirms stereotypical gender roles. As will become evident as we progress through the narrative, Luke "conveys a picture of a world divided by gender, of a culture and a mediation of tradition in which men and women, within the same community, nevertheless keep each to their own sphere of life."[75]

There are many parallels between Simeon and Anna: both are devout (2:25, 37), watching in expectation for the consolation (v. 25), salvation (v. 30), and redemption (v. 38) of their people. They embody those who hold traditional Jewish messianic hopes, including: "the return of Jews in exile to the land of Israel; the end of death, poverty, disease, and despair; a general resurrection of the dead; a final judgment; and the eternity of the messianic age."[76] Several Lukan episodes concretize the way that Jesus will fulfill these kinds of hopes for women: Simon's mother-in-law (4:38-39), a woman with hemorrhages (8:43-48), and a woman bent double for eighteen years (Luke 13:10-17) are healed of their infirmities; Jairus's daughter is raised from the dead (8:40-42, 49-56); a widow in Nain receives back her dead son alive (7:11-17); scribes who would take advantage of widows are condemned (21:1-4).

Both Simeon and Anna now see the "salvation" for which they longed (2:30, 38), a detail suggesting that here Luke identifies salvation with recognizing Jesus as Messiah rather than with an empirical change of circumstance. They both are said to praise God (2:28, 38) and speak out about the

74. Andrés García Serrano, "Anna's Characterization in Luke 2:36-38: A Case of Conceptual Allusion?," *CBQ* 76 (2014): 464–80. See also Jane Kopas, "Jesus and Women: Luke's Gospel," *ThTo* 43 (1986): 192. For García Serrano the dividing lines of gender, race, class, and age disappear with the advent of the Messiah (475 n. 50).

75. Seim, *Double Message*, 24. See Veronica Koperski, "Is 'Luke' a Feminist or Not? Female-Male Parallels in Luke–Acts," in *Luke and His Readers: Festschrift A. Denaux*, ed. Reimund Bieringer, Gilbert van Belle, and Joseph Verheyden, BETL 182 (Leuven: Leuven University Press, 2005), 25–48, for a detailed evaluation of various scholarly positions on Lukan gender pairs. See Sara Parks, *Gender in the Rhetoric of Jesus: Women in Q* (Lanham, MD: Fortress Academic, 2019), who argues that sayings in Q in gender pairs were an innovation of Jesus, unprecedented in Jewish or Hellenistic literature. She concludes that they function to convey the same message to women and men, thus pointing to intellectual and religious equality, but not social equality. Gendered social expectations were not disrupted.

76. Levine and Witherington, *The Gospel of Luke*, 65.

child (2:29-32, 38), but Luke conveys the content only of Simeon's speech. Like Mary, Simeon declares himself the Master's slave (δοῦλος, "servant" in NRSV),[77] who is now being freed (ἀπολύεις, literally "you are freeing," rendered in NRSV: "you are dismissing"). This declaration of liberation creates a frame with verse 38, where Anna is said to speak about the child to all who were looking for the redemption of Jerusalem. Again, though the word for redemption is λύτρωσιν, a noun used for the buying back of the freedom of slaves, no explanation of the content of redemption is given. In view of the ubiquity of parables involving slaves in Luke, whatever redemption Anna has seen does not involve literal freeing of slaves.[78]

Simeon and Anna, like Moses before them (Exod 33:11), come face to face with the divine. Simeon says, "my eyes have seen your salvation" (2:30), and Anna is the daughter of Phanuel, a name meaning "face of God," a variation of Peniel, the place where Jacob saw God face to face (Gen 32:30). Both Simeon and Anna have been awaiting the salvation of Israel (2:32, 38), but Simeon, expressing Jewish hopes, widens the radius of the saving revelation to the Gentiles (2:31-32). Such universalism, a strong theme in Luke, builds on the kind of hope expressed in texts such as Zechariah 14:9, that all nations would worship the one God.[79]

While verses 29-32 of Simeon's speech are addressed to God, the last part is directed to Mary (vv. 34-35). Verse 34 ("This child is destined for the falling and the rising of many in Israel") anticipates the split between Jews who follow Jesus and Jews who do not. The verse not only predicts a schism but also holds the more ominous message that those who do not accept the child will "fall." In relation to the destruction of Jerusalem (see commentary on Luke 19:41-44; 21:20-24; and 23:27-33 and below),

---

77. See comments above at 1:48 on the slave-master metaphor.

78. See Excursus on the Moral Problem of Slavery in Luke at 17:7-10. See Luke 24:21, where Cleopas and his companion say to the not yet recognized risen Christ, "we had hoped that he was the one to redeem [λυτροῦσθαι] Israel" (cf. Acts 1:6). The dashing of hopes in this verse that Jesus's ministry involves political redemption is a key passage for those who argue that Luke is an apologist for Christians to Rome. See the classic work of Hans Conzelmann, *The Theology of St. Luke* (New York: Harper, 1960), and, more recently, Seyoon Kim, *Christ and Caesar: The Gospel and the Roman Empire in the Writings of Paul and Luke* (Grand Rapids: Eerdmans, 2008).

79. Levine and Witherington, *The Gospel of Luke*, 66. See Malka Zeiger Simkovich, *The Making of Jewish Universalism: From Exile to Alexandria* (Lanham, MD: Lexington Books, 2017); "The Origins of Jewish Universalism: What It Is and Why It Matters," *The Lehrhaus*, October 6, 2016, https://www.thelehrhaus.com/scholarship/the-origins -of-jewish-universalism-what-it-is-and-why-it-matters/.

Rome's destruction of the city is caused by Jerusalem's rejection of Jesus. Simeon's final words to Mary, "and a sword will pierce your own soul too" (2:35), indicate that Mary is not exempt from needing to choose whether or not to accept the mission of her son.[80] The next time Mary appears in the gospel (8:19-21), Luke implies she is among those who hear the word of God as Jesus proclaims it and act on it.

At the completion of Simeon's speech, Luke turns to the prophet Anna. Her name and her prayer again recollect Hannah, the mother of Samuel (1 Sam 1). Anna is the only woman the New Testament calls προφῆτις, "prophet," aside from a "woman Jezebel, who calls herself a prophet" (Rev 2:20). The verb προφητεύω is used of Philip's "four unmarried daughters who had the gift of prophecy [προφητεύουσαι, literally 'who prophesied']" (Acts 21:9), but, like Anna, Luke does not preserve their words.[81] As we have shown in our commentary on chapter 1, both Elizabeth and Mary are depicted in ways that align them with prophets. But Luke does not use the term προφῆτις to describe them.[82] The only other prophets in Luke's Gospel are Zechariah (1:67), John the Baptist (1:76; 3:2; 7:26; 20:6), and Jesus, who is depicted as prophet more strongly in this gospel than in any other.[83]

Anna has impeccable credentials. She has passed through the first two and is now in the third of the traditional three stages of a woman's life: virgin, wife,[84] and wise elder woman. The RSV (1971) makes these three stages more evident with its literal translation of verse 36: ζήσασα μετὰ ἀνδρὸς ἔτη ἑπτὰ ἀπὸ τῆς παρθενίας αὐτῆς, "having lived with her husband seven years from her virginity." Anna's constant worshiping, fasting, and praying mirror the many times Luke portrays Jesus

---

80. Verse 35 is not talking about the pain that Mary would experience at seeing her son crucified; only in John's Gospel is Jesus's mother said to be at the foot of the cross (19:25-27). There is also a contrast in v. 35 between "the inner thoughts of many will be revealed" and Mary's keeping everything in her heart (2:19, 51).

81. There are also women who prophesy in the Corinthian assembly (1 Cor 11:2-16).

82. See comments above on 1:26-38.

83. See commentary on 4:18 on the Lukan portrayal of Jesus as prophet. In the Pentecost scene in Acts, Peter, using the words of the prophet Joel (3:1-5), pronounces that God will pour out the Spirit "upon all flesh, and your sons and your daughters shall prophesy" (2:17). But the Acts narrative does not include depictions of daughters prophesying. A female slave prophesies at 16:16 but she is a prophet of Pythia. For a reading of this Pentecost prophecy against the grain, see Matthews, *The Acts of the Apostles*, 73–91.

84. Luke does not say whether Anna was a mother.

praying and fasting.[85] This persistent vigilance prepares her to discern the moment that God's liberating action breaks forth in the gift of the awaited child.

TRANSLATION MATTERS

The phrase ἕως ἐτῶν ὀγδοήκοντα τεσσάρων in 2:37 can mean either that Anna's age is eighty-four (so NRSV) or that she has been a widow for eighty-four years. A symbolic meaning is that Anna's age signals perfection, completeness. In the Bible, seven is a number for fullness (e.g., seven days of creation, Gen 2:2; the necessity to forgive seven times a day, Luke 17:4) as is twelve (e.g., twelve tribes of Israel, twelve apostles). Anna lived a full married life (seven years) and an even more perfect widowhood (seven times twelve years).[86] Anna the aged widow is an exemplary figure whose words are to be taken to heart.

Ministering Widows

Anna is the first of many widows to appear in Luke's two volumes. Luke has more episodes that feature widows than any other evangelist, many of them unique to this gospel, including the widow of Zarephath (4:25-26), the widow at Nain (7:11-17), and the parable of the widow and the judge (18:1-8). Shared with Mark are the warnings about exploiting widows (Luke 20:47; Mark 12:40) and the widow who gives her whole life to the temple (Luke 21:1-4; Mark 12:41-44). Acts recounts an episode involving the widows of the Hellenists (6:1-6) and another where widows are present at the death of Dorcas (9:36-43). Although their marital status is not identified, it is possible that some of the Galilean women who follow Jesus in Luke 8:1-3

85. Luke 3:21; 5:16; 6:12; 9:18, 28-29; 10:21-23; 22:32, 39-46; 23:46. Jesus's disciples will also be in constant prayer and fasting: Acts 2:42, 46; 3:1; 24:53. Though fasting is a sign of true piety in Luke's narrative, we recognize that within Christian history fasting has taken on complex meaning for women and can sometimes be linked to eating disorders. See, for instance, Carolyn Walker Bynum, *Holy Feast and Holy Fast: The Religious Significance of Food to Medieval Women* (Berkeley: University of California Press, 1988); Lisa Isherwood, *The Fat Jesus: Feminist Explorations in Boundaries and Transgressions* (London: Darton, Longman and Todd, 2007).

86. See Bonnie Bowman Thurston, "Who Was Anna? Luke 2:36-38," *PRSt* 28 (2001): 47–55, here 49–50, who shows that remaining unmarried after being widowed was considered virtuous.

are widows, as well as Tabitha/ Dorcas (Acts 9:36-43), Mary (Acts 12:12), and Lydia (Acts 16:11-15).

Luke's widows are often seen to be part of his emphasis on care for those who are poor and vulnerable.[87] But most episodes featuring widows in Luke and Acts show them as ministering to the community, like Anna, not as destitute recipients of charity. Luke's widows are prototypes of what would develop into a clerical order of consecrated widows whose ministries included praying, fasting, visiting and laying hands on the sick, making clothes, and doing other good works.[88] The many widows in the Gospel and Acts may reflect the growing numbers and importance of widows in the ministry of the church of Luke's time.[89]

Anna is not a harmless widow whose pious practices don't disturb anyone. Her worshiping (λατρεύουσα) in the temple has a public character.[90] As a prophet, she watches night and day, keeping hope alive for people who have been waiting long years with expectation. She kept thanking God and kept speaking (the verbs ἀνθωμολογεῖτο and ἐλάλει in v. 38 are in the imperfect, connoting repeated past action) to all. Like Mary Magdalene, Joanna, Mary the mother of James, and the other women with them at the tomb who kept telling (ἀπήγγειλαν, also in the imperfect) the good news to the others (24:9), Anna's is not a one-time proclamation. In the early Christian communities, prophets rank with apostles and teachers as esteemed leaders (Eph 4:11-13).[91]

---

87. Brown, *Birth of the Messiah*, 466–67; Thurston, "Who Was Anna?," 48.

88. These are listed in the *Didascalia Apostolorum* (c. 230 CE). See R. Hugh Connolly, ed., *Didascalia Apostolorum* (Oxford: Clarendon, 1929; reprinted 1969), 132–45.

89. See the qualifications and restrictions placed on widows in 1 Tim 5:3-16: only those who are sixty years or more and without children, grandchildren, or other means of support are to be enrolled as "real" widows, eligible for support from the church for their ministry. Linda M. Maloney, "The Pastoral Epistles," in *Searching the Scriptures*, vol. 2: *A Feminist Commentary*, ed. Elisabeth Schüssler Fiorenza with the assistance of Ann Brock and Shelly Matthews (New York: Crossroad, 1994), 373, sees that the strategy of the author of this letter is to marginalize the widows' order and isolate it "from the 'regular' ministries of which he approves, those that correspond to the leadership roles in the Greco-Roman household." See also Annette Bourland Huizenga, *1–2 Timothy, Titus*, WCS 53 (Collegeville, MN: Liturgical Press, 2016), 52–65; Bonnie Bowman Thurston, *The Widows: A Women's Ministry in the Early Church* (Minneapolis: Fortress, 1989).

90. Thurston, "Who Was Anna?," 51–52.

91. Ibid., 50.

Despite acknowledging Anna as a prophetic figure, Luke diminishes her importance by withholding her words. Unlike Mary, Zechariah, and Simeon, whose canticles have become part of the daily liturgical prayer of Christians, Anna's words are lost. Nor does Luke tell of any reaction to her message, in contrast to the declaration of Simeon, which causes amazement (2:33; see also 1:63; 2:18). Even so, a number of women writers in the early nineteenth century found in Anna an example of an evangelizer who provided a basis to justify women's call to preach.[92]

Anna Justifying Women's Call to Preach

Sarah Hale (1788–1879), an editor and writer from Newport, New Hampshire, is most famous as the author of the nursery rhyme "Mary Had a Little Lamb." Hale's most ambitious project was a biographical dictionary of women, beginning with those who appear in the Scriptures. She sees Anna as superior to Simeon in bearing testimony to the Messiah: "The good old Simeon had no clearer revelation than the aged devout Anna. Both were inspired servants of the Most High; but here the characteristic piety of the woman is shown to excel. Simeon dwelt 'in Jerusalem,' probably engaged in secular pursuits; Anna 'departed not from the temple but served God with fasting and prayers night and day.'"[93]

Elizabeth Baxter (1837–1926), an English evangelist, author, traveling teacher and preacher, emphasized Anna's vocation of prayer as preparation for a ministry of proclamation: "Living continually face to face with God, drinking in perpetually the thoughts which he would impart to her . . . there must have been a light upon the countenance of Anna which was a study in itself, for God and heaven shone there." She then stresses Anna's impulse to proclaim came from "the same instinct from on high" that prompted Simeon to prophesy. She concludes with the wish that God "raise up praying Annas in our day."[94]

92. Marion Ann Taylor and Heather E. Weir (*Women in the Story of Jesus: The Gospels Through the Eyes of Nineteenth-Century Female Biblical Interpreters* [Grand Rapids: Eerdmans, 2016], 125–37) give examples of four women and their preaching about Anna.

93. Sarah Hale, *Woman's Record; or, Sketches of All Distinguished Women from the Creation to A.D. 1854* (New York: Harper & Brothers, 1855), 71–72, quoted in Taylor and Weir, *Women in the Story of Jesus*, 127.

94. Elizabeth Baxter, *The Women in the Word: A Few Simple Hints from Bible Portraits of Women*, 2nd ed. (London: Christian Herald, 1897), 203–5, quoted in Taylor and Weir, *Women in the Story of Jesus*, 129–30.

Elizabeth Wilson, an activist for women's rights in Ohio, found in Anna a witness that supported women's public preaching ministry, countering prohibitions of women's speaking such as 1 Corinthians 14:34.[95] One other Anglo-Catholic woman author, known only as M. G., holds up Anna in one of her published sermons (1893) as an example to widows to speak to everyone they can about Jesus.[96]

Mary's Precocious Son (2:41-52)

The infancy narratives conclude with a unique vignette from the life of the adolescent Jesus. Again, Mary and Joseph, faithful Jews, make the annual Passover pilgrimage to Jerusalem. The exchanges between Mary, Jesus, and Joseph in Luke 2:48-50 paint one of the few pictures of the Holy Family in early Christian literature that emphasizes the tension between them as all too human. Consider Mary's exasperated question, "Child, why have you treated us like this?" (v. 48), and the parents' lack of understanding of what their child might mean (v. 50). Fortunately for the parents' sake, the tension is resolved with the reassurance that after this incident Jesus remains obedient to his family (v. 51),[97] but in a sense they have already lost him as he goes about his Father's (God's, not Joseph's) business. The three-day search points forward to Jesus's being raised on the third day (9:22; 18:33; 24:7, 21, 46).

In the temple, all are amazed (ἐξίσταντο) at Jesus's penetrating answers.[98] His parents are likewise astonished (ἐξεπλάγησαν, v. 48), though, in their case, it is more a sense of being dumbfounded from lack of understanding

95. See her book *A Scriptural View of Women's Rights and Duties, in All the Important Relations of Life* (Philadelphia: Wm. S. Young, 1849), 231, 235, 237.

96. See Taylor and Weir, *Women in the Story of Jesus,* 131–37, for excerpts of Wilson, *A Scriptural View of Women's Rights and Duties,* and M. G., *Women Like Ourselves: Short Addresses for Mother's Meetings, Bible Classes, Etc.* (London: SPCK, 1893).

97. On this incident and also on the apocryphal gospels that feature Jesus and his family, see Christopher A. Frilingos, *Jesus, Mary, and Joseph: Family Troubles in the Infancy Gospels,* Divinations: Reading Late Ancient Religion (Philadelphia: University of Pennsylvania Press, 2017).

98. Fitzmyer, *The Gospel According to Luke I–IX,* 442, notes that συνέσει καὶ ἀποκρίσεσιν (lit. "his comprehension and his answers") is a hendiadys (the expression of a single idea by two words connected with "and"), better expressed by "penetrating answers."

Luke 2:41-52

⁴¹Now every year his parents went to Jerusalem for the festival of the Passover. ⁴²And when he was twelve years old, they went up as usual for the festival. ⁴³When the festival was ended and they started to return, the boy Jesus stayed behind in Jerusalem, but his parents did not know it. ⁴⁴Assuming that he was in the group of travelers, they went a day's journey. Then they started to look for him among their relatives and friends. ⁴⁵When they did not find him, they returned to Jerusalem to search for him. ⁴⁶After three days they found him in the temple, sitting among the teachers, listening to them and asking them questions. ⁴⁷And all who heard him were amazed at his understanding and his answers. ⁴⁸When his parents saw him they were astonished; and his mother said to him, "Child, why have you treated us like this? Look, your father and I have been searching for you in great anxiety." ⁴⁹He said to them, "Why were you searching for me? Did you not know that I must be in my Father's house?" ⁵⁰But they did not understand what he said to them. ⁵¹Then he went down with them and came to Nazareth, and was obedient to them. His mother treasured all these things in her heart.

⁵²And Jesus increased in wisdom and in years, and in divine and human favor.

(v. 50). Notices of Jesus's growth in wisdom and divine and human favor (χάρις, 2:40 and 2:52) encase this last scene and echo what is said of John the Baptist (1:80) and of Samuel (1 Sam 2:26). From growing in wisdom (2:52), Jesus will speak of himself as Wisdom incarnate at 7:35.⁹⁹

Luke 1–2: A Refutation of Marcion?

The contents of Luke 1 and 2, unique among the canonical gospels, are distinct even in comparison to the remainder of the Third Gospel. These two chapters have a high concentration of vocabulary not otherwise used in Luke; further, these chapters are closely related to the Septuagint,

99. The theme of Jesus as Wisdom incarnate is stronger in the Gospels of Matthew (8:18-22; 11:16-19, 25-26; 22:1-14) and John (1:1-18; and the I AM sayings), but there is an occasional glimmer of it in Luke. See Celia Deutsch, *Lady Wisdom, Jesus, and the Sages: Metaphor and Social Context in Matthew's Gospel* (Valley Forge, PA: Trinity Press International, 1996); Elaine M. Wainwright, *Shall We Look for Another? A Feminist Reading of the Matthean Jesus*, The Bible and Liberation (Maryknoll, NY: Orbis Books, 1998), 67–83; Martin Scott, *Sophia and the Johannine Jesus*, JSNTSup 71 (Sheffield: JSOT, 1992); Sharon H. Ringe, *Wisdom's Friends: Community and Christology in the Fourth Gospel* (Louisville: Westminster John Knox, 1999); Judith Lieu, "Scripture and the Feminine in John," in *A Feminist Companion to the Hebrew Bible in the New Testament*, ed. Athalya Brenner, FCB 10 (Sheffield: Sheffield Academic, 1996), 225–40.

both in terms of Greek vocabulary and themes (e.g., the importance of priestly service in the temple, infertile women who give birth, circumcision and purity).

These elements can lead to the conclusion that Luke 1–2 stand apart from the rest of the gospel. For example, Joseph Fitzmyer regards Luke 1–2 to have been composed after Luke 3–24: "The Lucan infancy narrative was composed with the hindsight not only of the gospel tradition prior to Luke, but also of the Lucan Gospel proper."[100] It is plausible not only that Luke 1–2 were composed later than the bulk of canonical Luke but also that they were composed for the specific purpose of countering the teachings associated with Marcion, a popular second-century Christian teacher who was later deemed a heretic.[101]

Marcion taught that the "High God" of the New Testament was not the same as the Creator God of the Jewish Scriptures, whom he regarded as lesser a god, associated with the material world rather than the spiritual realm. He argued that the High God who sent Jesus was associated only with love, mercy, and peace, while the Creator God promoted violence and vengeance. He claimed that Jesus and his sole apostle Paul had nothing to do with "Jewish things," such as the temple, the priesthood, the Jewish Scriptures, or even the "Jewish apostles," that is, Peter and the rest of the Twelve.

Further, Marcion associated these Jewish things with the "flesh" while emphasizing the superiority of the spiritual realm from which Jesus descended. He went so far as to argue that Jesus never experienced the indignity of gestation, birth, and infancy but rather had descended from the heavens as an adult, appearing on the earth during the "fifteenth year of the reign of the Emperor Tiberius" (Luke 3:1).[102]

Marcion used only one gospel, one quite similar to what we now know as canonical Luke 3–24. While it was once common to understand Marcion as having possessed canonical Luke, from which he lopped

---

100. Fitzmyer, *The Gospel According to Luke I–IX*, 306.

101. See Joseph B. Tyson, *Marcion and Luke–Acts: A Defining Struggle* (Columbia: University of South Carolina Press, 2006), reviving a theory first introduced by John Knox; Andrew Gregory, *The Reception of Luke and Acts in the Period before Irenaeus*, WUNT 2.169 (Tübingen: Mohr Siebeck, 2003), 173–209; Jason D. BeDuhn, *The First New Testament: Marcion's Scriptural Canon* (Salem, OR: Polebridge, 2013), 78–92; F. F. Bruce, "Some Thoughts on the Beginning of the New Testament Canon," *BJRL* 65 (1983): 37–60, esp. 54.

102. The debate over the fleshly nature of Jesus continues into subsequent centuries. Tertullian is a particularly notable champion of the incarnation, as seen, for example, in his *On the Flesh of Christ*.

off chapters 1 and 2, we see viability in the thesis that Marcion and the author of canonical Luke both had a version of Luke 3–24 and that Luke 1 and 2 were composed later to refute Marcion's teachings.[103]

A plethora of narrative details in these first two chapters do indeed contradict Marcion's teaching. While Marcion insisted that Jesus was not Jewish, the Jewishness of Jesus's advent is emphasized through the Septuagintal features. The centrality of the Jerusalem temple appears in the story of Zechariah (1:5-23), in the travels of the Holy Family (2:41-52), and in Jesus's speaking of the temple as his "Father's" house (v. 49). Further, Luke is the only gospel mentioning the circumcision of Jesus (2:21), a clear signal of his identity as a Jewish male.

Luke also emphasizes physical gestation. The angel Gabriel announces to Mary that "you will conceive *in your womb*" (1:31). The speech recorded in the meeting of Mary and Elizabeth offers references to the womb and the child within the womb (1:41-45). And while the circumcision is a sign of Jesus's Jewishness, performed on the eighth day it signals also his circumcision *as an infant*, a rebuttal to the proposal that Jesus descended to earth as an adult.

Feminist concerns arise in Luke's depictions both of Jewish practice and of Jesus's birth. Marcion's rejection of Judaism, and his assertion of distinct Gods for Christians, on the one hand, and for Jews, on the other, appears as a particularly virulent form of anti-Judaism. It thwarts attempts at rapprochement through focusing on common religious heritage and situating Jesus and Paul fully *within* Judaism.[104] Because "spirit," has typically been valued above "flesh" in Western culture, a move Marcion embraced, and because the female became associated primarily with the lesser-valued flesh, Luke's first two chapters, with their focus on the sexual and the corporeal, reclaim feminist concerns. In contrast to Marcion's denigration of women's reproductive capacity, Luke privileges two pregnant female protagonists, Mary and Elizabeth.

---

103. However, we disagree with those who explain Luke 24 as a refutation of Marcionite thinking. See Shelly Matthews, "Does Dating Luke–Acts into the Second Century Affect the Q Hypothesis?," in *Gospel Interpretation and the Q-Hypothesis*, ed. Mogens Müller and Heike Omerzu, LNTS 573 (London: Bloomsbury T&T Clark, 2018), 243–63.

104. For renewed focus on the Jewishness of the central figures of early Christianity, see, for instance, several of the essays with emphasis on Jewish context within Amy-Jill Levine, Dale C. Allison Jr., and John Dominic Crossan, eds., *The Historical Jesus in Context*, Princeton Readings in Religion (Princeton: Princeton University Press, 2006); Mark D. Nanos and Magnus Zetterhom, eds., *Paul within Judaism: Restoring the First-Century Context to the Apostle* (Minneapolis: Fortress, 2015). For evaluation of the various forms of anti-Judaism in Marcion, Luke, and orthodox Christianity, see Matthews, *Perfect Martyr*, 36.

Luke 3:1-38

Beloved Son of God and All God's Children

The Voice of One Crying in the Wilderness (3:1-20)

Following two chapters in which Mary, Elizabeth, Zechariah, Simeon, and Anna speak prophetically, one more formidable prophet paves the way for the one who is more powerful still. Elizabeth disappears as Luke introduces John as the son of Zechariah (3:2). Male lineage continues as John speaks of "father" Abraham and his children (3:8) and as the genealogy lists only male ancestors of Jesus (3:23-38).

The list of Roman rulers and high priests in 3:1-2 underscores the danger of prophetic ministry. Herod (Antipas), the son of Herod the Great mentioned at 1:5, appears again as the employer (or perhaps owner, since Chuza may be a slave) of Joanna's husband (8:3); in 9:7-8 Antipas, after beheading John, is dangerously curious about Jesus; later, Antipas apparently wants to kill Jesus (13:31). In 23:6-12, Pilate sends Jesus to Antipas, the tetrarch who interrogates and mocks Jesus before returning him to Pilate, who then hands Jesus over to be crucified (23:13-25). In 13:1, Luke notes Pilate's own brutality in a reference to the Galilean blood he spilt. Although Luke's passion narrative does not mention the high priests Annas and Caiaphas (3:2) by name (contrast John 18:13, 14,

Luke 3:1-20

3:1In the fifteenth year of the reign of Emperor Tiberius, when Pontius Pilate was governor of Judea, and Herod was ruler of Galilee, and his brother Philip ruler of the region of Ituraea and Trachonitis, and Lysanias ruler of Abilene, 2during the high priesthood of Annas and Caiaphas, the word of God came to John son of Zechariah in the wilderness. 3He went into all the region around the Jordan, proclaiming a baptism of repentance for the forgiveness of sins, 4as it is written in the book of the words of the prophet Isaiah,

"The voice of one crying out in the wilderness:

'Prepare the way of the Lord,
	make his paths straight.
5Every valley shall be filled,
	and every mountain and hill
		shall be made low,

and the crooked shall be made straight,
	and the rough ways made smooth;
6and all flesh shall see the salvation of God.'"

7John said to the crowds that came out to be baptized by him, "You brood of vipers! Who warned you to flee from the wrath to come? 8Bear fruits worthy of repentance. Do not begin to say to yourselves, 'We have Abraham as our ancestor'; for I tell you, God is able from these stones to raise up children to Abraham. 9Even now the ax is lying at the root of the trees; every tree therefore that does not bear good fruit is cut down and thrown into the fire."

10And the crowds asked him, "What then should we do?" 11In reply he said to them, "Whoever has two coats must

24, 28), Jesus is taken to the high priest's house immediately after his arrest (22:54). In Acts 4:6, Annas and Caiaphas are named among those of the high priestly family, rulers, elders, and scribes who interrogate Peter and John.

By framing John's proclamation with the list of rulers (3:1-2) and the notice of his confrontations with Herod and his imprisonment (3:19-20), Luke anticipates Jesus's own deathly encounters with political figures. Unlike Mark (6:14-29) and Matthew (14:1-12), Luke does not recount the fuller story of John's confrontation with Herod over Herodias and his subsequent beheading at the request of Herodias's daughter at her mother's instigation. In Luke, there is merely the statement made by Herod at 9:9 that he has beheaded John. Luke's omission of the grizzly details surrounding John's death masks the fact that women can be as murderous as men; but depicting women this way does not fit Luke's idealized portraits of women (see further comments in the authors' introduction on Luke and women).

share with anyone who has none; and whoever has food must do likewise." [12]Even tax collectors came to be baptized, and they asked him, "Teacher, what should we do?" [13]He said to them, "Collect no more than the amount prescribed for you." [14]Soldiers also asked him, "And we, what should we do?" He said to them, "Do not extort money from anyone by threats or false accusation, and be satisfied with your wages."

[15]As the people were filled with expectation, and all were questioning in their hearts concerning John, whether he might be the Messiah, [16]John answered all of them by saying, "I baptize you with water; but one who is more powerful than I is coming; I am not worthy to untie the thong of his sandals. He will baptize you with the Holy Spirit and fire. [17]His winnowing fork is in his hand, to clear his threshing floor and to gather the wheat into his granary; but the chaff he will burn with unquenchable fire."

[18]So, with many other exhortations, he proclaimed the good news to the people. [19]But Herod the ruler, who had been rebuked by him because of Herodias, his brother's wife, and because of all the evil things that Herod had done, [20]added to them all by shutting up John in prison.

Christians whose only access to first-century Jews comes through reading the New Testament might be surprised to learn that John the Baptist was a more popular figure in his own day than Jesus. The Jewish historian Josephus knows John, portrays him as a sympathetic figure concerned with righteousness, justice, and piety, and indicates that Jews regarded his death at Herod's hands as an injustice (*Ant.* 18.116–19).[1] The gospel authors also know that John the Baptist was more significant than Jesus in some quarters, as is clear from the many ways they work to assert the primacy of Jesus over John to an audience that apparently needs this clarification.[2]

1. Josephus says considerably more about John than Jesus, and what is recorded about Jesus in his *Antiquities* is largely the result of later scribal interpolation by Christian apologists. See *Ant.* 118.63–64, and John P. Meier, "Jesus in Josephus: A Modest Proposal," *CBQ* 52 (1990): 76–103.

2. Consider the threefold insistence in the first chapter of the Gospel of John that John the Baptist *is not* the Messiah: "There was a man sent from God, whose name was John. He came as a witness to the light. . . . He himself was not the light" (John 1:6–8); "John testified to him . . . . 'This was he of whom I said, "He who comes after me ranks ahead of me"'" (John 1:15); "[John] confessed and did not deny it, but confessed, 'I am not the Messiah'" (John 1:20).

Luke subordinates John to Jesus in chapter 1, by setting their birth stories side by side and marking Jesus's birth as more miraculous than John's.[3] Here he underscores Jesus's superiority as Mark and Matthew do, by emphasizing that John is merely a forerunner, paving the way for a greater one to come (Luke 3:4, 16; see Mark 1:2-3, 7; Matt 3:3, 11).

As we noted already in the introduction, Luke subjects the characterization of John he finds in his Markan source to a good polishing, in keeping with his purpose of reassuring Theophilus about the respectability of the movement. Gone are the scratchy camelhair garments and the ascetic diet of bugs that might suggest a wild man on the loose (Mark 1:14). Here instead John declaims as a good Old Testament prophet would, calling for repentance, citing the ancient prophet Isaiah at length, and threatening imminent judgment. Further, his origins are not in the wilderness but squarely within the priestly lineage of Zechariah and Anna. With these details Luke sculpts a court prophet, not an unsettling outsider.

John's wilderness location (3:2) recalls the wilderness wandering after the exodus from Egypt, which was a time of both testing (Num 14:1-12) and God's providential care (Exod 15:25; 16:1-36). The starkness of the desert also contrasts with the plush palaces of the Roman rulers[4] and the high priests named in 3:1-2. That he hears the word of God in the wilderness and baptizes in the Jordan are also clues that the message of the historical John the Baptist might have been more politically charged than Luke allows here. "Crossing the Jordan," of course, is the culmination of Israel's long journey from slavery in Egypt into the promised land. If John understood his baptisms in the Jordan to be charged with the political symbolism of exodus and conquest, then he stands in a line of sign-prophets protesting Roman rule mentioned in Josephus. Like them, John evokes exodus imagery, attracts crowds, and subsequently meets death at the hands of a ruler charged with keeping the peace.[5]

---

3. John Dominic Crossan, *Jesus: A Revolutionary Biography* (San Francisco: Harper-SanFrancisco, 1994), 5–10.

4. Herod Antipas, for example, had winter palaces in Jericho and atop Masada, in addition to ones in Machaerus and in Jerusalem.

5. Consider Theudas (*Ant.* 20.97–98; see also Acts 5:36), "the Egyptian" (*Ant.* 20.168–72; see also Acts 21:38), and Richard A. Horsley, "'Like One of the Prophets of Old': Two Types of Popular Prophets at the Time of Jesus," *CBQ* 47 (1985): 435–63.

Josephus on the Prophets of Deliverance

Two of the sign-prophets Josephus depicts in his story of the political agitation in Judea in the decades leading up to the Jewish war with Rome are Theudas and "The Egyptian." Of Theudas, he writes:

> During the period when Fadus was procurator of Judea, a certain magician named Theudas persuaded the majority of the masses to take up their possessions and to follow him to the Jordan River. He stated that he was a prophet and that at his command the river would be parted and would provide them an easy passage. With this talk he deceived many. Fadus, however, did not permit them to reap the fruit of their folly, but sent against them a squadron of cavalry. These fell upon them unexpectedly, slew many of them and took many prisoners. Theudas himself was captured, whereupon they cut off his head and brought it to Jerusalem. (*Ant.* 20:97–98)

Of "The Egyptian," he writes:

> At this time there came to Jerusalem from Egypt a man who declared that he was a prophet and advised the masses of the common people to go out with him to the mountain called the Mount of Olives, which lies opposite the city at a distance of five furlongs. For he asserted that he wished to demonstrate from there that at his command Jerusalem's walls would fall down, through which he promised to provide them an entrance into the city. When Felix heard of this he ordered his soldiers to take up their arms. Setting out from Jerusalem with a large force of cavalry and infantry, he fell upon the Egyptian and his followers, slaying four hundred of them and taking two hundred prisoners. The Egyptian himself escaped from the battle and disappeared. (*Ant.* 20.169–72)

Luke attributes the imprisonment of John to his rebuke of Herod for marrying his brother's wife, as well as to "all the evil things that Herod had done" (v. 19). Because we recognize the parallels between John's behavior and that of the sign-prophets, we regard Josephus's account of John's death as better reflecting Herod's likely motive. Josephus writes that Herod became alarmed because John attracted crowds. Such crowds are dangerous to the powers that be, as he explains:

Eloquence that had so great an effect on humankind might lead to some form of sedition, for it looked as if they would be guided by John in everything that they did. Herod decided therefore that it would be much better to strike first and be rid of him before his work led to an uprising. (*Ant.* 18:118)

Under Roman imperial expectations that their clients keep the peace, anyone who attracted crowds and inspired them as John did would best be killed. Reading Luke's more sanitized version of the ministry and death of John the Baptist against Josephus helps us to see the political contours of the first-century movements of John and of Jesus. As we have noted previously, Luke's overarching concern to reassure Theophilus involves numerous assertions that followers of the way do not challenge political structures. But here we catch a glimpse of an "eloquence" that may have moved some to "sedition."[6]

Children of Abraham (3:7-9)

In 3:7-9 John declares that repentance cannot be only a change of mind but must be visible in deeds: "Bear fruits worthy of repentance" (3:8a).[7] Nor is claiming lineage from Abraham sufficient, since "God is able from these stones to raise up children to Abraham" (3:8b).

The verses likely allude to Isaiah 51:1-2:[8]

> Listen to me, you that pursue righteousness,
>   you that seek the LORD.
> Look to the rock from which you were hewn,
>   and to the quarry from which you were dug.
> Look to Abraham your father
>   and to Sarah who bore you;
> for he was but one when I called him,
>   but I blessed him and made him many.

As Amy-Jill Levine has noted, appealing to Abraham (v. 8) may reflect the notion developed in rabbinic literature (e.g., b. Shabb. 55a) that one

---

6. For an important argument on the danger of stirring up crowds under the Roman imperial system, using both John and Jesus as examples, see Ellis Rivkin, "What Crucified Jesus," in *Jesus's Jewishness: Exploring the Place of Jesus in Early Judaism*, ed. James H. Charlesworth (New York: Crossroad, 1996), 226–57.

7. Similarly, Jesus, schooled by John, will emphasize both hearing and acting on the word, e.g., 6:49; 8:21.

8. Amy-Jill Levine and Ben Witherington III, *The Gospel of Luke*, NCBC (Cambridge: Cambridge University Press, 2018), 87.

might draw from the surplus "merits of the father" to cover for one's own failings. Insofar as this appeal, while "always available," is insufficient, and thus "each generation needs to add its own meritorious conduct,"[9] John stands in basic agreement with this Jewish notion. Merely being a child of Abraham[10] does not exempt one from the need to repent and do good works. Given the proto-supersessionist tendencies in Luke, the words may have a more ominous overtone in this gospel: if, in John's view, Abrahamic ancestry can as easily be attributed to stones[11] as to a people who have long traced their descent from the patriarch, Lukan readers might conclude there is no special standing for the Jews in Luke's narrative who reject messianic claims for Jesus.[12]

As feminists, we reject the use of harsh insults and violent images of judgment as a means to invite repentance (3:7-9). First, John calls the crowds that came to be baptized a "brood of vipers" (v. 7). Vipers are poisonous snakes that can catch their victims unawares and cause great bodily harm, even death. The ancients believed that vipers were birthed through force, by eating through their mother's stomach.[13] Then John likens those not bearing fruit to trees that will be chopped up and burned (v. 9). This violence is mirrored in John's promise that Jesus himself comes to clear the threshing floor and will burn the chaff in "unquenchable fire" (v. 17). Such threats of hell's torments, while common in some strains of Christian preaching, have done damage to countless believers, who have been paralyzed by fear of their own inadequacy and belief that such torturous punishment might be deserved. Feminists resonate more strongly with preaching that stresses the love of God for all created beings and urges responsible care for all who are part of the interconnected web of life through acts of justice and mercy, including restorative justice, rather than vindictive punishments for those who have done harm.

9. Ibid., 86–87.

10. Abraham appears much more often in the Third Gospel than in the others (Mark once; Matthew six times; John nine times; compared to fourteen times in Luke and eight times in Acts). Unlike Isa 51:2, Luke never mentions Sarah with Abraham. His androcentric focus erases her part in fulfilling the promises God makes to Abraham.

11. Amy-Jill Levine, "The Gospel of Luke," in *The Jewish Annotated New Testament*, ed. Amy-Jill Levine and Marc Zvi Brettler, 2nd ed. (New York: Oxford University Press, 2017), 116–17, notes that there is a wordplay between "stones" and "children" in both Aramaic (*avnayya . . . benayya*) and Hebrew (*avanim . . . banim*).

12. Here we see departure in Luke from the theology of Paul, who repeatedly insists in his letter to the Romans on the primacy of the Jews as God's chosen people and the irrevocability of their gift and calling. See especially Rom 1:16; 9:4-5; 11:28-29.

13. Levine, "The Gospel of Luke" in *The Jewish Annotated New Testament*, 6.

What Should We Do? (3:10-14)

The dialogue between John and those who come to him for baptism (3:10-14) is unique to Luke. The crowds, tax collectors,[14] and soldiers all ask a variation of the same question: what should we do? John's answers are practical, essentially the same, and each tailored to the social setting of the questioners. John insists that no one is to have excess when another is wanting. Tax collectors and soldiers[15] are not to take advantage of their positions to exact more money than what is prescribed. But we note that John's message, while charitable, is essentially nonpolitical. He does not urge the radical step of complete personal divesting, of leaving behind occupation or family or goods, as Jesus does (5:1-11, 27-28; 18:18-30). Tax collectors and soldiers both need to behave better, but John does not criticize the Roman imperial systems of taxation and military power. Feminists such as we say that more than personal conversion and charity is needed to bring about equity; changes in systems and institutions that inscribe inequality must be made.

The Coming One (3:15-18)

As we described above, in certain quarters John was a more prominent figure than Jesus. Addressing those who still wonder whether John might be the Messiah (ὁ χριστός, "the Christ"),[16] Luke puts a definitive answer on the lips of John: one more powerful is coming who will baptize not with water but by the Holy Spirit and fire. The imagery of fire and the Spirit evokes both purification (as in Isa 4:4-5; Ezek 36:25-26; Mal 3:2-4) and vivification (as in Isa 32:15; 44:3; Ezek 36:25-26). John expects that the coming one will continue the same kind of fiery message he himself preaches, threatening destruction for those who do not repent. As the gospel progresses, Jesus's preaching will center on repentance[17] as did John's, and at times he will use the same fiery rhetoric threatening vio-

---

14. For more on tax collectors, see comments at 5:27.

15. Laurie Brink, *Soldiers in Luke–Acts*, WUNT 2.362 (Tübingen: Mohr Siebeck, 2014), notes that the soldiers could be mercenaries of Herod Antipas, but if they are envisioned as Roman soldiers, then they point ahead to the baptism of Cornelius in Acts 10 (99–100). Brink shows that John's admonition to them is accurate: soldiers were notorious bullies who would extort money from the provincials (101). She notes that Luke does not narrate that the soldiers were actually baptized; at 3:14 he is merely planting in the mind of the reader the possibility that soldiers were capable of repentance, a notion that will come to actuality in Acts 10 (102). See 7:1-10 and 23:47 where centurions feature.

16. On the meaning of χριστός, see comments at 2:11.

17. E.g., 5:32; 10:13; 11:32; 13:1-5; 24:47.

lent punishment (10:14, 15; 13:3, 5), but his ministry will also diverge from that of John. Jesus goes out to people, rather than remain stationary and have people come to him, and his ministry will expand to include healings, exorcisms, and other miracles.

John the Baptizer appears in only one other scene in Luke, where he sends two of his disciples to ask Jesus, "Are you the one who is to come, or are we to wait for another?" (7:19). This scene provides one more instance for Luke to assert that Jesus is the coming one (see also 20:1-8 and Acts 19:1-7).[18]

In his historical reconstruction of the relationship between John and Jesus, John Meier asserts that John was the person who had the greatest single influence on Jesus; "in a sense, Jesus never was without John."[19] Based on the criteria of multiple attestation and of embarrassment,[20] he shows that Jesus was baptized by John, remained ministering with him as his disciple, and eventually separated (amicably) from him.[21] Jesus continued to baptize, though the gospels suppress this part of Jesus's

---

18. For a feminist argument that resists framing Jesus and John the Baptist as rivals, see Melanie Johnson-DeBaufre, *Jesus among Her Children: Q, Eschatology, and the Construction of Christian Origins*, HTS 55 (Cambridge, MA: Harvard University Press, 2005) and commentary on Luke 20:1-8.

19. John P. Meier, *A Marginal Jew: Rethinking the Historical Jesus*, vol. 2: *Mentor, Message, and Miracles*, ABRL (New York: Doubleday, 1994), 9.

20. Meier uses the following criteria to determine historicity: "(1) the criterion of embarrassment pinpoints Gospel material that would hardly have been invented by the early church, since such material created embarrassment or theological difficulties for the church even during the NT period (e.g., the baptism of Jesus by John); (2) The criterion of discontinuity focuses on words or deeds of Jesus that cannot be derived either from the Judaism(s) of Jesus's time or from the early church (e.g., Jesus's rejection of voluntary fasting); (3) the criterion of multiple attestation focuses on sayings or deeds of Jesus witnessed in more than one independent literary source (e.g., Mark, Q, Paul, or John) and/or more than one independent literary form or genre; (4) the criterion of coherence is brought into play only after a certain amount of historical material has been isolated by other criteria. The criterion of coherence holds that other sayings and deeds of Jesus that fit in well with the preliminary 'data base' established by the other criteria have a good chance of being historical" (*A Marginal Jew*, 2:5).

21. Meier (*A Marginal Jew*, 2:129) thinks that John 1:35-42 depicts a likely historical happening that some of John's followers became Jesus's disciples. The scenario of Jerome Murphy-O'Connor, "John the Baptist and Jesus: History and Hypotheses," *NTS* 36 (1990): 359–74, is very similar to that proposed by Meier. In addition, he posits that John and Jesus had a coordinated campaign in which Jesus remained baptizing in Judea, while John took the more difficult territory in Samaria (John 3:22-24), then eventually moved into the Galilee, where he was arrested by Herod Antipas. Jesus then takes up ministry in the Galilee (Mark 1:14; Matt 4:12), picking up where John left off.

ministry so that Jesus comes into the spotlight, out from the shadow of John.[22] In Acts there are frequent references to the baptism of new adherents to the Jesus movement (2:38, 41; 8:12, etc.), a practice that continues until today. The easiest explanation for why the early church used baptism to incorporate new members is that they were continuing Jesus's practice. It is more difficult to explain why the early church would have reinstituted the practice of John's baptism with a different meaning if Jesus had broken with it.[23]

Developments in the Theology of Baptism and a Feminist Critique

There has been ongoing development in the theology of baptism. In Acts, as in Luke, it continues to be connected with the forgiveness of sins and reception of the Spirit (3:28). Metaphors in Paul's letters describe baptism as dying and rising with Christ, dying to sin, purifying hearts as well as bodies, the beginning of a new life in Christ Jesus, and membership in the one body of believers (e.g., Rom 6:3-4; 1 Cor 12:13; Gal 3:27-28; Col 2:12).[24] Forms of administering baptism vary from immersion, to dipping, to simply pouring water over the forehead of the candidate. There have also been variations in the length and process of the preparation of catechumens for reception of baptism. In some Christian denominations, parents have their children baptized as infants, as they, along with the whole church, pledge to nurture them into a life of discipleship. Other denominations consider the decision to live a life of

---

22. With the exception of John 3:22-26; 4:1, which is then contradicted by 4:2, "it was not Jesus himself but his disciples who baptized," the gospels do not depict Jesus as continuing to baptize. Many scholars (e.g., Raymond E. Brown, *The Gospel According to John I–XII*, AB 29 [New York: Doubleday, 1966], 164; Francis J. Moloney, *The Gospel of John*, SP 4 [Collegeville, MN: Liturgical Press, 1998], 119–20; Meier, *A Marginal Jew*, 2:121–22) regard John 4:2 as evidence of another hand, different from the one who composed 3:22-26; 4:1. Meier (*A Marginal Jew*, 2:196) advances that the author of John 4:2, like the Synoptic writers, suppresses Jesus's baptizing ministry because it put Jesus too much in the shadow of John. Another reason for the correction in 4:2 is to cohere with the Johannine theme of the giving of the Spirit, which happens after Jesus's death (19:30; 20:22), not something that occurred during his lifetime through his baptizing.

23. Meier, *A Marginal Jew*, 2:129. Murphy-O'Connor, "John the Baptist and Jesus," 372, also thinks that Jesus continued to baptize and that Herod's identification of Jesus with John in Luke 9:7 was not simply because Jesus was known as John's disciple but because he had continued to baptize as did John.

24. On the development of the pastoral-liturgical tradition, see Kathleen Hughes, "Baptism," in *The Collegeville Pastoral Dictionary of Biblical Theology*, ed. Carroll Stuhlmueller (Collegeville, MN: Liturgical Press, 1996), 70–74.

committed discipleship one that cannot be made by someone else; it is a mature choice, and thus they delay baptism until adulthood.

Feminists have critiqued baptism as an initiation into Christianized patriarchy[25] and have denounced churches that baptize infants as desiring "to take control of people's lives from infancy."[26] Some feminists, we included, think it is possible to redeem baptism, finding that "the source of our oppression is also the source of our power."[27] Insofar as infant baptism is a sign of God's grace operative in one's life even before one is able to recognize it, we do not find it as necessarily patriarchal or controlling.

Furthermore, we are intrigued by the argument that Rosemary Radford Ruether advances that the church can be "the community of liberation from patriarchy"[28] and that baptism should be a ritual undergone in adulthood, during which one explicitly disaffiliates from patriarchy. A ritual for infants could have a signing and naming ceremony in which the child's life could be claimed for the journey into freedom, a claim that the person would need to own and appropriate in the future as an adult. She proposes the elements and structure of a feminist baptismal rite, including a litany for disaffiliating from patriarchal powers.[29]

Another aspect of the rite that can be disturbing to Christian feminists is the formula that names the triune God in patriarchal terms. The candidate is baptized "in the name of the Father and of the Son and of the Holy Spirit" (taken from Matt 28:19). One strategy is to use alternative formulae with female or gender-neutral names for the Trinity.[30] Another is to retain the traditional formula but augment it, for example, "I baptize you in the name of the Father and of the Son and of the Holy Spirit, One

25. Mary Daly, *Gyn/ecology: The Metaethics of Radical Feminism* (Boston: Beacon, 1978), 37, goes so far as to call it "a rite of entrance into the State of Possession."

26. Rosemary Radford Ruether, *Women-Church: Theology and Practice of Feminist Liturgical Communities* (San Francisco: Harper & Row, 1986), 127.

27. Catherine Mowry LaCugna, "The Baptismal Formula, Feminist Objections, and Trinitarian Theology," *JES* 26 (1989): 239, adapting this statement about the Bible from Elisabeth Schüssler Fiorenza, *In Memory of Her: A Feminist Theological Reconstruction of Christian Origins* (New York: Crossroad, 1984), 33.

28. Ruether, *Women-Church*, 127.

29. Ibid., 128–30.

30. See, e.g., Ruth C. Duck, *Gender and the Name of God: The Trinitarian Baptismal Formula* (New York: Pilgrim, 1991). Duck proposes changing the formula to three questions, to which the candidates for baptism and the congregation respond: "I believe": Do you believe in God, the Source, the fountain of life? Do you believe in Christ, the offspring of God embodied in Jesus of Nazareth and in the church? Do you believe in the liberating Spirit of God, the wellspring of new life? (185).

God, Mother of us all."[31] The Vatican has declared that formulae that remove the male names for God, such as "I baptize you in the name of the Creator, and of the Redeemer, and of the Sanctifier," or "I baptize you in the name of the Creator, and of the Liberator, and of the Sustainer," are invalid and undermine faith in the Trinity.[32] Some Protestant churches, for example, Episcopalians and United Methodists, agree with the Vatican, while others, for example, the United Church of Christ (USA), question the use of exclusively male language.[33] We agree that naming members of the Trinity by their functions is not a fully adequate strategy (see further excursus at 11:2 on calling God Father). Nor does augmenting the traditional formula with female images adequately offset the effects of the patriarchal language. For many Christian feminists, naming the Trinity in ways that include female reality does not undermine faith but makes it more possible. We hope that the quest for more adequate language for naming God in public prayer continues.

Mentoring

While many Christians think of Jesus as knowing everything from the start about what he needed to do in his ministry, we find the portraits sketched by Jerome Murphy-O'Connor and John Meier of Jesus being mentored by John helpful for understanding the development of the human Jesus. Moreover, the experience of mentoring resonates with many women for whom the guidance of another, particularly a senior woman, has been crucial for enabling her abilities to lead.

The importance of having a mentor[34] has been widely recognized. It is especially critical for women, particularly for those who work in male-dominated fields. In a study done in 2017 of women in

---

31. This formula is used by James F. Kay at Riverside Church in New York, as he explains in "Critic's Corner: In Whose Name? Feminism and the Trinitarian Baptismal Formula," *ThTo* 49 (1993): 524–33, here 531.

32. https://zenit.org/articles/holy-see-rejects-feminist-baptism/.

33. See Duck, *Gender and the Name of God*, 195–97.

34. The word "mentor" comes from Homer's epic *The Odyssey*. While Odysseus was away from home fighting and journeying for twenty years, he left his infant son Telemachus under the supervision of Mentor, an old trusted friend. https://www.merriam-webster.com/dictionary/mentor.

leadership in theological schools,[35] for example, of 516 women chief academic officers and presidents, 70% reported having a mentor. Those who had well-positioned mentors (some women had more than one) who strongly advocated for their leadership (76% had male advocates; 51% had female) considered this advocacy important for their professional journey (96% of those with men advocates; 95% of those with women advocates). They reported that having a mentor makes a difference in networking, building social capital, grant writing, fundraising, navigating organizational politics, conflict management, and mediation. As Stephanie Buckhanon Crowder elaborates (at 1:38-45, "Another View of Community Mothering"), such encouragement is akin to that offered by Elizabeth to Mary in 1:39-45. In Luke 1–3, by contrast, the mentoring of Jesus by John and their coordination of the baptizing ministry (see n. 22 above) is overshadowed by the evangelist's intent to distinguish Jesus from John and to subordinate the latter.[36] Today, both women and men in ministry and other arenas of work can find themselves in situations of rivalry and power struggles, as Luke depicts between John and Jesus. Feminists advocate for collaboration that enables the full flourishing of all, even as we recognize that women are equally capable as men of behavior that is domineering and subjugating.

You Are My Beloved (3:21-22)

The baptism of Jesus may have posed questions for those hearing this story, since presumably one who baptizes is superior to the one being baptized. The Gospel of Matthew addresses this question directly and makes clear that the act of baptizing does not imply any subordination on Jesus's part. In Matthew, John's objection, "I need to be baptized by you, and do you come to me?" is met by Jesus's reply, "Let it be so now;

35. This research was led by Debbie Gin, director of research and faculty development at the Association of Theological Schools, in the twentieth-anniversary year of the ATS initiative to promote women leaders in theological education. See https://www.ats.edu/uploads/resources/research/WIL-20th-anniversary-presentation--180301.pdf.

36. John's self-declaration "I am not worthy" has an echo at 7:6 when the centurion makes the same pronouncement. See comments at 7:6 on women who act from a false sense of unworthiness.

²¹Now when all the people were baptized, and when Jesus also had been baptized and was praying, the heaven was opened, ²²and the Holy Spirit descended upon him in bodily form like a dove. And a voice came from heaven, "You are my Son, the Beloved; with you I am well pleased."

for it is proper for us in this way to fulfill all righteousness" (3:14-15). Luke's narrative order, in which he first places John in prison (v. 20) and then immediately speaks of Jesus's baptism in the passive voice (v. 21), retains the tradition that Jesus was baptized without drawing attention to the agency of John in doing the deed.

Jesus's baptism sets the foundation for his ministry to follow, and the descent of the Spirit[37] along with the voice from the heavens authorizes that ministry.[38] Many contemporary women and gender nonconforming people who become ministers find that they too must first come to understand themselves as beloved children of God. Given the weight of patriarchal Scriptures and traditions that can instill in wo/men the belief that they are secondary and subservient to men and even that God's will is for them to suffer and to serve others, it is profoundly transformative for them to come to an understanding of themselves as beloved by God who only desires wellbeing for them and all creation. In their programs at CEDIMSE (Centro de Desarrollo Integral de las Mujeres, Santa Escolástica) in Torreón, México, for example, the Benedictine sisters first work with women on self-esteem and conscientization about their rights and dignity before delving into study of Scripture.[39]

37. There are particular resonances with the messianic prophecies of Isaiah: "the Spirit of the LORD shall rest upon him" (11:2; see also 61:1).

38. See 9:28-36, another critical turning point in Jesus's mission, where there is a similar divine manifestation and message in response to Jesus's prayer that will impel him toward Jerusalem. In Luke, the voice from heaven is directed to Jesus alone: "You are my Son, the Beloved" (3:22), as also in Mark 1:11; in Matthew the revelation is public: "This is my Son, the Beloved" (3:17). Luke and Mark emphasize the personal impact of the experience on Jesus.

39. CEDIMSE was founded by Benedictine sisters in 1992. It is a space for encounter, reflection, dialogue, prayer, and celebration that attends especially to issues of gender justice. See https://www.scribd.com/doc/104877977/Filosofia-y-Mapa-de-Cedimse. Two of the sisters, Patricia Henry Ford and Maricarmen Bracamontes, have authored a book to help the women in this regard: *Mujeres y Derechos Humanos. Perspectivas y Alternativas. Aportes Sociales y Eclesiales*, 3rd rev. ed. (Mexico, D.F.: Ediciones Schola, CEDIMSE, 2001).

The Spirit as the "Feminine Face of God"

As feminists critique the overwhelming male imagery and language for God and its impact on sustaining kyriarchal structures, some theologians have responded by suggesting that the Spirit, a feminine noun in Hebrew, רוח, is the expression of "the feminine dimension of God."[40] Most feminists, however, insist that the whole of the divinity must be imaged as female, not as basically masculine with a feminine side.[41] Moreover, the Greek word for Spirit, πνεῦμα, is neuter gender. Even so, grammatical gender is irrelevant for describing the nature of a thing. Alice Walker, who coined the term "womanist," says that the Spirit is neither male nor female: it is divine energy that permeates every entity in creation. On the lips of her character Shug in her novel *The Color Purple*, Walker says: "God ain't a he or a she, but a It. . . . It ain't something you can look at apart from anything else, including yourself."[42]

Feminists highlight the immanency of God in the Spirit. Whereas the Spirit had long been considered the most abstract and otherworldly person of the Trinity, for Christian feminists, the Spirit has come to mean the most intimate, powerful, and creative presence of God in all created beings. Transcending gender, it is the sacred power that gives life and energy for fighting against anything that opposes full flourishing of life for all.[43]

40. E.g., Helen Schüngel-Straumann, "The Feminine Face of God," in *The Many Faces of the Divine*, ed. Johann Baptist Metz and Hermann Häring, Concilium (London: SCM; and Maryknoll, NY: Orbis Books, 1995), 93–101. Mary has also been called the "feminine face of God" (e.g., Leonardo Boff, *El rostro materno de Dios: Ensayo interdisciplinario sobre lo femenino y sus formas religiosas*, 3rd ed. [Madrid: Paulinas, 1981]). Elizabeth A. Johnson ("Don't Make Mary the Feminine Face of God," *U.S. Catholic*, originally published April 1994, reprinted May 2016, http://www.uscatholic.org/articles/201605/don't-make -mary-feminine-face-god-30644, and "Mary and the Female Face of God," *TS* 50 [1989]: 500–526) critiques the attribution of feminine characteristics to Mary, such as mothering, nurturing, and being intuitive and sensitive so that she functions as the maternal face of God turned toward the world. She shows this to be a detrimental approach, in that it stereotypes feminine and masculine characteristics, does not resolve the problem of male-dominated imagery for God but rather leaves it intact, and forgets that all language about God is analogical or symbolic, not literal. Moreover, this more benevolent divine image, made more acceptable by feminine traits but still essentially patriarchal, actually functions to justify the priority of male rule while blocking women from full participation.

41. See also excursus at 11:2 on "Calling God Father."

42. Alice Walker, *The Color Purple* (New York: Harcourt Brace Jovanovich, 1982), 177–78.

43. Sallie McFague, "Holy Spirit," in *Dictionary of Feminist Theologies*, ed. Letty M. Russell and J. Shannon Clarkson (Louisville: Westminster John Knox, 1996), 146–47.

The Spirit from a Feminist Perspective

English poet Ann Lewin, reflecting on the divine Spirit, says:

Dare us to try new steps, explore
new patterns and new partnerships: release us from
old routines
to swing in abandoned joy
and fearful adventure.[44]

Feminist theologians have responded to Lewin's suggestion by offering new perspectives on God's Spirit. In her work on the Trinity, *She Who Is*, North American theologian Elizabeth A. Johnson explores God first as Spirit-Sophia, then as Jesus-Sophia, and ultimately as divine mystery, Mother-Sophia.[45]

We thank Johnson and many women whose scholarship on the Holy Spirit has been a fruit of the Spirit. Johnson's creativity reminds readers that human glimpses into the mystery of God are dependent on the Spirit who nudges human beings and who is the source of creativity.

The Spirit is often linked with life-giving. Genesis 1:2 describes "a wind from God" sweeping over the face of the waters, as God creates order from a watery chaos. At both the origins of the biblical story and of human birthing "water" signals life.

Once fourth-century patristic theologians[46] wrestled to describe the Spirit, one early title became "Life-Giver." This title continues. While Johnson depicts the Spirit as One who "empowers, lures, prods, dances on ahead,"[47] British ecofeminist theologian Mary Grey describes the Spirit as One who "anoint[s] into life, the playful, the joyful and ecstatic aspects of

---

44. Ann Lewin, "Jeu d'esprit," in *Watching for the Kingfisher: Poems and Prayers* (Norwich: Canterbury Press, 2009). © Ann Lewin, 2004, 2006 and 2009. Published by Canterbury Press. Used by permission. rights@hymnsam.co.uk.

45. Elizabeth A. Johnson, *She Who Is: The Mystery of God in Feminist Theological Discourse* (New York: Crossroad, 1992). "The symbol of God functions. Neither abstract in content nor neutral in its effect, speaking about God sums up, unifies, and expresses a faith community's sense of ultimate mystery, the world view and expectation of order devolving from this, and the concomitant orientation of human life and devotion" (4). Thus she seeks language for God that draws on both traditional language of Scripture and new language from feminist theology to shape emancipatory speech about the mystery of God.

46. E.g., Cyril of Jerusalem (c. 315–386), Athanasius (c. 295–373), Hilary of Poitiers (c. 315–367), Basil of Caesarea (c. 330–379), Gregory of Nyssa (c. 335–395). For easily accessible excerpts of their works, see J. Patout Burns and Gerald M. Fagin, *The Holy Spirit*, Message of the Fathers of the Church 3 (Wilmington, DE: Glazier, 1984), 90–154. See also excerpts from fifth-century theologians who spoke of the Spirit as "Lord and Giver of Life," 155–204.

47. Elizabeth A. Johnson, *Women, Earth, and Creator Spirit* (New York: Paulist Press, 1993), 44.

our personalities."[48] Feminist understandings of the Spirit include enrichment, surprise, and fullness of living.

From the context of Aotearoa New Zealand, I am aware of the deep sense of connectedness experienced by Indigenous Māori who honor relationships not only among their immediate and extended families (*whanau*) but also with the land of their forebears. For Māori, such relationships express their sense of belonging and a deep sense of self.

Māori are deeply aware of the Spirit and that all persons express their own *wairua* or spirit. Thus, the concept of *wairua* has deep spiritual and emotional connotations, and it is often the task of women to bring these elements to expression.

When Māori gather for special occasions, therefore, it is important to follow the protocol of ancestors. For example, at the start of formal gatherings it is women who initiate proceedings. This is not to suggest that all Māori women necessarily name themselves feminists! Nonetheless, women's roles are highly regarded within Māori communities. As people gather outside the communal meeting house, it is women who with their continuous chanting invite both family (*whanau*) and guests into the sacred meeting space—the *marae* and meeting house. A woman completes her welcoming role only when all guests have been properly received into the meeting house on the *marae*.

Our final focus is on the Spirit as the gift of the risen Jesus who continues to form prophetic communities throughout the world. During Easter we hear the encouraging words "Set us aflame with the fire of your love and bring us to the radiance of your heavenly glory!"[49] Attention to the risen Jesus and to God's Spirit intertwine as many present-day Christians struggle to be givers of Life. We conclude with one example.

Recent global intervention by thousands of people supporting the courageous stance of Asia Bibi, a Pakistani Christian woman, eventually secured her justice. Claiming innocence from committing blasphemy while offering water to Muslim farm coworkers, Bibi was released after many years of imprisonment in Pakistan. She now lives with her family in Canada.

We conclude with North American feminist theologian

48. Mary Grey, "Where Does the Wild Goose Fly To? Seeking a New Theology of Spirit for Feminist Theology," *New Blackfriars* 72 (1991): 93.
49. Roman Catholic Liturgy of Easter Vigil. See http://www.oremus.org/liturgy/lhwe/easter.html.

Nancy Victorin-Vangerud offering an image of God's Spirit as "the Raging Hearth."[50] The latter is a place where truth may be strongly contested yet ultimately warm embers remain! There is a time for such a Spirit-image. There is also, however, a time for Johnson's "Spirit-Sophia." Feminist theologians will continue to flourish with assistance from the same Spirit!

Helen Bergin

All God's Children (3:23-38)

Jesus's genealogy, an attestation of his identity and status, is not a historical record; it is a stylized listing with a christological purpose. The seventy-eight names including Jesus and God suggest seventy-seven generations, a perfect number.[51] Tracing Jesus's ancestry to God and Adam aligns with Luke's emphasis that Jesus's significance extends to all God's children.[52]

Absent from the list are Jesus's foremothers. In contrast to Matthew, who includes Tamar (1:3), Rahab (1:5), Ruth (1:5), the wife of Uriah (1:6), and Mary (1:16), Luke gives no hint of Jesus's maternal ancestors in his genealogy.[53] Although many of the names of the women ancestors who

50. Nancy M. Victorin-Vangerud, *The Raging Hearth: Spirit in the Household of God* (St. Louis: Chalice Press, 2000).

51. In the Bible, seven is a number for fullness, e.g., seven days of creation, Gen 2:2; the necessity to forgive seven times a day, Luke 17:4. See above at 2:36-37 on Anna's seven-year marriage and her age (7 x 12).

52. Though Matthew's Gospel, especially in its final charge to the disciples in 28:19, also is universal in scope, Matthew's genealogy traces Jesus's ancestors back only to Abraham (Matt 1:1–17).

53. For feminist analyses of Matthew's genealogy, see Amy-Jill Levine, "Gospel of Matthew," in *Women's Bible Commentary*, ed. Carol A. Newsom, Sharon H. Ringe, and Jacqueline E. Lapsley, 3rd ed. (Louisville: Westminster John Knox, 2012), 467–68; Amy-Jill Levine, "The Gospel of Matthew: Between Breaking and Continuity," in *Gospels: Narrative and History*, ed. Mercedes Navarro Puerto, Marinella Perroni, and Amy-Jill Levine (English ed.), The Bible and Women: An Encyclopedia of Exegesis and Cultural History, New Testament 2.1 (Atlanta: SBL Press, 2015), 121–44, esp. 132–36; Elaine M. Wainwright, "The Gospel of Matthew," in *Searching the Scriptures, vol. 2: A Feminist Commentary*, ed. Elisabeth Schüssler Fiorenza with Ann Brock and Shelly Matthews (New York: Crossroad, 1994), 641–44; Beverly Roberts Gaventa, *Mary: Glimpses of the Mother of Jesus*, Studies on Personalities of the New Testament (Columbia: University of South Carolina Press, 1995).

23 Jesus was about thirty years old when he began his work. He was the son (as was thought) of Joseph son of Heli, 24 son of Matthat, son of Levi, son of Melchi, son of Jannai, son of Joseph, 25 son of Mattathias, son of Amos, son of Nahum, son of Esli, son of Naggai, 26 son of Maath, son of Mattathias, son of Semein, son of Josech, son of Joda, 27 son of Joanan, son of Rhesa, son of Zerubbabel, son of Shealtiel, son of Neri, 28 son of Melchi, son of Addi, son of Cosam, son of Elmadam, son of Er, 29 son of Joshua, son of Eliezer, son of Jorim, son of Matthat, son of Levi, 30 son of Simeon, son of Judah, son of Joseph, son of Jonam, son of Eliakim, 31 son of Melea, son of Menna, son of Mattatha, son of Nathan, son of David, 32 son of Jesse, son of Obed, son of Boaz, son of Sala, son of Nahshon, 33 son of Amminadab, son of Admin, son of Arni, son of Hezron, son of Perez, son of Judah, 34 son of Jacob, son of Isaac, son of Abraham, son of Terah, son of Nahor, 35 son of Serug, son of Reu, son of Peleg, son of Eber, son of Shelah, 36 son of Cainan, son of Arphaxad, son of Shem, son of Noah, son of Lamech, 37 son of Methuselah, son of Enoch, son of Jared, son of Mahalaleel, son of Cainan, 38 son of Enos, son of Seth, son of Adam, son of God.

are related to the men named in 3:23-38 are known, Luke keeps in view only the male forebears. Luke has devoted significant attention to Jesus's mother and to Elizabeth in chapters 1–2, but he considers only the male predecessors as the ones who provide Jesus with status and identity. Luke's androcentric focus continues throughout the gospel as he foregrounds the role of the male disciples of Jesus, even though he includes women disciples at key junctures (see the authors' introduction on Luke's depiction of women). Having established Jesus's identity and status, Luke has paved the way for the beginning of Jesus's public ministry.

Jesus's Female Ancestors

Most of the men named as Jesus's forebears are known from other genealogical lists in the Old Testament (Gen 5:1-32; 11:10-26; 1 Chr 1–3); thirty-six are otherwise unknown. The names of some of the women related to these men are known and include the following: Bath-shua, daughter of Ammiel was the mother of Nathan (Luke 3:31) and Tamar was his sister (1 Chr 3:5, 9). Bath-shua is probably an alternate form of Bathsheba.[54] Jesse (Luke 3:32) fathered not only sons, the seventh of whom was David (Luke 3:31), but also two daughters: Zeruiah and Abigail (1 Chr 2:16). The wife of Boaz (Luke 3:32) was Ruth (Ruth 2–4). His father Sala (Luke 3:32), Salmon in Matthew's genealogy, was married to Rahab (Matt 1:4). While the name of the wife of Nahshon (Luke 3:32) is not known, his sister's is: Elisheba, the daughter of Amminadab (Luke 3:33), who married Aaron, the brother of Moses (Exod 6:23). The wife of Hezron (Luke 3:33) was Abijah (1 Chr 2:24). Judah (Luke 3:33) had three sons by Bath-shua (this is a different Bath-shua from the one in 1 Chr 3:5, who is one of David's wives), a Canaanite woman, and two by his daughter-in-law Tamar, one of whom was Perez (Luke 3:33; 1 Chr 2:2-4). Jacob (Luke 3:34) married Leah and Rachel (Gen 29:15-35); Leah is the mother of Judah (Luke 3:33). Jacob is the son of Isaac (Luke 3:34) and Rebekah (Gen 24:64-67); Isaac's father Abraham (Luke 3:34) was married to Sarah (Gen 17:15-22). According to the genealogy in Genesis 11:10-32, the male ancestors listed from Terah to Shem (Luke 3:34-36) all had daughters as well as sons, but their names are not given. The name of the wife of Lamech (Luke 3:36) is not found in the Old Testament, but her name appears as Bit-Enosh in a Qumran document (1QapGen 2:3, 19; 5:4, 10, 25, 26). Like the ancestors in Genesis 11, so too those listed in Genesis 5, Lamech to Adam (Luke 3:36-38) all had daughters as well as sons who remain unnamed (Gen 5:1-31). The name of Adam's partner was Eve (Gen 3:21).

54. See Adele Berlin, "Bath-shua 2," in *Women in Scripture: A Dictionary of Named and Unnamed Women in the Hebrew Bible, the Apocryphal/Deuterocanonical Books, and the New Testament,* ed. Carol Meyers, Toni Craven, and Ross Shepard Kraemer (Grand Rapids: Eerdmans, 2000), 59.

Luke 4:1-44

Prophetic Mission Declared; Divided Responses

Testing in the Wilderness (4:1-13)

In the gospel's opening chapters, John the Baptizer (1:15, 80), Mary (1:35), Elizabeth (1:41), Zechariah (1:67), and Simeon (2:25, 26, 27) are all filled with and directed by the Spirit. After his baptism (3:22), Jesus becomes the sole character filled with and directed by the Spirit. There are no more female prophets like Mary, Elizabeth, and Anna. In the Pentecost scene (Acts 2:1-13), Peter, quoting the prophet Joel (3:1-5), declares "your sons and your daughters shall prophesy." We hear no prophecy from women in the rest of the narrative, however, as male voices, primarily those of Peter and Paul, take over, just as Jesus's does from Luke 4 forward in the gospel. Luke does note that Philip has four daughters with the gift of prophecy (Acts 21:9), but we never hear what they have to say[1] (see further comments on Luke and women at the end of the authors' introduction).

---

1. There is also a female slave whom Paul and Silas meet in Philippi (Acts 16:16) who had "a spirit of divination" (πνεῦμα πύθωνα, lit. "a Pythian spirit," connecting her to the oracle of Apollo at Delphi), but she is not a Jesus-follower and Paul casts out the spirit. Ivoni Richter Reimer, *Women in the Acts of the Apostles: A Feminist Liberation Perspective*, trans. Linda M. Maloney (Minneapolis: Fortress, 1995), 151–94, sketches

Luke 4:1-13

⁴:¹Jesus, full of the Holy Spirit, returned from the Jordan and was led by the Spirit in the wilderness, ²where for forty days he was tempted by the devil. He ate nothing at all during those days, and when they were over, he was famished. ³The devil said to him, "If you are the Son of God, command this stone to become a loaf of bread." ⁴Jesus answered him, "It is written, 'One does not live by bread alone.'"

⁵Then the devil led him up and showed him in an instant all the kingdoms of the world. ⁶And the devil said to him, "To you I will give their glory and all this authority; for it has been given over to me, and I give it to anyone I please. ⁷If you, then, will worship me, it will all be yours." ⁸Jesus answered him, "It is written,

'Worship the Lord your God,
    and serve only him.'"

The Spirit leads Jesus into the wilderness,² where, not unlike the Israelites during their forty years in the desert, he faces a time of testing.³ Whereas at his baptism the divine voice asserted, "You are my Son, the beloved," now the devil⁴ challenges Jesus to doubt the authenticity of this experience by taunting: "If you are the Son of God . . ." (4:3, 9). The devil assails Jesus with three tests: "temptations to self-interest and

---

the vulnerable situation of the slave once she is no longer of use to her owners. Richter Reimer proposes that if the slave girl finds a welcome in the Christian community, perhaps among those who gathered at Lydia's house (Acts 16:40), then her story has a liberating ending. That there were slaves and freed persons in the Philippian community Richter Reimer surmises from Paul's greetings from those of "all the saints" and "especially those of the emperor's household" (Phil 4:22). She reads "those of the emperor's household" as slaves and freed persons, not members of the imperial family, who feel a close connection to those who were also slaves in Philippi. We appreciate Richter Reimer's attention to the fate of the slave girl. This is a feminist move that runs counter to Luke's program, as his focus is only on the consequences for the male heroes Paul and Silas after they enraged the girl's owners (16:19-24).

2. See comments above on 3:3 for the significance of desert.

3. The number forty days evokes this connection: Deut 8 outlines the ways that God cared for Israel during their forty-year desert sojourn. Forty may also allude to the number of days Moses (Exod 24:18; 34:28) and Elijah (1 Kgs 19:8) spent on Mounts Sinai and Horeb, respectively. Susan R. Garrett notes that the testing of Jesus stands in the tradition of the tests of faith and obedience undergone by other righteous individuals, especially Abraham and Job (*The Demise of the Devil: Magic and the Demonic in Luke's Writings* [Minneapolis: Fortress, 1989], 127 n. 2).

4. Throughout this episode, the tempter is called ὁ διάβολος, "the devil" (cf. Σατανᾶ, "Satan," at Mark 1:13). Satan appears at Luke 10:18; 11:18; 13:16; 22:3, 31.

⁹Then the devil took him to Jerusalem, and placed him on the pinnacle of the temple, saying to him, "If you are the Son of God, throw yourself down from here, ¹⁰for it is written,

'He will command his angels
concerning you,
to protect you,'

¹¹and

'On their hands they will bear you
up,
so that you will not dash your
foot against a stone.'"

¹²Jesus answered him, "It is said, 'Do not put the Lord your God to the test.'" ¹³When the devil had finished every test, he departed from him until an opportune time.

expedience; temptations of power and glory gained by false worship; and temptations of invulnerability, self-importance, and entitlement."[5] Each test corrects a false understanding of Jesus's mission and so is specific to Jesus.[6] Yet there is a sense in which all disciples of Jesus face similar temptations.

What constitutes temptation to sin depends in part on one's social location. Although there is a certain essentializing[7] in her approach, Valerie Saiving Goldstein made a groundbreaking contribution in 1960 in her article "The Human Situation: A Feminine View." She was one of the first to challenge the way that theologians have regarded male experience as universal and thus identified the primordial sin as "pride, will-to-power, exploitation, self-assertiveness, and the treatment of others as objects rather than persons."[8] She argued:

The temptations of woman as woman are not the same as the temptations of man as man, and the specifically feminine forms of sin—"feminine" not because they are confined to women because women are incapable

5. Amy-Jill Levine and Ben Witherington III, *The Gospel of Luke*, NCBC (Cambridge: Cambridge University Press, 2018), 111.

6. Joseph A. Fitzmyer, *The Gospel According to Luke I–IX*, AB 28 (Garden City, NY: Doubleday, 1981), 509.

7. Essentializing makes universal claims for an entity, such as women. Rather than assert there is an "essence" that all women share, most feminists today recognize that what it means to be a woman is socially constructed and varies with historical and cultural context. See Ellen T. Armour, "Essentialism," in *Dictionary of Feminist Theologies*, ed. Letty M. Russell and J. Shannon Clarkson (Louisville: Westminster John Knox, 1996), 88.

8. Valerie Saiving Goldstein, "The Human Situation: A Feminine View," *JR* 40 (1960), 100–112, here 107.

of sinning in other ways but because they are outgrowths of the basic feminine character structure—have a quality which can never be encompassed by such terms as "pride" and "will-to-power." They are better suggested by such items as triviality, distractibility, and diffuseness; lack of an organizing center or focus; dependence on others for one's own self-definition; tolerance at the expense of standards of excellence; inability to respect the boundaries of privacy; sentimentality, gossipy sociability, and mistrust of reason—in short, underdevelopment or negation of the self.[9]

Expanding on her work, Judith Plaskow and Susan Nelson Dunfee[10] among other feminists examined the cultural circumstances that cause women to fear and fail to take the steps toward self-definition. Feminist theologians have consistently looked more at sinful social structures than individual personal sin. Women's sin is thus the internalization of feelings of unworthiness and failure to oppose sinful structures that devalue and defile women and Earth.[11] Womanist theologian Delores S. Williams calls attention to the gravest kind of social sin: "The defilement of Black women's bodies and the resulting attack upon their spirits and self-esteem. . . . Thus, elevating and healing Black women's self-esteem figures into womanist notions of what constitutes salvation for the oppressed African American community."[12] The tests Jesus faces concerning his identity and mission have some intersections with but also disjunctions from the kinds of temptations many women face.

Jesus's first test is to foreground his needs and feed himself first. This would not be as strong a temptation for many women, especially those from cultures where feeding others is considered their prime responsibility. A greater temptation would be to neglect their own selves as they ensure that everyone else is fed. For women with scarce resources, this means giving the best portions of food to their husband and children while taking only scraps for themselves. The ideal the *Magnificat* articulates is that all have enough to eat (1:53). Jesus, the one placed in a food trough at his

---

9. Ibid., 108–9.

10. Judith Plaskow, *Sex, Sin, and Grace: Women's Experience and the Theologies of Reinhold Niebuhr and Paul Tillich* (Washington, DC: University Press of America, 1980); Susan Nelson Dunfee, "The Sin of Hiding: A Feminist Critique of Reinhold Niebuhr's Account of the Sin of Pride," *Soundings* 65 (1982): 25–35.

11. Marjorie Hewitt Suchocki, "Sin," in Russell and Clarkson, *Dictionary of Feminist Theologies*, 261–62.

12. Delores S. Williams, "A Womanist Perspective on Sin," in *A Troubling in My Soul: Womanist Perspectives on Evil and Suffering*, ed. Emilie M. Townes, The Bishop Henry McNeal Turner Studies in North American Black Religion 8 (Maryknoll, NY: Orbis Books, 1993), 130–49, here 145.

birth (2:7), puts this ideal into practice as he feeds more than five thousand hungry people (9:10-17) and offers his own body for nourishment (22:19).

In the second test, the devil shows Jesus all the kingdoms (πάσας τὰς βασιλείας) of the world and offers him glory (δόξα) and power (ἐξουσία). The devil's offer stands in contrast to the kingdom of God (βασιλεία τοῦ θεοῦ) Jesus was sent to proclaim (4:43). The glory Jesus embraces, having nothing to do with self-aggrandizement, is manifested in his death (9:26, 31, 32; 19:38; 24:26). His power (ἐξουσία) is demonstrated in his words (4:32), his ability to cast out unclean spirits (4:36), and his effecting forgiveness and healing (5:24).[13] He shares this power with the disciples he sends out (9:1; 10:19). Following his action in the temple, the chief priests, scribes, and elders demand to know by what authority (ἐξουσία) Jesus is doing these things (20:2). The contrast between his power and that of the political authorities is manifest when at his arrest Jesus says, "This is your hour, and the power [ἐξουσία] of darkness!" (22:53).

While women are not exempt from seeking and using power in destructive ways, as Valerie Saiving Goldstein and others have shown, the will-to-power tends to be a stronger temptation for men than for most women. A more prevalent shortcoming for women is failure to claim and exercise our power or unwillingness to challenge the systems that limit our power. Another temptation for some women is to regard power as a bad thing, something we shouldn't try to grab, rather than see it as collaborative energy to accomplish good (see the excursus "Feminist Understandings of Power").

The Kingdom of God

The phrase ἡ βασιλεία τοῦ θεοῦ, usually translated "the kingdom of God," appears thirty-two times in the Gospel of Luke and six times in Acts. Some people misunderstand "kingdom of God" to mean a locale with fixed boundaries, whereas ἡ βασιλεία τοῦ θεοῦ signifies divine "kingly rule" or "reign," not "kingdom" in a territorial sense. It is not so much a place as a way of being in which divine power works through people who act as Torah and Jesus instruct. It is already present in Jesus's preaching and healing (Luke 17:21) though it has yet to come to fullness (Luke 22:18).

Another difficulty is that this phrase presents an image of God

---

13. In several instances (4:36; 9:1; 10:19), ἐξουσία is paired with another word for power, δύναμις.

as king, who rules according to a male monarchical model, making unilateral top-down decisions. The image is also problematic for believers who live in countries with democratic governance for whom kingship is foreign to their experience. There are people who romanticize monarchies, forgetting that kings can be despotic, not kindly patriarchs whose prime concern is the well-being of their people.[14] Whatever kind of king one may envision, there is still the problem that "kingdom of God" upholds the dominant image of God as male, leaving women unable to see themselves as made in God's image and likeness.[15]

It is also important to remember that in a first-century Mediterranean context the term βασιλεία recollects the Roman imperial system of domination and exploitation. Jesus's annunciation of the βασιλεία of God offered an alternative vision to that of the empire of Rome, one in which there is no victimization or domination. This βασιλεία was already present incipiently in Jesus's healings, teachings, and the inclusive table sharing of his followers. The political threat that Jesus's rival βασιλεία presented to Rome is clear from their execution of him.[16]

Feminist scholars experiment with alternative terms to convey the sense of ἡ βασιλεία τοῦ θεοῦ as God's authoritative power and empowerment by God-with-us, a saving power over all creation, already inaugurated in a new way with the incarnation and ministry of Jesus, continued in the faithful ministry of the believing community, but not yet fully manifest. These expressions include "kin-dom," "rule," "reign," "realm," "empire," "domain," and "commonweal." Because each of these choices has its drawbacks—for example, some are difficult to pronounce and some are associated with meanings other than what we intend—our preference is to leave βασιλεία untranslated and use the transliteration *basileia*.

14. Recall, for example, the cruelty of King Herod, who ordered the massacre of all the infants two years and younger (Matt 2:16-18).

15. Despite there being queens in the Bible (e.g., Esther, the Queen of Sheba, 1 Kgs 10:1) and in societies ancient and modern, "king" refers only to males. On feminist images of God, see Sallie McFague, *Models of God: Theology for an Ecological, Nuclear Age* (Philadelphia: Fortress, 1987); Elizabeth A. Johnson, *She Who Is: The Mystery of God in Feminist Theological Discourse* (New York: Crossroad, 1992); Linda A. Moody, *Women Encounter God: Theology across the Boundaries of Difference* (Maryknoll, NY: Orbis Books, 1996).

16. Elisabeth Schüssler Fiorenza, *Jesus: Miriam's Child, Sophia's Prophet: Critical Issues in Feminist Christology* (New York: Continuum, 1994), 92-93. See also Elisabeth Schüssler Fiorenza, "The Basileia Vision of Jesus as the Praxis of Inclusive Wholeness," in *In Memory of Her: A Feminist Theological Reconstruction of Christian Origins* (New York: Crossroad, 1983), 118–30.

Feminist Understandings of Power

Understanding power and how it is exercised is a complex endeavor. There is more involved than simply contrasting "power over," which results in exploitive domination, with "power to," which effects good. Nor is it adequate to cast men as the ones who hold all power and women as powerless. These dualistic contrasts consider neither the diverse realities due to race and class and other social markers nor the differences that exist in particular social, cultural, and historical settings. As Denise Ackermann points out: "Definitions of power need to take into account the fact that power is evidenced in diverse and interrelated ways: as power over, power to, power for, power with; as related to knowledge, love, difference, violence, resistance, and embodiment. Power is present in the very fabric of our lives, in political, social, economic, and religious structures and it has both internal and external aspects." She offers: "A conventional understanding of power is the ability or means to accomplish ends. Ideally, power is reciprocal, collaborative energy that engages us personally and communally with God, with one another, and with all of creation in such a way that power becomes synonymous with the vitality of living fully and freely."[17]

An example of a young woman who has used this kind of power to raise consciousness and galvanize countless people to work with renewed fervor toward combatting climate change is Greta Thunberg.[18] The Swedish teenager, nominated in 2019 for the Nobel Peace Prize, has gained the attention of heads of nations as well as children in hundreds of countries who are emulating her actions. In an interview with William Brangham of PBS (Public Broadcasting Service) on September 13, 2019, she described how she hopes the movement she has started will empower others: "Everyone can make a huge difference. We should not underestimate ourselves, because if lots of individuals go together then we can accomplish almost anything."[19]

17. Denise M. Ackermann, "Power," in Russell and Clarkson, *Dictionary of Feminist Theologies*, 219–20.

18. See Sam Knight, "The Uncanny Power of Greta Thunberg's Climate-Change Rhetoric," *The New Yorker*, April 24, 2019, https://www.newyorker.com/news/daily-comment/the-uncanny-power-of-greta-thunbergs-climate-change-rhetoric.

19. William Brangham, "Climate Activist Greta Thunberg on the Power of a Movement," *PBS NewsHour*, September 13, 2019, https://www.pbs.org/newshour/show/climate-warrior.

In the United States, a key example of such activism and marshalling of power is the Black Lives Matter movement, founded by three Black women, Alicia Garza, Patrisse Cullors, and Opal Tometi, in response to the acquittal of the man who shot and killed the Black teenager, Trayvon Martin, as he walked home from a convenience store in Sanford, Florida. This grassroots movement, focused on state-sanctioned violence and anti-Black racism, has flowered into a global force for justice.[20]

The third test (4:9-11) revolves around the notion that God would never let any harm come to the beloved Son. The temptation is to consider himself invulnerable and so not fully embrace his humanity. It introduces the question of theodicy: how could a loving and all-powerful God allow harm to come to any beloved child, especially Jesus? The devil tempts Jesus to prove his status by provoking a sign of God's power.[21] Jesus refuses, relying on Deuteronomy, as he does in all three temptations.[22] The temptation to consider oneself invulnerable, self-important, or entitled to special protection takes on a different contour for most women and other members of minoritized communities. It is also colored by our social location. Women who are socialized always to put men's needs and aims before their own rarely are tempted to self-importance; just the opposite. And those who live with a batterer or who struggle daily against poverty know how very vulnerable they are and would not be tempted to think otherwise. In cultures where men think of themselves as protectors of women, a woman can be tempted to accede to special treatment and not claim her own agency and power.

The scene closes on an ominous note: the devil departs from Jesus "until an opportune time" (4:13). Luke signals that the temptations were not an ordeal that Jesus finished definitively after this forty-day trial. Rather, discerning the true nature of his mission was a lifelong endeavor. In one instance, opponents intent on testing (πειράζοντες, the same verb as at 4:2) him keep demanding a sign from heaven (11:16), which Jesus refuses (11:29). That Jesus has experienced testing throughout his ministry is evident when he says to his disciples at the Last Supper: "You are those who

---

20. For information, see the website: https://blacklivesmatter.com/.
21. See comments at 1:8-23 on asking for a sign from God.
22. Jesus's response in v. 4 is from Deut 8:3; in v. 8 from Deut 6:13 and 10:20; in v. 12 from Deut 6:16.

have stood by me in my trials [πειρασμοῖς]" (22:28). Echoes of the devil's tempting Jesus to question his identity as Son and temptations to false manifestations of his mission reverberate in the passion narrative as the elders, chief priests, and scribes interrogate Jesus, "Are you, then, the Son of God?" (22:70), and as they scoffed at him on the cross, "He saved others; let him save himself if he is the Messiah of God, his chosen one!" (23:35).[23] As in the first temptation, where Jesus relies on the power of the Spirit and the word (Deut 8:3; 6:13, 16), so in his final ordeal, the words of Scripture (Ps 31:5) sustain him as he prays: "Father, into your hands I commend my spirit" (23:46). While Luke makes no mention of prayer in 4:1-13, Jesus prays throughout the rest of the gospel,[24] especially at critical points, as he seeks to know the way forward as Son of God.[25] He also teaches his disciples to pray not to be brought to the time of trial (πειρασμόν, 11:4) and reminds them twice on the Mount of Olives to pray in the way that he does as he himself implores the Father and seeks his will (22:39-46).

The very human depiction of Jesus in this scene invites believers to identify with him and to emulate the ways that he overcomes each temptation. While the kinds of temptations women and other vulnerable persons face are often very different, even opposite those endured by Jesus, we can appropriate his manner of dealing with them: claiming the power of the Spirit[26] and using the Scriptures to speak rightly of God. The devil quotes Psalm 91:11-12 when he is tempting Jesus to throw himself down from the pinnacle of the temple and to call on God to rescue him (4:10-11). Feminists can resonate with the way Jesus unmasks the devil's manipulation of Scripture and then quotes it rightly. We find this akin to the way feminist biblical scholars denounce interpretations of the Bible that fuel kyriarchy and reinterpret it in ways that promote flourishing of all humans and creation.

One way that believers misinterpret this scene is when they use it to explain that God is testing them when they are undergoing difficulties. We find such an image of God troubling and without support in this scene of Jesus's temptations. It is not God but the devil who tests Jesus (4:2 ; see also Jas 1:13). God's Holy Spirit fills him and leads him (4:1), and the word of God in Scripture is what gives Jesus the ability to withstand the temptations posed by the devil.

23. See further comments in chaps. 22–23 on the dangerous implications of casting the Jewish leaders as the devil.

24. See excursus at 11:2 on the prevalence of prayer in Luke.

25. See further comments at 9:28-36.

26. See excursus on feminist understandings of the Spirit in chap. 1.

Good News and Liberation (4:14-30)

Teaching in Synagogues (4:14-15)

Having let the Spirit lead him in the wilderness, Jesus is filled with the power of the Spirit and returns to the Galilee (4:14). He is teaching[27] in synagogues, and news about him begins to spread (4:14; 4:37). The synagogue was not only the gathering place for prayer but also the space for "public gatherings, communal meals, the storage of monies and sacred scrolls, the administration of justice, . . . manumission procedures, charitable activities, and a range of educational functions."[28] Following the communal reading of the Torah and Nevi'im (Prophets), there would be teaching and open discussion about the meaning of the text.[29] Jesus teaches and debates in these gatherings as a key strategy for advancing

---

27. The NRSV translation takes the verb ἐδίδασκεν in 4:15 as incipient: "he began to teach." The imperfect tense, however, is better translated "was teaching," indicating repeated actions. See Levine and Witherington, *The Gospel of Luke*, 112; Robert C. Tannehill, *Luke*, ANTC (Nashville: Abingdon, 1996), 90. For other instances of διδάσκειν, see 5:3, 17; 11:1; 12:12; 13:22, 26; 19:47; 20:1, 21; 21:37; 23:5.

28. Lee I. Levine, "The Synagogue," in *The Jewish Annotated New Testament*, ed. Amy-Jill Levine and Marc Zvi Brettler, 2nd ed. (New York: Oxford University Press, 2017), 662–66, here 663. The origin of the synagogue and whether there were any single-purpose synagogue buildings in the first century remain question of debate. See Leslie J. Hoppe, "Synagogue," in *The Collegeville Pastoral Dictionary of Biblical Theology*, ed. Carroll Stuhlmueller (Collegeville, MN: Liturgical Press, 1996), 969–71; Leslie J. Hoppe, *The Synagogues and Churches of Ancient Palestine* (Collegeville, MN: Liturgical Press, 1993); Mordechai Aviam, "People, Land, Economy, and Belief in First-Century Galilee and Its Origins: A Comprehensive Archaeological Synthesis," in *The Galilean Economy in the Time of Jesus*, ed. David A. Fiensy and Ralph K. Hawkins, ECL 11 (Atlanta: SBL, 2013), 5–48, esp. 37–41; Jordan J. Ryan, *The Role of the Synagogue in the Aims of Jesus* (Minneapolis: Fortress, 2017); James D. G. Dunn, "Did Jesus Attend the Synagogue?," in *Jesus and Archaeology*, ed. James H. Charlesworth (Grand Rapids: Eerdmans, 2006), 206–22; Lee I. Levine, *The Ancient Synagogue: The First Thousand Years* (New Haven, CT: Yale University Press, 2000).

29. According to Carl Mosser ("Torah Instruction, Discussion, and Prophecy in First-Century Synagogues," in *Christian Origins and Hellenistic Judaism: Social and Literary Contexts for the New Testament*, ed. Stanley E. Porter and Andrew W. Pitts, Texts and Editions for New Testament Study 10 [Leiden: Brill, 2013], 523–51), "anyone could offer insights or dispute the interpretive claims of others" (550). The Theodotos Inscription, which likely dates to the early first century, lists the study of the Torah and teaching as primary functions of the synagogue. See John S. Kloppenborg, "The Theodotos Synagogue Inscription and the Problem of First-Century Synagogue Buildings," in Charlesworth, *Jesus and Archaeology*, 236–82.

Luke 4:14-30

[14]Then Jesus, filled with the power of the Spirit, returned to Galilee, and a report about him spread through all the surrounding country. [15]He began to teach in their synagogues and was praised by everyone.

[16]When he came to Nazareth, where he had been brought up, he went to the synagogue on the sabbath day, as was his custom. He stood up to read, [17]and the scroll of the prophet Isaiah was given to him. He unrolled the scroll and found the place where it was written:

[18]"The Spirit of the Lord is upon me, because he has anointed me to bring good news to the poor.
He has sent me to proclaim release to the captives
and recovery of sight to the blind,
to let the oppressed go free,
[19]to proclaim the year of the Lord's favor."

[20]And he rolled up the scroll, gave it back to the attendant, and sat down. The eyes of all in the synagogue were fixed on him. [21]Then he began to say to them, "Today this scripture has been fulfilled in your hearing." [22]All spoke well

his mission (see also 4:31; 6:6; 13:10).[30] In Acts, Paul and his companions continue this practice.[31]

Though many scholars engaged in questions concerning the historical Jesus and his followers imagine them as illiterate, or semiliterate at best, Luke drops the reference to Jesus being a carpenter (τέκτων) from his source (Mark 6:3) and depicts Jesus as having a high literacy level. Jesus is able to unroll the scroll (or possibly, to "open the codex") to the precise passage he seeks and to read without hesitancy. Presenting Jesus as having scribal

30. All four gospels depict Jesus as teaching in synagogues: Mark 1:38-39; Matt 4:23; Luke 4:15-16; 4:43-44; John 18:20. Jordan Ryan (*The Role of the Synagogue*, 141) notes that Jesus's strategy differed from that of John the Baptist, who stayed in a fixed area. Ryan argues that "the synagogue was intrinsic rather than incidental to the aims of Jesus, and that it was both the vehicle and the means by which he intended to bring the Kingdom of God, as he conceived of it, into existence" (18). In Mark and Matthew, Jesus does not teach again in a synagogue after being rejected in Nazareth. In Luke, Jesus teaches three other times in a synagogue on the sabbath. In each instance, he heals a person, evoking amazement and approval from the crowds (4:37; 13:17) but opposition from the scribes and Pharisees (6:11) and a synagogue leader (13:14).

31. Acts 9:20; 13:5, 14, 42-44; 14:1; 17:1-2, 10, 17; 18:4, 19; 19:8. See also 18:26, where Apollos teaches in the synagogue.

of him and were amazed at the gracious words that came from his mouth. They said, "Is not this Joseph's son?" [23]He said to them, "Doubtless you will quote to me this proverb, 'Doctor, cure yourself!' And you will say, 'Do here also in your hometown the things that we have heard you did at Capernaum.'" [24]And he said, "Truly I tell you, no prophet is accepted in the prophet's hometown. [25]But the truth is, there were many widows in Israel in the time of Elijah, when the heaven was shut up three years and six months, and there was a severe famine over all the land; [26]yet Elijah was sent to none of them except to a widow at Zarephath in Sidon. [27]There were also many lepers in Israel in the time of the prophet Elisha, and none of them was cleansed except Naaman the Syrian." [28]When they heard this, all in the synagogue were filled with rage. [29]They got up, drove him out of the town, and led him to the brow of the hill on which their town was built, so that they might hurl him off the cliff. [30]But he passed through the midst of them and went on his way.

literacy[32] makes sense in view of the author's concern to depict the movement in reassuring ways to Theophilus, the ideal reader. Book culture comes to be an increasingly important sign of status in the late first and early second century.[33] Polishing the portrait of Jesus in this way, to align him with those with access to formal scribal education, removes him from the bottom rungs of social standing. Though Luke's Jesus advocates for the poor and marginalized in verses 18-19, it is clear he does so from a superior station.[34] The question of Jesus's level of literacy raises christological issues. In particular, it impacts how one views Jesus

32. "Scribal literacy" refers to "literate skills that allow some educated individuals to function as authoritative interpreters of texts." This includes scribes responsible for documents in civil government (e.g., marriage contracts, land deeds, bills of sale) and religious authorities who are experts in sacred texts. Scribes referred to in the gospels are recognized authoritative readers, copyists, and teachers of the law. Chris Keith, *Jesus' Literacy: Scribal Culture and the Teacher from Galilee*, Library of Historical Jesus Studies 8, LNTS 413 (New York: T&T Clark, 2011), 110.

33. Roger S. Bagnall, "Jesus Reads a Book," *JTS* 51 (2000): 577–88. For observations on depicting early Christians as engaged in book culture, see John S. Kloppenborg, "Literate Media in Early Christ Groups: The Creation of a Christian Book Culture," *JECS* 22 (2014): 21–59.

34. As we noted in chap. 1, Greg Carey observes that though the Gospel is "designed to challenge insiders and welcome outsiders, Luke does so from the perspective of the prosperous, the male, the religious insider, and the righteous person" (*Luke: An Introduction and Study Guide; All Flesh Shall See God's Salvation*, T&T Clark's Study Guides to the New Testament [London: Bloomsbury T&T Clark, 2017], 88).

as a teacher and, thus, how one interprets the controversies with other teachers.[35] As feminists with low christologies who do not believe that the historical Jesus was omniscient, we are not troubled at the thought that Jesus shared with the majority of his contemporaries a lack of scribal literacy. Furthermore, we do not equate the lack of literacy with a lack of intelligence.

We expect that there were women in the Nazareth synagogue gathering. There is no evidence that the prayer spaces for women and men were separate or that there was a women's balcony at the time of Jesus.[36] In several episodes in Luke and Acts there are women present in the synagogue. At Luke 13:10-17 a woman who had been bent for eighteen years comes into the synagogue on the sabbath while Jesus is teaching. In Acts 16:12-14, when Paul and Silas look for a place of prayer (προσευχὴν, v. 13),[37] they find a group of women, among whom was Lydia. In Acts 17:4, "not a few of the leading women" hear Paul and Silas preach in the synagogue in Thessalonica and join them. And finally, in Acts 18:26, Priscilla and her husband Aquila hear Apollos preaching in a synagogue in Ephesus and take him aside to explain the Way of God more accurately to him.[38]

That women would have been able to read from the Torah as Jesus did and carry out other functions in the synagogue service is very likely.

---

35. Keith, *Jesus' Literacy*, 23. Keith shows that there were two different ways that the early church remembered Jesus: as a scribal-literate teacher (as Luke presents him) and as a teacher who did not hold scribal literacy (e.g., Mark 6:1-5 // Matt 13:54-58) but managed to convince many in his audiences that he did. The differing versions of the Nazareth synagogue scene are illustrative: in Mark and Matthew, the townspeople reject Jesus because he is a common artisan without scribal education and is not qualified to teach in the synagogue. In Luke, Jesus is a scribal-literate; they reject him because he will not perform miracles for them. Keith concludes that most likely Jesus did not hold scribal literacy but was perceived to be a scribal-literate teacher by some members of his audiences. The controversy narratives, then, are not in-house debates between equally qualified/authoritative teachers but "attempts on the part of the scribal-literate authorities to expose Jesus as an imposter to the position of interpretive authority" (191).

36. See Bernadette J. Brooten, *Women Leaders in the Ancient Synagogue: Inscriptional Evidence and Background Issues*, BJS 36 (Chico, CA: Scholars Press, 1982), 103–38; Lee I. Levine, "The Synagogue," 663.

37. Προσευχή is the equivalent of συναγωγή (BDAG, 878); see Martin Hengel, "Proseuche und Synagoge. Jüdische Gemeinde, Gotteshaus und Gottesdienst in der Diaspora und in Palästina," in *Festschrift Karl George Kuhn. Tradition und Glaube: das frühe Christentum in seiner Umwelt. Festgabe für Karl Georg Kuhn zum 65. Geburtstag*, ed. Gert Jeremias, Heinz-Wolfgang Kuhn, and Hartmut Stegemann (Göttingen: Vandenhoeck & Ruprecht, 1971), 157–84.

38. See Brooten, *Women Leaders in the Ancient Synagogue*, 140–41, for examples in rabbinic literature that also speak of women participating in synagogue services.

Some women would have had the education to do so (see the excursus "Women's Authorship in Antiquity" in the authors' introduction), and Priscilla is depicted as teaching (ἐξέθεντο) Apollos in the synagogue at Ephesus (Acts 18:26).[39] Bernadette Brooten has shown that women bore titles such as "head of synagogue," "leader," "elder," "mother of the synagogue," and "priest" and argues that the women assumed the same functions that their male counterparts with those titles had. Brooten sketches the following possibilities: women heads of synagogues had an administrative role, were knowledgeable in Torah, and taught and exhorted their congregations; as elders, they could have been part of the council of elders, exercising oversight of the finances and sitting in front during the synagogue service facing the people; elders might also have been scholars and may have had some say about the reading of the Scriptures in the synagogue; and as priests, they may have had a cultic function or perhaps a synagogue function such as reading from the Torah. Women donors and patrons of synagogues may also have taken on these kinds of roles as they exercised influence in the workings of the synagogue.[40]

At the conclusion of this chapter, Jesus continues proclaiming the message (ἦν κηρύσσων)[41] in the synagogues of Judea (4:44).[42] Jesus's initial teaching draws universal praise (4:15), but this will quickly change.

---

39. It is also possible to read προσελάβοντο αὐτὸν, "they took him aside," to mean that they took him outside the synagogue.

40. Ibid., 32, 55, 99, 141–44.

41. This verb is used of John the Baptizer's preaching at 3:3 and of Jesus's preaching at 4:18, 19; 8:1. At 8:39, the man healed of a demon "went away proclaiming [κηρύσσων] throughout the city how much Jesus had done for him." Jesus sends the Twelve out to proclaim (κηρύσσειν) the basileia of God (9:2). At 12:3 Jesus tells his disciples "what you have whispered behind closed doors will be proclaimed [κηρυχθήσεται] from the housetops." The risen Christ instructs the eleven and their companions (24:33) "that repentance and forgiveness of sins is to be proclaimed [κηρυχθῆναι] in his name to all nations, beginning from Jerusalem" (24:47). In Acts, those who proclaim (κηρύσσειν) are Peter (10:41-42), Philip (8:5), and Paul (9:20; 19:13; 20:25; 28:31). No women are explicitly told to proclaim or are said to do so.

42. Here "Judea" can be understood in a comprehensive sense: all the country of the Jews (as at 1:5; 6:17; 7:17; 23:5; Acts 10:37). It is not until 9:51 that Jesus begins to journey toward Jerusalem, and his first appearance in a Judean synagogue is at 13:10. Luke says, however, that Jesus's fame had spread to Judea earlier: 5:17; 6:17; 7:17. John S. Kloppenborg, "Luke's Geography: Knowledge, Ignorance, Sources, and Spatial Conception," in *Luke on Jesus, Paul, and Christianity: What Did He Really Know?*, ed. Joseph Verheyden and John S. Kloppenborg, BTS 29 (Leuven: Peeters, 2017), 101–43, shows this to be one of many instances in which Luke is fuzzy on the geography of interior Syro-Palestine.

Rejected Prophet (4:16-30)

Jesus comes to his hometown, Nazareth (4:16), the setting for Mary's prophetic call (1:26-38).[43] Luke cast Elizabeth, Zechariah, Simeon, Anna, and John as prophets;[44] henceforth Jesus takes that role. Citing Isaiah,[45] he presents himself as a prophet upon whom the Spirit rests, anointed[46] by God to bring good news (εὐαγγελίσασθαι)[47] to the poor, release to captive and oppressed persons, recovery of sight to those unable to see, and to proclaim a year of God's favor (4:18-19). Like Elijah (1 Kgs 13:1-6; 17:17-24) and Elisha (2 Kgs 4:8-37; 5:1-19), Jesus's prophetic mission involves not only proclamation of good news but also healing,[48] which makes visible the inbreaking of God's reign.

Good News to the Poor

The Lukan Jesus has more to say about riches and poverty than in any other gospel.[49] His Sermon on the Plain (6:17-49) begins with "Blessed are you who are poor" (6:20) and "woe to you who are rich" (6:24). He declares that a person cannot serve both God and mammon[50] (16:13).

---

43. See comments on Mary as prophet at 1:26-30, 46-56. Luke has expanded considerably on the Markan version of this scene (6:1-6). The setting and the substance are the same: a reference to Jesus's parentage, a proverb, and an initial positive reaction, then negative. Luke's additions underscore Jesus's identity as prophet, aligning him with Isaiah, Elijah, and Elisha.

44. See comments on Elizabeth's prophetic speaking at 1:24-25, 39-45, 57-66; Zechariah at 1:8-23, 67-80; Simeon at 2:22-35; Anna at 2:36-38; John at 3:1-17.

45. The text Jesus reads is a combination of Isa 61:1a; 58:6; 61:2a; and 42:7. Levine and Witherington (*The Gospel According to Luke*, 115) note that this combination is unusual; unlike Christian lectionaries that select and combine sections of a book, synagogue readings do not combine or omit verses. Jordan J. Ryan (*Synagogue*, 176) proposes that this combination may be an instance of the hermeneutical method *gĕzērâ šāwâ*, which fuses together two different passages of Scripture that have similar words of phrases. In this instance, שלח, "to send," and רצון, "acceptable," occur in the MT of both Isa 58:5-6 and 61:1-2, as does ἄφεσις in the LXX.

46. See comments at 2:11 on *Christos*, "anointed one."

47. See comments at 2:10 on good news. See 4:43; 7:22; 8:1; 16:16; 20:1 for Jesus's proclaiming good news (εὐαγγελίζομαι).

48. See John J. Pilch, *Healing in the New Testament: Insights from Medical and Mediterranean Anthropology* (Minneapolis: Fortress, 2000), 94–103, who shows Jesus to be a folk healer, in contrast to a professional physician, ἰατρός (4:23; 5:31; 8:43). For comments on women healers, see below at 4:38-39.

49. See excursus "Luke and Riches" at 16:1.

50. Mammon is "material wealth or possessions especially as having a debasing influence" (*Merriam-Webster*: https://www.merriam-webster.com/dictionary/mammon).

When a rich official is unable to leave everything to follow Jesus as Peter, James, John (5:11), and Levi (5:18) did, Jesus speaks about how difficult it is for a rich person to enter the kingdom of God (18:25). He tells the crowds, "none of you can become my disciple if you do not give up all your possessions" (14:33). He calls his disciples' attention to the gift of a poor widow, contrasting it with gifts of the rich who give from their abundance (21:1-4). In two of the parables unique to Luke, the rich fool (12:16-21) and the rich man and Lazarus (16:19-23), Jesus paints the dire consequences of accumulating riches for oneself.

Each of these stories and sayings adds weight to the seriousness with which followers of Jesus must grapple with questions concerning their use of possessions and care for those who are poor. In 4:18, as elsewhere in Luke, Jesus is not speaking about those who are "poor in spirit" (cf. Matt 5:3); πτωχοῖς, "poor," refers primarily to those who are economically impoverished. As has always been the case, the majority of poor people are women and children (see the excursus "Women and Poverty"). Not only does Jesus teach about the danger of riches, but his disciples model various ways in which they use material goods to bring good news. Some, such as Simon Peter, James, John, and Levi, leave everything to follow Jesus (5:11, 28). Others retain their possessions but place them at the service of Jesus's mission, as Mary Magdalene, Joanna, Susanna, and other Galilean women do with their financial resources (8:1-3). Zacchaeus, a wealthy chief tax collector, gives half his possessions to the poor (19:1-10). The nascent community of Jesus's followers held all things in common and "would sell their possessions and goods and distribute the proceeds to all, as any had need" (Acts 2:44) so that "there was not a needy person among them" (Acts 4:34).[51] As we remarked at 1:53, Christian communities of women and men religious today still try to live in this manner. In Israel, kibbutzim (plural of kibbutz, קיבוץ, "gathering, clustering"), collective communities, also have a similar aim. The gospel gives no uniform way to respond personally and does not propose

---

51. For analysis of this theme in each section of the Bible, see Leslie J. Hoppe, *There Shall Be No Poor among You: Poverty in the Bible* (Nashville: Abingdon, 2004). On the Lukan theme, see John Gillman, *Possessions and the Life of Faith: A Reading of Luke–Acts, Zacchaeus Studies*, New Testament (Collegeville, MN: Liturgical Press, 1991); Luke T. Johnson, *The Literary Function of Possessions in Luke–Acts*, SBLDS 39 (Missoula: Scholars Press, 1977); Christopher M. Hays, *Luke's Wealth Ethics: A Study in Their Coherence and Character*, WUNT 2.275 (Tübingen: Mohr Siebeck, 2010); Christopher M. Hays, *Renouncing Everything: Money and Discipleship in Luke* (New York: Paulist Press, 2016).

a comprehensive economic system. In Jesus's declaration at 4:18, Luke plants the hope of finding a way for equitable distribution, still a great challenge in our own times.

Women and Poverty

On the twentieth anniversary of the Beijing Declaration and Platform for Action, adopted by 189 member states in 1995, the United Nations Entity for Gender Equality and the Empowerment of Women reports:[51]

The last few years have seen historic achievements in reducing the number of people who are poor, making the end of extreme poverty possible in the coming generation. That requires cutting the multiple roots of impoverishment. One of the deepest is gender discrimination, which imposes a disproportionate burden on women.

When women are poor, their rights are not protected. They face obstacles that may be extraordinarily difficult to overcome. This results in deprivation in their own lives and losses for the broader society and economy, as women's productivity is well known as one of the greatest generators of economic dynamism.

While both men and women suffer in poverty, gender discrimination means that women have far fewer resources to cope. They are likely to be the last to eat, the ones least likely to access healthcare, and routinely trapped in time-consuming, unpaid domestic tasks. They have more limited options to work or build businesses. Adequate education may lie out of reach. Some end up forced into sexual exploitation as part of a basic struggle to survive.

And while women at large have not yet achieved an equal political voice, women in poverty face extra marginalization. Their voices are rarely heard, for example, in decisions on managing an economy, or sharing benefits and costs.

The Beijing Declaration and Platform for Action, adopted by 189 Member States in 1995, . . . reflects the urgency around women and

---

52. United Nations Entity for Gender Equality and the Empowerment of Women, "The Beijing Platform for Action Turns 20," http://beijing20.unwomen.org/en/in-focus /poverty.

poverty by making it the first of 12 critical areas of concern. Actions under any of these, whether education, the environment, and so on, help women build better lives. But measures targeted to reducing women's poverty are critical too.

Governments agreed to change economic policies to provide more opportunities for women, improve laws to uphold economic rights, and boost access to credit.[52]

They are committed to collecting better information to track how poverty affects women differently, as knowing any problem is essential for solving it.

Since Beijing, much progress has been made in these areas.[53] There is still far to go. Ending extreme poverty will come within reach only by fully involving women and respecting their rights—at every step along the way.

Release, Sight, and Freedom

Next Jesus proclaims release (ἄφεσιν) to people who are captive (αἰχμαλώτοις), recovery of sight to those who are blind,[55] and freedom for those who are oppressed (τεθραυσμένους). The meaning of the middle phrase is clear. Luke reports that Jesus did give sight to many who were blind (7:21), and he tells the story of Jesus healing a man near Jericho who begged Jesus to let him see again (18:35-43). The meaning of the other two phrases and how the freedom or release will be accomplished is less clear. The word ἄφεσις, "release," appears in both phrases. The

---

53. One example is Professor Muhammad Yunus, who established the Grameen Bank in Bangladesh to help people escape from poverty by providing loans without collateral to support income-generating activities. From its modest beginnings in 1976, today the Grameen Bank is the forefront of a burgeoning world movement toward eradicating poverty through microlending. Ninety-seven percent of its 8.4 million borrowers are women. It has lent over USD 8.4 billion with a near 100 percent repayment rate. See https://beijing20.unwomen.org/en/news-and-events/stories/2014/10/oped-muhammad-yunus.

54. For stories of girls who are being taught income-earning skills and women farmers who are learning about nutrition, modern agricultural techniques, and business skills and creating cooperatives in Rwanda, Malawi, Egypt, Guatemala, and Ecuador, see https://beijing20.unwomen.org/en/in-focus/poverty.

55. Scholars working in the area of disability studies urge that people who have disabilities not be identified by their disability and to put their personhood ahead of their disability, e.g., to say "a man who is blind" instead of saying "a blind man."

word αἰχμαλώτοις, "captives," ordinarily refers to those who have been taken as prisoners of war.[56] Luke's readers in Asia Minor might think of the scores of images of Barbarian captives, subdued by Roman emperors, that featured in the cityscapes and coins of that region. Here, for instance, is an image of a Roman emperor with a kneeling Barbarian at his feet.[57]

In the Lukan Jesus's context, "captives" can refer to political prisoners, such as John, whom Herod had put in prison for having rebuked him because of Herodias, his brother's wife (3:19-20). Josephus says that Herod imprisoned John in his fortress at Machaerus, a rocky mountaintop on the east side of the Dead Sea (*Ant.* 18.5.2). In biblical times, people were not imprisoned as a punishment; they were put in detention when awaiting

56. BDAG, 32.
57. Picture by Katherine A. Shaner. Statue is located in the Istanbul Archaeological Museum. Used with photographer's permission.

trial or the execution of a sentence. Jesus does not say how he intended to release such captives. John the Baptist dies in prison (Matt 14:10 // Mark 6:27), and Jesus himself is executed after his arrest. Ironically, Barabbas, who was put in prison for insurrection and murder, is released instead of Jesus (23:19, 25). Rather than take Jesus's declaration in 4:18 as a literal outline for Jesus's missionary program, we agree with Fred Danker that "the political language of the text is unmistakable. Greco-Roman auditors would associate with these prophetic words the kinds of expectations that were pronounced at the beginning of an imperial reign."[58]

There are a number of scenes in Acts where Jesus's disciples are imprisoned for preaching about Jesus and then released. A Spirit-filled defense and fear of the people lead to Peter and John's release (4:8, 21, 31); twice a nocturnal visit of an angel of the Lord procures Peter and the apostles' freedom (5:17-19; 12:6-11); an earthquake opens the doors of the prison and unfastens the chains for Paul and Silas (16:19-36). Perhaps Luke intends Jesus's proclamation at 4:18 to reassure any disciple who preaches in his name that they can expect divine intervention to free them (see 21:12-19). But what of James, the brother of John, who is killed by Herod (Acts 12:2)? And what of Paul, who despite numerous defense speeches and appeals is still, after years of detention, imprisoned at the end of Acts. Beyond the accounts of Luke, we know that both Peter and Paul were eventually martyred. It seems that Jesus's declaration in 4:18 must be taken in a spiritual or metaphorical sense, as when he tells the disciples in Luke 21:16-18: "they will put some of you to death. . . . But not a hair of your head will perish."

Women Captives Today

There are many ways in which people are held captive today. Here we name only some that involve women. One of the most widely known incidents in our time is the kidnapping of 276 girls by Boko Haram,[58] from a school in Chibok, Nigeria, in April 2014. Frustrated with the slow and unsuccessful response of the government, concerned citizens organized under the banner Bring Back Our Girls,

---

58. Frederick W. Danker, *Jesus and the New Age: A Commentary on St. Luke's Gospel*, rev. and expanded ed. (Philadelphia: Fortress, 1988), 107.

59. Boko Haram is a jihadist terrorist organization based in northeastern Nigeria that began in 2002. They target schools because they believe Western education corrupts the values of Muslims.

"advocating for speedy and effective search and rescue of all abducted girls and for a rapid containment and quelling of insurgency in Nigeria."[59] As of 2019, 57 have escaped, 107 were released in exchange for Boko Haram militants, and 112 of them are still missing. Some are thought to have died; many have been forced to marry their captors. Because of the global outcry and the efforts of the International Committee of the Red Cross, who brokered the release of some of the girls, a portion of the captives have been freed. But not all cases are so high profile. In 2015 Amnesty International estimated that some two thousand women and girls had been taken captive since 2014, many of whom were forced into sexual slavery.[60] This number does not include boys who have been taken and forced to become soldiers. The trauma for the girls taken captive does not end with their release. The challenges of reintegrating into their families and towns are oftentimes insurmountable, as a documentary about the stolen daughters shows.[61]

Human trafficking is another form of captivity today. This expression refers to a variety of ways that people are held against their will and forced into work. The International Organization for Migration estimates that globally in 2016 approximately 24.9 million people are trapped in forced labor. Of those people, 16 million are exploited in the private sector, doing work such as domestic, construction, or agriculture; 4.8 million persons are in forced sexual exploitation; and 4 million persons are in forced labor imposed by state authorities. An additional 15.4 million are in forced marriage. Because of the hidden nature of these crimes, it is difficult to give accurate numbers. But what is known is that women and girls are disproportionately affected. They account for 99 percent of victims in the commercial sex

60. See their website: https://bringbackourgirls.ng/.

61. BBC News, "Nigeria Chibok Abductions: What We Know," May 8, 2017: https://www.bbc.com/news/world-africa-32299943. Another one hundred girls were taken in February 2018 from the northeastern town of Dapchi. The government once again was slow and unsuccessful in their response. See Tara John, "Boko Haram Has Kidnapped Dozens of Schoolgirls, Again: Here's What to Know," *TIME*, February 26, 2018, https://time.com/5175464/boko-haram-kidnap-dapchi-schoolgirls/.

62. Amanda Holpuch, "Stolen Daughters: What Happened after #BringBackOurGirls?," *The Guardian*, October 22, 2018: https://www.theguardian.com/tv-and-radio/2018/oct/22/bring-back-our-girls-documentary-stolen-daughters-kidnapped-boko-haram.

industry, and 58 percent in other sectors.[62]

One response to this reality is International Network of Religious Against Trafficking in Persons, which was launched in Rome in October 2007 by a group of thirty women religious leaders from twenty-six different countries. A similar group of US Catholic Sisters Against Human Trafficking (USCSAHT) has organized with the following aims:[63]

- Advocate for national legislation that:
  - addresses the evil of human rights violations against trafficked persons
  - allocates resources for human trafficking victims' essential services
- Build positive relationships with legislators and their staffs, other advocates in coalitions, and USCSAHT members
- Meet regularly with legislators and their staff members, in district and on the Hill
- Encourage USCSAHT members to be in regular contact with legislators and their staff members
- Provide legislative and policy updates for inclusion on USCSAHT's website, including action alerts for response by members and others
- Participate in events or actions addressing human trafficking as appropriate
- Collaborate with other USCSAHT working groups

Success stories can be found in their monthly reflection, such as "Pathway to a Better Life" by Sister of Mercy Jeanne Christensen who works in Haiti, written March 5, 2020.[64] She describes an eighteen-month program with a 96-percent graduation rate in which women who are among the poorest and most vulnerable are provided education and resources to help them create a better life and reduce the risk of them falling victim to trafficking.[65]

There are also political prisoners around the globe, many of whom are women. Some suffer horrific abuses, including sexual abuse,

63. International Labor Organization, "Forced Labor, Modern Slavery and Human Trafficking," https://www.ilo.org/global/topics/forced-labour/lang—en/index.htm.

64. See their website: https://www.sistersagainsttrafficking.org/about/who-we-are/.

65. Jeanne Christensen, RSM, in collaboration with Dale Jarvis, RSM, "Pathway to a Better Life," https://www.sistersagainsttrafficking.org/2020/03/05/march-2020-monthly-reflection/.

66. This information is from the International Labour Organization, "Forced Labour, Modern Slavery, and Human Trafficking," http://www.ilo.org/global/topics/forced-labour/lang--en/index.htm.

medical neglect, humiliation, and deprivation of basic necessities.[66] Working to release political prisoners are groups such as Amnesty International, Human Rights Watch, and many national organizations. Their actions include investigating and exposing facts, lobbying governments, educating people, and telling the stories of detainees to reveal the truth and to mobilize supporters.[67]

More than physical release is needed. Artistic expression in painting, drawing, sculpture, film, and books, such as the project "The Art of Resistance in Iran," frees former captives from other ways in which they remain bound while simultaneously raising consciousness about their plight.[68]

The final phrase of 4:18, "to let the oppressed go free," is less specific about who are "the oppressed" and how Jesus might send them off (ἀποστεῖλαι) in freedom (ἐν ἀφέσει). The allusion to the Jubilee Year, "the year of the Lord's favor," in 4:19 leads us to read 4:18 in that light.[70] As Anne Elvey describes the Jubilee:

Here ἄφεσις interrupts the usual social cycles with freedom upon the land/earth for all its inhabitants (ἐπὶ τῆς γῆς πᾶσιν τοῖς κατοικοῦσιν αὐτήν; Lev 25:10 LXX). Agricultural labour is suspended (Lev 25:11) and from the open country (ἀπὸ τῶν πεδίων) the people are to eat the land's products (τὰ γενήματα αὐτῆς; Lev 25:12). Moreover, ἄφεσις extends to the way the people buy and sell the land and its produce; the Jubilee interrupts the capacity for anyone to own the land (Lev 25:13-17). On the principle that the land belongs to YHWH (Lev 25:23), the people are tenants who must keep the land (Lev 25:23-24) in such a way that they enable the divine blessing to be effective in the season of Jubilee (Lev 25:18-22). They must provide for the redemption of the land (Lev 25:24-28), so that all can return to their ancestral holdings as to a gift. In this dispensation of liberation (ἄφεσις), kin who fall into difficulty are not to be treated as

---

67. See the Fact Sheet from Amnesty International: https://www.prisonpolicy.org/scans/women_prison.pdf.

68. See "What Does Amnesty Do?," https://www.amnesty.org/en/who-we-are/; Human Rights Watch provides news on individual political prisoners around the globe: https://www.hrw.org/tag/political-prisoners#; as also Alliance for Global Justice: https://afgj.org/politicalprisonersusa.

69. See "The Art of Resistance in Iran": https://womenpoliticalprisoners.com/.

70. See Lev 25:8-55 for how the Jubilee was to be carried out every fiftieth year. See also Christopher J. H. Wright, "Jubilee, Year of," ABD 3.1025–29.

slaves, but to be paid workers, who are released from the authority of the house in the Jubilee, returning to their ancestral holdings (Lev 25:40-41).[71]

There is no evidence that the Jubilee Year was ever practiced, but the ideals it offers for equitable distribution of the land and resources and the release from debt remain timely. The Lukan Jesus's teachings about the dangers of accumulating riches echo these Jubilee ideals, and his disciples attempt equitable distribution of their resources (Acts 2:44; 4:34; see comments above on Good News for the Poor).

In every other instance in Luke and Acts, ἄφεσις means release from sin,[72] and perhaps that is how we should read it in 4:18. In that case, Jesus fulfills that part of his mission program when he declares forgiven a man who was paralyzed (5:20) and a woman who anoints his feet (7:47, 48) and prays for God to forgive his executioners (23:34). He teaches his disciples to forgive (6:37; 11:4; 17:3-4), and his final instruction to them is to proclaim repentance and forgiveness of sins in his name to all nations (24:47). Peter and Paul carry out that commission in Acts.[73] Jesus also sets people free from demons (4:33-35, 41; 8:2, 26-39; 9:37-43; 11:14; 13:32)[74] and sickness, but Luke does not describe these acts as "freeing." An exception is at 13:12, where Jesus tells the woman bent for eighteen years, "you are set free from your ailment," but in this case the verb is ἀπολέλυσαι, not ἀφίημι.

Jesus's proclamation of good news to the poor, release for captives, sight for the blind, and freedom for the oppressed begins to be fulfilled by Jesus's and his disciples' teaching, preaching, and actions. To try to enact these ideals is still a challenge for subsequent generations of believers. Feminists can hear in Jesus's declaration a rallying cry to work toward eradicating poverty, which primarily affects women and children (see excursus "Women and Poverty"). It urges us to work to free girls and wo/men who are captive and trafficked. It compels us to educate those who are blind to practices and systems that oppress wo/men and to work to change those patterns and structures. Such actions bring to fulfillment the ideals voiced by Leviticus 25, the prophet Isaiah, and Jesus.

---

71. Anne Elvey, "Can There Be a Forgiveness That Makes a Difference Ecologically? An Eco-Materialist Account of Forgiveness as Freedom (ἄφεσις) in the Gospel of Luke," *Pacifica* 22 (2009): 148–70, here 163.

72. The noun ἄφεσις, "release," is used for release from sin at 1:77; 3:3; 24:47; the verb ἀφίημι, meaning forgiveness for sin, occurs at 5:20, 21, 23, 24; 7:47, 48, 49; 11:4; 12:10; 17:3, 4; 23:34; Acts 2:38; 5:31; 8:22; 10:43; 13:38; 26:18.

73. Peter at Acts 2:38; 5:31; 8:22; 10:43; Paul at 13:38; 26:18.

74. Joel B. Green, *The Gospel of Luke*, NICNT (Grand Rapids: Eerdmans, 1997), 212.

The Matter of the Text and *Aphesis*: Luke 4:16-30 in (Post-)Colonial Context

At a moment in the gospel, the Lukan Jesus takes matter into his hands by unrolling parchment or papyrus, animal skin or plant fiber, to read, touching the text (4:17).[74] As I encounter this text in Australia, I read and write as a descendent of settler-migrant-convict-invaders of a land whose many First Nations' cultures are tens of thousands of years older than the biblical texts of Isaiah from which Luke has Jesus read. Traditionally, scholars interpret Luke 4:16-30 as a programmatic text in which two passages from Isaiah (58:6; 61:1-2), two prophetic songs, entwine in a proclamation of freedom (*aphesis*, Luke 4:18-19). Luke derives and weaves the wisdom of *aphesis* from Leviticus 25:10 and the notion of Jubilee, a period of release for enslaved people and land.[75] *Aphesis* can refer to release from debt and debt slavery but also in Luke to forgiveness, in parallel with material freedom from debt (Luke 7:41-42, 47-49). The materiality of Lukan *aphesis* becomes relevant in what will become the nation of Australia when the colonizers arrive in the late eighteenth century with guns and smallpox, sheep and cattle, rabbits and rats, Bibles and crosses, blankets and beads, and their willed blindness to the Indigenous occupiers' claims to, and deeply embedded relationships with, land, sea, and sky. Here too, a little over two centuries later, politicians can win elections on cruel policies of offshore detention in the service of border control.[76] In what some Indigenous writers are calling "The Colony," not only the tragedy of young lives ended too soon, but resistance, resilience, and recognition are keynotes of First Nations' living under the ongoing system of invasion.[77]

As a material thing (a scroll) in the hands of the Lukan Jesus, a text opens through the breathy materiality of speaking both to the materialities of

74. For a more detailed engagement with the materiality of the text in the hands of the Lukan Jesus, see Anne Elvey, *The Matter of the Text: Material Engagements between Luke and the Five Senses* (Sheffield: Sheffield Phoenix, 2011), 44–53.

75. Elvey, "Can There Be a Forgiveness?," 148–70, esp. 162–65.

76. Mark G. Brett, *Political Trauma and Healing: Biblical Ethics for a Postcolonial World* (Grand Rapids: Eerdmans, 2016), 164.

77. On invasion as a structure rather than an event, see Patrick Wolfe, "Settler Colonialism and the Elimination of the Native," *Journal of Genocide Research* 8 (2006): 387–409, here 388; Tony Birch, "'We've Seen the End of the World and We Don't Accept It': Protection of Indigenous Country and Climate Justice," in *Places of Privilege: Interdisciplinary Perspectives on Identities, Change and Resistance*, ed. Nicole Oke, Christopher Sonn, and Alison Baker (Leiden: Brill, 2018), 139–52, here 141.

ancient lives under policies and practices of debt slavery[78] and the materialities of contemporary cries for freedom from the ongoing oppression of colonizing (kyriarchal) structures. The materialities of text and voice, touched (4:17) and heard (4:23, 28), not only speak to the desire for *aphesis* (4:18) but also provoke rejection (4:29). At the same time, the text challenges the hearer to risk witnessing to the life-denying worlds to which the promise of *aphesis* responds.

Behrouz Boochani, a Kurdish journalist and refugee from Iran, held in an Australian-run detention center on Manus Island in Papua New Guinea for over six years, describes the way, through nonviolent protest over three weeks in November 2017, he and the other detainees claimed their freedom while remaining in detention, a moment in which, I suggest, a kind of desire for and understanding of something like *aphesis* spoke back to the system imprisoning them.[79] Boochani continues to write and speak from detention, using Elisabeth Schüssler Fiorenza's term "kyriarchy" to critique the Kyriarchal System that underwrites what he calls Manus Prison.[80] Feminist biblical scholarship provides a term "kyriarchy" that, decades later, a man, oppressed by a nation from which he sought refuge, employs to analyze his situation and that of his codetainees.

While Luke 4:16-30 does not explicitly name women, the breath (*pneuma*, 1:47) with which Mary proclaims the reversals flows into the breath with which the Lukan Jesus proclaims

---

79. See the parable in Matt 18:23-34 that presumes that one can be taken into bondage to pay off a debt. In the Old Testament, debtors in utmost need who sold themselves could be held in slavery for only six years, after which they should be set free without any pay (Exod 21:2; Deut 15:12; Jer 34:14). Jews regarded any enslavement of Jews by Jews as improper because they had all become "slaves of God" through their liberation from Egyptian bondage (Lev 25:55). See Muhammad A. Dandamayev, "Slavery: Old Testament," ABD 6.62–65; and S. Scott Bartchy, "Slavery: New Testament," ABD 6.65–73.

80. Behrouz Boochani, "All We Want Is Freedom —Not Another Prison Camp," *The Guardian*, November 13, 2017, https://www.theguardian.com/commentisfree/2017/nov/13/all-we-want-is-freedom-not-another-prison-camp; Anne Elvey, "From Cultures of Violence to Ways of Peace: Reading the *Benedictus* in the Context of Australia's Treatment of Asylum Seekers in Offshore Detention," in *Things That Make for Peace: Traversing Text and Tradition in Christianity and Islam*, ed. Anthony Rees (Lanham, MD: Lexington, 2020).

81. Behrouz Boochani, *No Friend but the Mountains: Writing from Manus Prison*, trans. Omid Tofighian (Sydney: Picador, 2018); Omid Tofighian, "Translator's Tale: A Window to the Mountains," in Boochani, *No Friend but the Mountains*, xi–xxxiv, esp. xxvii; Elisabeth Schüssler Fiorenza, *But She Said: Feminist Practices of Biblical Interpretation* (Boston: Beacon, 1992), 8, 123. On kyriarchy, see above, xli.

release/freedom (*aphesis*), a
release that emerges through a
visitation of divine hospitality,
judgment, and compassion (1:68,
77-78; 19:41-44).[81] Although the
auspices of empire, of kyriarchy,
infect a Lukan imaginary,
the desire for and promise of
aphesis envisions cultures of
compassion and hospitality.
How we read, how we write,
how we attune ourselves to the
prophetic voices of our *kairos*
(12:56), cultivates the ground for
such cultures.

Aphesis
after Luke 4:16-20

Hands unroll
papyrus

worked from pith

and custom. Entwining

two ancient
songs, the reader

breathes the possible
even

as hearing, you
know that bound

hearts enchain
bodies. They

are sea-rent
and borne, arriving

against
any odds. Held

too long, their
singing is

as old as the plaint
of prophets.[82]

Anne F. Elvey

Fulfillment of Scripture

The theme of fulfillment of Scripture appears here for the first time (4:21) and weaves throughout the gospel. There are both allusions as well as direct quotations of the Septuagint (LXX, the Greek translation of the Hebrew Scriptures). Luke explicitly calls attention to the motif with the verb πληρόω, "to fulfill," and δεῖ, "it is necessary."[84] The theme comes to a climax in the last chapter of the gospel when the risen Christ says to Cleopas and his companion (who could have been a woman) on the road to Emmaus, "Oh, how foolish you are, and how slow of heart to believe all that the prophets have declared! Was it not necessary [ἔδει] that the Messiah should suffer these things and then enter into his glory?" (24:25-26). He then interprets for them everything about him in all the

82. On the interplay of divine visitation, hospitality, forgiveness, and compassion, see Brendan Byrne, *The Hospitality of God: A Reading of Luke's Gospel* (Strathfield, NSW: St Pauls, 2000).

83. Anne Elvey, *On Arrivals of Breath: Poems and Prayers* (Montrose, VIC: Poetica Christi Press, 2019). Used by permission.

84. πληρόω appears at Luke 1:20; 3:5; 4:21; 7:1; 9:31; 21:24; 22:16; 24:44; δεῖ at Luke 2:49; 4:43; 9:22; 11:42; 12:12; 13:14, 16, 33; 15:32; 17:25; 18:1; 19:5; 21:9; 22:7, 37; 24:7, 26, 44.

Scriptures (24:27). Luke is intent on showing that the Jesus movement is in continuity with all that God has done in the past. God who acted with power and mercy on behalf of Israel (1:49-55, 68-79) is the same faithful God who acts with salvific power through Christ. From a feminist perspective, continuity with the past is valuable when it concerns appropriating divine power and mercy in present-day contexts. When it comes to kyriarchal attitudes and structures from the past, it is necessary to leave these behind and replace them with egalitarian ones.[85]

Divided Responses

Jesus's prophetic proclamation evokes amazement and approval. As the gospel progresses, there will continue to be people who are lifted up through Jesus's words and deeds and who will be amazed at him (4:22) and praise him (4:15). At the same time, there will be authorities whose power, privilege, and status are threatened by him and who will work to do away with him. But the people in his hometown synagogue are not these authorities who will eventually execute him. They are faithful Jews who know him as Joseph's son (4:22) and who have heard about what he has been saying in other synagogues around the Galilee (4:14-15). They are amazed at his gracious words and are eager to hear more.

The mood shifts as Jesus says out loud what he imagines they might say: that they expect him to do at home for them what he has been doing in other places like Capernaum (4:23).[86] This imagined request sounds akin to the misguided sign-seekers whom Jesus denounces at 11:29. Jesus asserts that his neighbors in Nazareth will not accept him by making an implicit comparison between them and those who rejected the messages of Elijah and Elisha (4:25-27). The anger of the assembly is not because they hear Jesus praise Gentiles, such as the widow at Zarephath[87] and

---

85. For more on the problems of *appropriating* the past, and the potential anti-Judaism in Luke's assertion that *all* of the Scriptures are fulfilled in Jesus, see commentary on Luke 24.

86. Luke 4:23 is the first mention of Capernaum (see also 4:31; 7:1; 10:15). In the Gospel of Mark, Jesus has already performed many healings in Capernaum before the scene in the synagogue at Nazareth. This verse also has the first of many Lukan parables (παραβολὴν). In this instance, it is a short proverb. See the excursus at 6:39 on parables.

87. For a feminist perspective on the widow of Zarephath, see Jan Tarlin, "Toward a 'Female' Reading of the Elijah Cycle: Ideology and Gender in the Interpretation of 1 Kings 17–19, 21 and 2 Kings 1–2.18," in *A Feminist Companion to Samuel and Kings*, ed. Athalya Brenner, FCB 5 (Sheffield: Sheffield Academic, 1994), 208–17.

Naaman the Syrian (4:26-27),[88] or because they oppose an outreach to Gentiles; their rage is at Jesus's implication that they are like the unresponsive Israelites in the time of Elijah and Elisha.[89] Jesus's walking through their midst and going on his way when they are about to hurl him off the cliff recalls the way that Elijah escaped the murderous attempts of Ahab and Jezebel (1 Kgs 19:3).

The Widow at Zarephath and Naaman the Syrian	The chapter opens with Elijah predicting a drought and being fed by ravens and drinking from the Wadi Cherith until it dries up (1 Kgs 17:1-8). Then God directs him to go to Zarephath in Sidon, where God has commanded a widow to feed him. He finds her gathering sticks and asks her for water and bread. Invoking Elijah's God, she swears she has no food; she has only a handful of meal and a little oil, which she was about to make into a final meal for herself and her son before they die. Elijah instructs her to do as she planned, but first to make him a little cake and afterward feed herself and her son. To feminist ears,
Jesus invokes the widow at Zarephath and Naaman the Syrian to drive home his point that a prophet is not accepted in his hometown.[90] Both the widow and Naaman were foreigners who, contrary to Israelites who resisted the prophets Elijah and Elisha, accepted the word of the prophet and acclaimed YHWH as God (1 Kgs 17:12, 24; 2 Kgs 5:14, 15).	
There are two parts to the story of Elijah and the widow of Zarephath in 1 Kings 17: the miraculous feeding (vv. 8-16) and the resuscitation of the widow's son (vv. 17-24).	

88. In her reading of Luke 4:25-30, Amy-Jill Levine exposes the fallacies of commentators who interpret the references to the widow of Zarephath and Naaman the Syrian as "designed to explode Jewish patriarchy, purity, xenophobia, and class consciousness." Such readings are based on misunderstanding and negative stereotypes of Judaism and fuel replacement theology, that is, the notion that the covenant with Israel has been abrogated and Gentile followers of Jesus have taken their place. She suggests instead that "Luke, the (likely) gentile writer, critiques Jesus' Jewish contemporaries, and the Jewish contemporaries of Luke's own readers, for not believing in Jesus. Insider critique becomes outsider polemic" (Levine and Witherington, *The Gospel of Luke*, 120–21).

89. John C. Poirier, "Jesus as an Elijianic Figure in Luke 4:16-30," *CBQ* 69 (2007): 349–63; similarly, Levine and Witherington, *The Gospel of Luke*, 119–24; Michael F. Patella, "The Gospel According to Luke," in *New Collegeville Bible Commentary: New Testament*, ed. Daniel Durken (Collegeville, MN: Liturgical Press, 2009), 229.

90. See comments at 2:21-40 on Gender Pairs.

this demand of Elijah seems outrageously self-centered and is the opposite response Jesus makes when tempted by the devil to feed himself first (4:3-4). The widow's initial refusal to give Elijah the last of what she had to eat is surprising. She swears by Elijah's God (v. 12), who has commanded her to feed him (v. 9), but she prioritizes her son and her own needs, seemingly against God's directive.[91] Only after Elijah assures her that God will see that the jar of meal and the jug of oil never go empty does the widow do as Elijah said. Ironically, the widow who was supposed to feed the prophet is now fed along with her son and the prophet by his God.[92]

In the second scene, the widow's son becomes ill and dies. She accuses the prophet of causing his death: "What have you against me, O man of God? You have come to me to bring my sin to remembrance, and to cause the death of my son!" (v. 18). Anthropologist Susan Starr Sered observes that "bereaved mothers often feel responsible for the deaths of their children and guilty that they did not prevent them."[93] The widow may think she has verbally condemned her son when she declared that he would die after the meal she thought would be their last (v. 12). Or perhaps she thinks she has brought upon herself and her son the wrath of Elijah's God for having initially refused to feed the prophet.[94] Elijah then takes her son and carries him upstairs, lays him on his own bed, invokes God, then stretches himself upon the child three times. This unconventional action is a means of transferring life force to the boy (also used by Elisha in reviving the Shunammite woman's son in 2 Kgs 4:34). The widow acclaims Elijah as "a man of God" and affirms "that the word of the LORD in your mouth is true" (v. 24).

The story of Naaman the Syrian in 2 Kings 5:1-19 is also one in which a foreigner acclaims an Israelite prophet and professes allegiance to his God. In contrast to the needy widow, he is "commander of the army of the king of Aram," a "great man in high favor with his master," a "mighty warrior" who was victorious in battle (vv. 1, 2). But he is afflicted with leprosy. A young girl who had been taken captive from Israel[95] and who serves Naaman's wife sets the story in motion as she urges them to seek the help of Elisha. The king of Aram sends Naaman

---

91. Amy Kalmanofsky, "Women of God: Maternal Grief and Religious Response in 1 Kings 17 and 2 Kings 4," *JSOT* 36 (2011): 63.

92. Ibid.

93. Ibid., 64, citing Susan Starr Sered, "Mother Love, Child Death and Religious Innovation: A Feminist Perspective," *JFSR* 12 (1996): 5–23, here 8–9.

94. Kalmanofsky, "Women of God," 64.

95. See excursus at 4:18 on Women Captives Today.

with a letter and large amounts of money and garments to the king of Israel to ask for the cure. The latter thinks this a trick, but Elisha urges the Israelite king to send Naaman to him "that he may learn that there is a prophet in Israel" (v. 8). So Naaman goes "with his horses and chariots" (v. 9) to Elisha's house. The display of power by Naaman and his king is unnecessary. Elisha will not accept any gifts and simply directs Naaman to wash in the Jordan seven times. The commander becomes enraged; he expected the prophet to "stand and call on the name of the LORD his God, and wave his hand over the spot, and cure the leprosy" (v. 11). Moreover, if washing were the cure, he was sure the rivers at home in Damascus were better. His servants intervene and convince him to do as Elisha directed, and he is cured, causing Naaman to declare before Elisha, "Now I know that there is no God in all the earth except Israel" (v. 15).

Both the widow and Naaman initially resisted the directives of the prophet, but then acquiesced, experienced miraculous feeding and healing, and ended by acclaiming the prophet and

his God. Both stories have resonances with how prophet Jesus will miraculously feed people from meager provisions (9:10-17), resuscitate a widow's only son (7:11-17), and heal people with leprosy (5:12-16; 7:22; 17:11-19), deeds that are meant to evoke acclamation of him as God's prophet (as at 7:16). This is the response that the Lukan Jesus seeks from his neighbors in Nazareth, but it is not forthcoming. By invoking these stories, Luke maintains the focus on Jesus as prophet, just as the stories involving Elijah and Elisha keep them and their God in the spotlight. The widow of Zarephath and Naaman the Syrian are grateful recipients of the prophet's ministrations, just as Luke depicts the widows and people with leprosy to whom Jesus ministers. Widows appear frequently in Luke's two volumes and reflect their growing numbers as ministers in the early church. But Luke minimizes their contribution as prophets and ministers, portraying them more often as needy objects of compassion as he expects us to see the widow at Zarephath (see the excursus "Ministering Widows" at 2:21-40).

The Rejection at Nazareth, Luke and the Jews

The depiction of Jesus's synagogue opponents foreshadows the many instances in the gospel and Acts where Jewish leaders, other subgroups of Jews, or "the Jews" writ large, exhibit similar rage against Jesus and his followers. As we note in our introduction (see lix–lxi), scholars are divided on whether this rift here in Nazareth should be read as *intra-*

Jewish (an instance of a prophet scorned by his own people) or as a sign of Luke's proto-supersessionism (an instance in which Jesus, the [Christian] Messiah is violently attacked by "the Jews"). Such differing interpretations are represented in the commentary on Luke coauthored by Amy-Jill Levine and Ben Witherington III. Levine's position is: "Replacement theology coupled with the negative depictions of Jewish gatherings is part of Luke's literary strategy. For Luke, the synagogue is a place to be avoided." Witherington, in contrast, sees Luke's presentation of successful missions in the synagogues in Acts and "finds Luke's theology to be one of inclusion in Christ—Jews and gentiles united in Christ." For him, there is no point in Acts at which there is a complete turning away from Jews, not even in Acts 28.[96] For Levine, the citation of Isaiah at the end of Acts 28 concerning a people who will not listen, indicates a direct turning to the Gentiles, who are the ones who will listen. Shelly agrees with Levine; furthermore, *pace* Witherington, she feels that communities united in Christ are more accurately described as exclusive, rather than inclusive, insofar as they deem salvation available *only* to those who convert to Christ belief/Christianity.[97] Barbara is not as sure about Luke's intention, but both of us insist that Christians must not read the gospel in a way that fuels anti-Judaism, whether reading with or against Luke's intent.

At the time we wrote initial drafts of this chapter, the United States was reeling from the massacre of eleven Jews on October 27, 2018, at the Tree of Life Synagogue in Pittsburgh. That was not an isolated incident; the Anti-Defamation League reported "a 57 percent rise in anti-Semitic incidents in the United States in 2017, compared to the previous year—including bomb threats, assaults, vandalism, and anti-Semitic posters and literature found on college campuses."[98] Since then, we have witnessed

96. Christian scholars often elide the language of supersessionism in Luke and Acts, preferring to speak of Luke "holding out hope" that the Jews "might turn or repent," without making explicit that in Luke's soteriology to turn or repent is to convert to Christ belief. For examples of this scholarly framing, see Shelly Matthews, *Perfect Martyr: The Stoning of Stephen and the Construction of Christian Identity* (New York: Oxford University Press, 2010), 30–36.

97. Levine and Witherington, *The Gospel of Luke*, 122.

98. Laurie Goodstein, " 'There Is Still So Much Evil': Growing Anti-Semitism Stuns American Jews," *The New York Times*, October 29, 2018, https://www.nytimes .com/2018/10/29/us/anti-semitism-attacks.html. The statistics for anti-Semitic attacks in the United States in 2018, according to the Anti-Defamation League, are somewhat lower in 2018 than in 2017 but still at historic highs: https://www.adl .org/2018-audit-S.

further violent incidents, including the murder of participants in the Poway Synagogue in California on April 27, 2019, by a man who was a member of a Presbyterian church and who posted an open letter blaming Jews for the "meticulously planned genocide of the European race."[99] He quoted the Bible and named Jesus and Paul among those who inspired him. There has also been a spate of murderous attacks against Jews in New York in the last quarter of 2019.[100] The leader of a right-wing Christian news source, who once opined on his radio show that "when Jews take over a country, they kill millions of Christians," has just received White House Press credentials for a trip to Davos in January 2020.[101]

When Christian preachers and teachers encounter assertions in Luke that Jews harbor murderous intentions toward Jesus and his followers, they must make clear for their audiences what was the meaning in Luke's historical context and what the ramifications are in reading his text in contemporary contexts. Luke could not foresee how his small band of "Followers of the Way" would become a dominant world religion, with power to wield the sword against their enemies. Thus, he could not anticipate how polemical narrative depictions in his gospel would inspire acts of physical violence in centuries beyond his own. Christians today must recognize Luke's depictions as part of his polemic generated at a time when there was increasing separation and animosity between those who followed Jesus and those who did not, and not as a historically accurate reflection of early Jewish behaviors toward Jesus believers. Furthermore, Christians must not extrapolate from Luke's depictions to the Jewish people as a whole. We must clearly denounce

99. Not all attacks on Jews have been by White nationalists; the killings in a Jewish kosher deli in New Jersey on December 11, 2019, were carried out by an African American man and woman.

100. Michael Davis, "The Anti-Jewish Manifesto of John T. Earnest, the San Diego Synagogue Shooter," May 15, 2019, *Middle East Research Institute*, Inquiry and Analysis Series, No. 1454, https://www.memri.org/reports/anti-jewish-manifesto-john-t-earnest-san-diego-synagogue-shooter; Jane Coaston, "The Conspiracy Theories behind the Anti-Semitic Violence in New York," *Vox*, January 3, 2020, https://www.vox.com/2020/1/3/21039446/anti-semitism-anti-orthodox-farrakhan-conspiracy-theories-bipartisan.

101. Michael M. Grynbaum, "Site That Ran Anti-Semitic Remarks Got Passes for Trump Trip," *New York Times*, January 26, 2020, https://www.nytimes.com/2020/01/26/business/media/trunews-white-house-press-credentials.html?smtyp=cur&smid=fb-nytimes&fbclid=IwAR2knY0OJerXNi5q7ZFja8KRQTD_IXxRGaq6FwMgLGkZCYrRR5x3ALomRcI.

all contemporary forms of Christian anti-Judaism as abhorrent. As seminary professors and New Testament scholars, we try to do this through our teaching, preaching, lectures, and writing, especially as we shape the next generation of biblical interpreters and ministers. Having Jewish colleagues and dialogue partners is an important way for Christians to learn about Judaism and increase our mutual respect and collaboration. Barbara appreciates the importance that her school (Catholic Theological Union at Chicago) has placed on having a Jewish member of the Bible faculty since the school's founding in 1968. Students take courses in Scripture and in Jewish studies as a required part of their program of studies. In addition, CTU has an endowed chair in Catholic-Jewish studies, thrice-yearly lecture series and an annual conference given by Jewish scholars, and sustained involvement in interreligious dialogue. Shelly also works at a Christian divinity school where Jewish studies are part of the curriculum. While she regularly draws attention to anti-Judaism in her introductory course on the New Testament, she has come to feel the inadequacy of those efforts. Thus, she has recently developed a course focusing solely on anti-Judaism in the New Testament designed for students training for ministry. The Gospel of John receives considerable attention as a gospel that is anti-Jewish.[102] We suggest that passages such as the rejection of Jesus in Nazareth in Luke also merit "warning labels" as potentially inciting dangerous behavior toward Jews today.

A Confrontation Between Holy and Unclean Spirits (4:31-37)

Following the potentially deadly conflict in the synagogue at Nazareth, Jesus goes to teach in the synagogue at Capernaum, some thirty miles away. Located on the northwest shore of the Sea of Galilee, Capernaum was at an important juncture on the Via Maris.[103] The "way of the sea" was the ancient trade route that extended from Syria to Egypt, passing through Capernaum, Migdal, and Hazor before swerving west to follow the Mediterranean coastline. Jesus's choice of Capernaum for evangeliz-

---

102. See, most recently, Adele Reinhartz, *Cast Out of the Covenant: Jews and Anti-Judaism in the Gospel of John* (Lanham, MD: Lexington Books/Fortress Academic, 2018); Adele Reinhartz, ed., *The Gospel of John and Jewish-Christian Relations* (Lanham, MD: Lexington Books/Fortress Academic, 2018).

103. See Sharon Lea Mattila, "Revisiting Jesus' Capernaum: A Village of Only Subsistence-Level Fishers and Farmers?," in Fiensy and Hawkins, *The Galilean Economy in the Time of Jesus*, 75–138, who shows from the archaeological evidence that in Jesus's day, at least some of the villagers in Capernaum had wealth beyond subsistence and enjoyed imported Roman glassware, among other things.

31He went down to Capernaum, a city in Galilee, and was teaching them on the sabbath. 32They were astounded at his teaching, because he spoke with authority. 33In the synagogue there was a man who had the spirit of an unclean demon, and he cried out with a loud voice, 34"Let us alone! What have you to do with us, Jesus of Nazareth? Have you come to destroy us? I know who you are, the Holy One of God." 35But Jesus rebuked him, saying, "Be silent, and come out of him!" When the demon had thrown him down before them, he came out of him without having done him any harm. 36They were all amazed and kept saying to one another, "What kind of utterance is this? For with authority and power he commands the unclean spirits, and out they come!" 37And a report about him began to reach every place in the region.

ing would have exposed him to many travelers as well as locals. Although the people in Nazareth (4:23) refer to the things Jesus did at Capernaum, this is the first time in the narrative that Jesus appears there. Jesus returns to Capernaum at 7:1, where he will heal a centurion's slave, but unlike the Gospel of Mark (2:1), Luke does not call Capernaum Jesus's home. Later, Jesus will excoriate Capernaum for its lack of repentance (10:15).

In the Capernaum synagogue, Jesus's teaching once again produces astonishment, as he speaks with authority. As noted above, from this point forward, Jesus becomes the primary speaker, as he teaches (διδάσκω), preaches (κηρύσσω), and evangelizes (εὐαγγελίζομαι),[104] giving instruction, telling parables, addressing people in need, and sparring verbally with opponents. There are no more prophetic proclamations such as those by Mary, Elizabeth, Zechariah, Simeon, or John the Baptist. No more female characters speak except to be corrected by Jesus (10:41-42; 11:27-28; 23:28) or to be disbelieved (24:11).[105] No characters, male or female, whether follower or opponent of Jesus, speak at any length and what they say is most often corrected or challenged by him.[106] Only Jesus speaks, and he

---

104. Jesus teaches (διδάσκω): 5:3, 17; 6:6; 11:1; 13:10, 22; 19:47; 20:1, 21; 21:37; 23:5; preaches (κηρύσσω): 4:18, 19, 44; 8:1; evangelizes (εὐαγγελίζομαι): 4:19, 43; 7:22; 8:1; 16:16; 20:1. The verb λαλέω, "to speak," refers to Jesus eight times; λέγω, "to say," approximately 103 times.

105. Mary Rose D'Angelo, "Women in Luke–Acts: A Redactional View," *JBL* 111 (1992): 441–61, here 452.

106. A few exceptions are when Jesus speaks words of affirmation to persons who ask him for healing. For a detailed analysis of all the characters who speak in the Third Gospel, see Barbara E. Reid, "The Gospel of Luke: Friend or Foe of Women Proclaimers of the Word?," *CBQ* 78 (2016): 1–23.

does so with authority. The "authority" (ἐξουσία) Jesus exercises is evident when he commands unclean spirits and they come out of people who were possessed (4:35; 8:29; 9:42), when he declares sins forgiven (5:20; 7:48), and when he speaks to people seeking healing (5:24; 6:10; 8:48, 54; 13:12). When Jesus is teaching in the temple in Jerusalem, the chief priests, scribes, and elders demand to know by what authority he is doing so, a question he deflects (20:1-8).

Female readers of the gospel search in vain for any gender specific validation of their preaching, teaching, or healing. Jesus bestows power and authority (ἐξουσία) only on the twelve male apostles to expel demons, to cure diseases, to proclaim the *basileia* of God, and to heal (9:1-2). To the further seventy sent out, whom Luke likely envisions as male, he gave authority (ἐξουσία) "to tread on snakes and scorpions, and over all the power of the enemy" (10:19). In Acts, the male appropriation of ἐξουσία continues, as Peter and Paul do almost all the speaking, exorcising, and healing.

The question of authority is a very important one for feminists. As Letty Russell describes, "Authority can be understood as legitimated power. It is a form of power, or the ability to accomplish desired ends. Authority in a religious community usually includes social power to affect the behavior of another group or individual. Human beings look for guidance and a sense of security and turn to authorities in their lives to fill those needs. Those in authority accomplish their ends by evoking the assent of the respondents."[107] Feminists question the prevailing paradigm in patriarchal religious and cultural traditions in which elite males are at the top exercising their authority through domination. A feminist liberationist paradigm locates authority within community, where the needs of those who are at the bottom of the kyriarchal pyramid are given priority and where all "participate in the common task of creating an interdependent community of humanity and nature."[108] Russell sees such a construal of authority as consistent with that of Jesus as articulated in Luke 4:16-30. While we agree with Russell's insights about reframing the model of authority, we see the Lukan Jesus as exercising his authority more like a male at the top of the kyriarchal pyramid. He is the prime possessor of authority who shares it only with select males. Feminists who seek to construct a different model may be able to base it on the Lukan Jesus's words, but not on his manner of dictating.

---

107. Letty M. Russell, "Authority," in Russell and Clarkson, *Dictionary of Feminist Theologies*, 18–19, here 19.
108. Ibid., 19.

As at the synagogue in Nazareth (4:16-30), conflict erupts, but this time the confrontation is between the spirit of an unclean demon and Jesus, conceived (1:35) and empowered by the Holy Spirit (3:21; 4:1, 14, 18). In Luke, spirits, demons,[109] and Satan take a larger role than in the other gospels.[110] Jesus's healings and exorcisms are cast as battles between these malevolent forces and God's Spirit.

The man who is possessed calls Jesus by name and identifies him as the Holy One of God. This naming is an attempt to gain control over Jesus. The one who speaks with authority (4:32) now silences demons with a word and heals people who are possessed (see also 4:41; 6:18; 8:26-39; 9:37-43; 11:14; 13:10-17). Amazement at Jesus's power and authority (in contrast to that which the devil offered, 4:6) continues to build. Jesus shares with the Twelve this power and authority over demons when he sends them out to cure diseases, proclaim the *basileia* of God, and to heal (9:1-2). Questions about the source of Jesus's power and accusations of him being an agent of Beelzebul surface at 11:14-23.

Simon's Mother-in-Law: Healed and Serving (4:38-41)

In the Gospel of Mark, Jesus had already called Simon to follow him (Mark 1:16-20) before he enters his house and heals his mother-in-law (Mark 1:29-31). Luke provides no indication that Jesus and Simon have met previously. It may be that Simon, in accord with Jewish tradition, invites the stranger, Jesus, to his home to share a Sabbath meal with his family. Or, having seen Jesus heal the man who was possessed, he is hoping Jesus may also be able to help his mother-in-law.[111] Whatever

---

109. On Daimons/Demons in Greco-Roman Antiquity, see Wendy Cotter, *Miracles in Greco-Roman Antiquity: A Sourcebook for the Study of New Testament Miracle Stories* (New York: Routledge, 1999), 75–105. For gender analysis of Luke's approach to demons, see especially commentary on 8:1-3, and chapters 10 and 11.

110. As John Pilch notes, "In addition to the spirit-related illness episodes reported by other evangelists (Luke 4:33-37; 8:26-39; 9:37-43a, 49; 11:14-15, 24-26), Luke adds these reports: disciples against demons (10:17); Satan entered Judas (22:3); Satan wants to sift Simon (22:31-34)." He also observes that in Luke's descriptions of ailments afflicting women (4:38; 8:2-3, 58; 13:10, 16), the spirit is also given a prominent place (*Healing in the New Testament*, 99). See also Garrett, *The Demise of the Devil*. For correlations between the exorcism stories in the gospels and epigraphic sources dating from the Hellenistic and early Roman periods, see Esther Eshel, "Jesus the Exorcist in Light of Epigraphic Sources," in Charlesworth, *Jesus and Archaeology*, 178–85.

111. Levine and Witherington, *The Gospel of Luke*, 126.

Luke 4:38-41

³⁸After leaving the synagogue he entered Simon's house. Now Simon's mother-in-law was suffering from a high fever, and they asked him about her. ³⁹Then he stood over her and rebuked the fever, and it left her. Immediately she got up and began to serve them.

⁴⁰As the sun was setting, all those who had any who were sick with various kinds of diseases brought them to him; and he laid his hands on each of them and cured them. ⁴¹Demons also came out of many, shouting, "You are the Son of God!" But he rebuked them and would not allow them to speak, because they knew that he was the Messiah.

⁴²At daybreak he departed and went into a deserted place. And the crowds were looking for him; and when they reached him, they wanted to prevent him from leaving them. ⁴³But he said to them, "I must proclaim the good news of the kingdom of God to the other cities also; for I was sent for this purpose." ⁴⁴So he continued proclaiming the message in the synagogues of Judea.

---

the case, they intercede[112] with Jesus for her, and when he rebukes (ἐπετίμησεν) the fever, it leaves her. The healing of Simon's mother-in-law is not only an act that benefits her individually; it has an impact on all those around her.[113]

There is little development of Simon's mother-in-law as a character in her own right. Nameless, she is identified only through her relation to her son-in-law.[114] She resides within his home, but Luke does not say why or who else lived there. Perhaps she was a widow with no children to care for her. Perhaps Simon's wife is dead and her mother has taken over responsibility for the household. There is no mention of Simon's wife anywhere in the gospel tradition, although Paul speaks of Cephas (Aramaic for Peter)[115] and other apostles being "accompanied by a believing wife" (ἀδελφὴν γυναῖκα, lit. a "sister wife," 1 Cor 9:5). Some of the church fathers (e.g., Jerome, *Ad. Jovinian* 1.26; Clement of Alexandria, *Stromata* 3.6) read this expression to mean not a wife but a woman minister who would assist with baptisms of women, for example. Clement

---

112. Luke does not specify who is "they." In Mark 1:29-30, it is Simon, Andrew, James, and John. The verb ἠρώτησαν, "asked," has more the sense of imploring him to do something for her than simply informing him about her. See John 17:9 for a similar use of the verb ἐρωτάω.

113. Pilch, *Healing in the New Testament*, 97.

114. No character in a healing story is named. See comments on naming at 1:5-7.

115. For comments on Simon's name changing to Peter, see 5:1-11.

also preserves a tradition that Peter, when he saw his wife being led to her death in Rome, encouraged her to remember the Lord (*Stromata* 7.11).

Simon's mother-in-law does not speak directly to Jesus, nor does she give voice to her own suffering. But in the final verse, her actions following her healing link her to Jesus in two important ways. She arises (ἀναστᾶσα), the same verb used of Jesus's resurrection (ἀναστῆναι ἐκ νεκρῶν, 24:46),[116] and she serves (διηκόνει), the same term that Jesus uses of his own actions at Luke 22:27, "I am among you as one who serves [ὁ διακονῶν]." The verb διηκόνει in the imperfect tense can be translated either "she began to serve" or "she kept on serving."

The setting of the story points to Simon's mother-in-law's service as domestic, probably involving a meal. This is not, however, the only connotation of the verb διακονεῖν or of the noun διακονία, "service." In many instances in the New Testament, including Luke and Acts, these terms refer to ministerial service of various kinds.[117] Following is a brief list; see commentary at each occurrence for a fuller explanation.

- Luke 8:3: Mary Magdalene, Joanna, Susanna, and the other Galilean women "provided for" (διηκόνουν) Jesus and the Twelve out of their financial resources

- Luke 10:40: Martha is concerned about "much ministry" (πολλὴν διακονίαν)[118]

- Luke 12:37: Jesus tells his disciples: "Blessed are those slaves whom the master finds alert when he comes; truly I tell you, he will fasten his belt and have them sit down to eat, and he will come and serve [διακονήσει] them."

---

116. See also Luke 14:14; 20:27, 33, 35, 36.

117. In secular Greek, the first known instance of διακονεῖν is by fifth-century historian Herodotus (*Herod.* 4.154.3). He and other classical Greek writers use it to mean "to wait at table" (also Aristoph. *Ach.* 1015–16; Diod. *S.*, 5.28.4). It can also mean "to provide or care for" and is often used of the work of women (Plat. *Leg.* 7.805e; Plut. *Adulat.* 22.2.63d). The verb does not occur in the LXX. Josephus uses it in three senses: "to wait at table" (*Ant.* 6.52; 11.163); "to serve" with the meaning "to obey" (*Ant.* 9.25; 17.140); and "to render priestly service" (*Ant.* 7.365; 10.72). See Hermann W. Beyer, "διακονέω, διακονία, διάκονος," *TDNT* 2 (1964): 81–93. In his exhaustive study, John N. Collins, *DIAKONIA: Re-interpreting the Ancient Sources* (New York: Oxford University Press, 1990), shows that the basic meaning in non-Christian sources is to act as a "go-between," being another person's agent, implementing their intentions or desires. In New Testament texts where διακονία refers to ministry, the meaning flows from earlier Greek usage, so that the sense is "a sacred obligation, . . . a charge put upon someone," by church authorities or, in a few instances, received directly from God (258).

118. NRSV renders πολλὴν διακονίαν as "many tasks." See discussion at 10:38-42.

- Luke 17:8: Jesus instructs his disciples about serving, using the example of a slave who prepares supper and then serves (διακόνει) it to the master

- Luke 22:26: Jesus instructs his disciples that the leader must be as one who serves (ὁ διακονῶν), as is he himself (22:27)

- Acts 1:25: The apostles pray to be shown Judas's replacement "in this apostolic ministry" (τῆς διακονίας ταύτης καὶ ἀποστολῆς)[119]

- Acts 6:2, 4: Seven Greek speakers are chosen for "ministry of the table" (διακονεῖν τραπέζαις; NRSV: "wait on tables") while the Twelve devote themselves to "ministry of the word" (διακονίᾳ τοῦ λόγου; NRSV: "serving the word")

- Acts 11:29; 12:25: Barnabas and Saul's relief mission (διακονία) for the community in Judea

- Acts 20:24; 21:19: διακονία encompasses the whole of Paul's ministerial service

The range of ministerial meanings of διακονεῖν and διακονία and their occurrence in reference to the Galilean women who followed and ministered to/with Jesus (Mark15:41; Matt 27:55) have led a number of feminist interpreters to propose this meaning for Simon's mother-in-law's service, seeing her as ministering to Jesus or an example of an early disciple.[120] For example, in her analysis of the Markan version of the episode (1:29-31), Elaine M. Wainwright[121] proposes that the restoration of Simon's mother-in-law can be interpreted on two levels within the Markan community. At first they might understand her service as domestic, as offering hospitality to guests. But the imperfect form of διακονεῖν and repeated hearing of the gospel with faithful women ministering

---

119. The expression τῆς διακονίας ταύτης καὶ ἀποστολῆς rendered by NRSV as "in this ministry and apostleship" is a hendiadys, i.e., a single idea expressed with two words.

120. For such interpretations of Mark 1:29-31, see, e.g., Mary Ann Tolbert, "Mark," in *The Women's Bible Commentary*, ed. Carol A. Newsom and Sharon H. Ringe (Louisville: Westminster John Knox, 1992), 267; Luise Schottroff, *Let the Oppressed Go Free: Feminist Perspectives on the New Testament* (Louisville: Westminster John Knox, 1993), 80–118; Marla Selvidge, "'And Those Who Followed Feared' (Mark 10:32)," *CBQ* 45 (1983): 396–400; Elisabeth Meier Tetlow, *Women and Ministry in the New Testament: Called to Serve* (Lanham, MD: University Press of America, 1985), 97; Schüssler Fiorenza, *In Memory of Her*, 320–21.

121. Elaine M. Wainwright, *Women Healing/Healing Women: The Genderization of Healing in Early Christianity*, BibleWorld (London: Equinox, 2006), 111.

(διηκόνουν) to Jesus (15:41) would lead them to see her as a disciple, possibly among those at the foot of the cross or among those who, like the Twelve, were commissioned to heal others (Mark 6:12-13).

In Wainwright's analysis of Matthew's version (8:14-15), she proposes that the original account was a call story with a healing motif, but in the final form, the healing story masks the call story.[122] She outlines the verbal and formal similarities between the call of Matthew (Matt 9:9) and the story of Simon's mother-in-law (Matt 8:14-15). In both, Jesus takes the initiative, a feature of call stories, in contrast to healing stories, where ordinarily the ill person or an advocate for them takes the initiative. Jesus sees each of them, εἶδεν (8:14; 9:9). Simon's mother-in-law directs her response to Jesus alone (αὐτῷ, 8:15), as does Matthew (9:9; contrast Luke's plural αὐτοῖς, "them," 4:39).

We appreciate these ways of reading ministering women back into the story of early Christianity and the efforts to read between the lines and to connect the dots. We agree, however, with Deborah Krause, who shows that, in the case of Simon's mother-in-law, the context of Mark 1:31 demands a different meaning for διακονέω than in Mark 15:41.[123] Simon's mother-in-law is inside a house, providing table service and hospitality to Simon, Andrew, James, and John (named in 1:29), in contrast to the women who are witnessing the crucifixion outdoors and who had been following (ἠκολούθουν) Jesus and had provided for him (διηκόνουν αὐτῷ) when he was in the Galilee (15:40-41). "Following" is associated with discipleship, and Jesus (αὐτῷ, "him") is the object of their serving, in contrast to "them" (αὐτοῖς) in 1:31. Krause is right when she proposes that "Mark's Gospel preserves traditions that reveal women in traditionally bound roles of domestic servitude, while at the same time preserving traditions that reveal women in liberated roles of equal discipleship."[124]

We come to a similar conclusion for the meaning Luke intended for διηκόνει in 4:39; the domestic context and the plural αὐτοῖς, "them" (unspecified in Luke), point toward Simon's mother-in-law providing

---

122. Elaine M. Wainwright, *Towards a Feminist Critical Reading of the Gospel According to Matthew*, BZNW 60 (Berlin: de Gruyter, 1991), 177–91. See also Wainwright, *Women Healing/Healing Women*, 143–46.

123. Deborah Krause, "Simon Peter's Mother-in-Law—Disciple or Domestic Servant? Feminist Biblical Hermeneutics and the Interpretation of Mark 1.29-31," in *A Feminist Companion to Mark*, ed. Amy-Jill Levine with Marianne Blickenstaff, FCNTECW 2 (Sheffield: Sheffield Academic, 2001), 37–53.

124. Ibid., 50. Krause also revisits the work of Winsome Munro, who had previously made a similar argument in "Women Disciples in Mark?," CBQ 44 (1982): 225–41.

hospitality, likely involving a meal. That διηκόνουν has a different meaning at Luke 8:3, where Mary Magdalene, Joanna, Susanna, and the other Galilean women "were providing for" (διηκόνουν) Jesus and the Twelve (αὐτοῖς), is clear from the added phrase ἐκ τῶν ὑπαρχόντων αὐταῖς, "out of their monetary resources." The context as well is outside their homes, accompanying Jesus and the Twelve as he was preaching in cities and villages in the Galilee. Unlike Mark (15:41) and Matthew (27:55), Luke does not refer to their ministry in the crucifixion scene. Moreover, at the cross, it is not only the women who had followed Jesus from Galilee who are watching everything but also "all his acquaintances" (23:49). Recognizing that the gospels preserve traditions that show women both as active ministers in the Jesus movement and as constrained within patriarchally organized gender roles leads us to renewed efforts to challenge the latter. We question the inequities, for example, when the bulk of unpaid domestic labor falls on the shoulders of women in many cultures yet today, even as we recognize that the strategies for changing entrenched attitudes about women's domestic service vary in each context.

Women Healers

Luke depicts the following accounts of women who are healed: Simon's mother-in-law (4:38-39); Mary Magdalene, Joanna, Susanna, and many others "who had been cured of evil spirits and infirmities" (8:1-3); Jairus's daughter (8:40-42, 49-56); a woman with a hemorrhage (8:43-48); and a woman with a spirit that had crippled her for eighteen years (13:10-17). We may also imagine women among the multitudes Jesus healed (4:40-41; 6:18; 7:22). In the first two instances, the healed women respond by ministering (4:39; 8:3), and the latter group of women continue to follow Jesus to Jerusalem (24:10). There are no accounts in Luke and Acts, however, of women exercising a ministry of healing. Jesus gives the Twelve "power and authority over all demons and to cure diseases," he sends them out "to proclaim the kingdom of God and to heal" (9:1-2), and they do cure diseases everywhere (9:6). Then he appoints seventy others to cure the sick in whatever town they enter (10:9). If women were in this group of apostles, Luke does not say.[124] Acts depicts only male disciples as healing: Peter (3:1-10 [along with John]; 5:15-16; 9:32-35), Philip (8:7), Ananias (9:17), and Paul (14:8-10; 19:12; 28:8-9).

---

125. See comments in chap. 10, where we will argue that Luke sees this as a mission for men.

Given the association of women with the healing arts,[125] that women followers of Jesus are not included among those participating in this healing ministry is a point of suspicion. While this lack of women healers may owe to Luke's tendency to minimize women's roles, it may also reflect the male domination of the developing profession of medicine. As treatises by professional healers like Dioscorides (c. 40–90 CE), Soranus (c. 98–138 CE), and Galen (c. 129–216 CE) appeared, questions arise as to what effect this had on female folk practitioners of medicine: "Did they continue to develop their knowledge and skill and to whom did they offer healing? How, too, was their source of income affected by the much broader availability of their particular knowledge and art with its accompanying healing power and authority?"[126]

In antiquity, healing was intimately intertwined with religion, as people sought the power of divine figures to cure them. Rituals, incantations, and formulae were used to obtain healing.[127] The most popular healing god from the fifth century BCE to well into the Christian era was Asclepius, son of the god Apollo and a human mother. Both women[128] and men would go on pilgrimage to the temples of Asclepius and make offerings; sleeping in the *abaton*, the enclosure attached to the temple, they would pray to be visited by the god during the night and be healed. Of particular importance is Hygieia, the daughter of Asclepius, who also had healing power. She is frequently represented at Asclepius's side and sometimes

---

126. Wainwright (*Women Healing/Healing Women*, 75) notes, "There existed across the Greek and Roman worlds, a dominant literary trope of the woman who deals in herbs and drugs as well as chants and incantations," though they are not always portrayed positively. "Women's knowledge of drug lore, a power shared with divine figures, is a source of fear among men" (ibid., 76). Consider, for example, women who are characterized as witches in Apuleius's *Metamorphosis*, including Meroe (1.8–12) and Pamphile (2.5). Carole R. Fontaine ("Disabilities and Illness in the Bible: A Feminist Perspective," in *A Feminist Companion to the Hebrew Bible in the New Testament*, ed. Athalya Brenner, FCB 10 [Sheffield: Sheffield Academic, 1996], 286–300) notes that feminist readers miss in the gospel "the midwife, the wise woman, the folk healer, the mothers, wives, sisters and daughters who routinely nurse the ailing members of the traditional household" (298).

127. Wainwright, *Women Healing/Healing Women*, 80.

128. For example, the Greek magical papyri, found in Egypt, which date from 100 BCE to approximately 400 CE. See further, Garrett, *Demise of the Devil*, 13.

129. See Wainwright, *Women Healing/Healing Women*, 83–88, for data and analysis of inscriptions and dedications made by women supplicants at the Asclepieia at Athens and Epidaurus.

independently of him. Like Asclepius, she is acclaimed as Savior, ΣΩΤΕΙΡΗ, in one of the inscriptions found at Epidauros. Hygieia may have both modeled and authorized female healing in the late Hellenistic and early Roman period when women were becoming more active in the public profession of healing. Her presence alongside Asclepius may also account for the equal number of women supplicants at the healing shrines in Athens and Epidauros.[129]

Another important female healing god was Isis, whose religion originated in ancient Egypt and spread through the Greco-Roman world. In hymns to her, she designates herself as patroness of women, who has given to women power equal to that of men.[130] She is particularly celebrated for her motherly devotion to Horus and her love for her brother-husband Osiris, whom she restored to life. Pregnant women implored her protection as dispenser of life.

The numerous models of female healing goddesses and women who exercised the healing arts in both the professional and folk sectors in the Greco-Roman world provide a stark contrast with the lack of women healers in the New Testament. There are, however, many women throughout history, both Jewish and Christian, who are known to have been doctors, midwives, and healers. One notable example is Hildegard of Bingen, who was born around 1098 in Germany.[131] She was a sickly child and at eight years of age her parents gave her to the care of a Benedictine nun, Blessed Jutta, who taught her to read and sing the psalms in Latin. As a young adult, Hildegard began to experience visions and became renowned for her piety. At the age of eighteen she became a nun and after Jutta's death became the abbess of the community. In addition to her extensive knowledge of herbs and medicinal arts, she was also a gifted writer, composer, philosopher, and mystic. Although she had been recognized as a saint for centuries, Pope Benedict XVI formally declared her so and on October 7, 2012, named her a Doctor of the Church, only the fourth woman to be so named. One of the reasons why Hildegard's practices as a

130. Wainwright, *Women Healing/Healing Women*, 89–92.

131. Sharon Kelly Heyob, *The Cult of Isis among Women in the Graeco-Roman World*, EPRO 51 (Leiden: Brill, 1975), 52. For aretologies and inscriptions recognizing Isis as healer and giver of immortality, see Cotter, *Miracles in Greco-Roman Antiquity*, 30–34.

132. On Jewish women doctors from the same period, see Cheryl Tallan, "Doctors: Medieval," in *The Encyclopedia of Jewish Women*: https://jwa.org/encyclopedia/article /doctors-medieval.

healer are so well known is that she wrote two volumes that explain her theories and practices. In one, *Physica*, she describes the scientific and medicinal properties of various plants, stones, fish, reptiles, and animals. The other, *Causae et Curae*, focuses on the human body, showing its interconnectedness to the rest of the natural world and detailing the causes and cures of various diseases.[132] Hildegard is one of the few medical practitioners who provide such documentation from medieval times. There were many other women healers at the time, but most did not know how to write in Latin.[133] Hildegard is attractive to contemporary ecofeminists for the way that she relates human beings to the rest of the cosmos and for emphasizing the vital connection between the "greening power," *viriditas*, of the natural world and the holistic health of the human person.

Oxyrhynchus Hymn to Isis

The following hymn is found in the Oxyrhynchus papyri that were discovered in the late nineteenth and early twentieth centuries near the Egyptian town by that name. The papyrus containing this hymn dates to the early second century CE, but the text was likely composed a century earlier, probably during the reign of Augustus. Only about half of the original hymn survives.[134] What draws our attention is the line "you made the power of women equal to that of men." We wonder how that assertion affected Isis's female devotees. Furthermore, what might have attracted women to

133. See further Hildegard von Bingen, *Causae et Curae (Holistic Healing)*, ed. Mary Palmquist and John Kulas, trans. Manfred Pawlik and Patrick Madigan (Collegeville, MN: Liturgical Press, 1994); Hildegard von Bingen, *Physica*, trans. Priscilla Throop (Rochester, VT: Healing Arts Press, 1998); Bruce W. Hozeski, trans., *Hildegard's Healing Plants: From Her Medieval Classic Physica* (Boston: Beacon, 2001).

134. See the work of Mélanie Lipinska (1865–1933), a Polish physician, who studied at the University of Paris medical school. Her doctoral thesis on the history of women in medicine (*Histoire des femmes médecins*), including the writings of Hildegard, was presented in 1900.

135. This translation from the Greek text of P.Oxy. 1380, available at http://www.attalus .org/poetry/isis_hymns.html#6, is adapted from *The Oxyrhynchus Papyri*, vol. 11, nos. 1351–1404, ed. Bernard P. Grenfell and Arthur S. Hunt. Graeco-Roman memoirs 14 (London: Egypt Exploration Society, 1915), 190–220, accessible at https://archive.org /stream/oxyrhynchuspapyr11gren#page/202/mode/2up.

seek healing from Jesus instead of Isis? We notice that the only woman in Luke who deliberately approaches Jesus for healing is a woman with a hemorrhage (8:43-48); in the case of Simon's mother-in-law (4:38-39) and Jairus's daughter (8:40-42, 49-56), it is a male relative who brings Jesus to the woman or girl who needs healing. It might have been that some men would be more inclined to seek a male healer, and in this way their women would be introduced to Jesus. In the case of the woman who was crippled for eighteen years (13:10-17), there is no indication that she is looking to Jesus for healing; he initiates it. As for Mary Magdalene, Joanna, Susanna, and many others "who had been cured of evil spirits and infirmities" (8:1-3), Luke gives no details about who did the healing nor whether the women asked for it.

> Lady Isis, greatest of the gods,
>   first of names, Io Sothis;
> you rule over the mid-air and
>   the immeasurable;
> you devise the weaving of . . .;
> it is also your will that women
>   in health come to anchor
>   with men;
> all the elders at E . . . ctus
>   sacrifice;
> all the maidens who . . .
> at Heracleopolis turn (?) to
>   you and dedicated the
>   country to you;
> you are seen by those who
>   invoke you faithfully;
> from whom . . . in virtue of
>   the 365 combined days;
> gentle and merciful is
>   the favour of your two
>   ordinances;
> you bring the sun from rising
>   unto setting, and all the
>   gods are glad;
> at the risings of the stars
> the people of the country
>   worship you unceasingly
> you established your son
>   Horus Apollo
> everywhere the youthful lord
>   of the whole world
> and . . . for all time;
> you made the power of
>   women equal to that of men;
> and in the sanctuary you did
>   . . . nations . . .

Healing Everyone, Preaching Everywhere (4:40-44)

With the sun setting, the Sabbath[136] concludes, and people are now able to carry their sick to Jesus. Healing by laying on of hands (4:40) is not

---

136. Although the healing of the man with a demon and Simon's mother-in-law take place on a sabbath, the issue of healing on a sabbath is not a source of controversy until 6:6-11. There is no law that forbids healing on the sabbath; the controversy is whether healing is work that is prohibited on the sabbath.

found in the Old Testament.[137] In Acts 9:17, Ananias lays his hands on Paul and restores his sight (9:17), and in Acts 28:8, Paul heals the father of Publius by laying hands on him. Today, there is general recognition of the healing power of touch that can channel energy and well-being. In the gospels, Jesus's touching of sick people is an act of compassion and has nothing to do with transgressing purity.[138] Commentators who see Jesus as violating purity laws—there is no law forbidding a healer from touching anyone—not only misunderstand his actions but also take the focus away from the healthcare itself.

Chapter 4 begins with Jesus being led by the Spirit into the wilderness; it concludes with his departure to a deserted place. Luke does not give the reason for Jesus's seeking seclusion from the crowds at 4:42; the Markan parallel (1:35) says that Jesus went to a deserted place and prayed, something that the Lukan Jesus does at 5:16. Jesus then continues on his program of proclaiming the good news to other cities.

137. Levine and Witherington (*The Gospel of Luke*, 127) note that there is a Qumran text, 1QapGen 20:28-29, that refers to Abraham laying hands on Pharaoh and exorcising a demon from him. In Acts of the Apostles, the laying on of hands is part of the ritual of commissioning ministers: Acts 6:6; 8:17; 13:3; 19:6. See also 1 Tim 4:14; 2 Tim 1:6; Heb 6:2.
138. See further Levine and Witherington, *The Gospel of Luke*, 127.

Luke 5:1-39

Male Disciples Called; Female Disciples in the Shadows

The Call of the First Male Disciples (5:1-11)

At the conclusion of chapter 4, Jesus had left Simon's house at Capernaum on the northwest shore of the Sea of Galilee to proclaim the good news to other cities (4:43). He continues to do this in synagogues (4:44), as at Nazareth (4:16-30) and Capernaum (4:31-37). Now he is back at the shore of the lake,[1] and the crowd is clambering to hear him. For the first time, Jesus's teaching is said to be "the word of God" (5:1).[2]

---

1. Lake Gennesaret is another name for the "Sea of Galilee," which is a freshwater lake, approximately thirteen miles long and seven miles across at its widest point. Gennesaret was a fertile plain south of Capernaum. Because the shape of the lake resembles a harp (*kinor*, כנר), it is also called "Kinneret," the name used in present-day Israel. Luke more properly calls it a lake, λίμνη (5:1; 8:22, 23, 33), while in Matthew and Mark it is the Sea (θάλασσα) of Galilee (Matt 4:18; 15:29; Mark 1:16; 7:31). In John's Gospel, it is the Sea of Tiberias (6:1; 21:1) for the city constructed by Antipas and named for Emperor Tiberius in 20 CE.

2. At 4:22, Jesus's words are gracious; at 4:32, authoritative; and at 4:36, his utterance (ὁ λόγος) is with authority and power. "Word of God" occurs also at 8:11, 21; 11:28.

Luke 5:1-11

⁵:¹Once while Jesus was standing beside the lake of Gennesaret, and the crowd was pressing in on him to hear the word of God, ²he saw two boats there at the shore of the lake; the fishermen had gone out of them and were washing their nets. ³He got into one of the boats, the one belonging to Simon, and asked him to put out a little way from the shore. Then he sat down and taught the crowds from the boat. ⁴When he had finished speaking, he said to Simon, "Put out into the deep water and let down your nets for a catch." ⁵Simon answered, "Master, we have worked all night long but have caught nothing. Yet if you say so, I will let down the nets." ⁶When they had

Simon's call story has the same elements as the call stories of several Old Testament prophets and the call of Jesus's mother at 1:26-38.³ God's messenger issues a commission, followed by an objection, an assurance, and an admonition not to fear; the messenger provides a sign, and the person commissioned assents. In Luke, contrary to Mark and Matthew, Simon's family has a prior encounter with Jesus (it is not clear that Simon was at home when his mother-in-law was healed, 4:38-39), so that it is not unreasonable that Jesus gets into Simon's boat and asks him to head out from the shore.⁴ The dialogue and miraculous catch of fish in 5:4-10 are unique to Luke's account.⁵

Simon Peter's⁶ declaration that he is a sinful man (ἀνὴρ ἁμαρτωλός) is Luke's way of introducing a major gospel theme: Jesus's association with sinners, something for which the Pharisees will frequently criticize him (5:30; 7:34; 15:2; 19:7).⁷ Sinners are those who deliberately break God's

3. See above on 1:26-38.

4. Contrast Mark 1:16-20; Matt 4:18-22, where Jesus calls Simon and Andrew, James and John away from their nets and boats. In Mark (1:29-31) and Matthew (8:14-15), the healing of Simon's mother-in-law occurs after his call.

5. There are, however, thematic parallels between this story of Peter's calling and the resurrection appearance to Peter and the disciples in John 21:4-8.

6. The name Peter appears alongside Simon for the first time in Luke 5:8 (see 6:14), but without the explanation found in Matt 16:18 of how he becomes associated with "rock," πέτρος.

7. In each of these instances Jesus's opponents criticize him for associating with tax collectors as well as sinners (see further comments below at 5:30). Commentators often say that Jesus is criticized for his association with "outcasts." There is no such formulation in the gospel.

done this, they caught so many fish that their nets were beginning to break. [7]So they signaled their partners in the other boat to come and help them. And they came and filled both boats, so that they began to sink. [8]But when Simon Peter saw it, he fell down at Jesus' knees, saying, "Go away from me, Lord, for I am a sinful man!" [9]For he and all who were with him were amazed at the catch of fish that they had taken; [10]and so also were James and John, sons of Zebedee, who were partners with Simon. Then Jesus said to Simon, "Do not be afraid; from now on you will be catching people." [11]When they had brought their boats to shore, they left everything and followed him.

commandments as revealed in the Torah.[8] Twice in the gospel, Jesus affirms that keeping the commandments leads to eternal life (10:25-28; 18:18-20).[9] Jesus justifies his association with sinners, saying, "I have come to call not the righteous but sinners to repentance" (5:32).

Repentance (μετάνοια) features prominently in Jesus's preaching, as it did in John the Baptizer's (3:3, 8). Μετάνοια, "a change of mind," a "turning about,"[10] means returning to God and observing the Torah. This is not a new message; the Old Testament prophets frequently called Israel to "return," שוב, to God (e.g., Isa 44:22; Jer 3:12; Hos 14:1), who is "gracious and merciful, slow to anger, and abounding in steadfast love" (Joel 2:13). What is new in John's and Jesus's preaching of repentance is the urgency: the *basileia* of God is already here (3:9; 10:9, 11; 17:21). In a number of instances, Jesus gives warnings about dire consequences for those who do not repent (10:13; 11:32; 13:3, 5; 16:30). But like the prophets before him, Jesus also stresses God's mercy (6:36; 18:13),[11] and he likens the delight of finding a lost sheep or a lost coin to the joy in heaven over one sinner who repents (15:7, 10). He teaches his disciples not only to seek God's forgiveness but also to forgive a brother or sister who repents (17:3-4). The stress on repentance continues until the risen Christ gives

8. See Paula Fredriksen, *Sin: The Early History of an Idea* (Princeton: Princeton University Press, 2012), on the development of Christian concepts of sin. Notions such as original sin or that human beings are born sinful are not central to Jewish understandings of sin.
9. See also 1:6, Elizabeth and Zechariah are "righteous before God, living blamelessly according to all the commandments and regulations of the Lord."
10. BDAG, 640-41.
11. So also 1:50, 54, 58, 72, 78.

this final instruction to his disciples: "repentance and forgiveness of sins is to be proclaimed in his name to all nations, beginning from Jerusalem" (24:47). Peter and Paul carry out this command in Acts (2:38; 3:19; 8:22; 17:30; 20:21; 26:20).

Luke does not show the complexities of processes of repentance, forgiveness, and reconciliation. He gives the impression that simply hearing a preacher like John or Jesus causes people to repent and live a new life. Modern studies show that processes of reconciliation most often begin with the aggrieved party offering forgiveness to the perpetrator of the wrongdoing.[12] In an ideal situation, the wrongdoer acknowledges their offense and makes whatever restitution may be possible, and the two persons can begin to construct a new relationship.[13] But what happens when the wrongdoer does not acknowledge what they have done? What if the wrongdoer does not or cannot make restitution? What if the wrongdoing is collective, not individual? What happens when a change in behavior does not accompany "repentance," as in situations of domestic violence, where the cycle of abuse continues after the batterer expresses regret and repeatedly breaks promises to reform? What of women who falsely accept blame and "repent" for what their partners say they made them do?[14] The gospel answers none of these questions directly, but reflecting on the biblical texts can open ways toward finding solutions.

Luke does not specify what kinds of sins Peter committed, and biblical commentators rarely speculate about them. Some point ahead to Peter's denial of Jesus (22:54-62), but that does not explain his declaration in 5:8. By contrast, commentaries on 7:36-50 are rife with speculation about the sorts of sins the woman "who was a sinner" (7:37) committed. More often than not, they conclude, without evidence, that she was a prostitute. There is both a male bias and some voyeuristic tendencies at play when people are fascinated with female sinners but not male.

---

12. E.g., Robert J. Schreiter, *Reconciliation: Mission and Ministry in a Changing Social Order* (Maryknoll, NY: Orbis Books, 1992), 15.

13. See, e.g., Robert J. Schreiter, *The Ministry of Reconciliation: Spirituality and Strategies* (Maryknoll, NY: Orbis Books, 1998); John Paul Lederach, *Reconcile: Conflict Transformation for Ordinary Christians* (Harrisonburg, VA: Herald Press, 2014); Avis Clendenen, *Forgiveness: Finding Freedom through Reconciliation* (New York: Crossroad, 2002); Maria Mayo, *The Limits of Forgiveness: Case Studies in the Distortion of a Biblical Ideal* (Minneapolis: Augsburg Fortress, 2015).

14. While the majority of instances of domestic abuse are by males toward females, sometimes the reverse is the case. See Roxanne Dryden-Edwards, "Domestic Violence," MedicineNet Newsletters, https://www.medicinenet.com/domestic_violence/article.htm. See further comments at 17:3-4.

Jesus tells Peter not to be afraid and that from now on his work will be "catching people." The NRSV translation "people" accurately reflects the inclusive meaning of ἄνθρωπος: human beings, both male and female, in contrast to ἀνήρ, "man" (5:8), that refers only to males. Jesus will spell out the nature of this work when he sends out Peter and eleven others to proclaim the kingdom of God and to heal (9:1-6). The dialogue in 5:8-10 is between Jesus and Peter, but Luke notes that James and John, his partners, were among all those amazed at the catch of fish. The brothers then join Peter in leaving everything[15] to follow Jesus (5:11). This divesting also marks the response of Levi at 5:28.

The text does not tell what became of Simon's mother-in-law (4:38-39), his wife, and children, if he had any. How did they manage once Peter gave up his fishing business to follow an itinerant teacher? While Mark (2:1; 9:33) notes that Jesus made a home in Capernaum, Luke's Jesus has no home; it appears that neither does Peter.[16]

In the remainder of the gospel, the only persons who declare their sinfulness are male characters in parables: the younger son who returns and declares to his father, "I have sinned against heaven and before you" (15:21), and the tax collector who prays, "God, be merciful to me, a sinner!" (18:13). The father's exuberant welcome of the returned son (15:20-24), the justification of the tax collector (18:14), along with Jesus's calling of the sinful Peter (5:10) conveys to the reader that admission of one's sins leads to reconciliation, justification, and in some instances, a commission to draw others to Jesus. While women readers may be able to stretch to hear themselves included in the assurance of reconciliation and justification in these scenes with male protagonists, we doubt, however, that Luke intends for females to identify with Peter's commission to "fish for people." Jesus tells the only woman in the gospel who was identified as a sinner "Your faith has saved you; go in peace" (7:50). He sends her away without a mission and we hear nothing more of her.

15. Leaving everything is not the only possible response of a disciple. See above at 4:18 on the relationship between discipleship and the use of possessions.

16. See comments on Peter's wife at 4:38. The Coptic fragment of the apocryphal Acts of Peter preserved in a fourth- to fifth-century papyrus manuscript tells of Peter's daughter who has palsy and lies helpless, stretched out in a corner. After Peter heals a multitude of other sick people, a person in the crowd questions him as to why he has not healed his own daughter. Peter then does so to prove he can, but afterward returns her to her palsied state, saying that he had been told in a vision that this daughter would bring hurt to many souls if her body continued whole. See "The Acts of Peter" from *The Apocryphal New Testament*, trans. M. R. James (Oxford: Clarendon, 1924), http://www.earlychristianwritings.com/text/actspeter.html.

A Man with Leprosy Touched and Healed (5:12-16)

The scene shifts to "one of the cities," where Jesus encounters a man with leprosy. We do not know whether his ailment was what is known today as Hansen's disease or whether he suffered from some other kind of skin disorder such as psoriasis. His condition is severe—he is "covered with leprosy"—and when he sees Jesus he bows his face to the ground,[17] either out of respect or out of a desire to hide his disfigured face, or both. Like Simon (v. 8), he addresses Jesus as κύριε, "Lord" or "Sir,"[18] and hopes he will heal him. He believes Jesus is able to cure him; what is questionable is whether Jesus will choose to do so.

The question is not whether Jesus will incur ritual impurity through contact with the man. A Jew needed to be ritually pure only when going to the temple. This episode is set in the Galilee, far from Jerusalem. Commentators frequently misinterpret this scene, saying that the man with leprosy transgresses the Law by not remaining apart from Jesus or that Jesus transgresses purity laws by touching the leper. The latter interpretation cannot be maintained since Jesus restores the man to purity[19] and instructs him to complete the ritual prescribed in the Law (5:13-14, alluding to Lev 13–14). As for the supposed isolation of people with leprosy, Myrick Shinall, in a detailed study of biblical and extrabiblical sources, shows that exclusionary practices toward people with leprosy varied over time and space and that many texts show people with leprosy to be integrated into society.[20] One notable example is Naaman, the Syrian commander whom Luke names at 4:27. In 2 Kings 5:1-19, Naaman is not isolated when he has leprosy; he is a mighty warrior who commands an army, he has a wife, and he has personal access to the kings of Aram and Israel. Likewise, the man with leprosy in 5:12-16 is not ostracized; he is in the city, mingling with other people, when he and Jesus encounter one another.

---

17. Literally "falling on his face," πεσὼν ἐπὶ πρόσωπον, the same gesture as Abraham toward God in Gen 17:3, 17. See also 1 Cor 14:25.

18. See comments on κύριε at 1:46.

19. The verb καθαρίζω, "make clean" (vv. 12, 13), and the noun καθαρισμός, "cleansing" (v. 14), refer to the removal of ritual impurity, not to any "dirtiness" of the disease. On Christian misperceptions of Jewish purity, see Amy-Jill Levine, *The Misunderstood Jew: The Church and the Scandal of the Jewish Jesus* (San Francisco: HarperSanFrancisco, 2006), 172–77.

20. Myrick C. Shinall Jr., "The Social Condition of Lepers in the Gospels," *JBL* 137 (2018): 915–34. Similarly, John J. Pilch (*Healing in the New Testament: Insights from Medical and Mediterranean Anthropology* [Minneapolis: Fortress, 2000], 51) notes that "in none of the synoptic contexts is there a hint that the leper is quarantined. He seems to be in a public place, mingling with others, and has rather easy access to Jesus."

[12]Once, when he was in one of the cities, there was a man covered with leprosy. When he saw Jesus, he bowed with his face to the ground and begged him, "Lord, if you choose, you can make me clean." [13]Then Jesus stretched out his hand, touched him, and said, "I do choose. Be made clean." Immediately the leprosy left him. [14]And he ordered him to tell no one. "Go," he said, "and show yourself to the priest, and, as Moses commanded, make an offering for your cleansing, for a testimony to them." [15]But now more than ever the word about Jesus spread abroad; many crowds would gather to hear him and to be cured of their diseases. [16]But he would withdraw to deserted places and pray.

Jesus's willingness to touch the man full of leprosy is both a means of transmitting power[21] and an act of profound compassion. Modern studies show the critical importance of touch for well-being. Failure to touch and hold babies, for instance, results in sensory deprivation that impedes their development. Likewise, solitary confinement has lasting deleterious effects, especially to mental health. Practitioners of modern Healing Touch therapy use their hands to work with human energy fields to help restore balance and harmony for people suffering from a variety of ailments.[22]

There are many examples of Christians who have followed Jesus's example in providing healing touch to people with leprosy. Saint Francis of Assisi (1181/1182–1226) famously kissed a man with leprosy and associated with other persons so afflicted as a dramatic illustration of his conversion. Saint Catherine of Siena (1347–1380) cared for a woman named Cecca, who had leprosy, even though Cecca cursed her violently whenever Catherine ministered to her.[23] Closer to our day, Dutch missionary Damien DeVeuster (1840–1889) spent sixteen years on the island of Molokai ministering to people suffering from Hansen's disease. Tending to their medical,

21. Pilch (*Healing in the New Testament*, 52) notes, "Touching is the way power is transmitted, so that Jesus' touch is an effective conduit for healing power." At 4:40, Jesus lays his hands on many sick people and cures them. For other instances in which Jesus touches people, see 6:19; 7:14, 39; 8:44, 45, 46, 47; 18:15; 22:51. For the risen Christ's invitation to his disciples to touch him to see that he is not a ghost, see 24:39. There are times, however, when Jesus heals without touching, e.g., 7:1-10.

22. See https://discover.healingtouchprogram.com/htp-home.

23. See Sigrid Undset, *Catherine of Siena*, trans. Kate Austin-Lund (New York: Sheed and Ward, 1954), 70–71.

spiritual, and emotional needs, he did not hesitate to touch them and to share life with them, until he himself succumbed to the disease. Likewise, Mother Teresa of Calcutta (1910–1997), founder of the Missionaries of Charity, spent her life tending to those who were in the most desperate straits, including people suffering from leprosy. In the 1950s she established Shanti Nagar, "Town of Peace," near the city of Asansol in India, for people with leprosy. These saints not only exemplify the healing power of touch but also testify to the profound effect it has on their own lives as they become one with the persons to whom they minister.

Miriam's Leprosy

A disturbing episode in Numbers 12 recounts how God afflicted Miriam, the sister of Moses and Aaron, with leprosy as a punishment for speaking against Moses for marrying a Cushite woman and challenging his leadership, "Has the LORD spoken only through Moses? Has he not spoken through us also?" (Num 12:2). Hearing their critique, God tells Aaron and Miriam that while other prophets receive dreams and visions, only Moses receives face-to-face communication. Afterward, Miriam becomes leprous, "as white as snow" (Num 12:10, NRSV, see critique of this translation below). Aaron then pleads with Moses, who intercedes with God to heal her. Nevertheless, God insists that she be shut out of the camp for seven days.

Feminists, beginning with Elizabeth Cady Stanton, have seen in Numbers 12 a classic example of a double standard: only Miriam and not Aaron is punished for speaking out.[24] Elisabeth Schüssler Fiorenza sees this as the central theological question for Jewish and Christian feminists: "Did G*d

24. Elizabeth Cady Stanton, *The Woman's Bible* (Amherst, NY: Prometheus Books, 1999 [1897]), 102. For a list of other feminist works on Miriam, see Wendy Zierler, "'On Account of the Cushite Woman That Moses Took': Race and Gender in Modern Hebrew Poems about Numbers 12," *Nashim: A Journal of Jewish Women's Studies & Gender Issues* 19 (Spring 2010): 34–61, esp. 60, n. 39. Katharine Doob Sakenfeld, "Numbers," in *Women's Bible Commentary*, ed. Carol A. Newsom, Sharon H. Ringe, and Jacqueline E. Lapsley, 3rd ed. (Louisville: Westminster John Knox, 2012), 84, offers an explanation for why Aaron is not punished: as a priest, he must maintain ritual cleanness and be free of physical blemishes (Lev 21–22). As the paradigmatic priestly figure, the narrator cannot conceive of presenting him as contracting a skin disease. Masha Turner, "Criticizing Moses: Miriam, Aaron, and the Cushite Woman (12:1-16)," in *The Torah: A Women's Commentary*, ed. Tamara Cohn Eskenazi and Andrea L. Weiss (New York: URJ Press and Women of Reform Judaism, The Federation of Temple Sisterhoods, 2008), 859–60, points out that the verb "spoke" in v. 1 is feminine singular, indicating that Miriam is the chief spokesperson, thus she is the one who is punished.

not also speak with us wo/men? Does G*d punish wo/men who claim their own authority, their own power, and their own leadership potential and exercise these actively?"[25]

Beginning in the 1990s there was a surge of interest in Miriam, especially by Jewish feminists who creatively rewrote her story using poetry, artwork, and song. Some focused on her prophetic power that flowed from her own initiative. Others celebrated her liturgical leadership in women's music and dance, as in Exodus 15.[26] Pesha Joyce Gertler imagines Miriam's response to her punishment with leprosy "by organizing the women to hold secret meetings, practice guerilla theatre, write poems for their descendants, and anticipate the time that 'not Moses, but I will / descend from Mt. Sinai with 2 new Commandments: / Welcome the Return of Women. / And listen when they speak.'"[27] Wendy Zierler reframes the seven-day banishment of Miriam. Whereas God treats Miriam like a daughter who has heinously disrespected male authority (Num 12:14), Zierler imagines a conversation between Moses and Miriam (based on Exod 4:6-7) as he comes to her alone and looking uneasy late on the seventh day of her exile. He confesses that he never wanted the job and tried to tell the voice in the burning bush, but the voice said, "'"If you want to see My powers as expressed in you, put your hand into your bosom and then pull it out." And there it was before me: covered with snowy scales! Don't you see? God has now spoken to you, too, from a cloud. Beware of what you ask for, my sister. God has answered you and etched the power of prophecy onto your skin. Now you too must bear the burden of this people, whom I have neither fathered nor mothered, but nevertheless, I carry on my back.' Miriam looked at her arm, and behold, the scales were healed. Her arm tingling, she followed her brother Moses back to the camp.

25. Elisabeth Schüssler Fiorenza, "Has G*d Not Spoken with Us Also?," in *Empowering Memory and Movement: Thinking and Working across Borders* (Minneapolis: Fortress, 2014), 141. On the use of G*d, see "Language for God," pp. xxxvi–xxxvii in the general editor's introduction. On wo/men, see the authors' introduction, p. xlv n. 9.

26. Rivkah M. Walton, "Lilith's Daughters, Miriam's Chorus: Two Decades of Feminist Midrash," *Religion & Literature* 43 (2011): 122. Walton traces how in the 1980s the figure of Lilith commanded feminist attention as a woman who demanded equality from the place of a subordinated outsider. By the mid-1990s, as attention shifted to socio-political goals for women's leadership, Miriam became the figure who could help women actualize such power.

27. Pesha Joyce Gertler, "Miriam: Not an American Success Story," *Bridges: A Jewish Feminist Journal* 12 (2007): 72–73, quoted in Walton, "Lilith's Daughters, Miriam's Chorus," 122.

Reverently, the people waited as she gathered her things, and took her place at the head of the line."[28]

Another feminist approach is exemplified by Katharine Doob Sakenfeld. She first recognizes the unfairness of Miriam's treatment as "a painful signal of the patriarchal perspective underlying the narrative."[29] But then she expands the lens to the wider biblical tradition in which God stands with and defends those who have been put on the outside, such as Hagar (Gen 21), the exiles (Isa 40–55), and Jesus, crucified outside the city (Heb 13:12). She concludes, "The starkness of Numbers 12 must not be undercut, but Miriam outside the camp may point us not only to the painful arbitrariness of her situation but also, however indirectly and allusively, to God's presence beyond the camp and even to the suffering of God in the face of human injustice."[30]

Attending to both the racial and the gender dynamics in Numbers 12, Mukti Barton points out that many interpreters overlook verse 1, where Miriam and Aaron speak against Moses "because of the Cushite woman he had married." The word כשית, "Cushite," means black color, dark-skinned; it also is a place, Ethiopia.[31] Barton advances that ancient Ethiopia included Midian and that the unnamed Cushite woman of Numbers 12:1 is Zipporah from Midian whom Moses married in Exodus 2:15-22. She notes that the Hebrews had many marriages with Black African people; there is nothing unusual in Moses having a Black wife. Nor should we envision Miriam and Aaron and Moses as White. "It is difficult to know who among the Hebrews were black or how black, but it is clear that they were not white."[32] She sees in Numbers 12:1 an unusual incidence of color prejudice. She calls attention to the ironic twist that Miriam's harassment of her sister-in-law due to the color of her Black skin results in her becoming "white as snow"—one of the few times in the Bible when white is not equated with something good.[33]

28. Wendy Zierler, "For Days Miriam Sat Outside," in Eskenazi and Weiss, *The Torah*, 868. See 866–68 for other poems on Numbers 12. On rabbinic interpretations of Miriam's leprosy, see Tal Ilan, "Post-biblical Interpretations," in Eskenazi and Weiss, *The Torah*, 862–64.

29. Sakenfeld, "Numbers," 84.

30. Ibid.

31. Robert Houston Smith, "Ethiopia (Place)," AYBD 2.665.

32. Mukti Barton, "The Skin of Miriam Became as White as Snow: The Bible, Western Feminism and Colour Politics," *FT* 27 (2001), 68–80, here 73.

33. Similarly, Rodney S. Sadler, "Can a Cushite Change His Skin? Cushites, 'Racial Othering,' and the Hebrew Bible," *Int* 60 (2006): 386–403: "It is plausible that the chapter is intentionally anti-racialist in its orientation, that it seeks to preclude any

Barton also advances that Miriam and Aaron should have had empathy for Moses's Cushite wife as a resident alien (so Exod 23:9). Miriam's seven-day exclusion gives her the opportunity to understand the heart of the one she wanted to exclude. Moreover, had Miriam cultivated a relationship with Zipporah, she could have learned from her something about shared leadership and thus have influenced Moses. Zipporah's father was the one who persuaded Moses to share his leadership in Exodus 18:17-18; his daughter would have learned his collaborative ways. Barton ends with a plea for White feminists similarly to cultivate empathy for their Black and Asian sisters who "dance with both patriarchy and racism" on their backs.[34]

A difficulty with Barton's analysis is that if racial prejudice was not usual among the ancient Hebrews, then how is it that Miriam exhibits it with regard to Moses's Cushite wife?[35] Womanist scholar Wilda C. Gafney points out that interpreters' contemporary experiences of race relations color how they read Numbers 12, including how verse 10 is translated (NRSV: "Miriam had become leprous, as white as snow").[36] She rightly points out that the word "white" is not in the text; מצרעת כשלג is literally "leprous as snow," which can mean "flaky/scaly like snowflakes," "cold/dead as snow," or "wet as snow."[37] Gafney interprets Miriam's challenge to Moses not to involve race but to be about his divorcing and abandoning Zipporah and her children (Exod 18) and marrying the Cushite woman. Moses's behavior is problematic and potentially disqualifies him from preeminent prophet status.

---

notion that Cushites were ontologically different from Hebrews, and that it symbolically transcends perceived otherness by placing YHWH's seal of approval on Moses' union with a Cushite woman."

34. Barton, "The Skin of Miriam Became as White as Snow," 80. See also Zierler, "'On Account of the Cushite Woman That Moses Took,'" who analyzes three modern Hebrew poems on Numbers 12 from the perspectives of both race and gender.

35. In Jewish circles, a popular midrash has Miriam protesting on behalf of the Cushite wife (Zipporah), with whom Moses was no longer having sexual relations as he was remaining in a state of ritual purity while in perpetual communion with God. See Amy-Jill Levine and Douglas A. Knight, *The Meaning of the Bible: What the Jewish Scriptures and Christian Old Testament Can Teach Us* (New York: HarperOne, 2012), 276.

36. Wilda C. Gafney, *Daughters of Miriam: Women Prophets in Ancient Israel* (Minneapolis: Fortress, 2008), 83.

37. Ibid., 84.

While YHWH's response[38] and the ongoing traditions about Moses's leadership show her to have transgressed, the account of Miriam's death in Numbers 20 and her remembrance as a leader along with Moses and Aaron in Micah 6:4 attest to her status in the community.

We appreciate the work of these feminists and womanists in critiquing Miriam's affliction with leprosy from both gender and racial perspectives. Furthermore, we problematize the idea of leprosy as a punishment from God. We wonder how a person who suffers from Hansen's disease or other skin ailments can feel themselves beloved, not punished by God. And what of a person who pleads to be healed but, unlike the man in Luke 5:12, is not? Other biblical texts, such as Lamentations 3, that assure of God's steadfast and unceasing love (v. 22) even when "my flesh and my skin waste away" (v. 4) will need to provide those answers.

After Jesus heals the man with leprosy, word about him continues to spread (see also 4:14, 37), and crowds continue to gather to hear him and be healed (see also 4:40, 42; 5:1). This episode points forward to 7:22, where healing people with leprosy is part of the evidence John's disciples are to report to the imprisoned Baptizer in response to his query whether Jesus is the one to come. Later, in another episode, unique to Luke, Jesus heals ten people of leprosy (17:11-19). Jesus continues to go apart to deserted places to pray,[39] a critical necessity for replenishing his energies and for ongoing discernment concerning his mission. Today, a common difficulty for busy ministers and caregivers is to carve out time to retreat for prayer and rest. Jesus's practice models that self-care is needed by anyone who wants to be a healer for others.

A Man Who Was Paralyzed Forgiven and Healed (5:17-26)

Numerous readers of this and other gospel healing stories think of a person with a disability as helpless, dependent, and destitute. Frequently, they identify the man in this story only by his disability: "the paralytic." Feminist disability studies help us to see other ways of envisioning him. First, disability activists urge the use of people-first language: in

38. Gafney (ibid., 83–85) advances that Aaron was also punished with a skin afflic-tion and that it was possibly Moses, not YHWH, who caused the suffering.
39. See comments above at 4:14 and the excursus at 11:2, "Prominence of Prayer in Luke."

Luke 5:17-26

¹⁷One day, while he was teaching, Pharisees and teachers of the law were sitting near by (they had come from every village of Galilee and Judea and from Jerusalem); and the power of the Lord was with him to heal. ¹⁸Just then some men came, carrying a paralyzed man on a bed. They were trying to bring him in and lay him before Jesus; ¹⁹but finding no way to bring him in because of the crowd, they went up on the roof and let him down with his bed through the tiles into the middle of the crowd in front of Jesus. ²⁰When he saw their faith, he said, "Friend, your sins are forgiven you." ²¹Then the scribes and the Pharisees began to question, "Who is this who is speaking blasphemies? Who can forgive sins but God alone?" ²²When Jesus perceived their questionings, he answered them, "Why do you raise such questions in your hearts? ²³Which is easier, to say, 'Your sins are forgiven you,' or to say, 'Stand up and walk'? ²⁴But so that you may know that the Son of Man has authority on earth to forgive sins"—he said to the one who was paralyzed—"I say to you, stand up and take your bed and go to your home." ²⁵Immediately he stood up before them, took what he had been lying on, and went to his home, glorifying God. ²⁶Amazement seized all of them, and they glorified God and were filled with awe, saying, "We have seen strange things today."

this case we do better to speak of "a man with paralysis" rather than "the paralytic." The people-first language underscores "that disability is one characteristic of that individual but not the defining variable. A person should not be reduced to his or her disability."[40] Next, rather than presume the man to be helpless, we note, instead, his resourcefulness.[41] Like most people with disabilities, he and his caregivers have to be creative and assertive in gaining access to venues where the obstacles are daunting—in this case, coming through the roof when they could not get past the crowd. We can also envision the man as able to earn a good living, despite his needing to be carried. Anna Rebecca Solevåg notes analogously, "Plutarch mentions a lame engineer of siege engines, Artemos, who acquired the nickname Periphoretus because he was carried everywhere on a litter (φορεῖων, *Per.* 27.3–4)."[42] The man with paralysis has sufficient money to own a home (vv. 24-25), possibly with a wife and children. If the men who help him (v. 18) are hired servants or slaves,

---

40. Anna Rebecca Solevåg, *Negotiating the Disabled Body: Representations of Disability in Early Christian Texts*, ECL 23 (Atlanta: SBL Press, 2018), 33–34.
41. This section follows Solevåg, *Negotiating the Disabled Body*, 36–39.
42. Quoted in ibid., 37.

rather than relatives or friends, this would be another indicator of financial status. Such a re-visioning of the man as resourceful, employed, having economic resources, owning slaves,[43] and maintaining a home helps us to see a complex figure beyond his paralysis.

Rosemarie Garland-Thomson observes:

> Seldom do we see disability presented as an integral part of one's embodiment, character, life, and way of relating to the world. Even less often do we see disability presented as part of the spectrum of human variation, the particularization of individual bodies, or the materialization of an individual body's history. Instead we learn to understand disability as something that is wrong with someone, as an exceptional and escapable calamity rather than as what is perhaps the most universal of human experiences. After all, if we live long enough, we will all become disabled. A feminist disability perspective suggests that we are better off learning to accommodate disabilities, appreciate disabled lives, and create a more equitable environment than trying to eliminate disability.[44]

We appreciate these insights of Garland-Thomson. We, however, would not see as mutually exclusive an appreciation of disabilities and attempts to eliminate them. We hope that when medical advances allow, persons with physical and other challenges could seek treatments, if they wish. We would also set aside the term "disabled" in favor of an expression such as "alternately abled" or "differently abled."

Faith and Forgiveness

This episode, like 7:36-50, links faith with forgiveness. In both instances, Jesus declares "your sins are forgiven" (ἀφέωνταί, 5:20; 7:48). The passive voice of the verb points to God doing the forgiving, but in both stories, Jesus's critics understand him to be appropriating the power to himself. Jesus's reply (v. 24) is that he is an earthly agent of God with authority to remit sins for God.[45] Divine forgiveness is only one aspect of reconciliation; healing of relationships on a human level is also needed and requires processes that can be lengthy and complex (see above on

---

43. On the problematic aspects of slavery, see comments at 1:38, 48 and excursus on Luke and Slavery at 17:7-10.

44. Rosemarie Garland-Thomson, "Feminist Disability Studies," *Signs* 30 (Winter 2005): 1557–87, here 1568.

45. In a text from Qumran, 4QPrNab 1:3-4, a Jewish exorcist remits the sins of an ailing man named Nabonidus "for Him" (i.e., for God), showing that some Jews thought that a human being on earth could remit sins for God.

5:1-11). An encounter with Jesus can be a catalyst for accepting the gift of divine forgiveness and for one who has done wrong to put in motion human processes of repentance and reconciliation. Believers who practice sacramental reconciliation find there the grace to pursue what needs to be done to restore broken relationships.[46]

A novel element in this story is that the faith of the companions is what prompts Jesus's declaration of forgiveness. Faith in this instance seems to refer to their confidence that Jesus can do something to help the paralyzed man.[47]

TRANSLATION MATTERS

In Luke 5:20 and 12:14 the NRSV translates Ἄνθρωπε, the vocative form of ἄνθρωπος, as "Friend." This is not accurate, as the word for "friend" is φίλος.[48] The NKJV translates Ἄνθρωπε at 5:20, "Man"; NRSV translates it this way at 22:58. We surmise that the NRSV is avoiding gender-exclusive language, as it also does at 6:41-42 where ἀδελφός, literally "brother," occurs three times. The first two times NRSV translates it as "neighbor"; the third as "friend." The NAB similarly avoids gender-exclusive language at 5:20 by rendering Ἄνθρωπε "as for you."

We appreciate translators' efforts at gender inclusivity, but in 5:18 it is clearly a man who is paralyzed (παραλελυμένος, "paralyzed" is a masculine participle) and those carrying him are male (ἄνδρες, "men," means males, unlike ἄνθρωποι, which is inclusive of men and women). Translating Ἄνθρωπε in verse 20 as "Friend" also leads some interpreters to call the caregivers "friends," when they may well be slaves, hired servants, or relatives.

Disability, Sin, and Forgiveness

The juxtaposition of forgiveness and healing in this episode can imply that there is a causal link between sinning and the man's paralysis.[49] This

---

46. See comments at 17:4 on the dangers of repeatedly forgiving, which can fuel cycles of violence and victimization. See also 6:37 and 11:4 where there is also a connection between divine and human forgiveness.

47. See also 7:9; 8:48-50; 17:19; 18:42 where faith is connected with healing.

48. Luke 7:9, 34; 11:5 [2x], 6, 8; 12:4; 14:10, 12; 15:6, 9, 29; 16:9; 21:16; 23:12.

49. Amos Yong, *The Bible, Disability, and the Church: A New Vision of the People of God* (Grand Rapids: Eerdmans, 2011), 61, reads it differently: he sees Jesus's forgiveness and healing as two distinct acts: the first was for the sake of the person with paralysis; the second was a sign for the scribes and Pharisees. Thus, for him it is a mistake to read a causal relationship between sin and disability in this passage.

connection reflects a common assumption in the ancient world and is still held by some people today.[50] The insights of Sharon Ringe are helpful:

> Even though such an assumption [that disease is a consequence of sin] may have been held by biblical authors (or even by Jesus), we cannot ignore what science has taught us about the physical causes of disease and of various physical disabilities. To ignore such knowledge, and to heap guilt on people who are suffering by implying that they have caused their own condition, is clearly inappropriate. On the other hand, modern medicine is only beginning to explore the connections between spiritual, emotional, or psychological health (or lack of it) and physical illness or well-being. Thus, if the paralyzed person felt a connection between the physical paralysis and his or her "sin," an effort to heal the latter without attention to the former might well be in vain. If indeed that was the person's understanding, Jesus's words of forgiveness (5:20b) and healing (5:24c) together might have enabled that person to be restored to health.[51]

Pharisees in Luke

The Pharisees appear for the first of sixteen episodes in 5:17-26. To most Christians, the word "Pharisee" connotes a person who is "marked by hypocritical censorious self-righteousness."[52] Such a misperception rests on the gospels' portraits of them, which reflect the increasing tensions between followers of Jesus and other Jews in a post-70s context. In addition to the New Testament, we can turn to Josephus, the Dead Sea Scrolls, and rabbinic literature, each of which give us limited information.[53] The Pharisees began to gain influence in Hasmonean times (152–63 BCE) as part of the council of elders and became the dominant voice

50. See, e.g., John 9:2, where Jesus's disciples ask him whose sins caused the man to be born blind: his or his parents'. Jesus says neither (9:3). In the same gospel, however, Jesus does voice a connection between sin and paralysis when he says to the man whom he healed at the pool of Bethesda, "See, you have been made well! Do not sin any more, so that nothing worse happens to you" (John 5:14). In the book of Job, the friends insist that Job's sins brought on the deaths and diseases that plagued him. At the end of the book, God rejects this claim.

51. Sharon H. Ringe, *Luke*, Westminster Bible Companion (Louisville: Westminster John Knox, 1995), 80–81.

52. Pharisaical" in *Merriam-Webster* 2018 online dictionary: https://www.merriam-webster.com/dictionary/pharisaical.

53. See analyses of each of these literary sources as well as contributions from archaeology in *In Quest of the Historical Pharisees*, ed. Jacob Neusner and Bruce D. Chilton (Waco, TX: Baylor University Press, 2007). See also Justin R. Howell, *The Pharisees and*

in the council during the reign of Salome Alexandra (76–67 BCE). Josephus states that during Herodian times they numbered about six thousand (*Ant.* 17.42), and he speaks about their popularity among the people (*Ant.* 13.298; 18.15). This popularity, along with their approach to the Law that combined adherence to the written Torah with adaptations based on what would come to be called the oral Law (laws and customs passed down through the generations), enabled Judaism to adapt and survive after the destruction of the temple in 70 CE.

Luke's portrayal of the Pharisees is mixed. For the most part, they appear antagonistic toward Jesus, accusing him of speaking blasphemies (5:21) and criticizing him for his table fellowship (5:30; 15:2), for his failure to fast (5:33), and for violating the sabbath (6:1-5, 6-11). They invite Jesus to dinners, but at each one he points out their shortcomings: the inability to recognize or seek forgiveness (7:29-30, 36-50),

neglecting justice and the love of God (11:42), seeking seats of honor (14:7-11), and not inviting people who are poor, crippled, lame, or blind (14:12-14). He warns his disciples that they are hypocrites (12:1) and regard others with contempt (18:9). He calls them lovers of money and self-righteous (16:14-15; 18:9). Some of the interactions of Pharisees with Jesus can be read in a positive way: they warn Jesus that Herod is trying to kill him (13:31), they ask about when the kingdom of God will come, possibly out of genuine interest (17:20), and they urge Jesus to stop his disciples from acclaiming him as king, perhaps to avoid Roman reprisal (19:39). Given the overall negative portrayal of the Pharisees, Luke likely intends these three incidents to be read as the Pharisees' misunderstanding and attempting to derail Jesus from his mission rather than having genuine concern for him and the *basileia* he proclaims.[54] On a positive note, Pharisees are absent from Luke's passion narrative, where the chief

_____

Figured Speech in Luke–Acts, WUNT 2.456 (Tübingen: Mohr Siebeck, 2017), chap. 3: "Scholarship on the Historical Pharisees," 39–60; Lawrence H. Schiffman, "Pharisees," in *The Jewish Annotated New Testament*, ed. Amy-Jill Levine and Marc Zvi Brettler, 2nd ed. (New York: Oxford University Press, 2017), 619–22; and the proceedings from a conference held in 2019 in Rome titled *"Jesus and the Pharisees: An Interdisciplinary Reappraisal,"* forthcoming from Eerdmans Press and available online at https://www .jesusandthepharisees.org.

54. Amy-Jill Levine, "Pharisees in Luke," in Levine and Brettler, eds., *Jewish Annotated New Testament*, 121–22; see also Amy-Jill Levine, "Luke's Pharisees," in Neusner and Chilton, *In Quest of the Historical Pharisees*, 113–30.

priests, scribes, and elders are those seeking to put Jesus to death.[55] In Acts 5:34-43, a Pharisee named Gamaliel succeeds in persuading the council to leave Jesus's followers alone, and at 15:5 some Pharisees are among the believers. Paul continues to claim his identity as a Pharisee (23:6).

We consider it important to recognize how Luke's portrayal of the Pharisees contributes to the enduring denigration and persecution of Jews. It is incumbent on preachers, teachers, and ministers to do all in their power to correct such negative stereotypes.

Women Members and Supporters of the Pharisees

In Luke's writings, the only Pharisees who seem to be in view are males, but Tal Ilan has demonstrated that women were also adherents and supporters of the Pharisaic movement.[56] Ilan examines texts from Josephus and rabbinic literature about Queen Shelamzion Alexandra (*J.W.* 1.107–19; *Ant.* 13.398–432), Pheroras's Wife (*Ant.* 15:369–70; 17.42), Queen Helene of Adiabene (*Ant.* 20.17–96; m. Nazir 3:6; t. Sukkah 1:1; m. Yoma 3:10), Martha bat Boethus (b. Bava Batra 21a; m. Yoma 3:9, among others), and the daughter of Naqadimon ben Gurion (Sifre Deut 305).[57] She finds evidence that these wealthy and royal

55. The chief priests, scribes, and elders become the prime opponents of Jesus at Luke 20:1, 19, 39, 46; 22:2, 52, 66; 23:4, 13. Sadducees appear at 20:27.

56. Tal Ilan, "The Attraction of Aristocratic Jewish Women to Pharisaism during the Second Temple Period," HTR 88 (1995): 1–33, which also appears in her book *Integrating Women into Second Temple History* (Tübingen: Mohr Siebeck, 1999), 11–42; Ilan, "Gender," in Levine and Brettler, *The Jewish Annotated New Testament*, 611–14.

57. Queen Shelamzion (also called Salome) Alexandra (76–67 BCE), was wife and successor of King Alexander Yannai (Jannaeus) (c. 126–76 BCE). She was the only Jewish queen to hold power during the Second Temple period. She is praised in rabbinic literature (Sifre Deut. 42) for having put the Pharisees in power. Pheroras (c. 68 BCE–c. 5 BCE) was the youngest son of Antipater I (the founder of the Herodian dynasty) and his wife, Cypros. Pheroras's wife, whose name is unknown, was accused after his death of poisoning him. Queen Helene was the sister and wife of Monabazus Bazaeus, king of Adiabene (a Persian province at the northern end of Tigris River, modern-day Erbil, Iraqi Kurdistan) at the beginning of the first century CE, who converted to Judaism with other members of her family. She made a pilgrimage to Jerusalem in 46–47 CE and purchased large quantities of grain and figs from Egypt for Jews of the city suffering from famine (*Ant.* 20.17–96). She also made donations to the temple (m. *Yoma*

women financially supported the Pharisees, sometimes against their husbands' wishes. Ilan sees similarities between these Jewish women supporters of the Pharisees and women participants in the Jesus movement such as Mary Magdalene, Joanna, and Susanna (8:1-3), the sisters Mary and Martha (10:38-42), and Mary the mother of John Mark (Acts 12:12), who provided financial support and hospitality. Ilan thinks that through their financial contributions, women supporters of the Pharisees and of the Jesus movement not only demonstrated their financial independence but also may have influenced decision- and policy-making in the parties they chose to support.[58]

Son of Man

The enigmatic expression ὁ υἱὸς τοῦ ἀνθρώπου, "the Son of Man," occurs for the first of twenty times at Luke 5:24. It is found in all four gospels and only on the lips of Jesus, relating to his earthly ministry, his passion, and his return as eschatological judge.[59] To avoid exclusively male terminology, some feminists use "Son of Humanity" or "the Human One," underscoring the fact that ἄνθρωπος means "human being" rather than "man."

Both these choices convey one of the possible meanings for the expression: "a human being," "a certain person," or "someone." But it does not adequately represent another meaning, which is likely at 12:8 ("And I tell you, everyone who acknowledges me before others, the Son of Man also will acknowledge before the angels of God"), where Jesus appears to be talking about someone other than himself, a future supernatural figure who would vindicate his present ministry.

3:10). She and her son Izotus were buried in Jerusalem. Martha bat Boethus was the wife of the high priest Joshua ben Gamla (m. Yevamot 6:4), a priestly family that rose to prominence during Herod's time and enjoyed a position of power until the temple was destroyed. Naqadimon ben Gurion was a wealthy Jewish man who lived in Jerusalem in the first century CE. In t. Ketub. 5:9-10, his daughter is portrayed as a spoiled princess.

58. Ilan, *Integrating Women*, 33.

59. In reference to his earthly ministry, see Luke 5:24; 6:5, 22; 7:34; 9:58; 11:30; 12:10; 19:10; in regard to his passion, see 9:22, 44; 18:31; 22:22, 48; 24:7; in reference to his future coming, see 9:26; 12:8; 17:22, 24, 26, 30; 18:8; 21:27, 36; 22:69. See further Lawrence M. Wills, "Son of Man," in Levine and Brettler, eds., *The Jewish Annotated New Testament*, 74; Géza Vermes, "The Son of Man Debate Revisited (1960–2010)," *JJS* 61 (2010): 193–206.

Calling a Tax Collector (5:27-32)

The Lukan Jesus has a predilection for dining with tax collectors and sinners, for which the Pharisees repeatedly criticize him (see also 7:34; 15:1-2; 19:1-10). Jesus defends his practice by comparing himself to a doctor (see also 4:23) whose work it is to heal sick people. By dining with sinners, he establishes a relationship that can open the way for them to repent. Luke does not specify of what Levi needed to repent. John the Baptizer implies that tax collectors were prone to extortion: "Collect no more than the amount prescribed for you" (3:13). John does not demand that tax collectors leave their position, only that they carry out their work honestly. Levi, however, leaves everything and follows Jesus, as did Peter, James, and John (5:11).[60]

The banquet scene in 5:29-32 stands in tension with the assertion that Levi left everything. His portrait is more like that of Mary Magdalene, Joanna, Susanna, and many other Galilean women (8:1-3), Mary the mother of John Mark (Acts 12:12), and Lydia (Acts 16:15, 40), who use their wealth to advance Jesus's mission and to host gatherings of Jesus and his followers.

Female Disciples

The term "disciples" occurs for the first time of thirty-seven instances at 5:30. The term μαθητής (sing.) means "pupil, apprentice, adherent."[61] In Luke's Gospel, the term almost always occurs in the plural, οἱ μαθηταί. In sayings directed to disciples, the Lukan Jesus articulates these criteria: following Jesus (14:27),[62] the willingness to suffer for doing so (14:27; 21:12, 16-17), giving up family and possessions (14:26, 33), becoming like the teacher (6:40), and serving (22:26-27). In the gospel and Acts, women fulfill all of these criteria. Mary Magdalene, Joanna, Mary the mother of James, and other women (24:10) follow Jesus (συνακολουθοῦσαι αὐτῷ, 23:49) from Galilee[63] and witness his crucifixion (23:49) and burial (23:55). In addition to following,

---

60. Zacchaeus, another tax collector with whom Jesus dines, gives half his belongings to the poor (see comments at 19:8).

61. BDAG, 609.

62. Similar to 14:27 is 9:23-24.

63. That Mary Magdalene, Joanna, Susanna, and other Galilean women followed Jesus is also implied at 8:1-3 as they are with him as he goes through cities and villages proclaiming the good news.

²⁷After this he went out and saw a tax collector named Levi, sitting at the tax booth; and he said to him, "Follow me." ²⁸And he got up, left everything, and followed him.

²⁹Then Levi gave a great banquet for him in his house; and there was a large crowd of tax collectors and others sitting at the table with them. ³⁰The Pharisees and their scribes were complaining to his disciples, saying, "Why do you eat and drink with tax collectors and sinners?" ³¹Jesus answered, "Those who are well have no need of a physician, but those who are sick; ³²I have come to call not the righteous but sinners to repentance."

Mary Magdalene, Joanna, Susanna, and other Galilean women place their financial possessions at the service of Jesus's mission (8:3). While no disciple in the gospel is depicted as suffering for following Jesus, in Acts, Saul/Paul imprisons both women and men who do so (8:3; 9:1-2). In Luke's Sermon on the Plain, Jesus declares that a disciple will be like the teacher (6:40). In the gospel, only Jesus teaches, but in Acts, Priscilla, along with her husband Aquila, teaches Apollos, an eloquent teacher and preacher (18:26).[64] Finally, discipleship means being like Jesus as one who serves (ὁ διακονῶν, Luke 22:26-27).[65] The only characters with whom the verb διακονεῖν and the noun διακονία are used in the gospel are women: Simon's mother-in-law (διηκόνει, 4:39); Mary Magdalene, Joanna, Susanna, and the other Galilean women (διηκόνουν, 8:3); and Martha (διακονεῖν, 10:40). In addition to showing women as fulfilling the qualifications for discipleship, in Acts 9:36, Luke explicitly names Tabitha as a disciple, μαθήτρια.[66]

Luke restricts the role of "apostle" to twelve men and, in his second work, makes explicit

---

64. The verb is ἐκτίθημι, "to convey information by careful elaboration, explain, expound" (BDAG, 310), rather than διδάσκω, "tell, instruct" (BDAG, 241), the verb used in the other citations.

65. Luke 22:14 says that at the Last Supper Jesus gathers with apostles (ἀπόστολοι), whom Luke identifies with the twelve men chosen from a larger group of disciples (6:13; 9:1 with 9:10; see also 17:5; 22:14; 24:10). Shelly reads the entire supper and Gethsemane scene in Luke as involving only Jesus and the twelve men. But Barbara points to the use of οἱ μαθηταί at 22:11 and 22:39 to suggest that a larger group of followers is in view at the Passover and the Mount of Olives.

66. The only other disciples in Luke and Acts identified by name are James and John (Luke 9:54) and Timothy (Acts 16:1).

that the replacement for Judas among the Twelve must also be a man (ἀνήρ, Acts 1:21-22).[67] When most readers encounter "the disciples," they envision these twelve male apostles (Luke 6:12-16; 9:1-6).[68] But even though Luke continually foregrounds the men in the Jesus movement, relegating women disciples to silent, passive roles,[69] his concept of discipleship is broader than his concept of apostleship, and thus, we may read the masculine plural οἱ μαθηταὶ, "the disciples," as an "androcentric inclusive" phrase, that is, one that includes women as well as men. This reading strategy is important for correcting the false impression that Jesus had only male disciples and that only they exercised important ministerial roles in Jesus's day and in the early church. Continued exclusion of women from certain ministries and leadership positions rests in part on this false understanding.

Fasting and Feasting (5:33-39)

The conflict at Levi's table continues as they (presumably the Pharisees and scribes of 5:30) shift their criticism from Jesus's dining companions to his disciples' eating and drinking. Jesus fasted forty days in the desert (4:2), but the rest of the gospel frequently depicts Jesus and his disciples eating and drinking.[70] Jesus's critics do not state why they expect Jesus's disciples to fast.[71] Jesus's explanation for not fasting first centers on timing and then on incompatibility. He likens the present time to a wedding feast with himself as the bridegroom, a time when joyous eating and drinking is expected. The Old Testament prophets used this image (e.g., Hos 2:19;

---

67. Luke's concern to restrict the title "apostle" to the Twelve leads him to deny the title to Paul in the Acts of the Apostles (except at 14:14), in spite of Paul's repeated self-identification as an apostle in his own epistles. Further, Paul in his epistles demonstrates recognition of a broader definition of apostle than Luke, even recognizing the woman Junia as apostle in Rom 16:7. For the significance of restricting the designation of apostle to the twelve men in Luke and Acts, see Shelly Matthews, "Fleshly Resurrection, Authority Claims, and the Scriptural Practices of Lukan Christianity," *JBL* 136 (2017): 163–83. For Junia, see Yii-Jan Lin, "Junia: An Apostle before Paul," *JBL* 139 (2020): 191–209.

68. See further discussion on apostles in Luke at 9:1-6; 22:24-34; 24:36-43.

69. See comments on Luke and Women in the authors' introduction.

70. Luke 7:36-50; 9:10-17; 11:37-54; 14:1-24; 19:1-10; 22:4-38; 24:29-32.

71. The Old Testament associates fasting with mourning and repentance (2 Sam 1:2; 3:36; 1 Kgs 21:27), making prayer of supplication more efficacious (2 Sam 12:13-25; Ps 35:13-14) and opening an individual to divine revelation (Dan 10:3). In the other two references to fasting in the gospel, Luke does not give a motive for why Anna (2:37) or the Pharisee (18:12) do so.

Luke 5:33-39

33Then they said to him, "John's disciples, like the disciples of the Pharisees, frequently fast and pray, but your disciples eat and drink." 34Jesus said to them, "You cannot make wedding guests fast while the bridegroom is with them, can you? 35The days will come when the bridegroom will be taken away from them, and then they will fast in those days." 36He also told them a parable: "No one tears a piece from a new garment and sews it on an old garment; otherwise the new will be torn, and the piece from the new will not match the old. 37And no one puts new wine into old wineskins; otherwise the new wine will burst the skins and will be spilled, and the skins will be destroyed. 38But new wine must be put into fresh wineskins. 39And no one after drinking old wine desires new wine, but says, 'The old is good.'"

Isa 54:3-6; 62:5; Jer 2:2; Ezek 16) to portray YHWH as the faithful groom or the husband of the people of the covenant calling them back to himself. We resist the trope of casting the wife as the unfaithful one, first, because in many cases it is the husband who is untrue to his wife rather than vice versa.[72] In addition, the stereotype of the unfaithful wife can be quite dangerous, as when a husband is a batterer and falsely accuses his wife of betraying him. In Luke 5:34-35 there is no overt mention of faithfulness and repentance, but with Luke's frequent references to repentance and the pervasive way the bridegroom image functions in the Old Testament, a call to turn and adhere to the bridegroom may be implied.

Parables and the Art of Storytelling

The Gospel of Luke has more parables than Mark and Matthew; there are no parables in John.[73] The term παραβολή indicates figurative speech of various kinds: a proverb such as "Doctor, cure yourself" (4:23); a wisdom saying, such as that

72. The 2006 American General Social survey showed that nearly twice as many married men as women admitted to having had sexual relations with someone other than their spouse. A survey done in 2000 in the United Kingdom found that 15 percent of men had had "overlapping" relationships in the previous year, but only 9 percent of women had, https://www.bbc.com/news/magazine-18233843.

73. Most scholars count twenty-five in Luke, compared to seventeen in Matthew and nine in Mark. Neither the term παραβολή, "parable," nor the kinds of parabolic stories found in the Synoptic Gospels occur in the Fourth Gospel, though παροιμία, "figure of speech," occurs three times (John 10:6; 16:25, 29).

in 5:37-38; or a comparison, as when Jesus compares the *basileia* of God to a woman hiding yeast in bread dough (13:20-21). Parables can also be longer stories, such as one about the Samaritan traveler who helps a man on the road to Jericho (Luke 10:29-37).

Jesus's parables use everyday images and true-to-life situations to draw in the listener with their familiarity. But there is usually something unexpected, a twist that leaves one puzzling, "What does this mean?" Jesus's parables, for the most part, remain open-ended and so challenge hearers to finish the story. They are not stories that confirm the status quo; like parables in the Old Testament,[74] they lead hearers to change their way of thinking or acting.

Storytelling is an ancient art that has often been the domain of women. In the Old Testament, there are two notable examples. The wise[75] woman of Tekoa (2 Sam 14:1-20) acts out a parable to get David to change his mind and let Absalom return to Jerusalem. Another wise woman, this time in Abel Beth-maacah (2 Sam 20:14-22), uses a proverb and her rhetorical skill to dissuade Joab, David's general, from attacking the whole city while in pursuit of the rebellious Sheba, son of Bichri.[76]

In Native American cultures, such as the Lakota, grandmothers in the past were the primary educators of the children while the men would go to hunt and the mothers worked on tasks that required younger, stronger hands. Through their stories, still today, the women pass on the core values and the culture's spiritual practices.[77] In modern times when there is a high rate of alcoholism, depression, and suicide among Native peoples, Stella Long, who is Choctaw, tells healing stories that seek to connect people through experience and thought, to help mend hearts and minds. Other modern modes of storytelling include rap music, such as that

74. In the Old Testament, the prophet Nathan told a parable to King David to bring him to repentance (2 Sam 12:1-12). Isaiah's parable of an unproductive vineyard was a vivid way to denounce social injustices in Israel (Isa 5:1-7). Jotham confronts the lords of Shechem who made Abimelech king with a parable of trees (Judg 9:7-15).

75. As Claudia V. Camp notes, "One defining attribute of 'wisdom,' in the biblical tradition, is skill in rhetoric (Prov 1:5-6 and *passim*)" ("Wise Woman of Tekoa," in *Women in Scripture: A Dictionary of Named and Unnamed Women in the Hebrew Bible, The Apocryphal/Deuterocanonical Books, and the New Testament*, ed. Carol Meyers, Toni Craven, and Ross Shepard Kraemer [Grand Rapids: Eerdmans, 2000], 263.

76. See further, Claudia V. Camp, "Wise Woman of Abel of Beth-maacah," in Meyers, Craven, and Kraemer, *Women in Scripture*, 266–67.

77. See Shannon Smith, "Native Storytellers Connect the Past and the Future," http://cojmc.unl.edu/nativedaughters/storytellers/native-storytellers-connect-the-past-and-the-future.

by Hope Brings Plenty, who lives on the Pine Ridge Reservation.[78] Valerie Red Horse uses drama; Virginia Driving Hawk Sneve from the Rosebud Reservation in South Dakota is passing on the rich heritage of oral storytelling in her numerous published works, particularly children's books. Ecofeminists find common ground with Native American storytellers such as Kenneth Little Hawk, who stress connectedness with and care for Earth.[79]

Increased attention in recent years to the use of storytelling for empowering women and other disadvantaged persons has spawned numerous groups and blogs. The digital storytelling project Women Win, for example, teaches young women from around the globe how to tell their stories using multimedia and so trains them to be leaders and agents

of change.[80] A Lebanese social media training program "Shou Osstik?," Arabic for "What's your story?," likewise aims to educate women in digital storytelling and social media and so empowers them with tools for communicating their messages.[81] Black women use storytelling as a powerful form of activism; they insist on the need to tell their own stories and not to let men or White women speak for them.[82] Muslim Women's Story Lab mobilizes Muslim women to reclaim Islam's legacy of inclusivity and women's empowerment. It also aims to undermine false ideas about Muslim women by telling counternarratives.[83] African women are claiming their stories as a basis for theologizing, both as individuals and collectively.[84] Indian women are making breakthroughs in becoming

78. See "Native Women Bring Traditional Art into the 21st Century," http://cojmc .unl.edu/nativedaughters/artists/native-women-bring-traditional-art-into-the-21st -century.

79. Kenneth Little Hawk, *"Care for the Earth": Native American Stories of Respect for All Life* (Little Hawk Productions, 2010).

80. See http://womenwin.org/stories/digital-storytelling-project.

81. See SMEX, "Shou Osstik? Storytellers Graduate," October 4, 2012, https:// smex.org/shou-osstik-participants-it-is-only-the-beginning/.

82. See, e.g., Briana Perry, "The Power of Black Women's Storytelling in Activist Work," March 11, 2015, http://www.forharriet.com/2015/03/the-power-of-black -womens-storytelling.html#axzz4EIjX4oBA.

83. See Arsalan Suleman, "Amplifying Muslim Women's Voices through Storytell- ing Platforms," posted March 30, 2016, on the official blog site of the US State Depart- ment: http://2007-2017-blogs.state.gov/stories/2016/03/30/amplifying-muslim -women-s-voices-through-storytelling-platforms.html.

84. Musimbi R. A. Kanyoro, *Introducing Feminist Cultural Hermeneutics: An African Perspective*, IFT (Cleveland: Pilgrim Press, 2002), 23–24.

public storytellers, long the domain of men.[85]

Even organizations that coach people to be successful corporate leaders use storytelling to teach women and other disadvantaged persons to become successful communicators among high-level business executives.[86] Courses on women and storytelling are also being taught in universities,[87] and such courses counter the notion that women's stories are "old wives' tales" (1 Tim 4:7) or petty gossip.

The desire to bring more stories into the archives of what it means to be human is felt not just by women but extends into trans and gender-diverse communities as well. The organization TRUTH (TRransgender yoUTH), has a mission of liberation through storytelling, providing a platform for gender-nonconforming young people and their families, in an effort to build empathy and understanding.[88] In the United States, the National Center for Transgender Equality, organized in 2003, recognizes the importance of storytelling to change public policy.[89] In 2015, the *New York Times* initiated a series on transgender experiences, which at the time of this writing is still soliciting stories.[90]

85. See Anasuya Basu's BBC report of July 12, 2016, "How India's Female Storytellers Fought to Be Heard," http://www.bbc.com/news/world-asia-india-36648490.

86. See, for example, "Corporate Storytelling: Communicating with Credibility for Women Leaders," taught by Cheryl Chartier, a corporate storyteller for Articulus, who specializes in coaching women to success in high-stakes communications: https://www.articulus.com/training/communicate-w-credibility-women/.

87. E.g., Caren S. Neile, PhD, MFA, a faculty member in the School of Communication and Multimedia Studies at Florida Atlantic University in Boca Raton, teaches a course on women and storytelling. She is also producer and cohost, with Michael Stock, of *The Public Storyteller* on 91.3 FM Miami public radio WLRN. She is also the former chair of the National Storytelling Network and a founding editor of the international academic journal *Storytelling, Self, Society*. See https://storynet.org/groups/healing-story-alliance-hsa/stories-for-social-justice/periodicals/. At Columbia University, Frank Rose teaches strategic storytelling, instructing students in the essential elements of any story and explains how to assemble these elements for maximum impact in a digital world. See http://www8.gsb.columbia.edu/execed/program-pages/details/831/DSS?utm_source=bing&utm_medium=cpc&utm_term=storytelling&utm_content=Digital_Storytelling&utm_campaign=Core_Marketing.

88. https://ourtranstruth.org/mission-history/. See also Phi Wagner-Hecht, ed., *The Poetry on Our Arms: Poems by Young Trans, Nonbinary and GNC Writers* (Independently Published, September 30, 2018).

89. Voices for Trans Equality, https://transequality.org/voices-for-trans-equality.

90. Transgender Lives: Your Stories, https://www.nytimes.com/interactive/2015/opinion/transgender-today.

The transformative potential of storytelling both on individuals and society is attested by the research of StoryCorps, whose listeners report a high rate of increase in understanding and feeling of connection with people different from themselves; these results also lead them to think about social issues and policy changes.[91] The tagline from Jewish Women's Archive reflects this same truth: "Sharing Stories, Inspiring Change."[92]

Not all stories are parables, and not all of these contemporary movements correlate with the aims of Jesus's parables. What they all have in common is the recognition that stories have power to shape people's thinking and actions. Who tells the tale is of utmost importance, as this African story illustrates:[93]

The young boy went to his grandfather and said,

"Grandfather, is it true that the lion is the king of the jungle?"

"Yes," said the old man, "but why do you ask?"

"Well," said the boy, "in all the stories that I read and even in the ones I hear, man will always defeat the lion. So, how can this be true?"

The old man looked his grandson in the eyes and said, "It will always be that way, my son, until the lion tells the story."

The teller of all the parables in the gospels is the male Jesus,[94] and most of the parables foreground male experience from first-century Galilee and Judea. In Luke, there are three notable exceptions: the woman hiding leaven in dough (13:20-21); the woman searching for the lost coin (15:8-10); and the widow confronting an unjust judge (18:1-8). They are told,

91. StoryCorps' mission "is to preserve and share humanity's stories in order to build connections between people and create a more just and compassionate world." See https://storycorps.org/about/.

92. http://jwa.org.

93. Madafo Lloyd Wilson, "African and African American Storytelling," https://www.ncpedia.org/culture/stories/african-american.

94. Regarding the authenticity of Jesus's parables, Klyne R. Snodgrass asserts, "Virtually everyone grants that they are the surest bedrock we have of Jesus' teaching" (*Stories with Intent: A Comprehensive Guide to the Parables of Jesus* [Grand Rapids: Eerdmans, 2008], 31). By contrast, John P. Meier, *A Marginal Jew: Rethinking the Historical Jesus*, vol. 5: *Probing the Authenticity of the Parables*, ABRL (New Haven, CT: Yale University Press, 2016), finds that only four parables meet the criteria for authenticity: the mustard seed, the evil tenants of the vineyard, the talents/pounds, and the great supper. See above chap. 3 n. 20 on his criteria for historical authenticity.

however, through a male lens, as Luke has reshaped them to advance his message.[95] Contemporary storyteller movements call attention to the importance of telling one's own story—individually and collectively—from one's particular experience in all its complexity.[96]

In 5:36-39 two parabolic sayings stress the incompatibility of the old with the new. Pheme Perkins notes that the ones envisioned as patching old garments or putting new wine into wineskins were poor persons, either female or male, an adult tradesperson, or a child apprentice.[97] Only poor people patched clothing. Only poor persons stored wine in skins; rich people used leak-proofed jars. The sayings envision foolish mistakes made by a young or inept apprentice. The resulting loss of a necessary garment and skin of wine had much more dire consequences for poor persons.

Given the controversy with the Pharisees' disciples, Perkins understands verses 36-39 as a satirical response intended to shame those attempting to dishonor Jesus and his disciples. Jesus discredits his opponents by comparing them with poor people and showing them to be no better than rich fools. No one but the absurdly rich, who have hoards of cloth, would foolishly tear a piece of cloth off a new garment to sew

95. For a collection of feminist interpretations of parables in the canonical gospels and the Gospel of Thomas, see Mary Ann Beavis, ed. *The Lost Coin: Parables of Women, Work and Wisdom*, BibSem 86 (London: Sheffield Academic, 2002). The volume concludes with a modern-day feminist parable by Christin Lore Weber, "Gathering: A Mythic Parable," 308–12. See also Antoinette Clark Wire, *Holy Lives, Holy Deaths: A Close Hearing of Early Jewish Storytellers*, SBLStBL (Atlanta: SBL, 2002), who analyzes 129 stories drawn from apocryphal and pseudepigraphical literature, early Jewish historians, Christian texts, the Mishnah, and early Talmudic writings dating from 150 BCE to 150 CE. While the writers of these stories were men—rabbis, scribes, apostles, and evangelists—Wire invites her readers to consider that women storytellers were among those who shaped and transmitted these traditions.

96. See, for example, Natalia Imperatori-Lee, *Cuéntame. Narrative in the Ecclesial Present* (Maryknoll, NY: Orbis Books, 2018), who shows the importance of storytelling in Latinx theology, in particular in constructing a more adequate and inclusive ecclesiology.

97. Pheme Perkins, "Patched Garments and Ruined Wine: Whose Folly? (Mk. 2.21-22; Mt. 9.16-17; Lk. 5.36-39)," in Beavis, *The Lost Coin*, 124–35.

it onto an old. And no one but a stingy rich man[98] prefers new wine to a vintage aged one. "When the poor drink old wine, it is sour, spoiled, or the dregs of the vat. For such persons, new wine would always be preferable."[99] A rich man is a fool if he drinks new wine, saving his huge supply of fine aged wine, so that it sours by the time he opens it. Perkins concludes: "No one takes the part of fool . . . except those whose ignorance is equivalent to that of the terrified young apprentice."[100] The impact of the parable is that it is foolish not to take up the new way that Jesus offers. These sayings do not urge the replacement of the "old" Judaism with the "new" Christianity. Jesus's movement was a renewal movement within Judaism.

From a feminist perspective, this parable can serve as a vehicle for reflection on the need to completely revamp structures in the church and world to achieve equality for women and other disadvantaged persons. It is not sufficient to patch the existing systems, to just "add women and stir." The very nature of hierarchical structures and clerical thinking impedes egalitarian ways of relating. New wineskins are needed for new wine.

98. Horace, *Satire*, 2.2–3, satirizes such a man.
99. Perkins, "Patched Garments and Ruined Wine," 132.
100. Ibid., 135.

Luke 6:1-49

Multitudes of Women and Men Are Healed and Hear

Sabbath Observance (6:1-11)

On a previous sabbath, Jesus healed a man with an unclean spirit and Simon's mother-in-law (4:31-39), and no one criticized him for the healings. Now, Pharisees and scribes accuse him and his disciples of breaking the sabbath by picking grain and healing.[1] Because of such controversy stories (see also 13:10-17 and 14:1-6), some Christians think that sabbath observance was a burden and that Jesus deliberately overturned the law.[2] Sabbath is not a burden; it is a gift, and Jesus observes it (4:16), as do his followers (23:56). Jesus does not seek to do away with sabbath restrictions. Rather, he and his opponents debate how properly to interpret the command to honor the sabbath. In 6:1-5, Jesus cites a biblical precedent to justify plucking grain; in 6:6-11, he relies on the principle that saving life takes precedence over all else.[3]

---

1. The scene is fanciful. Pharisees did not lurk in grain fields on the sabbath looking for sabbath violators.

2. See, e.g., Witness Lee, "Jesus Intentionally Breaks the Sabbath," in *Christ Versus Religion*, composed of messages given by Lee in Los Angeles, July 1970 (Living Stream Ministry): http://www.ministrysamples.org/excerpts/JESUS-INTENTIONALLY-BREAKS-THE-SABBATH.HTML.

3. Texts that support such a principle include "You shall keep my statutes and my ordinances; by doing so one shall live" (Lev 18:5); "I gave them my statutes and showed them my ordinances, by whose observance everyone shall live" (Ezek 20:11).

Luke 6:1-11

⁶ː¹One sabbath while Jesus was going through the grainfields, his disciples plucked some heads of grain, rubbed them in their hands, and ate them. ²But some of the Pharisees said, "Why are you doing what is not lawful on the sabbath?" ³Jesus answered, "Have you not read what David did when he and his companions were hungry? ⁴He entered the house of God and took and ate the bread of the Presence, which it is not lawful for any but the priests to eat, and gave some to his companions?" ⁵Then he said to them, "The Son of Man is lord of the sabbath."

⁶On another sabbath he entered the synagogue and taught, and there was a man there whose right hand was withered. ⁷The scribes and the Pharisees watched him to see whether he would cure on the sabbath, so that they might find an accusation against him. ⁸Even though he knew what they were thinking, he said to the man who had the withered hand, "Come and stand here." He got up and stood there. ⁹Then Jesus said to them, "I ask you, is it lawful to do good or to do harm on the sabbath, to save life or to destroy it?" ¹⁰After looking around at all of them, he said to him, "Stretch out your hand." He did so, and his hand was restored. ¹¹But they were filled with fury and discussed with one another what they might do to Jesus.

Jesus ends the debate in 6:1-5 by asserting that he is the authoritative interpreter of the commandments.

Sabbath observance is still of supreme value, though its implications vary according to one's context. In a culture where people struggle with burnout and exhaustion, addictive overworking, unbridled production and consumerism, sabbath can be a means of breaking such rhythms and restoring balance. It can also be an act of resistance to the pressures to produce and consume, not just a pause that refreshes, but the pause that transforms.[4] Sabbath can open up space for those with abundant resources to attend to those in need and to become energized to work for justice to ensure that all people have dignified work with just recompense and rightful rest. In these ways, the command given in Deuteronomy 5:12-15 is fulfilled: to remember Israel's liberation from slavery in Egypt, thus ensuring that no one will work as did the slaves in Egypt, without a chance to rest. The command in Exodus 20:8-11 is to observe sabbath because God rested at the culmination of creation (Gen 1:1–2:4). From an ecofeminist perspective, observing this command allows participation

---

4. Walter Brueggemann, *Sabbath as Resistance: Saying No to the Culture of Now* (Louisville: Westminster John Knox, 2017), 45.

in the divine delight in all creation, perceiving the beauty and fragility of Earth and its ecosystems. Observing sabbath can lead to lifestyle choices based on reverence for Earth, ensuring sustainability and just distribution. Sabbath observance also has a gendered dimension: the majority of those exploited by injustice in the workplace and who stand to benefit most from sabbath are women.[5] And in welcoming the sabbath on Friday nights in Jewish homes, it is traditionally a woman's role to light the candles, symbolizing the life and light that women bring to their families and to the world.

Twelve Male Apostles Chosen (6:12-16)

Jesus's disciples (μαθηταί) first appeared at Levi's banquet (5:30, 33) and again in the grainfields (6:1). In these instances, Luke gives no specifics about their gender or number (see the excursus at 5:30, "Female Disciples"). From the disciples, Jesus chooses twelve men, whom he also names apostles (ἀπόστολοι, "ones sent"). The number twelve is significant, in that it evokes the twelve tribes of Israel. Jesus's calling of the Twelve is a prophetic gesture, symbolizing and putting into motion the eschatological reconstitution of a fragmented Israel.[6] For Luke, the importance of the twelve apostles will be tied especially to their exclusive role as witnesses to the bodily resurrection of Jesus (see commentary on Luke 24).

> ### Women Apostles in Early Christian Tradition
>
> Only Luke among the evangelists equates the Twelve and the (male) apostles (6:13; 9:1, 10).[7] Because of this, many Christians have the idea that historically, there were only twelve male apostles. Further, they justify restricting women from certain ministries and leadership positions based on this narrow reading. But Luke views apostleship more narrowly than many early Christians did, including Paul

---

5. See, e.g., Focus on Labour Exploitation, "Women Workers and Exploitation: The Gender Pay Gap Is Just the Beginning," August 3, 2017, https://www.labourexploitation.org/news/women-workers-and-exploitation-gender-pay-gap-just-beginning.

6. John P. Meier, *A Marginal Jew: Rethinking the Historical Jesus*, vol. 3: *Companions and Competitors*, ABRL (New York: Doubleday, 2001), 148–54.

7. For more on Luke's distinctive understanding of apostleship, such that, in his reckoning, Paul himself does not count as an apostle, see commentary on Luke 24.

Luke 6:12-16

[12]Now during those days he went out to the mountain to pray; and he spent the night in prayer to God. [13]And when day came, he called his disciples and chose twelve of them, whom he also named apostles: [14]Simon, whom he named Peter, and his brother Andrew, and James, and John, and Philip, and Bartholomew, [15]and Matthew, and Thomas, and James son of Alphaeus, and Simon, who was called the Zealot, [16]and Judas son of James, and Judas Iscariot, who became a traitor.

himself.[8] There are numerous other apostles named in Pauline letters, including one woman, Junia. Paul says that Andronicus and Junia are his relatives who were in prison with him, that they "are prominent among the apostles," and that they were in Christ before he was (Rom 16:7).

Debate about Romans 16:7 occurs on two fronts: (1) the gender of Ἰουνίαν, and (2) the interpretation of ἐπίσημοι ἐν τοῖς ἀποστόλοις, whether it means "prominent among the apostles" or "well known to the apostles." On the first question, whether Ἰουνίαν is the feminine name Junia or the masculine Junias, the evidence is overwhelmingly in favor of the feminine. The masculine name has not been found in any Latin or Greek inscriptions or in any ancient literature, whereas the feminine Junia is well attested. Moreover, early commentators on the letter to the Romans all took Junia to be a woman. Not until the thirteenth century did commentators begin to interpret the name as masculine, beginning with Aegidius of Rome (1245–1316).[9] On the meaning of ἐπίσημοι ἐν τοῖς ἀποστόλοις, Hellenistic Greek literary works, papyri, inscriptions, and artifacts all show without exception that ἐπίσημοι ἐν plus the plural dative has the sense "notable among." This is also the meaning reflected in the interpretations of all patristic commentators.[10] The careful work of feminist biblical

---

8. Paul frequently calls himself an apostle (e.g., Rom 1:1; 11:13; 1 Cor 1:1; 9:1, 2), along with Apollos (1 Cor 4:6, 9), Barnabas (1 Cor 9:5-6), Epaphroditus (Phil 2:25), Sylvanus and Timothy (1 Thess 1:1 with 2:7), James (Gal 1:19), and Andronicus and Junia (Rom 16:7).

9. See Bernadette J. Brooten, "'Junia . . . Outstanding among the Apostles' (Romans 16:7)," in *Women Priests: A Catholic Commentary on the Vatican Declaration*, ed. Leonard Swidler and Arlene Swidler (New York: Paulist Press, 1977), 141–44; Eldon Jay Epp, *Junia: The First Woman Apostle* (Minneapolis: Fortress, 2005); Rena Pederson, *The Lost Apostle: Searching for the Truth about Junia* (San Francisco: Jossey-Bass, 2006); Yii-Jan Lin, "Junia: An Apostle before Paul," *JBL* 139 (2020): 191–209, esp. 192–94.

10. Linda L. Belleville, "Ἰουνίαν . . . ἐπίσημοι ἐν τοῖς ἀποστόλοις: A Re-examination of Romans 16:7 in Light of Primary Source Materials," *NTS* 51 (2005): 231–49.

scholars has uncovered false translations and interpretations based on presumptions that there could be no women apostles. Seeing the larger picture of women included in the ranks of the apostles undercuts Luke's agenda to reinforce a male-only leadership.[11]

We also note that early church fathers remembered women in the gospels as apostles. Hippolytus of Rome calls Mary Magdalene and her companions "apostles to the apostles, having been sent by Christ."[12] Origen (ca. 185–253/54) refers to the Samaritan woman as an apostle and evangelist.[13] Similarly, Theophylact of Bulgaria (ca. 1050– 1108) calls the Samaritan woman an apostle, as well as "anointed with priesthood."[14] A chant from Byzantine tradition names her Photina, "enlightened one," and calls her "equal to the apostles":

> Thou wast illumined by the Holy Spirit
> and refreshed by the streams of Christ the Saviour.
> Having drunk the Water of Salvation
> thou didst give copiously to the thirsty.
> O holy Great Martyr Photina,
> Equal-to-the Apostles,
> entreat Christ our God that our souls may be saved.[15]

Similarly, Epp, *Junia*, 78; Lin, "Junia," 194–201. Both Belleville and Lin show the shortcomings of the argument by Michael H. Burer and Daniel B. Wallace ("Was Junia Really an Apostle? A Re-examination of Rom 16.7," *NTS* 47 [2001]: 76–91) that "ἐπίσημοι ἐν τοῖς ἀποστόλοις almost certainly means 'well known to the apostles.'" Their interpretation goes contrary to standard Greek lexicons and grammars, is based on a small pool of texts and some misrepresentations of the Greek text, assumes a conclusion not based on the evidence, and is contrary to the way all the patristic interpreters understood Rom 16:7. Lin adds a new convincing line of interpretation by noting that Paul's care to situate Andronicus and Junia as apostles who were "in Christ before" him makes sense in terms of his self-understanding as the "last" apostle.

11. See Judette Gallares, "And She Will Speak: Junia, the Voice of a Silenced Woman Apostle," in *Ecclesia of Women in Asia: Gathering the Voices of the Silenced*, ed. Evelyn Monteiro and Antoinette Gutzler (Delhi: ISPCK, 2005), 89–107, for an example of how Junia functions as a paradigm for Filipina Christian women ministers.

12. *Comm. Song of Songs* 25.6, 7. Mary Ann Beavis ("Reconsidering Mary of Bethany," *CBQ* 74 [2012]: 281–97) argues that Hippolytus is more likely thinking of Mary and Martha of Bethany.

13. *Comm. S. Jean* 4.26–27.

14. *Joan.* 4.28–30; PG 123:1241D.

15. Menologion for the Twenty-sixth Day of the Month of February, http://www .orthodox.cn/saints/menologia/2-26_en.htm. See also Ute E. Eisen, *Women Office-holders in Early Christianity: Epigraphical and Literary Studies*, trans. Linda M. Maloney (Collegeville, MN: Liturgical Press, 2000).

Second- and third-century Christians regarded other women as apostles. In Orthodox tradition, Thecla has been venerated as "apostle and protomartyr among women" and "equal to the apostles in sanctity."[16] The *Acts of Thecla*,[17] written in Asia Minor in the late second century, recounts how Thecla, a rich aristocratic woman, renounced her family, fortune, and fiancé to accompany Paul in his missionary work. Devotion to Saint Thecla became widespread throughout Asia Minor and Egypt. Her image has been found painted on walls of tombs, stamped on clay flasks and oil lamps, and engraved on bronze crosses.[18]

Another woman, Nino, is also venerated in the Orthodox Church as "equal of the apostles" as well as "enlightener of Georgia."[19] The traditions about her are varied. One is that she received her theological education from a woman, Sara Niaphor, to whose care her parents entrusted her after they moved to Jerusalem when Nino was twelve years old. Subsequently, Juvenal, the first patriarch of Jerusalem (451–458), gave her a cross and commissioned her to evangelize wherever she might go. Another tradition says that during the reign of Constantine she traveled throughout Georgia, where she preached the Gospel as a prisoner of war.

Traditions about apostolic women such as Thecla and Nino going out to preach and heal abound. Whether these were historical characters or not, the veneration of such women shows that many Christians, from early centuries until now, found no obstacle in a woman being an apostle. Such resistance to the direction Luke sets by depicting a male-only group of twelve apostles is still necessary for unleashing women's full gifts in the church.

16. "Protomartyr and Equal of the Apostles Thekla" in Orthodox Church in America (September 24, 2020), https://www.oca.org/saints/lives/2020/09/24/102715-proto martyr-and-equal-of-the-apostles-thekla.

17. See Sheila E. McGinn, "The Acts of Thecla," in *Searching the Scriptures*, vol. 2: *A Feminist Commentary*, ed. Elisabeth Schüssler Fiorenza with the assistance of Ann Brock and Shelly Matthews (New York: Crossroad, 1994), 800–828, and her forthcoming monograph *Exploring the Acts of Thecla* in the Rhetoric of Religious Antiquity series from SBL Press. See also Susan E. Hylen, *A Modest Apostle: Thecla and the History of Women in the Early Church* (New York: Oxford University Press, 2015).

18. See Stephen J. Davis, *The Cult of St. Thecla: A Tradition of Women's Piety in Late Antiquity*, OECS (New York: Oxford University Press, 2001).

19. "Saint Nino (Nina), Equal of the Apostles, Enlightener of Georgia" in Orthodox Church in America (January 14, 2019), https://www.oca.org/saints/lives/2019 /01/14/100191-saint-nino-nina-equal-of-the-apostles-enlightener-of-georgia.

Multitudes of Women and Men are Healed and Hear (6:17-19)

Luke 6:17-19 introduces a series of sayings traditionally called the Sermon on the Plain.[20] There are three sections: blessings and woes (6:20-26), exhortation to love enemies (6:27-36), and maxims (6:37-49). The multitudes have come not only to be healed[21] but also to hear Jesus. The audience for the teaching is not only Jesus's disciples (6:20) but also a larger group of people (τοῦ λαοῦ, 7:1).[22]

Blessings and Woes (6:20-26)

Four beatitudes begin the teaching.[23] The adjective μακάριος, "blessed," is a favorite of Luke,[24] first appearing on the lips of Elizabeth (1:45) and Mary (1:48).[25] A pronouncement using μακάριος does not confer a blessing; rather, it recognizes an existing state of happiness[26] and so is translated "happy are." Rhetorically, such declarations serve to persuade the hearer to imitate what is being praised.[27] These kinds of utterances are found in wisdom literature and the Psalms, where they express desires for things such as wisdom (Prov 3:13; Sir 14:20; 25:10), prosperity (Ps 49:18), a good wife (Sir 25:8; 26:1), a friend (Sir 25:9). Also frequent are pronouncements of happiness of those who fear God (Ps 128:1), trust in God (Pss 40:4; 84:12), and keep God's ways (Ps 119:1; Prov 8:32).

Luke's beatitudes differ from the sayings in wisdom literature in that their subject is not simple human desires such as prosperity or a good wife or friend. Moreover, they are paradoxical: who would wish to be poor or hungry, to weep or be hated? The gospel beatitudes speak of a present state of blessedness because God's action is already manifest in Jesus and points to a future state of happiness when this action is brought to its fullness. Beatitudes are ordinarily expressed in the third person, "Blessed are

---

20. The parallel in Matthew's Gospel (5:1–7:29) is from a mountaintop.

21. On healing touch, see comments at 5:12-16; on feminist understandings of power, see 4:1-13; on the expression "power came out from him," see 8:46.

22. On the significance of ὁ λαός, "the people," in Luke, see Clifard Sunil Ranjar, *Be Merciful Like the Father: Exegesis and Theology of the Sermon on the Plain (Luke 6,17-49)*, AnBib 219 (Rome: Gregorian and Biblical Press, 2017), 26–27.

23. By contrast, Matt 5:1-11 has eight beatitudes.

24. It occurs eleven other times: 1:45; 7:23; 10:23; 11:27, 28; 12:37, 38, 43; 14:14, 15; 23:29.

25. At 1:48 it is the verb μακαρίζω rather than the adjective μακάριος.

26. L. John Topel, *Children of a Compassionate God: A Theological Exegesis of Luke 6:20-49* (Collegeville, MN: Liturgical Press, 2001), 62.

27. Dennis Hamm, *The Beatitudes in Context: What Luke and Matthew Meant*, Zacchaeus Studies: New Testament (Wilmington, DE: Glazier, 1990), 12.

Luke 6:17-26

¹⁷He came down with them and stood on a level place, with a great crowd of his disciples and a great multitude of people from all Judea, Jerusalem, and the coast of Tyre and Sidon. ¹⁸They had come to hear him and to be healed of their diseases; and those who were troubled with unclean spirits were cured. ¹⁹And all in the crowd were trying to touch him, for power came out from him and healed all of them.

²⁰Then he looked up at his disciples and said:

"Blessed are you who are poor,
     for yours is the kingdom of God.
²¹"Blessed are you who are
     hungry now,
     for you will be filled.
"Blessed are you who weep now,
     for you will laugh.
²²"Blessed are you when people hate you, and when they exclude you, revile you, and defame you on account of the Son of Man. ²³Rejoice in that day and leap for joy, for surely your reward is great in heaven; for that is what their ancestors did to the prophets.
²⁴"But woe to you who are rich,
     for you have received your
         consolation.
²⁵"Woe to you who are full now,
     for you will be hungry.
"Woe to you who are laughing now,
     for you will mourn and weep.
²⁶"Woe to you when all speak well
         of you,
     for that is what their ancestors
         did to the false prophets."

they who." In Luke 6:20-26, however, Jesus addresses his audience in the second-person plural, which has a greater rhetorical impact.

The first beatitude, "Blessed are you who are poor,"²⁸ is easy to romanticize by those who are not poor. Those who have enough material resources can turn away from the misery of those who live in poverty, thinking that God has a special love for people who suffer or that God will reward in the next life those who are in dire straits now. Such an interpretation is counter to Jesus's mission of bringing good news to the poor (4:18). There is nothing good or romantic about poverty. Good news would be its eradication.

The beatitude has different implications depending on whether the one hearing it is poor or not. People who are poor might hear hope for an end to their misery with the coming *basileia*. God hears their cries (Ps 34:6) and responds. Divine response takes concrete shape when those who have economic means do everything possible to change the desperate condition of the poor both through charity and by working for

_____

28. By contrast, Matthew says, "Blessed are the poor in spirit" (5:3).

systemic change.[29] Luke's intended audience is the more well-to-do, like Theophilus (1:4), and Luke continually stresses that discipleship involves divestment and sharing. He shows a variety of ways that Jesus's followers do this (see comments at 4:16-30) and points to the ideal that there be no needy person (Acts 4:34; similarly, Deut 15:4).[30] The woe in verse 24 calls attention to the consequences for the rich who hold on to their goods.

In declaring woes in verses 24-26, Jesus speaks as did the Old Testament prophets who uttered warnings and calls to repentance (e.g., Isa 5:8-23; Hab 2:6-19).[31] The woes are meant to prompt a change of mind and heart that leads to life. There is nothing in Luke's Gospel that would support contemporary preachers of a "prosperity gospel"—that is, the belief that God rewards Christians who live faithful lives with blessings of good health and material wealth.[32]

The second beatitude concerns those that are chronically starving, not simply those who get hungry at mealtime. The verb "will be filled" (χορτασθήσεσθε, v. 21) points to this meaning, as it is also found in two Lukan parables with this sense. In one, a young son who squanders his inheritance on dissolute living is "dying of hunger" (15:17) and longs to fill himself (χορτασθῆναι, 15:16) with the pods the pigs were eating. In the other, a rich man feasts sumptuously every day while a poor man, Lazarus, sat at his gate and "longed to satisfy his hunger [χορτασθῆναι] with what fell from the rich man's table" (16:21). Like the beatitude in verse 21 and its matching woe in verse 25, the second parable makes a connection between the desperately hungry and the rich. Mary's acclamation that God "has filled the hungry with good things, and sent the rich away empty" (1:53) also makes this link.

---

29. See, e.g., Michael Griffin and Jennie Weiss Block, eds., *In the Company of the Poor: Conversations with Dr. Paul Farmer and Fr. Gustavo Gutiérrez* (Maryknoll, NY: Orbis Books, 2013), for how the stance of preferential option for the poor and concomitant actions can lead to transformation.

30. See Leslie J. Hoppe, *There Shall Be No Poor among You: Poverty in the Bible* (Nashville: Abingdon, 2004), who shows that throughout the Bible poverty is shown to be caused by human decisions and is not God's will. God sides with the poor and acts on their behalf because God did not intend people to be poor.

31. See other woes at Luke 10:13; 11:42-52; 17:1; 21:23; 22:22. On our resistance to damning threats as a means of evangelization, see comments at 3:7-9.

32. The prosperity gospel movement originated in the United States after World War II as an offshoot of Pentecostalism. With the rise of televangelism in the 1980s it has become widespread among revivalist and charismatic churches and now has spread internationally.

As with the first beatitude, there is no blessedness in starvation; God's blessing occurs in its alleviation. There is a constant challenge to the rich readers of Luke's Gospel, like Theophilus (1:4), to make this blessing a reality in the present.

A Hermeneutics of Hunger

In her book *The Silent Cry: Mysticism and Resistance*,[33] German feminist theologian and activist Dorothee Soelle (1929–2003) advocates that, in addition to a hermeneutics of suspicion developed by feminist scholars,[34] a hermeneutics of hunger is needed. It is not enough to critique texts, traditions, and institutions that legitimize systems of domination. Also necessary is an investigation of what drives people as they yearn to live a different kind of life. For people who are poor, the alleviation of physical hunger is primary; for those who are rich, spiritual hunger is central.

But for Soelle, no spirituality that involves fleeing the world and ignoring the plight of the suffering poor is genuine. Those who are well off must see and hear those who hunger, which leads them to social and political engagement toward working for the well-being of all.

Kathleen M. O'Connor took up Soelle's plea for a hermeneutics of hunger in her presidential address to the Catholic Biblical Association of America (CBA) in 2009.[35] This address then inspired a volume of essays, produced by the CBA's Feminist Biblical Hermeneutics Task Force,[36] which explores the socio-historical contexts of select

33. Dorothee Soelle, *The Silent Cry: Mysticism and Resistance*, trans. Barbara and Martin Rumscheidt (Minneapolis: Fortress, 2001).

34. A feminist hermeneutics of suspicion is a deconstructive reading strategy that "locates the means by which a text signals underlying ideological stances by seeking contradictions, gaps, projections, and silences. It then moves beyond such identification to more complete historical reconstructions and more inclusive modern appropriations" (Amy-Jill Levine, "Hermeneutics of Suspicion," in *Dictionary of Feminist Theologies*, ed. Letty M. Russell and J. Shannon Clarkson [Louisville: Westminster John Knox, 1996], 140–41, here 141). See also Elisabeth Schüssler Fiorenza, *Wisdom Ways: Introducing Feminist Biblical Interpretation* (Maryknoll, NY: Orbis Books, 2001), 175–77.

35. Kathleen M. O'Connor, "Let All the Peoples Praise You: Biblical Studies and a Hermeneutics of Hunger," *CBQ* 72 (2010): 1–14.

36. Sheila E. McGinn, Lai Ling Elizabeth Ngan, and Ahida Calderón Pilarski, eds., *By Bread Alone: The Bible through the Eyes of the Hungry* (Minneapolis: Fortress, 2014). The Task Force is composed of scholars from diverse ethnic, racial, and religious contexts, who explore the chosen texts with this diversity in view.

biblical texts[37] with an eye to the realities of the hungry, both in biblical and contemporary times. These feminist scholars aim to help First-World readers "develop a different field of vision for the biblical texts—one that *sees* and *hears* those who hunger, both those mentioned or intimated in the texts and those in our own world today" so that they "shift the interpretive center of gravity to begin reading in solidarity with the hungry."[38]

While the third beatitude does not specify the cause of weeping (6:21b), the context implies that it accompanies poverty and starvation. When that misery is alleviated then comes laughter. The joy comes not only to those who were in misery but also to those whose empathy causes them to weep with others who are destitute and hungry (in Rom 12:15, Paul advised to "weep with those who weep"). The corresponding woe (6:25b) warns those whose laugh now (like the rich fool who makes merry in 12:19) but remain oblivious to the suffering of those around them. No authentic joy exists for those who ignore the weeping of others.

These first beatitudes have a gendered dimension, as they foreground the experience of women, who are the majority of the world's poor and hungry (see the excursus "Women and Poverty" at 4:16-30).[39] The final beatitude (6:22) shifts to experiences specific to disciples, whether female[40] or male: exclusion, revilement, and defamation on account of following Jesus. Jesus's instruction to "rejoice" (χάρητε) and "leap for joy" (σκιρτήσατε) is not an invitation to take pleasure in suffering; rather, it is to delight in these indications that God's saving work is being accomplished. Jesus likens the disciples' experience to that of the prophets who always provoke opposition (see comments at 4:16-30). Although "in that day" has eschatological overtones (so also 10:12; 17:31; 21:34), the disciples experience the joy already now in the present.

---

37. One of the essays is on a Lukan text: Linda Maloney, "The Friend at Midnight (Luke 11:1-10)," 129–34.

38. Lai Ling Elizabeth Ngan, Ahida Calderón Pilarski, and Sheila E. McGinn, "Introduction: The Bible through the Eyes of the Hungry," in *By Bread Alone*, 6. On hunger and environmental sustainability, see David Alexander, "Feeding the Hungry and Protecting the Environment," in *All Creation Is Groaning: An Interdisciplinary Vision for Life in a Sacred Universe*, ed. Carol J. Dempsey and Russell A. Butkus (Collegeville, MN: Liturgical Press, 1999), 77–98.

39. See World Food Program USA, which chronicles how in countries facing famine, extreme conflict, and hunger, women often eat last and least: https://www.wfpusa.org/women-hunger/.

40. See the excursus at 5:30, "Female Disciples."

This joy causes reviled disciples to "leap" or "spring about" (σκιρτάω), as did John in Elizabeth's womb (1:41, 44). In the LXX, the psalmist sings of delight at the exodus that causes mountains to skip (σκιρτάω) like rams and the hills like lambs (Ps 114:4, 6), and Malachi prophesies that on the great day of the Lord, those who revere his name "shall go out leaping like calves from the stall" (Mal 4:2). John Topel suggests, "Given its LXX background of leaping animals and mountains, σκιρτήσατε may well depict graphically the disciples' dancing participation in the salvific joy of animals and the whole cosmos."[41]

Mechtilde of Magdeburg, *The Flowing Light of the Godhead*[42]

Mechtilde of Magdeburg (c. 1207–c. 1282/1294) was a medieval Christian mystic, who described her visions of God in her book *The Flowing Light of Divinity* (originally in German: *Das fließende Licht der Gottheit*). Mechtilde was a Beguine, a member of a movement founded in the Netherlands in the thirteenth century in which women lived in ascetic and philanthropic communities but not with vows. In this excerpt, her image of leaping with abandon and leaping into love evokes Luke 6:23.

I cannot dance, Lord,
unless you lead me.
If you want me to leap with
    abandon,
you must intone the song.
Then I shall leap into love,
from love into knowledge,
and from enjoyment
beyond all human
    sensations.
There I want to remain
yet want also to circle
    higher still.

Love Everyone—No Exceptions (6:27-38)

The command to love enemies goes contrary to the normal response to acts of enmity, which is to retaliate. The ancient world was steeped in the notion of talionic justice, the belief that one who does harm should receive a corresponding harm in return. Greek plays, for example, feature characters who retaliate with violence, including females. One example

---

41. Topel, *Children of a Compassionate God*, 110.
42. https://www.bing.com/videos/search?q=mechtild+in+the+dance+i+am+the+dancer&&view=detail&mid=7F30F049A442CE614D6A7F30F049A442CE614D6A&&FORM=VRDGAR.

27"But I say to you that listen, Love your enemies, do good to those who hate you, 28bless those who curse you, pray for those who abuse you. 29If anyone strikes you on the cheek, offer the other also; and from anyone who takes away your coat do not withhold even your shirt. 30Give to everyone who begs from you; and if anyone takes away your goods, do not ask for them again. 31Do to others as you would have them do to you.

32"If you love those who love you, what credit is that to you? For even sinners love those who love them. 33If you do good to those who do good to you, what credit is that to you? For even sinners do the same. 34If you lend to those from whom you hope to receive, what credit is that to you? Even sinners lend to sinners, to receive as much again. 35But love your enemies, do good, and lend, expecting nothing in return. Your reward will be great, and you will be children of the Most High; for he is kind to the ungrateful and the wicked. 36Be merciful, just as your Father is merciful.

37"Do not judge, and you will not be judged; do not condemn, and you will not be condemned. Forgive, and you will be forgiven; 38give, and it will be given to you. A good measure, pressed down, shaken together, running over, will be put into your lap; for the measure you give will be the measure you get back."

is Hecuba in Euripides's play by that name who takes violent revenge on the murderer of her son. Mary Lefkowitz comments: "When Greek women turn the other cheek upon being wronged, it is only because they have no better choice."[43] Passages in both the Old and New Testaments also contain expressions of desire for vengeance against enemies. A large number of those expressions are present in the New Testament, where apocalyptic longings, combined with a belief in hell, lead to desires for enemies to be punished in perpetuity (see especially the book of Revelation, but also, for instance, 1 Cor 15:24; 2 Thess 1:5-10).

But our Scriptures also contain more elevated ethical views, enjoining love toward an enemy as the better choice, even as it goes against natural inclinations.[44] In 1 Samuel 24, for example, when David has the

43. Mary R. Lefkowitz, "Did Ancient Women Write Novels?," in *"Women Like This": New Perspectives on Jewish Women in the Greco-Roman World*, ed. Amy-Jill Levine, EJL 1 (Atlanta: Scholars Press, 1991), 207.
44. On love of neighbor in Jewish thought, see Michael Fagenblat, "The Concept of Neighbor in Jewish and Christian Ethics," in *The Jewish Annotated New Testament*, ed. Amy-Jill Levine and Marc Zvi Brettler, 2nd ed. (New York: Oxford University Press, 2017), 645–50.

opportunity to kill Saul, who was seeking his life, he refrains from doing so, despite the urging of his men. David tells Saul how he spared him. He then exclaims, "who has ever found an enemy, and sent the enemy safely away?" (1 Sam 24:19). There are also maxims in the book of Proverbs that advise acts of love toward enemies, such as: "Do not rejoice when your enemies fall, and do not let your heart be glad when they stumble" (24:17). Furthermore, in rabbinic thought the principle of neighbor love in Leviticus 19:18 was often interpreted expansively to include love of enemies as well.[45]

The Relationship of Enemy Love to Vengeance: Some Early Christian Views

Many early Christians, including Clement of Rome (2 Clem. 13.4) and Justin Martyr (*Apol.* 1.15.9), asserted that enemy love was a teaching unique to Jesus. But perhaps no greater champion of the idea that Jesus's teaching on enemy love defined Christianity as a new revelation was Marcion, who taught that Jesus's message from the High God to love even enemies demonstrated the wide gulf between this God and the vengeful God of the Jews.[46]

Marcion's Christian opponents vehemently fought against the view that Jesus's teaching contradicted the teaching of the Old Testament, but not as we do here, when we emphasize that both the Old and New Testaments contain teaching on how to love enemies. Rather, they stressed that God was consistently vengeful across the Old and New Testaments, interpreting Jesus's counsel on enemy love, not as an *overturning* of vengeance, but rather merely as a *delay* of vengeance. For interpreters such as Tertullian, enemy love was only an interim step, a request for human patience until God would administer the vengeance due (cf. Deut 23.35).[47] Such a sentiment likely accounts for Paul's teaching in Romans 12:19-21, where counsel to feed and provide water to enemies is joined with the reminder that vengeance on them belongs to God (cf. Prov 25:21-22).

---

45. Ibid., 648.

46. The importance of Jesus's teaching on enemy love in Marcion's thought is reconstructed from Tertullian's attacks against him. See *Marc.* 4.16.1–8 and 2.28.2. For more on Marcion's teaching, see commentary on Luke 2 under the heading, "Luke 1–2: A Refutation of Marcion?"

47. As Tertullian argues in *Marc.* 4.16.4 concerning the teaching to turn the other cheek, "He teaches patience in expectation of vengeance [*patientiam docet vindicate expectatricem*]."

Recognizing the shape of these early Christian arguments helps us to see both the lingering influence of Marcion (many Christians today still mistakenly assume that Jesus's teaching on enemy love is both unique and somehow antithetical to Old Testament ethics) and the logic of vengeance that permeated the thinking of some early Christians, even as they encountered some of Jesus's most merciful teachings. In her commentary on the forgiveness prayer of Jesus from the cross at Luke 23:34, Shelly will take up that logic in more detail, as she shows how that merciful petition calls into question the certainty that evildoers will be punished. That is, Jesus's prayer to God from the cross for the forgiveness of his persecutors is an example of enemy love with no expectation of ultimate vengeance.

Love involves not only feelings but also actions; it can arise in response to a benevolent act or from a commitment, such as to the covenant. Love is not manifest only in individual acts; in 6:27, "you" (ὑμᾶς) is plural and so suggests that doing good, blessing, and praying are collective. Each action that a wronged person or group can take makes possible the breaking of the cycle of retaliation and initiating a positive counteraction. Rabbi Jonathan Sacks observes, "An ethic that commands us to love our enemies, without any hint as to how we are to achieve this, is simply unlivable."[48] He shows how the Torah sets forth a realistic program for how to approach someone who has done us harm by speaking, conversing, challenging, and remonstrating with that one. In such a way it is possible to achieve reconciliation—"not always, to be sure, but often."[49] Jesus likewise offers concrete examples of how to love an enemy in 6:27-30.

Blessing those who curse you and praying for those who abuse you has the potential to stop the abusers when their action does not achieve its desired effect. Praying for an abuser, however, must not be read as the only action to take. Jesus is not asking for allowing abuse to continue. A woman who is repeatedly beaten by her husband, for example, shows love when she seeks help for both herself and her husband to break the cycle of violence. Prayer alone is not sufficient. Prayer can strengthen a person who is abused to take other actions needed as she sees herself as beloved by God and rejects the insults of her attacker. It can also allow

48. Rabbi Jonathan Sacks, "Love and Hate": https://www.chabad.org/parshah/article_cdo/aid/2186228/jewish/Love-and-Hate.htm.
49. Ibid.

her to see her batterer as more than his despicable actions—as also a beloved child of God—and someday allow for a healed relationship.

The concrete examples in 6:29-30 concern individual actions; here "you" is in the singular. Offering the other cheek and giving to everyone, positive actions, are balanced by two ways to refrain from acting: do not withhold and do not ask. Being struck on the cheek signals a situation of humiliation. Offering the other cheek and inviting the aggressor to strike a second time is neither an act of weakness nor an indication of submission to abuse. The verb παρέχω, "offer," "give as a gift,"[50] indicates that an opportunity is being given. Offering the other cheek is an act of provocation: it challenges aggressors to reflect on their action and change their course in relation to the other.

The situation envisioned in the second example could be either robbery or a judicial proceeding. If it is the first, a robber who takes one's outer garment (ἱμάτιον) may go so far as to strip the victim of the inner garment (χιτών) as well. It is difficult to see how giving one's shirt shows love toward the attacker. It appears to be simply a means of avoiding injury, along the line of "surrender your wallet rather than risk a bullet." Hans Dieter Betz offers a cogent interpretation: "If the robber proves to be 'generous,' in that he is only after the victim's overcoat, he is outdone by the even greater generosity of the victim. . . . The paradoxical reaction of the victim counters the violence by making a gift, no doubt a challenge to respond in kind."[51]

If the situation is a judicial proceeding, a creditor is taking the cloak as a pledge for a debt (see Deut 24:12-13). If the debtor strips off an undergarment as well and stands naked before the creditor, the debtor shames the creditor into recognizing the injustice of taking the garment.[52] Several present-day examples of such actions taken by women illustrate that this tactic is sometimes effective. In the 1980s a group of Black South African women in a squatter's village were ordered by soldiers with bulldozers to clear out within two minutes. With their men away at work and no other means to protect themselves, they stood in front of the bulldozers

---

50. BDAG, 776–77.

51. Hans Dieter Betz, *The Sermon on the Mount: A Commentary on the Sermon on the Mount, Including the Sermon on the Plain (Matthew 5:3–7:27 and Luke 6:20-49)*, Hermeneia (Minneapolis: Fortress, 1995), 597.

52. Walter Wink, *Engaging the Powers: Discernment and Resistance in a World of Domination* (Minneapolis: Fortress, 1992), 177–79.

and stripped naked. The soldiers turned and fled, and the community retained its little portion of land.[53] Filipina women used a similar tactic to stop the building of an electric power generation project, the Chico River Dam, on the island of Luzon. Local residents protested for two decades because if the river were dammed, it threatened to inundate villages of the native Kalinga people. One of the actions that finally shut down the proposed project was when the women took off their blouses in front of the construction crew.[54]

The third saying (v. 30) has two parts. The first, "Give to everyone who begs from you," seems less related to loving enemies; it is a simple admonition to charity. The NRSV translation of παντὶ αἰτοῦντί, "everyone who begs from you," gives the impression that the giving is only to those reduced by poverty to begging. The NABRE more accurately reads: "Give to everyone who asks of you"—the request for money or possessions from anyone is to be granted. Such a directive is acceptable when the addressee has sufficient means to share and when the person requesting is in genuine need.[55] But a perversion of Jesus's saying can happen, such as when poor retirees give their hard-earned savings to greedy televangelists who ask for support.

In the first part of verse 30, the person giving is in control, but the second part seems to involve taking one's goods without consent. It is difficult to see how not asking for the goods back is commendable or even how it might relate to love of enemies. A woman whose bank account is emptied by her partner, for example, may choose not to report the crime out of fear, but it is hard to see how not asking for her money back could be an act of love for the one who wronged her. Loving action toward a criminal would be to stop the offensive behavior.

A general maxim, "Do to others as you would have them do to you" (6:31), sums up the reason why people should act in the ways 6:27-30 describe. Commonly called "the Golden Rule," it advises: as you would want people (οἱ ἄνθρωποι) to do to you, so you should likewise do to

53. As recounted to Wink (ibid., 235) by Sheena Duncan, November 6, 1989.
54. As retold by feminist theologian Sr. Mary John Mananzan in *Call To Action News*, December 1999, p. 3. See also the account by one of the women, Leticia Bula-at of Innabuyog, presented at the NGO Forum of the Fourth World Conference on Women 1995: http://cpcabrisbane.org/Kasama/1996/V10n2/Innabuyog.htm.
55. Luke does not specify whether the situation is one of genuine need or one of greed. If the latter, it is difficult to see why Jesus would advocate enabling greed.

them.[56] Verses 32-34 move beyond the motivation of wanting treatment in kind from others. To reciprocate is typical: we love those who love us, we do good to those who do good to us, we lend to those who are able to lend back to us. Even sinners act this way. There is no graciousness (χάρις) in equal reciprocity.

TRANSLATION MATTERS

The NRSV translation of the thrice-repeated question ποία ὑμῖν χάρις ἐστίν, "what credit is that to you?" (6:32, 33, 34), obscures an important wordplay with ἀχάριστος (NRSV: "ungrateful") in 6:35. The word χάρις signifies "grace, favor, graciousness,"[57] not "credit." In 6:35, the α- (*alpha privative*) before χάρις makes it the opposite of gracious. "Credit" implies accounting of what is due; χάρις is about "grace," unmerited favor.

In 6:32-36, Jesus exhorts his disciples to act in gracious ways: loving enemies, doing good, and lending without expectation of return, not only because they would want to be so treated (6:31), but because this is the manner in which God acts (6:36). To those who are ungracious (ἀχάριστος, NRSV: "ungrateful") and wicked (πονηρός), God is kind (χρηστός) (6:35). Those who heed Jesus are likewise to be merciful (οἰκτίρμων) to all. Acting like the "Father," as "children of the Most High," is not done simply to gain a heavenly reward (v. 35). Acts of mercy set into motion dynamics that redound already in the present to both the persons who do them and those at whom they are directed.

---

56. Jesus was not the first or only one to pronounce such a rule. Hillel the Elder, Jesus's contemporary, said, "What is hateful to you, do not do to your fellow" (b. Shabb. 31a). Proverbs 24:29 has a similar maxim: "Do not say, 'I will do to others as they have done to me; I will pay them back for what they have done.'" Similarly, Tobit 4:15: "what you hate, do not do to anyone." See also Lev 19:18, 34; Deut 10:19. The Greek orator and rhetorician Isocrates (436–338 BCE) said, "Do not do to others that which angers you when they do it to you" (*Ad Nic.*, 61). Similarly, the Greek Stoic Philosopher Epictetus (c. 50–135 CE) wrote: "For this too is a very pleasant strand woven into the Cynic's pattern of life; he must needs be flogged like an ass, and while he is being flogged he must love the men who flog him, as though he were the father or brother of them all" (*Discourses* 3.22.54).

57. BDAG, 1079.

Often in feminist analysis we speak of seeking justice for women and all disadvantaged persons and for the cosmos. Seldom do we speak in terms of mercy. Many persons think of justice and mercy as two opposites and that God sets aside justice or tempers it when acting mercifully toward sinners. In fact, justice and mercy are not opposed to one another, but are two dimensions of a single reality.[58] As we continue to advocate for justice, we see mercy as an inherent and necessary component.

Further examples of how to act mercifully in imitation of God follow in 6:37-38: foregoing judgment, refusing to condemn, offering forgiveness, and giving. These verses also elaborate on payment (μισθός) that comes to the actors. Beyond receiving back in kind what they give, disciples who imitate God's extravagant mercy will find themselves overwhelmed with immeasurable benefits. The image is a vivid one of grain being poured into a container, patted down, and shaken so that all the space is filled tightly, and still the grain continues to be poured, overflowing into one's garment, as when Boaz pours six measures of barley into Ruth's cloak (Ruth 3:15).[59] We are reminded of the widow of Zarephath whose jar of meal never emptied while Elijah was with her (1 Kgs 17:16).

We need to be alert, though, to pitfalls in these sayings. Not judging does not mean to forego sharpening skills of critical decision-making Misplaced forgiveness, for example, of a partner who asks for forgiveness without changing abusive behavior, can fuel cycles of victimization (see comments at 5:17-26 and 17:1-4). Excessive giving, while neglecting one's own care and well-being, is dangerous.

Seeing Clearly, Good Fruit, and a Firm Foundation (6:39-49)

A series of parabolic sayings concludes this section of teaching.[60] The saying about blind guides has many well-known variations in ancient literature.[61] The way the questions are posed in Luke 6:39 makes it obvious what answer is expected. The first question, "Can a blind person guide a

---

58. See further comments above on p. 57.
59. Amy-Jill Levine and Ben Witherington III, *The Gospel of Luke*, NCBC (Cambridge: Cambridge University Press, 2018), 183.
60. See the excursus "Parables and the Art of Storytelling" at 5:36.
61. See Frederick W. Danker, *Jesus and the New Age: A Commentary on St. Luke's Gospel*, rev. and expanded ed. (Philadelphia: Fortress, 1988), 153–55.

[39]He also told them a parable: "Can a blind person guide a blind person? Will not both fall into a pit? [40]A disciple is not above the teacher, but everyone who is fully qualified will be like the teacher. [41]Why do you see the speck in your neighbor's eye, but do not notice the log in your own eye? [42]Or how can you say to your neighbor, 'Friend, let me take out the speck in your eye,' when you yourself do not see the log in your own eye? You hypocrite, first take the log out of your own eye, and then you will see clearly to take the speck out of your neighbor's eye.

[43]"No good tree bears bad fruit, nor again does a bad tree bear good fruit; [44]for each tree is known by its own fruit. Figs are not gathered from thorns, nor are grapes picked from a bramble bush. [45]The good person out of the good treasure of the heart produces good, and

blind person?" begins with Μήτι, an emphatic interrogative particle that expects the answer "surely not!" The second question, "Will not both fall into a pit?" starts with οὐχί, which expects the answer "of course!" But the fact that the answers to these questions seem obvious should not cloud our own recognition that blind persons, both then and now, are often most capable of leading and teaching. In the ancient world blindness was attributed to some of the most revered bards (Homer) and seers (Tiresias). One of the most well-known women in the modern era who was blind and deaf and who became an extraordinary author, lecturer, and political activist is Helen Keller (1880–1968).[62] An art teacher in the Bronx named Jessica Jones, who lost her sight to type 1 diabetes, has been a brilliant guide for many years for her students who are also blind.[63] In Kerala, India, Baby Girija, blind from birth, is a Braille teacher at the Government School for Visually Handicapped, where in her spare time she is transcribing thousands of books for her students into Braille.[64] These are only a few of countless exemplary contemporary "blind guides."

The point in 6:39-42, however, is about not physical sight but insight. Luke frequently uses seeing as a metaphor for spiritual understanding,

---

62. Jamie Berke, "Biography of Helen Keller," https://www.verywellhealth.com /helen-kellers-biography-1046171.

63. Amy Freeze, "Blind Woman Teaches Art to Blind Students in the Bronx," https://abc7ny.com/education/blind-woman-teaches-art-to-blind-students-in-the -bronx/3338760/.

64. R. Ayyappan, "Blind Teacher with a Vision on a Priceless Mission," https:// english.manoramaonline.com/women/on-a-roll/2019/03/08/blind-teacher-baby -girija-braille-books-kerala.html.

the evil person out of evil treasure produces evil; for it is out of the abundance of the heart that the mouth speaks.

46"Why do you call me 'Lord, Lord,' and do not do what I tell you? 47I will show you what someone is like who comes to me, hears my words, and acts on them. 48That one is like a man building a house, who dug deeply and laid the foundation on rock; when a flood arose, the river burst against that house but could not shake it, because it had been well built. 49But the one who hears and does not act is like a man who built a house on the ground without a foundation. When the river burst against it, immediately it fell, and great was the ruin of that house."

especially for leaders. Sensitivity toward those who are sight impaired causes us to ask how we might recast such formulations. The sayings about seeing conclude with the hyperbolic comment about specks and logs; it drives home the point about needing to have insight into one's own shortcomings before instructing others about theirs (6:41-42).

In 6:43-45, the metaphor shifts to trees and their fruit. The sayings point not only to the importance of the good fruit but to the way in which the fruit reveals the nature of the plant that produces it. In 6:45, Jesus states that the heart is the central place from which all else flows. In biblical times, the heart was regarded as the seat of the desires, emotions, thoughts, and plans.[65] It is the place where one encounters God and treasures everything like Mary (2:19, 51).[66] The image of an honest and good heart that bears fruit is reprised in 8:15.

Addressing Jesus as "Lord"

New Testament texts use the term "Lord" for both God and Jesus. According to Exodus 3:14, the name YHWH was revealed by God to Moses; Jews do not pronounce the name out of reverence.[67] In oral reading

---

65. See Luke 1:51, 66; 2:35; 3:15; 5:22; 9:47; 12:34, 45; 21:14, 34; 24:38.
66. See Luke 1:17; 8:12, 15; 10:27; 16:15; 24:25, 32. See Thomas P. McCreesh, "Heart," in *The Collegeville Pastoral Dictionary of Biblical Theology*, ed. Carroll Stuhlmueller (Collegeville, MN: Liturgical Press, 1996), 422–24.
67. Likewise, Pope Benedict XVI reiterated a directive on June 29, 2008, that Catholics should refrain from pronouncing the divine name in prayers and hymns and replace it with "Lord" or a word "equivalent in meaning" in the local language.

of a text where YHWH is written, Jews traditionally read "Adonai," "My Lord." New Testament texts often refer to God as "Lord" (κύριος). Jesus, for example, addresses God as "Father, Lord [κύριε] of heaven and earth" (10:21).

The followers of Jesus applied the same term to Jesus.[68] The address κύριε does not, however, always carry a religious significance. It was a term of respect, proper for speaking to teachers. People who call Jesus κύριε during his earthly ministry are using a polite form of address, such as "Sir"; no connotations of divinity are necessary.[69] In a number of instances the evangelists retroject this postresurrection title into Jesus's earthly life. It is likely that the title was first applied to Jesus in reference to his return at the parousia (as in Matt 24:42: "Keep awake therefore, for you do not know on what day your Lord is coming"). We see this use in the early Aramaic prayer, Μαράνα θά, "Our Lord come!" preserved in Greek in 1 Corinthians 16:22.[70]

For Christians today, "Lord" remains a popular term of address both for God and for Jesus. Yet today there are serious difficulties with this address.[71] The term evokes feudal times replete with lords and ladies. We must ask: what are the effects of using this language for God and Christ?

68. E.g., in 3:4; 4:12, Luke applies to Jesus texts from Isaiah and Deuteronomy where "Lord" refers to God.

69. Consequently, the NRSV translates κύριε as "Sir," not "Lord," when addressed to Jesus in Mark 7:28; John 4:11, 15, 19, 49; 5:7; 12:21. Along with these instances the NABRE translates κύριε as "Sir" in John 6:34; 8:11; 9:36; 20:15. See further Larry Hurtado, *One God, One Lord: Early Christian Devotion and Ancient Jewish Monotheism*, Cornerstones, 3rd ed. (London: Bloomsbury T&T Clark, 2015). Jason A. Staples ("'Lord, Lord': Jesus as YHWH in Matthew and Luke," *NTS* 64 [2018]: 1–19) shows that the double κύριος formula in 6:46 would have been familiar to a first-century, Greek-speaking Jewish audience as signaling the Tetragrammaton, thus here Luke represents Jesus as applying the name YHWH to himself.

70. As a christological title, "Lord" was a favorite of the apostle Paul: it occurs some 250 times in the letters attributed to him. On the background of the title, see further Joseph A. Fitzmyer, "New Testament *Kyrios* and *Maranatha* and Their Aramaic Background," in *To Advance the Gospel: New Testament Studies* (New York: Crossroad, 1981), 218–35; Fitzmyer, "The Semitic Background of the New Testament *Kyrios*-Title," in *A Wandering Aramean: Collected Aramaic Essays*, SBLMS 25 (Chico, CA: Scholars Press, 1979), 115–42.

71. Gail Ramshaw, *God Beyond Gender: Feminist Christian God-Language* (Minneapolis: Fortress, 1995), 47–58.

The Anglo-Saxon word "lord" denoted the male authority figure who was obligated to provide food and protection for his community. In the Middle Ages it acquired its connotation of feudal power. Thus, the term "lord" is androcentric, archaic, and domination-oriented. Conversely, the divine name YHWH, or "I will be what I will be," has no gender. Moreover, "Lord" derives from an economic system in which a powerful man provided for his subservients. More often in medieval times the reverse was true: lords consumed disproportionately the produce of peasants. The question is not, however, whether lords were benevolent or abusive. The problem is that "Lord" reinforces patterns of inequality and domination.

Our challenge is to create language that expresses the idea of divine providence, mercy, and power in ways that do not support systems of domination and submission. One proposal, offered by the National Council of Churches, is to use "the SOVEREIGN ONE" to render the Hebrew YHWH and "the Sovereign Jesus Christ" for κύριος.[72] Another proposed title is "the Living One."[73] This phrase has the advantage of not reinscribing divine gender as male, and it captures the life-giving and life-sustaining power of "I will be what I will be." Further, it speaks of God's power to release all from suffering and death, expressed in and exercised by Christ, who is also well-named "the Living One" (24:5). Another possibility is simply "the Name" or "I AM."[74]

Each of these proposals has its advantages, although they all share the disadvantage of being less familiar and less easy to pronounce than "Lord." Moreover, some Christians have found it important to emphasize the Lordship of Jesus *as opposed to* earthly powers, as a way to diminish the hold of those earthly powers over their lives. For example, for some African Americans recalling the long legacy of antebellum slavery, calling Jesus or God "Lord," rather than

72. See the NCC's comments in their inclusive language revision of the Revised Standard Version: *An Inclusive-Language Lectionary*, ed. the Inclusive-Language Lectionary Committee, Division of Education and Ministry, National Council of the Churches of Christ in the USA (Atlanta: John Knox, 1984), 10–11.

73. Ramshaw, *God Beyond Gender*, 54–57.

74. Ibid., 57–58.

White men in authority, is liberating.[75] Still, the gender and power implications beg for resolution.[76]

The final verses in the Sermon on the Plain drive home the importance of not simply hearing Jesus's words but acting on them. Jesus criticizes those who call him "Lord," which usually happens when they need something from him (5:12; 7:6; 10:40; 11:1; 12:41; 17:5; 18:41), but then do not act on his words. His comments echo Exodus 24:7, where hearing and doing are required of Israel at Sinai (similarly, Deut 31:11-12). The emphasis now is on hearing and acting on Jesus's interpretation of the Law (the pronoun μου, "my," is in an emphatic position, preceding τῶν λόγων, "words" in 6:47).

Women Builders

The person building a house in Luke 6:48-49 is usually envisioned as male (reinforced by the translation of ἄνθρωπος[77] as "man" [2x] in the NRSV), but other sources associate women with construction. The second-century *The Shepherd of Hermas* offers a vision of a tower being

---

75. Jacquelyn Grant ("Womanist Theology: Black Women's Experience as a Source for Doing Theology, with Special Reference to Christology," *The Journal of the Interdenominational Theological Center* 13 [1986]: 195–212) cites prayers of Black slaves who call Jesus "Massa," such as this one of a woman who affirmed the contribution of Abraham Lincoln to the emancipation of Blacks, but rejected Mr. Lincoln as her real or ultimate master: "Dear Massa Jesus, we all uns beg Ooner [you] come make us a call dis yere day. We is nutting but poor Etiopian women and people ain't tink much 'bout we. We ain't trust any of dem great high people for come to we church, but do you is de one great Massa, great too much dan Massa Linkum, you ain't shame to care for we African people" (205, taken from Harold A. Carter, *The Prayer Tradition of Black People* [Valley Forge: Judson Press, 1976], 50). Dr. C. Vanessa White affirmed in conversation with Barbara that "Lord" is still an important way to address Jesus in the African American religious experience. M. Shawn Copeland notes: "In the witness of African American religious experience, Jesus of Nazareth *is* Lord and Christ, he is freedom enfleshed" (*Knowing Christ Crucified: The Witness of the African American Religious Experience* [Maryknoll, NY: Orbis Books, 2018], 149).
76. Some womanists speak of God without an articulated gender or in the feminine. See Wilda C. Gafney, *Womanist Midrash: A Reintroduction to the Women of the Torah and the Throne* (Louisville: Westminster John Knox, 2017), 15–19.
77. The Greek ἄνθρωπος denotes a human being without specifying gender.

built (*Sim.* 9.2–9), which is the church. It is built on a rock, signifying the Son of God (*Sim.* 9.3.1; 9.12.1-8).[78] Twelve young women carry the stones with which the tower is to be built and hand them to the men doing the building.

A fresco in the catacomb of San Gennaro in Naples dating to the early third century (restored in 1985) depicts this scene of the women bringing stones to build the tower.[79] As Carolyn Osiek describes, "Three women with bound hair and bare shoulders, in long dresses of dark colors, bring stones for the tower. The woman on the right carefully carries a square stone. Other stones lie around on the ground. The middle woman stands behind the tower and is either putting stones into its wall or handing them through a door that is not shown. The turreted tower is out of proportion to the women, who are almost as tall as it is."[80]

There is also evidence that wealthy Roman women in the first and second centuries were involved in brickmaking.[81] The names of owners, contractors,

78. Carolyn Osiek, *Shepherd of Hermas: A Commentary*, Hermeneia (Minneapolis: Fortress, 1999), 220.

79. Image is from https://commons.wikimedia.org/wiki/File:Catacombe_di_San_Gennaro_052.jpg.

80. Osiek, *Shepherd*, 7.

81. E.g., Claudia Marcellina (*CIL* 15.934–36), Sergia Paulina (*The Roman Brick Stamps*, ed. Herbert Bloch [Rome: L'Erma de Bretschneider, 1967], 147). See Susan E. Hylen, *Women in the New Testament World*, Essentials of Biblical Studies (Oxford: Oxford University Press, 2019), 123; Päivi Setälä, "Women and Brick Production—Some New Aspects," in *Women, Wealth and Power in the Roman Empire*, ed. Päivi Setälä, et al. (Rome: Instituti Romani Finlandiae, 2002), 187.

and production managers stamped on the bricks make evident that approximately one-third of the owners were women, and some 6 percent were contractors or production managers. While women may not have done the actual labor, they were involved in the production of the materials and the commissioning and supervising of building projects.

Luke 7:1-50

Wisdom's Children Justified

"Lord, I Am Not Worthy" (7:1-10)

The widening of the radius of the saving revelation to the Gentiles was first announced by Simeon (2:31-32). It now takes concrete form in this healing story. In previous healing stories (4:31-44; 5:12-26; 6:6-11; 17-19), the supplicants are Jewish and they have face-to-face encounters with Jesus. Here the petitioner is a centurion, a Gentile military officer. A centurion, as the name indicates, was a leader of a Roman company of one hundred men. As is fitting for someone of his status, he communicates with Jesus, not face-to-face, but through intermediaries: first, Jewish elders (v. 3); then, unspecified friends (v. 6). The episode portrays not only cooperation between Romans and Jews but also collaboration between Jewish leaders and Jesus, a very different picture from that painted in the passion narrative.

The pericope contains several details that defy verisimilitude, beginning with the fact that no Roman troops were stationed in the Galilee in Jesus's day.[1] Furthermore, the narrative contains a number of surprising

---

1. Those looking for a historical basis for a centurion in the Galilee at this time note that such an official may have been in the service of Herod Antipas as the leader of mercenary troops or serving in police or customs work. It is also possible that a centurion on retirement may have taken up residence in Capernaum.

7:1After Jesus had finished all his sayings in the hearing of the people, he entered Capernaum. 2A centurion there had a slave whom he valued highly, and who was ill and close to death. 3When he heard about Jesus, he sent some Jewish elders to him, asking him to come and heal his slave. 4When they came to Jesus, they appealed to him earnestly, saying, "He is worthy of having you do this for him, 5for he loves our people, and it is he who built our synagogue for us." 6And Jesus went with them, but when he was not far from the house, the centurion sent friends to say to him, "Lord, do not trouble yourself, for I am not worthy to have you come under my roof; 7therefore I did not presume to come to you. But only speak the word, and let my servant be healed. 8For I also am a man set under authority, with soldiers under me; and I say to one, 'Go,' and he goes, and to another, 'Come,' and he comes, and to my slave, 'Do this,' and the slave does it." 9When Jesus heard this he was amazed at him, and turning to the crowd that followed him, he said, "I tell you, not even in Israel have I found such faith." 10When those who had been sent returned to the house, they found the slave in good health.

reversals of social expectation. While literary works (histories, satires, comedies) most often portray centurions as brutal toward their subordinates and "unjust and unconcerned with the rights of civilians,"[2] this centurion cares deeply for his slave and is on such good terms with the Jews of Capernaum that he built their synagogue[3] and has advocates among the elders. That the centurion sends φίλοι, "friends" (v. 6), demonstrates atypically good relationships between the centurion and the provincials. The use of πρεσβυτέροι, "elders," and ἀπέστειλεν, "sent" (v. 3), suggests that the centurion is sending an embassy to Jesus, a formal protocol typically initiated by subjects before their rulers, and not vice versa.[4] This portrayal of the centurion as friendly to the Jews and deferential to Jesus fits with Luke's aim to show that the values of the Jesus movement align with those of the empire. Theophilus may find it par-

2. Laurie Brink, *Soldiers in Luke–Acts*, WUNT 2.362 (Tübingen: Mohr Siebeck, 2014), 139.

3. Evidence for Gentiles who were patrons of synagogues is known from inscriptions. For references, see Amy-Jill Levine and Ben Witherington III, *The Gospel of Luke*, NCBC (Cambridge: Cambridge University Press, 2018), 199; Brink, *Soldiers*, 144 n. 49. Brink also notes that, in addition to providing funds, centurions may have used their soldiers' labor in constructing buildings (144 n. 50).

4. Brink, *Soldiers*, 141–46.

ticularly reassuring that this high-standing Roman official recognizes Jesus as a superior.[5]

Some recent studies have suggested that the implied relationship between the centurion and his slave (δοῦλος, 7:2) was romantic.[6] They find support for this interpretation in the description of the slave as ἔντιμος, "precious" (7:2), and the use of the word παῖς, "boy" or "servant" (7:7), a word that can be used for the partner of a superior male in sexual relationships.[7] Theodore Jennings and Tat-Siong Benny Liew interpret the reluctance of the centurion to have Jesus enter his house as his fear "that the centurion's new patron (Jesus) has the authority to tell him, as a client, what to do, and to order the centurion's subordinates (including his beloved) to come to Jesus and abandon the centurion."[8]

This reading is problematic for a number of reasons, beginning with the assumption that Luke is presenting this narrative as related to sexual partners. The slave's value, as indicated by the word ἔντιμος (7:2), rests in his monetary worth[9] and the service he renders, which need not be

---

5. Other positive depictions of centurions occur in the crucifixion scene at 23:47 and in Acts 10, where the devout and godfearing (φοβούμενος τὸν θεὸν, Acts 10:2) Cornelius becomes the first Gentile convert. God-fearers are those who were attracted to Jewish faith and synagogue worship but did not seek full membership. Unlike Cornelius, the centurion in 7:1-10 is not said to be a convert or God-fearer. But in a gesture of subservience even more radical than this centurion's, Cornelius bows to Peter, prepared to worship him as a god (Acts 10:25). On the strong parallels between the centurion in Luke 7 and Cornelius, see Brink, *Soldiers*, 135, 148–62. In addition to the positive portrayal of centurions, Luke also shows soldiers as open to John the Baptizer's message (3:14).

6. The most notable of these studies, published in the flagship journal of the Society of Biblical Literature, focuses on Matthew's version: Theodore W. Jennings Jr. and Tat-Siong Benny Liew, "Mistaken Identities but Model Faith: Rereading the Centurion, the Chap, and the Christ in Matthew 8:5-13," *JBL* 123 (2004): 467–94. See also David B. Gowler, "Text, Culture and Ideology in Luke 7:1-10: A Dialogic Reading," in *Fabrics of Discourse: Essays in Honor of Vernon K. Robbins*, ed. David B. Gowler, L. Gregory Bloomquist, and Duane F. Watson (Harrisburg, PA: Trinity Press International, 2003), 89–125. See also the rejoinder by D. B. Saddington, "The Centurion in Matthew 8:5-13: Consideration of the Proposal of Theodore W. Jennings, Jr., and Tat-Siong Benny Liew," *JBL* 125 (2006): 140–42; and Christopher B. Zeichmann, "Rethinking the Gay Centurion: Sexual Exceptionalism, National Exceptionalism in Readings of Matt. 8:5-13 // Luke 7:1-10," *The Bible and Critical Theory* 11 (2015): 35–54; Christopher B. Zeichmann, "Gender Minorities in and under Roman Power: Race and Respectability Politics in Luke–Acts," in *Luke–Acts*, ed. James P. Grimshaw, Texts@Contexts (London: T&T Clark, 2019), 61–73.

7. Jennings and Liew, "Mistaken Identities," 472–73.

8. Ibid., 485.

9. BDAG, 340.

sexual. The centurion's reluctance to have Jesus come under his roof relates to his expression of submission to Jesus's authority, not a desire to keep him from finding out the true nature of his relationship to his slave. As a man who understands chains of command, he is placing himself in a subservient position of an unworthy supplicant who looks to a higher authority to grant his request. Jesus affirms how the centurion has positioned himself and heals the slave from a distance.[10]

Furthermore, as Christopher Zeichmann has shown, those who have read the pericope as LGBT-friendly have problematically assigned to Jesus an "exceptional" view of sexuality, vis-à-vis the locals. That is, Jesus is read as one who tolerates queer sexual relations, and his tolerance is painted against the backdrop of an otherwise monolithic Judaism depicted as completely closed-minded and homophobic.[11]

With respect to the historical situation of Roman officers and their slaves at the time of Jesus, it is also important to point out that while sexual relationships between centurions and their slaves would have been common, those relationships were exploitative, even if couched in the language of sentimentality and affection. Because the power differential prevents the relationship from being consensual,[12] the better word for Roman soldiers engaged in sexual relations both with slaves in the military and with vulnerable persons—male and female—in the local populations is rape, not romance.[13] Gender of those raped by conquering soldiers was inconsequential. Consider Tacitus's remark on rape during Roman military conquest: "Whenever a young woman or

---

10. For reasons why Luke omits the account of the Syrophoenician/Canaanite woman's daughter who is healed at a distance (Mark 7:24-31; Matt 15:21-28), see comments at 10:38-42.

11. Zeichmann, "Rethinking," 42–48; "Gender Minorities," 65–67. In this evaluation, Zeichmann engages the concept "homonationalism" coined by the theorist of gender and sexuality, Jasbir Puar. Central to this concept is the notion of cosmopolitan, queer-friendly Western nation-states, that need to battle terror-states, which are depicted as violently anti-queer. See Jasbir Puar, *Terrorist Assemblages: Homonationalism in Queer Times* (Durham: Duke University Press, 2007).

12. Zeichmann, "Rethinking," 37.

13. This is not to say that feelings of affection between these partners could never have been present. But especially in terms of the master-slave relationship, affection can always be overridden by the master's force. See, for example, Mitzi J. Smith, "Unity, Fraternity, and Reconciliation: Ancient Slavery as a Context for the Return of Onesimus," in *Onesimus Our Brother: Reading Religion, Race, and Culture in Philemon,* ed. Matthew V. Johnson, James A. Noel, and Demetrius K. Williams, Paul in Critical Contexts (Minneapolis: Fortress, 2012), 47–58.

a handsome youth fell into their hands, they were torn to pieces by the violent struggles of those who tried to secure them" (*Hist.* 3.33 [Moore, LCL]).[14] Finally, since soldiers stationed in the Galilee during the Herodian period would have been locals, it would have been less likely for them to have taken local boys as sex slaves; they would have sought more acceptable outlets, such as sex workers.[15]

Because of feminist concern for the most vulnerable in society, it is unsettling that we hear nothing from the slave's point of view. We do not know if he wants to be healed. Perhaps he would prefer to die rather than be trapped in this relationship from which he has no power to escape.[16] Alternatively, if he had heard about Jesus's proclamation of release to captives (4:18), he may have hoped Jesus would free him from his slavery. Such hopes are not realized, as Jesus returns him to health and to service. In no gospel text does Jesus free slaves or challenge directly the system of slavery.[17] The work of dismantling slavery would fall to people of much later generations.[18]

A further unsettling aspect of this episode is that it presents as normal a model of authority based on command and control. The centurion knows his place under his superiors in the chain of command. To soldiers and slaves under his authority, all he need do is issue a word of command and they obey (7:8). He expects Jesus to act the same way: to "only speak the word" (7:7). Here Jesus does not contradict the centurion's articulation of how power works. But Barbara sees evidence in other episodes, particularly at the Last Supper, where Jesus instructs his disciples and models for them a different kind of leadership and exercise of authority. He contrasts the manner in which the kings of the Gentiles and those in authority lord it over their subjects with the way his disciples are to lead: as one who serves, just as Jesus is among them as one who serves (22:25-27).[19]

---

14. Cited by both Jennings and Liew, "Mistaken Identities," 475; and Zeichmann, "Rethinking," 49.

15. Zeichmann, "Rethinking," 50.

16. Levine and Witherington, *The Gospel of Luke*, 201–2.

17. Though see critiques of power and authority, especially as expressed in Mark 10:41-45, where the one who would be great must be "slave of all."

18. See further comments on slavery and human trafficking at 1:38, 48, and excursus on Luke and Slavery at 17:7-10.

19. Shelly agrees that it would be possible to read Luke 22:25-27 in this way but sees this saying as modifying a more radical saying concerning power (Mark 10:42-44), in the direction that a centurion might appreciate. See commentary on Luke 22:25-30.

Nonhierarchical Models of Leadership

Recent studies on leadership show models of command and control to be ineffective. Leadership theorists now study quantum physics, the science of self-organizing systems, and chaos theory to show the need for new models of leadership that are attuned to the rhythms of the cosmos.[20] Leaders can bring about collective transformation by focusing on possibility, generosity, and gifts, rather than problem solving, fear, and retribution.[21] In the face of changing realities, adaptive leadership works best by valuing diversity over central management and by risking experimentation.[22] Building circles of friends and fostering networks of compassion is another approach to leadership that generates new ideas and new ways of responding to the mission.[23]

These approaches to leadership and authority resonate with feminist ways of thinking and acting, which stress cooperation, interconnectedness, and inclusivity.[24] The Women-Church movement, for example, a global, ecumenical movement that began in 1983, is composed of ad hoc women's groups that are redefining church through their construction of new rituals and patterns of organization. There is no central or permanent leadership. Women-Church aims to dismantle clericalism and hierarchical distinctions between clergy and laity. In contrast to

---

20. E.g., Margaret J. Wheatley, *Leadership and the New Science: Discovering Order in a Chaotic World*, 3rd ed. (San Francisco: Berrett-Koehler, 2006), outlines the shift away from a Newtonian mechanistic and materialistic view of the universe, where it was thought that studying the parts leads to understanding the whole, and focusing on what can be known through our physical senses brought comprehension of our world. New science focuses on wholism rather than parts and gives attention to relationship and connectedness of all creation. Another insight from new science is that the world is inherently orderly and continues to create systems of great scope, capacity, and diversity through a self-organizing process. Chaos theory contributes the insight that no great change and new ordering is possible without chaos.

21. Peter Block, *Community: The Structure of Belonging* (San Francisco: Berrett-Koehler, 2008).

22. Ronald Heifetz, Alexander Grashow, and Marty Linsky, *The Practice of Adaptive Leadership: Tools and Tactics for Changing Your Organization and the World* (Boston: Harvard Business Press, 2009).

23. Donna J. Markham, *Spiritlinking Leadership: Working through Resistance to Organizational Change* (New York: Paulist Press, 1999).

24. See the excursus "Feminist Understandings of Power" at 4:1-13 and comments on authority at 4:31-37.

top-down structures in which clergy dispense all the teaching, preaching, and sacraments and hold all the leadership positions, Women-Church stresses that ministries, including leadership, originate from within the community.[25] Other examples of experimentation with circular models of leadership can be found in the ways that communities of Catholic women religious have made adaptations following the directives of Vatican II (1962–1965). Many communities have changed from unilinear hierarchical patterns and now have structures of shared leadership among the elected leaders and the members.

In 7:9, Jesus is amazed, not at the way in which the centurion exercises his authority (cf. 4:32, 36; 5:24, 26, where Jesus's authority evokes amazement), but at his faith.[26] The centurion's faith would seem to refer only to his belief that Jesus can heal. Luke makes no mention of whether there is any ongoing relationship that would lead the centurion to believe in Jesus as something more than a healer—that is, unless he follows Jesus to Jerusalem and is the centurion that declares Jesus's innocence at the crucifixion (23:47).[27]

The declaration "Lord, I am not worthy" (7:6) is troublesome from a feminist point of view. In many cultures, women are socialized in ways that undermine their sense of self-worth and emphasize their subordination to their fathers, brothers, and husbands. A first step in the Bible study with the women of CODIMUJ,[28] for example, is to work on the self-esteem of the women and to teach them their value in God's eyes. The women probe texts like Genesis 1:27 (the creation of male and female, at the same time, as equals) and stories in the New Testament where Jesus heals women and where female disciples are featured. Likewise, at CEDIMSE, in Torreón, México, the Benedictine sisters first work with

25. See, e.g., Rosemary Radford Ruether, *Women-Church: Theology and Practice of Feminist Liturgical Communities* (San Francisco: Harper & Row, 1986).
26. Other instances in which faith is connected with healing are 5:20; 7:50; 8:48, 50; 17:19; 18:42. In each instance, faith appears to have a causal effect toward healing. Cf. 9:41, where the disciples' lack of faith makes them unable to heal. On lack of faith, see also 8:25; 17:5-6; 18:8; 22:32.
27. Levine and Witherington, *The Gospel of Luke*, 202.
28. On CODIMUJ, see excursus above, p. 34.

women on knowing their dignity and their human rights, both social and ecclesial, before delving more deeply into the study of Scripture and theology.[29] It is not only women but other marginalized persons who are made to feel unworthy. For Roman Catholics, it is particularly difficult to sustain a hard-won sense of dignity and worth when at the eucharistic liturgy, just before Communion, the congregation prays the words, "Lord, I am not worthy that you should enter under my roof, but only say the word and my soul shall be healed."[30] It would be a welcome change to replace the emphasis on unworthiness with prayers of gratitude, acknowledging that faith and the call to follow Jesus are gifts; they are never earned or deserved.

Widows and Power over Death (7:11-17)

This episode, unique to Luke, is set in Nain, a town a few miles southwest of Nazareth. Two large crowds come face to face: the one following Jesus (7:11) and the one comprising the funeral procession (7:12). Both crowds are likely composed of women and men.[31] Although it is commonly thought that mourning the dead was primarily women's business,[32] Nicola Denzey assesses the evidence correctly: "Friezes from sarcophagi and wall paintings depict both men and women doing funerary work: offering sacrifices, visiting the grave, mourning, singing, acting as pantomimes. . . . All that can safely be deduced from the ancient evidence is that both men and women cared for and lamented the dead, sometimes in gender-specific ways (for example, women might

29. See above, p. 110.

30. See Mark Etling, "Lord, Why Am I not Worthy?," *National Catholic Reporter*, July 13–26, 2018, https://www.ncronline.org/news/opinion/soul-seeing/lord-why -am-i-not-worthy, who argues that no one is unworthy; all are created in the image of God, who is love (Gen 1:27; 1 John 4:16), and even our sin does not tarnish that. He cites Jesus's practice of eating with, healing, commissioning, and giving authority to women and men without regard for their "worthiness." Finally, "Jesus didn't die to restore us to 'worthy' status; he died because we are worthy of his supreme sacrifice."

31. Disciples (7:11) includes women and men. See the excursus "Female Disciples" at 5:30.

32. Kathleen E. Corley, *Maranatha: Women's Funerary Rituals and Christian Origins* (Minneapolis: Fortress, 2010), 46–47. Jeremiah 9:17-22 speaks of professional women mourners who taught their daughters the skills of lamenting.

Luke 7:11-17

[11]Soon afterwards he went to a town called Nain, and his disciples and a large crowd went with him. [12]As he approached the gate of the town, a man who had died was being carried out. He was his mother's only son, and she was a widow; and with her was a large crowd from the town. [13]When the Lord saw her, he had compassion for her and said to her, "Do not weep." [14]Then he came forward and touched the bier, and the bearers stood still. And he said, "Young man, I say to you, rise!" [15]The dead man sat up and began to speak, and Jesus gave him to his mother. [16]Fear seized all of them; and they glorified God, saying, "A great prophet has risen among us!" and "God has looked favorably on his people!" [17]This word about him spread throughout Judea and all the surrounding country.

cry while men might orate), but sometimes in non-gender-specific ways (for example, both men and women might prepare a body for burial)."[33]

The pathos of the scene is heightened when we learn that the dead man is his mother's only son and that she is a widow.[34] While most readers think of biblical widows as poor and needy, that is not the way Luke characterizes them.[35] The widow Anna is a vigilant prophet who voices expectations for redemption (2:36-38); the widow in the parable at 18:1-8 relentlessly faces off with an unjust judge until she achieves justice; another widow gives her whole life to the temple (21:1-4); widows are engaged in daily ministry (Acts 6:1-7);[36] and possibly the widows

33. Nicola Denzey Lewis, review of Kathleen E. Corley, *Maranatha: Women's Funerary Rituals and Christian Origins* (Philadelphia: Fortress, 2010), CBQ 74 (2012): 594–96, here 596.

34. In two other episodes Luke heightens the distress of the parents by adding that Jairus's ill daughter is his only daughter (8:42; cf. Mark 5:23) and that the son who suffers from a spirit that makes him convulse is the man's "only begotten" (μονογενής, Luke 9:38; cf. Mark 9:17).

35. See the excursus "Ministering Widows" at 2:21-40. See also Robert M. Price, *The Widow Traditions in Luke–Acts: A Feminist-Critical Scrutiny*, SBLDS 155 (Atlanta: Scholars Press, 1997).

36. Barbara argues that the widows in Acts 6:1-7 were not the object of the daily διακονία, "ministry" (misleadingly translated by NRSV as "distribution of food"), but were being overlooked in not being given their role in the ministerial service. See Barbara E. Reid, "The Power of the Widows and How to Suppress It (Acts 6:1-7)," in *A Feminist Companion to the Acts of the Apostles*, ed. Amy-Jill Levine with Marianne Blickenstaff, FCNTECW 8 (London: T&T Clark, 2004), 71–88.

with Tabitha/Dorcas in Acts 9:39 were ministering through their textile work.[37] Given these other widows, we may imagine that there is more to the widow in 7:11-17 than being a silent object of pity.

While Luke does not say how her son died or how the widowed mother acts at the funeral, we might imagine her as taking up a protest against his death like many contemporary women do. Lamentation for the dead not only expresses sorrow at the loss; when the death is caused by an injustice, dirges contain elements of protest, accusation, a call for justice.[38] Lament can serve a socio-political purpose when it denounces abusive power.[39] It can serve as a source of strength by lifting up "portraits of courageous resistance amid the rubble of misogynist landscapes."[40] Contemporary examples of women who protest unjust deaths abound. Mamie Till Bradley, for example, demanded that the coffin be open and the mutilated body of her fourteen-year-old son Emmett be displayed for all to see after he was lynched in Mississippi in August 1955. The funeral and the images broadcast in the news fueled further actions in the Civil Rights movement. The Madres de la Plaza de Mayo in Buenos Aires, Argentina, marched every Thursday from 1977 to 2006, demanding to know the fate of their "disappeared" husbands, fathers, brothers, and sons during Argentina's "dirty war" during the military dictatorship from 1976 to 1983. They now continue their advocacy for justice on a range of issues.[41] The Women in Black was formed in the wake of the First Intifada by Israeli women in Jerusalem in 1988 to protest violations of human rights by Israeli soldiers toward Palestinians in the Occupied Territories. Standing in silent vigil every Friday, they wore black as a sign of mourning for all the victims. Women in many other

---

37. It is not clear whether Tabitha/Dorcas was herself a widow, what her relationship was to the widows mourning her death, whether the clothing they made was given out as part of Tabitha's charitable works (Acts 9:36), or whether this work was her means of support. See Amy-Jill Levine, "Tabitha/Dorcas: Spinning Off Cultural Criticism," in *Delightful Acts: New Essays on Canonical and Non-canonical Acts*, ed. Harold W. Attridge, Dennis R. MacDonald, Clare K. Rothschild, WUNT 391 (Tübingen: Mohr Siebeck, 2017), 41–65.

38. Nancy C. Lee, "Lamentations and Polemic: The Rejection/Reception History of Women's Lament . . . and Syria," *Int* 67 (2013): 155–83, here 160–61.

39. Ibid., 157.

40. Gina Hens-Piazza, *Lamentations*, WCS 30 (Collegeville, MN: Liturgical Press, 2017), xliii.

41. See "Speaking Truth to Power: Madres of the Plaza de Mayo," Women in World History, http://www.womeninworldhistory.com/contemporary-07.html.

countries have followed their lead.[42] The midwives Shiphrah and Puah provide a biblical example of women whose bold protest successfully deterred Pharaoh from murdering the sons of the Hebrews (Exod 1:15-22).

Whether the death of the son in Luke 7:11-17 was a violent one or caused by injustice, the text does not say. Nor does it tell us if the mother's weeping is in angry protest, heartbroken grief, or both. By not giving any details about the widow and making her voiceless, as Luke does with other women, he keeps the stereotype of the silent, needy widow in place. She is dependent on Jesus's compassion,[43] much as Tabitha/Dorcas is dependent on Peter in Acts 9:36-43.

We pause at Jesus's instruction to the widow not to weep and wonder that his gut-felt compassion does not cause him to weep with her as he does with Mary and the others grieving at the death of Lazarus in John 11:33-35. Rather than see Jesus's response in Luke 7:13 as a psychologically damaging admonition not to cry at the loss of a loved one,[44] we interpret it as pointing to death being overcome. The impact of the episode is to affirm Jesus as a great prophet (7:16), which leads into the discussion about Jesus's identity with John's disciples in the next episode, followed by the exchange with Simon (7:36-50), which also focuses on Jesus's identity as a prophet.

Wisdom's Children Justified (7:18-35)

A central question in this section (7:18-35) and the next (7:36-50) is Jesus's identity as a prophet. In 7:18-23, the imprisoned John the Baptizer (see 3:20) questions whether Jesus is the awaited one. Jesus's list of what John's disciples have seen and heard[45] echoes his proclamation in 4:18 of his mission, which casts him in the mold of the prophet Isaiah (61:1-2). It also parallels the signs of the messianic age in Isaiah 35:5-6. What John's

---

42. See Lee, "Lamentations," 176–77, for other such examples.

43. The verb ἐσπλαγχνίσθη (7:13) means to feel "gut-felt compassion." Σπλάγχνον refers to the inward parts of the body, especially the viscera (BDAG, 938), which were thought to be the seat of the emotions (as today we would say of the heart). See also 1:78; 10:33; 15:20.

44. Levine and Witherington, *The Gospel of Luke*, 203–4, rightly point out that to confront grieving parents with Jesus's command not to weep is a misuse of the text.

45. Luke shows Jesus healing people who are blind (18:35-43), paralyzed (5:17-26), leprous (5:12-16; 17:11-19), and deaf and mute (11:14-15); raising the dead (7:11-17; 8:40-56); and proclaiming good news (4:43; 8:1).

Luke 7:18-35

[18]The disciples of John reported all these things to him. So John summoned two of his disciples [19]and sent them to the Lord to ask, "Are you the one who is to come, or are we to wait for another?" [20]When the men had come to him, they said, "John the Baptist has sent us to you to ask, 'Are you the one who is to come, or are we to wait for another?'" [21]Jesus had just then cured many people of diseases, plagues, and evil spirits, and had given sight to many who were blind. [22]And he answered them, "Go and tell John what you have seen and heard: the blind receive their sight, the lame walk, the lepers are cleansed, the deaf hear, the dead are raised, the poor have good news brought to them. [23]And blessed is anyone who takes no offense at me."

[24]When John's messengers had gone, Jesus began to speak to the crowds about John: "What did you go out into the wilderness to look at? A reed shaken by the wind? [25]What then did you go out to see? Someone dressed in soft robes? Look, those who put on fine clothing and live in luxury are in royal palaces. [26]What then did you go out to see? A prophet? Yes, I tell you, and more than a prophet. [27]This is the one about whom it is written,

'See, I am sending my messenger ahead of you,

disciples have seen and what they have heard in the Scriptures provides them the answer that Jesus is the prophet issuing in the messianic era.

The theme of seeing and believing, particularly pronounced in the Gospel of Luke,[46] is central to each of the four units in 7:18-50. While restoring physical sight is part of Jesus's mission (4:18), seeing is also a metaphor for perceiving the word of God.[47] The questions "what have you seen?" (7:18-23), the thrice repeated "What did you go out to see?" (7:24, 25, 26), and the implied "Where are you looking?" (7:24, 25) can prompt feminist reflection on the importance of evaluating the source of interpretations of life and Scripture that appear to be "obvious." Who does the seeing, what they perceive from their point of view, what presuppositions they have that color what they see, and where they look for answers are all questions that point to the fact that truth is multivalent

---

46. See Stephen D. Moore, *Mark and Luke in Poststructuralist Perspectives: Jesus Begins to Write* (New Haven, CT: Yale University Press, 1992), esp. chap. 6, "Look-Acts: Seeing Is Believing."

47. See R. Alan Culpepper, "Seeing the Kingdom of God: The Metaphor of Sight in the Gospel of Luke," *CurTM* 21 (1994): 434–43.

who will prepare your way
before you.'
28I tell you, among those born of women no one is greater than John; yet the least in the kingdom of God is greater than he." 29(And all the people who heard this, including the tax collectors, acknowledged the justice of God, because they had been baptized with John's baptism. 30But by refusing to be baptized by him, the Pharisees and the lawyers rejected God's purpose for themselves.)

31"To what then will I compare the people of this generation, and what are

they like? 32They are like children sitting in the marketplace and calling to one another,

'We played the flute for you, and
you did not dance;
we wailed, and you did not
weep.'

33For John the Baptist has come eating no bread and drinking no wine, and you say, 'He has a demon'; 34the Son of Man has come eating and drinking, and you say, 'Look, a glutton and a drunkard, a friend of tax collectors and sinners!' 35Nevertheless, wisdom is vindicated by all her children."

and can be approximated only when insight from diverse perspectives is shared.

The curious parable in 7:31-32 regarding the "people of this generation [γενεᾶς ταύτης]"[48] concerns, as 7:33-35 clarifies, the refusal of the people of Jesus's time to accept either the ascetic John's "dirge" or the profligate Jesus's "flute." How one responds to the invitations of John and Jesus is not a game; heeding their call is the way to righteousness (see comments on the meaning of righteousness at 1:6). The verb δικαιόω ("to demonstrate to be morally right," "to show justice," "to vindicate")[49] frames the parable, but the NRSV translation masks this, rendering ἐδικαίωσαν τὸν θεόν as "acknowledged the justice of God" (7:29, lit. "justified God") and ἐδικαιώθη as "vindicated" (7:35). The sense is this: those who accepted John's baptism accepted God's way of righteousness (7:29), and those who heed Jesus likewise show themselves to be Wisdom's children, proving her way to be right. There is an allusion to Proverbs 8:32-36, where Woman Wisdom exhorts:

48. The expression γενεᾶς ταύτης, "this generation," generally has a pejorative connotation in Luke. See 9:41; 11:29-32, 50-51; 17:25. At 1:50, however, Mary sings of how God offers mercy "from generation to generation [εἰς γενεὰς καὶ γενεὰς] to those who fear [φοβουμένοις] him."
49. BDAG, 249.

And now, my children, listen to me:
  happy are those who keep my ways.
Hear instruction and be wise,
  and do not neglect it.
Happy is the one who listens to me,
  watching daily at my gates,
  waiting beside my doors.
For whoever finds me finds life
  and obtains favor from the LORD;
but those who miss me injure themselves;
  all who hate me love death.

In 7:35 Luke evokes traditions in the books of Job, Proverbs, Sirach, Wisdom of Solomon, and Baruch that portray Wisdom as the female personification of God's creative and saving action in the world. While all language for God is metaphorical, analogical, or symbolic,[50] it matters whether we use male, female, or gender-neutral language and images that speak of LGBTQIA experience to address God and to speak of the Divine. Deconstructing the dominant male imagery of God undermines patriarchal power and allows all to see themselves as equally made in the image of God and to see the divine revealed in their experience.[51]

---

50. Metaphor compares a figure of speech in which a word or phrase is applied to an object or action to which it is not literally applicable (https://www.merriam-webster.com/dictionary/metaphor). In theological metaphors, there is always an is/is not quality, e.g., "God is a rock," that is, God is like a rock but is not a rock. See Sallie McFague, *Metaphorical Theology: Models of God in Religious Language* (Philadelphia: Fortress, 1982). Analogy is a comparison of two otherwise unlike things based on resemblance of a particular aspect (https://www.merriam-webster.com/dictionary/analogy). Analogy does not have the "is not" quality, e.g., "God is good." Symbol is something that stands for or suggests something else by reason of relationship, association, convention, or accidental resemblance (https://www.merriam-webster.com/dictionary/symbol). In theological terms, symbol (from the Greek συνβάλλω, "to throw together") throws one into the experience, participates in what it signifies. See Roger Haight, *Jesus, Symbol of God* (Maryknoll, NY: Orbis Books, 1999).
51. See Mary C. Grey, *Introducing Feminist Images of God*, IFT 7 (Cleveland: Pilgrim, 2001); Elizabeth A. Johnson, *She Who Is: The Mystery of God in Feminist Discourse* (New York: Crossroad, 1992); Gail Ramshaw, *God Beyond Gender: Feminist Christian God-Language* (Minneapolis: Fortress, 1995); Kim Jeong Ja Leo, "God Our Ma/Father's Korean Women's Church," in *Ecclesia of Women in Asia: Gathering the Voices of the Silenced*, ed. Evelyn Monteiro and Antoinette Gutzler (Delhi: ISPCK, 2005), 162–83; Kwok Pui-lan, *Introducing Asian Feminist Theology*, IFT (Cleveland: Pilgrim, 2000), esp. chap. 5 "Speaking about God," 65–78; Satoko Yamaguchi, "Father Image of G*d and Inclusive Language: A Reflection in Japan," in *Toward a New Heaven and a New Earth:*

Jesus as Wisdom Incarnate

In several instances in Luke, John and Jesus act in ways that Woman Wisdom does. Just as Wisdom called out to invite all to her banquet (Prov 9:3), so John called out his invitation in the desert (3:4) and Jesus calls out his message for anyone with ears to hear (8:8). Wisdom's invitation, like that of YHWH (Isa 25:6; 55:1; Ps 23:5), is to eat her bread and drink her wine (Prov 9:5), much as Luke associates Jesus with banqueting.[52] And just as Wisdom is rejected by the foolish (Sir 15:7-8), so too John (7:33) and Jesus (4:28-29; 7:34; 11:15). Portraying Jesus as Wisdom incarnate can undermine gender dualism, showing that he integrates divine femaleness with human maleness.[53] Wisdom Christology also makes clear that the saving significance of Christ does not reside in his maleness.[54]

Further, it can allow females and any who do not identify as male to see themselves as fully able to embody the Christ. There are, however, pitfalls to this approach. Wisdom Christology can romanticize and divinize patriarchal notions of femininity, thereby unwittingly reinscribing gender dualism.[55] Extolling the feminine qualities of Woman Wisdom can paint femininity as superior and transcendent, thus divinizing patriarchal notions of cultural femininity. As a consequence, one does not question the sociopolitical implications of ways gender construction keeps kyriarchy intact. In addition, wisdom literature originated in elite male circles. Its function was to give instruction to the paterfamilias, legitimate male authority, and advance kyriarchal agenda.[56] Finally, when the male Jesus takes on the persona of Wisdom,

Essays in Honor of Elisabeth Schüssler Fiorenza, ed. Fernando F. Segovia (Maryknoll, NY: Orbis Books, 2003), 199–224. See also the excursus "Calling God Father" at 11:2.

52. Luke 5:30, 33; 7:36-50; 10:7; 11:37; 12:19, 22, 29, 45; 13:26; 14:7-24; 15:2; 17:8, 27, 28; 22:7-20, 30; 24:43.

53. See Elaine M. Wainwright, *Shall We Look for Another? A Feminist Rereading of the Matthean Jesus*, The Bible and Liberation (Maryknoll, NY: Orbis Books, 1998), 77–78; Elisabeth Schüssler Fiorenza, *Sharing Her Word: Feminist Biblical Interpretation in Context* (Boston: Beacon, 1998), 160–83; Elisabeth Schüssler Fiorenza, *Jesus: Miriam's Child, Sophia's Prophet: Critical Issues in Feminist Christology* (New York: Continuum, 1994); Celia Deutsch, *Lady Wisdom, Jesus, and the Sages: Metaphor and Social Context in Matthew's Gospel* (Valley Forge, PA: Trinity Press International, 1996); Judith E. McKinlay, *Gendering Wisdom the Host: Biblical Invitations to Eat and Drink*, JSOTSup 216 (Sheffield: Sheffield Academic, 1996).

54. See the excursus "Can a Male Savior Save Women?" at 2:9.

55. Schüssler Fiorenza, *Sharing Her Word*, 177.

56. Schüssler Fiorenza, *Jesus*, 155–62.

it co-opts femaleness and casts gender in the binary male/female, keeping out of view other constructions of gender. Nonetheless, reflection on Jesus's

identification with Woman Wisdom can open space for reflection on the function of gendered language for God and the Christ.

The identification of Jesus with Wisdom is stronger in the Matthean parallel to Luke 7:35: "Yet wisdom is vindicated by her deeds" (Matt 11:19). It is Jesus who will be proved right by his deeds. In Luke, the saying applies to both John and Jesus (and to any who heed Jesus). Jesus is not equated with Wisdom, but he and John are her children. There is much less development of Wisdom Christology in Luke; it is more evident in the Gospels of Matthew (8:18-22; 11:19, 28-30; 23:34-39) and John (1:1-18; 7:27-34).[57]

57. For a fuller treatment of Matt 11:19, see Barbara E. Reid, "Wisdom's Children Justified (Mt. 11.16-19; Lk. 7.31-35)," in *The Lost Coin: Parables of Women, Work and Wisdom*, ed. Mary Ann Beavis, BibSem 86 (London: Sheffield Academic, 2002), 287–305, esp. 298–300. On parallels between Wisdom and the *Logos* in John 1:1-18 and the I AM sayings, see Raymond E. Brown, *The Gospel According to John I–XII*, AB 29A (Garden City, NY: Doubleday, 1966), cxxv, 521–23, 533–38; Ingrid Rosa Kitzberger, "Transcending Gender Boundaries in John," in *A Feminist Companion to John*, vol. 1, ed. Amy-Jill Levine with Marianne Blickenstaff, FCNTECW 4 (London: Sheffield Academic, 2003), 171–207, esp. 192–93; Judith Lieu, "Scripture and the Feminine in John," in *A Feminist Companion to the Hebrew Bible in the New Testament*, ed. Athalya Brenner, FCB 10 (Sheffield: Sheffield Academic, 1996), 225–40; Sally Douglas, *Early Church Understandings of Jesus as the Female Divine: The Scandal of Particularity*, LNTS 557 (London: Bloomsbury T&T Clark, 2016); and Eva Günther, *Wisdom as a Model for Jesus' Ministry: A Study on the "Lament over Jerusalem" in Matt 23:37-39 Par. Luke 13:34-35*, WUNT 2.513 (Tübingen: Mohr Siebeck, 2020). Pauline evocations of Christ as Wisdom include the following: "the power of God and the wisdom of God" (1 Cor 1:22-24); "the one through whom all things were made" (1 Cor 8:6); and "he is the image of the invisible God" (Col 1:15). On the Christ hymn in Colossians, see Cynthia Briggs Kittredge and Claire Miller Colombo, "Colossians," in *Philippians, Colossians, Philemon*, by Elsa Tamez et al., WCS 51 (Collegeville, MN: Liturgical Press, 2017), 149–52. See also Daniel Boyarin, "Logos, A Jewish Word: John's Prologue as Midrash," in *The Jewish Annotated New Testament*, ed. Amy-Jill Levine and Marc Zvi Brettler, 2nd ed. (New York: Oxford University Press, 2017), 688–91; Adele Reinhartz, "Children of God and Aristotelian Epigenesis in the Gospel of John," in *Creation Stories in Dialogue: The Bible, Science, and Folk Traditions; Radboud Prestige Lectures by R. Alan Culpepper*, ed. R. Alan Culpepper and Jan G. van der Watt (Leiden: Brill, 2016), 243–52, who argues that epigenesis provides a key to comprehending the revelatory function that Jesus plays in the world but at the same time poses difficult problems for feminist theology by focusing attention on the masculinity of both God and Jesus.

Do You See This Woman? (7:36-50)

Jesus's question in verse 44, "Do you see this woman?" prompts us to interrogate not only the differing perceptions of Simon and Jesus in the text but also the ways Luke and biblical interpreters see the woman, leaving a legacy of misperceptions that redound negatively toward actual women.[58]

First, what does Luke see? All four gospels have an episode of a woman who anoints Jesus. In Mark (14:3-9) and Matthew (26:6-13), an anonymous woman anoints Jesus on the head just before the passion narrative. Some object, but Jesus defends her action as anointing his body beforehand for burial. The episode takes place in Bethany, in the home of Simon who had leprosy. In John 12:1-8, the setting is also Bethany, but in the home of Lazarus. His sister Mary anoints Jesus's feet. The one who objects is Judas. Jesus defends Mary's purchase of the costly ointment, "that she might keep it for the day of my burial" (12:7). Luke has recrafted the story, deliberately eliminating this image of a woman performing a prophetic action.[59] The redactional seams from Luke's omission are evident in Luke 22 (see further comments there). Even though Luke has portrayed Mary, Elizabeth, and Anna as prophets in chapters 1–2, and he will mention Philip's four daughters who were prophets in Acts 21:9 (without giving them any voice), Luke features only male apostles as proclaiming and preaching throughout his gospel and Acts.[60] Luke sees women as disciples, but he restricts them to traditional roles.

Second, what do Simon and Jesus see? The conflict in the text centers on their two different perceptions of the woman. Jesus sees a woman who has been freed from her sins (see below on the timing of the forgiveness) and who is extravagant in her gestures of love. Simon sees a sinner, and because that is all he sees, he is convinced Jesus is not a prophet (7:39). Jesus tries to change Simon's perception. As he often does in conflictual situations, he tells a parable (7:41-42). Its point is easy to grasp and Simon

---

58. On seeing as a metaphor for insight in Luke, see comments at 6:39-42.
59. The anointing on the head is similar to Samuel anointing Saul (1 Sam 10:1) and David as king (1 Sam 16:13). For a persuasive argument linking all of these stories of women anointing Jesus to a common oral tradition, see Marianne Sawicki, *Seeing the Lord: Resurrection and Early Christian Practices* (Minneapolis: Fortress, 1994), 149–54.
60. For more details see Barbara E. Reid, *Choosing the Better Part? Women in the Gospel of Luke* (Collegeville, MN: Liturgical Press, 1996), 30–34. See comments on Luke's overall treatment of women in the authors' introduction.

Luke 7:36-50

[36]One of the Pharisees asked Jesus to eat with him, and he went into the Pharisee's house and took his place at the table. [37]And a woman in the city, who was a sinner, having learned that he was eating in the Pharisee's house, brought an alabaster jar of ointment. [38]She stood behind him at his feet, weeping, and began to bathe his feet with her tears and to dry them with her hair. Then she continued kissing his feet and anointing them with the ointment. [39]Now when the Pharisee who had invited him saw it, he said to himself, "If this man were a prophet, he would have known who and what kind of woman this is who is touching him—that she is a sinner." [40]Jesus spoke up and said to him, "Simon, I have something to say to you." "Teacher," he replied, "speak." [41]"A certain creditor had two debtors; one owed five hundred denarii, and the other fifty. [42]When they could not pay, he canceled the debts for both of them. Now which of them will love him more?" [43]Simon

gets it (7:43). Then Jesus points Simon back to the situation at hand: "Do you see this woman?" (7:44). Jesus then says what he sees, contrasting the woman's lavish loving actions with Simon's lack of hospitality. He interprets the woman's actions as evidence of her great love that results from forgiveness (see Translation Matters on 7:47). Whether Jesus has persuaded Simon to see the woman as Jesus sees her and then to perceive Jesus correctly remains unanswered. The whole episode functions as an open-ended parable that confronts the hearer both then and now with making a decision to see as Jesus sees.

Next, we look at what interpreters of this text see. A glance at the way Bible editors title the passage is revealing (there are no titles in the Greek text). Many editors keep the reader's view firmly fixed on the woman's sin: "The Pardon of a Sinful Woman" (NAB); "The Woman Who Was a Sinner" (NJB); "A Sinful Woman Forgiven" (NRSV). *La Nueva Biblia Latinoamericana* mistakenly makes her "La mujer pecadora de Magdala," "The sinful woman from Magdala"![61] We have yet to find a version of the Bible that places the focus on "A Woman who Showed Great Love," which is the way Jesus characterizes her in the text.

In kyriarchal ideology, while men are understood to be complex, varied, and capable of an array of deeds both good and bad, women tend to be defined under one of two poles, either the good woman/wife or

61. For how the woman in Luke 7:36-50 comes to be associated with Mary Magdalene, see our commentary on 8:1-3.

answered, "I suppose the one for whom he canceled the greater debt." And Jesus said to him, "You have judged rightly." [44]Then turning toward the woman, he said to Simon, "Do you see this woman? I entered your house; you gave me no water for my feet, but she has bathed my feet with her tears and dried them with her hair. [45]You gave me no kiss, but from the time I came in she has not stopped kissing my feet. [46]You did not anoint my head with oil, but she has anointed my feet with ointment. [47]Therefore, I tell you, her sins, which were many, have been forgiven; hence she has shown great love. But the one to whom little is forgiven, loves little." [48]Then he said to her, "Your sins are forgiven." [49]But those who were at the table with him began to say among themselves, "Who is this who even forgives sins?" [50]And he said to the woman, "Your faith has saved you; go in peace."

the bad woman/whore. Thus, while commentators rarely conjecture about the nature of Simon Peter's sins (5:7), which could be multiple and varied, the most common interpretation of the woman in Luke 7 is that she is a prostitute, the catch-all term for any woman who sins.[62] Interpreters who assume she is a prostitute tend to focus on her being

62. Consider the insightful reflection of Jane Schaberg, who is both circumspect about women who work in the sex industry, considering "the dynamics of the sex industry in peace and in war, the process of scapegoating, controlling and abuse, the economic conditions and gender stereotypes that make prostitution a reasonable choice for some women," and cautious that "every woman—transgressive or not—is vulnerable to the whore stigma which the prostitute embodies. . . . Demonizing whores blurs the social reality that wives and whores can be seen as the respective legitimized and illegitimized prototypes of a common female condition" (*The Resurrection of Mary Magdalene: Legends, Apocrypha, and the Christian Testament* [New York: Continuum, 2004], 104–5).

No gospel indicates explicitly that Jesus had repentant prostitutes among his followers. This notion comes from one saying, unique to Matthew, where Jesus tells the chief priests that "the tax collectors and the prostitutes are going into the kingdom of God ahead of you. For John came to you in the way of righteousness and you did not believe him, but the tax collectors and the prostitutes believed him; and even after you saw it, you did not change your minds and believe him" (Matt 21:31-32; the saying is absent from the parallel verses, Luke 7:29-30). As Levine and Witherington (*The Gospel of Luke*, 210–11) note, "The only time Luke mentions prostitutes is in the parable of the prodigal son, in which the older brother accuses the prodigal of 'devouring [the father's] property with prostitutes' (15:30). That is, the prostitutes in Luke exist only in the imagination of the elder brother and the reader."

known in the city, her loosened hair, her expensive alabaster flask of ointment, and her sensual way of touching Jesus's feet. Typically, they project much more onto the story concerning her "prostitute lifestyle" than the details of the story allow.

Consider, for instance, the sermon of Pope Gregory the Great (sixth century) that links Mary Magdalene to the "sinner" of Luke 7 and suggests that the oil she uses on Jesus's feet was "previously used . . . to perfume her flesh in forbidden acts."[63] Kathleen Corley asserts that the combination of "sinner" with being known in the city "makes it more than likely that Luke intends for his readers to identify her as a prostitute"[64] and, further, that the "erotic overtones of the story are obvious" in the woman's anointing and "fondling" of Jesus's feet.[65] Joel Green sees the woman's letting down her hair on a par with "appearing topless in public."[66] Furthermore, he sees the touching of feet as the kind of fondling that slave girls performed on guests at dinner parties as a prelude to sexual favors, though he does not give any evidence for such a practice.[67] Kenneth Bailey asserts (without giving a source) that women were known to wear a flask with perfume around the neck that hung down below the breast, used to sweeten the breath and perfume the person. He remarks, "It does not take much imagination to understand how important such a flask would be to a prostitute."[68]

Luke himself does not explicitly name the woman's sin as sexual, and many of the details in this passage can be explained in other ways. That Luke locates her "in the city" need not connote sexual looseness. The urban location may simply reflect Luke's predilection for cities (sixteen references in the gospel and forty in Acts). Loose hair is sometimes associated with sexual impropriety, as many criticisms of women worshipers of Dionysos reveal,[69] but unbound hair has other connotations as well. It was customary for unmarried women to wear loose hair. A woman

---

63. *Homily* 33 (PL 76:1239–40). See further our commentary on 8:1-3.

64. Kathleen E. Corley, *Private Women, Public Meals: Social Conflict in the Synoptic Tradition* (Peabody: Hendrickson, 1993), 124. Similarly, François Bovon, *Luke 1: A Commentary on the Gospel of Luke 1:1–9:50*, trans. Christine M. Thomas, Hermeneia (Minneapolis: Fortress, 2002), 293.

65. Corley, *Private Women, Public Meals*, 125.

66. Joel B. Green, *The Gospel of Luke*, NICNT (Grand Rapids: Eerdmans, 1997), 309.

67. Ibid., 309–10.

68. Kenneth E. Bailey, *Poet and Peasant and through Peasant Eyes*, 2 vols. in 1 (Grand Rapids: Eerdmans, 1976), 2.8.

69. See, for instance, Tacitus, *Ann.* 11.31.2, for the association of maenads (female worshipers of Dionysos), loose hair, and sexual promiscuity.

might also unbind her hair as an expression of "grief, gratefulness, propitiation, or pleading."[70]

The expensive flask of oil might be a detail Luke includes in keeping with his high regard for women who had money. The perfume could have been purchased with her earnings. Greco-Roman women were employed as weavers, midwives, doctors, hairdressers, wet nurses, masseuses, attendants, and musicians, to name a few.[71] In Acts we have two references to working women: Lydia, who dealt in purple goods (16:14), and Prisca, who was a leatherworker (18:3).

Washing or anointing feet is not necessarily inappropriate or erotic. In this passage it is an expected act of hospitality, as Jesus's remarks to Simon in 7:44 indicate. While the woman who washes and anoints Jesus's feet in 7:36-50 is judged deviant, the same judgment is not typically made when Mary anoints Jesus's feet in John 12:3 or when Jesus washes his disciples' feet in John 13:5. In the Lukan text, none of the characters sees the woman's actions as sexually provocative; Simon observes (to himself)[72] that Jesus would have to be a prophet to know that she is a sinner (7:39).

Finally, what can feminist readers see in this text? There is more than one feminist way to read this story, each of which can open up new possibilities toward dignity and equality for women and other disadvantaged persons.

A common feminist reading is to mourn the fact that Luke has transformed the relatively positive story of a woman who anointed Jesus on the head (see Mark 14:3-9, and our comments on Luke 22:1-6) to a story of a woman who is depicted as subservient and sinful. From this reading perspective, we see that once again there is an unnamed woman who is an object of discussion among two male characters who have a name and identity and who take center stage. The woman never speaks, although her actions say volumes. The one to whom Jesus directs most of his speech is Simon. Even when Jesus turns to the woman (7:44), he is speaking to Simon. Only at 7:48 and 7:50 does Jesus address her directly.

70. Charles H. Cosgrove, "A Woman's Unbound Hair in the Greco-Roman World, with Special Reference to the Story of the 'Sinful Woman' in Luke 7:36-50," *JBL* 124 (2005): 675–92, here 688, 691.

71. Jane Gardner, *Women in Roman Law and Society* (Bloomington: Indiana University Press, 1986), 233–55. See below on 8:3 on sources of women's income.

72. On Lukan interior monologues, see Melissa Harl (née Philip) Sellew, "Interior Monologue as a Narrative Device in the Parables of Luke," *JBL* 111 (1992): 239–53; Michal Beth Dinkler, "The Thoughts of Many Hearts Shall Be Revealed: Listening in on Lukan Interior Monologues," *JBL* 134 (2015): 373–99. For Dinkler, interior monologues reveal the equivocation of the characters who are speaking to themselves and invite readers to a change in their thinking.

From a different angle of vision, a more positive portrait emerges. Barbara sees in this text that a woman who has been forgiven many sins (the imperfect verb ἦν, "was" [7:37], describes past habitual action; she "used to be" a sinner) has found release and expresses gratitude to Jesus with extravagant gestures (see Translation Matters on 7:47: the loving gestures are a consequence of the forgiveness). What kinds of sins she committed does not matter. The woman is forgiven before the banquet, most likely by Jesus (the perfect passive verb ἀφέωνται, "have been forgiven," in 7:47 and 7:48 indicates that the forgiveness took place prior to the banquet). She seeks Jesus out and expresses her love with profuse tears and kisses and perfume. She stands behind him as he is reclining at table,[73] not crawling under the table like a dog, as in paintings such as "Feast in the House of Simon the Pharisee" by Peter Paul Rubens (ca. 1618). She accepts Jesus's public reaffirmation that she has been forgiven (7:48),[74] that her trust (πίστις, NRSV: "faith")[75] in him has saved and healed her (the verb σέσωκέν in 7:50 means both "saved" and "healed"; NRSV translates it "made you well" at 8:48 and 17:19; and "saved" at 7:50 and 18:42), and that she can be at peace.

TRANSLATION MATTERS

The conjunction ὅτι in the phrase ὅτι ἠγάπησεν πολύ (7:47) is ambiguous. It can be translated either in a causal sense, "because she has shown great love" (as in KJV: "for she loved much"; The Living Bible: "for she loved me much"), or in a consecutive sense, "hence she has shown great love" (NRSV, NABRE). The parable in 7:41-43 and the conclusion in 7:47c, "But the one to whom little is forgiven, loves little," indicates that the meaning of ὅτι in 7:47 is "hence," or "therefore." The woman's great love follows as a consequence of her having experienced forgiveness. The forgiveness is not earned because she showed great love.

---

73. The verb κατεκλίθη, rendered by NRSV "took his place at the table" (7:36), means "he reclined at table," indicating a banquet, where diners reclined on couches with their feet extending out behind them.

74. Alfred Plummer, *The Gospel According to S. Luke*, 5th ed., ICC (Edinburgh: T&T Clark, 1981), 214, understands ἀφέωνται in 7:48 to mean "have been and remain forgiven." "There is nothing either in the word or in the context to show that her sins were not forgiven until this moment: the context implies the opposite." In 7:48 Jesus confirms and publicly declares her forgiveness.

75. Levine and Witherington, *The Gospel of Luke*, 215, note that here "faith" does not mean adherence to particular doctrinal views but to trust that Jesus would grant forgiveness, just as God is always ready to do. See comments at 5:17-26 on the connection between faith and forgiveness.

What Luise Schottroff sees is that the woman is a prostitute, but one who is not repentant; she has experienced and has given love but remains a prostitute out of economic necessity. For Schottroff, the story is not about prostitution that can be overcome by Christian repentance but is one of mercy and respect toward prostitutes exhibited by Jesus in contrast with Simon's prejudice against them.[76] She calls this narrative "a sign of hope for feminist theology of sexuality and sensuality,"[77] as it values female eroticism and as Jesus accepts her love, not distinguishing between what she shares with him and what she may have shared with some of her "johns." Though "Jesus does not explicitly mention the patriarchal misuse of women and of love, . . . the story makes it clear that he knows about this misuse and stands up against it."[78] Schottroff sees that there are not only sexist but also anti-Jewish biases in some interpretations that paint the Pharisee as blind and unable to overcome "legalistic Judaism" to accept the unconditional forgiveness offered by the gospel of Christ.[79]

From another angle, Teresa Hornsby sees in this story a possible threat to Jesus's masculinity as he takes the passive role of being anointed. But by labeling the woman as sinner, deviant, Luke makes her "a type of lightning rod that attracts all the power and danger (represented by her female and/or the eroticized body) away from the body of Jesus so that the edifice of his masculinity remains secure."[80] Jesus reasserts his role as active male as he forgives the woman's sins and bests Simon in the verbal sparring. After showing that interpreters choose time and time again the reading that most denigrates the woman, thus disarming a potentially powerful biblical figure, Hornsby suggests: "Perhaps the time has come to celebrate rather than denigrate this woman: she shows initiative; she has her own economic resources; she is unconcerned with social perception; she is unashamed of her physicality; and her actions prompt

---

76. Luise Schottroff, "Through German and Feminist Eyes: A Liberationist Reading of Luke 7.36-50," in Brenner, *A Feminist Companion to the Hebrew Bible in the New Testament*, 332–41.

77. Ibid., 341.

78. Ibid., 340–41.

79. She cites as examples of such readings Walter Grundmann, *Das Evangelium nach Lukas*, 5th ed. (Berlin: Evangelische Verlagsanstalt, 1969), 170; and François Bovon, *Das Evangelium nach Lukas*, vol. 1, EKK 3 (Zürich: Benziger, 1989), 393, 396.

80. Teresa J. Hornsby, "The Woman Is a Sinner/The Sinner Is a Woman," in *A Feminist Companion to Luke*, ed. Amy-Jill Levine with Marianne Blickenstaff, FCNTECW 3 (London: Sheffield Academic, 2002), 121–32, here 131–32.

Jesus's positive recognition. Perhaps as well the time has come to revision Jesus's masculinity and so those constructed views of appropriate male and female behavior that continue to influence our own culture."[81]

While there have been many readings of this woman that rest on sexist presuppositions, feminist lenses allow us to see liberative possibilities instead. The text leaves us yet with many questions. We do not know whether Simon was able to see the woman as Jesus sees her and thus perceive Jesus correctly. We do not know how the question of the others at table gets answered: "Who is this who even forgives sins?" (7:49). This query raises other questions about who should forgive and when and how the complex processes of repentance, restitution, and reconciliation get worked out and how they can go awry (see comments at 5:17-26 and 17:1-4). We do not know what happened to the woman after this banquet, whether she continued to follow Jesus or not. We do not know if she was one of the "many" Galilean women who accompanied Jesus and the Twelve, ministering with her monetary resources (8:1-3; 23:49). The story remains to be finished.

A Potentially Humorous Turn in Luke 7:44

In Luke 7:44, Jesus critiques Simon for his lackluster hosting skills while turning to face the woman who had anointed his feet. This movement has been chronically omitted from major commentaries on the interaction—including the other Synoptic versions of the story—yet at no other point in the gospels does Jesus physically turn away from his conversation partner. I contend that this detail, when seen through the lens of choreography and a study of comparanda, reveals the possibility of humor. While there are many obstacles in the way of a humorous reading of Scripture—tradition favors serious interpretations, and translation itself obscures original humor—I argue that Jesus's turn in Luke could be deliberately humorous, a chance for readers to laugh *with*, not *at*, the story.[82]

While scholars have long observed theatrical elements of this scene, only recently have voices like Harold Attridge positioned readers as directors. Attridge notes that like a dramatic director, readers "have

---

81. Ibid., 132.

82. Esther Fuchs, "Laughing with/at/as Women: How Should We Read Biblical Humor?," in *Are We Amused? Humour about Women in the Biblical World*, ed. Athalya Brenner, JSOTSup 383 (New York: T&T Clark, 2003), 127–36, here 128.

made choices about how the part should be played, how the character works. While all have some foundation in the text, what the various directors bring to the text strongly influences what they see in it."[83] The turns envisioned by each reader for Luke 7:44 might range from a subtle turn, similar to those in modern British period dramas, to a slapstick-style half-turn, in which Jesus's back is entirely to Simon as he issues his rebuke.

Within examples of similar choreography among the comparanda—such as in *The Life of Aesop*—the act of turning is repeatedly tied to humor. In this text, a merchant turns to laugh at Aesop, a slave (14.1). In the following passage, Aesop causes a number of other humorous turns while disrupting social order by actively marketing his own sale (15.8). Further along in the narrative, Xanthus, a slave owner, has already turned to leave the market but returns to purchase Aesop, whom he had previously dismissed as too ugly to buy (24.16). Classically, these turns symbolize a decision that is later reversed. There is also, however, an element of humor in the hyperbole of Xanthus's initial refusal compared to the outcome of paying for the very slave he had rejected. Reversals of power dynamics like those caused by Aesop in these examples were characteristic of humor in the ancient world. Humor in the Roman context came at a cost to those in lower social positions, which Mary Beard underscores by pointing out that "for every laugh in the face of autocracy, there was another laugh by the powerful at the expense of the weak."[84] More specifically, reversals of the otherwise strict social hierarchies were prime material for ancient humor, potentially informing Jesus's turn to the sinful woman, away from Simon.

The placement of Jesus's turn within a symposium setting also lends further potential for humorous readings. A symposium typically included a number of elements, including an event that sparks conversation and argumentation, a philosophically minded guest whose perspective triumphs, and a host who facilitates the conversation and perhaps even challenges the guest himself. While humorous dialogue in symposia has been routinely noted, records of physical humor

83. Harold Attridge, "The Samaritan Woman: A Woman Transformed," in *Character Studies in the Fourth Gospel: Narrative Approaches to Seventy Figures in John*, ed. Steven A. Hunt, D. Francois Tolmie, and Ruben Zimmermann (Grand Rapids: Eerdmans, 2016), 268–81, here 270.

84. Mary Beard, *Laughter in Ancient Rome: On Joking, Tickling, and Cracking Up* (Berkeley: University of California Press, 2014), 6.

also exist.[85] Diogenes Laertius reports Cynic sage Diogenes of Sinope not only criticizing Plato's appetite for olives at a banquet but also trampling on his carpets and berating Plato's pride. He was, however, bested when Plato remarked that the trampling demonstrated its own sort of pride—the lessons conveyed were both verbal and physical.[86] This particular symposium scene in Luke 7 is a bit short on words for the dialogue to flow as heavily as the Cynics' conversations, but the main players and the opportunities for reversals are clear. Like Diogenes, Jesus is not confined to the traditional and narrative expectation of facing his dialogue partner. Rather, he directs his attention to the one he deems greater than the one he addresses, defying the social order in both the physical and verbal realms. His physical act transgresses the typical symposium boundaries just as the woman's action has already done, playing into the social inversion-based humor previously referenced.

While far from conclusive, the evidence within my analysis reclaims the possibility of intentionally humorous physicality within Luke 7:44. Regardless of the gospel author's intent in the construction of this specific passage, our disciplinary aversion to the idea of humor forecloses potentially fruitful analyses. Luke 7:44 provides a clear model of social inversion with plausible humor, by which we might come to better interpret other passages as well.

Acacia Chan

85. Terri Bednarz, *Humor in the Gospels: A Sourcebook for the Study of Humor in the New Testament, 1863–2014* (Lanham, MD: Lexington Books, 2015), 177.
86. Diogenes Laertius, *Lives of Eminent Philosophers*, vol. 2, trans. Robert Drew Hicks (Cambridge, MA: Harvard University Press, 1925), 27–29.

Luke 8:1-56

Galilean Women Followers and Financiers

Mary Magdalene and Companions (8:1-3)

Though the Synoptic Gospels feature a cast of male protagonists—Jesus, John the Baptist, the twelve male disciples—they also acknowledge groups of women as centrally involved in the movement. Mark reserves his first explicit acknowledgment of women's centrality for his passion narrative, where he credits the women as the only associates of Jesus to witness the crucifixion (15:40–41; cf. Matt 27:55).[1] These verses placed near the very end of Mark's Gospel remind us that the women had been there all along, as those who had followed (ἠκολούθουν), served (διηκόνουν),[2] and traveled up with (συναναβᾶσαι) Jesus to Jerusalem. Luke asserts a similar acknowledgment that "women were there too" early in the ministry, well before the passion. Like Mark, Luke credits the women with serving (διηκόνουν, 8:3),[3] while adding the distinctly Lukan qualification that the service was out of their own

---

1. The names of the women vary. See n. 13 below.
2. These verbs are in the imperfect tense, indicating repeated ongoing action.
3. For διακονεῖν see comments on 4:39.

247

Luke 8:1-3

^{8:1}Soon afterwards he went on through cities and villages, proclaiming and bringing the good news of the kingdom of God. The twelve were with him, ²as well as some women who had been cured of evil spirits and infirmities: Mary, called Magdalene, from whom seven demons had gone out, ³and Joanna, the wife of Herod's steward Chuza, and Susanna, and many others, who provided for them out of their resources.

resources: ἐκ τῶν ὑπαρχόντων αὐταῖς.[4] The noun ὑπαρχόντων, "resources," means possessions, property, money, or goods in Luke and Acts.[5] That the resources belonged to the women is clear from the feminine plural pronoun αὐταῖς, "their."

Whether we imagine these women characters as relatively wealthy (something that is suggested by the inclusion of a woman linked to Herod's court, v. 3) or merely as scrappy enough to have accumulated a measure of resources they are willing to share,[6] it is clear that Luke depicts them as "givers," whose support is rooted in their healing and

4. Amy-Jill Levine and Ben Witherington III (*The Gospel of Luke*, NCBC [Cambridge: Cambridge University Press, 2018], 225) note that grammatically "it is indeterminate whether the 'many others' served Jesus, the Twelve, *and the three named women*, or whether the named women and the 'many others' were the ones who served. . . . If there is a grammatical break such that the three named women are among those who were served by the others, then the three named women should be grouped with Jesus and the Twelve, who also evangelized" (italics in the original). It seems more likely to us that Luke means to group all of these women together, as having been healed from evil spirits and as serving the men in the group. Luke does not depict women as evangelists.

5. Luke 11:21; 12:15, 33, 44; 14:33; 16:1; 19:8; Acts 4:32. BDAG, 1029.

6. Claudia Janssen and Regene Lamb ("The Gospel of Luke: The Humbled Will Be Lifted Up," in *Feminist Biblical Interpretation: A Compendium of Critical Commentary on the Books of the Bible and Related Literature*, ed. Luise Schottroff and Marie-Theres Wacker, trans. Lisa E. Dahill, Everett R. Kalin, Nancy Lukens, Linda M. Maloney, Barbara Rumscheidt, Martin Rumscheidt, and Tina Steiner [Grand Rapids: Eerdmans, 2012], 654–55) suggest that their resources "included not only money, but also their capacity for work, for providing accommodations, their solidarity, faith, imagination, vision, and hopes." Levine and Witherington (*The Gospel of Luke*, 225) note that the Galilean women's service "could have been paying for whatever the entourage needed—food, housing, footwear, and so on—as well as perhaps using social capital to open doors," and they conclude that "this type of patronage does not require that the women be 'rich' per se."

directed inward, toward Jesus and the Twelve. The details concerning the women contrast starkly with those concerning the Twelve, whose presence with Jesus is legitimated through an explicit calling (6:12-16) and who will be commissioned to proclaim the Gospel and participate in the healing ministry (9:1-2).

Even though Luke subordinates the women to Jesus and the Twelve, he credits the women's support to their own initiative, providing no hint that it is contingent on the approval of fathers, brothers, or husbands. Furthermore, though the text does not explicitly describe such travel, the fact that they are depicted *with* Jesus and the Twelve may lead readers to assume that they traveled along with the group.[7] Pointing especially to the issue of women's itineracy, John Meier characterizes Luke 8:1-3 as a "potentially shocking picture of women," one that goes against the grain of Luke's aim to present "Christianity as a 'respectable religion.'"[8] We do not think this depiction disrupts Luke's orderly narrative, neither with respect to benefaction nor with respect to travel.

Based on women's legitimate involvement in financial matters in the Roman world, we conclude that Luke regards women taking initiative to finance a religious movement as an acceptable practice. As already noted (see the excursus "Women Members and Supporters of the Pharisees," Luke 5:17-26), the Pharisees received considerable financial support from elite women, sometimes independently from the religious and political leanings of their spouses. Phoebe is acknowledged in Romans 16:2 as Paul's benefactor (προστάτις). Inscriptional evidence in Asia Minor provides ample indication that elite women served as patrons in civic contexts. A second-century inscription from a synagogue in the city of Smyrna hails the Jewish woman Rufina as a patron.[9] Examples such as these show that Luke's mention of women financially supporting Jesus

---

7. Amy-Jill Levine argues that the women were likely homebound supporters rather than unchaperoned itinerants. See "Women, Itineracy and the Criteria of Authenticity in John Meier's *Marginal Jew*," in *The Figure of Jesus in History and Theology: Essays in Honor of John Meier*, ed. Vincent Skemp and Kelley Coblentz-Bautch, CBQ Imprints (Washington, DC: CBA, 2020), 90–113.

8. John P. Meier, *A Marginal Jew: Rethinking the Historical Jesus*, vol. 3: *Companions and Competitors*, ABRL (New York: Doubleday, 2001), 76. Meier stresses that the shock lies in the fact that the women are assumed to be unchaperoned.

9. For recent work on women patrons, see Katherine Bain, *Women's Socioeconomic Status and Religious Leadership in Asia Minor in the First Two Centuries C.E.* (Minneapolis: Fortress, 2014); Carolyn Osiek, "Women Patrons in the Life of House Churches," in *A Woman's Place: House Churches in Earliest Christianity*, by Carolyn Osiek, Margaret Y. MacDonald, with Janet H. Tulloch (Minneapolis: Fortress, 2006), 194–219.

and the Twelve, independently from male relatives or guardians, would not set off alarm bells for Theophilus.[10]

While women's unchaperoned travel would have been regarded as scandalous in the ancient Roman world, Luke seems unconcerned to defend his protagonists here, or elsewhere, from any accusation that they have violated this particular social norm. This is most clear in the (unaccompanied?) travel Mary makes from Nazareth to visit Elizabeth in the hill country of Judea (1:39), a trip that would have been a four-days' journey by foot. While travel is the necessary means by which the movement spreads in Luke and Acts from the Galilee to Jerusalem and then on to Rome, Luke seems to have little concern for verisimilitude, that is, for making the travel scenes "realistic."[11] That Luke does not explicitly defend the practice of women traveling along with the men in 8:1-3 could mean that he expects his readers to understand that these were uncontroversial "day trips from home bases."[12] Alternately, the logistics of traveling the Galilee, and the implications of invoking a mixed-gender group following Jesus in those travels, might not have been a concern to him or his first readers.

10. These women may be categorized in Luke–Acts within a considerable line-up of the well-to-do supporters, including Zacchaeus (Luke 19:1-10); Barnabas (Acts 4:36-37); a eunuch with oversight of the treasury of the queen of the Ethiopians (Acts 8:27); Mary, the mother of John Mark, who had a house large enough to host the disciples in Jerusalem (Acts 12:12); Lydia, a dealer in luxury items (Acts 16:14); prominent women in Thessalonica (Acts 17:4); influential Greek women and men in Beroea (Acts 17:12); Prisca and Aquila, who hosted Paul in Corinth (Acts 18:1-11) and who had the means to travel with Paul to Ephesus to establish a new mission base there (Acts 18:18-28).

11. John S. Kloppenborg observes: "[Luke's] opening representations of Mary's apparently uncomplicated travel to Judaea to visit Elizabeth, and then Jesus' family trips from Nazareth to Jerusalem and back are in striking contrast to the realities of life in premodern villages, where it is hardly unusual to find large portions of the inhabitants not having travelled more than a few kilometers from their village during an entire lifetime. Yet Luke treats movement—of Mary, Jesus, the apostles, and Paul—as unproblematic and 'normal.' This says more about Luke's social location than it does about the family of Jesus" ("Luke's Geography: Knowledge, Ignorance, Sources, and Spatial Conception," in *Luke on Jesus, Paul, and Christianity: What Did He Really Know?*, ed. Joseph Verheyden and John S. Kloppenborg, BTS 29 [Leuven: Peeters, 2017], 101–43, here 136). We add that this says more about the author's social location than it does about the first followers of Jesus.

12. Jane D. Schaberg and Sharon H. Ringe, "Gospel of Luke," in *Women's Bible Commentary*, ed. Carol A. Newsom, Sharon H. Ringe, and Jacqueline E. Lapsley, 3rd ed. (Louisville: Westminster John Knox, 2012), 506.

Mary, Joanna, Susanna

Like his Synoptic counterparts Luke singles out three women by name with Mary Magdalene leading the list. Along with Mary, Luke notes Joanna, the wife of a steward in the court of Herod Antipas, and Susanna.[13] The fact that named women are grouped in lists of three at several points in gospel tradition may simply be a product of popular narration. In folklore, fables, and jokes, groupings of three are common. The three women may function as counterparts to the three male disciples who seem to comprise an inner circle—Peter, John, and James (8:51; 9:28; cf. Gal 2:9)—but the fact that the three female names do not stabilize shows that recognition does not coalesce for the women as it does for the men. The importance of Peter, James, and John comes to be firmly established in developing Christian tradition, both in canonical and extracanonical materials.[14] No comparable traditions survive for most of the women in these lists of three. Joanna, Susanna, Salome, the mother of the sons of Zebedee, and Mary wife of Clopas leave virtually no trace in Christian memory. Mary the mother of Jesus, of course, has a long and complex tradition history (see commentary on chaps. 1 and 2). We analyze in detail below the one additional woman in these lists who features significantly in developing Christian tradition, Mary Magdalene. But first, we consider the question related to all of the women here, including Mary: what significance attaches to their healing from evil spirits?

13. A different grouping of three women is featured in Luke's resurrection scene—Mary Magdalene, Joanna, and Mary the mother of James (24:10). The Gospel of Mark places Mary Magdalene, Mary the mother of James and Joses, and Salome both at the cross and the tomb (15:40; 16:1). Matthew counts Mary Magdalene, Mary the mother of James and Joseph, and the mother of the sons of Zebedee (James and John) at the cross (27:26). The Fourth Gospel names Mary the mother, Mary's sister, Mary (wife of Clopas), and Mary Magdalene and places them near the cross with the Beloved Disciple (John 19:25-27). The variation among the lists is reduced if we recognize the mother of James and Joses (Mark 15:40, 16:1), and mother of James (Luke 24:10), the mother of James and Joseph (Matt 27:26) as Mary the mother of Jesus (cf. the names of Jesus's brothers given at Mark 6:3)

14. For example, the following literary sources are associated with *Peter*: Acts 1–15, the epistles of 1 and 2 Peter, the Acts of Peter, the Apocalypse of Peter, the Pseudo-Clementine Homilies; with *James*: Acts 15, 21, the epistle of James, Hegesippus (the martyrdom of James), the Pseudo-Clementine Homilies; with *John*: the Gospel of John, the epistles 1, 2, 3 John, the Acts of John. John of Patmos also comes to be associated with John the Apostle.

The Women and Their Demons

Luke is rife with stories of exorcising demons. Typically, Jesus is depicted as the exorcist in chief (8:26-39; 9:37-43; 11:14), though exorcists outside of the Jesus group are acknowledged (9:49). The seventy-two sent out in mission return to Jesus rejoicing in their own exorcising abilities (10:17). While sometimes interactions with demons are depicted in language of the battlefield and outmuscling an aggressive opponent (see commentary on 10:1–20; 11:14-23; 22:31-32), the primary mode of demonic presence in Luke is bodily invasion.[15]

Though Luke does not explicitly name Jesus as the one who has exorcised the demons from the women in 8:2-3, context suggests that he, rather than an anonymous exorcist, is responsible for the healing. The structure of the sentence makes it unclear whether the healed include only the named women (Mary Magdalene, Joanna, and Susanna) or the named women along with "the many others." Given Luke's penchant to denigrate women in the movement, this passage may well be a broad brushstroke, painting *all* of the women connected to the Galilean ministry as having once been possessed of demons.

Understanding how bodily penetration maps onto Roman hierarchies of gender and sexuality helps to clarify the implications of demon possession in Luke in general and of this story of the women Jesus has healed of evil spirits in particular.[16] Ancient Roman ideas of gender and sexuality were organized around the binaries of active-passive, penetrator-penetrated. These binaries, which obtained both in the symbolic realm and in the realm of physical sexual encounters, coded active and penetrating agents as masculine, and passive and receiving subjects as feminine. Moreover, these binaries were understood neither as permanently fixed nor as rigidly correlated with one's gender assignment at birth. Masculinity was the

---

15. Loren T. Stuckenbruck, *The Myth of Rebellious Angels: Studies in Second Temple Judaism and New Testament Texts* (Tübingen: Mohr Siebeck, 2014), 174–75, proposes that New Testament literature stands out both from Jewish sources predating it and from Greco-Roman sources in general by depicting corporal indwelling, rather than attack, as the primary mode of demonic activity. Shelly's own work on the Gospel of Luke suggests demonic attack also features in this gospel. See comments on Luke 10, 11, and 22.

16. This section is drawn largely from Shelly Matthews, "'I Have Prayed for You . . . Strengthen Your Brothers' (Luke 22:32): Jesus's Proleptic Prayer for Peter and Other Gendered Tropes in Luke's War on Satan," in *Petitioners, Penitents, and Poets: On Prayer and Praying in Second Temple Judaism*, ed. Timothy J. Sandoval and Ariel Feldman, BZAW 524 (Berlin: de Gruyter, 2020), 231–46.

measure of humanity, but it was not merely given to all possessing male genitalia. Rather, it was a prized possession that had to be earned and for which elite males continually strove. Slaves, the weak, the morally undisciplined, and even elite males deemed to have failed at the contest for the masculine prize were denigrated as feminine and perceived as ideal targets of penetration.[17]

Because ancients assigned gender and sexuality according to questions of insertion and reception, it is not surprising to find stories of women's bodily penetration by demons explicitly described as sexual penetration. The Acts of Thomas (third century CE) describes the demonic penetration of a woman drawn to the teachings of Thomas in these terms. The woman testifies:

> In that night he [the demon] came in to me and made me share in his foul intercourse. . . . According to his wont, he came at night and abused me. . . . I have been tormented by him for five years, and he has not departed from me. (Acts Thom. 43 [Elliott])

Note here that bodily penetration by the demon is described as a repeated rape. The woman is forcibly made to share "in his foul intercourse" by night. Another example of the conceptual association of demonic invasion with sexual penetration is the temptation of Eve by Satan, which is widely assumed in writings from this time period to be a form of sexual "seduction" (*Life of Adam and Eve* 9–11; 4 Macc 18:7-8; 2 En. 31:6; 2 Cor 11:3). Luke does not explicitly say that those experiencing bodily penetration by demons are sexually violated. But readers attuned to this logic could have made this connection readily. Indeed, the conceptual overlap between the shame of sexual violation and corporeal inhabitation by demons might help to explain what comes to be a pervasive tradition in early Christianity and beyond, that Mary Magdalene, once possessed of seven demons, was a prostitute (see commentary below).

---

17. Maud Gleason, *Making Men: Sophists and Self-Presentation in Ancient Rome* (Princeton: Princeton University Press, 1995); Colleen M. Conway, *Behold the Man: Jesus and Greco-Roman Masculinity* (Oxford: Oxford University Press, 2008). Elite women could be coded as possessing masculine traits (See Philo, *Embassy* 319–20, on the maleness of the empress Livia's "reasoning power"). Because of the centrality of penetration to the sexual act for ancient Greek and Latin authors, those who imagined female homoeroticism invariably assume a "phallus-like appendage" has to have been involved. See Bernadette J. Brooten, *Love Between Women: Early Christian Responses to Female Homoeroticism* (Chicago: University of Chicago Press, 1996), 6–8, 54, 152–54.

Another assumption within ancient demonology is that those who have been penetrated by demons are vulnerable to a demon's reentry.[18] This threat is made explicit in the Acts of Thomas when, after Thomas compels the demon to leave the woman he has inhabited, the demon warns:

> Remain in peace since you have taken refuge with one greater than I. I will go away, and seek one like you; and if I find her not, I shall return again to you. (Acts Thom. 46 [Elliott])[19]

The idea that one who has been exorcized is vulnerable to repossession is expressed also in Luke 11:24-26, an ominous threat that a demon once expelled will return to inhabit that body, bringing seven more demons along. Since Luke 11:24-26 is the only passage in the gospel to speak of seven demons after 8:2, readers might remember Mary when they come upon this ominous threat (see commentary on 11:24-26).

These assumptions concerning ancient demonology shed light on the claim in 8:2-3 that (all of?) the women in the group with Jesus had been cured of evil spirits. Readers who share this general understanding of the vulnerability of those once possessed might assume that these women mentioned in 8:1-3 are damaged goods, susceptible to a demon's reentry. This vulnerability is most pronounced in the case of Mary Magdalene, singled out as having been possessed by no fewer than seven demons, a condition of grave depravity. Luke 8:2, along with the Markan appendix, 16:9, a late addition to Mark that draws on Luke 8:2, are the earliest sources for this tradition that Mary Magdalene was penetrated by seven demons before she is healed by Jesus. No other passages in the New Testament, or in the early Christian materials commonly categorized as gnostic that feature Mary, assert that Mary was a demoniac before Jesus healed her. Against scholars such as John Meier who find in this story of Mary's possession a kernel of historical truth, we side with Jane

---

18. Both Loren Stuckenbruck (*The Myth of Rebellious Angels*, 181–85) and Joel Marcus ("The Beelzebul Controversy and the Eschatologies of Jesus," in *Authenticating the Activities of Jesus*, ed. Bruce Chilton and Craig A. Evans [Leiden: Brill, 1999], 247–77) note that exorcism is typically a matter of relocation, rather than of the destruction of demons, and that bodies once inhabited by a demon or demons are thus vulnerable to a repossession.

19. As the story continues, the woman begs the apostle to "give her the seal," which she understands as apotropaic, that is, as preventing the demon from entering her again (Acts Thom. 49).

Schaberg, who sees here not historical reminiscence but rhetorical character defamation.[20]

Excavating Migdal/Reconstructing Mary

Throughout the gospels, Mary is identified with the city Magdala, a name that derives from the Hebrew word מגדל, *migdal*, "tower." Located on the northwest corner of the Sea of Galilee, Magdala was known for its processing of fish by salting, thus the Greek name of the village: Tarichaea ("salted fish"). It was destroyed in 67 CE by Vespasian during the First Jewish Revolt.

In 2004, when Jane Schaberg published her landmark work on Mary Magdalene, *The Resurrection of Mary Magdalene*, Midgal was a site neglected by archaeologists, a "place of high walls and weeds." Ever rueful that Peter, who infamously betrayed Jesus, fared so much better in Christian reception than Mary, who stayed with Jesus to the end and "who did not cease to love the dead,"[21] Schaberg used the neglected site of Migdal as an entry point for a feminist reflection on archaeology, place, and the historical reconstruction of women. Wanting an excavation at Migdal that was less androcentric than the excavation at Capernaum devoted to Peter, she invoked a feminist social archaeology and imagined an expansive village scene:

> The streets and buildings, the promenade and shops filled with women and children and men, the elderly and the young, wealthy and the poor, the marginal and respected. . . . a garden . . . and . . . a place to sit and commune with ghosts, to consider the dominance of male interests, and the agency of women and wo/men. . . . In this artistic and intellectual community all are at table, in the discussion.[22]

In 2006, the Legion of Christ acquired land in Magdala and have constructed a pilgrim house and guest center. Extensive archaeological excavations at the site have revealed important finds from the first-century town, including a synagogue and a structure with several mikvahs.[23]

---

20. See Jane Schaberg, *The Resurrection of Mary Magdalene: Legends, Apocrypha, and the Christian Testament* (New York: Continuum, 2004), 77. For more on Mary Magdalene, see commentary on Luke 24:1-12.

21. Ibid., 16.

22. Ibid., 62.

23. See https://www.magdala.org/. On the remains of a building that is being called a synagogue, see David A. Fiensy and Ralph K. Hawkins, eds., *The Galilean Economy in the Time of Jesus*, ECL 11 (Atlanta: SBL, 2013), 37–41; Jordan J. Ryan, *The Role of the Synagogue in the Aims of Jesus* (Minneapolis: Fortress, 2017).

While the site is of value to any who are interested in the archaeology of the Galilee, it is far from the feminist center for learning that Schaberg had imagined. Of the several chapels in the guest center, only one features an image of Mary Magdalene. The mosaic in this chapel does not draw from the story of John 20 to depict her as a visionary or even in her recognized role as "Apostle to the Apostles."[24] Rather, it draws from the Lukan story we have lamented here—memorializing Mary Magdalene as the woman once possessed of seven devils.

Schaberg herself had predicted that the site would be built over with a resort hotel. But she promised in her book that she would continue to visit the site and to ask historical questions of it.[25] She was firm in her conviction of the importance for doing so:

> Even though certainty always eludes us, the possibilities and the probabilities of women's historical contributions should be honored by examination, enjoyment, use, imagination; and their lack of historical contributions, where that can be shown, should be mourned and imagined. Both the contributions and the lack of contributions, and the images of contribution and of lack, have shaped how historical actors in the past and present live their lives. They shape us.[26]

Mary Magdalene in Reception History

Many myths have developed about Mary Magdalene, both laudatory and pejorative.[27] She is often confused with other gospel Marys and

24. In the early third century, Hippolytus of Rome calls the women who met the risen Christ "apostles to the apostles" in his commentary on the Song of Songs (25.6, 7). In June 2016, Pope Francis recognized this tradition and elevated the memorial of Mary Magdalene on July 22 to a feast day in the Catholic Church's liturgical calendar. Mass on that day now also includes a preface titled "Apostle of the apostles." See further commentary on Luke 24:1-12.

25. Schaberg was in the process of organizing a feminist tour of Migdal when, lamentably, she was diagnosed with a recurrence of cancer that would eventually result in her death.

26. Schaberg, *Resurrection of Mary Magdalene*, 63.

27. Many books in recent years try to unravel the myths and to reconstruct the biblical Mary Magdalene and her importance for Christianity. See, e.g., Ann Graham Brock, *Mary Magdalene, the First Apostle: The Struggle for Authority*, HTS 51 (Cambridge, MA: Harvard University Press, 2003); Esther de Boer, *Mary Magdalene: Beyond the Myth*, trans. John Bowden (Harrisburg, PA: Trinity Press International, 1997); Boer, *The Mary Magdalene Cover-Up: The Sources Behind the Myth*, trans. John Bowden (London: T&T Clark, 2007); Susan Haskins, *Mary Magdalen: Myth and Metaphor* (New York:

other unnamed women: Mary of Bethany (John 12:1-8) and the anonymous women of Mark 14:3-10 and Matthew 26:6-13 who anoint Jesus for burial, the woman who loved greatly (Luke 7:36-50), the unknown woman caught in adultery (John 7:53–8:11), and the nameless woman healed of hemorrhaging (Luke 8:43-48).[28] No gospel text makes any reference to her having been a sinner or a prostitute.[29]

Even the name "Magdalene" has come to be associated with institutions for prostitutes. Some have been as abusive toward the women as when they were trapped in the sex trade, such as the "Magdalene Laundries" or "Magdalene Asylums" in Ireland in the eighteenth to twentieth centuries. Others, like Magdalene House in Chicago, offer a place of healing for women who have survived trafficking, prostitution, addiction, and homelessness.

Mary Magdalene as a Sinful Prostitute: Connecting the Dots

The first textual evidence associating Mary Magdalene with prostitution is a sixth-century homily by Pope Gregory the Great. By several imaginative leaps, he connects the story of the woman "who was a sinner" (Luke 7:36-50) and the first mention of Mary Magdalene in Luke 8:2. The through-line involves the myrrh the woman uses to anoint Jesus's feet: for Gregory, the woman procured the myrrh through

---

Riverhead Books, 1995); Holly E. Hearon, *The Mary Magdalene Tradition: Witness and Counter-Witness in Early Christian Communities* (Collegeville, MN: Liturgical Press, 2004); Katherine Ludwig Jansen, *The Making of the Magdalen: Preaching and Popular Devotion in the Later Middle Ages* (Princeton: Princeton University Press, 2000); Karen L. King, *The Gospel of Mary of Magdala: Jesus and the First Woman Apostle* (Santa Rosa, CA: Polebridge, 2003); Marinella Perroni and Cristina Simonelli, *Mary of Magdala: Revisiting the Sources*, trans. Demetrio S. Yocum (New York: Paulist Press, 2019); Schaberg, *The Resurrection of Mary Magdalene*.

28. Some combine confusion of the various biblical characters with fanciful invention, such as Carsten and Sylvi Johnsen, *The Writing in the Sand: The Part of the Story That You Were Never Told about Mary Magdalene* (New York: Vantage, 1984).

29. See Jane Schaberg, "How Mary Magdalene Became a Whore," *BibRev* 8 (1992): 30–37, 51–52; Schaberg, "Thinking Back through Mary Magdalene," *Continuum* 1 (1991): 71–90.

selling her body. In his homily, he denigrates the woman by imagining her motives and practices before her repentance:

> She whom Luke calls the sinful woman [Luke 7:37] . . . we believe to be Mary from whom seven devils were cast out [Luke 8:2]. . . . And what did these devils signify, if not all the vices. . . . It is clear, brothers, that the woman previously used the unguent to perfume her flesh in forbidden acts. What she therefore displayed more scandalously, she was now offering to God in a more praiseworthy manner. She had coveted with earthly eyes, but now through penitence these are consumed with tears. She displayed her hair to set off her face, but now her hair dries her tears. She had spoken proud things with her mouth, but in kissing the Lord's feet, she now planted her mouth on the Redeemer's feet. For every delight, therefore, she had had in herself, she now immolated herself. She turned the mass of her crimes to virtues, in order to serve God entirely in penance, for as much as she had wrongly held God in contempt. (*Homily* 33 [PL 76:1239–40])[30]

This reception history, which waivers between ambivalence and outright hostility toward Mary Magdalene, seems to us as of a piece with the way Mary is featured in Luke 8:1-3. One way to counter this history is through consideration of alternate ancient sources. These include both the story of Mary as first witness to the resurrection in John 20:1-18 and the many extracanonical sources commonly categorized as gnostic that suggest Mary's prominence. Among these, the Gospel of Mary holds a place of particular interest (see our commentary on Luke 24). All of these sources require reading with a feminist lens, one that incorporates suspicion and the willingness to read against the grain. But they allow us to counter Luke's image of a woman who came to the movement in a state of severe debilitation, plagued by the seven demons.

---

30. Cited in Schaberg, *Resurrection of Mary Magdalene*, 82.

"If Not for the Women": The Gift and Sisterhood of Women

The strength of women who bond together for a common goal or journey is striking. Stories within the Black tradition that focus on the relationships of women, such as the story of Celie and Shug in *The Color Purple*,[31] attest to how women support one another in times of trouble. What resources do women have when they come together? What power emerges from their sisterhood? What do we as women do when we come together? Womanist scholar Emilie Townes describes ways that African American women have survived in a "society based on inequalities rather than justice."[32] We stretch what we have to provide what is needed for the community. We are daughters, mothers, sisters, wives, partners, aunts, grandmothers, play mothers, godmothers, all nurturing and providing comfort to those who are challenged in their day-to-day living and experiencing those times of trouble. While we may inhabit traditional roles of preparing the meals, praying, listening, and nurturing, we are also models of strength and inner power and resource that is needed to provide for the survival of our communities.

In reading the story of the Galilean women, we encounter diverse women who came together with various needs to witness and support the

Hearing, Holding Fast, Bearing Fruit (8:4-18)

Building on the theme introduced at 4:20-30 and that reenters at 7:24-35, Jesus tells a parable about differing responses to the word of God (8:4-8), comments on the importance of acting on what one hears (8:9-15), and concludes with a saying about sharing what one hears (8:16-18).

While most parables are open-ended,[33] leaving the hearer to puzzle out the meaning, this one has an allegorical explanation (8:11-15) that focuses attention on the varying kinds of soil and their receptivity to the

31. *The Color Purple* by Alice Walker (New York: Harcourt Brace Jovanovich, 1982) won the 1983 Pulitzer Prize for Fiction and the National Book Award for Fiction. Steven Spielberg directed the 1985 film. While we admire Walker's contributions to womanist scholarship, we lament her anti-Semitic stances. See Alexandra Alter, "Alice Walker, Answering Backlash, Praises Anti-Semitic Author as 'Brave,' " *New York Times*, December 21, 2018, https://www.nytimes.com/2018/12/21/arts/alice-walker-david-icke-times.html.

32. Emilie Townes, *In a Blaze of Glory: Womanist Spirituality as Social Witness* (Nashville: Abingdon, 1995), 10.

33. On the dynamics of parables, see above at 5:36.

ministry of Jesus. Not only were Mary Magdalene, Joanna, and Susanna mentioned by name but the text clearly states there were many others. Who were these other women? Were they women with families? Were they single women or widowed? While their voices may not have been heard or remembered, their presence was felt in the fact that they are mentioned four times, first in this text and later as witnesses to Jesus's death (23:49), to his burial (23:55), and to the empty tomb (24:1-10).

These women, these sisters in their everyday lives, provided resources for Jesus and the Twelve to continue in their work. While it may be assumed that some of the women were wealthy, the text does not clearly state this as fact. What does it mean to provide from their resources? What resources do women have when they come together? What power emerges from their sisterhood?

If we reflect on women today, what do we as women do when we come together? What wisdom or counsel is shared? How have women survived in a society that is based on inequalities and patriarchy in many parts of the world?

Furthermore, if we look at what women do and continue to do, we may exclaim "If not for the women, we would not have a church." If not for women and their bond of sisterhood, what would Jesus and the Twelve have been able to accomplish? Jesus and the Twelve had need of the gifts that these women provided as they moved closer to Jerusalem and what awaited Jesus there. He had need of the special sisterhood of women that offered their strength and resources. These very women remained committed and stayed with Jesus when many of the Twelve deserted him. Yes, if not for the women![34]

C. Vanessa White

seed (identified as the word of God in 8:11). The stress is on the importance of not only listening to and responding positively to the word (8:8) but also a disciplined cultivation of a life of discipleship that bears fruit. Deep roots are needed beyond an initial superficial joyous acceptance.

From an ecofeminist perspective, the fruitfulness of the divine word is closely linked with the fertility of Earth, not only in the gospels, but also in the Old Testament.[35] At creation, for example, God's word brings forth every kind of vegetation, plants yielding seed of every kind and

34. See Cheryl Townsend Gilkes, *If It Wasn't for the Women: Black Women's Experience and Womanist Culture in Church and Community* (Maryknoll, NY: Orbis Books, 2001).
35. The following insights are from Anne F. Elvey, *An Ecological Feminist Reading of the Gospel of Luke: A Gestational Paradigm* (Lewiston, NY: Edwin Mellen, 2005), 160–63.

⁴When a great crowd gathered and people from town after town came to him, he said in a parable: ⁵"A sower went out to sow his seed; and as he sowed, some fell on the path and was trampled on, and the birds of the air ate it up. ⁶Some fell on the rock; and as it grew up, it withered for lack of moisture. ⁷Some fell among thorns, and the thorns grew with it and choked it. ⁸Some fell into good soil, and when it grew, it produced a hundredfold." As he said this, he called out, "Let anyone with ears to hear listen!"

⁹Then his disciples asked him what this parable meant. ¹⁰He said, "To you it has been given to know the secrets of the kingdom of God; but to others I speak in parables, so that

'looking they may not perceive,
   and listening they may not
      understand.'

¹¹"Now the parable is this: The seed is the word of God. ¹²The ones on the

bearing every kind of fruit (Gen 1:11-12). Isaiah links the fruitfulness of the watered Earth, singing mountains, and clapping trees with the effectiveness of God's word in rehabilitating the people (Isa 55:10-13). Similarly, Luke characterizes the efficacious divine word as good and fruitful earth (8:15). Holding the word fast with patient endurance before bearing fruit (8:15) is a multilayered image: Earth keeps the seed within, giving it time to sprout, grow, and produce fruit, just as Mary does with the word (2:19, 51) and the blessed fruit of her womb (1:42). Disciples, similarly, are to nurture the word with rhythms akin to Earth. Something to resist is Luke's characterization of Earth in four different levels of receptivity, implying that "Earth ought to be universally fertile, or alternatively, as if a failure of fertility—because of the diversity of the Earth Community (which includes rocks and thorns and weeds)—is improper."[36]

Between the parable (8:4-8) and its interpretation (8:9-15) Jesus explains to his disciples why some heed his word and some do not. From a worldview in which God causes everything that happens, the disciples' ability to understand the mysteries (μυστήρια, 8:10, NRSV: "secrets") of the *basileia* of God is a divine gift (the passive "has been given" is a circumlocution that indicates God is the giver). To explain why others do not understand, Jesus quotes Isaiah 6:9, aligning himself with the prophet[37] whose mission it was to warn Israel to heed the word of God

---

36. Ibid., 161.
37. As also at 4:18, when Jesus uses Isa 61:1 to announce his mission.

Luke 8:4-18 (cont.)

path are those who have heard; then the devil comes and takes away the word from their hearts, so that they may not believe and be saved. ¹³The ones on the rock are those who, when they hear the word, receive it with joy. But these have no root; they believe only for a while and in a time of testing fall away. ¹⁴As for what fell among the thorns, these are the ones who hear; but as they go on their way, they are choked by the cares and riches and pleasures of life, and their fruit does not mature. ¹⁵But as for that in the good soil, these are the ones who, when they hear the word, hold it fast in an honest and good heart, and bear fruit with patient endurance.

¹⁶"No one after lighting a lamp hides it under a jar, or puts it under a bed, but puts it on a lampstand, so that those who enter may see the light. ¹⁷For nothing is hidden that will not be disclosed, nor is anything secret that will not become known and come to light. ¹⁸Then pay attention to how you listen; for to those who have, more will be given; and from those who do not have, even what they seem to have will be taken away."

and to "turn and be healed" (Isa 6:10). Both Isaiah's and Jesus's preaching result[38] in some people refusing to see and hear. It is not that Jesus speaks in parables to keep people from understanding or that God has given the gift to only a select few (the sower in the parable scatters the seed on all kinds of soil), but people's own unwillingness prevents them from hearing and heeding. The disciples do not understand everything at once about Jesus and the *basileia*; it is only gradually revealed (8:17). Especially hidden is the meaning of Jesus's passion and death; the disciples do not understand (9:45; 18:34) until after the resurrection (24:27; Acts 1:3).

In the gospel, the sower of the word is Jesus, but in a postresurrection context, disciples take up this role and illumine others (8:16). In Luke's view, however, only male disciples need apply. Peter and Paul are the main sowers of the word in Acts; Paul even uses the same quotation from Isaiah 6:9 when some to whom he preaches are convinced and others refuse to believe (Acts 28:26-27).[39] Other sowers of the word in Acts are Philip (8:4-40; 21:8), John (4:1-22; 8:25), some men of Cyprus and Cyrene (11:20), and Barnabas (13:13–14:28). Luke's prejudice against

---

38. The conjunction ἵνα, "so that" (8:10), has a consecutive sense, i.e., "with the result that," rather than purpose.

39. Luke's final pronouncement is that "this salvation of God has been sent to the Gentiles; they will listen" (Acts 28:28).

female sowers of the word is still deeply implanted in many Christians. Feminist preachers, teachers, and biblical scholars experience resistance and worse.[40]

Jesus's Mother and Sisters and Brothers (8:19-21)

By placing these verses about Jesus's family after the parable (in Mark and Matthew they come before), Luke softens the distinction between his new family of disciples and his blood kin, even allowing that his mother (who was already shown to be a model of hearing and acting on the word in chaps. 1–2) and siblings[41] exemplify those who hear the word of God and put it into practice.[42]

This is the only mention of Jesus's siblings[43] in the gospel; they, along with Mary, reappear in Acts 1:14, where they are in Jerusalem, praying with the Eleven and some of the women. It is likely Luke intends only male siblings with the masculine plural ἀδελφοί (NRSV: "brothers") in 8:19-21. When he wants to include sisters, he does so explicitly, as at 14:26 where Jesus tells a crowd, "Whoever comes to me and does not hate father and mother, wife and children, brothers and sisters [τοὺς ἀδελφοὺς καὶ τὰς ἀδελφάς], yes, and even life itself, cannot be my disciple." Luke commends women disciples for hearing the word (10:38-42), but for him, their way of acting on it differs from men (see comments on Luke's treatment of women in the authors' introduction).

Who Is This? (8:22-25)

The remainder of this chapter shows Jesus's authority over nature, demonic spirits, illness, and death. The first episode ends with the question "Who is this?" (8:25), one that is initially voiced by the scribes and

40. See examples in the excursus in chap. 1: "Jane Schaberg, The Illegitimacy of Jesus, Feminist Courage, Patriarchal Backlash" and further comments at 24:1-10.

41. See excursus at 2:7: "Jesus: The Only Child of a Perpetual Virgin or a Boy with Siblings?"

42. By contrast, Mark draws a sharp distinction between Jesus's blood relations, who remain outside, while the disciples around him are his new family (Mark 3:21, 31-35). Luke also eliminates the motive for Jesus's family seeking to see him; in Mark, they were trying to restrain him, thinking he had gone out of his mind (3:21).

43. Unlike Mark (6:3) and Matthew (13:55), Luke never names Jesus's siblings, save James, Jesus's brother (Gal 1:19), who becomes the leader of the community of believers in Jerusalem (Acts 12:17; 15:13; 21:18). Mark and Matthew also note Jesus's sisters but do not give their names.

[19]Then his mother and his brothers came to him, but they could not reach him because of the crowd. [20]And he was told, "Your mother and your brothers are standing outside, wanting to see you." [21]But he said to them, "My mother and my brothers are those who hear the word of God and do it."

[22]One day he got into a boat with his disciples, and he said to them, "Let us go across to the other side of the lake." So they put out, [23]and while they were sailing he fell asleep. A windstorm swept down on the lake, and the boat was filling with water, and they were in danger. [24]They went to him and woke him up, shouting, "Master, Master, we are perishing!" And he woke up and rebuked the wind and the raging waves; they ceased, and there was a calm. [25]He said to them, "Where is your faith?" They were afraid and amazed, and said to one another, "Who then is this, that he commands even the winds and the water, and they obey him?"

Pharisees (5:21), then by Simon's guests (7:49), and finally by Herod (9:9). Luke starts to answer the question in 8:22-25 when the episode is read in light of texts such as Psalm 107:29 that acclaim God who "made the storm be still, and the waves of the sea were hushed" (similarly Pss 65:7; 89:9). The answer comes more fully at 9:20, where Peter declares Jesus to be "the Messiah of God."

From an ecofeminist perspective, Jesus's mastery over nature raises concerns about what that communicates to his followers in terms of our relationship to the rest of the cosmos. While the parable in 8:4-15 bespeaks a symbiotic relationship between nature and human beings, 8:22-25 emphasizes Jesus's control over the wind and sea. Jesus promises this same ability to conquer nature to his apostles, saying that if they had faith the size of a mustard seed, they could say to a mulberry tree, "Be uprooted and planted in the sea," and it would obey them (17:6). In an age when there is heightened awareness of the disastrous effects of the exploitation of Earth and its resources by human beings, 8:22-25 can prompt reflection on how to understand all life in the cosmos as interrelated and interdependent and to read our texts and our lives from the point of view of the whole creation rather than from our human perspective alone.[44]

44. Theodore Hiebert, "Rethinking Dominion Theology," *Direction* 25 (Fall, 1996): 16–25. See also Elizabeth A. Johnson, *Ask the Beasts: Darwin and the God of Love* (London: Bloomsbury, 2014).

Returning the Homeless One to His Home (8:26-39)

Jesus and his disciples arrive at the eastern side of the lake, in Gentile territory,[45] where they encounter a demon-possessed man. The man's situation is abject.[46] On the one hand, he is bereft of the basic elements of human civilization—possessing neither clothing nor shelter, alternating between the spaces of the graveyard and the wilderness. On the other hand, humans watch over him, subjecting him to harsh disciplinary measures. While the agents policing him are unnamed, we are told that he is guarded (φυλασσόμενος, v. 29) and bound in chains and shackles (ἐδεσμεύετο ἁλύσεσιν καὶ πέδαις, v. 29).

In our own time, stories of persons deprived of basic human necessities while subject to punitive disciplinary measures bring to mind scenes of torture and neglect by imperialist invaders, rogue actors, or insensitive bureaucrats—Abu Ghraib, a detention center for undocumented immigrants, or a mismanaged institution for the mentally ill. In Luke, the torment owes to demon possession.

The depiction of demons as invading human bodies and subjecting those bodies to torture features prominently in the Synoptic Gospels.[47] The story assumes common features of ancient demonology: the demons are bodiless, parasitic on the bodies of other living beings, and fearful of being deprived of an embodied host.[48] The exchange between the demons and Jesus is both vivid and strange. The demons negotiate an exit strategy, pleading not to be sent back into the abyss (ἄβυσσον, 8:30), the abode of the dead (Ps 107:26; Rom 10:7). At first glance, Jesus seems to oblige them by granting them permission to enter a large herd of pigs (8:32). But, given that the swine then plunge into the lake and drown, they land in a watery grave, without a bodily host in short order (8:33).

Because the demon is named "Legion," a word for a Roman military unit, interpreters often see an anti-Roman polemic: Jesus's exorcism of the demon reflects the desire of an occupied territory to be freed from

---

45. On the confusion concerning the location, see Kloppenborg, "Luke's Geography," 105–6.

46. Sharon H. Ringe (*Luke*, Westminster Bible Companion [Louisville: Westminster John Knox, 1995], 120) observes, "The story is marked by such grotesque and fantastic descriptions that it is like a caricature drawn in primary colors."

47. For further discussion of bodily invasion by demons in Luke, see commentary on 8:1-3; 9:37-43; 11:14-26, 22:1-6, 31-32.

48. For an introduction to demonology in extracanonical texts of Second Temple Judaism, see Stuckenbruck, *The Myth of Rebellious Angels*.

Luke 8:26-39

[26]Then they arrived at the country of the Gerasenes which is opposite Galilee. [27]As he stepped out on land, a man of the city who had demons met him. For a long time he had worn no clothes, and he did not live in a house but in the tombs. [28]When he saw Jesus, he fell down before him and shouted at the top of his voice, "What have you to do with me, Jesus, Son of the Most High God? I beg you, do not torment me"—[29]for Jesus had commanded the unclean spirit to come out of the man. (For many times it had seized him; he was kept under guard and bound with chains and shackles, but he would break the bonds and be driven by the demon into the wilds.) [30]Jesus then asked him, "What is your name?" He said, "Legion"; for many demons had entered him. [31]They begged him not to order them to go back into the abyss.

[32]Now there on the hillside a large herd of swine was feeding; and the demons begged Jesus to let them enter these. So he gave them permission. [33]Then the demons came out of the man and entered the swine, and the

its oppressors.[49] But a number of considerations cast doubt on this interpretation, including the fact that the story is not set in the province of Judea (there are no Roman legions in Galilee), and that the people from the surrounding territory do not celebrate the healing as a sign of their release from oppression. Instead, they ask Jesus to leave. Furthermore, especially in the case of the Lukan version, it is difficult to square an "anti-Roman military" reading of this pericope with the multiple instances in which Luke casts the Roman military in a positive light.[50]

A better understanding of how a demon-possessed man might come to the name "Legion" for the occupiers of his body is to recognize how frequently demonic possession is described in terms of military warfare.

49. Scholars taking up this interpretation typically focus on the Markan version of the story. See, e.g., Richard A. Horsely, *Jesus and Empire: The Kingdom of God and the New World Disorder* (Minneapolis: Fortress, 2003), 100–103; Brian J. Incigneri, *The Gospel to the Romans: The Setting and Rhetoric of Mark's Gospel*, BibInt 65 (Leiden: Brill, 2003), 190–94; Hans Leander, *Discourses of Empire: The Gospel of Mark from a Postcolonial Perspective*, SemeiaSt 71 (Atlanta: SBL, 2013), 201–19.

50. See our commentary on Luke 7:1-10; Laurie Brink, *Soldiers in Luke–Acts*, WUNT 2.362 (Tübingen: Mohr Siebeck, 2014); Alexander Kyrychenko, *The Roman Army and the Expansion of the Gospel: The Role of the Centurion in Luke–Acts*, BZNW 203 (Berlin: DeGruyter, 2014). On this particular passage, see Christopher Zeichmann, *The Roman Army and the New Testament* (Lanham, MD: Lexington Books/Fortress Academic, 2018), 50–57, 79.

herd rushed down the steep bank into the lake and was drowned.

³⁴When the swineherds saw what had happened, they ran off and told it in the city and in the country. ³⁵Then people came out to see what had happened, and when they came to Jesus, they found the man from whom the demons had gone sitting at the feet of Jesus, clothed and in his right mind. And they were afraid. ³⁶Those who had seen it told them how the one who had been possessed by demons had been healed. ³⁷Then all the people of the surrounding country of the Gerasenes asked Jesus to leave them; for they were seized with great fear. So he got into the boat and returned. ³⁸The man from whom the demons had gone begged that he might be with him; but Jesus sent him away, saying, ³⁹"Return to your home, and declare how much God has done for you." So he went away, proclaiming throughout the city how much Jesus had done for him.

Consider, for example, the saying concerning the binding of the strong man, which Luke casts in the language of battle (see commentary on Luke 11:14-22), or the way the mission of the seventy to heal and exorcise is couched in military terms (see commentary on 10:17-19). To name the demons "Legion" is to describe one's possession as akin to being in the grip of Satan's army. In contrast to readings that see here anti-Roman polemic, this reading "compares the demons to the Roman army, and not vice versa." Such a reading "attends to the way in which the civilians' experience of the military was internalized and became a part of their conception of related matters—power-by-proxy and cosmic dualism. . . . [R]ather than a face-to-face encounter between God and Satan, Jesus engages Satan's demonic subordinates taking the form of Legion."[51] In this pericope, as in all Lukan passages where Jesus directly engages the demons, he prevails as the stronger one.

From our feminist perspective, we read with some ambivalence. The dead pigs inject a macabre element into the scene. Their destruction seems a needless loss of animal life.[52] We are puzzled by Jesus's role in

---

51. Zeichmann, *The Roman Army*, 55–56.
52. For a feminist analysis of the Markan version of the pericope in terms of the phenomenon of mass suicide as political protest in India, see Sharon Jacob, "Jauhar, Mass-Suicide, and the Spectacle of Death: A Reading of Mark 5:1-20," *FSR* (blog), February 12, 2020, https://www.fsrinc.org/jauhar-mass-suicide-and-the-spectacle-of-death-a-reading-of-mark-51-20/.

this killing. Furthermore, though we abhor practices of isolation and restraint such as those endured by the tormented man in this pericope, we do not operate with a worldview in which such torments owe to the machinations of demonic agents from an otherworldly realm. While these features complicate our search for a saving proclamation in the pericope, we affirm this overarching message: Jesus is concerned to heal even the most tormented and socially ostracized human beings from their misery, to clothe the naked, to soothe the distraught (v. 35), and to bring them into human community (v. 39a: "Return to your home").

Daughters Healed and Resuscitated (8:40-56)

Two intertwined stories[53] with verbal and thematic links feature women who are restored to health: the woman who has endured an illness for twelve years and the twelve-year-old daughter of Jairus whom Jesus raises from the dead. The woman who approaches Jesus from within the crowds is nameless, introduced simply as "the woman with a flow of blood," γυνὴ οὖσα ἐν ῥύσει αἵματος. We take this affliction as key to her characterization, noting with Adele Reinhartz that the "principal effect of the absence of a proper name is to focus the reader's attention on the role designations that flood into the gap that anonymity denotes."[54] Luke does not specify the source of the blood flow, but we are led to think that it is vaginal, because the description compares closely to language concerning women with irregular vaginal flows in Leviticus 15:25 (γυνὴ ἐὰν ῥέῃ ῥύσει αἵματος ἡμέρος πλείους) as well as to language found in ancient Greek medical handbooks.[55] A further clue concerning this

---

53. Luke has essentially taken these over from Mark (5:21-43), who is known for his literary technique of intercalation, that is, interrupting one story with another and then returning to complete the first.

54. Adele Reinhartz, "Why Ask My Name?" Anonymity and Identity in Biblical Narrative (New York: Oxford University Press, 1998), 188. Cited in Susan Haber, "A Woman's Touch: Feminist Encounters with the Hemorrhaging Woman in Mark 5:24-34," JSNT 26 (2003): 171–92, esp. 173. Compare also Elaine M. Wainwright, Women Healing/Healing Women: The Genderization of Healing in Early Christianity, BibleWorld (London: Equinox, 2006), 117: "The woman is described or introduced into the narrative . . . in somatic language. She carries in her body a debilitating disease. It is almost as if she is her disease." See further comments on naming at 1:5-7.

55. Annette Weissenrieder, "The Plague of Uncleanness? The Ancient Illness Construct 'Issue of Blood' in Luke 8:43-48," in The Social Setting of Jesus and the Gospels, ed. Wolfgang Stegemann, Bruce J. Malina, and Gerd Theissen (Minneapolis: Fortress, 2002), 207–27.

Luke 8:40-56

40Now when Jesus returned, the crowd welcomed him, for they were all waiting for him. 41Just then there came a man named Jairus, a leader of the synagogue. He fell at Jesus' feet and begged him to come to his house, 42for he had an only daughter, about twelve years old, who was dying.

As he went, the crowds pressed in on him. 43Now there was a woman who had been suffering from hemorrhages for twelve years; and though she had spent all she had on physicians, no one could cure her. 44She came up behind him and touched the fringe of his clothes, and immediately her hemorrhage stopped. 45Then Jesus asked, "Who touched me?" When all denied it, Peter said, "Master, the crowds surround you and press in on you." 46But Jesus said, "Someone touched me; for I noticed that power had gone out from me." 47When the woman saw that she could not remain hidden, she came trembling; and falling down before him, she declared in the presence of all the

woman's twelve-year ailment is provided by the age of the daughter of Jairus. A twelve-year-old girl is on the brink of menarche and, according to Roman law, of marriage. The symmetry between the stories bound by the catchword "twelve" suggests that, as for the older woman whose bleeding is unceasing, the disease of Jairus's daughter that has led to her death is a womb that is closed.[56]

We consider each of the stories in turn, beginning with the bleeding woman.

Claiming Her Power for Healing

Because misunderstanding of Jewish purity laws continues to plague Christian readings of this passage, we underscore that the plight of the bleeding woman should not be interpreted as suffering due to an oppressive Jewish purity system, from which the enlightened Jesus frees her.[57] Because there is no evidence that women with irregular vaginal

56. Both Mary Rose D'Angelo ("Gender and Power in the Gospel of Mark: The Daughter of Jairus and the Woman with the Flow of Blood," in *Miracles in Jewish and Christian Antiquity: Imagining Truth*, ed. John C. Cavadini, Notre Dame Studies in Theology 3 [Notre Dame, IN: University of Notre Dame Press, 1999], 83–109, esp. 95–96), and Wainwright (*Women Healing/Healing Women*, 115–16) have marshalled the evidence of ancient medical handbooks to suggest that readers would have recognized in the case of Jairus's daughter an instance in which disease was caused by the retention of blood flow in the uterus.

57. This reading, put forth by Marla Selvidge in 1984 ("Mark 5:25-34 and Leviticus 14:19-20: A Reaction to Restrictive Purity Regulations," *JBL* 103 [1984]: 619–23), has

people why she had touched him, and how she had been immediately healed. [48]He said to her, "Daughter, your faith has made you well; go in peace."

[49]While he was still speaking, someone came from the leader's house to say, "Your daughter is dead; do not trouble the teacher any longer." [50]When Jesus heard this, he replied, "Do not fear. Only believe, and she will be saved." [51]When he came to the house, he did not allow anyone to enter with him, except Peter, John, and James, and the child's father and mother. [52]They were all weeping and wailing for her; but he said, "Do not weep; for she is not dead but sleeping." [53]And they laughed at him, knowing that she was dead. [54]But he took her by the hand and called out, "Child, get up!" [55]Her spirit returned, and she got up at once. Then he directed them to give her something to eat. [56]Her parents were astounded; but he ordered them to tell no one what had happened.

discharges were socially ostracized in Second Temple Judaism, proposals that the woman is oppressed by the community because they regard her as a pollutant are misguided. The emphasis in the story is on a physical ailment from which the woman is healed, not on an impurity from which she must be cleansed.[58]

---

been widely critiqued. See Shaye J. D. Cohen, "Menstruants and the Sacred in Judaism and Christianity," in *Women's History and Ancient History*, ed. Sarah B. Pomeroy (Chapel Hill: University of North Carolina Press, 1991), 273–99; Amy-Jill Levine, "Discharging Responsibility: Matthean Jesus, Biblical Law, and Hemorrhaging Woman," in *Treasures New and Old: Recent Contributions to Matthean Studies*, ed. David R. Bauer and Mark Alan Powell (Atlanta: Scholars Press, 1996), 379–97, reprinted in Amy-Jill Levine with Marianne Blickenstaff, eds., *A Feminist Companion to Matthew*, FCNTECW 1 (Sheffield: Sheffield Academic, 2001), 70–87; Charlotte Fonrobert, "The Woman with a Blood-Flow (Mark 5:24-34) Revisited: Menstrual Laws and Jewish Culture in Christian Feminist Hermeneutics," in *Early Christian Interpretation of the Scriptures of Israel: Investigations and Proposals*, ed. Craig A. Evans and James A. Sanders, JSNTSup 148, SSEJC 5 (Sheffield: Sheffield Academic, 1997), 121–40; Haber, "A Woman's Touch"; D'Angelo, "Gender and Power."

In spite of the many persuasive arguments that this story is not about Jewish purity laws and the plight of a "polluted" woman, the inaccurate assumption persists. See, for example, David F. Watson, "Luke–Acts," in *The Bible and Disability: A Commentary*, ed. Sarah J. Melcher, Mikeal C. Parsons, and Amos Yong, Studies in Religion, Theology, and Disability (Waco, TX: Baylor University Press, 2017), 303–32, esp. 313–14.

58. Contrast, for instance, the story of the healing of the man with leprosy, Luke 5:12-14, where the language of cleansing is used and Jesus instructs the man to make an offering in the temple because of the cleansing.

Vaginal Blood, Front and Center

Ancient medical handbooks include discussions of both menstruation and irregular blood flows, and a wide range of Greek and Roman authors with interest in science, magic, and/or medicine indicate awareness of the purported qualities of vaginal blood.[59] Still, these accounts in the Synoptic Gospels stand out as rare instances in ancient *narrative* in which a bleeding woman appears as a sympathetic character.[60]

Consider first the positive characterization of the woman in Mark.[61] Because she, and not Jesus, initiates the transfer of power by reaching out and touching his garment, we may regard her as an agent of her own healing. The Gospel of Mark enhances this characterization of the woman by drawing attention to her self-awareness in three passages. First, the woman explains her motivation through direct speech (presumably to herself): "If I but touch his clothes, I will be made well" (Mark 5:28). Further, Mark mentions the woman's awareness of the healing: "she recognized in her body that she was healed of her disease." Finally, her self-awareness is stressed again in Mark's version at 5:33, where she comes to kneel before Jesus, "knowing what had happened to her."

Focusing on the woman's agency and self-awareness in Mark's version, both Elaine Wainwright and Mary Rose D'Angelo have suggested that this story bespeaks a healing practice in the ancient *basileia*

59. See, for instance, Hippocrates, *Diseases of Women*; Soranus, *Gynecology* 1.6; 3.40–42, and discussions in D'Angelo, "Gender and Power," 85–96; Wainwright, *Women Healing/Healing Women*, 112–23.

60. For an additional instance of ancient narrative, beyond the gospels, that features discussion of women's menses, consider the novel by Achilles Tatius, *Leucippe and Clitophon* 4.7, in which the heroine makes excuses that she is unable to have sex with her captor because she is menstruating.

61. Much feminist analysis of this story has focused on Mark's version, which contains the fullest characterization of this woman. Haber, "A Woman's Touch"; D'Angelo, "Gender and Power"; Wainwright, *Women Healing/Healing Women*; Musa W. Dube, "Fifty Years of Bleeding: A Storytelling Feminist Reading of Mark 5:24-43," in *Other Ways of Reading: African Women and the Bible*, ed. Musa W. Dube (Atlanta: SBL, 2001), 11–17; Wendy Cotter, "Mark's Hero of the Twelfth-Year Miracles: The Healing of the Woman with the Hemorrhage and the Raising of Jairus's Daughter (Mk 5:21–43)," in *A Feminist Companion to Mark*, ed. Amy-Jill Levine with Marianne Blickenstaff, FCNTECW 2 (Sheffield: Sheffield Academic, 2001), 54–78; Brigitte Kahl, "Jairus und die verlorenen Töchter Israels: Sozioliterarische Überlegungen zum Problem der Grenzüberschreitung in Mk 5, 21–43," in *Von der Wurzel getragen: Christlich-feministische Exegese in Auseinandersetzung mit Antijudaismus*, ed. Luise Schottroff and Marie-Theres Wacker, BibInt 17 (Leiden: Brill, 1996), 61–78.

movement that need not be understood kyriocentrically—as concentrated solely on the actions of Jesus. Wainwright poses a question linked to the project of historical retrieval, wondering whether we find here a trace of the existence of women healers: "Healed of her disease, healed as a result of her own initiative, does this woman point to female healing power that seems to be obscured in the Markan text, but available in the Markan world?"[62] D'Angelo stresses the "high estimation of the believer's and therefore the early Christian reader's share in the spirit" in this miracle story, noting that Mark has a "christology of shared spiritual power, one in which Jesus' power is active through the participation of others."[63]

Luke clips from Mark each of these three references to the woman's self-awareness. He omits the interior monologue by the woman in Mark 5:28, which provides the rationale for her approach of Jesus;[64] he stresses only Jesus's recognition that power has gone from him, rather than balancing Jesus's recognition with the woman's own (Luke 8:46; compare Mark 5:29-30); the woman comes forth after Jesus calls in Luke 8:47, but instead of reminding us of her own experience of healing (cf. Mark 5:33), the text explains that she comes forward because she recognizes that she cannot remain hidden (v. 47; cf. v. 17).

In spite of these redactions, the woman with the flow of blood still remains the agent of her own healing in Luke's version. She is the one who initiates the healing, by reaching out to touch the garment (v. 44), thus drawing the power out of Jesus (v. 46). Though Luke does not allow her direct speech, she is still said to have spoken before the entire crowd, explaining her reason for touching and the result of her effort (v. 47). At the close of the scene Jesus affirms that it is the woman's own faith that has saved her (ἡ πίστις σου σέσωκέν σε, v. 48).[65]

---

62. Wainwright, *Women Healing/Healing Women*, 120. For more on women healers, see commentary at Luke 4:38-39.

63. D'Angelo, "Gender and Power," 101. See also Candida Moss, "The Man with the Flow of Power: Porous Bodies in Mark 5:25-34," *JBL* 129 (2010): 507–19, who argues that Jesus is portrayed in this pericope as feminine, having a porous body from which power leaks.

64. Melissa Harl (née Philip) Sellew ("Interior Monologue as a Narrative Device in the Parables of Luke," *JBL* 111 [1992]: 239–53) notes that in Luke, Jesus is the primary narrator of interior monologue, a literary device that serves to underscore Jesus's "especially sharp and penetrating insight."

65. The verb σώζω means both "save" and "heal." See note at 7:50.

Thus, we conclude that even if Luke's redactional aim is to muffle Mark's story of a woman taking initiative for her own healing, this aim is not highly successful. The insights concerning ancient women healers and shared spiritual power within the *basileia* movement may be more easily drawn from the Markan pericope, as Wainwright and D'Angelo have shown. But readers can glimpse them in Luke's version of the story as well.[66]

Though the story is of irregular vaginal discharge, rather than menstrual blood, it can still serve as a springboard for feminist reflection on menstruation, given that menstruation is widely understood as a negative bodily function, akin to disease.[67] Feminists across the globe have argued for a greater acceptance of menstruation as a healthy bodily process and for greater accessibility and affordability of menstrual hygiene products.[68] This story of a bleeding woman determined to get what she needs to be whole might serve as inspiration to those engaged in this work. In ecclesial contexts, preachers and teachers can use this pericope as an invitation to normalize talk about gynecological health.

---

66. In this instance, the Gospel of Matthew, rather than Luke, has done the most to deflect from the concept of shared spirit and power between the woman and Jesus. See D'Angelo, "Gender and Power," 101–2.

67. In a contextual reading of this passage with impoverished women in South Africa, Malika Sibeko and Beverley Haddad reported that these women were prompted by the story of the bleeding woman to explore their own experiences of oppression correlated with menstruation. These experiences included male leaders of the African Independent Church refusing to lay hands on a menstruant and the prohibition against women sitting in designated worship space while menstruating. See Malika Sibeko and Beverley Haddad, "Reading the Bible 'with' Women in Poor and Marginalized Communities in South Africa," *Semeia* 78 (1997): 83–92.

Insofar as the woman bleeding for twelve years evokes situations of long-term suffering and vulnerability, the passage has also inspired contextual readings with respect to HIV and AIDS in Africa. See Mmapula Lefa, "Reading the Bible Amidst the HIV and AIDS Pandemic in Botswana," in *African and European Readers of the Bible in Dialogue: In Quest of a Shared Meaning*, ed. J. H. de Wit and Gerald O. West, Studies on Religion in Africa 32 (Leiden: Brill, 2008), 285–303.

68. See, for instance, the US-based organization PERIOD, whose mission includes "serving menstruators in need by distributing tampons, pads and menstrual cups; running educational workshops to change the way people think, talk, and learn about periods; and fighting for systemic change towards menstrual equity" (https://www .period.org/). As another example, consider the award-winning 2018 documentary short film directed by Rayka Zehtabchi, *Period. End of Sentence*, which follows local women in Hapur, India, as they create a small business to manufacture and sell sanitary pads at affordable prices to women in India.

Jairus's Daughter, Raised from the Dead

From the open-air setting of the crowds, where the woman with the flow of blood has been healed, the scene shifts to Jairus's house.[69] In the presence of her parents and Peter, John, and James, Jesus takes the daughter by the hand and calls her to arise. In raising the child from the dead, Jesus evokes the prophets Elijah and Elisha, who also resuscitated children for bereft parents (1 Kgs 17:17-24; 2 Kgs 4:8-37).[70] His ability to raise the dead also confirms Jesus's messianic identity, as has been announced to the disciples of John in 7:22.[71]

Miracle narratives in ancient literature often require translation for contemporary readers whose worldviews do not allow for direct divine intervention. This may be especially true of stories of dead children raised to life, given the unspeakably tragic nature of such deaths. Considered in the context of those grieving the death of children, Jesus's response when told that the child has died (v. 50: "Do not fear. Only believe, and she will be saved"; cf. v. 52), may ring empty, if not cruel. A better strategy for eliciting meaning from the passage in contemporary contexts is to shift to a metaphorical plane. Consider, for instance, the literary analysis of Charles Hedrick (offered with explicit reference to Mark's version of the story):

69. In 8:41 Jairus is identified as ἄρχων τῆς συναγωγῆς, "a leader of the synagogue." Three Greek inscriptions, dating from the second to the fifth century, name women who bear the title of ἀρχισυνάγογος or ἀρχισυνάγογισσα, "head of synagogue": Rufina, Sophia, and Theopempte. There is no evidence to suggest that there were differences between women and men who exercised this role. See Bernadette J. Brooten, *Women Leaders in the Ancient Synagogue: Inscriptional Evidence and Background Issues*, BJS 36 (Chico, CA: Scholars Press, 1982), 57–72.

70. See Thomas L. Brodie, *The Crucial Bridge: The Elijah–Elisha Narrative as an Interpretive Synthesis of Genesis–Kings and a Literary Model for the Gospels* (Collegeville, MN: Liturgical Press, 2000). For an argument that this story also alludes to the sacrifice of the daughter of Jephthah in Judges 11:34-40, see Mary Ann Beavis, "The Resurrection of Jephthah's Daughter: Judges 11:34-40 and Mark 5:21-24, 35-43," *CBQ* 72 (2010): 46–62.

71. At the time of this writing, we have been unable to access Janine Luttick, "'Little Girl, Get Up!' (and Stand on Your Own Two Feet!): A Reading of Mark 5:21-24, 35-43 with an Awareness of the Role and Function of the Body" (PhD diss., Australian Catholic University, 2017). This work analyzes a wide range of literary and material data from the early Roman Empire and late Second Temple Judaism to explain how the bodies of women and female children were depicted and what those images conveyed. Luttick is currently revising the dissertation for publication.

This story holds open the possibility that even in an apparently closed world, things may be other than they seem. Hence the story contrasts two ways of viewing the world: a closed system in which death is inevitable and always the victor—represented by those mourners who laughed at Jesus. And a system slightly open in which the inevitabilities of the closed system have become mere possibilities—represented by Jesus and Jairus's daughter. Hence the story, by affirming the mystery of death and holding open the possibility of life, calls all people to the courage of an irrational faith, a faith that holds out for the possibility of new beginnings in spite of the "obvious" inevitability of conclusions that militate against hope.[72]

72. Charles W. Hedrick, "Miracle Stories as Literary Compositions: The Case of Jairus's Daughter," *PRSt* 20 (1993): 217–33, here 133.

Luke 9:1-62

The Cross That Should Not Be Taken Up

Disciples Made Apostles (9:1-6)

Jesus had called twelve male disciples out of the larger group (6:12-16) and named ἀπόστολοι, "apostles" (6:13), envoys, messengers. He now sends them out with his power and authority[1] to preach and to heal. He directs them not simply to travel lightly but to take nothing. Μηδέν, "nothing," is in an emphatic position as the first word of the instruction. The apostles are totally dependent on the hospitality of others.[2] The model of mission is a two-way exchange of gifts. Hospitality extended to apostles is as important as the itinerant preaching and healing. For Luke, the latter is reserved to males and the former to females (e.g., Martha in 10:38-42; Mary, the mother of John Mark in Acts 12:12; Lydia in Acts 16; Prisca in Acts 18:1-3). Other strands of Christian tradition preserve the memory of women apostles as well as men other than the Twelve (see excursus at 6:13). Unique to Luke is the sending of

---

1. See the excursus at 4:1-13, "Feminist Understandings of Power," and comments on authority at 4:31-37.
2. See 22:35 where they affirm that they lacked for nothing.

⁹:¹Then Jesus called the twelve together and gave them power and authority over all demons and to cure diseases, ²and he sent them out to proclaim the kingdom of God and to heal. ³He said to them, "Take nothing for your journey, no staff, nor bag, nor bread, nor money—not even an extra tunic. ⁴Whatever house you enter, stay there, and leave from there. ⁵Wherever they do not welcome you, as you are leaving that town shake the dust off your feet as a testimony against them." ⁶They departed and went through the villages, bringing the good news and curing diseases everywhere.

a further seventy (11:1-12; see commentary on this passage). While they are nameless and their gender is not specified, it is most likely that Luke also envisions these apostles as male.

Herod's Ominous Question (9:7-9)

When sending out his apostles, Jesus warned that not everyone would receive them (9:5); he has not yet told his followers that their lives may be in danger. That will come at 9:21-27. Herod's question, "who is this?" (cf. 5:21; 7:49; 8:25; 9:20), is ominous: he is assessing what kind of threat Jesus poses and whether he needs to dispose of him as he did John.[3] He will not actually see Jesus until Pilate sends him to him at 23:8.

Feeding Five Thousand Men and Countless Women (9:10-17)

Sandwiched between Herod's ominous question (9:9) and Jesus's first prediction of his death (9:21-22), this feeding story provides another indicator of Jesus's identity. Jesus emulates God's provision of manna in the desert for the Israelites (Exod 16:1-36), building toward the identification of him as God's anointed (9:20) chosen son (9:35). The scene also points ahead to the Last Supper (22:14-23) and prepares disciples for Jesus's death and the possibility of their own. While contemporary readers speculate about *how* the multiplication of the loaves occurred (a miracle? a sharing of provisions?), the focus for Luke is *who* Jesus is. Questions about gender roles in hosting meals and serving food also

---

3. See comments at 3:19-20 on Herod's imprisonment of John and Luke's omission of the fuller story of John's beheading at the instigation of Herodias.

[7]Now Herod the ruler heard about all that had taken place, and he was perplexed, because it was said by some that John had been raised from the dead, [8]by some that Elijah had appeared, and by others that one of the ancient prophets had arisen. [9]Herod said, "John I beheaded; but who is this about whom I hear such things?" And he tried to see him.

[10]On their return the apostles told Jesus all they had done. He took them with him and withdrew privately to a city called Bethsaida. [11]When the crowds found out about it, they followed him; and he welcomed them, and spoke to them about the kingdom of God, and healed those who needed to be cured.

[12]The day was drawing to a close, and the twelve came to him and said, "Send the crowd away, so that they may go into the surrounding villages and countryside, to lodge and get provisions; for we are here in a deserted

emerge. The answers to the latter set of questions have implications for Christian ministry.

The scene opens with Jesus taking the apostles to Bethsaida after their first foray into preaching and healing. Luke gives no details about how long they were gone or whether they met opposition. While Luke does not say what is the purpose of the trip to Bethsaida (in Mark 6:31 it is to rest),[4] the Lukan literary context suggests that Jesus wants to escape Antipas (9:7-9) by going into the territory ruled by Philip, another of Herod the Great's sons.[5] As John 1:44 notes, Philip, Peter, and Andrew were from Bethsaida.[6] They may still have had family and friends there who would provide them hospitality. Had Jesus intended to escape no-

4. In Mark 6:45, Bethsaida is the destination after the feeding of the five thousand.
5. Bethsaida was part of the tetrarchy of Philip, who ruled from 4 BCE until his death in 34 CE. In 30 CE Philip renamed the city Julias in honor of Livia-Julia, the wife of Emperor Augustus and mother of Tiberius (*Ant.* 18.2.1 §28). The location of Bethsaida is a matter of some debate. Excavations begun in 1987 have identified it with et-Tell, at the northeast corner of the Galilee, about a mile and a half away from the present shoreline. The archaeological finds from the Iron Age are extensive; they are more modest for Hellenistic and early Roman times. See the report of Rami Arav, leader of the excavation, "Bethsaida," in *Jesus and Archaeology*, ed. James H. Charlesworth (Grand Rapids: Eerdmans, 2006), 145–66. At 10:13-16 Jesus denounces Bethsaida along with Capernaum and Chorazin for their unrepentance.
6. Jerome Murphy-O'Connor ("Fishers of Fish, Fishers of Men," *BibRev* [1999]: 22–27, 48–49) offers that the fishermen were savvy businessmen who may have moved to Capernaum for a tax break.

place." ¹³But he said to them, "You give them something to eat." They said, "We have no more than five loaves and two fish—unless we are to go and buy food for all these people." ¹⁴For there were about five thousand men. And he said to his disciples, "Make them sit down in groups of about fifty each." ¹⁵They did so and made them all sit down. ¹⁶And taking the five loaves and the two fish, he looked up to heaven, and blessed and broke them, and gave them to the disciples to set before the crowd. ¹⁷And all ate and were filled. What was left over was gathered up, twelve baskets of broken pieces.

tice, the crowds put an end to that. Jesus welcomes them, talks (ἐλάλει, "spoke," is in the imperfect tense, meaning ongoing action) about the kingdom of God, and heals.[7]

As night descends, the Twelve advise Jesus to send the crowd away to get provisions and find lodging. While Jesus had told the devil, "One does not live by bread alone" (4:3-4; Deut 8:3), he also knows that people cannot be receptive to his teaching, let alone survive, without eating.

Luke numbers the people who were fed as "about five thousand men [ἄνδρες]" (9:14). The NRSV accurately renders the word ἄνδρες as "men"; unlike ἄνθρωποι, which is inclusive of women and men, ἄνδρες refers to males only.[8] Matthew also puts the number at five thousand men but then adds: "besides women and children" (Matt 14:21). Matthew, like contemporary feminists, remembers to count the women and children. Even if they are not mentioned in the text, we presume they were present and active.

Here at 9:10-17 and again at the Last Supper (22:14-23), Jesus and his male disciples[9] adopt a role traditionally belonging to women and slaves:

---

7. See similar summaries at 4:40; 5:15; 6:18.

8. On Luke's use of ἀνήρ (singular of ἄνδρες), see Mary Rose D'Angelo, "The ANHP Question in Luke–Acts: Imperial Masculinity and the Deployment of Women in the Early Second Century," in *A Feminist Companion to Luke*, ed. Amy-Jill Levine with Marianne Blickenstaff, FCNTECW 3 (London: Sheffield Academic, 2002), 44–69.

9. Narratively, it appears that the "the disciples" (μαθηταῖς) at 9:16 refers to the same group that is designated "apostles" (οἱ ἀπόστολοι, 9:10) and the Twelve (οἱ δώδεκα) at 9:12. For Luke, οἱ ἀπόστολοι and οἱ δώδεκα are males (6:12-16). We think it unlikely, contrary to Sharon H. Ringe, that Luke envisions female disciples as well as male at 9:16: "All the followers, and not just an elite group of leaders, share in the serving" (*Luke*, Westminster Bible Companion [Louisville: Westminster John Knox, 1995], 133).

serving food (see 4:39; 10:40; 12:37; 17:8).[10] One way of reading this is to see a leveling of gender roles leading to egalitarianism. We see instead male leaders coopting a traditionally female role. And at 22:25-26 Luke clearly diminishes the potential for reading the saying about greatness and serving as solidarity from below. In line with Luke, as presiding at the eucharistic table emerges as the key ministerial function, it becomes restricted to males.[11]

Women and Waiting at Table

Food and drink sustain physical life, and table-companionship promotes group identity. These themes influence Luke's characterization of Jesus's roles at table vis-à-vis the other characters (5:27-39; 7:36-50; 9:10-17; 10:38-42; 11:37-54; 14:1-24; 19:1-10; 22:14-38; 24:13-35; and 24:36-43).

In Galilee, Jesus is first depicted as being served at table by Simon's mother-in-law, whom he healed (4:39). He is also guest of two opposite characters: Levi, a tax collector (5:29), and Simon, a law-abiding Pharisee (7:37). Does this imply that Jesus can also be the guest of those who fall in between? As the Galilean ministry ends, the Lukan Jesus transitions from being a guest to being the host of a hungry multitude in an outdoor meal setting (9:15).

As Jesus journeys to Jerusalem, he is portrayed only as a guest: of Martha, albeit with a puzzlingly strong remark against her table-service (10:38-42); of another Pharisee (11:37-54); of a ruler of the Pharisees (14:1-24); and of a chief tax collector, Zacchaeus (19:1-10). The last two intensify his being guest of seeming opposites (Pharisees and tax collectors) as in Galilee. On the journey, Jesus addresses direct antagonism from those he dines with (11:53-54; 14:1) and from others who disapprove of his brand of meal sharing (15:2; 19:7).

Despite the disapproval, Jesus continues his table-fellowship with the only repast in Jerusalem, a Passover meal, commonly regarded as his farewell meal or the last of his suppers (22:14-38). Jesus plays host to his disciples that include one who will betray him, another who will deny him (22:14-23, 31-34), and a group who, ironically, argue about the

---

10. See discussion at 10:38-42 where we advance that Martha's service is ministe-rial. In the Lukan meal scenes, the hosts are all males (5:29; 7:36; 11:37; 14:1; 19:1-10; 22:14-23) as are the guests (5:29; 14:15; 22:14).

11. For evidence of women presbyters/priests in early Christianity, see chap. 1 n. 26.

greatest while at table even in this poignant setting (22:24-26). Jesus's correction reiterates that, at table, he is among them as one who serves (22:27).

After the crucifixion, the risen Jesus reveals himself in Emmaus as he acts like a host even if he was primarily a guest (24:13-35). The joyful but disbelieving disciples in Jerusalem also recognize him when he asks for food (24:41-43).

Jesus has a cyclic role with respect to table in Luke, moving from guest to host, to food-and-drink, to servant at table, and to guest again. Yet, on a closer look, what does this mean for women? Without assuming that women are absent from Jesus's meals because they are not cited, three women are mentioned in Jesus's table-companionship. One is the unwelcomed, unnamed, but affirmed woman who anointed Jesus (7:36-50). Simon's mother-in-law (4:39) and Martha (10:38-42) are described as serving (at table). Yet if Martha was criticized by Jesus for being busy in her table-serving, why does Jesus identify himself as one who serves at table at the end of his ministry? Does it respect women's role at table? Or does it result in the usurpation of this role? In Acts 6:1-6, the Twelve say, "It is not right that we should neglect the word of God in order to wait on tables," and only men were appointed.

How do these insights matter today? This challenge of cyclically changing roles at table is even more pressing in the Filipino setting. One of the most common expressions of Filipino hospitality is table-companionship with friends and family, expected and unexpected visitors, and even with strangers. It is summed up in the greeting, *"Kain tayo!"* (Let's eat) that expresses the basic desire to share food and drink with others because one is a *kapwa* (the other is a person like one's self).

The Filipino level of social cohesion is noticeable in table-fellowship through the kind of food and drink served, the tableware used, and the relationship between guests and hosts. *Pakikipagkapwa* is the highest level of humanness: the *kapwa* (other) is *sarili na rin* (oneself). Shared inner self and recognition of shared identity are the roots of *pakikipagkapwa*. *Kapwa* embraces both the categories of *ibang tao* (outsiders) and *hindi ibang tao* (insiders).

Filipino table-companionship reveals the level of relationship among the partakers. The *ibang tao* ("other," outsider) category moves from *pakikitungo* (level of amenities) to *pakikibagay* (level of conforming) and *pakikisama* (level of adjusting). Afterward, the parties move toward *hindi ibang tao* ("not-other," insider) category, which includes two levels: *pakikipagpalagayang-loob* (level of mutual trust) and *pakikiisa* (level of fusion, oneness and full of trust). The progression from outsider to insider is evident in the quality of relationships expressed in the meals, with *pakikitungo* as the shallowest and *pakikiisa* as the deepest. The food and drink served gradually changes from elaborate and expensive ones in outsider category when the tablemates try to gain each other's confidence to that of being able to serve daily fare in the insider category. The tableware changes from those reserved for special occasions to those used daily as the partakers become more at home with each other. Consequently, one sees how a visitor grows from being a guest toward becoming a cohost with the host and a coservant at table when the deepest level of relationship has been achieved. The role transformation enables the former guest to be one with the host and to help serve the new guests. This role transformation is most obvious among women who tend to be charged with the food-and-drink task for families and communities.

These Filipino cultural insights reflect some of what I see in Jesus's table-companionship in Luke. While everyone begins as guest (receiver of food and drink), each must also transition to being host or servant at table or become metaphorical food and drink as everyone goes through life. Jesus's cyclically changing role as guest-host-servant-food-and-drink at table consequently challenges Christians to follow what seems like Jesus's meal ministry that proclaims a facet of God's kingdom as a banquet for all, responding to those who are hungry in many ways (as expressed in Mary's song, 1:53).

Jesus's changing roles at table challenge his followers then and now to be cognizant of their own role whenever they have table-companionship. For me, these cyclical roles pose questions as to how one responds to the Filipino cultural challenge of changing roles at table vis-à-vis the task of promoting physical sustenance and communal interrelationship as manifested in the components of the United Nations Sustainable Development Goals #2 (no hunger) and #6 (clean water). Christians and Christian communities need to be active respondents to these urgent and complex issues by contributing in ways that uphold economic, political, and socio-cultural rights that affect the food and drink security, sufficiency, and sovereignty of peoples. Active participation respectful of gender identity and roles but also cognizant and critical of cultural context, however, needs to be incorporated into daily life and into the symbolic levels like the liturgical and ecclesial life. In this way, Jesus's meal ministry and the cyclical roles at table and the vision of a banquet for all will be meaningful and life-giving for Christians today.

Ma. Marilou S. Ibita

Taking up the Cross (9:18-27)

The question "Who is this?" has been posed in various forms by John the Baptist (7:19), the disciples (8:25), and Herod (9:9). Now Jesus asks his disciples, female[12] and male, what the crowds are saying. Their answer echoes Herod's musings in 9:7-9. Jesus narrows the focus, asking for their own response to the question.

Peter, whom Luke regards as primary among the disciples, answers for the group: the "Messiah of God."[13] Jesus orders the disciples not to tell anyone[14] and then elaborates on what kind of Messiah he is: one rejected by the elders, chief priests, and scribes, who will suffer, be killed, and be raised. He expounds further: suffering is not his fate alone but also that of any who choose to follow him. The "cross" that disciples are to take up encompasses whatever hardships and suffering befall them as a direct result of following him ("for my sake," v. 24) and holding fast to his words (v. 26). The cross that disciples are to take up is not suffering that comes from abuse and injustice (see excursus: "The Cross That Should Not Be Taken Up"). Those kinds of sufferings Jesus tried to alleviate, not accept. Moreover, Jesus is speaking with disciples (9:18) who can choose whether or not to follow him. People caught in systems of abuse and who consequently suffer often do not have such a choice. Finally, the choice to expose oneself to suffering as a disciple is not made once and for all; it is a daily[15] decision.

In order to make such a choice, followers must be willing to reject a self-centered existence. Denial of self (9:23) does not mean denying certain pleasures but a radical self-identification with Jesus. A free person who has a healthy sense of self can choose self-denial; people so battered or mentally abused that they have lost their authentic sense of self may not have the ability to make such a choice.

---

12. As Turid Karlsen Seim observes (*The Double Message: Patterns of Gender in Luke–Acts* [Nashville: Abingdon, 1994], 151), 24:6-7 demonstrates how women disciples were among those who heard Jesus's words about suffering and the cross (both at 9:21-22 and 17:22-37).

13. In John 11:27 this declaration is made by Martha. See above at 2:8-20 for the meaning of χριστός, "Christ," "Anointed One" of "Messiah."

14. See comments at 8:56, where Jesus issues the same command to Jairus and his wife, but contrast with 8:39. Luke has retained some traces of Mark's theme of "messianic secret," where Jesus's identity is not fully revealed until the crucifixion. In Luke, Jesus is already revealed as χριστός, "Messiah," at his birth (2:11).

15. The expression καθ' ἡμέραν, "daily," is a Lukan addition to the saying; compare Mark 8:34; Matt 16:24.

[18]Once when Jesus was praying alone, with only the disciples near him, he asked them, "Who do the crowds say that I am?" [19]They answered, "John the Baptist; but others, Elijah; and still others, that one of the ancient prophets has arisen." [20]He said to them, "But who do you say that I am?" Peter answered, "The Messiah of God."

[21]He sternly ordered and commanded them not to tell anyone, [22]saying, "The Son of Man must undergo great suffering, and be rejected by the elders, chief priests, and scribes, and be killed, and on the third day be raised."

[23]Then he said to them all, "If any want to become my followers, let them deny themselves and take up their cross daily and follow me. [24]For those who want to save their life will lose it, and those who lose their life for my sake will save it. [25]What does it profit them if they gain the whole world, but lose or forfeit themselves? [26]Those who are ashamed of me and of my words, of them the Son of Man will be ashamed when he comes in his glory and the glory of the Father and of the holy angels. [27]But truly I tell you, there are some standing here who will not taste death before they see the kingdom of God."

The Cross That Should Not Be Taken Up

As I (Barbara) was doing research for my book *Taking Up the Cross*,[16] I heard a number of chilling stories of women who had internalized Jesus's directive to "take up their cross" in ways that only increased their suffering and kept them trapped in abusive situations. A student of mine who worked in a shelter for women who were being battered by their partners told me that time after time, when women would finally break the silence about the abuse, they would go to their priest or minister. More often than not, he would advise the woman to go home and endure this suffering as her way of carrying the cross. In recent years there are concerted efforts among some pastors to help ministers and parishioners recognize the signs of domestic violence and know where to direct victims to receive professional help. Also important are preaching about domestic violence and interpreting the cross in ways

16. Barbara E. Reid, *Taking Up the Cross: New Testament Interpretations through Latina and Feminist Eyes* (Minneapolis: Fortress, 2007); Spanish translation: *Reconsiderar la Cruz. Interpretación latinoamericana y feminista del Nuevo Testamento*, Aletheia 5 (Estella [Navarro], España: Editorial Verbo Divino, 2009).

that do not fuel cycles of violence and victimization.[17]

In LaPaz, Bolivia, I met a woman who explained the strong cross-centered piety and its consequences in the Indigenous cultures of Aymara and Quechua:

> Our women identify strongly with the crucified Christ and his sufferings. When beaten or abused, we identify with Mary, the mother of Jesus, who kept all these sufferings in her heart. There is a strong sense of submission in our Aymara and Quechua cultures. Women submit to sexual abuse from their fathers, uncles, and husbands, with a strong sense of resignation. Women identify with the suffering servant in Isaiah; what we lack is a sense that we need to struggle against the causes of these sufferings. And women have the capacity to fight injustice. They are very strong. They can move the whole city to action when they put their mind to it. But in their own homes women are like meek doves who submit to their husband's beatings. What is necessary is space for women to reflect with other women. When they are united with others, then they can work for change.[18]

The ways in which persons who are suffering abuse interiorize such a misdirected understanding of the gospel causes us to search for liberative interpretations and strategies, such as those offered above, that set free those who are so unjustly bound.

Discerning the Way Forward (9:28-36)

The Lukan version of this episode has a number of unique elements that cannot be explained by Lukan redaction of Mark.[19] These point to a separate source, one that focuses on how Jesus discerns the way forward to fulfill his mission. Mark (9:1-8) and Matthew (17:1-8) focus

17. See, e.g., the Archdiocese of Chicago Domestic Violence Outreach program spearheaded by Fr. Chuck Dahm: https://pvm.archchicago.org/human-dignity-solidarity/domestic-violence-outreach.

18. Reid, *Taking Up the Cross*, 22. For African American scholarship, including womanist, on the problems of sacrifice as a model of discipleship, see commentary on Luke 22:7-13.

19. For details, see Barbara E. Reid, *The Transfiguration: A Source- and Redaction-Critical Study of Luke 9:28-36*, CahRB 32 (Paris: Gabalda, 1993).

²⁸Now about eight days after these sayings Jesus took with him Peter and John and James, and went up on the mountain to pray. ²⁹And while he was praying, the appearance of his face changed, and his clothes became dazzling white. ³⁰Suddenly they saw two men, Moses and Elijah, talking to him. ³¹They appeared in glory and were speaking of his departure, which he was about to accomplish at Jerusalem. ³²Now Peter and his companions were weighed down with sleep; but since they had stayed awake, they saw his glory and the two men who stood with him. ³³Just as they were leaving him, Peter said to Jesus, "Master, it is good for us to be here; let us make three dwellings, one for you, one for Moses, and one for Elijah"—not knowing what he said. ³⁴While he was saying this, a cloud came and overshadowed them; and they were terrified as they entered the cloud. ³⁵Then from the cloud came a voice that said, "This is my Son, my Chosen; listen to him!" ³⁶When the voice had spoken, Jesus was found alone. And they kept silent and in those days told no one any of the things they had seen.

more on what the disciples experienced. For some commentators this episode is a resurrection appearance story that has been retrojected into the Galilean ministry; others think it was a vision (as Matt 17:9 states) of the glorified Christ given to the disciples to sustain them through the difficulties ahead. Still others think it was not a supernatural occurrence but an experience of a mountaintop sunrise illuminating Jesus or a night storm with lightning and thunder that the disciples interpret as a divine manifestation. For Luke's account, none of these explanations satisfies.

Mark and Matthew do not say why Jesus went up the mountain; in Luke (9:28) it is to pray, as at other turning points in the gospel (6:12; 22:39-46).[20] As Jesus has continued to gather many crowds in the Galilee, he contemplates whether he should direct his efforts now to Jerusalem. He is aware of the growing opposition, and he knows full well the danger should he do so (9:22); Jerusalem kills prophets (13:33-34). As he prays to discern the way forward, he receives the answer, and his face changes (9:29). Mark and Matthew, by contrast, say that "he was transfigured," μετεμορφώθη, a word Luke does not use.[21] Instead, Luke describes a change in the appearance of Jesus's face, like Moses, whose face was

---

20. On the frequency of prayer in Luke, see 11:2.
21. Paul uses this verb to mean the inner change of a Christian being conformed to Christ: 1 Cor 3:18; Rom 12:2.

radiant after his encounter with God on Mount Sinai (Exod 34:29-30), and like Hannah, whose face was no longer downcast after she received an answer to her prayer for a son (1 Sam 1:9-18).

Two heavenly messengers interpret the meaning for the reader.[22] The conversation among Jesus, Moses, and Elijah (a detail unique to Luke) reveals what Jesus has come to understand in his prayer. They speak about his ἔξοδος, *exodos*, "departure," that he is about to accomplish in Jerusalem. The word ἔξοδος has a double meaning: departure from among the living (cf. 2 Pet 1:15) and the exodus from Egypt (Pss 104:38; 113:1). Jesus discerns that he is to go to Jerusalem, be put to death there, but his death will not be the end of his mission. Rather, it will accomplish a new "exodus" for his people, a liberating movement that will be continued by his disciples (see comments at 4:18 on Jesus's mission to free people and chap. 22 on the Last Supper and the exodus). And so he will "set his face" to go to Jerusalem (9:51).

As occurred at Jesus's baptism (3:22), symbols of the divine presence confirm what he has discerned. The cloud evokes the pillar of cloud that led the Israelites during the exodus (Exod 13:21-22; Num 14:14), and the voice reaffirms Jesus's identity as beloved Son. At Jesus's baptism, the voice was directed to Jesus alone (3:22); here it addresses the disciples, pointing to Jesus not only as Son but also as "my Chosen" (ἐκλελεγμένος). Disciples are to anticipate that being God's chosen one does not exempt Jesus from suffering, as the scoffers at the crucifixion expect: "He saved others; let him save himself if he is the Messiah of God, his chosen one!" (23:35). Rather, election by God entails a mission that includes suffering, just as it did for others designated ἐκλεκτός, "chosen one": Moses (Ps 106:23), David (Ps 89:19), and the servant of God (Isa 42:1). There are Christians who declare that "God sent his Son to die for our sins." Such a formulation cannot be sustained from the Gospel of Luke. In Luke, Jesus's death is that of a rejected prophet, not an atonement for sin. As chosen one, Jesus also chooses. He chooses to continue his mission by going to Jerusalem. (See further comments at 1:38 on agency and free choice and chap. 22.)

Oscar Romero, martyred bishop of El Salvador,[23] rightly saw the "transfiguration" not as a glimpse of Jesus's eschatological glory but as a happening that had profound implications for followers of Jesus both

---

22. At key moments, heavenly messengers in Luke and Acts give the divine perspective on the happenings: 1:8-20, 26-38; 2:8-20; 24:1-9; Acts 1:10-11; 10:1-8.
23. Romero was canonized October 14, 2018; his feast day is March 24.

then and now: disciples must be made anew; the church, societies and nations, and history itself must be transfigured. And the way to this transfiguration is the same as it was for Jesus: the way of the cross.[24]

A Demon Submits to the One Who Is Stronger (9:37-43)

A desperate father seeking a cure for his child shouts (ἐβόησεν, v. 38) from the crowd and then begs (δέομαι, v. 38) Jesus to take a look at his son; he explains that he had previously begged (ἐδεήθην, v. 40) his disciples to cast out the demon. Instead of consoling the father, Jesus hurls an insult at "this generation" and expresses impatience at having to deal with the crowds (9:41). Though Christians often sentimentalize Jesus as the exemplar of compassion, in this response, present also in Matthew 17:17 and Mark 8:19, Jesus provides no model for pastoral care. The concern of the narrative is less on the interaction between Jesus and a worried parent than on the cruelty of the demon and on Jesus's marvelous ability to cast the demon out.

The boy's symptoms, convulsions and foaming at the mouth, have been assessed in modern medical parlance as "consistent with the epileptic syndrome now known as generalized tonic-clonic seizures."[25] But disability scholars working on ancient texts caution against imposing modern medical terminology on these sources, arguing instead that we should seek to understand these stories within the classificatory frames of the ancient world.[26] Luke, drawing on an understanding of illness typical in his day, presents the cause of the malady not in medical terms but as demon possession. The father identifies the agent inside his son as a "spirit" (v. 39); the conclusion of the pericope clarifies that the spirit is "unclean" and uses "demon" as a synonym (v. 42).

The father's lament that Jesus's disciples were not able to exorcise his son (v. 40) will be the last mention of the failing of Jesus's true followers vis-à-vis the demonic in Luke–Acts. The seventy report victory over the

24. Michael Kibbe, "Light That Conquers the Darkness: Oscar Romero on the Transfiguration of Jesus," in *ThTo* 75 (2019): 447–57.

25. Nicole Kelley, " 'The Punishment of the Devil Was Apparent in the Torment of the Human Body': Epilepsy in Ancient Christianity," in *Disability Studies and Biblical Literature*, ed. Candida R. Moss and Jeremy Schipper (New York: Palgrave MacMillan, 2011), 205–21, here 209.

26. Anna Rebecca Solevåg, *Negotiating the Disabled Body: Representations of Disability in Early Christian Texts*, ECL 23 (Atlanta: SBL Press, 2018), 11.

[37]On the next day, when they had come down from the mountain, a great crowd met him. [38]Just then a man from the crowd shouted, "Teacher, I beg you to look at my son; he is my only child. [39]Suddenly a spirit seizes him, and all at once he shrieks. It convulses him until he foams at the mouth; it mauls him and will scarcely leave him. [40]I begged your disciples to cast it out, but they could not." [41]Jesus answered, "You faithless and perverse generation, how much longer must I be with you and bear with you? Bring your son here." [42]While he was coming, the demon dashed him to the ground in convulsions. But Jesus rebuked the unclean spirit, healed the boy, and gave him back to his father. [43]And all were astounded at the greatness of God.

demons in 10:17-19; Peter withstands the attack of Satan during Jesus's passion (22:31-32); both Peter and Paul will have victories over emissaries of Satan (Acts 8:9-24; 19:11-20).[27] But here there is no doubt that Jesus is the mightiest exorcist, and his apostles are only exorcists-in-training.

In Luke's depiction of Jesus's battle with the demons, he often emphasizes the physical force used by demons against the bodies they inhabit and the necessary force required in turn to subdue them. Luke describes the demon's agency over the boy as involving "seizing" (λαμβάνει, v. 39); "convulsing" or "tearing apart" (σπαράσσει, v. 39; συνεσπάραξεν, v. 42); "crushing" (συντρῖβον, v. 39); and "breaking" (ἔρρηξεν, v. 42). These are signs that the demon is a "strong one" who requires a "stronger one" to vanquish him (cf. 11:21-22).[28]

We lament how the ancient association of seizures with demonic possession in this pericope was read in subsequent centuries to stigmatize people with epilepsy and other related developmental disabilities. Sometimes this stigmatization has led to the death of children, even in modern times. For example, in the Faith Temple Church of the Apostolic Faith in Milwaukee in 2003, a boy with autism died during a prayer service, after having been repeatedly restrained. The pastor defended the church's treatment of the boy, saying they were only "asking God to take this

---

27. On the victory of Jesus and his followers over the demonic in Luke–Acts, see Susan R. Garrett, *The Demise of the Devil: Magic and the Demonic in Luke's Writings* (Minneapolis: Fortress, 1989). On the gendered nature of that battle, see commentary on Luke 8:1-3.

28. See also commentary on the significance of the name "Legion" for the demons inhabiting the Gerasene, Luke 8:26-39.

spirit that was tormenting this little boy to death."[29] Disability studies call into question such stigmatization, as well as the socially constructed nature of both the "stigmatized" and the "normate" subject position.[30]

Welcoming the Child (Luke 9:43b-48)

Despite Jesus's teaching about the cross, the disciples still do not understand (9:45). Their argument over which one of them was the greatest poses a stark contrast to Jesus's words about his coming betrayal. Jesus interrupts their jostling for status and places a little child, παιδίον, beside him. The term is the diminutive of παῖς, a word that can also be used of a slave,[31] as at 7:7. In the first-century Roman world, children were loved and valued, as they ensured the family's economic survival.[32] At the same time, they were physically not powerful, economically dependent, of no account politically, and subject to violence. It is alongside such a one that Jesus situates himself. He instructs his followers to welcome such people. Jesus's lesson might have been easier for female

---

29. http://news.bbc.co.uk/2/hi/americas/3179789.stm. Cited in Kelley, "The Punishment of the Devil, " 206.

30. On demon possession and disability studies, see especially Solevåg, *Negotiating the Disabled Body*, 95–116.

31. Carolyn Osiek, Margaret Y. MacDonald, with Janet H. Tulloch, *A Woman's Place: House Churches in Earliest Christianity* (Minneapolis: Fortress, 2006), 72–73, note that children and slave children in the Roman world often played together and were nursed by the same women slaves. See also Beryl Rawson, *Children and Childhood in Roman Italy* (Oxford: Oxford University Press, 2003); Beryl Rawson, ed., *A Companion to Families in the Greek and Roman Worlds* (Chichester: Wiley-Blackwell, 2011). On children and the perspective of the child in the New Testament, e.g., Thomas Wiedemann, *Adults and Children in the Roman Empire* (New Haven, CT: Yale University Press, 1989); W. A. Strange, *Children in the Early Church: Children in the Ancient World, the New Testament and the Early Church* (Carlisle: Paternoster, 1996); Marcia J. Bunge, ed., *The Child in Christian Thought* (Grand Rapids: Eerdmans, 2001); Peter Balla, *The Child-Parent Relationship in the New Testament and Its Environment*, WUNT 155 (Tübingen: Mohr Siebeck, 2003); James M. M. Francis. *Adults as Children: Images of Childhood in the Ancient World and the New Testament*, Religions and Discourse 17 (Oxford: Peter Lang, 2006); Marcia J. Bunge, Terence E. Fretheim, and Beverly Roberts Gaventa, *The Child in the Bible* (Grand Rapids: Eerdmans, 2008); Cornelia B. Horn and John W. Martens, "Let the Little Children Come to Me": *Childhood and Children in Early Christianity* (Washington, DC: The Catholic University of America Press, 2009); Sharon Betsworth, *Children in Early Christian Narratives* (New York: Bloomsbury T&T Clark, 2015).

32. Judith M. Gundry-Volf, "The Least and the Greatest: Children in the New Testament," in Bunge, *The Child in Christian Thought*, 29–60, here 31–32.

Luke 9:43b-48

While everyone was amazed at all that he was doing, he said to his disciples, [44]"Let these words sink into your ears: The Son of Man is going to be betrayed into human hands." [45]But they did not understand this saying; its meaning was concealed from them, so that they could not perceive it. And they were afraid to ask him about this saying.

[46]An argument arose among them as to which one of them was the greatest. [47]But Jesus, aware of their inner thoughts, took a little child and put it by his side, [48]and said to them, "Whoever welcomes this child in my name welcomes me, and whoever welcomes me welcomes the one who sent me; for the least among all of you is the greatest."

disciples, especially widows, who often took in and cared for abandoned or orphaned children.[33] The disciples will still be struggling to take in this teaching when, at the end of the journey to Jerusalem, they try to prevent Jesus from welcoming children (18:15-17).[34]

In the context of the two passion predictions (9:21-22, 43b-45), Jesus's declaration, "Whoever welcomes this child in my name welcomes me" (9:48), reminds us that children both then and now are exposed to violence in many forms (e.g., infanticide, exposure,[35] sexual exploitation, and other physical abuse).[36] Like these children, so Jesus is the Child of God who will be tortured and killed.[37] Unlike them, he makes choices that result in his suffering and death. Abuse of children is completely antithetical to what Jesus teaches, and his followers must be ever vigilant for the protection and well-being of those who are most vulnerable.

33. Osiek and MacDonald, *A Woman's Place*, 76–77, speculate that widows were often the ones who cared for others' children (see 1 Tim 5:10).

34. For how 9:46-48 and 18:15-17 frame the whole journey narrative, see Jerome Kodell, "Luke and the Children: The Beginning and End of the Great Interpolation (Luke 9:46-56; 18:9-23)," *CBQ* 49 (1987): 415–30.

35. Gundry-Volf, "The Least and the Greatest," 33, notes that females were especially vulnerable to exposure. A husband writing to his pregnant wife around 100 CE says: "If by chance you bear a child, if it is a boy, let it be, if it is a girl, cast it out" (POxy IV 744, cited by John L. White, *Light from Ancient Letters* [Philadelphia: Fortress, 1986], 111–12).

36. See chap. 6, "Exposing Children to Violence," in Horn and Martens, "*Let the Little Children Come to Me*," 213–51.

37. Gundry-Volf, "The Least and the Greatest," 44–46.

Another Exorcist (9:49-50)

This short exchange concerns the question of in-group versus out-group. John, an in-group member, assumes that an exorcist who uses Jesus's name but who does not "follow with" the disciples should be stopped. Jesus's view is more expansive: "whoever is not against you is for you." The saying stands in direct conflict with the saying attributed to Jesus in 11:23a, also in the context of teaching concerning exorcism: "Whoever is not with me is against me." Since feminists typically do not concern themselves with exorcising demons, we have no obvious ethical takeaway from these enigmatic aphorisms concerning proper allegiance for those engaged in the practice. In very general terms, we might affirm Jesus's rebuttal to John as an articulation of the principle that alliances among groups concerned for justice are better forged through an expansive philosophy rather than through a restrictive one. Of course, since the saying is Christocentric, it cannot serve as a guidepost in inter-religious conversations.

Reacting to Rejection (9:51-62)

The lengthy journey narrative (9:51–19:28) begins as Jesus sets his face toward Jerusalem. His apostles (17:5; 22:14) and disciples, including the Galilean women (23:49), follow. Between the Galilee and Jerusalem lies Samaria. Jews going to Jerusalem could avoid passing through Samaria by crossing over to the east side of the Jordan River, then crossing again near Jericho before proceeding to Jerusalem (see Mark 10:1, 46). The enmity between the Jews and Samaritans[38] was centuries old, and it was still very much alive in Jesus's day. Josephus recounts one incident that occurred when Coponius was procurator of Judea (6–9 CE) in which Samaritans strewed human bones in the temple in Jerusalem to make it ritually impure for Passover (*Ant.* 18.29). Another time, when Cumanus was governor (48–52 CE), Samaritans killed Jewish pilgrims attempting to cross through Samaria on their way to the temple in Jerusalem (*War* 2.232–35; *Ant.* 20.118).[39] Luke does not explain why Jesus wants to go through Samaria. It is no surprise that the Samaritans do not receive him.

38. See Robert T. Anderson, "Samaritans," AYBD 5.940–43.
39. Cited by Amy-Jill Levine and Ben Witherington III, *The Gospel of Luke*, NCBC (Cambridge: Cambridge University Press, 2018), 268.

⁴⁹John answered, "Master, we saw someone casting out demons in your name, and we tried to stop him, because he does not follow with us." ⁵⁰But Jesus said to him, "Do not stop him; for whoever is not against you is for you."

⁵¹When the days drew near for him to be taken up, he set his face to go to Jerusalem. ⁵²And he sent messengers ahead of him. On their way they entered a village of the Samaritans to make ready for him; ⁵³but they did not receive him, because his face was set toward Jerusalem. ⁵⁴When his disciples James and John saw it, they said, "Lord, do you want us to command fire to come down from heaven and consume them?" ⁵⁵But he turned and rebuked them. ⁵⁶Then they went on to another village.

James and John are understandably disturbed, but their violent solution (echoing the destruction of Sodom and Gomorrah for their lack of hospitality in Gen 19:24) shows that they have not understood or have forgotten Jesus's previous teaching to simply shake the dust from their feet if any town would not welcome them (9:5) and to love their enemies (6:35).[40] In coming episodes, there are positive portrayals of Samaritans (10:25-37; 17:11-19). In Acts, Jesus includes Samaria in the mission program (1:8), which is successfully taken up by Philip (8:4-13), Peter, and John (8:14, 25).

A twist on the call to discipleship occurs in 9:57-62. Call stories ordinarily begin with Jesus taking the initiative (see 5:1-11, 27-28; 9:59). In 9:57 and 9:61, two different individuals approach Jesus. His response to the first (9:58) underscores his itinerancy, but it is not clear if the potential disciple joins the movement. Luke does not tell us whether the second and third persons shift their priorities and follow Jesus. It is also not clear whether the one who wants to bury his father seeks to wait until his father dies, whether the burial is imminent, or whether the issue is secondary burial in an ossuary. If the cost of discipleship means foregoing filial duties and abandoning one's family,[41] it is a steep one indeed. At 14:26 and 18:28-29, it is clear that Jesus has male disciples in mind when he includes one's wife among those whom a disciple must leave.

40. See Dale C. Allison Jr., "Rejecting Violent Judgment: Luke 9:52-56 and Its Relatives," *JBL* 121 (2002): 459–78, who shows the long tradition of understanding God as merciful and forbearing in the OT and in rabbinic literature.

41. Luke 9:61-62 alludes to 1 Kgs 19:19-21: Elisha asks to kiss his father and mother before following Elijah, and he allows it.

57As they were going along the road, someone said to him, "I will follow you wherever you go." 58And Jesus said to him, "Foxes have holes, and birds of the air have nests; but the Son of Man has nowhere to lay his head." 59To another he said, "Follow me." But he said, "Lord, first let me go and bury my father." 60But Jesus said to him, "Let the dead bury their own dead; but as for you, go and proclaim the kingdom of God." 61Another said, "I will follow you, Lord; but let me first say farewell to those at my home." 62Jesus said to him, "No one who puts a hand to the plow and looks back is fit for the kingdom of God."

We wonder what happens to the women, children, and other family members left behind. The gospel is silent on who takes over their care if the head of the household abandons them. Perhaps the male disciples, like the women at 8:1-3, left home only temporarily, engaging in day trips with Jesus and returning to their homes at night. The point is to prioritize response to Jesus over all else.

Works Cited

Aboud, Hosn. "'*Idhan Maryam Nabiyya*' ('Hence Maryam Is a Prophetess'): Muslim Classical Exegetes and Women's Receptiveness to God's Verbal Inspiration." In *Mariam, the Magdalene, and the Mother*, edited with an introduction by Deirdre Good, 183–96. Bloomington: Indiana University Press, 2005.

Ackermann, Denise M. "Power." In *Dictionary of Feminist Theologies*, edited by Letty M. Russell and J. Shannon Clarkson, 219–20. Louisville: Westminster John Knox, 1996.

Aguilar, Grace. *The Women of Israel*. England, 1845; New York: D. Appleton, 1872.

Alexander, David. "Feeding the Hungry and Protecting the Environment." In *All Creation Is Groaning: An Interdisciplinary Vision for Life in a Sacred Universe*, edited by Carol J. Dempsey and Russell A. Butkus, 77–98. Collegeville, MN: Liturgical Press, 1999.

Alexander, Loveday. "The Acts of the Apostles as an Apologetic Text." In *Apologetics in the Roman Empire: Pagans, Jews, and Christians*, edited by Mark Edwards, Martin Goodman, Simon Price, and Christopher Rowland, 15–44. Oxford: Oxford University Press, 1999.

———. "Luke's Preface in the Context of Greek Preface Writing." *NovT* 28 (1986): 48–74.

———. *The Preface to Luke's Gospel: Literary Convention and Social Context in Luke 1.1-4 and Acts 1.1*. SNTSMS 78. Cambridge: Cambridge University Press, 1993.

———. "What if Luke Had Never Met Theophilus?" *BibInt* 8 (2000): 161–70.

Alliance for Global Justice. "Political Prisoners in the USA." https://afgj.org/politicalprisonersusa.

Allison, Dale C., Jr. "Rejecting Violent Judgment: Luke 9:52-56 and Its Relatives." *JBL* 121 (2002): 459–78.

Alter, Alexandra. "Alice Walker, Answering Backlash, Praises Anti-Semitic Author as 'Brave.'" *New York Times.* December 21, 2018. https://www.nytimes.com/2018/12/21/arts/alice-walker-david-icke-times.html.

Amnesty International. "What Does Amnesty Do?" https://www.amnesty.org/en/who-we-are/.

———. "Women in Prison: A Fact Sheet." https://www.prisonpolicy.org/scans/women_prison.pdf.

Anderson, Janice Capel, and Stephen D. Moore, eds. *Mark and Method: New Approaches in Biblical Studies.* 2nd ed. Minneapolis: Fortress, 2008.

Anderson, Robert T. "Samaritans." AYBD 5.940–43.

Andrade, Kevin G. "Fear of Census Common for Immigrants in R. I." *Providence Journal.* July 5, 2018. https://www.providencejournal.com/news/20180705/fear-of-census-common-for-immigrants-in-ri.

Anti-Defamation League. "Audit of Anti-Semitic Incidents: Year in Review 2018." https://www.adl.org/2018-audit-S.

Aquino, María Pilar, and María José Rosado-Nunes, eds. *Feminist Intercultural Theology: Latina Explorations for a Just World.* Studies in Latino/a Catholicism. Maryknoll, NY: Orbis Books, 2007.

Aquino, María Pilar, Daisy L. Machado, and Jeanette Rodríguez, eds. *A Reader in Latina Feminist Theology.* Austin: University of Texas Press, 2002.

Arav, Rami. "Bethsaida." In *Jesus and Archaeology,* edited by James H. Charlesworth, 145–66. Grand Rapids: Eerdmans, 2006.

Archdiocese of Chicago Domestic Violence Outreach. https://pvm.archchicago.org/human-dignity-solidarity/domestic-violence-outreach.

Armour, Ellen T. "Essentialism." In *Dictionary of Feminist Theologies,* edited by Letty M. Russell and J. Shannon Clarkson, 88. Louisville: Westminster John Knox, 1996.

Articulus. "Corporate Storytelling: Communicating with Credibility for Women Leaders." https://www.articulus.com/training/communicate-w-credibility-women/.

Associated Press. "The Murder of Her Son Jordan Davis Prompted Her Activism, Now She's Won the Congressional Primary in Georgia." *Atlanta Black Star.* July 27, 2018. https://atlantablackstar.com/2018/07/27/the-murder-of-her-son-jordan-davis-prompted-her-activism-now-shes-won-the-congressional-primary-in-georgia/.

Astell, Mary. *Some Reflections upon Marriage.* New York: Source Book Press, 1970. Reprint of the 1730 edition; earliest ed. 1700.

Attridge, Harold. "The Samaritan Woman: A Woman Transformed." In *Character Studies in the Fourth Gospel: Narrative Approaches to Seventy Figures in John,* edited by Steven A. Hunt, D. Francois Tolmie, and Ruben Zimmermann, 268–81. Grand Rapids: Eerdmans, 2016.

Atwood, Margaret. *The Handmaid's Tale.* New York: Alfred A. Knopf, 2006.

Aviam, Mordechai. "People, Land, Economy, and Belief in First-Century Galilee and Its Origins: A Comprehensive Archaeological Synthesis." In *The Gali-*

lean Economy in the Time of Jesus, edited by David A. Fiensy and Ralph K. Hawkins, 5–48. ECL 11. Atlanta: SBL, 2013.

Ayyappan, R. "Blind Teacher with a Vision on a Priceless Mission." https://english .manoramaonline.com/women/on-a-roll/2019/03/08/blind-teacher-baby -girija-braille-books-kerala.html.

Bach, Alice, ed. *Women in the Hebrew Bible: A Reader*. New York: Routledge, 1999.

Baden, Joel S. "The Nature of Barrenness in the Hebrew Bible." In *Disability Studies and Biblical Literature*, edited by Candida R. Moss and Jeremy Schipper, 13–27. New York: Palgrave Macmillan, 2011.

Bagnall, Roger S. "Jesus Reads a Book." *JTS* 51 (2000): 577–88.

Bailey, Kenneth E. *Poet and Peasant and through Peasant Eyes*. 2 vols. in 1. Grand Rapids: Eerdmans, 1976.

Bain, Katherine. *Women's Socioeconomic Status and Religious Leadership in Asia Minor in the First Two Centuries C.E.* Minneapolis: Fortress, 2014.

Bal, Mieke. *Death and Dissymmetry: The Politics of Coherence in the Book of Judges*. Chicago: University of Chicago Press, 1988.

———. *Lethal Love: Feminist Literary Readings of Biblical Love Stories*. Bloomington: Indiana University Press, 1987.

Balla, Peter. *The Child-Parent Relationship in the New Testament and Its Environment*. WUNT 155. Tübingen: Mohr Siebeck, 2003.

Barry, Dan, Serge F. Kovaleski, Campbell Robertson, and Lizette Alvarez. "Race, Tragedy and Outrage Collide after a Shot in Florida." *The New York Times*. April 1, 2012. https://www.nytimes.com/2012/04/02/us/trayvon -martin-shooting-prompts-a-review-of-ideals.html.

Barry, Emily Reimer. "On Women's Health and Women's Power: A Feminist Appraisal of *Humane Vitae*." *TS* 79 (2018): 818–40.

Bartchy, S. Scott. "Slavery: New Testament." *ABD* 6.65–73.

Barton, Mukti. "The Skin of Miriam Became as White as Snow: The Bible, Western Feminism and Colour Politics." *FT* 27 (2001): 68–80.

Baskin, Judith R. "Women and Post-Biblical Commentary." In *The Torah: A Women's Commentary*, edited by Tamara Cohn Eskenazi and Andrea L. Weiss, xlix–lv. New York: URJ Press and Women of Reform Judaism, The Federation of Temple Sisterhoods, 2008.

Basu, Anasuya. "How India's Female Storytellers Fought to Be Heard." BBC. July 12, 2016. http://www.bbc.com/news/world-asia-india-36648490.

Bauckham, Richard. *Jude and the Relatives of Jesus in the Early Church*. London: T&T Clark, 2004.

Baxter, Elizabeth. *The Women in the Word: A Few Simple Hints from Bible Portraits of Women*. 2nd ed. London: Christian Herald, 1897.

BBC News. "Nigeria Chibok Abductions: What We Know." May 8, 2017. https:// www.bbc.com/news/world-africa-32299943.

Beard, Mary. *Laughter in Ancient Rome: On Joking, Tickling, and Cracking Up*. Berkeley: University of California Press, 2014.

Beattie, Tina. "Catholicism, Choice, and Consciousness: A Feminist Theological Perspective on Abortion." *International Journal of Public Theology* 4 (2010): 51–75.

———. *God's Mother, Eve's Advocate: A Marian Narrative of Women's Salvation.* London: Continuum, 2002.

Beavis, Mary Ann, ed. *The Lost Coin: Parables of Women, Work and Wisdom.* BibSem 86. London: Sheffield Academic, 2002.

———. "Reconsidering Mary of Bethany." *CBQ* 74 (2012): 281–97.

———. "The Resurrection of Jephthah's Daughter: Judges 11:34-40 and Mark 5:21-24, 35-43." *CBQ* 72 (2010): 46–62.

Bednarz, Terri. *Humor in the Gospels: A Sourcebook for the Study of Humor in the New Testament, 1863–2014.* Lanham, MD: Lexington Books, 2015.

BeDuhn, Jason D. *The First New Testament: Marcion's Scriptural Canon.* Salem, OR: Polebridge, 2013.

Belleville, Linda L. "Ἰουνίαν . . . ἐπίσημοι ἐν τοῖς ἀποστόλοις: A Re-examination of Romans 16.7 in Light of Primary Source Materials." *NTS* 51 (2005): 231–49.

Benjamin, Mara H. "Tracing the Contours of a Half Century of Jewish Feminist Theology." *JFSR* 36 (2020): 11–31.

Berke, Jamie. "Biography of Helen Keller." https://www.verywellhealth.com /helen-kellers-biography-1046171.

Berlin, Adele. "Bath-shua 2." In *Women in Scripture: A Dictionary of Named and Unnamed Women in the Hebrew Bible, the Apocryphal/Deuterocanonical Books, and the New Testament,* edited by Carol Meyers, Toni Craven, and Ross Shepard Kraemer, 59. Grand Rapids: Eerdmans, 2000.

Betsworth, Sharon. *Children in Early Christian Narratives.* New York: Bloomsbury T&T Clark, 2015.

Betz, Hans Dieter. *The Sermon on the Mount: A Commentary on the Sermon on the Mount, Including the Sermon on the Plain (Matthew 5:3–7:27 and Luke 6:20-49).* Hermeneia. Minneapolis: Fortress, 1995.

Beyer, Hermann W. "διακονέω, διακονία, διάκονος." *TDNT* 2 (1964): 81–93.

Billings, Drew W. *Acts of the Apostles and the Rhetoric of Roman Imperialism.* Cambridge: Cambridge University Press, 2018.

Birch, Tony. " 'We've Seen the End of the World and We Don't Accept It': Protection of Indigenous Country and Climate Justice." In *Places of Privilege: Interdisciplinary Perspectives on Identities, Change and Resistance,* edited by Nicole Oke, Christopher Sonn, and Alison Baker, 139–52. Leiden: Brill, 2018.

Bird, Phyllis A. *Missing Persons and Mistaken Identities: Women and Gender in Ancient Israel.* Minneapolis: Fortress, 1997.

Black Lives Matter. https://blacklivesmatter.com/.

Bleeker, C. J. "Isis as Saviour Goddess." In *The Saviour God: Comparative Studies in the Concept of Salvation,* edited by S. G. F. Brandon. Manchester: Manchester University Press, 1963.

Bloch, Herbert, ed. *The Roman Brick Stamps.* Rome: L'Erma de Bretschneider, 1967.

Block, Peter. *Community: The Structure of Belonging.* San Francisco: Berrett-Koehler, 2008.

Boer, Esther de. *Mary Magdalene: Beyond the Myth.* Translated by John Bowden. Harrisburg, PA: Trinity Press International, 1997.

——. *The Mary Magdalene Cover-Up: The Sources Behind the Myth.* Translated by John Bowden. London: T&T Clark, 2007.

Boer, Roland, and Christina Petterson. *Time of Troubles: A New Economic Framework for Early Christianity.* Minneapolis: Fortress, 2017.

Boff, Leonardo. *El rostro materno de Dios: Ensayo interdisciplinario sobre lo femenino y sus formas religiosas.* 3rd ed. Madrid: Paulinas, 1981.

Bonz, Marianne Palmer. *The Past as Legacy: Luke–Acts and Ancient Epic.* Minneapolis: Fortress, 2000.

Boochani, Behrouz. "All We Want Is Freedom—Not Another Prison Camp." *The Guardian.* November 13, 2017. https://www.theguardian.com/commentisfree/2017/nov/13/all-we-want-is-freedom-not-another-prison-camp.

——. *No Friend but the Mountains: Writing from Manus Prison.* Translated by Omid Tofighian. Sydney: Picador, 2018.

Bovon, François. *Luke 1: A Commentary on the Gospel of Luke 1:1–9:50.* Translated by Christine M. Thomas. Hermeneia. Minneapolis: Fortress, 2002.

——. *Das Evangelium nach Lukas.* Vol. 1. EKK 3. Zürich: Benziger, 1989.

Bowean, Lolly. "Hadiya Pendleton's Parents Reflect on the Trial, Their Losses, Their Lives." *Chicago Tribune.* August 27, 2018. https://www.chicagotribune.com/news/local/breaking/ct-met-hadiya-pendleton-mother-father-20180827-story.html.

Boyarin, Daniel. "*Logos,* A Jewish Word: John's Prologue as Midrash." In *The Jewish Annotated New Testament,* edited by Amy-Jill Levine and Marc Zvi Brettler, 688–91. 2nd ed. New York: Oxford University Press, 2017.

Brangham, William. "Climate Activist Greta Thunberg on the Power of a Movement." *PBS NewsHour.* September 13, 2019. https://www.pbs.org/newshour/show/climate-warrior.

Brenner, Athalya. "Female Social Behavior: Two Descriptive Patterns within the 'Birth of the Hero' Paradigm." *VT* 36 (1986): 257–73.

——. *The Israelite Woman: Social Role and Literary Type in Biblical Narrative.* London: Bloomsbury, 2014.

Brett, Mark G. *Political Trauma and Healing: Biblical Ethics for a Postcolonial World.* Grand Rapids: Eerdmans, 2016.

Bring Back Our Girls. https://bringbackourgirls.ng/.

Brink, Laurie. *Soldiers in Luke–Acts.* WUNT 2.362. Tübingen: Mohr Siebeck, 2014.

Brock, Ann Graham. *Mary Magdalene, the First Apostle: The Struggle for Authority.* HTS 51. Cambridge, MA: Harvard University Press, 2003.

Brodie, Thomas L. *The Crucial Bridge: The Elijah–Elisha Narrative as an Interpretive Synthesis of Genesis–Kings and a Literary Model for the Gospels.* Collegeville, MN: Liturgical Press, 2000.

Brooke, George J. "A Long-Lost Song of Miriam." *BAR* 20 (1994): 62–65.

Brooten, Bernadette J. "'Junia . . . Outstanding among the Apostles' (Romans 16:7)." In *Women Priests: A Catholic Commentary on the Vatican Declaration*, edited by Leonard Swidler and Arlene Swidler, 141–44. New York: Paulist Press, 1977.

———. *Love Between Women: Early Christian Responses to Female Homoeroticism.* Chicago: University of Chicago Press, 1996.

———. *Women Leaders in the Ancient Synagogue: Inscriptional Evidence and Background Issues.* BJS 36. Chico, CA: Scholars Press, 1982.

Brown, Raymond E. "The Annunciation to Zechariah, the Birth of the Baptist, and the Benedictus (Luke 1:5-25, 57-30)." *Worship* 62 (1988): 482–96.

———. *The Birth of the Messiah: A Commentary on the Infancy Narratives in Matthew and Luke.* Garden City, NY: Doubleday, 1977.

———. *The Gospel According to John I–XII.* AB 29. New York: Doubleday, 1966.

———. "Gospel Infancy Narrative Research from 1976 to 1986: Part I (Matthew)." *CBQ* 48 (1986): 468–83.

———. "Gospel Infancy Narrative Research from 1976 to 1986: Part II (Luke)." *CBQ* 48 (1986): 660–80.

Brown, Raymond E., Karl P. Donfried, Joseph A. Fitzmyer, and John Reumann. *Mary in the New Testament: A Collaborative Assessment by Protestant and Roman Catholic Scholars.* Philadelphia: Fortress; New York: Paulist Press, 1978.

Bruce, F. F. "Some Thoughts on the Beginning of the New Testament Canon." *BJRL* 65 (1983): 37–60.

Brueggemann, Walter. *Sabbath as Resistance: Saying No to the Culture of Now.* Louisville: Westminster John Knox, 2017.

Bula-at, Leticia. "Indigenous Women's Struggles: The Chico Dam Project and the Kalinga Women." Edited and translated by Bernice See. http://cpcabrisbane.org/Kasama/1996/V10n2/Innabuyog.htm.

Bunge, Marcia J., ed. *The Child in Christian Thought.* Grand Rapids: Eerdmans, 2001.

Bunge, Marcia J., Terence E. Fretheim, and Beverly Roberts Gaventa, eds. *The Child in the Bible.* Grand Rapids: Eerdmans, 2008.

Burer, Michael H., and Daniel B. Wallace. "Was Junia Really an Apostle? A Reexamination of Rom 16.7." *NTS* 47 (2001): 76–91.

Burns, J. Patout, and Gerald M. Fagin, eds. *The Holy Spirit.* Message of the Fathers of the Church 3. Wilmington, DE: Glazier, 1984.

Burns, Rita J. *Has the Lord Indeed Spoken Only Through Moses? A Study of the Biblical Portrait of Miriam.* SBLDS 84. Atlanta: Scholars Press, 1987.

Bynum, Carolyn Walker. *Holy Feast and Holy Fast: The Religious Significance of Food to Medieval Women.* Berkeley: University of California Press, 1988.

Byrne, Brendan. *The Hospitality of God: A Reading of Luke's Gospel.* Strathfield, NSW: St. Pauls, 2000.

Cadbury, H. J. *The Style and Literary Method of Luke.* HTS 6/1. Cambridge, MA: Harvard University Press, 1920.

Cady Stanton, Elizabeth. *The Woman's Bible*. Amherst, NY: Prometheus Books, 1999 (original 1897).

Camp, Claudia V. "Wise Woman of Abel of Beth-maacah." In *Women in Scripture: A Dictionary of Named and Unnamed Women in the Hebrew Bible, The Apocryphal/ Deuterocanonical Books, and the New Testament*, edited by Carol Meyers, Toni Craven, and Ross Shepard Kraemer, 266–67. Grand Rapids: Eerdmans, 2000.

———. "Wise Woman of Tekoa." In *Women in Scripture: A Dictionary of Named and Unnamed Women in the Hebrew Bible, The Apocryphal/Deuterocanonical Books, and the New Testament*, edited by Carol Meyers, Toni Craven, and Ross Shepard Kraemer, 263. Grand Rapids: Eerdmans, 2000.

Cannon, Katie G. "The Emergence of Black Feminist Consciousness." In *Feminist Interpretation of the Bible*, edited by Letty M. Russell, 30–40. Philadelphia: Westminster, 1985.

Carey, Greg. *Luke: An Introduction and Study Guide; All Flesh Shall See God's Salvation*. T&T Clark's Study Guides to the New Testament. London: Bloomsbury T&T Clark, 2017.

Carroll, Robert P. "Coopting the Prophets: Nehemiah and Noadiah." In *Priests, Prophets, and Scribes: Essays on the Formation of Heritage of Second Temple Judaism in Honour of Joseph Blenkinsopp*, edited by Eugene Ulrich, 87–99. JSOTSup 149. Sheffield: JSOT, 1992.

Carter, Harold A. *The Prayer Tradition of Black People*. Valley Forge: Judson Press, 1976.

Carter, Warren. *The Gospel of Matthew in Its Roman Imperial Context*. London: T&T Clark, 2005.

———. *The Roman Empire and the New Testament: An Essential Guide*. Nashville, TN: Abingdon, 2006.

Cassidy, Richard S. *Society and Politics in the Acts of the Apostles*. Maryknoll, NY: Orbis Books, 1987.

Castelli, Elizabeth. "*Les Belles Infidèles*/Fidelity or Feminism? The Meanings of Feminist Biblical Translation." In *Searching the Scriptures*, vol. 1: *A Feminist Introduction*, edited by Elisabeth Schüssler Fiorenza with the assistance of Shelly Matthews, 189–204. New York: Crossroad, 1993.

Centro de Desarrollo Integral de las Mujeres, Santa Escolástica. https://www.scribd.com/doc/104877977/Filosofia-y-Mapa-de-Cedimse.

Charlesworth, James H. *Jesus and Archaeology*. Grand Rapids: Eerdmans, 2006.

Christensen, Jeanne, in collaboration with Dale Jarvis. "Pathway to a Better Life." https://www.sistersagainsttrafficking.org/2020/03/05/march-2020-monthly-reflection/.

The Church of England. "The Churching of Women." http://anglicanhistory.org/liturgy/old_catholic_ritual/churching.html.

Claassens, L. Juliana, and Carolyn J. Sharp, eds. *Feminist Frameworks and the Bible: Power, Ambiguity, and Intersectionality*. LHBOTS 630. London: Bloomsbury T&T Clark, 2017.

Clendenen, Avis. *Forgiveness: Finding Freedom through Reconciliation*. New York: Crossroad, 2002.

Coaston, Jane. "The Conspiracy Theories behind the Anti-Semitic Violence in New York." *Vox*. January 3, 2020. https://www.vox.com/2020/1/3/21039446/anti -semitism-anti-orthodox-farrakhan-conspiracy-theories-bipartisan.

CODIMUJ (Coordinación Diocesana de Mujeres). *Con Mirada, Mente y Corazón de Mujer*. México, D.F.: CODIMUJ, 1999.

Cohen, Shaye J. D. "Menstruants and the Sacred in Judaism and Christianity." In *Women's History and Ancient History*, edited by Sarah B. Pomeroy, 273–99. Chapel Hill: University of North Carolina Press, 1991.

Coleridge, Mark. *The Birth of the Lukan Narrative: Narrative as Christology in Luke 1–2*. JSNTSup 88. Sheffield: JSOT, 1993.

Collins, John N. *DIAKONIA: Re-interpreting the Ancient Sources*. New York: Oxford University Press, 1990.

Columbia University Business School. "Strategic Storytelling." http://www8.gsb .columbia.edu/execed/program-pages/details/831/DSS?utm_source =bing&utm_medium=cpc&utm_term=storytelling&utm_content=Digital _Storytelling&utm_campaign=Core_Marketing.

Connolly, R. Hugh, ed. *Didascalia Apostolorum*. Oxford: Clarendon, 1929; re-printed 1969.

Conway, Colleen M. *Behold the Man: Jesus and Greco-Roman Masculinity*. Oxford: Oxford University Press, 2008.

Conzelmann, Hans. *The Theology of St. Luke*. New York: Harper, 1960.

Copeland, M. Shawn. *Knowing Christ Crucified: The Witness of the African American Religious Experience*. Maryknoll, NY: Orbis Books, 2018.

Corley, Kathleen E. *Maranatha: Women's Funerary Rituals and Christian Origins*. Minneapolis: Fortress, 2010.

———. *Private Women, Public Meals: Social Conflict in the Synoptic Tradition*. Pea-body, MA: Hendrickson, 1993.

Corrington, Gail Paterson. *Her Image of Salvation: Female Saviors and Formative Christianity*. Gender and the Biblical Tradition. Louisville: Westminster John Knox, 1992.

Cosgrove, Charles H. "A Woman's Unbound Hair in the Greco-Roman World, with Special Reference to the Story of the 'Sinful Woman' in Luke 7:36-50." *JBL* 124 (2005): 675–92.

Cotter, Wendy. "Mark's Hero of the Twelfth-Year Miracles: The Healing of the Woman with the Hemorrhage and the Raising of Jairus's Daughter (Mk 5:21-43)." In *A Feminist Companion to Mark*, edited by Amy-Jill Levine with Marianne Blickenstaff, 54–78. FCNTECW 2. Sheffield: Sheffield Academic, 2001.

———. *Miracles in Greco-Roman Antiquity: A Sourcebook for the Study of New Tes-tament Miracle Stories*. New York: Routledge, 1999.

Creech, Mark H. "What if Mary Had Known about Abortion?" *Christian Post*. December 17, 2012. https://www.christianpost.com/news/what-if-mary -had-known-about-abortion.html.

Crenshaw, Kimberlé. *On Intersectionality: Essential Writings*. New York: The New Press, 2000.

Crossan, John Dominic. *God and Empire: Jesus against Rome, Then and Now*. San Francisco: HarperSanFrancisco, 2007.

——. *The Historical Jesus: The Life of a Mediterranean Jewish Peasant*. San Francisco: HarperSanFrancisco, 1991.

——. *Jesus: A Revolutionary Biography*. San Francisco: HarperSanFrancisco, 1994.

——. "'Like One of the Prophets of Old': Two Types of Popular Prophets at the Time of Jesus." *CBQ* 47 (1985): 435–63.

Crowder, Stephanie Buckhanon. *When Momma Speaks: The Bible and Motherhood from a Womanist Perspective*. Louisville: Westminster John Knox, 2016.

Croy, N. Clayton, and Alice E. Connor. "Mantic Mary? The Virgin Mother as Prophet in Luke 1.26-56 and in the Early Church." *JSNT* 34 (2011): 254–76.

Culpepper, R. Alan. "Seeing the Kingdom of God: The Metaphor of Sight in the Gospel of Luke." *CurTM* 21 (1994): 434–43.

D'Angelo, Mary Rose. "The ANHP Question in Luke–Acts: Imperial Masculinity and the Deployment of Women in the Early Second Century." In *A Feminist Companion to Luke*, edited by Amy-Jill Levine with Marianne Blickenstaff, 44–69. FCNTECW 3. Sheffield: Sheffield Academic, 2002.

——. "Gender and Power in the Gospel of Mark: The Daughter of Jairus and the Woman with the Flow of Blood." In *Miracles in Jewish and Christian Antiquity: Imagining Truth*, edited by John C. Cavadini, 83–109. Notre Dame Studies in Theology 3. Notre Dame, IN: University of Notre Dame Press, 1999.

——. "(Re)Presentations of Women in the Gospel of Matthew and Luke–Acts." In *Women and Christian Origins*, edited by Ross Shepard Kraemer and Mary Rose D'Angelo. New York: Oxford University Press, 1999.

——. "Women in Luke–Acts: A Redactional View." *JBL* 109 (1990): 441–61.

——. "Women Partners in the New Testament." *JFSR* 6 (1990): 65–86.

Daly, Mary. *Beyond God the Father: A Philosophy of Women's Liberation*. Boston: Beacon, 1973.

——. *Gyn/ecology. The Metaethics of Radical Feminism*. Boston: Beacon, 1978.

Dandamayev, Muhammad A. "Slavery: Old Testament." ABD 6.62–65.

Danker, Frederick W. *Benefactor: Epigraphic Study of a Graeco-Roman and New Testament Semantic Field*. St. Louis: Clayton, 1982.

——. *Jesus and the New Age: A Commentary on St. Luke's Gospel*. Rev. and exp. ed. Philadelphia: Fortress, 1988.

Davies, Stevan L. *The Revolt of the Widows: The Social World of the Apocryphal Acts*. Carbondale: Southern Illinois University, 1980.

Davis, Andrew. "The End of Humiliation in LXX Isa 40:2." In *Forget Not God's Benefits (Ps 103:2): A Festschrift in Honor of Leslie J. Hoppe, OFM*. CBQ Imprints. Washington, DC: CBA, forthcoming.

Davis, Michael. "The Anti-Jewish Manifesto of John T. Earnest, the San Diego Synagogue Shooter." May 15, 2019. *Middle East Research Institute*. Inquiry and Analysis Series, No. 1454. https://www.memri.org/reports/anti-jewish-manifesto-john-t-earnest-san-diego-synagogue-shooter.

Davis, Stephen J. *The Cult of St. Thecla: A Tradition of Women's Piety in Late Antiquity*. OECS. New York: Oxford University Press, 2001.

Davison, Lisa Wilson. *Preaching the Women of the Bible*. St. Louis: Chalice, 2006.

Deissmann, Adolf. *Light from the Ancient East: The New Testament Illustrated by Recently Discovered Texts of the Graeco-Roman World*. Translated by Lionel R. M. Strachan. London: Hodder & Stoughton, 1910.

Denzinger, Heinrich. *Enchiridion symbolorum: definitionum et declarationum de rebus fidei et morum*. 34th ed. Barcinone: Herder, 1965.

Deutsch, Celia. *Lady Wisdom, Jesus, and the Sages: Metaphor and Social Context in Matthew's Gospel*. Valley Forge, PA: Trinity Press International, 1996.

Dinkler, Michal Beth. *Literary Theory and the New Testament*. AYBRL. New Haven: Yale University Press, 2019.

———. "The Thoughts of Many Hearts Shall Be Revealed: Listening in on Lukan Interior Monologues." *JBL* 134 (2015): 373–99.

Diogenes Laertius. *Lives of Eminent Philosophers*. Vol. 2. Translated by Robert Drew Hicks. Cambridge, MA: Harvard University Press, 1925.

Douglas, Sally. *Early Church Understandings of Jesus as the Female Divine: The Scandal of Particularity*. LNTS 557. London: Bloomsbury T&T Clark, 2016.

Dryden-Edwards, Roxanne. "Domestic Violence." MedicineNet Newsletters. https://www.medicinenet.com/domestic_violence/article.htm.

Dube, Musa W. "Fifty Years of Bleeding: A Storytelling Feminist Reading of Mark 5:24-43." In *Other Ways of Reading: African Women and the Bible*, edited by Musa W. Dube, 11–17. Atlanta: SBL, 2001.

———. *Postcolonial Feminist Interpretation of the Bible*. Atlanta: Chalice, 2000.

Duck, Ruth C. *Gender and the Name of God: The Trinitarian Baptismal Formula*. New York: Pilgrim, 1991.

Duff, Nancy J. "Mary, Servant of the Lord." In *Blessed One: Protestant Perspectives on Mary*, edited by Beverly Roberts Gaventa and Cynthia L. Rigby, 59–70. Louisville: Westminster John Knox, 2002.

Dunfee, Susan Nelson. "The Sin of Hiding: A Feminist Critique of Reinhold Niebuhr's Account of the Sin of Pride." *Soundings* 65 (1982): 25–35.

Dunn, James D. G. "Did Jesus Attend the Synagogue?" In *Jesus and Archaeology*, edited by James H. Charlesworth, 206–22. Grand Rapids: Eerdmans, 2006.

Eagleton, Terry. *Ideology: An Introduction*. London: Verso, 2007.

———. *Literary Theory: An Introduction*. 3rd ed. Minneapolis: University of Minnesota Press, 2008.

Edwards, Denis. *Breath of Life: A Theology of the Creator Spirit*. Maryknoll, NY: Orbis Books, 2004.

Edwards, Jason. *Eve Kosofsky Sedgwick*. Routledge Critical Thinkers. New York: Routledge, 2009.

Einat, Ramon. "Ritual: A Feminist Approach." *Jewish Women: A Comprehensive Historical Encyclopedia*. March 1, 2009. Jewish Women's Archive. https://jwa.org/encyclopedia/article/ritual-feminist-approach.

Eisen, Ute E. *Women Officeholders in Early Christianity: Epigraphical and Literary Studies*. Translated by Linda M. Maloney. Collegeville, MN: Liturgical Press, 2000.

Elkins, Kathleen Gallagher. *Mary, Mother of Martyrs: How Motherhood Became Self-Sacrifice in Early Christianity*. Indianapolis: FSR Books, 2018.

Elliott, J. K. *The Apocryphal New Testament: A Collection of Apocryphal Christian Literature in English Translation*. New York: Oxford University Press, 2006.

Elvey, Anne F. *An Ecological Feminist Reading of the Gospel of Luke: A Gestational Paradigm*. Lewiston, NY: Edwin Mellen, 2005.

_____. "Can There Be a Forgiveness That Makes a Difference Ecologically? An Eco-Materialist Account of Forgiveness as Freedom (ἄφεσις) in the Gospel of Luke." *Pacifica* 22 (2009): 148–70.

_____. "From Cultures of Violence to Ways of Peace: Reading the *Benedictus* in the Context of Australia's Treatment of Asylum Seekers in Offshore Detention." In *Things That Make for Peace: Traversing Text and Tradition in Christianity and Islam*, edited by Anthony Rees. Lanham, MD: Lexington, 2020.

_____. *The Matter of the Text: Material Engagements between Luke and the Five Senses*. Sheffield: Sheffield Phoenix, 2011.

_____. *On Arrivals of Breath: Poems and Prayers*. Montrose, VIC: Poetica Christi Press, 2019.

Epp, Eldon Jay. *Junia: The First Woman Apostle*. Minneapolis: Fortress, 2005.

Eshel, Esther. "Jesus the Exorcist in Light of Epigraphic Sources." In *Jesus and Archaeology*, edited by James H. Charlesworth, 178–85. Grand Rapids: Eerdmans, 2006.

Eskenazi, Tamara Cohn, and Andrea L. Weiss, eds. *The Torah: A Women's Commentary*. New York: URJ Press and Women of Reform Judaism, The Federation of Temple Sisterhoods, 2008.

Etling, Mark. "Lord, Why Am I not Worthy?" *National Catholic Reporter*. July 13–26, 2018. https://www.ncronline.org/news/opinion/soul-seeing/lord-why-am-i-not-worthy.

Exum, J. Cheryl. "Second Thoughts about Secondary Characters: Women in Exodus 1.8–2.10." In *A Feminist Companion to Exodus to Deuteronomy*, edited by Athalya Brenner, 75–97. FCB 6. Sheffield: Sheffield Academic, 1994.

Exum, J. Cheryl, and David J. A. Clines, eds. *The New Literary Criticism and the Hebrew Bible*. Valley Forge, PA: Trinity Press International, 1993.

Fagenblat, Michael. "The Concept of Neighbor in Jewish and Christian Ethics." In *The Jewish Annotated New Testament*, edited by Amy-Jill Levine and Marc Zvi Brettler, 645–50. 2nd ed. New York: Oxford University Press, 2017.

Fell, Margaret. *Women's Speaking Justified, Proved and Allowed by the Scriptures*. London, 1667.

Feminists for Life. https://www.feministsforlife.org/.

Feminist Sexual Ethics Project. https://www.brandeis.edu/projects/fse/about /index.html.

Fewell, Danna Nolan, and David M. Gunn. *Gender, Power, and Promise: The Subject of the Bible's First Story.* Nashville: Abingdon, 1993.

Fiensy, David A. "Assessing the Economy of Galilee in the Late Second Temple Period: Five Considerations." In *The Galilean Economy in the Time of Jesus,* edited by David A. Fiensy and Ralph K. Hawkins, 165–86. ECL 11. Atlanta: SBL, 2013.

Fischer, Irmtraud, Adriana Valerio, Mercedes Navarro Puerto, Christiana de Groot, and Mary Ann Beavis. *The Bible and Women: An Encyclopaedia of Exegesis and Cultural History.* http://www.bibleandwomen.org.

Fitzmyer, Joseph A. *The Gospel According to Luke I–IX.* AB 28. Garden City, NY: Doubleday, 1981.

———. "New Testament *Kyrios* and *Maranatha* and Their Aramaic Background." In *To Advance the Gospel: New Testament Studies,* 218–35. New York: Crossroad, 1981.

———. "The Semitic Background of the New Testament *Kyrios*-Title." In *A Wandering Aramean: Collected Aramaic Essays,* 115–42. SBLMS 25. Chico, CA: Scholars Press, 1979.

———. "The Virginal Conception of Jesus in the New Testament." *TS* 34 (1973): 567–70.

Focus on Labour Exploitation. "Women Workers and Exploitation: The Gender Pay Gap Is Just the Beginning." August 3, 2017. https://www.labour exploitation.org/news/women-workers-and-exploitation-gender-pay -gap-just-beginning.

Foerster, Werner. "σωτήρ." *TDNT* 7 (1971): 1004–5.

Fonrobert, Charlotte. "The Woman with a Blood-Flow (Mark 5:24-34) Revisited: Menstrual Laws and Jewish Culture in Christian Feminist Hermeneutics." In *Early Christian Interpretation of the Scriptures of Israel: Investigations and Proposals,* edited by Craig A. Evans and James A. Sanders, 121–40. JSNTSup 148. SSEJC 5. Sheffield: Sheffield Academic, 1997.

Fontaine, Carole R. "Disabilities and Illness in the Bible: A Feminist Perspective." In *A Feminist Companion to the Hebrew Bible in the New Testament,* edited by Athalya Brenner, 286–300. FCB 10. Sheffield: Sheffield Academic, 1996.

Ford, Josephine Massyngbaerde. *Redeemer—Friend and Mother: Salvation in Antiquity and in the Gospel of John.* Minneapolis: Fortress, 1997.

Ford, Patricia Henry, and Maricarmen Bracamontes. *Mujeres y Derechos Humanos. Perspectivas y Alternativas. Aportes Sociales y Eclesiales.* 3rd rev. ed. Mexico, D.F.: Ediciones Schola, CEDIMSE, 2001.

Foskett, Mary F. *A Virgin Conceived: Mary and Classical Representations of Virginity.* Bloomington: Indiana University Press, 2002.

———. "Virginity as Purity in the *Protoevangelium of James.*" In *A Feminist Companion to Mariology,* edited by Amy-Jill Levine with Maria Mayo Robbins, 67–76. FCNTECW 10. Edinburgh: T&T Clark, 2005.

Francis, James M. M. *Adults as Children: Images of Childhood in the Ancient World and the New Testament*. Religions and Discourse 17. Oxford: Peter Lang, 2006.

Francis, Pope. "Address to the Central American Bishops." Panama. January 24, 2019. http://www.vatican.va/content/francesco/en/speeches/2019/january/documents/papa-francesco_20190124_panama-vescovi-centroamericani.html.

———. *Evangelii Gaudium*. Apostolic Exhortation. November 24, 2013. http://www.vatican.va/content/francesco/en/apost_exhortations/documents/papa-francesco_esortazione-ap_20131124_evangelii-gaudium.html.

———. "Homily, Chrism Mass." March 28, 2013. http://www.vatican.va/content/francesco/en/homilies/2013/documents/papa-francesco_20130328_messa-crismale.html.

———. Letter of His Holiness Pope Francis to the Grand Chancellor of the "Pontificia Universidad Católica Argentina" for the One Hundredth Anniversary of the Founding of the Faculty of Theology. http://www.vatican.va/content/francesco/en/letters/2015/documents/papa-francesco_20150303_lettera-universita-cattolica-argentina.html.

———. *Misericordiae Vultus*. Papal Bull. http://w2.vatican.va/content/francesco/en/apost_letters/documents/papa-francesco_bolla_20150411_misericordiae-vultus.html.

———. "No Longer Slaves But Brothers and Sisters." World Day of Peace. January 1, 2015. http://www.vatican.va/content/francesco/en/messages/peace/documents/papa-francesco_20141208_messaggio-xlviii-giornata-mondiale-pace-2015.html.

Fredriksen, Paula. *Sin: The Early History of an Idea*. Princeton: Princeton University Press, 2012.

Freeze, Amy. "Blind Woman Teaches Art to Blind Students in the Bronx." https://abc7ny.com/education/blind-woman-teaches-art-to-blind-students-in-the-bronx/3338760/.

Frilingos, Christopher A. *Jesus, Mary, and Joseph: Family Troubles in the Infancy Gospels*. Divinations: Reading Late Ancient Religion. Philadelphia: University of Pennsylvania Press, 2017.

Frymer-Kensky, Tikva. "Deborah 2." In *Women in Scripture: A Dictionary of Named and Unnamed Women in the Hebrew Bible; The Apocryphal/Deuterocanonical Books, and the New Testament*, edited by Carol Meyers, Toni Craven, and Ross Shepard Kraemer, 67. Grand Rapids: Eerdmans, 2000.

———. *Reading the Women of the Bible*. New York: Schocken, 2002.

Fuchs, Esther. "Laughing with/at/as Women: How Should We Read Biblical Humor?" In *Are We Amused? Humour about Women in the Biblical World*, edited by Athalya Brenner, 127–36. JSOTSup 383. New York: T&T Clark, 2003.

———. "The Literary Characterization of Mothers and Sexual Politics in the Hebrew Bible." In *Women in the Hebrew Bible: A Reader*, edited by Alice Bach, 127–40. New York: Routledge, 1999.

G., M. *Women Like Ourselves: Short Addresses for Mother's Meetings, Bible Classes, Etc.* London: SPCK, 1893.

Gafney, Wilda C. *Daughters of Miriam: Women Prophets in Ancient Israel.* Minneapolis: Fortress, 2008.

———. *Womanist Midrash: A Reintroduction to the Women of the Torah and the Throne.* Louisville: Westminster John Knox, 2017.

Gallares, Judette. "And She Will Speak: Junia, the Voice of a Silenced Woman Apostle." In *Ecclesia of Women in Asia: Gathering the Voices of the Silenced,* edited by Evelyn Monteiro and Antoinette Gutzler, 89–107. Delhi: ISPCK, 2005.

García-Rivera, Alejandro. "The Whole and the Love of Difference: Latino Metaphysics as Cosmology." In *From the Heart of Our People: Latino/a Explorations in Catholic Systematic Theology,* edited by Orlando O. Espín and Miguel H. Díaz, 54–83. Maryknoll, NY: Orbis Books, 1999.

García Serrano, Andrés. "Anna's Characterization in Luke 2:36-38: A Case of Conceptual Allusion?" *CBQ* 76 (2014): 464–80.

Gardner, Jane. *Women in Roman Law and Society.* Bloomington: Indiana University Press, 1986.

Garland-Thomson, Rosemarie. "Feminist Disability Studies." *Signs* 30 (Winter 2005): 1557–87.

Garrett, Susan R. *The Demise of the Devil: Magic and the Demonic in Luke's Writings.* Minneapolis: Fortress, 1989.

Gaventa, Beverly Roberts. "'All Generations Will Call Me Blessed': Mary in Biblical and Ecumenical Perspective." In *A Feminist Companion to Mariology,* edited by Amy-Jill Levine with Maria Mayo Robbins, 121–29. Cleveland: Pilgrim Press, 2005.

———. *Mary: Glimpses of the Mother of Jesus.* Studies on Personalities of the New Testament. Columbia: University of South Carolina Press, 1995.

Gaventa, Beverly Roberts, and Cynthia L. Rigby, eds. *Blessed One: Protestant Perspectives on Mary.* Louisville: Westminster John Knox, 2002.

Gebara, Ivone, and Maria Clara L. Bingemer. *María, Mujer Profética. Ensayo teológico a partir de la mujer y de América Latina.* Madrid: Ediciones Paulinas, 1988.

Gertler, Pesha Joyce. "Miriam: Not an American Success Story." *Bridges: A Jewish Feminist Journal* 12 (2007): 72–73.

Getty-Sullivan, Mary Ann. *Women in the New Testament.* Collegeville, MN: Liturgical Press, 2001.

Gilkes, Cheryl Townsend. *If It Wasn't for the Women: Black Women's Experience and Womanist Culture in Church and Community.* Maryknoll, NY: Orbis Books, 2001.

Gilligan, Carol. *In a Different Voice: Psychological Theory and Women's Development.* Cambridge, MA: Harvard University Press, 1982.

Gillman, Florence Morgan. *1 Thessalonians.* WCS 52. Collegeville, MN: Liturgical Press, 2016.

Gillman, John. *Possessions and the Life of Faith: A Reading of Luke–Acts.* Zacchaeus Studies, New Testament. Collegeville, MN: Liturgical Press, 1991.

Gin, Deborah H. C., and Jo Ann Deasy. "In Your Own Words." Association of Theological Schools Women in Leadership in Theological Education Twentieth Anniversary. March 1, 2018. https://www.ats.edu/uploads/resources/research/WIL-20th-anniversary-presentation--180301.pdf.

Glancy, Jennifer. *Slavery in Early Christianity.* New York: Oxford University Press, 2002.

Gleason, Maud. *Making Men: Sophists and Self-Presentation in Ancient Rome.* Princeton: Princeton University Press, 1995.

Golani, Shira. "Is There a Consensus That a Census Causes a Plague?" https://thetorah.com/is-there-a-consensus-that-a-census-causes-a-plague/.

Goldstein, Valerie Saiving. "The Human Situation: A Feminine View." *JR* 40 (1960): 100–112.

Gonzalez, Michelle A. "Latina Feminist Theology: Past, Present, and Future." *JFSR* 25 (2009): 150–55.

Good, Deirdre J. "Reading Strategies for Biblical Passages on Same-Sex Relations." *Theology and Sexuality* 7 (1997): 70–82.

———. "What Does It Mean to Call Mary Mariam?" In *A Feminist Companion to Mariology,* edited by Amy-Jill Levine with Maria Mayo Robbins, 99–106. FCNTECW 10. Edinburgh: T&T Clark, 2005.

Goodacre, Mark. *The Case against Q: Studies in Markan Priority and the Synoptic Problem.* Harrisburg, PA: Trinity Press International, 2002.

Goodstein, Laurie. "'There Is Still So Much Evil': Growing Anti-Semitism Stuns American Jews." *The New York Times.* October 29, 2018. https://www.nytimes.com/2018/10/29/us/anti-semitism-attacks.html.

Gowler, David B. "The Chreia." In *The Historical Jesus in Context,* edited by Amy-Jill Levine, Dale C. Allison Jr., and John Dominic Crossan, 132–48. Princeton Readings in Religion. Princeton: Princeton University Press, 2006.

———. "Text, Culture and Ideology in Luke 7:1-10: A Dialogic Reading." In *Fabrics of Discourse: Essays in Honor of Vernon K. Robbins,* edited by David B. Gowler, L. Gregory Bloomquist, and Duane F. Watson, 89–125. Harrisburg, PA: Trinity Press International, 2003.

Grant, Jacquelyn. "The Sin of Servanthood and the Deliverance of Discipleship." In *A Troubling in My Soul: Womanist Perspectives on Evil and Suffering,* edited by Emilie M. Townes, 199–218. The Bishop Henry McNeal Turner Studies in North American Black Religion 8. Maryknoll, NY: Orbis Books, 1993.

———. "Womanist Theology: Black Women's Experience as a Source for Doing Theology, with Special Reference to Christology." *The Journal of the Interdenominational Theological Center* 13 (1986): 195–212.

Green, Joel B. *The Gospel of Luke.* NICNT. Grand Rapids: Eerdmans, 1997.

———. "Setting the Context: Roman Hellenism." In *The World of the New Testament: Cultural, Social and Historical Contexts,* edited by Joel B. Green and Lee Martin McDonald. Grand Rapids: Baker, 2013.

———. "The Social Status of Mary in Luke 1,5–2,52: A Plea for Methodological Integration." *Bib* 73 (1992): 457–72.

Gregersen, Niels Henrik, ed. *Incarnation: On the Scope and Depth of Christology.* Minneapolis: Fortress, 2015.

Gregory, Andrew. *The Reception of Luke and Acts in the Period before Irenaeus.* WUNT 2.169. Tübingen: Mohr Siebeck, 2003.

Grenfell, Bernard P., and Arthur S. Hunt, eds. *The Oxyrhynchus Papyri.* Vol. 11. Nos. 1351–1404. Graeco-Roman Memoirs 14. London: Egypt Exploration Society, 1915. https://archive.org/stream/oxyrhynchuspapyr11gren#page/202/mode/2up.

Grey, Mary C. *Introducing Feminist Images of God.* IFT 7. Cleveland: Pilgrim, 2001.

———. "Where Does the Wild Goose Fly To? Seeking a New Theology of Spirit for Feminist Theology." *New Blackfriars* 72 (1991): 89–96.

Griffin, Michael, and Jennie Weiss Block, eds. *In The Company of the Poor: Conversations with Dr. Paul Farmer and Fr. Gustavo Gutiérrez.* Maryknoll, NY: Orbis Books, 2013.

Grimké, Sarah. *Letters on the Equality of the Sexes and the Condition of Woman.* Boston: Isaac Knapp, 1838.

Grundmann, Walter. *Das Evangelium nach Lukas.* 5th ed. Berlin: Evangelische Verlagsanstalt, 1969.

Grynbaum, Michael M. "Site That Ran Anti-Semitic Remarks Got Passes for Trump Trip." *New York Times.* January 26, 2020. https://www.nytimes.com/2020/01/26/business/media/trunews-white-house-press-credentials.html?smtyp=cur&smid=fb-nytimes&fbclid=IwAR2knY0OJerXNi5q7ZFja8KRQTD_lXxRGaq6FwMgLGkZCYrRR5x3ALomRcI.

Guest, Deryn. *When Deborah Met Jael: Lesbian Feminist Hermeneutics.* London: SCM, 2011.

Gundry-Volf, Judith M. "The Least and the Greatest: Children in the New Testament." In *The Child in Christian Thought*, edited by Marcia J. Bunge, 29–60. Grand Rapids: Eerdmans, 2001.

Günther, Eva. *Wisdom as a Model for Jesus' Ministry: A Study on the "Lament over Jerusalem" in Matt 23:37-39 Par. Luke 13:34-35.* WUNT 2.513. Tübingen: Mohr Siebeck, 2020.

Gutiérrez, Gustavo. *The God of Life.* Translated by Matthew J. O'Connell. Maryknoll, NY: Orbis Books, 1991. Originally published as *El Dios de la vida.* Lima, Perú: Instituto Bartolomé de las Casas, 1989.

———. *A Theology of Liberation: History, Politics, and Salvation.* Maryknoll, NY: Orbis Books, 1973.

Habel, Norman C., and Peter Trudinger. *Exploring Ecological Hermeneutics.* SymS 46. Atlanta: SBL, 2008.

Haber, Susan. "A Woman's Touch: Feminist Encounters with the Hemorrhaging Woman in Mark 5:24-34." *JSNT* 26 (2003): 171–92.

Haight, Roger. *Jesus, Symbol of God.* Maryknoll, NY: Orbis Books, 1999.

Hale, Sarah. *Woman's Record; or, Sketches of All Distinguished Women from the Creation to A.D. 1854.* New York: Harper & Brothers, 1855.

Hamm, Dennis. *The Beatitudes in Context: What Luke and Matthew Meant.* Zacchaeus Studies: New Testament. Wilmington, DE: Glazier, 1990.

Harris, William V. *Ancient Literacy.* Cambridge, MA: Harvard University Press, 1989.

Harrison Beverly Wildung. *Our Right to Choose: Toward a New Ethic of Abortion.* Boston: Beacon, 1983.

Haskins, Susan. *Mary Magdalen: Myth and Metaphor.* New York: Riverhead Books, 1995.

Havrelock, Rachel. "The Myth of Birthing the Hero: Heroic Barrenness in the Hebrew Bible." *BibInt* 16 (2008): 154–78.

Hayes, Diana L. *And Still We Rise: An Introduction to Black Liberation Theology.* New York: Paulist Press, 1996.

——. "And When We Speak: To Be Black, Catholic, and Womanist." In *Taking Down Our Harps: Black Catholics in the United States,* edited by Diana L. Hayes and Cyprian Davis, 102–19. Maryknoll, NY: Orbis Books, 1998.

Hayes, Diana L., and Cyprian Davis, eds. *Taking Down Our Harps: Black Catholics in the United States.* Maryknoll, NY: Orbis Books, 1998.

Hays, Christopher M. *Luke's Wealth Ethics: A Study in Their Coherence and Character.* WUNT 2.275. Tübingen: Mohr Siebeck, 2010.

——. *Renouncing Everything: Money and Discipleship in Luke.* New York: Paulist Press, 2016.

Healing Touch Program. https://discover.healingtouchprogram.com/htp-home.

Hearon, Holly E. *The Mary Magdalene Tradition: Witness and Counter-Witness in Early Christian Communities.* Collegeville, MN: Liturgical Press, 2004.

Hearon, Holly E., and Philip Ruge-Jones, eds. *The Bible in Ancient and Modern Media: Story and Performance.* Eugene, OR: Cascade, 2009.

Hedrick, Charles W. "Miracle Stories as Literary Compositions: The Case of Jairus's Daughter." *PRSt* 20 (1993): 217–33.

Heifetz, Ronald, Alexander Grashow, Marty Linsky. *The Practice of Adaptive Leadership: Tools and Tactics for Changing Your Organization and the World.* Boston: Harvard Business Press, 2009.

Hendel, Ronald S. *The Epic of the Patriarch: The Jacob Cycle and the Narrative Traditions of Canaan and Israel.* HSM 42. Atlanta: Scholars Press, 1987.

Hengel, Martin. "Proseuche und Synagoge. Jüdische Gemeinde, Gotteshaus und Gottesdienst in der Diaspora und in Palästina." In *Festschrift Karl George Kuhn. Tradition und Glaube: das frühe Christentum in seiner Umwelt. Festgabe für Karl Georg Kuhn zum 65. Geburtstag,* edited by Gert Jeremias, Heinz-Wolfgang Kuhn, and Hartmut Stegemann, 157–84. Göttingen: Vandenhoeck & Ruprecht, 1971.

Hens-Piazza, Gina. *Lamentations.* WCS 30. Collegeville, MN: Liturgical Press, 2017.

——. *The New Historicism.* GBS, Old Testament Series. Minneapolis: Fortress, 2002.

Heyob, Sharon Kelly. *The Cult of Isis among Women in the Graeco-Roman World.* Études préliminaires aux religions orientales dans l'Empire romain 51. Leiden: Brill, 1975.

Hezser, Catherine. *Jewish Literacy in Roman Palestine.* TSAJ 81. Tübingen: Mohr Siebeck, 2001.

Hiebert, Theodore. "Rethinking Dominion Theology." *Direction* 25 (Fall 1996): 16–25.

Hirschfeld, Gustav, ed. *The Collection of Ancient Greek Inscriptions in the British Museum.* Part IV. London, 1893.

Hobart, W. K. *The Medical Language of St. Luke.* London: Longmans Green, 1882.

Hoke, Jimmy. *Under God? Romans in Feminist and Queer Assemblages.* ECL. Atlanta: SBL Press, forthcoming.

Holpuch, Amanda. "Stolen Daughters: What Happened after #BringBackOur-Girls?" *The Guardian.* October 22, 2018. https://www.theguardian.com/tv-and-radio/2018/oct/22/bring-back-our-girls-documentary-stolen-daughters-kidnapped-boko-haram.

hooks, bell. *Feminist Theory: From Margin to Center.* Boston: South End Press, 1984.

Hoppe, Leslie J. "Synagogue." In *The Collegeville Pastoral Dictionary of Biblical Theology,* edited by Carroll Stuhlmueller, 969–71. Collegeville, MN: Liturgical Press, 1996.

———. *The Synagogues and Churches of Ancient Palestine.* Collegeville, MN: Liturgical Press, 1993.

———. *There Shall Be No Poor among You: Poverty in the Bible.* Nashville: Abingdon, 2004.

Horn, Cornelia B., and John W. Martens. *"Let the Little Children Come to Me": Childhood and Children in Early Christianity.* Washington, DC: The Catholic University of America Press, 2009.

Hornsby, Teresa J. "The Woman Is a Sinner/The Sinner Is a Woman." In *A Feminist Companion to Luke,* edited by Amy-Jill Levine with Marianne Blickenstaff, 121–32. FCNTECW 3. London: Sheffield Academic, 2002.

Hornsby, Teresa, and Ken Stone, eds. *Bible Trouble: Queer Readings at the Boundaries of Biblical Scholarship.* Atlanta: SBL, 2011.

Horsley, Richard A. *Jesus and Empire: The Kingdom of God and the New World Disorder.* Minneapolis: Augsburg Fortress, 2003.

———. *Jesus and the Spiral of Violence: Popular Jewish Resistance in Roman Palestine.* San Francisco: Harper & Row, 1987.

———. *The Liberation of Christmas: The Infancy Narratives in Social Context.* New York: Crossroad, 1989.

———. "'Like One of the Prophets of Old': Two Types of Popular Prophets at the Time of Jesus." *CBQ* 47 (1985): 435–63.

Hospodar, Blaise. "*META SPOUDES* in Lk 1.39." *CBQ* 18 (1956): 14–18.

Howell, Justin R. *The Pharisees and Figured Speech in Luke–Acts.* WUNT 2.456. Tübingen: Mohr Siebeck, 2017.

Hozeski, Bruce W., trans. *Hildegard's Healing Plants: From Her Medieval Classic Physica*. Boston: Beacon, 2001.

Hughes, Kathleen. "Baptism." In *The Collegeville Pastoral Dictionary of Biblical Theology*, edited by Carroll Stuhlmueller, 70–74. Collegeville, MN: Liturgical Press, 1996.

Huizenga, Annette Bourland. *1–2 Timothy, Titus*. WCS 53. Collegeville, MN: Liturgical Press, 2016.

Human Rights Watch. https://www.hrw.org/tag/political-prisoners#.

Hurtado, Larry. *One God, One Lord: Early Christian Devotion and Ancient Jewish Monotheism*. Cornerstones. 3rd ed. London: Bloomsbury T&T Clark, 2015.

Hylen, Susan E. *A Modest Apostle: Thecla and the History of Women in the Early Church*. New York: Oxford University Press, 2015.

———. *Women in the New Testament World*. Essentials of Biblical Studies. Oxford: Oxford University Press, 2019.

Ilan, Tal. "The Attraction of Aristocratic Jewish Women to Pharisaism during the Second Temple Period." *HTR* 88 (1995): 1–33.

———. "Gender." In *The Jewish Annotated New Testament*, edited by Amy-Jill Levine and Marc Zvi Brettler, 611–14. 2nd ed. New York: Oxford University Press, 2017.

———. *Integrating Women into Second Temple History*. Tübingen: Mohr Siebeck, 1999.

———. *Jewish Women in Greco-Roman Palestine*. Peabody, MA: Hendrickson, 1996.

———. "Notes on the Distribution of Jewish Women's Names in Palestine in the Second Temple and Mishnaic Periods." *JJS* 40 (1989): 186–200.

———. "Post-biblical Interpretations." In *The Torah: A Women's Commentary*, edited by Tamara Cohn Eskenazi and Andrea L. Weiss, 862–64. New York: URJ Press and Women of Reform Judaism, The Federation of Temple Sisterhoods, 2008.

Imperatori-Lee, Natalia. *Cuéntame: Narrative in the Ecclesial Present*. Maryknoll, NY: Orbis Books, 2018.

Incigneri, Brian J. *The Gospel to the Romans: The Setting and Rhetoric of Mark's Gospel*. BibInt 65. Leiden: Brill, 2003.

International Labour Organization. "Forced Labour, Modern Slavery, and Human Trafficking." http://www.ilo.org/global/topics/forced-labour/lang--en/index.htm.

Irarrázaval, Diego, Susan Ross, and Marie-Theres Wacker, eds. *The Many Faces of Mary*. Concilium 2008, no. 4. London: SCM, 2008.

Isasi-Díaz, Ada María. *Mujerista Theology: A Theology for the Twenty-first Century*. Maryknoll, NY: Orbis Books, 1996.

Isherwood, Lisa. *The Fat Jesus: Feminist Explorations in Boundaries and Transgressions*. London: Darton, Longman and Todd, 2007.

Jacob, Sharon. "Jauhar, Mass-Suicide, and the Spectacle of Death: A Reading of Mark 5:1-20." *FSR* (blog). February 12, 2020. https://www.fsrinc.org/jauhar-mass-suicide-and-the-spectacle-of-death-a-reading-of-mark-51-20/.

———. *Reading Mary Alongside Indian Surrogate Mothers: Violent Love, Oppressive Liberation, and Infancy Narratives.* The Bible and Cultural Studies. New York: Palgrave Macmillan, 2015.

James, M. R., trans. "The Acts of Peter." In *The Apocryphal New Testament.* Oxford: Clarendon, 1924. http://www.earlychristianwritings.com/text/actspeter.html.

Jansen, Katherine Ludwig. *The Making of the Magdalen: Preaching and Popular Devotion in the Later Middle Ages.* Princeton: Princeton University Press, 2000.

Janssen, Claudia, and Regene Lamb. "Gospel of Luke: The Humbled Will Be Lifted Up." In *Feminist Biblical Interpretation: A Compendium of Critical Commentary on the Books of the Bible and Related Literature,* edited by Luise Schottroff and Marie-Theres Wacker, translated by Lisa E. Dahill, Everett R. Kalin, Nancy Lukens, Linda M. Maloney, Barbara Rumscheidt, Martin Rumscheidt, and Tina Steiner, 645–61. Grand Rapids: Eerdmans, 2012.

Janzen, J. Gerald. "Song of Moses, Song of Miriam: Who Is Seconding Whom?" *CBQ* 54 (1992): 211–20.

Jennings, Theodore W., Jr., and Tat-Siong Benny Liew, "Mistaken Identities but Model Faith: Rereading the Centurion, the Chap, and the Christ in Matthew 8:5-13." *JBL* 123 (2004): 467–94.

Jewish Lifecycle. "Brit Banot." http://jewishwebsight.com/lifecycle/brit.html.

Jewish Women's Archive. http://jwa.org.

Jobling, David. *The Sense of Biblical Narrative: Three Structural Analyses in the Old Testament.* JSOTSup 7. Sheffield: University of Sheffield Press, 1978.

Jobling, David, and Tina Pippin, eds. *Ideological Criticism of Biblical Texts.* Semeia 59. Atlanta: Scholars Press, 1992.

John, Tara. "Boko Haram Has Kidnapped Dozens of Schoolgirls, Again. Here's What to Know." *TIME.* February 26, 2018. https://time.com/5175464/boko-haram-kidnap-dapchi-schoolgirls/.

Johnsen, Carsten, and Sylvi Johnsen. *The Writing in the Sand: The Part of the Story That You Were Never Told about Mary Magdalene.* New York: Vantage, 1984.

Johnson, Elizabeth A. *Ask the Beasts: Darwin and the God of Love.* London: Bloomsbury, 2014.

———. *Creation and the Cross: The Mercy of God for a Planet in Peril.* Maryknoll, NY: Orbis Books, 2018.

———. "Don't Make Mary the Feminine Face of God." *U.S. Catholic.* Originally published April 1994; reprinted May 2016. http://www.uscatholic.org/articles/201605/don't-make-mary-feminine-face-god-30644.

———. "God." In *Dictionary of Feminist Theologies,* edited by Letty M. Russell and J. Shannon Clarkson, 128–30. Louisville: Westminster John Knox, 1996.

———. "Mary and the Female Face of God." *TS* 50 (1989): 500–526.

———. *She Who Is: The Mystery of God in Feminist Theological Discourse.* New York: Crossroad, 1992.

———. "The Symbolic Character of Theological Statements about Mary." *JES* 22 (1985): 312–35.

————. *Truly Our Sister: A Theology of Mary in the Communion of Saints*. New York: Continuum, 2003.

————. *Women, Earth, and Creator Spirit*. New York: Paulist Press, 1993.

Johnson, Luke T. *The Literary Function of Possessions in Luke–Acts*. SBLDS 39. Missoula: Scholars Press, 1977.

Johnson-DeBaufre, Melanie. *Jesus among Her Children: Q, Eschatology, and the Construction of Christian Origins*. HTS 55. Cambridge, MA: Harvard University Press, 2005.

Joshel, Sandra R., and Sheila Murnaghan. *Women and Slaves in Greco-Roman Culture: Differential Equations*. London: Routledge, 1998.

Jung, Patricia Beattie. "Abortion: An Exercise in Moral Imagination." *Reproductive Health Matters* 1 (1993): 84–86.

Junior, Nyasha. *An Introduction to Womanist Biblical Interpretation*. Louisville: Westminster John Knox, 2015.

————. "Womanist Biblical Interpretation." In *Engaging the Bible in a Gendered World: An Introduction to Feminist Biblical Interpretation in Honor of Katharine Doob Sakenfeld*, edited by Linda Day and Carolyn Pressler, 37–46. Louisville: Westminster John Knox, 2006.

Kaaland, Jennifer T. *Reading Hebrews and 1 Peter with the African American Great Migration: Diaspora, Place, Identity*. London: Bloomsbury T&T Clark, 2019.

Kahl, Brigitte. "Jairus und die verlorenen Töchter Israels: Sozioliterarische Überlegungen zum Problem der Grenzüberschreitung in Mk 5, 21–43." In *Von der Wurzel getragen: Christlich-feministische Exegese in Auseinandersetzung mit Antijudaismus*, edited by Luise Schottroff and Marie-Theres Wacker, 61–78. BibInt 17. Leiden: Brill, 1996.

————. "Reading Luke against Luke: Non-Uniformity of Text, Hermeneutics of Conspiracy and the 'Scriptural Principle' in Luke 1." In *A Feminist Companion to Luke*, edited by Amy-Jill Levine with Marianne Blickenstaff, 70–88. FCNTECW 3. Sheffield: Sheffield Academic, 2002.

Kamanofsky, Amy. "Women of God: Maternal Grief and Religious Response in 1 Kings 17 and 2 Kings 4." *JSOT* 36 (2011): 55–74.

Kamitsuka, Margaret D. "Unwanted Pregnancy, Abortion, and Maternal Authority: A Prochoice Theological Argument." *JFSR* 34 (2018): 41–57.

Kanyoro, Musimbi R. A. *Introducing Feminist Cultural Hermeneutics: An African Perspective*. IFT. Cleveland: Pilgrim Press, 2002.

Karris, Robert J. "Women and Discipleship in Luke." *CBQ* 56 (1994): 1–20.

Kasper, Walter. *The God of Jesus Christ*. New York: Crossroad, 1984.

Kay, James F. "Critic's Corner: In Whose Name? Feminism and the Trinitarian Baptismal Formula." *ThTo* 49 (1993): 524–33.

Keith, Chris. *Jesus' Literacy: Scribal Culture and the Teacher from Galilee*. Library of Historical Jesus Studies 8. LNTS 413. New York: T&T Clark, 2011.

————. *Literacy: New Testament*. Oxford Bibliographies Online. New York: Oxford University Press, 2015.

Kelley, Nicole. "'The Punishment of the Devil Was Apparent in the Torment of the Human Body': Epilepsy in Ancient Christianity." In *Disability Studies and Biblical Literature*, edited by Candida R. Moss and Jeremy Schipper, 205–21. New York: Palgrave MacMillan, 2011.

Kibbe, Michael. "Light That Conquers the Darkness: Oscar Romero on the Transfiguration of Jesus." *ThTo* 75 (2019): 447–57.

Kim, Seyoon. *Christ and Caesar: The Gospel and the Roman Empire in the Writings of Paul and Luke*. Grand Rapids: Eerdmans, 2008.

King, Karen L. *The Gospel of Mary of Magdala: Jesus and the First Woman Apostle*. Santa Rosa, CA: Polebridge, 2003.

Kinzer, Mark. *Jerusalem Crucified, Jerusalem Risen*. Eugene, OR: Cascade, 2018.

Kittredge, Cynthia Briggs, and Claire Miller Colombo. "Colossians." In *Philippians, Colossians, Philemon*, by Elsa Tamez, Cynthia Briggs Kittredge, Claire Miller Colombo, and Alicia J. Batten. WCS 51. Collegeville, MN: Liturgical Press, 2017.

Kitzberger, Ingrid Rosa, ed. *Autobiographical Biblical Interpretation: Between Text and Self*. Leiden: Deo, 2002.

———. "Transcending Gender Boundaries in John." In *A Feminist Companion to John*. vol. 1, edited by Amy-Jill Levine with Marianne Blickenstaff, 171–207. FCNTECW 4. London: Sheffield Academic, 2003.

Kizley, Benedict. "Estimating the Number of Homeless in America." *The Data Face*. January 21, 2018. http://thedataface.com/2018/01/public-health/american-homelessness.

Kloppenborg, John S. "Conceptual Stakes in the Synoptic Problem." In *Gospel Interpretation and the Q-Hypothesis*, edited by Mogens Müller and Heike Omerzu, 13–42. LNTS 573. London: Bloomsbury T&T Clark, 2018.

———. "Literate Media in Early Christ Groups: The Creation of a Christian Book Culture." *JECS* 22 (2014): 21–59.

———. "Luke's Geography: Knowledge, Ignorance, Sources, and Spatial Conception." In *Luke on Jesus, Paul, and Christianity: What Did He Really Know?*, edited by Joseph Verheyden and John S. Kloppenborg, 101–43. BTS 29. Leuven: Peeters, 2017.

———. "On Dispensing with Q? Goodacre on the Relation of Luke to Matthew." *NTS* 49 (2003): 210–36.

———. "The Theodotos Synagogue Inscription and the Problem of First-Century Synagogue Buildings." In *Jesus and Archaeology*, edited by James H. Charlesworth, 236–82. Grand Rapids: Eerdmans, 2006.

Knight, Sam. "The Uncanny Power of Greta Thunberg's Climate-Change Rhetoric." *The New Yorker*. April 24, 2019. https://www.newyorker.com/news/daily-comment/the-uncanny-power-of-greta-thunbergs-climate-change-rhetoric.

Kochenash, Michael. "Review Essay: Taking the Bad with the God; Reconciling Images of Rome in Luke–Acts." *RelSRev* 41 (2015): 43–51.

Kodell, Jerome. "Luke and the Children: The Beginning and End of the Great Interpolation (Luke 9:46-56; 18:9-23)." *CBQ* 49 (1987): 415–30.

Koester, Helmut. *Introduction to the New Testament*. Vol. 1: *History, Culture and Religion of the Hellenistic Age*. 2nd ed. New York: DeGruyter, 1995.

Kopas, Jane. "Jesus and Women: Luke's Gospel." *ThTo* 43 (1986): 192–202.

Koperski, Veronica. "Is 'Luke' a Feminist or Not? Female-Male Parallels in Luke–Acts." In *Luke and His Readers: Festschrift A. Denaux*, edited by Reimund Bieringer, Gilbert van Belle, and Joseph Verheyden, 25–48. BETL 182. Leuven: Leuven University Press, 2005.

Kraemer, Ross Shepard. *Her Share of the Blessings: Women's Religions Among Pagans, Jews, and Christians in the Greco-Roman World*. New York: Oxford University Press, 1992.

———. "Monastic Jewish Women in Greco-Roman Egypt: Philo Judaeus on the Therapeutrides." *Signs* 14 (1989): 342–70.

———. *Unreliable Witnesses: Religion, Gender, and History in the Greco-Roman Mediterranean*. Oxford: Oxford University Press, 2011.

———. "Women's Authorship of Jewish and Christian Literature in the Greco-Roman Period." In *"Women Like This": New Perspectives on Jewish Women in the Greco-Roman World*, edited by Amy-Jill Levine, 221–42. EJL 1. Atlanta: Scholars Press, 1991.

Kraemer, Ross Shepard, and Mary Rose D'Angelo, eds. *Women and Christian Origins*. New York: Oxford University Press, 1999.

Krause, Deborah. "Simon Peter's Mother-in-Law—Disciple or Domestic Servant? Feminist Biblical Hermeneutics and the Interpretation of Mark 1.29-31." In *A Feminist Companion to Mark*, edited by Amy-Jill Levine with Marianne Blickenstaff, 37–53. FCNTECW 2. Sheffield: Sheffield Academic, 2001.

Kuhn, Karl Allen. "Deaf or Defiant? The Literary, Cultural, and Affective-Rhetorical Keys to the Naming of John (Luke 1:57-80)." *CBQ* 75 (2013): 486–503.

Kümmel, Werner Georg. *Einleitung in das Neue Testament*. 17th ed. Heidelberg: Quelle und Meyer, 1973.

Kyrychenko, Alexander. *The Roman Army and the Expansion of the Gospel: The Role of the Centurion in Luke–Acts*. BZNW 203. Berlin: DeGruyter, 2014.

LaCugna, Catherine Mowry. "The Baptismal Formula, Feminist Objections, and Trinitarian Theology." *JES* 26 (1989): 235–50.

———. *God for Us: The Trinity and Christian Life*. San Francisco: Harper Collins, 1991.

Laffey, Alice L. "Images of Mary in the Christian Scriptures." In *All Generations Shall Call Me Blessed*, edited by F. A. Eigo, 39–71. Villanova, PA: Villanova University Press, 1994.

Leander, Hans. *Discourses of Empire: The Gospel of Mark from a Postcolonial Perspective*. SemeiaSt 71. Atlanta: SBL, 2013.

LeClaire, Jennifer. "What if Mary Had Chosen Abortion?" *Charism News*. December 18, 2015. https://www.charismanews.com/opinion/watchman-on-the-wall/53920-what-if-mary-had-chosen-abortion.

Lederach, John Paul. *Reconcile: Conflict Transformation for Ordinary Christians*. Harrisonburg, VA: Herald Press, 2014.

Lee, Nancy C. "Lamentations and Polemic: The Rejection/Reception History of Women's Lament . . . and Syria." *Int* 67 (2013): 155–83.

Lee, Witness. "Jesus Intentionally Breaks the Sabbath." In *Christ Versus Religion*. Living Stream Ministry. http://www.ministrysamples.org/excerpts/JESUS-INTENTIONALLY-BREAKS-THE-SABBATH.HTML.

Lefa, Mmapula. "Reading the Bible Amidst the HIV and AIDS Pandemic in Botswana." In *African and European Readers of the Bible in Dialogue: In Quest of a Shared Meaning*, edited by J. H. de Wit and Gerald O. West, 285–303. Studies on Religion in Africa 32. Leiden: Brill, 2008.

Lefkowitz, Mary R. "Did Ancient Women Write Novels?" In *"Women Like This": New Perspectives on Jewish Women in the Greco-Roman World*, edited by Amy-Jill Levine, 199–219. EJL 1. Atlanta: Scholars Press, 1991.

Lefkowitz, Mary R., and Maureen B. Fant. *Women's Life in Greece and Rome: A Sourcebook in Translation*. 2nd ed. Baltimore: Johns Hopkins University Press, 1992.

Leo, Kim Jeong Ja. "God Our Ma/Father's Korean Women's Church." In *Ecclesia of Women in Asia: Gathering the Voices of the Silenced*, edited by Evelyn Monteiro and Antoinette Gutzler, 162–83. Delhi: ISPCK, 2005.

Lerner, Gerda. *Creation of Feminist Consciousness: From the Middle Ages to Eighteen-Seventy*. New York: Oxford University Press, 1993.

Levine, Amy-Jill. "Anti-Judaism and the Gospel of Matthew." In *Anti-Judaism and the Gospels*, edited by William R. Farmer, 9–36. Harrisburg, PA: Trinity Press International, 1999.

———. "Christian Privilege, Christian Fragility, and the Gospel of John." In *The Gospel of John and Jewish-Christian Relations*, edited by Adele Reinhartz, 87–111. Lanham, MD: Lexington Press, 2018.

———. "Discharging Responsibility: Matthean Jesus, Biblical Law, and Hemorrhaging Woman." In *Treasures New and Old: Recent Contributions to Matthean Studies*, edited by David R. Bauer and Mark Alan Powell, 379–97. Atlanta: Scholars Press, 1996. Reprinted in *A Feminist Companion to Matthew*, edited by Amy-Jill Levine with Marianne Blickenstaff, 70–87. FCNTECW 1. Sheffield: Sheffield Academic, 2001.

———. "The Gospel of Matthew: Between Breaking and Continuity." In *Gospels: Narrative and History*, edited by Mercedes Navarro Puerto, Marinella Perroni, and Amy-Jill Levine (English ed.), 121–44. The Bible and Women: An Encyclopedia of Exegesis and Cultural History. New Testament 2.1. Atlanta: SBL Press, 2015.

———. "Gospel of Matthew." In *Women's Bible Commentary*, edited by Carol A. Newsom, Sharon H. Ringe, and Jacqueline E. Lapsley, 465–77. 3rd ed. Louisville: Westminster John Knox, 2012.

_____. "Hermeneutics of Suspicion." In *Dictionary of Feminist Theologies*, edited by Letty M. Russell and J. Shannon Clarkson, 140–41. Louisville: Westminster John Knox, 1996.

_____. "Introduction." In *A Feminist Companion to Luke*, edited by Amy-Jill Levine with Marianne Blickenstaff, 1–22. FCNTECW 3. Sheffield: Sheffield Academic, 2002.

_____. "Luke's Pharisees." In *In Quest of the Historical Pharisees*, edited by Jacob Neusner and Bruce D. Chilton, 113–30. Waco, TX: Baylor University Press, 2007.

_____. *The Misunderstood Jew: The Church and the Scandal of the Jewish Jesus*. San Francisco: HarperSanFrancisco, 2006.

_____. "Pharisees in Luke." In *The Jewish Annotated New Testament*, edited by Amy-Jill Levine and Marc Zvi Brettler, 121–22. 2nd ed. New York: Oxford University Press, 2017.

_____. *Short Stories by Jesus: The Enigmatic Parables of a Controversial Rabbi*. New York: HarperOne, 2014.

_____. "Tabitha/Dorcas: Spinning Off Cultural Criticism." In *Delightful Acts: New Essays on Canonical and Non-canonical Acts*, edited by Harold W. Attridge, Dennis R. MacDonald, and Clare K. Rothschild, 41–65. WUNT 391. Tübingen: Mohr Siebeck, 2017.

_____. "Women, Itineracy and the Criteria of Authenticity in John Meier's *Marginal Jew*." In *The Figure of Jesus in History and Theology: Essays in Honor of John Meier*, edited by Vincent Skemp and Kelley Coblentz-Bautch, 90–113. CBQ Imprints. Washington, DC: CBA, 2020.

Levine, Amy-Jill, and Marc Zvi Brettler, eds. *The Jewish Annotated New Testament*. 2nd ed. New York: Oxford University Press, 2017.

Levine, Amy-Jill, and Douglas A. Knight, *The Meaning of the Bible: What the Jewish Scriptures and Christian Old Testament Can Teach Us*. New York: HarperOne, 2012.

Levine, Amy-Jill, and Ben Witherington III. *The Gospel of Luke*. NCBC. Cambridge: Cambridge University Press, 2018.

Levine, Amy-Jill, Dale C. Allison Jr., and John Dominic Crossan, eds. *The Historical Jesus in Context*. Princeton Readings in Religion. Princeton: Princeton University Press, 2006.

Levine, Amy-Jill, with Marianne Blickenstaff, eds. *A Feminist Companion to Luke*. FCNTECW 3. Sheffield: Sheffield Academic, 2002.

Levine, Lee I. *The Ancient Synagogue: The First Thousand Years*. New Haven, CT: Yale University Press, 2000.

_____. "The Synagogue." In *The Jewish Annotated New Testament*, edited by Amy-Jill Levine and Marc Zvi Brettler, 662–66. 2nd ed. New York: Oxford University Press, 2017.

Lewin, Ann. *Watching for the Kingfisher: Poems and Prayers*. Norwich: Canterbury Press, 2009.

Lewis, Naphtali, Yigael Yadin, and Jonas C. Greenfield. *The Documents from the Bar Kokhba Period in the Cave of Letter. I. Greek Papyri*. JDS. Jerusalem: Israel Exploration Society, 1989.

Lewis, Nicola Denzey. Review of Kathleen E. Corley, *Maranatha: Women's Funerary Rituals and Christian Origins* (Philadelphia: Fortress, 2010). In *CBQ* 74 (2012): 594–96.

Lieu, Judith. "Scripture and the Feminine in John." In *A Feminist Companion to the Hebrew Bible in the New Testament*, edited by Athalya Brenner, 225–40. FCB 10. Sheffield: Sheffield Academic, 1996.

Lin, Yii-Jan. "Junia: An Apostle before Paul." *JBL* 139 (2020): 191–209.

Lincoln, Andrew T. *Born of a Virgin? Reconceiving Jesus in the Bible, Tradition, and Theology*. Grand Rapids: Eerdmans, 2013.

Little Hawk, Kenneth. *"Care for the Earth": Native American Stories of Respect for All Life*. Little Hawk Productions, 2010.

Long, Asphodel. *In a Chariot Drawn by Lions: The Search for the Female in the Deity*. London: Women's Press, 1992.

Ludolph of Saxony. *Vita Domini nostri Jesu Christi ex quatuor evangeliis*. Mainz, fourteenth century. An English translation, *The Life of Jesus Christ*, is being translated by Milton Walsh and published in four volumes by Cistercian Publications.

Luttick, Janine. " 'Little Girl, Get Up!' (and Stand on Your Own Two Feet!): A Reading of Mark 5:21-24, 35-43 with an Awareness of the Role and Function of the Body." PhD diss., Australian Catholic University, 2017.

MacDonald, Dennis R. *The Legend and the Apostle: The Battle for Paul in Story and Canon*. Philadelphia: Westminster, 1983.

———. *Luke and Vergil: Imitations of Classical Greek Literature*. The New Testament and Greek Literature. Vol. 2. Lanham, MD: Rowman & Littlefield, 2015.

———. *Two Shipwrecked Gospels: The Logoi of Jesus and Papias's Exposition of Logia about the Lord*. ECL 8. Atlanta: SBL, 2012.

Madigan, Kevin, and Carolyn Osiek, eds. *Ordained Women in the Early Church: A Documentary History*. Baltimore: Johns Hopkins University Press, 2005.

Magdala. https://www.magdala.org/.

Maier, Cristl M., and Carolyn J. Sharp. *Prophecy and Power: Jeremiah in Feminist and Postcolonial Perspective*. London: Bloomsbury, 2013.

Maloney, Linda M. "The Friend at Midnight (Luke 11:1-10)." In *By Bread Alone: The Bible Through the Eyes of the Hungry*, edited by Sheila E. McGinn, Lai Ling Elizabeth Ngan, and Ahida Calderón Pilarski, 129–34. Minneapolis: Fortress, 2014.

———. "The Pastoral Epistles." In *Searching the Scriptures*, vol. 2: *A Feminist Commentary*, edited by Elisabeth Schüssler Fiorenza with the assistance of Ann Brock and Shelly Matthews, 361–80. New York: Crossroad, 1994.

Maloney, Linda M., Willie James Jennings, and Ivoni Richter Reimer. *Acts of the Apostles*. WCS 45. Collegeville, MN: Liturgical Press, forthcoming.

Marchal, Joseph A. "Queer Studies and Critical Masculinity Studies in Feminist Biblical Studies." In *Feminist Biblical Studies in the Twentieth Century: Scholarship and Movement*, edited by Elisabeth Schüssler Fiorenza, 261–80. The Bible and Women 9.1. Atlanta: Society of Biblical Literature, 2014.

Marcus, Joel. "The Beelzebul Controversy and the Eschatologies of Jesus." In *Authenticating the Activities of Jesus*, edited by Bruce Chilton and Craig A. Evans, 247–77. Leiden: Brill, 1999.

Markham, Donna J. *Spiritlinking Leadership: Working through Resistance to Organizational Change*. New York: Paulist Press, 1999.

Marshall, Jill E. *Women Praying and Prophesying in Corinth: Gender and Inspired Speech in First Corinthians*. WUNT 2.448. Tübingen: Mohr Siebeck, 2017.

Martin, Clarice J. "Womanist Interpretations of the New Testament: The Quest for Holistic and Inclusive Translation and Interpretation." In *I Found God in Me: A Womanist Biblical Hermeneutics Reader*, edited by Mitzi J. Smith, 19–41. Eugene, OR: Cascade, 2015.

Matthews, Shelly. *The Acts of the Apostles: An Introduction and Study Guide; Taming the Tongues of Fire*. T&T Clark Study Guides to the New Testament. London: Bloomsbury T&T Clark, 2017.

———. *The Acts of the Apostles: Taming the Tongues of Fire*. Phoenix New Testament Guides. Sheffield: Sheffield Phoenix, 2013.

———. "Does Dating Luke–Acts into the Second Century Affect the Q Hypothesis?" In *Gospel Interpretation and the Q-Hypothesis*, edited by Mogens Müller and Heike Omerzu, 245–65. LNTS 573. London: Bloomsbury T&T Clark, 2018.

———. *First Converts: Rich Pagan Women and the Rhetoric of Mission in Early Judaism and Christianity*. Stanford, CA: Stanford University Press, 2001.

———. "Fleshly Resurrection, Authority Claims, and the Scriptural Practices of Lukan Christianity." *JBL* 136 (2017): 163–83.

———. "'I Have Prayed for You . . . Strengthen Your Brothers' (Luke 22:32): Jesus's Proleptic Prayer for Peter and Other Gendered Tropes in Luke's War on Satan." In *Petitioners, Penitents, and Poets: On Prayer and Praying in Second Temple Judaism*, edited by Timothy J. Sandoval and Ariel Feldman, 231–46. BZAW 524. Berlin: de Gruyter, 2020.

———. *Perfect Martyr: The Stoning of Stephen and the Construction of Christian Identity*. New York: Oxford University Press, 2010.

———. "The Weeping Jesus and the Daughters of Jerusalem: Gender and Conquest in Lukan Lament." In *Doing Gender—Doing Religion: Fallstudien zur Intersektionalität im frühen Judentum, Christentum und Islam*, edited by Ute E. Eisen, Christine Gerber, and Angela Standhartinger, 385–403. WUNT 302. Tübingen: Mohr, 2013.

Mattila, Sharon Lea. "Revisiting Jesus' Capernaum: A Village of Only Subsistence-Level Fishers and Farmers?" In *The Galilean Economy in the Time of Jesus*, edited by David A. Fiensy and Ralph K. Hawkins, 75–138. ECL 11. Atlanta: SBL, 2013.

Mayfield, D. L. "Mary's 'Magnificat' in the Bible Is Revolutionary: Some Evangelicals Silence Her." *Washington Post*. December 20, 2018. https://www.washingtonpost.com/religion/2018/12/20/marys-magnificat-bible-is-revolutionary-so-evangelicals-silence-it/.

Mayo, Maria. *The Limits of Forgiveness: Case Studies in the Distortion of a Biblical Ideal.* Minneapolis: Augsburg Fortress, 2015.

McClain, Dani. *We Live for the We: The Political Power of Black Motherhood.* New York: Bold Type Books, 2019.

McCollough, Thomas. "City and Village in Lower Galilee: The Import of the Archeological Excavations at Sepphoris and Khirbet Qana (Cana) for Framing the Economic Context of Jesus." In *The Galilean Economy in the Time of Jesus,* edited by David A. Fiensy and Ralph K. Hawkins, 49–74. ECL 11. Atlanta: SBL, 2013.

McCreesh, Thomas P. "Heart." In *The Collegeville Pastoral Dictionary of Biblical Theology,* edited by Carroll Stuhlmueller, 422–24. Collegeville, MN: Liturgical Press, 1996.

McFague, Sallie. "Holy Spirit." In *Dictionary of Feminist Theologies,* edited by Letty M. Russell and J. Shannon Clarkson, 146–47. Louisville: Westminster John Knox, 1996.

———. *Metaphorical Theology: Models of God in Religious Language.* Philadelphia: Fortress, 1982.

———. *Models of God: Theology for an Ecological, Nuclear Age.* Philadelphia: Fortress, 1987.

McGinn, Sheila E. "The Acts of Thecla." In *Searching the Scriptures,* vol. 2: *A Feminist Commentary,* edited by Elisabeth Schüssler Fiorenza with the assistance of Ann Brock and Shelly Matthews, 800–828. New York: Crossroad, 1994.

———. *Exploring the Acts of Thecla.* Rhetoric of Religious Antiquity. Atlanta: SBL Press, forthcoming.

McGinn, Sheila E., Lai Ling Elizabeth Ngan, and Ahida Calderón Pilarski, eds. *By Bread Alone: The Bible through the Eyes of the Hungry.* Minneapolis: Fortress, 2014.

McKinlay, Judith E. *Gendering Wisdom the Host: Biblical Invitations to Eat and Drink.* JSOTSup 216. Sheffield: Sheffield Academic, 1996.

———. *Reframing Her: Biblical Women in Postcolonial Focus.* Sheffield: Sheffield Phoenix, 2004.

McKnight, Edgar V., and Elizabeth Struthers Malbon, eds. *The New Literary Criticism and the New Testament.* Valley Forge, PA: Trinity Press International, 1994.

McLean, Kalbryn A. "Calvin and the Personal Politics of Providence." In *Feminist and Womanist Essays in Reformed Dogmatics,* edited by Amy Plantinga Pauw and Serene Jones, 107–24. Louisville: Westminster John Knox, 2006.

Mead, Francis. "The Women Shepherds of Somaliland." United Nations blogs. January 7, 2014. https://blogs.un.org/blog/2014/01/07/the-women -shepherds-of-somaliland/.

Mechtilde of Magdeburg. *The Flowing Light of the Godhead.* https://www.bing .com/videos/search?q=mechtild+in+the+dance+i+am+the+dancer&&vi ew=detail&mid=7F30F049A442CE614D6A7F30F049A442CE614D6A&&F ORM=VRDGAR.

Meier, John P. *A Marginal Jew: Rethinking the Historical Jesus.* 5 vols. ABRL. New York: Doubleday, 1991, 1994, 2001, 2009; New Haven: Yale University Press, 2016.

_____. "Jesus in Josephus: A Modest Proposal." *CBQ* 52 (1990): 76–103.

Melcher, Sarah J., Mikeal C. Parsons, and Amos Yong, eds. *The Bible and Disability: A Commentary.* Studies in Religion, Theology, and Disability. Waco, TX: Baylor University Press, 2017.

Menologion for the Twenty-sixth Day of the Month of February. http://www.orthodox.cn/saints/menologia/2-26_en.htm.

Merriam Webster Online Dictionary. "analogy." https://www.merriam-webster.com/dictionary/analogy.

_____. "mammon." https://www.merriam-webster.com/dictionary/mammon.

_____. "mentor." https://www.merriam-webster.com/dictionary/mentor.

_____. "metaphor." https://www.merriam-webster.com/dictionary/metaphor.

_____. "pharisaical." https://www.merriam-webster.com/dictionary/pharisaical.

_____. "symbol." https://www.merriam-webster.com/dictionary/symbol.

Meyers, Carol. *Discovering Eve: Ancient Israelite Women in Context.* New York: Oxford University Press, 1991.

_____. "Miriam, Music, and Miracles." In *Mariam, the Magdalen, and the Mother,* edited by Deirdre Good. Bloomington: Indiana University Press, 2005.

Meyers, Carol, Toni Craven, and Ross Shepard Kraemer, eds. *Women in Scripture: A Dictionary of Named and Unnamed Women in the Hebrew Bible, The Apocryphal/Deuterocanonical Books, and the New Testament.* Grand Rapids: Eerdmans, 2000.

Millard, Alan R. *Reading and Writing in the Time of Jesus.* Washington Square: New York University Press, 2000.

Miller, Amanda C. *Rumors of Resistance: Status Reversals and Hidden Transcripts in the Gospel of Luke.* Minneapolis: Fortress, 2014.

Miller-McLemore, Bonnie J. "'Pondering All These Things': Mary and Motherhood." In *Blessed One: Protestant Perspectives on Mary,* edited by Beverly Roberts Gaventa and Cynthia L. Rigby, 97–114. Louisville: Westminster John Knox, 2002.

Mojab, Shahrzad. "Political Prisoners: The Art of Resistance in Iran." https://womenpoliticalprisoners.com/.

Moloney, Francis J. *The Gospel of John.* SP 4. Collegeville, MN: Liturgical Press, 1998.

Moody, Linda A. *Women Encounter God: Theology Across the Boundaries of Difference.* Maryknoll, NY: Orbis Books, 1996.

Moore, Stephen D. *The Bible in Theory: Critical and Postcritical Essays.* Atlanta: SBL, 2010.

_____. *Mark and Luke in Poststructuralist Perspectives: Jesus Begins to Write.* New Haven, CT: Yale University Press, 1992.

_____. *Poststructuralism and the New Testament: Derrida and Foucault at the Foot of the Cross.* Minneapolis: Fortress, 1994.

Moss, Candida. "The Man with the Flow of Power: Porous Bodies in Mark 5:25-34." *JBL* 129 (2010): 507–19.

Moss, Candida R., and Jeremy Schipper, eds. *Disability Studies and Biblical Literature*. New York: Palgrave MacMillan, 2011.

Moss, Candida R., and Joel S. Baden. *Reconceiving Infertility: Biblical Perspectives on Procreation and Childlessness*. Princeton: Princeton University Press, 2015.

Mosser, Carl. "Torah Instruction, Discussion, and Prophecy in First-Century Synagogues." In *Christian Origins and Hellenistic Judaism: Social and Literary Contexts for the New Testament*, edited by Stanley E. Porter and Andrew W. Pitts, 523–51. Texts and Editions for New Testament Study 10. Leiden: Brill, 2013.

Moyano, María Elena. *The Autobiography of María Elena Moyano: The Life and Death of a Peruvian Activist*. A translation of *María Elena Moyano: en busca de una esperanza*. Edited by Diana Miloslavich Tupac. Translated by Patricia S. Taylor Edmisten. Gainesville: University Press of Florida, 2000. https://ufdcimages.uflib.ufl.edu/AA/00/01/16/41/00001/Autobiography Moyano.pdf.

Müller, Mogens, and Heike Omerzu, eds. *Gospel Interpretation and the Q-Hypothesis*. LNTS5 73. London: Bloomsbury T&T Clark, 2018.

Munro, Winsome. "Women Disciples in Mark?" *CBQ* 44 (1982): 225–41.

Murphy-O'Connor, Jerome. "Fishers of Fish, Fishers of Men." *BibRev* (1999): 22–27, 48–49.

———. "John the Baptist and Jesus: History and Hypotheses." *NTS* 36 (1990): 359–74.

Nanko-Fernández, Carmen. "Theological Reflections: Luke 2:1-14, (15-20)." *Lectionary Homiletics* (December 2011): 27–28.

Nanos, Mark D., and Magnus Zetterhom, eds. *Paul within Judaism: Restoring the First-Century Context to the Apostle*. Minneapolis: Fortress, 2015.

Narayan, Uma. *Dislocating Cultures: Identities, Traditions and Third World Feminism*. New York: Routledge Press, 1997.

National Center for Transgender Equality. https://transequality.org/voices-for-trans-equality.

National Council of Churches. Revised Standard Version: *An Inclusive-Language Lectionary*, edited by the Inclusive-Language Lectionary Committee, Division of Education and Ministry, National Council of the Churches of Christ in the USA. Atlanta: John Knox, 1984.

National Storytelling Network. https://storynet.org/groups/healing-story-alliance-hsa/stories-for-social-justice/periodicals/.

"Native Women Bring Traditional Art into the 21st Century." http://cojmc.unl.edu/nativedaughters/artists/native-women-bring-traditional-art-into-the-21st-century.

Neu, Diann L. *Women's Rites: Feminist Liturgies for Life's Journey*. Cleveland: Pilgrim Press, 2003.

Neusner, Jacob, and Bruce D. Chilton, eds. *In Quest of the Historical Pharisees*. Waco, TX: Baylor University Press, 2007.

Newman, Barbara. *Sister of Wisdom: St. Hildegard's Theology of the Feminine.* Berkeley: University of California Press, 1987.

Newsom, Carol A., Sharon H. Ringe, and Jacqueline E. Lapsley, eds. *Women's Bible Commentary.* 3rd ed. Louisville: Westminster John Knox, 2012.

Niditch, Susan. *"My Brother Esau Is a Hairy Man": Hair and Identity in Ancient Israel.* Oxford: Oxford University Press, 2008.

Nowell, Irene. *Women in the Old Testament.* Collegeville, MN: Liturgical Press, 1997.

Oakman, Douglas E. "Execrating? Or Execrable Peasants!" In *The Galilean Economy in the Time of Jesus,* edited by David A. Fiensy and Ralph K. Hawkins, 139–64. ECL 11. Atlanta: SBL, 2013.

———. *Jesus and the Economic Questions of His Day.* Studies in the Bible and Early Christianity 8. Lewiston, NY/Queenston, Ont.: Mellen, 1986.

O'Connor, Kathleen M. "Let All the Peoples Praise You: Biblical Studies and a Hermeneutics of Hunger." *CBQ* 72 (2010): 1–14.

Orthodox Church in America. "Protomartyr and Equal of the Apostles Thekla." https://www.oca.org/saints/lives/2020/09/24/102715-protomartyr-and-equal-of-the-apostles-thekla.

———. "Saint Nino (Nina), Equal of the Apostles, Enlightener of Georgia." https://www.oca.org/saints/lives/2019/01/14/100191-saint-nino-nina-equal-of-the-apostles-enlightener-of-georgia.

Osiek, Carolyn. *Shepherd of Hermas: A Commentary.* Hermeneia. Minneapolis: Fortress, 1999.

———. "The Women at the Tomb: What Are They Doing There?" *Ex Auditu* 9 (1993): 97–107. Reprinted in *A Feminist Companion to Matthew,* edited by Amy-Jill Levine with Marianne Blickenstaff, 203–20. FCNTECW 1. Sheffield: Sheffield Academic, 2001.

———. "Women Patrons in the Life of House Churches." In *A Woman's Place: House Churches in Earliest Christianity,* by Carolyn Osiek, Margaret Y. MacDonald, with Janet H. Tulloch, 194–219. Minneapolis: Fortress, 2006.

Osiek, Carolyn, Margaret Y. MacDonald, with Janet H. Tulloch. *A Woman's Place: House Churches in Earliest Christianity.* Minneapolis: Fortress, 2006.

O'Toole, Robert F. *The Unity of Luke's Theology: An Analysis of Luke–Acts.* GNS 9. Wilmington, DE: Glazier, 1984.

Ott, Kate M. "From Politics to Theology: Responding to Roman Catholic Ecclesial Control of Reproductive Ethics." *JFSR* 30 (2014): 138–47.

Owen, Amos. "Inside the White House Bible Study Group." *BBC NEWS.* April 8, 2018. http://www.bbc.com/news/world-us-canada-43534724.

Oxyrhynchus Hymn to Isis. http://www.attalus.org/poetry/isis_hymns.html#6.

Parker, D. C. *The Living Text of the Gospels.* Cambridge: Cambridge University Press, 1997.

Parks, Sara. *Gender in the Rhetoric of Jesus: Women in Q.* Lanham, MD: Fortress Academic, 2019.

Parsons, Mikeal C., and Richard I. Pervo. *Rethinking the Unity of Luke and Acts.* Minneapolis: Fortress, 1993.

Patella, Michael F. "The Gospel According to Luke." In *New Collegeville Bible Commentary: New Testament*, edited by Daniel Durken. Collegeville, MN: Liturgical Press, 2009.

Pederson, Rena. *The Lost Apostle: Searching for the Truth about Junia.* San Francisco: Jossey-Bass, 2006.

Penchansky, David. "Deconstruction." In *The Oxford Encyclopedia of Biblical Interpretation*, edited by Steven McKenzie, 196–205. New York: Oxford University Press, 2013.

Penner, Todd. *In Praise of Christian Origins: Stephen and the Hellenists in Lukan Apologetic Historiography.* New York: T&T Clark, 2004.

PERIOD. https://www.period.org/.

Perkins, Pheme. "Patched Garments and Ruined Wine: Whose Folly? (Mk. 2.21-22; Mt. 9.16-17; Lk. 5.36-39)." In *The Lost Coin: Parables of Women, Work and Wisdom*, edited by Mary Ann Beavis, 124–35. London: Sheffield Academic, 2002.

Perroni, Marinella. "Disciples, Not Apostles: Luke's Double Message." In *Gospels: Narrative and History*, edited by Mercedes Navarro Puerto, Marinella Perroni, and Amy-Jill Levine (English ed.), 173–213. The Bible and Women: An Encyclopedia of Exegesis and Cultural History. New Testament 2.1. Atlanta: SBL Press, 2015.

Perroni, Marinella, and Cristina Simonelli. *Mary of Magdala: Revisiting the Sources.* Translated by Demetrio S. Yocum. New York: Paulist Press, 2019.

Perry, Briana. "The Power of Black Women's Storytelling in Activist Work." March 11, 2015. http://www.forharriet.com/2015/03/the-power-of-black -womens-storytelling.html#axzz4EIjX4oBA.

Pervo, Richard I. *Acts.* Hermeneia. Minneapolis: Fortress, 2009.

———. *The Gospel of Luke.* The Scholars Bible. Salem, OR: Polebridge, 2014.

Peters, Rebecca Todd. *Trust Women: A Progressive Christian Argument for Reproductive Justice.* Boston: Beacon, 2018.

Pilch, John J. *Healing in the New Testament: Insights from Medical and Mediterranean Anthropology.* Minneapolis: Fortress, 2000.

Plaskow, Judith. "Anti-Judaism in Feminist Christian Interpretation." In *Searching the Scriptures*, vol. 1: *A Feminist Introduction*, edited by Elisabeth Schüssler Fiorenza with the assistance of Shelly Matthews, 117–29. New York: Crossroad, 1993.

———. *Sex, Sin, and Grace: Women's Experience and the Theologies of Reinhold Niebuhr and Paul Tillich.* Washington, DC: University Press of America, 1980.

Plummer, Alfred. *The Gospel According to S. Luke.* 5th ed. ICC. Edinburgh: T&T Clark, 1981; first ed. 1901.

Poirier, John C. "Jesus as an Elijianic Figure in Luke 4:16-30." *CBQ* 69 (2007): 349–63.

Pope, Michael. "Gabriel's Entrance and Biblical Violence in Luke's Annunciation Narrative." *JBL* 137 (2018): 701–10.

———. "Luke's Seminal Annunciation: An Embryological Reading of Mary's Conception." *JBL* 138 (2019): 791–807.

Powell, Mark Allan. *What Are They Saying about Luke?* New York: Paulist Press, 1989.

Praeder, Susan M. "Acts 17:1–28:16: Sea Voyages in Ancient Literature and the Theology of Luke–Acts." *CBQ* 46 (1984): 683–706.

Price, Robert M. *The Widow Traditions in Luke–Acts: A Feminist-Critical Scrutiny.* SBLDS 155. Atlanta: Scholars Press, 1997.

Puar, Jasbir. *Terrorist Assemblages: Homonationalism in Queer Times.* Durham, NC: Duke University Press, 2007.

Pui-lan, Kwok. *Introducing Asian Feminist Theology.* IFT. Cleveland, OH: Pilgrim, 2000.

———. *Postcolonial Imagination and Feminist Theology.* Louisville: Westminster John Knox, 2005.

Ramshaw, Gail. *God Beyond Gender: Feminist Christian God-Language.* Minneapolis: Fortress, 1995.

Ranjar, Clifard Sunil. *Be Merciful Like the Father: Exegesis and Theology of the Sermon on the Plain (Luke 6,17-49).* AnBib 219. Rome: Gregorian and Biblical Press, 2017.

Rawson, Beryl. *Children and Childhood in Roman Italy.* Oxford: Oxford University Press, 2003.

Rawson, Beryl, ed. *A Companion to Families in the Greek and Roman Worlds.* Chichester: Wiley-Blackwell, 2011.

Reeder, Caryn A. *Gendering War and Peace in the Gospel of Luke.* Cambridge: Cambridge University Press, 2019.

Reid, Barbara E. *Choosing the Better Part? Women in the Gospel of Luke.* Collegeville, MN: Liturgical Press, 1996.

———. "The Gospel of Luke: Friend or Foe of Women Proclaimers of the Word?" *CBQ* 78 (2016): 1–23.

———. "The Power of the Widows and How to Suppress It (Acts 6:1-7)." In *A Feminist Companion to the Acts of the Apostles,* edited by Amy-Jill Levine with Marianne Blickenstaff, 71–88. FCNTECW 8. London: T & T Clark, 2004.

———. "Prophetic Voices of Mary, Elizabeth, and Anna in Luke 1–2." In *New Perspectives on the Nativity,* edited by Jeremy Corley, 37–46. London: T&T Clark, 2009.

———. *Taking Up the Cross: New Testament Interpretations through Latina and Feminist Eyes.* Minneapolis: Fortress, 2007. Spanish translation: *Reconsiderar la Cruz. Interpretación latinoamericana y feminista del Nuevo Testamento.* Aletheia 5. Estella (Navarro), España: Editorial Verbo Divino, 2009.

———. *The Transfiguration: A Source- and Redaction-Critical Study of Luke 9:28-36.* CahRB 32. Paris: Gabalda, 1993.

———. "Wisdom's Children Justified (Mt. 11.16-19; Lk. 7.31-35)." In *The Lost Coin: Parables of Women, Work and Wisdom,* edited by Mary Ann Beavis, 287–305. BibSem 86. London: Sheffield Academic, 2002.

————. "Women Prophets of God's Alternative Reign." In *Luke–Acts and Empire: Essays in Honor of Robert L. Brawley*, edited by David Rhoads, David Esterline, and Jae Won Lee, 44–59. PTMS. Eugene, OR: Pickwick Papers, 2010.

Reinhartz, Adele. *Cast out of the Covenant: Jews and Anti-Judaism in the Gospel of John.* Lanham, MD: Lexington Books/Fortress Academic, 2018.

————. "Children of God and Aristotelian Epigenesis in the Gospel of John." In *Creation Stories in Dialogue: The Bible, Science, and Folk Traditions; Radboud Prestige Lectures by R. Alan Culpepper*, edited by R. Alan Culpepper and Jan G. van der Watt, 243–52. BibInt 139. Leiden: Brill, 2016.

————, ed. *The Gospel of John and Jewish-Christian Relations.* Lanham, MD: Lexington Books/Fortress Academic, 2018.

————. *"Why Ask My Name?" Anonymity and Identity in Biblical Narrative.* New York: Oxford University Press, 1998.

Ress, Mary Judith. *Ecofeminism in Latin America.* Women from the Margins. Maryknoll, NY: Orbis Books, 2006.

Richey, Lance Byron. *Roman Imperial Ideology and the Gospel of John.* CBQMS 43. Washington, DC: CBA, 2007.

Richter Reimer, Ivoni. *Women in the Acts of the Apostles: A Feminist Liberation Perspective.* Translated by Linda M. Maloney. Minneapolis: Fortress, 1995.

Ringe, Sharon H. *Luke.* Westminster Bible Companion. Louisville: Westminster John Knox, 1995.

————. *Wisdom's Friends: Community and Christology in the Fourth Gospel.* Louisville: Westminster John Knox, 1999.

Rivkin, Ellis. "What Crucified Jesus." In *Jesus' Jewishness: Exploring the Place of Jesus in Early Judaism*, edited by James H. Charlesworth, 226–57. New York: Crossroad, 1996.

RNZ. "A Tale of Three New Zealand Women Shepherds." *New Zealand Herald.* November 4, 2019. https://www.nzherald.co.nz/the-country/news/article.cfm?c_id=16&objectid=12282266.

Rocha, Zildo. *Helder, O Dom: uma vida que marcou os rumos da Igreja no Brasil.* Petrópolis: Editora Vozes, 2000.

Ross, Loretta, and Rickie Solinger. *Reproductive Justice: An Introduction.* Oakland: University of California Press, 2017.

Rossi, Mary Ann. "Priesthood, Precedent, and Prejudice: On Recovering the Women Priests of Early Christianity." *JFSR* 7 (1991): 73–94.

Rowe, C. Kavin. "Luke–Acts and the Imperial Cult: A Way Through the Conundrum?" *JSNT* 27 (2005): 279–300.

Ruether, Rosemary Radford. *Sexism and God-Talk: Toward a Feminist Theology.* Boston: Beacon, 1983.

————. *Women-Church: Theology and Practice of Feminist Liturgical Communities.* San Francisco: Harper & Row, 1986.

Russell, Letty M. "Authority." In *Dictionary of Feminist Theologies*, edited by Letty M. Russell and J. Shannon Clarkson, 18–19. Louisville: Westminster John Knox, 1996.

Russell, Letty M., and J. Shannon Clarkson. *Dictionary of Feminist Theologies.* Louisville: Westminster John Knox, 1996.

Rutledge, David. *Reading Marginally: Feminism, Deconstruction and the Bible.* BibInt 21. Leiden: Brill, 1996.

Ryan, Jordan J. *The Role of the Synagogue in the Aims of Jesus.* Minneapolis: Fortress, 2017.

Sacks, Jonathan. "Love and Hate." https://www.chabad.org/parshah/article_cdo/aid/2186228/jewish/Love-and-Hate.htm.

Saddington, D. B. "The Centurion in Matthew 8:5-13: Consideration of the Proposal of Theodore W. Jennings, Jr., and Tat-Siong Benny Liew." *JBL* 125 (2006): 140–42.

Sadler, Rodney S. "Can a Cushite Change His Skin? Cushites, 'Racial Othering,' and the Hebrew Bible." *Int* 60 (2006): 386–403.

Sadowski, Dennis. "Women Religious Vow Solidarity in Fight Against Human Trafficking." *America.* October 31, 2018. https://www.americamagazine.org/politics-society/2018/10/31/women-religious-vow-solidarity-fight-against-human-trafficking.

Sakenfeld, Katharine Doob. *Just Wives? Stories of Power and Survival in the Old Testament and Today.* Louisville: Westminster John Knox, 2003.

——. "Numbers." In *Women's Bible Commentary,* edited by Carol A. Newsom, Sharon H. Ringe, and Jacqueline E. Lapsley, 79–87. Rev. and updated ed. Louisville: Westminster John Knox, 2012.

Sawicki, Marianne. *Crossing Galilee: Architectures of Contact in the Occupied Land of Jesus.* Harrisburg, PA: Trinity Press International, 2000.

——. *Seeing the Lord: Resurrection and Early Christian Practices.* Minneapolis: Fortress, 1994.

Schaberg, Jane D. *The Death and Resurrection of the Author and Other Feminist Essays on the Bible.* Edited by Holly E. Hearon. The Bible in the Modern World 51. Sheffield: Sheffield Phoenix, 2012.

——. "How Mary Magdalene Became a Whore." *BibRev* 8 (1992): 30–37, 51–52.

——. *The Illegitimacy of Jesus: A Feminist Theological Interpretation of the Infancy Narratives.* San Francisco: Harper & Row, 1987; exp. 20th ann. ed., Sheffield: Sheffield Phoenix, 2006.

——. "Luke." In *The Women's Bible Commentary,* edited by Carol A. Newsom and Sharon H. Ringe, 275–92. Louisville: Westminster John Knox, 1992.

——. *The Resurrection of Mary Magdalene: Legends, Apocrypha, and the Christian Testament.* New York: Continuum, 2004.

——. "Thinking Back through Mary Magdalene." *Continuum* 1 (1991): 71–90.

Schaberg, Jane D., and Sharon H. Ringe. "Gospel of Luke." In *Women's Bible Commentary,* edited by Carol A. Newsom, Sharon H. Ringe, and Jacqueline E. Lapsley, 493–511. Rev. and updated ed. Louisville: Westminster John Knox, 2012.

Schaff, Philip, and Henry Wace, eds. *A Select Library of Nicene and Post-Nicene Fathers.* Vol. 7. Grand Rapids: Eerdmans, 1955.

Schiffman, Lawrence H. "Pharisees." In *The Jewish Annotated New Testament,* edited by Amy-Jill Levine and Marc Zvi Brettler, 619–22. 2nd ed. New York: Oxford University Press, 2017.

Schneiders, Sandra M. *The Revelatory Text: Interpreting the New Testament as Sacred Scripture.* Rev. ed. Collegeville, MN: Liturgical Press, 1999.

Scholz, Susanne. "From the 'Woman's Bible' to the 'Women's Bible': The History of Feminist Approaches to the Hebrew Bible." In *Introducing the Women's Hebrew Bible,* 12–32. IFT 13. New York: T&T Clark, 2007.

Schottroff, Luise. *Let the Oppressed Go Free: Feminist Perspectives on the New Testament.* Louisville: Westminster John Knox, 1993.

———. *Lydia's Impatient Sisters: A Feminist Social History of Early Christianity.* Translated by Barbara and Martin Rumscheidt. Louisville: Westminster John Knox, 1995. Originally published in German: *Lydias ungeduldige Schwestern: Feministische Sozialgeschichte des frühen Christentums.* Gütersloher: Kaiser/Gütersloher, 1994.

———. "Through German and Feminist Eyes: A Liberationist Reading of Luke 7.36-50." In *A Feminist Companion to the Hebrew Bible in the New Testament,* edited by Athalya Brenner, 332–41. FCB 10. Sheffield: Sheffield Academic, 1996.

Schottroff, Luise, and Marie-Theres Wacker, eds. *Feminist Biblical Interpretation: A Compendium of Critical Commentary on the Books of the Bible and Related Literature.* Translated by Lisa E. Dahill, Everett R. Kalin, Nancy Lukens, Linda M. Maloney, Barbara Rumscheidt, Martin Rumscheidt, and Tina Steiner. Grand Rapids: Eerdmans, 2012.

Schreiter, Robert J. *The Ministry of Reconciliation: Spirituality and Strategies.* Maryknoll, NY: Orbis Books, 1998.

———. *Reconciliation: Mission and Ministry in a Changing Social Order.* Maryknoll, NY: Orbis Books, 1992.

Schulte, Augustin Joseph. "Churching of Women." *The Catholic Encyclopedia.* Vol. 3. New York: Robert Appleton Company, 1908. http://www.newadvent.org/cathen/03761a.htm.

Schüngel-Straumann, Helen. "The Feminine Face of God." In *The Many Faces of the Divine,* edited by Hermann Häring and Johann Baptist Metz, 93–101. Concilium. London: SCM; and Maryknoll, NY: Orbis Books, 1995.

Schüssler Fiorenza, Elisabeth. *But She Said: Feminist Practices of Biblical Interpretation.* Boston: Beacon, 1992.

———. *Empowering Memory and Movement: Thinking and Working across Borders.* Minneapolis: Fortress, 2014.

———. *Ephesians.* WCS 50. Collegeville, MN: Liturgical Press, 2017.

———, ed. *Feminist Biblical Studies in the Twentieth Century: Scholarship and Movement.* The Bible and Women 9.1. Atlanta: Society of Biblical Literature, 2014.

_____. *In Memory of Her: A Feminist Theological Reconstruction of Christian Origins.* New York: Crossroad, 1983.

_____. *Jesus: Miriam's Child, Sophia's Prophet: Critical Issues in Feminist Christology.* New York: Continuum, 1994.

_____. *The Power of the Word: Scripture and the Rhetoric of Empire.* Minneapolis: Fortress, 2007.

_____. *Sharing Her Word: Feminist Biblical Interpretation in Context.* Boston: Beacon, 1998.

_____. " 'Waiting at Table': A Critical Feminist Theological Reflection on Diakonia." In *Diakonia: Church for the Others*, edited by N. Greinacher and N. Mette, 84–94. Concilium 198. Edinburgh: T&T Clark, 1988.

_____. *Wisdom Ways: Introducing Feminist Biblical Interpretation.* Maryknoll, NY: Orbis Books, 2001.

Schutte, P. J. W. "When *They, We,* and the Passive Become *I*—Introducing Autobiographical Biblical Criticism." *HTS Teologiese Studies / Theological Studies* 61 (2005): 401–16.

Scott, Martin. *Sophia and the Johannine Jesus.* JSNTSup 71. Sheffield: JSOT, 1992.

Seim, Turid Karlsen. *The Double Message: Patterns of Gender in Luke–Acts.* Nashville: Abingdon, 1994.

_____. "Feminist Criticism." In *Methods for Luke*, edited by Joel B. Green, 42–73. Methods in Biblical Interpretation. Cambridge: Cambridge University Press, 2010.

_____. "The Gospel of Luke." In *Searching the Scriptures*, vol. 2: *A Feminist Commentary*, edited by Elisabeth Schüssler Fiorenza with Ann Brock and Shelly Matthews, 728–62. New York: Crossroad, 1994.

Sellew, Melissa Harl (née Philip). "Interior Monologue as a Narrative Device in the Parables of Luke." *JBL* 111 (1992): 239–53.

Selvidge, Marla. " 'And Those Who Followed Feared (Mark 10:32)." *CBQ* 45 (1983): 396–400.

_____. "Mark 5:25–34 and Leviticus 14:19-20: A Reaction to Restrictive Purity Regulations." *JBL* 103 (1984): 619–23.

Sered, Susan Starr. "Mother Love, Child Death and Religious Innovation: A Feminist Perspective." *JFSR* 12 (1996): 5–23.

Setälä, Päivi. "Women and Brick Production—Some New Aspects." In *Women, Wealth and Power in the Roman Empire*, edited by Päivi Setälä, et al., 181–201. Rome: Instituti Romani Finlandiae, 2002.

Sherwood, Yvonne. *A Biblical Text and Its Afterlives: The Survival of Jonah in Western Culture.* Cambridge: Cambridge University Press, 2000.

_____. "Introduction." In *The Bible and Feminism: Remapping the Field.* New York: Oxford University Press, 2017.

Shinall, Myrick C., Jr. "The Social Condition of Lepers in the Gospels." *JBL* 137 (2018): 915–34.

Sibeko, Malika, and Beverley Haddad. "Reading the Bible 'with' Women in Poor and Marginalized Communities in South Africa." *Semeia* 78 (1997): 83–92.

Sievers, Joseph, and Amy-Jill Levine, eds. *Jesus and the Pharisees: An Interdisciplinary Reappraisal*. Grand Rapids, MI: Eerdmans Press, forthcoming. https://www.jesusandthepharisees.org.

Simkovich, Malka Zeiger. *The Making of Jewish Universalism: From Exile to Alexandria*. Lanham, MD: Lexington Books, 2017.

———. "The Origins of Jewish Universalism: What It Is and Why It Matters." *The Lehrhaus*. October 6, 2016. https://www.thelehrhaus.com/scholarship/the-origins-of-jewish-universalism-what-it-is-and-why-it-matters/.

SMEX. "Shou Osstik? Storytellers Graduate." October 4, 2012. https://smex.org/shou-osstik-participants-it-is-only-the-beginning/.

Smith, Mitzi J. "Unity, Fraternity, and Reconciliation: Ancient Slavery as a Context for the Return of Onesimus." In *Onesimus Our Brother: Reading Religion, Race, and Culture in Philemon*, edited by Matthew V. Johnson, James A. Noel, and Demetrius K. Williams, 47–58. Paul in Critical Contexts. Minneapolis: Fortress, 2012.

Smith, Mitzi J., and Jin Young Choi, *Minoritized Women Reading Race and Ethnicity: Intersectional Approaches to Constructed Identity and Early Christian Texts*. Lanham, MD: Lexington Books, 2020.

Smith, Robert Houston. "Ethiopia (Place)." AYBD 2.665.

Smith, R. R. R. *Aphrodisias VI: The Marble Reliefs from the Julio-Claudian Sebasteion at Aphrodisias*. Darmstadt: von Zabern, 2013.

Smith, Shannon. "Native Storytellers Connect the Past and the Future." http://cojmc.unl.edu/nativedaughters/storytellers/native-storytellers-connect-the-past-and-the-future.

Snodgrass, Klyne R. *Stories with Intent: A Comprehensive Guide to the Parables of Jesus*. Grand Rapids: Eerdmans, 2008.

Snyder, Jane McIntosh. *The Woman and the Lyre: Women Writers in Classical Greece and Rome*. Carbondale: Southern Illinois University Press, 1989.

Soelle, Dorothee. *The Silent Cry: Mysticism and Resistance*. Translated by Barbara and Martin Rumscheidt. Minneapolis: Fortress, 2001.

Sojourner Truth. "Ain't I a Woman?" Modern History Sourcebook. https://sourcebooks.fordham.edu/mod/sojtruth-woman.asp.

Solevåg, Anna Rebecca. *Negotiating the Disabled Body: Representations of Disability in Early Christian Texts*. ECL 23. Atlanta: SBL Press, 2018.

Spencer, F. Scott. *Salty Wives, Spirited Mothers, and Savvy Widows: Capable Women of Purpose and Persistence in Luke's Gospel*. Grand Rapids: Eerdmans, 2012.

Staples, Jason A. "'Lord, Lord': Jesus as YHWH in Matthew and Luke." *NTS* 64 (2018): 1–19.

StoryCorps. https://storycorps.org/about/.

Strange, W. A. *Children in the Early Church: Children in the Ancient World, the New Testament and the Early Church*. Carlisle: Paternoster, 1996.

Strelan, Rick. *Luke the Priest: The Authority of the Author of the Third Gospel.* Aldershot: Ashgate, 2008.

Stuckenbruck, Loren T. *The Myth of Rebellious Angels: Studies in Second Temple Judaism and New Testament Texts.* Tübingen: Mohr Siebeck, 2014.

Suchocki, Marjorie Hewitt. "Sin." In *Dictionary of Feminist Theologies,* edited by Letty M. Russell and J. Shannon Clarkson, 261–62. Louisville: Westminster John Knox, 1996.

Suleman, Arsalan. "Amplifying Muslim Women's Voices through Storytelling Platforms." http://2007-2017-blogs.state.gov/stories/2016/03/30/amplifying -muslim-women-s-voices-through-storytelling-platforms.html.

Taitz, Emily, Sondra Henry, Cheryl Tallan, eds. *JPS Guide to Jewish Women 600 B.C.E.–1900 C.E.* Philadelphia: JPS, 2003.

Tallan, Cheryl. "Doctors: Medieval." *The Encyclopedia of Jewish Women.* https://jwa .org/encyclopedia/article/doctors-medieval.

Tannehill, Robert C. "Israel in Luke–Acts: A Tragic Story." *JBL* 104 (1985): 69–85.

———. *Luke.* ANTC. Nashville: Abingdon, 1996.

Tarlin, Jan. "Toward a 'Female' Reading of the Elijah Cycle: Ideology and Gender in the Interpretation of 1 Kings 17–19, 21 and 2 Kings 1–2.18." In *A Feminist Companion to Samuel and Kings,* edited by Athalya Brenner, 208–17. FCB 5. Sheffield: Sheffield Academic, 1994.

Taylor, Marion Ann, and Agnes Choi, eds. *Handbook of Women Biblical Interpreters: A Historical and Biographical Guide.* Grand Rapids: Baker Academic, 2012.

Taylor, Marion Ann, and Heather E. Weir, eds. *Women in the Story of Jesus: The Gospels Through the Eyes of Nineteenth-Century Female Biblical Interpreters.* Grand Rapids: Eerdmans, 2016.

Tetlow, Elisabeth Meier. *Women and Ministry in the New Testament: Called to Serve.* Lanham, MD: University Press of America, 1985.

Thurston, Bonnie Bowman. "Who Was Anna? Luke 2:36-38." *PRSt* 28 (2001): 47–55.

———. *The Widows: A Women's Ministry in the Early Church.* Minneapolis: Fortress, 1989.

———. *Women in the New Testament.* New York: Crossroad, 1998.

Tiede, David. " 'Fighting Against God': Luke's Interpretation of Jewish Rejection of the Messiah Jesus." In *Anti-Semitism and Early Christianity: Issues of Polemic and Faith,* edited by Craig Evans and Donald Hagner, 102–12. Minneapolis: Fortress, 1993.

Tolbert, Mary Ann. "Mark." In *The Women's Bible Commentary,* edited by Carol A. Newsom and Sharon H. Ringe, 263–74. Louisville: Westminster John Knox, 1992.

———. "Social, Sociological, and Anthropological Methods." In *Searching the Scriptures,* vol. 1: *A Feminist Introduction,* edited by Elisabeth Schüssler Fiorenza with the assistance of Shelly Matthews, 255–71. New York: Crossroad, 1993.

Topel, L. John. *Children of a Compassionate God: A Theological Exegesis of Luke 6:20-49.* Collegeville, MN: Liturgical Press, 2001.

Townes, Emilie. *In a Blaze of Glory: Womanist Spirituality as Social Witness.* Nashville: Abingdon, 1995.

Traina, Cristina L. "Between a Rock and a Hard Place." *JRE* 46 (2018): 658–81.

Transgender Lives: Your Stories. https://www.nytimes.com/interactive/2015/opinion/transgender-today.

Transgender Today. *New York Times.* https://www.nytimes.com/interactive/2015/opinion/transgender-today.

TRans yoUTH. https://ourtranstruth.org/mission-history/.

Trible, Phyllis. "Bringing Miriam out of the Shadows." *BibRev* 5 (1989): 14–25.

———. *God and the Rhetoric of Sexuality.* OBT. Philadelphia: Fortress, 1978.

Turner, Masha. "Criticizing Moses: Miriam, Aaron, and the Cushite Woman (12:1-16)." In *The Torah: A Women's Commentary,* edited by Tamara Cohn Eskenazi and Andrea L. Weiss, 859–60. New York: URJ Press and Women of Reform Judaism, The Federation of Temple Sisterhoods, 2008.

Tyson, Joseph B., ed. *Luke–Acts and the Jewish People: Eight Critical Perspectives.* Minneapolis: Augsburg, 1988.

———. *Marcion and Luke–Acts: A Defining Struggle.* Columbia: University of South Carolina Press, 2006.

Undset, Sigrid. *Catherine of Siena.* Translated by Kate Austin-Lund. New York: Sheed and Ward, 1954.

United Nations Entity For Gender Equality and the Empowerment of Women. "The Beijing Platform for Action Turns 20." http://beijing20.unwomen.org/en/in-focus/poverty.

"U.S. Boy Dies During Exorcism." BBC News. August 25, 2003. http://news.bbc.co.uk/2/hi/americas/3179789.stm.

U.S. Catholic Sisters Against Human Trafficking. https://www.sistersagainsttrafficking.org/about/who-we-are/.

Vander Stichele, Caroline, and Todd Penner, eds. *Her Master's Tools? Feminist and Postcolonial Engagements of Historical-Critical Discourse.* Atlanta: SBL, 2005.

Vermes, Géza. "The Son of Man Debate Revisited (1960–2010)." *JJS* 61 (2010): 193–206.

Via, E. Jane. "Women in the Gospel of Luke." In *Women in the World's Religions: Past and Present,* edited by Ursula King, 49–50. New York: Paragon House, 1987.

Victorin-Vangerud, Nancy M. *The Raging Hearth: Spirit in the Household of God.* St. Louis: Chalice Press, 2000.

Voices for Trans Equality. https://transequality.org/voices-for-trans-equality.

von Bingen, Hildegard. *Causae et Curae (Holistic Healing).* Edited by Mary Palmquist and John Kulas. Translated by Manfred Pawlik and Patrick Madigan. Collegeville, MN: Liturgical Press, 1994.

———. *Physica.* Translated by Priscilla Throop. Rochester, VT: Healing Arts Press, 1998.

Wagner-Hecht, Phi, ed. *The Poetry on Our Arms: Poems by Young Trans, Nonbinary and GNC Writers*. Independently Published, September 30, 2018.

Wainwright, Elaine M. "The Gospel of Matthew." In *Searching the Scriptures*, vol. 2: *A Feminist Commentary*, edited by Elisabeth Schüssler Fiorenza with Ann Brock and Shelly Matthews, 635–77. New York: Crossroad, 1994.

———. *Shall We Look for Another? A Feminist Rereading of the Matthean Jesus*. The Bible and Liberation. Maryknoll, NY: Orbis Books, 1998.

———. *Towards a Feminist Critical Reading of the Gospel According to Matthew*. BZNW 60. Berlin: de Gruyter, 1991.

———. *Women Healing/Healing Women: The Genderization of Healing in Early Christianity*. BibleWorld. London: Equinox, 2006.

Walker, Alice. *The Color Purple*. New York: Harcourt Brace Jovanovich, 1982.

———. *In Search of Our Mothers' Gardens: Womanist Prose*. New York: Harcourt Brace Jovanovich, 1967, 1983.

Walters, Patricia. *The Assumed Authorial Unity of Luke and Acts: A Reassessment of the Evidence*. SNTSMS 145. Cambridge: Cambridge University Press, 2009.

Walton, Rivkah M. "Lilith's Daughters, Miriam's Chorus: Two Decades of Feminist Midrash." *Religion & Literature* 43 (2011): 115–27.

Walton, Steve. "The State They Were In: Luke's View of the Roman Empire." In *Rome in the Bible and the Early Church*, edited by Peter Oakes, 1–41. Grand Rapids: Baker Academic, 2002.

Watson, David F. "Luke–Acts." In *The Bible and Disability: A Commentary*, edited by Sarah J. Melcher, Mikeal C. Parsons, and Amos Yong, 303–32. Studies in Religion, Theology, and Disability. Waco, TX: Baylor University Press, 2017.

Weber, Christin Lore. "Gathering: A Mythic Parable." In *The Lost Coin: Parables of Women, Work and Wisdom*, edited by Mary Ann Beavis, 308–12. London: Sheffield Academic, 2002.

Weems, Renita. *Just a Sister Away: A Womanist Vision of Women's Relationships in the Bible*. San Diego: Lura Media, 1988.

Weissenrieder, Annette. "The Plague of Uncleanness? The Ancient Illness Construct 'Issue of Blood' in Luke 8:43-48." In *The Social Setting of Jesus and the Gospels*, edited by Wolfgang Stegemann, Bruce J. Malina, and Gerd Theissen, 207–27. Minneapolis: Fortress, 2002.

Wengst, Klaus. *Pax Romana: And the Peace of Jesus Christ*. Philadelphia: Fortress, 1987.

Wheatley, Margaret J. *Leadership and the New Science: Discovering Order in a Chaotic World*. 3rd ed. San Francisco: Berrett-Koehler, 2006.

White, John L. *Light from Ancient Letters*. Philadelphia: Fortress, 1986.

Wiedemann, Thomas. *Adults and Children in the Roman Empire*. New Haven, CT: Yale University Press, 1989.

Williams, Delores S. *Sisters in the Wilderness: The Challenge of Womanist God-Talk*. Anniversary ed. Maryknoll, NY: Orbis Books, 2013.

———. "A Womanist Perspective on Sin." In *A Troubling in My Soul: Womanist Perspectives on Evil and Suffering*, edited by Emilie M. Townes, 130–49. The

Bishop Henry McNeal Turner Studies in North American Black Religion 8. Maryknoll, NY: Orbis Books, 1993.

Williams, Margaret H. "Palestinian Jewish Personal Names in Acts." in *The Book of Acts in Its Palestinian Setting*, edited by Richard Bauckham, 79–113. Grand Rapids: Eerdmans, 1995.

Wills, Lawrence M. "Son of Man." In *The Jewish Annotated New Testament*, edited by Amy-Jill Levine and Marc Zvi Brettler, 74. 2nd ed. New York: Oxford University Press, 2017.

Wilson, Brittany E. "Masculinity in Luke–Acts: The Lukan Jesus and Muscular Christianity." In *Luke–Acts*, edited by James P. Grimshaw, 23–33. Texts@ Contexts. London: T&T Clark, 2019.

———. "Pugnacious Precursors and the Bearer of Peace: Jael, Judith, and Mary in Luke 1:42." *CBQ* 68 (2006): 436–56.

———. *Unmanly Men: Refigurations of Masculinity in Luke–Acts*. New York: Oxford University Press, 2015.

Wilson, Elizabeth. *A Scriptural View of Women's Rights and Duties, in All the Important Relations of Life*. Philadelphia: Wm. S. Young, 1849.

Wilson, Madafo Lloyd. "African and African American Storytelling." https://www.ncpedia.org/culture/stories/african-american.

Wink, Walter. *Engaging the Powers: Discernment and Resistance in a World of Domination*. Minneapolis: Fortress, 1992.

Wire, Antoinette Clark. *The Corinthian Women Prophets: A Reconstruction through Paul's Rhetoric*. Minneapolis: Fortress, 1990.

———. *Holy Lives, Holy Deaths: A Close Hearing of Early Jewish Storytellers*. SBLStBL. Atlanta: SBL, 2002.

Witherington, Ben, III. *The Acts of the Apostles: A Socio-Rhetorical Commentary*. Grand Rapids: Eerdmans, 1998.

Wolfe, Patrick. "Settler Colonialism and the Elimination of the Native." *Journal of Genocide Research* 8 (2006): 387–409.

Wolter, Michael. *Das Lukasevangelium*. HNT 5. Tübingen: Mohr Siebeck, 2008.

———. *The Gospel According to Luke: Volume I (Luke 1–9:50)*. Translated by Wayne Coppins and Christoph Heilig. Waco, TX: Baylor University Press, 2016.

Women in World History. "Speaking Truth to Power: Madres of the Plaza de Mayo." http://www.womeninworldhistory.com/contemporary-07.html.

Women Win. http://womenwin.org/stories/digital-storytelling-project.

Woods, Fiona. "Are Men Really More Unfaithful than Women?" BBC News. June 2, 2012. https://www.bbc.com/news/magazine-18233843.

World Food Program USA. https://www.wfpusa.org/women-hunger/.

Wright, Christopher J. H. "Jubilee, Year of." ABD 3.1025–29.

Wyler, Bea. "Mary's Call." In *A Feminist Companion to the Hebrew Bible in the New Testament*, edited by Athalya Brenner, 136–48. Sheffield: Sheffield Academic, 1996.

Yamaguchi, Satoko. "Father Image of G*d and Inclusive Language: A Reflection in Japan." In *Toward a New Heaven and a New Earth: Essays in Honor of Elisabeth*

Schüssler Fiorenza, edited by Fernando F. Segovia, 199–224. Maryknoll, NY: Orbis Books, 2003.

Yee, Gale, ed. *Judges and Method: New Approaches in Biblical Studies*. Minneapolis: Fortress, 1995.

Yong, Amos. *The Bible, Disability, and the Church: A New Vision of the People of God*. Grand Rapids: Eerdmans, 2011.

Zeichmann, Christopher B. "Gender Minorities in and under Roman Power: Race and Respectability Politics in Luke–Acts." In *Luke–Acts*, edited by James P. Grimshaw, 61–73. Texts@Contexts. London: T&T Clark, 2019.

———. "Rethinking the Gay Centurion: Sexual Exceptionalism, National Exceptionalism in Readings of Matt. 8:5-13 // Luke 7:1-10." *The Bible and Critical Theory* 11 (2015): 35–54.

———. *The Roman Army and the New Testament*. Lanham, MD: Lexington Books/Fortress Academic, 2018.

Zenit. "Holy See Rejects Feminist 'Baptism.'" February 28, 2009. https://zenit.org/articles/holy-see-rejects-feminist-baptism/.

Zierler, Wendy. "For Days Miriam Sat Outside." In *The Torah: A Women's Commentary*, edited by Tamara Cohn Eskenazi and Andrea L. Weiss, 868. New York: URJ Press and Women of Reform Judaism, The Federation of Temple Sisterhoods, 2008.

———. "'On Account of the Cushite Woman That Moses Took': Race and Gender in Modern Hebrew Poems about Numbers 12." *Nashim: A Journal of Jewish Women's Studies & Gender Issues* 19 (Spring 2010): 34–61.

Coauthor

Shelly Matthews holds a ThD from Harvard Divinity School and is professor of New Testament at Brite Divinity School, Fort Worth, Texas. She is the general editor for the SBL Press series Early Christianity and Its Literature and the cofounder and cochair of the SBL Program Unit Racism, Pedagogy and Biblical Studies. Her books include *Perfect Martyr: The Stoning of Stephen and the Construction of Christian Identity* (Oxford University Press, 2010) and *The Acts of the Apostles: An Introduction and Study Guide; Taming the Tongues of Fire* (T&T Clark, 2017). She is currently writing a monograph under the working title *A Feminist Guide to Early Christian Resurrection: Justice, Authority, Presence.*

Volume Editor

Amy-Jill Levine is university professor of New Testament and Jewish Studies, Carpenter Professor of New Testament Studies, and professor of Jewish Studies at Vanderbilt Divinity School and College of Arts and Science; she is also affiliated professor, Centre for the Study of Jewish-Christian Relations, Cambridge, United Kingdom. Her recent publications include *The Misunderstood Jew: The Church and the Scandal of the Jewish Jesus* (HarperSanFrancisco, 2006) and *Short Stories by Jesus: The Enigmatic Parables of a Controversial Rabbi* (HarperOne, 2014). Dr. Levine is also coeditor of *The Jewish Annotated New Testament* (Oxford University Press, 2011).

Coauthor and Series Editor

Barbara E. Reid, general editor of the Wisdom Commentary series, is a Dominican Sister of Grand Rapids, Michigan. She is the president of Catholic Theological Union and the first woman to hold the position. She has been a member of the CTU faculty since 1988 and also served as vice president and academic dean from 2009 to 2018. She holds a PhD in biblical studies from The Catholic University of America and was also president of the Catholic Biblical Association in 2014–2015. Her most recent publications are *Wisdom's Feast: An Invitation to Feminist Interpretation of the Scriptures* (Eerdmans, 2016) and *Abiding Word: Sunday Reflections on Year A, B, C* (3 vols.; Liturgical Press 2011, 2012, 2013).